THE CODES
GUIDEBOOK FOR
INTERIORS

THE CODES GUIDEBOOK FOR INTERIORS

Fifth Edition

Sharon Koomen Harmon, IIDA
Katherine E. Kennon, AIA

WILEY

John Wiley & Sons, Inc.

This book is dedicated to the memory of Anna Maria (Rita) Koomen, 1932–2010.

Copyright © 2011 by John Wiley & Sons, Inc. All rights reserved.
Published by John Wiley & Sons, Inc., Hoboken, New Jersey.
Published simultaneously in Canada.

For general information on our other products and services, or technical support, please contact our Customer Care Department within the United States at 800-762-2974, outside the United States at 317-572-3993 or fax 317-572-4002.

Wiley also publishes its books in a variety of electronic formats. Some content that appears in print may not be available in electronic books.

For more information about Wiley products, visit our Web site at http://www.wiley.com.

Library of Congress Cataloging-in-Publication Data:

Harmon, Sharon Koomen, 1964-
    Codes guidebook for interior projects / Sharon Koomen Harmon, Katherine E. Kennon.—5th ed.
      p.   cm.
    Rev. ed. of: The codes guidebook for interiors. 4th ed. c2008.
    Includes bibliographical references and index.
    ISBN 978-0-470-59209-0 (cloth : alk. paper); 978-0-470-93980-2 (ebk.); 978-0-470-93981-9 (ebk.);
    978-0-470-95099-9 (ebk.); 978-0-470-95116-3 (ebk.); 978-111-8-01074-7 (ebk.)
      1. Building laws—United States.   2. Buildings—Specifications—United States.
    3. Interior architecture—United States.   I. Kennon, Katherine E.   II. Harmon, Sharon Koomen, 1964- The codes guidebook for interiors.   III. Title.
    KF5701.H37 2011
    343.73′078624—dc22
                                                                              2010033327
Printed in the United States of America
10 9 8 7 6 5 4 3 2 1

CONTENTS

Note: A more detailed table of contents can be found on the companion Web site www .wiley.com/harmon

INSET INDEX

PREFACE

Codes and standards continue to change and evolve. Even federal regulations are amended and updated. Why does this seem like a never-ending process? Because the many organizations and individuals that develop the codes, standards, and federal regulations strive to make the built environment as safe as possible. We learn from recent events and apply this knowledge to our future buildings and spaces.

A wide variety of factors are taken into consideration. Recent building fires, natural disasters, and even acts of terrorism shed light on how building safety can be improved. Industry trends, such as new building products and improved technology, provide additional options in addressing building safety. Even the growing exchange of information world-wide has affected the concepts concerning building safety in recent years. For instance, performance codes were used in other countries before they were developed for use in the United States. In addition, we are already seeing sustainability and green practices incorporated into the codes, standards, and federal regulations and at a much faster rate than originally anticipated. All of these influences continue to lead to new opportunities for collaboration between various organizations and future changes to the codes and standards.

These ongoing changes challenge design professionals to stay up to date. This book concentrates on the interior of a building because the codes, standards, and federal regulations affect projects on the interior of a building as much as the building shell. The goal is to make the codes user-friendly and to provide a good overall understanding of the various codes, standards, and federal regulations.

What sets this book apart is that it does more than just repeat the code requirements; it explains how various requirements and concepts work together to create building safety. This book discusses the relationship of the various code publications and other related documents and how to incorporate the different requirements into a single project. Understanding the overall code process creates safer buildings. It also makes code research more efficient, which can save both time and money. This fifth edition of *The Codes Guidebook for Interiors* includes the most recent changes and updates to the codes, standards, and federal regulations. Below is a preview of what is included.

❏ Focuses on the most current and widely used building code, the 2009 *International Building Code (IBC)*, as well as other related International Code Council (ICC) codes, such as the 2009 *International Fire Code*.

❏ Discusses how to use the NFPA's 2009 *Life Safety Code (LSC)* in conjunction with the *IBC* in the various code topics presented, ranging from selecting occupancy classifications to determining means of egress and fire-resistant assemblies.

❏ Incorporates information on the many standards referenced by the codes or used by the building and interior industry.

❏ Discusses the relationship of the ANSI accessibility standard (2003 *ICC/ANSI 117.1*) and the *2010 ADA Standards* and how to use them in conjunction with the codes. The differences between the original *1991 Americans with Disabilities Act Accessibility Guidelines (ADAAG)* and the new *ADA-ABA Accessibility Guidelines* are also explained.

❏ Explains sustainability practices as they relate to the existing codes and the newly developed green codes and standards including the *International Green Construction Code (IGCC)* and the *ASHRAE/USGBC/IES 189.1, Standard for the Design of High-Performance Green Buildings except Low-Rise Residential Buildings*.

❏ Describes the relationship between the energy codes, such as the 2009 *International Energy Conservation Code (IECC)*, sustainability codes, and federal energy regulations to the *IBC*.

❏ Includes interior-related electrical code requirements based on the 2008 *National Electrical Code (NEC)*.

❏ Explains plumbing codes (and plumbing fixtures), using the 2009 *International Plumbing Code*, and mechanical codes as they pertain to interior projects.

❏ Discusses the newest information on finish and furniture standards and testing, including the most current sustainability and life safety issues.

❏ Presents the role of "alternative material and methods" and performance codes to allow creative options to prescriptive code requirements.

❏ Explains the terms, concepts, and requirements of the codes, standards, and federal regulations in a simple, organized format—explaining the differences, which ones to use, and how to use them together.

❏ Includes multiple examples and sample floor plans covering a wide variety of building types and occupancy classifications.

❏ Includes many diagrams combining code and accessibility-related requirements for items such as means of egress, toilet and bathing rooms, and finish and furniture-related items.

❏ Includes an updated checklist in each chapter.

❏ Includes the latest information on working with code officials and documenting your projects using prescriptive, performance, and/or sustainability codes.

❏ Addresses a variety of building and project types, both large and small, and includes information on existing buildings, historic buildings, and single-family homes.

❏ Supplementing the information in this book, a *Study Guide* is also available. It is a valuable resource to test your understanding of the terms, concepts, and requirements presented in the *Guidebook*.

We hope that this book is helpful to you.

Sharon Koomen Harmon, IIDA
Katherine E. Kennon, AIA

ACKNOWLEDGMENTS

Once again we would like to thank our husbands and families for their ongoing patience and constant support. We would also like to thank the many who helped us with the continued development of the book. Our ability to bring the most up-to-date information is heavily assisted by the following people.

Those at the International Code Council (ICC) for their continued help and support, especially Mark Johnson, President of ICC Evaluation Service, who was instrumental in coordinating people and resources. He and several others helped clarify new and upcoming information, including Mike Pfeiffer (I-codes), Hamid Naderi (sustainability and codes), Marion Weiler (ICC-ES), Drew Azzara (global market), Rick Okawa (performance codes), and Deborah Galey-Tucker (resources).

Those who contributed to the figures in the book, including Margi Leddin, Colleen Petry-Johnson, and Rick Carroll with ICC and Dennis Berry and Josiane Domenici with the National Fire Protection Association, as well as with the development of various graphics, such as Sandi Wake with Viking Group and Teresa Cox with APCO Graphics. Thank you also to Greg Hansen with Steelcraft Manufacturing, Susan Druktenis at Underwriters Laboratories, Sara Sheth with Maharam, and Janan Rabiah with ACT.

Those at John Wiley & Sons, Inc. who took on the tedious job of organizing, proofing, and editing the manuscript, such as Sadie Abuhoff, Editorial Assistant; Amy Odum, Senior Production Editor; and Suzanne Rapcavage, Copyeditor.

Those at John Wiley & Sons, Inc. who continue to believe in this project and the value it gives to the industry, including Amanda Miller, Vice President and Publisher, and Paul Drougas, Editor.

We would particularly like to thank our readers, who continue to buy and recommend the book. Your praise and support of the book continues to motivate us. And finally, thank you to the many code jurisdictions, educators, students, and design professionals we have had the pleasure to work with through the years. All of you continue to give us inspiration.

HOW TO USE THIS BOOK

Codes, standards, and federal regulations are an essential part of designing building interiors. Whether space planning the interior of a new building, designing a new tenant space in part of a building, or making some minor changes in an existing building, all of these requirements must be taken into consideration. They should become a natural part of every interior project.

The Codes Guidebook for Interiors is designed to help the process of knowing which codes and regulation apply to a project. This book is intended to help whether you are an architect, interior designer, engineer, building owner, or facility manager. Most of the code publications address the entire building—exterior and interior as well as the structure of the building itself. This book concentrates on the codes that pertain to the interior of a building, helping you to minimize your research time. It will make the many interior codes, standards, and federal regulations user-friendly.

In this fifth edition of the *Codes Guidebook*, each section has been updated to inform you of the most current interior-related codes, standards, and federal regulations. Using the 2009 edition of the codes, this book concentrates on the requirements of the *International Building Code* and the *Life Safety Code*, two of the most widely used codes. The most current accessibility and sustainability requirements are discussed as well, including the *2010 ADA Standards*. Some chapters also discuss interior-related information from the fire codes, the electrical and energy-related codes, and the plumbing and mechanical codes, including any pertinent information on performance and alternative requirements.

Explaining how the various codes, standards, and federal regulations must be used together, this book will assist you in your code research. It will provide you with multiple examples, explanatory diagrams, and checklists to help you to eliminate costly mistakes and time-consuming changes in a project.

DEFINITIONS

Below are some common terms used throughout this book. Additional terms are defined in the Glossary in the back of the book.

◀ Note

This book deals with interior codes only. Unless otherwise noted, it is assumed that the exterior walls—including doors and windows—and the existing shell of the building are either existing or already determined.

ACCESSIBLE: Unless otherwise noted, it refers to areas, products, or devices usable by persons with disabilities, as required by the codes, federal legislation such as the Americans with Disabilities Act, and accessibility standards.

AUTHORITY HAVING JURISDICTION (AHJ): Used by the code organizations to indicate organizations, offices, or individuals that administer and enforce the codes. In this book we designate these as code jurisdictions, code departments, and code officials, respectively.

CODE OFFICIAL: Also known as a building official, it is an employee of a codes department who has the authority to interpret, administer, and enforce the codes, standards, and regulations within that jurisdiction. A code official can have a number of different titles, including plans examiner, building inspector, and, sometimes, fire marshal. Also generally referred to as the AHJ by the codes.

CODES DEPARTMENT: A local government agency that administers and enforces the codes within a jurisdiction. Some small jurisdictions may have a codes department that consists of only one person or code official, while some large jurisdictions may consist of many different agencies and departments. Also generally referred to as the AHJ by the codes.

◀ Note

Sustainable design and green design are not the same; sustainable design is more comprehensive.

GREEN DESIGN: The practice of increasing the efficiency of a building so that less resources (e.g., materials, energy, water) are used, while reducing the building's impact on human health and the environment. (See also Sustainable Design.)

JURISDICTION: A determined geographical area that uses the same codes, standards, and regulations. Each jurisdiction passes a law specifying which codes and standards are required and how they will be regulated. A jurisdiction can be as small as a township or as large as an entire state. The code jurisdiction of a project is determined by the location of the building. Also generally referred to as the AHJ by the codes.

PERFORMANCE CODE: A code that is more generally described and gives you an objective but not specific instructions on how to achieve it. The focus is on the desired outcome, not a single solution, and compliance is based on meeting the criteria established by the performance code. (Engineering tools and methodologies are often used to substantiate the use of the code criteria.)

PRESCRIPTIVE CODE: A code that provides a specific requirement that must be met for the design, construction, and maintenance of a building. The focus is on a specific solution to achieve an objective or outcome based on historical experience and established engineering. Historically, codes in the United States have been prescriptive in nature.

SUSTAINABLE DESIGN: More encompassing than green design, sustainability typically includes three main tenets: environmental responsibility, economic strength, and social responsibility. Buildings and spaces that incorporate sustainable design are designed to lessen their impact on the environment (e.g., energy and resource efficiency), stimulate the economy (e.g., using local products and labor), and provide improvements to those who use and surround the building (e.g., minimizing VOCs and enhancing the natural environment).

◢Note

All codes can be divided into two types. In the past, most codes were considered *prescriptive type* codes. These codes require specific compliance. Today, more *performance type* codes are being developed, which allow more than one solution to achieve the same results.

USING CODES IN THE DESIGN PROCESS

The best time to research codes and use this book is in the early stages of a design project, preferably in the programming phase while the designs are still preliminary, before construction documents are started and construction costs are estimated. Figure I.1 summarizes how the various phases in the traditional design process relate to the typical steps taken during the code process. Refer to this chart as you work on a project to make sure you are covering the necessary code steps. (A more detailed flow chart of the code process is included in Chapter 10.) The *Codes Guidebook* is organized so that you can follow it while working on a design project from beginning to end—in the order in which you would typically research the codes.

ORGANIZATION OF THE BOOK

Chapter 1 in *The Codes Guidebook for Interiors* gives a brief history of codes and provides some background on each of the main code publications, federal regulations, and standards organizations. Although this edition concentrates on the International Codes® (I-Codes®) by the International Code Council (ICC), there

Design Process	Code Process	Description
Programming/ Predesign	Preliminary Research	• Determine applicable codes, standards, and federal regulations • Preliminary code research to determine important code issues such as occupancy type, occupancy load, etc. • Determine level of sustainability required: code, standard, rating system, and/or green building program
Schematic/ Conceptual Design		• Incorporate code, accessibility, and sustainability compliance into design, keeping in mind means of egress, rated walls, etc.
Design Development	Preliminary Review	• Meet with code official to review conflicting code requirements (optional unless using performance codes but could be helpful) • May also be done during Schematic Design Phase
Construction Documents		• Check specific technical requirements such as aisle widths, stair dimensions, clearances, finish classifications • Compare code, accessibility, and sustainability requirements • Incorporate requirements into final design • Specify and/or detail items as required to meet codes, standards, and federal requirements
Bidding Process	Permitting Process	• Contractor applies for building permit • Code officials review construction documents for compliance to codes and standards, including any incorporated performance and/or sustainability requirements (federal requirements are not reviewed unless adopted locally)
Purchasing		• As items are ordered, confirm compliance with applicable codes, standards, and federal regulations
Construction Administration	Inspection Process	• Code officials review construction work by contractor to confirm that work complies with approved construction documents
Client Move-in	Final Inspection	• Final code approval of construction must occur before client can move in
Post-Occupancy Evaluation		• Provide client with documentation necessary for them to maintain building and/or contents as required for codes and standards (including performance and sustainability items)

Figure I.1 Comparison of design and code process.

are other codes widely used such as the *Life Safety Code (LSC)* and the *National Electrical Code (NEC)*. Chapter 1 explains all of these codes and gives a brief description of the newer codes developed by the National Fire Protection Association (NFPA) codes. (First available in 2003, the newer NFPA codes are not as widely adopted as the ICC codes.) Chapter 1 is helpful in determining which codes and standards publications and which federal regulations are required for an interior project. Chapter 10, the last chapter in this book, discusses code officials and the code process. It describes how they work and how to work with them, as well as how to document the codes you research. If you are new to codes research, you may want to review this chapter to gain a basic understanding before reading the rest of the book.

Each of the remaining chapters pertains to a specific code concept and discusses the related code, standard, and federal requirements for that topic using the publications summarized in Chapter 1. The chapters have been organized in the order in which these issues are typically considered during an interior project. Once you have used Chapter 1 to determine which publications apply to your project, we suggest you research the codes and standards in the following order:

Occupancy Classifications and Loads (Chapter 2)

Construction Types and Building Sizes (Chapter 3)

Means of Egress (Chapter 4)

Fire and Smoke Resistant Assemblies (Chapter 5)

Fire Protection Systems (Chapter 6)

Plumbing and Mechanical Requirements (Chapter 7)

Electrical and Communication Requirements (Chapter 8)

Finish and Furniture Selection (Chapter 9)

Like the code publications, most of the chapters in this book build on and add to the preceding ones. For example, the occupancy classifications in Chapter 2 are important because many of the other codes are based on the occupancy of a building or space. Therefore, it is suggested that the first-time user read this book in the order in which it is written and use it as a guide while referencing the actual codes, standards, and federal publications. Each chapter in the book includes the most current code tables, realistic design examples, summary charts, helpful diagrams, and project checklists. Each chapter also includes relevant accessibility regulations, sustainability requirements, and performance code information.

An index is provided so that you can refer to specific topics of interest. As you become familiar with the codes, use the Index and the Contents to direct you

◀ Note

A project may be governed by more than one jurisdiction. For example, both a city and a state municipality may regulate a particular project.

◀ Note

When using the code tables, be sure to check all footnotes. They often specify extra conditions that can apply to a project.

to the section of the book that applies to a specific code issue. Then refer to the appropriate code, standard, and federal publication to get the specific details.

Appendix A provides more information on the Americans with Disabilities Act (ADA). (See the section Accessibility Regulations later in this Introduction.) Appendix B has been added in this edition to address the many concepts pertaining to sustainability that are not currently covered by the codes. (See the section Sustainability Requirements later in this Introduction.)

The interiors of existing and historic buildings are also discussed separately. Appendix C briefly describes these additional codes and regulations, concentrating on the requirements in the ICC *International Existing Building Code (IEBC)*. Special consideration must also be given to historic buildings, since they usually have additional regulations on a local level within the code jurisdiction or within the township of the building. Appendix D (relocated in this edition) briefly discusses codes relating to the interior of private residences, referred to by the codes as "one- and two-family dwellings." Compared to the number of codes for commercial and public buildings, there are relatively few interior regulations for private residences. Since private residences have a separate ICC code publication, titled the *International Residential Code (IRC)*, they have been addressed separately.

The Bibliography in the back of this book has been organized by topic to help you start or add to your personal reference library. The complete list can be found on the companion Web site, www.wiley.com/harmon.

◀Note

The Abbreviations (previously Appendix D) and the Code Resources (previously Appendix E) have been removed from this edition of the book. This information is now easily accessible on the Internet.

AVAILABLE CODES AND STANDARDS

There are currently two main code organizations: the International Code Council (ICC), which publishes a comprehensive set of codes known as the International Codes, or I-Codes, and the National Fire Protection Association (NFPA), which publishes another set of codes known as the C3-Codes. Since the last edition of this book, the I-Codes have become even more widely adopted, having been adopted by at least one code jurisdiction in every state. In addition, many of the jurisdictions that had custom codes have now adopted a new code based on the ICC codes. The newer NFPA codes have not been as widely adopted. (See Chapter 1.)

Overall, this fifth edition of *The Codes Guidebook for Interiors* concentrates on the requirements and code tables from the 2009 *International Building Code (IBC)*, as well as other current code publications from the ICC such as the *International Plumbing Code (IPC)* and the *International Energy Conservation Code (IECC)*. Because many jurisdictions also use NFPA's *Life Safety Code (LSC)* and *National Electrical Code (NEC)*, both of these codes are explained throughout this book in relation to the I-Codes. (See Chapter 1.)

◀Note

Many jurisdictions throughout the United States are using the *International Building Code (IBC)* or a code based on the *IBC*.

Many required standards are explained in this book as well. Some of them are explained in Chapter 1 as the various standards organizations are described. This includes standards by the ICC and the NFPA. Additional standards are discussed in other chapters based on the topic being discussed. Certain standards are referenced by the codes and, therefore, are required by a jurisdiction. Others have become standard practice to incorporate in a project, often for the health, safety, and/or welfare of the building occupants. With the introduction of many new sustainability standards, additional organizations are joining the standards developing process.

◀**Note**

Although the newer NFPA codes have not been widely adopted, NFPA's *Life Safety Code* and *National Electrical Code* continue to be widely used.

PRESCRIPTIVE AND PERFORMANCE

Both the ICC and the NFPA now include performance criteria in addition to prescriptive requirements in their codes. (See previous Definitions.) The NFPA includes the performance-based requirements as a separate chapter within many of their publications. By contrast, the ICC produces a separate performance code publication that can be used in conjunction with their other codes when recognized by the code jurisdiction. Where a jurisdiction has not adopted the performance code, you have the option of using sections in the *International Building Code* that allows for some flexibility from the prescriptive code. The most common is titled *Section 104.11, Alternative Materials, Design and Methods of Construction and Equipment*. (See the section Performance Codes in Chapter 1.)

◀**Note**

When discussing prescriptive codes, the term *requirements* is often used. However, performance codes typically set *criteria, goals,* or *objectives.*

The performance codes are meant to be used in conjunction with the prescriptive codes. A project with an unusual design may require the use of a performance code. Most often performance-based criteria will be used for a particular part of the project and the standard prescriptive codes will be used for the rest. It would be unusual for an entire project to be designed using only performance codes. When a performance code requirement is used, there is more responsibility on the designer. Not only do the performance-related criteria need to be correctly documented, but it also must be proven that these criteria are being met with the use of fire models, testing, etc.

Various performance codes will be mentioned in each chapter of this book as they relate to the corresponding prescriptive codes. Chapter 10 will discuss how to document the use of performance codes for codes review. Ultimately, the performance codes can be used to explore unique designs and allow for the use of new technology. Even if you do not typically use them, by becoming familiar with the various performance requirements you will gain more insight into the prescriptive codes. They will also give you insight to using the *IBC Section 104.11*.

ACCESSIBILITY REGULATIONS

Today, accessible design is required for the majority of interior projects. The building codes include accessibility requirements and reference the ICC/ANSI accessibility standard *ICC/ANSI A117.1*. In addition, federal laws require the use of other accessibility regulations. For example, the American's with Disabilities Act (ADA) legislation has required the use of the *ADA Accessibility Guidelines (ADAAG)* in many projects since the early 1990s. More recently, the 2004 *ADA-ABA Accessibility Guidelines* have been adopted by federal agencies. The ABA portion of these guidelines, which replaced the *Uniform Federal Accessibility Standards (UFAS)*, are referred to as the *ABA Standards* and are required on many federal projects. (See inset titled *ADA-ABA Accessibility Guidelines Enforcement* on page 461.) The ADA portion of the guidelines are referred to as the *2010 ADA Standards* and became the applicable guideline in September 2010. (Either the *ADAAG* or the *2010 ADA Standards* can be used until March 2012. See the section New ADA Standards in Appendix A for more information.) The ICC/ANSI standard and the various federally required accessibility regulations are summarized in Chapter 1.

Since accessibility affects all aspects of a design, accessibility standards and the ADA are discussed throughout this book as they relate to each relevant topic. (The information focuses on the 2003 ICC/ANSI standard and the *2010 ADA Standards*.) For example, accessible toilet facilities are discussed in the plumbing chapter (Chapter 7), and accessible ramps are discussed in the means of egress chapter (Chapter 4). Because the *ADA-ABA Accessibility Guidelines* have been closely coordinated with the more current editions of the ICC/ANSI standards, the requirements are often the same, but there are some differences. Appendix A elaborates on the compliance and enforcement issues of the ADA and the *ADA Standards*.

Like the codes discussed in this book, not every specific accessibility dimension and requirement has been mentioned. For specific requirements and additional information, you must still consult the ADA and its related guidelines or standards, specific chapters within the building codes, and any other accessibility regulations required by a jurisdiction. (When discrepancies are found between the ADA standards and ICC/ANSI standard, the strictest requirements are typically discussed.)

SUSTAINABILITY REQUIREMENTS

Sustainability (and green) codes and standards add a whole new dimension to the code process, affecting design as well as material, equipment, and product selection. (See previous Definitions.) Existing codes, standards, and federal regulations do address some issues of sustainability. For example, earlier I-Codes address energy efficiency, waterless urinals, and graywater recycling systems. However, as explained in Chapter 1, there are a number of green codes and standards that are now available or in the process of being completed. The two most prominent ones are the *ASHRAE/USGBC/IES 189.1, Standard for the Design of High-Performance Green Buildings Except Low-Rise Residential Buildings* and the *International Green Construction Code (IGCC)*, both of which are discussed throughout this book. In addition, the federal government continues to raise the minimal requirements for energy efficiency, and various organizations have recently completed and continue to collaborate to create new sustainable standards.

Chapter 1 summarizes these sustainable-related publications and federal laws. Actual sustainability requirements are discussed throughout this book (including the appendixes) as they pertain to the various code topics presented. In most cases these requirements can already be found in the codes. In some instances, industry standards that have become common practice are explained. Appendix B has been added in this edition to explain other sustainable topics that are used in the industry but are not necessarily part of the code process.

In addition, a number of code jurisdictions have created customized "green building programs" in order to fill the gap between the wide use of sustainable products and practices and the previously limited information in the codes. (See the section Code Enforcement in Chapter 10.) As more sustainable codes and standards are created and adopted, the differences between the jurisdictions should be corrected.

Note

Numerous jurisdictions have created customized green building programs, many of which incorporate a green rating system. (See Chapter 10 and Appendix B for more information.)

FIGURES IN THE BOOK

Many figures in this book have been updated since the last edition. All code tables are based on the 2009 edition of the codes. In the diagrams, metric numbers are shown in parentheses, as in other code and accessibility documents, and represent millimeter measurements unless noted otherwise.

Many of the diagrams include both code and accessibility requirements. For example, the means of egress diagrams in Chapter 4 include clearances and minimum dimensions as required in the building codes, the *ADA Standards*, and the ICC/ANSI standard. In each case, the most stringent requirements were used. In some instances, notes have been added to clarify conflicting requirements. When working on a project, however, be sure to consult the original document as required by the local jurisdiction.

Note

The codes and accessibility publications do not always use the same metric conversion for a particular dimension. When there is a discrepancy, the most restrictive metric number is used.

GETTING STARTED

◄Note

This book is not intended to be a substitute for any code, standard, or federal publication required by a jurisdiction. It should be used as a reference book to gain a better understanding of the codes and to guide you through the code process.

This book should be used as a guide to assist you in researching the codes and to help you organize your projects. It is not a substitute or replacement for the actual code publications. It would be impossible to discuss every specific code, standard, and federal regulation in one book. In addition, some jurisdictions may have modified some of the requirements. Therefore, this book must be used in conjunction with the code publications. A thorough investigation of the codes and standards may include working closely with code officials, engineers, and other professionals.

Before beginning a project, you need to know which codes, standards, and federal publications must be referenced. Use Chapter 1 to help you confirm which codes and standards are available. The local codes department can verify the publications that must be referenced and notify you of any required local codes or amendments. They should also be able to tell you if there are any state requirements you need to follow, and if there are any green building programs in place. Since federal publications are not typically regulated on a local level, you will need to keep abreast of the latest changes in the laws that may apply to a project. This book will explain how to do this as well. It is important for you to have the actual publications on hand during the project so that specific codes and regulations can be referenced and verified.

MINIMUM REQUIREMENTS

◄Note

Rather than viewing codes as restrictive or as a burden, remember that they allow people to feel safe as they live and work in the buildings you design.

Always remember that codes, standards, and federal regulations have been developed as *minimum* requirements. There may be equivalent solutions, and often superior alternatives and solutions are available. By working with your client, the building requirements, and the budget for the project, you can make informed design decisions. By using the creative thinking process and by working with the code officials and other professionals, the best design solutions can be developed.

CHAPTER 1

ABOUT THE CODES

A variety of codes regulate the design and construction of buildings and building interiors. In addition, there are a large number of standards and federal regulations that play a major role. The most nationally recognized codes, laws, and standards organizations are described in this chapter. Most of them are referenced and discussed throughout this book as they pertain to the interior of a building; and they are summarized in a checklist at the end of this chapter.

While reading about each of these codes, standards, and regulations, keep in mind that *not all of them will be enforced by every code jurisdiction.* (See Definitions in the Introduction.) The jurisdiction chooses which code publications to use and the edition of each publication. For example, a jurisdiction could decide to adopt the 2009 edition of the *International Building Code (IBC)* or continue to use the 2006 edition, or a jurisdiction could decide to adopt the *NFPA 101, Life Safety Code,* as a stand-alone document or to be used in conjunction with a building code. The jurisdiction could also make a variety of local amendments that add or delete clauses from a code. Knowing which codes are being enforced is necessary in order to research codes for a particular project. (See Chapter 10.)

In addition, each code publication references certain standards; therefore, the standards that need to be used depend on the required code publications. The code will indicate which edition is required. For example, all the standards referenced throughout the *IBC* are listed in the back of the code; this list includes the year of the publication. Other standards may not be referenced by a code. Instead, they may be individually required by a jurisdiction or they may be accepted as industry-wide standards. For example, some finish and sustainability standards are not *required* by a local jurisdiction, but may need to be followed for safety, health, and/or liability reasons. The only regulations that are consistent in every jurisdiction are the federal regulations that are made mandatory by law.

⊴Note

There are now two main sets of codes. The ICC codes and the NFPA codes. Many of the ICC codes, such as the *International Building Code (IBC),* are widely adopted. Popular NFPA codes include the *Life Safety Code (LSC)* and the *National Electric Code (NEC).* NFPA added a number of new codes in 2003; however, they have not yet been widely adopted.

A BRIEF HISTORY

The use of regulatory codes can be traced back as far as the eighteenth century BCE to the *Code of Hammurabi*, a collection of laws governing Babylonia. The *Code of Hammurabi* made the builder accountable for the houses he built. If one of his buildings fell down and killed someone, the builder would be put to death.

In the United States, the first codes addressed fire prevention. The first building law on record was passed in 1625 in what was then called New Amsterdam (now New York). It governed the types and locations of roof coverings to protect the buildings from chimney sparks. Then, in the 1800s, there were a number of large building fires, including the famous Chicago fire of 1871, which caused many fatalities. As a result, some of the larger U.S. cities developed their own municipal building *codes*. Some of these requirements are still in use today. In the mid-1800s, the National Board of Fire Underwriters was set up to provide insurance companies with information on which to base their fire damage claims. One of the results was the publication of the 1905 *Recommended Building Code*—a code that helped spark the original three model building codes. Another group that originally represented the sprinkler and fire insurance interests also formed, and in 1896 published the first standard for automatic sprinklers (later known as *NFPA 13*). This group went on to become the National Fire Protection Association (NFPA).

The growing awareness for building safety inspired the development of other organizations and additional codes. The first of the original three model code organizations formed in 1915. Later known as the Building Officials Code Administrators International (BOCA), it produced the *BOCA National Building Code* and other codes. The BOCA codes were generally used in the eastern and mideastern regions of the United States. In 1922, 13 building officials created what eventually became the International Conference of Building Officials (ICBO). These codes were used primarily in the western regions of the United States. A similar group of building officials met in 1940 to form the Southern Building Code Congress International (SBCCI), producing codes for the southern states. These three legacy organizations (BOCA, ICBO, and SBCCI) founded the International Code Council (ICC) in 1994, later consolidating and putting their effort into one set of codes. Each individual organization eventually stopped producing its own separate code publications.

Meanwhile, the federal government was also creating *regulations*. Many of these laws pertained to government-built and -owned buildings. Some were national laws that superseded other required codes. In 1973, in an attempt to control government intervention, Congress passed the *Consumer Product Safety Act* and formed the Consumer Product Safety Commission (CPSC). The goal of the

◀ Note

In addition to federal regulations, a state may also create their own regulations, which would be required within all jurisdictions of that state.

commission is to prevent the necessity of federal regulations by encouraging industry self-regulation and *standardization*. This resulted in the creation of a number of new standards-writing organizations and trade associations. Additional legislation since then has been used to promote this process. Individual states can create and mandate statewide regulations as well.

Today, there are various building-related codes in existence in the United States, a wide variety of federal and state regulations, and hundreds of standards organizations and regulatory and trade associations in almost every facet of the industry. Only the most widely recognized ones as they pertain to interior projects are described below to provide the groundwork as they are discussed throughout this book. (For more information, refer to the resources in the Bibliography.)

CODE PUBLICATIONS

Codes are a collection of regulations, ordinances, and other statutory requirements put together by various organizations. Each jurisdiction decides which codes it will follow and enforce. (See more on jurisdictions in Chapter 10.) Once certain codes are adopted, they become law within that jurisdiction.

The International Code Council (ICC) produces a complete set of codes, known as the *International Codes*—or *I-Codes*, for short. Many of the I-Codes are used throughout the United States and in other countries. The interior-related ICC code publications have been listed in Figure 1.1. These are the codes that will be discussed throughout this book.

More recently, the National Fire Protection Association (NFPA) broadened the scope of codes that it develops. In the past, NFPA concentrated on developing standards as well as a few codes such as the *Life Safety Code* and the *National Electrical Code*. Now it has a complete set of codes, some of which were created in collaboration with other industry organizations. This series of codes is called the *Comprehensive Consensus Codes*—or *C3-Codes*, for short. Currently, the NFPA's collaboration partners include the International Association of Plumbing and Mechanical Officials (IAPMO), the Western Fire Chiefs Association (WFCA), and the American Society of Heating, Refrigeration, and Air-Conditioning Engineers (ASHRAE). Several of the NFPA codes are summarized in Figure 1.1, although many of the newer ones have not yet been widely adopted.

The ICC and NFPA codes are organized differently. Most of the I-Codes are organized using the *Common Code Format*. The code is arranged by chapters that address various aspects of a building and include specific requirements for each

CODE AND STANDARDS CHANGES

Each code and standards organization has its own procedures for changing and updating the requirements in its publications. In the United States, most of them use a *consensus* process to revise their publications. Each organization has a membership that consists of a wide range of individuals. These could include code officials, design professionals, building users, academics, manufacturers, building owners, consumers, contractors, and others. These members make up the committees that oversee the proposed changes. However, both members and nonmembers can typically propose and comment on changes either in writing or in person at open public hearings.

Many standards organizations as well as the National Fire Protection Association (NFPA) use a consensus process developed by the American National Standards Institute (ANSI), called the ANS process. Once a code or standard is ready to be revised, a *call for proposals* is issued. For example, the NFPA will request proposals for changes to a code or standard. As the proposals are received, they are sent to a technical committee made up of NFPA members for review. The committee makes revisions if necessary and then reissues them for public comment. Typically, both members and nonmembers can submit comments. These comments are used to modify the proposal so that it can be presented for recommendation and discussion at one of NFPA's membership meetings. Here, the various change proposals are voted on by the membership for the purpose of making a recommendation to the overseeing Standards Council. This council takes the votes into consideration but makes the final decision.

The International Code Council (ICC) uses what it calls a governmental consensus process, or *open process,* when developing its codes. (This was also used by the legacy model code organizations.) Much of the process is the same as described above. The main difference is that the final decision is made by the "governmental" members of the ICC rather than by a small group or council. These governmental members consist of code officials and employees of the governmental agencies that administer and enforce the codes. Although this does not include all ICC members, it is a large part of their membership base. When developing its standards, the ICC uses the ANS consensus process as described above.

Once a proposed code or standard change is voted on and approved, it is adopted by the organization. Usually once a year, or as needed, the organization will publish the most current changes in an addendum or supplement. When the next full edition of the code or standard is published, it incorporates all the changes into one text.

occupancy or building type. The C3-Codes use the *Manual of Style,* where there are several key chapters at the beginning and end of the code and the rest of the chapters are divided by occupancy type. The occupancy chapters allow the code review to start in the chapter that pertains to the project's occupancy type, which then indicates when to reference other chapters.

ICC I-Codes®		NFPA C3-Codes	
IBC®	International Building Code®	**NFPA 5000®**	Building Construction and Safety Code®
ICC PC®	ICC Performance Code® for Buildings and Facilities		(performance requirements included in each code)
IFC®	International Fire Code®	**NFPA 1®**	Fire Code® (previously titled the Uniform Fire Code or UFC)
	(similar requirements found in IBC and IFC)	**NFPA 101®**	Life Safety Code® (LSC)
IPC®	International Plumbing Code®	**IAPMOs**	Uniform Plumbing Code® (UPC)
IMC®	International Mechanical Code®	**IAPMOs**	Uniform Mechanical Code® (UMC)
	(no longer has separate code—refers to NEC)	**NFPA 70®**	National Electrical Code® (NEC)
IECC®	International Energy Conservation Code®		(ASHRAE standards 90.1 and 90.2 referenced by NFPA 5000) (NFPA 900® Building Energy Code® not currently available as separate document)
IGCC®	International Green Construction Code®		(none)
IRC®	International Residential Code® for One- and Two-Family Dwellings		(residential requirements included in other codes)
IEBC®	International Existing Building Code®		(existing building requirements included in each code)

NOTE: This chart includes the main interior-related codes from each code organization. Other codes dealing with overall building or site-related items are not included.

Figure 1.1 Comparison of code publications. (This chart is a summary of 2009 publications from the International Code Council® and the National Fire Protection Association that pertain to interior projects. Neither the ICC® nor the NFPA assumes responsibility for the accuracy or completeness of this chart.) NFPA 101®, Life Safety Code®, and NFPA 5000®, Building Construction and Safety Code® are registered trademarks of the National Fire Protection Association, Quincy, MA.

In the past, the legacy codes catered to certain regions of the country. The current model codes by the ICC and NFPA now take into account the many regional differences found throughout the United States. For example, certain coastal states need more restrictive seismic building code provisions to allow for the many earthquakes in those areas, and the northern states need codes to allow for long periods of below-freezing temperatures. All these various requirements are now in the current building codes. In some cases, a code jurisdiction will add amendments to the code they adopt to create requirements unique to their area.

There are a few states and cities that continue to maintain their own set of codes. However, even the differences between these customized codes are becoming less obvious as more jurisdictions are working closely with the code organizations. For example, many states (and some cities) are working with the ICC to

◤**Note**

The custom codes developed through the ICC are listed as "custom regional codes" in their product catalog and Web site store.

☜Note

Both the ICC and NFPA also work with federal and state agencies for possible adoption. For example, the U.S. Department of Defense and the National Park Service currently use some I-Codes. The Department of Veterans Affairs and the Centers for Medicare and Medicaid Services refer to the *Life Safety Code*.

☜Note

When a code is updated, a vertical line in the margin indicates a change from the previous edition and an arrow or bullet in the margin signifies that a section was removed. This allows a quick scan for changes.

☜Note

When an ICC code is modified for a special edition, such as the *2009 IBC, New Jersey* edition, a double line indicates changes from the original *IBC*.

☜Note

Since the three legacy code organizations no longer publish their respective codes, they will not be discussed in this book.

☜Note

Since the *NFPA 5000* has not been widely adopted, this book will concentrate on the *International Building Code (IBC)* requirements and discuss how they are used with the *Life Safety Code (LSC)*. Many jurisdictions adopt both the *IBC* and the *LSC*.

revise the *International Building Code* (IBC) as required for their state. The ICC then reprints the code specifically for that state as a customized code. For instance, the state of California and the city of New York maintained their own set of codes until recently. Both now use codes based on the I-Codes. Some jurisdictions have a complete set of unique codes, while others may have just one or two special code publications and use one of the available codes for everything else.

Most codes are updated on a three-year cycle, but each jurisdiction has its own schedule of reviewing and adopting the new codes. Not only is it extremely important to know which codes and standards apply to a project, it is also important to know the edition. (See the inset titled *Reviewing New Code Editions* on page 437) Each of the codes produced by the ICC and NFPA, as they pertain to interior projects, is described in this section. The various standards are described later in this chapter. Be sure to contact the local jurisdiction to obtain a list of the approved code publications and any other special requirements or addendums. (See Chapter 10.) Go to both the ICC Web site (www.iccsafe.org) and the NFPA Web site (www.nfpa.org) to learn about the latest code adoptions.

Building Codes

Building codes stress the construction requirements of an entire building and place restrictions on hazardous materials or equipment used within a building. The principal purpose is to ensure the health, safety, and welfare of the people using these buildings. This includes structural, mechanical, electrical, plumbing, life safety (egress), fire safety (detection and suppression), natural light and air, accessibility standards, and energy conservation. Although other codes and standards may be referenced, the building codes cover each of these topics.

The most widely adopted building code is the *International Building Code (IBC)* published by ICC. It has been adopted at the state or local level in all 50 states and most state-specific building codes are now based on the *IBC*. It is also used in several other countries. (See the inset titled *Codes and Standards in Other Countries* on page 26.) The *IBC* was first published in 2000, with the most current edition published in 2009 and the next edition due in 2012. The NFPA first published the *Building Construction and Safety Code*®(*NFPA 5000*®) in 2003 and it has yet to be adopted by more than a handful of jurisdictions. Its most current edition is 2009. Both codes are typically revised on a 3-year cycle.

Although there are more than 30 chapters and 10 appendixes in the *IBC* and even more chapters in the *NFPA 5000*, not all of them pertain to the interior of a building. The building interior–related chapters in both the *IBC* and the *NFPA 5000* are summarized in the comparative list in Figure 1.2. The most common chapters required for interior projects are listed as follows and are discussed throughout this book. Certain projects may require other sections of the building code to be referenced as well. For example, the information in the chapters

IBC (2009) International Building Code		NFPA 5000 (2009) Building Construction and Safety Code		LSC (2009) Life Safety Code*	
Chapter 2	Definitions	Chapter 3	Definitions	Chapter 3	Definitions
Separate	References separate code: *ICC Performance Code for Buildings and Facilities (ICCPC)* OR *IBC Section 104.11*	Chapter 5	Performance-Based Option	Chapter 5	Performance-Based Option
Chapter 3	Use and Occupancy Classification	Chapter 6	Classification of Occupancy, Classification of Hazard of Contents, and Special Operations	Chapter 6	Classification of Occupancy and Hazard of Contents
		Varies	Multiple chapters (16–30), each on a different occupancy, classification	Varies	Multiple (even) chapters (12–42), each on a different new occupancy classification
Separate	References separate code: *International Residential Code (IRC)*	Chapter 22	One- and Two-Family Dwellings	Chapter 24	One- and Two-Family Dwellings
Chapter 4	Special Detailed Requirements Based on Use and Occupancy	Chapter 31	Occupancies in Special Structures	Chapter 11	Special Structures and High-Rise Buildings
		Chapter 32	Special Construction		
		Chapter 33	High-Rise Buildings		
Chapter 5	General Building Heights and Areas	Chapter 7	Construction Types and Height and Area Requirements		(none)
Chapter 6	Types of Construction	Chapter 7	Construction Types and Height and Area Requirements		(none)
Chapter 7	Fire and Smoke Protection Features	Chapter 8	Fire-Resistive Materials and Construction	Chapter 8	Features of Fire Protection
Chapter 8	Interior Finishes	Chapter 10	Interior Finish	Chapter 10	Interior Finish, Contents, and Furnishings
Chapter 9	Fire Protection Systems	Chapter 55	Fire Protection Systems and Equipment	Chapter 9	Building Service and Fire Protection Equipment
Chapter 10	Means of Egress	Chapter 11	Means of Egress	Chapter 7	Means of Egress
Chapter 11	Accessibility	Chapter 12	Accessibility		(none)
Chapter 12	Interior Environment	Chapter 49	Interior Environment		(none)
Chapter 13	Energy Efficiency	Chapter 51	Energy Efficiency		(none)
Chapter 24	Glass and Glazing	Chapter 46	Glass and Glazing		(none)
Chapter 26	Plastic	Chapter 48	Plastics		(none)
Chapter 27	Electrical	Chapter 52	Electrical Systems		(none)
Chapter 28	Mechanical Systems	Chapter 50	Mechanical Systems		(none)
Chapter 29	Plumbing Systems	Chapter 53	Plumbing Systems		(none)
Chapter 34	Existing Structures OR separate code: *International Existing Building Code (IEBC)*	Chapter 15	Building Rehabilitation	Chapter 43	Building Rehabilitation
				Varies	Multiple (odd) chapters (13–39), each on a different existing occupancy classification
Chapter 35	Referenced Standards	Chapter 2	Referenced Publications	Chapter 2	Referenced Publications

*NOTE: This chart includes interior-related chapters only. *The Life Safety Code* is not a building code, so it will not have all the same types of chapters, but it is often used in conjunction with a building code.

Figure 1.2 Comparison of building codes and *Life Safety Code*®. (This chart is a summary of information contained in the 2009 editions of the *International Building Code*®, the *NFPA 5000*®, and the *Life Safety Code*®. Neither the ICC nor the NFPA assumes responsibility for the accuracy or completeness of this chart.)

✎Note

Most codes contain appendixes or annexes with additional requirements. For example, one *IBC* appendix includes additional accessibility requirements. However, these appendixes or annexes are only required when specifically adopted by a jurisdiction.

✎Note

A more comprehensive list of code adoptions can be found on the ICC Web site (www.iccsafe.org) and the NFPA Web site (www.nfpa. org).

✎Note

The *International Building Code* is the most widely used building code in the United States.

on glass and glazing, plastic, or existing structures may also be required (see Figure 1.2).

Use or Occupancy Classifications

Special Use or Occupancy Requirements

Types of Construction

Fire and Smoke Protection Features

Interior Finishes

Fire Protection Systems

Means of Egress

Accessibility

Interior Environment

Plumbing Systems

To cover as much as possible, the building codes frequently reference other codes and standards. Other code publications include a plumbing code, a mechanical code, a fire prevention code, an energy conservation code, and an existing structures code, most of which are described later in this chapter. Although many of these same topics are listed as chapters in the building codes, these chapters typically refer to another code or standard. (Refer to Figure 1.1 for a full list of interior-related code publications.) Performance codes (described next) are also referenced within each building code. *NFPA 5000* includes a chapter within the text, while the *IBC* references a separate ICC performance code publication. In addition, other nationally recognized standards organizations and publications are referenced by each of the codes. The *IBC* lists all the codes and standards it references in Chapter 35 of the code. (See also the section Standards Organizations later in this chapter.) Since the *IBC* is the most widely used building code, it will be the one discussed throughout this book.

Performance Codes

Traditionally, codes have been primarily prescriptive in nature. A *prescriptive* code provides a precise requirement, explaining exactly what needs to be done to meet the code. A *performance* code, on the other hand, provides an objective but not the specifics of how to achieve it. Historically, some requirements in the prescriptive codes have included parameters for the use of alternate methods, materials, and systems that can be considered more performance-like. In the *IBC*, an example of this can be found in Section 104.11, which is titled "Alternative materials, design and methods of construction and equipment" (described as "*IBC Section 104.11*" throughout this book). These alternate methods allowed some flexibility; however, the traditional code does not describe how to show equivalency, which can make it hard to obtain approval from a code official. (See also the inset titled *ICC Evaluation Services* on page 20.) A performance-based code, instead, provides more structure by stating an objective and providing an administrative process to follow. It shows the designer how to meet these objectives, how to document the results, and how to work with the code official to obtain final approval.

A good example of the difference between a prescriptive code and a performance criterion can be found in the spacing of guardrail elements. In the *IBC*, the prescriptive requirement specifies that rail elements "shall not have openings which allow passage of a sphere 4 inches (102 mm) in diameter from the walking surface to the required guard height." This requirement was developed specifically with children in mind. The *ICC Performance Code* does not mandate this narrow spacing. Instead, it specifies "that the openings shall be of an appropriate size and configuration to keep people from falling through based upon the anticipated age of the occupants." If it can be shown that children are not expected to frequent the building, then different spacing of the guardrail elements may be allowed. An example might be a manufacturing facility.

The development of performance-based codes separate from prescriptive codes is fairly recent in the United States. Many other countries already regularly use performance-based codes. (See the inset titled *Codes and Standards in Other Countries* on page 26.) The ICC first published the *ICC Performance Code for Buildings and Facilities (ICCPC)* in 2001. Updated most recently in 2009, it is on a 3-year revision cycle. The *ICCPC* is meant to be used in conjunction with the *IBC*, as well as most of the other I-Codes. It addresses the overall scope of each of the I-Codes in performance-based language and describes how to use them together. However, the *ICCPC* cannot be used with the other I-Codes unless it is adopted by the code jurisdiction, and currently it has not yet been widely adopted in the United States. If it is not adopted, work with a code official using the *IBC Section 104.11* to integrate performance criteria into the design solution.

The NFPA, on the other hand, does not have a separate text for performance criteria. Instead, the most current NFPA codes include both performance requirements and prescriptive requirements. For example, the *Life Safety Code* has a Chapter 5 titled "Performance-Based Option." In addition, NFPA recommends referencing Chapter 4, which discusses some of the code's goals, assumptions, and objectives and provides additional insight in using prescriptive-type codes. Since a jurisdiction that adopts one of the NFPA codes does have the option to exclude Chapter 5, confirm that the performance requirements are allowed before using them.

The purpose of performance codes is to allow for more creative design solutions in the use of materials and systems of construction and to allow innovative

◁ Note

The *SFPE Engineering Guide to Performance-Based Fire Analysis and Design of Buildings* is a good resource when working with performance-based codes. In addition, the *ICC Performance Code* contains a User's Guide in its appendix.

◁ Note

The use of performance codes actually started in other countries. Australia was one of the first to use them. Other countries that use performance codes include Canada, Japan, the Netherlands, New Zealand, Sweden, and the United Kingdom.

✎Note

Typically, only a certain portion of a project will be based on a performance-based code or on the alternative materials, design, and methods section in the *IBC*. The rest of the project would then be designed using standard prescriptive code requirements.

engineering to meet code requirements in ways that can be specific to each project. In designing to meet the requirements of a performance code, there are a number of parameters or assumptions that must be determined at the beginning of a project. (See the inset titled *Risk Factors and Hazards in Occupancies* on page 52.) These assumptions are used to create performance guidelines that are followed throughout the design process. (Similar assumptions were used by the code organizations in the development of the prescriptive codes.)

When using performance codes (or alternative methods and materials such as those allowed by *IBC Section 104.11*), it becomes even more important to start working with the code official in the early stages of a project. An overall team approach is actually encouraged by the code. For the solution to be acceptable, the code official must agree that the design and the supporting documentation meet the intent of the code. Performance codes are intended to allow for creativity in design and engineering while still providing the necessary safety and welfare concerns of the code. This will need to be proven to the code official. (See Chapter 10 and the inset on page 452, *Performance Codes*, for additional information.) Performance codes may be applied to any design project if allowed by the code official. However, they may be most effective in unique situations, including the use of new technology, incorporating sustainable design, and the reuse of existing and historic buildings, which may not easily meet the strict requirement of the prescriptive codes. In most cases, performance codes will only apply to part of a project and will not totally replace the required prescriptive codes.

ICC EVALUATION SERVICES

ICC Evaluation Service (ICC-ES) is a subsidiary of the International Code Council (ICC). It evaluates new materials, methods of construction, and testing as they become available to make sure they comply with the I-Codes, as well as other codes in the United States. The ICC-ES works closely with various accredited testing laboratories and approved inspection agencies in order to accomplish this. These laboratories and agencies are reviewed and approved by the International Accreditation Services (IAS), another independent subsidiary of the ICC.

The request to evaluate a product or system often comes from the manufacturer, but others, such as builders, code officials, engineers, architects, and designers, can do so as well. For example, a manufacturer might request an evaluation for a new building product they created, or a designer might request a job-specific evaluation. The ICC-ES develops acceptance criteria to evaluate the characteristics of the product, the installation of the product, and the conditions of its use to verify that it meets or exceeds the requirements of the codes and standards. Once a product or system is approved, an ICC-ES Evaluation Report is issued and made available to the industry. (They can be accessed and downloaded for free at www.icc-es.org.)

Some interior-related examples include:

❏ ESR-1175, Staron Sinks and Lavatories by Cheil Industries, Inc. for solid-surface, one-piece acrylic fixtures

❏ ESR-1260, Acrylite Acrylic Sheets by Cyro Industries for use as light-transmitting plastic

❏ ESR-1409, Photoluminescent Exit Signs by Active Safety Corporation for use as means of egress identification

❏ ESR-1598, Altos Wall System by Teknion Furniture Systems for moveable floor-to-ceiling interior wall partition system

❏ ESR-1791, Pyro-Guard Fire-Retardant-Treated Wood by Hoover Treaded Wood Products, Inc. for fire-retardant-treated wood not exposed to weather/wetting

❏ ESR-2769, Glasroc Tile Backer by Certainteed Gypsum, Inc. for tile backer board in shower and tub areas

More recently, the ICC-ES has added other evaluation services. The ICC-ES Sustainable Attributes Verification and Evaluation (SAVE) Program, verifies that a sustainable product has been independently tested to meet the sustainable attributes described by a manufacturer. (See also Appendix B.) The ICC-ES PMG Listing Program determines product compliance with the codes specifically in the areas of plumbing, mechanical, and fuel gas (PMG), covering a wide range of innovative and sustainable as well as code-complying products.

All of these evaluation reports and product listings can then be used by designers to support the use of an innovative product. It is especially helpful as part of a performance-based design or when using the alternative materials, design, and methods sections in the *IBC*. When a designer specifies a product already approved by the ICC-ES, the report/listing provides a third-party validation that the product meets the minimum performance requirements of the IBC. This is helpful to the code official reviewing the project. (The code official still has to approve its use.) This process also allows manufacturers to gain national recognition of a new product.

Other evaluation services are available as well. For example, some states, such as California and Florida, have developed their own uniform requirements to meet their statewide codes. (Reports created by the older model code organizations are still available and are known as ICC-ES "Legacy Reports." As each report is updated, it becomes part of the I-Codes.)

⬚Note

ICC-ES Evaluation Reports, Product Listings, and SAVE Program provide evidence that a product meets code requirements and are helpful when using performance codes or alternative materials, design, and methods sections in the *IBC*.

Fire Codes

Both the ICC and the NFPA have a fire code. The first fire code produced by the ICC was in 2000 and is called the *International Fire Code (IFC)*. Like the other I-Codes, it is on a 3-year revision cycle, with newer editions in 2009 and 2012. In 2003, NFPA came out with a new fire code, which was developed in partnership with the Western Fire Chiefs Association (WFCA). Titled the *Uniform Fire Code® (UFC)* or *NFPA 1®*, it merged the old *NFPA 1* with a legacy code by the WFCA. The new version is organized similarly to the other C3-Codes and includes a chapter on performance-based design. It was revised again in 2009 and is now simply known as the *Fire Code* (or *NFPA 1*). Much of the *NFPA 1* is taken from various other codes and standards produced by NFPA, such as the *Life Safety Code*. When a specific requirement comes from another publication, the *NFPA 1* references the original document and section.

When adopted by a jurisdiction, the fire code is typically used in conjunction with a building code. The fire code addresses building conditions that are hazardous and could cause possible fire and explosions. This could be due to a number of reasons such as the type of occupancy or use of the space, the type of materials used or stored, and/or the way certain materials are handled. The fire code becomes more prevalent when working with a building type that may not be fully covered by the building code. For example, it includes specifics for a paint booth in a car shop, a commercial kitchen in a restaurant, and a dry-cleaning facility. However, a fire code also has additional general requirements that need to be met. For example, it includes information on fire extinguishers as well as interior elements not discussed in the building codes.

There are a few chapters or sections in the fire codes that will be referenced more frequently for interior projects. They include the following:

Means of Egress

Fire-Resistance-Rated Construction

Fire Protection Systems

Interior Finishes

Furnishings and Decorative Materials

These are similar to the chapters in the building codes. In addition, the fire codes include a chapter on emergency planning and preparedness, which addresses such things as evacuation plans and fire drills for each type of occupancy. Although this chapter is geared more toward building owners and fire departments, there are certain occupancy provisions that may also affect an interior project such as signage and keying requirements. Many of the various fire code requirements related to interiors and the chapters listed above will be mentioned throughout this book.

Life Safety Code®

The *Life Safety Code (LSC)* was one of the first codes published by the NFPA. It is also referred to as *NFPA 101*®. Like the building codes, the *LSC* is typically revised every 3 years. More current editions would include 2009 and 2012, yet a jurisdiction may still be using an older version. The *LSC* is not a building code. It is a life safety code that concentrates on problems involving the removal or evacuation of all persons from a building. The purpose of the code is to establish minimum requirements for the design, construction, operation, and maintenance of buildings as required to protect building occupants from danger caused by fire, smoke, and toxic fumes. The difference between the *LSC* and the building codes can also be seen in Figure 1.2. The *LSC* chapters correspond to those found in the building codes, but since it is not a building code, it does not address all the issues required for the construction of a building. For example, it does not include chapters on accessibility, glazing, or plumbing.

The *LSC* uses the NFPA's *Manual of Style* format. The first part of the *LSC* concentrates on the broad topics of occupancies, means of egress, fire protection, and interior-related items. The remainder is divided into chapters by occupancy classification for both new and existing buildings. For example, there is a chapter on new apartment buildings and existing apartment buildings. This distinction is made to provide older buildings with additional safety and protective devices so that they are virtually as safe as newly constructed buildings. (This is different from the *NFPA 5000*, which has only one chapter per occupancy and puts all existing requirements into one separate chapter.) Once the occupancy classification and if it is new or existing is determined, most of the research will be concentrated in one chapter of the *LSC*. The occupancy chapter will then refer to other chapters as required. (See Chapter 2 for more detail.)

Starting in 2000, the *LSC* also includes a chapter on alternative performance-based options. This provides the ability to select the requirements that best suit a specific project. (See the section Performance Codes earlier in this chapter and the inset titled *Performance Codes* on page 452.) Like other codes, the *LSC* also references additional code and standard publications. These are summarized in Chapter 2 of the *LSC*. (See also the section on the NFPA standards later in this chapter.)

The *LSC* is used throughout the United States and in several other countries. It is currently used in at least one jurisdiction in every state and has been adopted statewide by at least 43 states in the United States. (A map of the locations can be found on the NFPA Web site at www.nfpa.org.) It is not uncommon for a jurisdiction to adopt both the *IBC* and the *LSC*. When a jurisdiction requires both, the design must satisfy both sets of requirements. Sometimes a requirement in the *LSC* might conflict with one in the building code. When this occurs, the more restrictive requirement must be met. Or, if necessary, work with the local code official to determine the best way to satisfy the two codes. Throughout this book, many *LSC* requirements are discussed in relation to those found in the *IBC*.

◀ **Note**

The *Life Safety Code* does have another corresponding document, *NFPA 101A, Alternative Approaches to Life Safety.* A jurisdiction has the option of adopting this document with the *LSC* or in place of the *LSC*.

◀ **Note**

Beginning with the 2006 edition, the *LSC* now includes a new Chapter 43 titled "Building Rehabilitation."

Plumbing Codes

✎Note

The *IBC* also includes a chapter on plumbing fixtures that duplicates some of the information found in the *IPC*. This chapter and other plumbing requirements will be explained in Chapter 7 of this book.

The *International Plumbing Code (IPC)* was the first I-Code published by the ICC in 1995. The most current version of the *IPC* is 2009, and it will continue to be revised every 3 years. Also available in 2003 as part of NFPA's set of C3-Codes was the *Uniform Plumbing Code (UPC)*. Produced in conjunction with one of their partners, the International Association of Plumbing and Mechanical Officials (IAPMO), it was most recently updated and published by IAPMO in 2009. In addition, the Plumbing-Heating-Cooling Contractors Association is continuing to publish its *National Standard Plumbing Code (NSPC)*. The newest edition is 2009. Currently most code jurisdictions use the *IPC*.

Most of the chapters in the plumbing code are geared to the engineer and the licensed plumbing contractor. In a project requiring plumbing work, collaboration with a licensed engineer who will design the system is usually required. Notice in Figure 1.2 that both building codes have a chapter on plumbing systems as well. These chapters refer to the respective plumbing code. However, in the *IBC*, the plumbing chapter also includes the minimum plumbing facilities section of the *IPC* with the related table. (The 2009 *IBC* includes a section on toilet room requirements as well.) The plumbing fixture table and its related requirements found in the *IPC* will be discussed in this book. When designing interior projects, the plumbing code chapter is used to determine the minimum number and type of plumbing fixtures required for a particular occupancy classification. It also includes information on how to locate these fixtures in a building. These requirements as well as the code table will be discussed in more detail in Chapter 7.

Mechanical Codes

✎Note

The *Uniform Mechanical Code* was originally published as part of the legacy codes but has now been significantly modified and incorporated into NFPA's set of C3-Codes.

Similar to the plumbing codes, a mechanical code is also published by the same organizations. The *International Mechanical Code (IMC)* was first published by ICC in 1996. The more current editions include 2009 and 2012. It is widely accepted. In 2003 the *Uniform Mechanical Code (UMC)* became part of NFPA's set of C3-Codes. Published by IAPMO in partnership with NFPA, the *UMC* was originally published as part of the legacy codes but was significantly modified to meet the requirements of NFPA. Its newest edition is 2009. Jurisdictions may choose between the *IMC* and the *UMC*.

Again, as shown in Figure 1.2, each building code has a chapter on mechanical systems. However, this chapter refers to the respective mechanical code. The mechanical codes are geared to mechanical engineers and professional installers. A designer may rarely have to refer to the mechanical codes. However, familiarity with some of the general requirements and terminology is useful when designing an interior project. These are discussed in more detail in Chapter 7.

Electrical Codes

The *National Electrical Code (NEC)*, published by the NFPA, is one of the oldest codes. Originally published in the late 1800s, it is now part of the NFPA C3-Code set. The more current editions include 2008 and 2011. Also known as *NFPA 70*, the *NEC* is the most widely used electrical code and is the basis for electrical codes in almost all code jurisdictions. Even the ICC references this code. In 2000, the ICC published the first edition of the *ICC Electrical Code—Administrative Provisions (ICCEC)*. However, 2006 is the last edition and this document is being phased out by the ICC.

  The electrical chapter in the building codes (see Figure 1.2) references the *NEC*. In the *IBC*, this chapter also includes a section on emergency and standby power systems. (*IBC* editions prior to 2009 refer to the *ICCEC* which then references the *NEC*.) It is typically the responsibility of an engineer to design electrical systems using the *NEC*. On the other hand, when designing an interior project it is necessary to know certain basic electrical code requirements, especially when locating electrical outlets and fixtures and, when specifying light fixtures and other equipment. Therefore, it is important to have an understanding of this code (as well as the energy codes as explained next). The most common requirements are explained in Chapter 8.

> **◀ Note**
>
> The *ICCEC* is being phased out by the ICC; 2006 was the last edition. Now the electrical chapter in the *IBC* directly references the *NEC*.

> **◀ Note**
>
> Although some ISO standards are similar to standards found in the United States, there are often differences. They may seek similar results, for example, but use different equipment and/or means of measuring to determine the result.

Energy Codes

Both the ICC and the NFPA have an energy conservation code that establishes minimum requirements for energy-efficient buildings. The ICC has the *International Energy Conservation Code (IECC)*, which was first published in 1998; the most current edition is 2009. It includes prescriptive and performance-related provisions. It also covers both residential and commercial buildings, using an ASHRAE energy standard as an option for commercial requirements. A majority of states in the United States currently require the use of the *IECC*.

  In 2004 the NFPA came out with its first energy conservation code, titled *NFPA 900, Building Energy Code (BEC)*. Rather than creating a totally new code, the *NFPA 900* outlined the provisions required for administering and enforcing two ASHRAE energy standards. (Beginning in 2009, the *NFPA 900* has been incorporated into the National Fire Code Set and is no longer available as a stand-alone document.) The same requirements are also included in the *NFPA 5000*.

  The energy standards referenced by the ICC and NFPA codes are *ASHRAE 90.1, Energy Standard for Buildings Except Low-Rise Residential Buildings* (geared to commercial buildings) and *ASHRAE 90.2, Energy-Efficient Design of New Low-Rise Residential Buildings* (geared to residential homes). On a 3-year cycle, both standards were most recently updated in 2007 and 2010. For commercial buildings, the 2009

> **◀ Note**
>
> *ASHRAE 90.1* is a standard geared to energy efficiency in commercial buildings. As of December 2010, the DOE requires the use of the 2004 edition throughout the United States. (Newer editions might be required by a state or local code jurisdiction. See the section Energy Policy Act later in this chapter.)

CODES AND STANDARDS IN OTHER COUNTRIES

Building codes and standards are used throughout the world. Many countries and U.S. territories have developed their own set of building codes. Outside the United States, these codes are typically developed on a national level through government regulations and many are considered performance-based. (See the inset titled *Performance Codes* on page 452.) Other countries have worked with the International Code Council and/or the National Fire Protection Association to adopt one or more of their codes and standards. For example, the *International Building Code,* as well as various other I-Codes, has been adopted by Saudi Arabia, the Emirate of Abu Dhabi, Jamaica, the U.S. Virgin Islands, Puerto Rico, and Guam.

In an effort to globalize standard development and use, many of the U.S. standards organizations have facilities located in other countries. (See also the section Standards Organizations later in this chapter.) Examples include Underwriters Laboratories with offices in 17 countries and NSF International with 22 worldwide locations. In addition, ASTM International has signed a "Memorandum of Understanding" with over 60 countries which allows these countries to participate in the ASTM standards developing process.

One of the largest global standards-setting organizations, outside of the United States, is the International Organization for Standardization (ISO) with representation in more than 140 countries. For example, ISO standards are used extensively in Europe as well as Japan and China. Some ISO standards are referenced by codes in the United States. However, there is resistance to some ISO standards. Unlike U.S.-based standards which are approved by a wider membership base made up of individuals, the ISO global standards are approved on a national level with each country getting one vote. (Canada also produces standards on a national level using the Canadian Standards Organization.) In addition, certain ISO standards are considered "leadership standards" which potentially may exclude a majority of products and/or manufacturers in the market. (For more information see the insets titled *Codes and Standards Changes* on page 14 and *ISO Standards for Sustainability* on page 474.)

To help foster communication between various countries and code organizations, the Inter-jurisdictional Regulatory Collaboration Committee (IRCC) was formed in 1997. The IRCC provides a forum to exchange information on codes and to promote more inter-jurisdictional commerce, especially as it relates to performance-based codes. (To learn more go to www.irccbuildingregulations.org.)

IECC allows the use of Chapter 5 in the code or the 2007 edition of *ASHRAE 90.1*. In addition, the U.S. Department of Energy (DOE) has established this standard as a requirement under the federal Energy Policy Act (EPAct). In 2005, the DOE required all states to have energy codes in place that are at least as strict as the 2001 edition of the standard. By the end of 2010, all state energy codes must be at least as strict as the 2004 edition of the standard. (See the section Energy Policy Act later in this chapter.)

The building codes have a chapter on energy efficiency; however, the chapter simply references the respective energy code. Energy conservation codes address many sustainable aspects of a building, starting with the energy efficiency of the building envelope, which promotes adequate thermal resistance and low air leakage. For example, in an exterior wall the code will specify how much and what type of glass can be used and the rating of the wall insulation required. When designing the interior, the energy codes will include requirements to maximize the amount of daylight entering the space.

The energy codes also cover the design, selection, and installation of energy-efficient mechanical systems, water-heating systems, electrical distribution systems, and illumination systems. These requirements, as well as one of the codes tables in the *IECC*, will be further explained in Chapters 7 and 8. Other energy requirements related to the interior of a building will be mentioned throughout the book. (See also Appendix B for additional sustainability information.)

Sustainability Codes

Codes and standards dedicated to sustainable buildings is a fairly new concept in the United States. Building codes and standards have historically concentrated on the safety of a building and its occupants. Their purpose is to limit the potential hazards in the built environment. Sustainability codes and standards, however, focus on how the building affects the environment.

Some of the codes and standards discussed earlier in this chapter incorporate sustainability requirements. The energy codes are a strong example (see previous section). Other examples include the requirements for water-efficient fixtures and waterless urinals in the *International Plumbing Code (IPC)* and the various provisions for indoor air quality in several of the ICC codes. Various code jurisdictions have incorporated their own sustainable requirements as part of their code process. Some states even require the use of a sustainable rating system, such as LEED or Green Globes (see Appendix B), as part of the design and code process. (See Chapter 10 for more information.) As more jurisdictions and clients require sustainability measures to be incorporated into design and construction, additional sustainability code and standards will be developed.

The first comprehensive sustainability code was produced by the state of California. Adopted by the state in 2008, the *California Green Building Standards Code (CGBSC)* went into affect August of 2009. It applies to all types of occupancies and building types such as state buildings, housing, schools, hospitals, and correctional facilities. The *CGBSC* consists of multiple chapters, covering the

Note

The *IECC* includes both prescriptive requirements and performance criteria.

key sustainability features of a building. Some of the topics, such as water conservation and energy efficiency, are similar to requirements found in the energy codes. Other sections of the code introduce new requirements such as the use of life cycle assessments (LCAs) when selecting building products. (See Appendix B.) The monitoring of volatile organic compounds (VOCs) for a wide variety of building materials and finishes is also established. (See Chapter 9.) This code is unique because it references multiple Web sites, in addition to recognized standards, to set benchmarks that must be attained when selecting building materials and products. Sustainable product certifications are also referenced. (See Appendix B.) Application matrices and worksheets are provided to help implement and document the green aspects of the project while using the *CGBSC*.

The *CGBSC* was used by the ICC in the development of their new sustainable code. Available in early 2012 and titled the *International Green Construction Code (IGCC)*, it covers similar provisions as the *CGBSC*. (Prior to its final release, some jurisdictions adopted earlier drafts known as "public versions." Discussion of these requirements are included in this book.) Before creating their green code, the ICC collaborated with the National Association of Home Builders (NAHB) to create a sustainable standard. Released in 2008, it is known as *ICC 700, National Green Building Standard*. (See the section International Code Council later in this chapter.) However, this standard concentrates on residential occupancies. The *IGCC* is more comprehensive and covers a wide variety of occupancies and building types.

The ICC developed the *IGCC* to coordinate with the other I-Codes. As shown in Figure 1.3, it covers a wide range of topics from conservation of materials, water, and energy to land use and environmental quality. It also includes a chapter on existing buildings as well as building operations and owner education. Similar to the *CGBSC* it uses performance benchmarks throughout the code to emphasize the outcome instead of specific design mandates. What makes it unique from the other I-Codes is that it provides "compliance electives" within each chapter so that a jurisdiction can more easily customize the code to its needs, allowing for regional differences, variation in site locations, and advanced levels of performance. (Checklists are provided within the code so that the project designer can also select compliance electives.) In addition, the *IGCC* includes the sustainability standard *ASHRAE 189.1* as an alternate path of compliance. (See the section American Society of Heating, Refrigeration, and Air-Conditioning Engineers later in this chapter.)

This book will discuss the sustainable-related codes and standards, as they relate to the various topics and code provisions discussed throughout this book. (See the section Standards Organizations later in this chapter for information on various sustainable standards.)

ICC International Green Construction Code (2012)		ANSI/ASHRAE/USGBC/IES	
[based on Public Version 2—November 2010]		Standard 189.1 (2009)	
Chapter 1	Administration	**Section 1**	Purpose
		Section 2	Scope
		Section 4	Administration and Enforcement
Chapter 2	Definitions	**Section 3**	Definitions, Abbreviations, and Acronyms
Chapter 3	Jurisdictional Requirements and Project Electives	**Section 4**	Administration and Enforcement
Chapter 4	Site Development and Land Use	**Section 5**	Site Sustainability
Chapter 5	Material Resource Conservation and Efficiency	**Section 9**	The Building's Impact on the Atmosphere, Materials, and Resources
Chapter 6	Energy Conservation, Efficiency and Atmospheric Quality	**Section 7**	Energy Efficiency
Chapter 7	Water Resource Conservation and Efficiency	**Section 6**	Water Use Efficiency
Chapter 8	Indoor Environmental Quality and Comfort	**Section 8**	Indoor Environmental Quality (IEQ)
Chapter 9	Commissioning, Operation and Maintenance	**Section 10**	Construction and Plans for Operation
Chapter 10	Existing Buildings		
Chapter 11	Existing Building Site Development		
Chapter 12	Referenced Standards	**Section 11**	Normative References

Figure 1.3 Comparison of sustainability publications. (This chart is a summary of information contained in the ICC *International Green Construction Code* and the *ANSI/ASHRAE/USGBC/IES Standard 189.1*. The various organizations do not assume responsibility for the accuracy or completeness of this chart.)

Residential Codes

The *International Residential Code (IRC)*, published by the ICC, first became available in 1998. The more current editions include 2009 and 2012. It is the main code used for the construction of single-family and duplex residences and townhouses. It covers the typical residential home that is not more than three stories in height and has a separate means of egress. All other types of residential uses would be regulated by a building code. For example, if working on a house that is over three stories or an apartment building where there are more than two dwelling units, a building code would need to be used instead of the *IRC*. The *IRC* is a stand-alone code, meaning that it covers all construction aspects of the building without having to refer to other code documents. In addition to the typical building code chapters, it includes complete chapters on mechanical, electrical, plumbing, and energy requirements.

◄**Note**

Refer to Appendix D for more information on codes for single-family homes.

The NFPA does not have a separate residential code. Instead, it covers the building aspects of single-family homes in its other codes. For example, the *Life Safety Code* has an occupancy chapter titled "One- and Two-Family Dwellings." This chapter provides specific requirements and refers to other chapters in the text that provide exceptions for single-family homes. This chapter also refers to other NFPA codes as well as to multiple NFPA standards that are appropriate for one- and two-family dwellings. If a jurisdiction requires the *IRC* in addition to an NFPA code, the most restrictive requirements should be followed. (Although this book concentrates more on commercial projects, codes and standards specifically for residential homes are briefly discussed in Appendix D.)

Existing Building Codes

The building codes, as well as the *Life Safety Code*, dedicate an entire chapter to existing buildings. (The *LSC* also includes existing occupancy chapters throughout its text.) However, in 2003 the ICC published the first *International Existing Building Code (IEBC)*. The most current edition is 2009. It is dedicated entirely to existing buildings, providing requirements for reasonable upgrades and improvements, depending on the type and extent of the work.

If a jurisdiction has not adopted the *IEBC*, the appropriate chapter in the building code and/or *LSC* will apply. However, if the *IEBC* is allowed, the extent of work (i.e., repair, alteration, or addition) will determine the level of code compliance. In some cases, the requirements will be more lenient than those in the building code. The *IEBC* also includes both prescriptive and performance-related provisions. All of this is explained in more detail in Appendix C. (Although this book concentrates on codes for new construction, many of the same requirements apply to new work being done in existing buildings. For more detailed information on codes for historic and existing buildings, see Appendix C.)

⊟Note

Design and construction projects in existing buildings typically require the use of the building codes. However, a jurisdiction may also have the option of using the *IEBC*. See Appendix C for more information.

⊟Note

Government regulations can be required on a federal, state, or local level. Most of the regulations discussed in this book are federal regulations required throughout the United States. Check for required state and local regulations as well.

FEDERAL REGULATIONS

A number of federal agencies and departments work with trade associations, private companies, and the general public to develop federal laws for building construction. These regulations are published in the *Federal Register (FR)* and the *Code of Federal Regulations (CFR)*. The *FR* is published daily and includes the newest updates for each federal agency. However, not all rules published in the *FR* are enforceable laws. Typically, a federal agency must review the regulations published in the *FR* and make a formal ruling. Once the regulations are passed into law, they are published in the *CFR*. The *CFR* is revised annually to include all permanent agency rules.

The federal government plays a part in the building process in a number of ways. First, it regulates the building of its own facilities. These include federal buildings, Veterans Administration (VA) hospitals, and military establishments as well as other buildings built with federal funds. The construction of a federal building is usually not subject to state and local building codes and regulations. Instead, each federal agency has criteria and regulations that must be met when constructing a new building or renovating an existing one. For example, the Department of Defense or the Department of Transportation might have certain building requirements and regulations that are not required by the Department of Justice.

More recently, however, the federal government has begun to adopt more codes and standards from the private sector rather than create its own. This trend became more prevalent with the passing of the National Technology Transfer and Advancement Act (NTTAA) of 1995, which establishes the responsibility for federal agencies to use national voluntary consensus standards instead of developing their own, wherever practical. Many federal agencies have been working with the ICC and the NFPA as well as standards organizations such as the American National Standards Institute (ANSI) to adopt existing codes and standards. (See Standards Organizations later in this chapter.) For example, multiple federal agencies require the use of the *Life Safety Code (LSC)*, and the Department of Defense requires the use of the *International Building Code (IBC)*. In some cases, federal agencies collaborate with other organizations to develop new documents. Some of these are discussed in this chapter. When working on a federally owned or funded building, contact the appropriate federal agency to determine which codes and standards apply. Keep in mind that more than one federal agency could be involved.

Another way the federal government plays a part in the building process is by passing legislation creating a law that supersedes all other state and local codes and standards. Each piece of legislation is created by a specific federal agency. When passed into law, it becomes mandatory nationwide. This is typically done to create a uniform level of standards throughout the country. The Americans with Disabilities Act (ADA) is one example. Although there is a wide variety of legislation covering everything from energy to transportation, only the pertinent laws that pertain to the design of interiors are discussed in this section and throughout this book.

Note

The Occupational Safety and Health Act (OSHA) is another federal regulation affecting building interiors. It stresses the safe installation of materials and equipment to ensure a safe work environment for construction workers and building occupants. It must be strictly observed by building contractors.

Note

The NTTAA gives the National Institute of Standards and Technology (NIST) the authority to assist with coordination between federal agencies and the private sector. To find out more, go to www.nist.gov.

ACCESSIBILITY REQUIREMENTS COMPARED

There are multiple accessibility documents that may apply to an interior project. Although in many ways they are similar, none of them match exactly. It is important to know which document applies to a project. The documents are summarized here and explained in more detail throughout this chapter.

ANSI A117.1 was originally developed by the American National Standards Institute (ANSI) and was one of the first accessibility standards used throughout the United States. The 1998 edition, known as *ICCI/ANSI A117.1,* was developed in conjunction with the ICC. The more current 2003 and 2009 editions were developed by the ICC with the Access Board to be more consistent with the new *ADA-ABA Accessibility Guidelines.*

The *Americans with Disabilities Act Accessibility Guidelines (ADAAG)* was developed by the Access Board as guidelines for the ADA legislation. Originally based on the 1986 *ANSI A117.1,* only minor updates have been made to it since its inception. More recently, the Access Board developed a new document to replace the *ADAAG,* combining it with the *Uniform Federal Accessibility Standards (UFAS),* to create the new 2004 *ADA-ABA Accessibility Guidelines.* The new guidelines share technical requirements but provide separate scoping requirements for each legislation. The ADA portion of the new guidelines is known as the *2010 ADA Standards.* (See also Appendix A.)

The *UFAS* was originally developed as the guidelines for the ABA legislation and is based on the 1980 ANSI standard. This document applied to federal buildings. However, the *UFAS* has been replaced with the new *ABA Standards,* which is the ABA portion of the 2004 *ADA-ABA Accessibility Guidelines.* (See Appendix A.) A project that uses federal funding may be required to meet both ADA and ABA requirements. In the past, state and local governments had the option of using the *ADAAG* or the *UFAS;* however, the *2010 ADA Standards* replaces this option.

The *Fair Housing Accessibility Guidelines (FHAG)* was developed in 1991 as part of the Fair Housing Act (FHA). Based on the 1986 *ANSI A117.1,* it provides accessibility requirements specifically for multi-unit housing that consists of four or more dwelling units and can include apartments as well as other building types such as dormitories and assisted living facilities.

The building codes, such as the *International Building Code,* also include a chapter on accessibility. This chapter specifies when an accessible feature is required and then references the ICC/ANSI standard for the details. Both documents must be used together. In addition, starting in 2003, the *IBC* Chapter 11 has become more consistent with the standard as well as the new ADA-ABA guidelines.

Because the various agencies and organizations continue to work together, these separate accessibility documents are becoming more similar in scope and organization. However, each document still has some unique requirements and different characteristics. Although the ICC/ANSI standard is referenced in the building codes, the various federal laws are not. Therefore, all applicable documents must be reviewed for the most stringent accessibility requirements. In some cases, more than one federal document will apply to a project. There may also be additional and/or conflicting state or local accessibility codes that need to be considered.

Accessibility requirements are addressed throughout this book. Typically, the most restrictive requirements are used. Any conflicting requirements are explained.

Americans with Disabilities Act

The Americans with Disabilities Act (ADA) is a four-part federal law that was enacted on July 26, 1990, and became enforceable beginning in 1992. Prior to this, only federal buildings and federally funded projects had to comply with similar legislation under the Architectural Barriers Act (ABA) and its related *Uniform Federal Accessibility Standards* (as explained later). With the passing of the ADA, many other types of projects are required to meet accessibility guidelines as outlined by the various titles of the law.

The ADA is a comprehensive civil rights law that protects individuals with disabilities in the areas of employment (Title I), state and local government services and public transportation (Title II), public accommodations and commercial facilities (Title III), and telecommunication services (Title IV). The ADA was developed by the Department of Justice (DOJ) and the Department of Transportation (DOT).

The regulations that will apply most often to interior projects are found in Title II and Title III. However, Title IV also applies, since it requires telephone companies to provide telecommunication relay services for the hearing and speech impaired. When specifying public telephones, these requirements must be considered.

Title II would apply when working on state or local government buildings or public transportation facilities. Title III covers all other public accommodations (any facility that offers food, merchandise, or services to the public) and commercial facilities (nonresidential buildings that do business but are not open to the general public). The intent of Title III is to regulate the design and construction of buildings so that persons with disabilities can use them. These regulations were incorporated into the *Americans with Disabilities Act Accessibility Guidelines (ADAAG)* as developed by the Architectural and Transportation Barriers Compliance Board (ATBCB or U.S. Access Board) and first published in 1991. The *ADAAG* deals with architectural concerns, such as accessible routes and restrooms, and communication concerns, such as visible alarm systems and signage.

The Access Board continually works with other organizations to conduct research and create new documents. Some of the research is used to create proposed additions to the ADA guidelines, while other research is used to create guidance materials, such as checklists and technical bulletins, which can be used to gain additional insight. A few minor changes were incorporated into the *ADAAG* since 1991; however, with the adoption of the new *ADA-ABA Accessibility Guidelines*, the *ADAAG* can no longer be used as of March 2012. (See the section New *ADA Standards* in Appendix A for timelines for the use of the appropriate document.) To keep abreast of the latest changes and rulings, go to www.access-board.gov.

✒ Note

The Access Board, ICC, and NFPA have all created comparison documents of the accessibility requirements found in each of their respective publications. These documents can be found on their Web sites.

✒ Note

The Access Board researches accessibility needs and is responsible for updating the ADA guidelines and providing other guidance materials. To review materials available from the Access Board, go to www.access-board.gov.

✒ Note

The new *ADA-ABA Accessbility Guidelines* and the 2003 ICC/ANSI standard provide alternate accessible requirements for children. If designing a building or space to be used primarily by children 12 years of age or younger, consult these documents.

The Access Board worked with other agencies and organizations to combine the rquirements of the *ADAAG* with the *UFAS*, which is used for federal buildings, to create the *ADA-ABA Accessibility Guidelines*. This document was published in July 2004. It is currently required by most government agencies (see the section Architectural Barriers Act later in this chapter), as well as most public accommodations and commercial facilities. The ADA portion of these new guidelines are referred to as the *2010 ADA Standards*. (The original *ADAAG* is now referred to as the *1991 ADA Standards* by the Access Board. See also Appendix A.)

The most comprehensive revision to date, these requirements are organized to more closely correspond to the accessibility chapters in the building codes and other industry standards. The ICC worked closely with the Access Board to assist with its organization as well as reduce the differences in the accessibility provisions in its more current editions of the *IBC*. In fact, the 2010 *ADA Standards* references the *IBC* for means of egresses and references several other code-based standards. The newer editions of the ICC/ANSI standard, *ICC/ANSI A117.1*, have also been harmonized with the new document. (See the section International Code Council later in this chapter.)

Although ADA regulations are mandatory, they will not be the only guidelines for accessibility issues that need to be followed. Figure 1.4 summarizes the organization of the *2010 ADA Standards* as compared to the 1998 and 2003 ICC/ANSI standards and the accessibility chapter in the *IBC*. Note, however, that as each document is updated some discrepancies will continue to occur. In addition, some states, such as California and North Carolina, have adopted their own accessibility requirements. If using the *IBC*, these states typically elect not to use the accessibility chapter (Chapter 11) in the building code. Research, compare, and follow the most stringent requirements for a jurisdiction while maintaining the minimum federal requirements. (See the inset titled *Accessibility Requirements Compared* on page 32. Other aspects of ADA, such as the varying levels of compliance and responsibility for compliance, are discussed further in Appendix A.)

> **◢ Note**
>
> The *2010 ADA Standards* and the *ABA Standards* are derived from the *ADA-ABA Accessibility Guidelines*. These guidelines include separate scoping requirements for the ADA and the ABA but share the same technical requirements.

> **◢ Note**
>
> The 2009 editions of the ICC and NFPA codes reference the 2003 ICC/ANSI standard. They have also been written to harmonize with the 2004 *ADA-ABA Accessibility Guidelines*.

> **◢ Note**
>
> The Appendix of the original *ADAAG* provides additional guidelines that enhance and clarify the main text. The new *ADA-ABA Accessibility Guidelines* (and *2010 ADA Standards*) insert similar notes throughout the text. Although they are helpful, they are not binding.

Fair Housing Act

The Fair Housing Act (FHA) is federal legislation enforced by the Department of Housing and Urban Development (HUD) in partnership with the DOJ. Originally established in 1968, the FHA regulates fair housing and protects the consumer from discrimination in housing when buying or renting. In 1988, the FHA was expanded to include persons with disabilities. The FHA prohibits discrimination because of race, color, national origin, religion, sex, family status, or disability. Although the FHA is not specifically accessibility legislation, it does incorporate a number of provisions for people with disabilities and families with children.

ICC/ANSI A117.1 (2003) Accessibility Standard		ADA Standards (2010)		IBC (2009) Chapter 11: Accessibility	
Chapter 1	Application and Administration	Chapter 1	Application and Administration	Section 1101 Section 1102	General Definitions
Chapter 2	Scoping	Chapter 2	Scoping Requirements	Section 1103	Scoping Requirements
Chapter 3	Building Blocks	Chapter 3	Building Blocks (basic technical requirements)	(not included—references ICC/ANSI A117.1)	
Chapter 4	Accessible Routes	Chapter 4	Accessible Routes	Section 1104	Accessible Route
Chapter 5	General Site and Building Elements	Chapter 5	General Site and Building Elements	Section 1105 Section 1106	Accessible Entrances Parking and Passenger Loading Facilities
Chapter 6	Plumbing Elements and Facilities	Chapter 6	Plumbing Elements and Facilities	Section 1109	Other Features and Facilities
Chapter 7	Communication Elements and Features	Chapter 7	Communication Elements and Features	Section 1110 Sections 1108	Signage Special Occupancies
Chapter 8	Special Rooms and Spaces	Chapter 8	Special Rooms, Spaces, and Elements	Sections 1108	Special Occupancies
Chapter 9	Built-in Furnishings and Equipment	Chapter 9	Built-in Elements	Section 1109	Other Features and Facilities
Chapter 10	Dwelling Units and Sleeping Units		(distributed throughout other chapters)	Section 1107	Dwelling Units and Sleeping Units
	(not included)	Chapter 10	Recreation Facilities		(not included)

Figure 1.4 Comparison of accessibility publications. (This chart is a summary of information contained in the *ICC/ANSI A117.1* standard, the *ADA Standards*, and Chapter 11 of the *IBC*. The ICC, ANSI, and the Access Board do not assume responsibility for the accuracy or completeness of this chart.)

The FHA regulations may apply to private housing, private housing that receives federal financial assistance, and state and local government housing. The FHA typically pertains to residential housing that has four or more dwelling units, such as apartments and condominiums. The ADA generally covers the places of public accommodation in these facilities, such as the related sales and rental offices; the FHA covers additional accessibility requirements. In 1991, HUD developed the final *Fair Housing Accessibility Guidelines (FHAG)* to help clarify these requirements. Many of the interior aspects of a dwelling are regulated, such as the location of thermostats, electrical outlets, light switches, and maneuvering areas in hallways, bathrooms, and kitchens. In addition, at least the ground-floor units must be accessible and meet specific construction requirements. HUD also

◁**Note**

The 2003 and 2006 *IBC* and the 2003 *ICC/ANSI A117.1* were approved by HUD as "safe harbor" documents. The 2000 *IBC* when used with the 2001 *Supplement to the International Codes* is also considered a safe harbor document.

enforces Title II of the ADA when it relates to state and local public housing, housing assistance, and housing referrals; these types of projects may need to follow additional requirements based on the ADA requirements.

HUD also endorses other documents as being equivalent to the most current version of the *FHAG*. Once it is approved by HUD, the document is given a "safe harbor" status, which means that it meets or exceeds the requirements in the *FHAG*. The 2003 *IBC*, the 2006 *IBC* (with a January 31, 2007 erratum), and the 2003 *ICC/ANSI A117.1* have been approved as safe harbor documents. The 2009 *IBC* will most likely be approved as well. If using one of these safe harbor documents, the project should be in compliance with the *FHAG*.

Architectural Barriers Act

The Architectural Barriers Act (ABA), which became law in 1968, was the first federal legislation that addressed accessibility. It applies to a wide variety of federal buildings, such as post offices, social security offices, prisons, and national park facilities. It also applies to nongovernment facilities that are designed, built, altered, or leased with federal funds such as certain schools, public housing, and mass transit facilities.

The ABA created the Architectural and Transportation Barriers Compliance Board (ATBCB or U.S. Access Board) and charged it with the development of the *Uniform Federal Accessibility Standards (UFAS)* to be used as guidelines for the ABA. First issued in 1989, the *UFAS* provides minimum requirements for construction and alteration of facilities covered by the law. However, the *UFAS* has been replaced with the new *ABA Standards*. The *ABA Standards* are derived from the 2004 *ADA-ABA Accessibility Guidelines*. (See Appendix A.) The four agencies responsible for these standards include the General Services Administration (GSA) which is responsible for most federal buildings, as well as the Department of Defense (DOD) for military facilities, the Department of Housing and Urban Development (HUD) for government housing, and the U.S. Postal Service (USPS) for postal facilities.

Even though federal buildings are not currently required to conform to ADA regulations, a project that uses federal funding may be required to meet both the *ADA Standards* and the *ABA Standards*. In the past, state and local governments typically had the option of using the *ADAAG* or the *UFAS*; however, the *2010 ADA Standards* replaces this option. The new *ADA-ABA Accessibility Guidelines* share the technical requirements; although there are still separate scoping requirements for the ADA and the ABA legislation. Most federal agencies require the use of the *ABA Standards*. (See the inset titled *ADA-ABA Accessibility Guidelines Enforcement* on page 461.)

Energy Policy Act

The Energy Policy Act (EPAct) was enacted by the federal government in 1992 to promote energy efficiency and conservation. Among other things, it amended Title III of the Energy Conservation and Production Act (ECPA), mandating the use of the 1989 edition of the sustainability standard *ASHRAE/IESNA 90.1, Energy Standard for Buildings Except Low-Rise Residential Buildings* as the minimum standard for all new commercial and high-rise residential buildings. (See the section American Society of Heating, Refrigeration, and Air-Conditioning Engineers later in this chapter.) All states were required to adopt this standard or create an acceptable alternate energy model.

Enforced by the U.S. Department of Energy (DOE), the EPAct was updated again in 2005. In addition to requiring states to now use the 2001 edition of the *ASHRAE/IESNA 90.1* standard, the act includes other legislation such as labeling requirements for electrical devices, tax deduction provisions for commercial buildings, and specific requirements for federally built and/or funded buildings. For example, all new nonresidential federal buildings must exceed the 2001 standard by 30 percent. And, every energy-efficient product purchased by a federal agency is required to be either an ENERGY STAR® product or one designated by DOE's Federal Energy Management Program (FEMP). Beginning in 2011, the 2004 edition of the standard is required by the DOE. (See Chapter 8.)

Inspection and testing for building compliance is the responsibility of the U.S. Secretary of the Treasury and is still being developed. However, compliance with the EPAct is mandated at the state level, which means that jurisdictions will be required to use the 2004 (or newer) edition of *ASHRAE/IESNA 90.1* (or an energy code that references the appropriate edition). Compliance at the project level, therefore, is part of the code process. (See Chapter 10.)

✎Note

Another federal legislation titled the 2007 Energy Independence and Security Act requires all federal facilities to reduce energy use by 30 percent by 2015. It also gradually halts the use of inefficient incandescent lamps and requires improved energy standards on numerous products.

✎Note

The Department of Homeland Security (DHS) continues to encourage the development and adoption of standards which relate to national security. Standards that DHS adopts are not mandatory; however, they may be required if working on a building or space accepting DHS funds.

STANDARDS ORGANIZATIONS

A standard is a definition, a recommended practice, a test method, a classification, or a required specification that must be met. Standards are developed by trade associations, government agencies, and standards-writing organizations where members are often allowed to vote on specific issues. The size of these groups can range from a worldwide organization to a small trade association that develops one or two industry-related standards.

By themselves, standards have no legal standing. Instead, they are typically referenced by the codes. The standards become law when the code is adopted by a jurisdiction. (In some cases, a jurisdiction will adopt an individual standard which will then supplement the code. For example, some jurisdictions are

✎Note

Each code publication has a chapter listing the standards mentioned throughout its text. This list will indicate which edition of the standard is required. This required standard is sometimes referred to as the *active* standard.

adopting sustainable standards.) Typically, instead of giving all the details, a code will establish the minimum quality and performance criteria for a particular material or method. The code will then reference a standard, which sets the conditions or requirements for the material or method to meet. This allows the codes to provide specific instructions without going into great detail. For example, instead of setting specific fire extinguisher requirements, the *International Building Code (IBC)* references the *NFPA 10, Portable Fire Extinguishers*. *NFPA 10* then becomes a part of the enforced building code.

When a standard is referenced, the acronym of the standard organization and a standard number is called out. For example, *ASTM E84* is an American Society for Testing and Materials standard known as *E84*. It is a standard method of testing the burning characteristics of building materials. The reference also typically includes the year of the required edition (e.g., *ASTM E84-07* is the 2007 edition of the standard). When it is listed in a code publication, note the year to make sure the correct edition is being used and/or referenced. Although the year might not be used when mentioned within the text, each code publication includes a separate list of all the standards referenced within the text. This list will include the year or edition of the standard to be used.

The most common standards organizations that pertain to interior projects are described in this section. Each develops a wide variety of standards. Some may need to be examined in detail prior to designing an interior project. Others may only need mentioning in the specifications of the project. The most common standards that pertain to interior projects are discussed throughout this book. (See also the inset titled *Industry Standards* on page 380.)

American National Standards Institute

The American National Standards Institute (ANSI) publishes the *American National Standard (ANS)*. ANSI is a private corporation that was founded in 1918 as the American Engineering Standards Committee. It is a coordinator of voluntary standards development. ANSI does not develop standards. Rather it establishes a method by which standards can be developed and defined. This process is known as the ANS consensus process. (See also the inset titled *Code and Standards Changes* on page 14.)

Presently, there are more than 220 organizations that use the ANS process. Accredited organizations include code and standards organizations, industry trade associations as well as sustainable-related organizations. The ICC and NFPA, as well as most of the standards organizations described below, use this process to develop new standards. By representing virtually every facet of trade, commerce, organized labor, and the consumer, ANSI's approval procedures ensure a consensus of interests. They are widely accepted on an international level, and local jurisdictions often require compliance with ANSI standards.

One of the most common ANSI-designated standards used by designers for interior projects is *ANSI A117.1*. Its full title is *ICC/ANSI A117.1, Standard on Accessible and Usable Buildings and Facilities*. It was first published by ANSI in 1961; however, it is now updated and published by the ICC (see below). Although many standards organizations use the ANS process, using the ANSI designation as part of the standard's title is optional.

Overall, ANSI acts as a watchdog of the standards industry. In addition to maintaining a standardization process, it helps to establish priorities and avoid duplication between different standards. ANSI now also offers third-party certification which is an important part of sustainable codes and standards. (See Appendix B.)

≝Note

The ANS consensus process is used by many standards organizations, including the ICC for the development of its standards and the NFPA for the development of both its codes and standards.

National Fire Protection Association

The National Fire Protection Association (NFPA) was originally founded in 1896 to develop standards for the early use of sprinklers. Today it is one of the largest standards organizations. It develops and publishes more than 300 different standards, many of which are referenced in the codes and used internationally. Each document is available from NFPA in book or booklet form.

As mentioned earlier in this chapter, NFPA also publishes a full set of codes known as the C3-Codes. All of the NFPA codes, as well as those produced by the ICC, reference the NFPA standards in their text. Many of the NFPA standards are geared to fire protection. Generally, they are designed to reduce the extent of injury, loss of life, and destruction of property during a fire. Their testing requirements cover everything from textiles to fire-fighting equipment and means of egress design. The standards are developed by committees made up of NFPA members using the ANS process. (See the inset titled *Code and Standards Changes* on page 14.) They are reviewed and updated as needed. Similar to the C3-Codes, the newer standards and the most current editions of the existing standards have been formatted to meet NFPA's new *Manual of Style* format. Many of the NFPA standards as they relate to building interiors will be discussed throughout this book.

≝Note

When a code requirement varies from that of a standard referenced by the code, the code requirement takes precedence over the standard.

International Code Council

The International Code Council (ICC) is predominately known for its set of I-Codes. However, ICC can be considered a standards organization as well. It currently has six standards available. Known as I-Standards, the ICC uses the ANS process to create and update them. (See the inset titled *Code and Standards Changes* on page 14.) The most popular standard is *ICC/ANSI A117.1, Guidelines for the*

✍ Note

The IBC has a chapter dedicated to accessibility requirements, which references the *ANSI/ICC A117.1* accessibility standard. The 2009 edition of the code references the 2003 ICC/ANSI standard. (See Figure 1.4.)

✍ Note

In addition to its own standards, ICC now publishes four separate volumes of standards produced by other standards organizations to be used in conjunction with the I-Codes. These include standards by ASTM International, AWPA, NSF International, and UL.

✍ Note

When using the NGBS, the building must be designed to perform at the highest level in each section of the standard before the building as a whole can achieve the next level of recognition.

Accessible and Usable Buildings and Facilities (referred to as the "ICC/ANSI standard" throughout this book).

The ICC/ANSI standard concentrates on the accessibility features in the design of buildings and their interiors, allowing people with disabilities to achieve independence. It was the first standard written for accessibility and is the most widely known with various editions used as the basis for the *ADAAG*, the *UFAS*, and the *FHAG*. (See the inset titled *Accessibility Requirements Compared* on page 32.) The building codes reference it as well. In addition to the many requirements included in the standard, the ICC/ANSI standard refers to other industry standards for certain items such as power-operated doors, elevator/escalators, and signaling systems.

The 2003 edition of the ICC/ANSI standard was developed by the ICC in conjunction with the Access Board to create consistency between the accessibility chapter in the *IBC* and the 2004 *ADA-ABA Accessibility Guidelines*. A comparison of the various sections in the 2003 ICC/ANSI standard and *2010 ADA Standards* is shown in Figure 1.4. The figure also includes the comparable sections of the 2009 *IBC* which references the 2003 ICC/ANSI standard. (Note that there is a newer edition of the standard, which became available in early 2011, known simply as *2009 ICC A117.1*, that some states may adopt. Some states may have their own accessibility requirements as well.)

Other ICC standards are more building-type specific, such as the *ICC 300, Bleachers, Folding and Telescopic Seating, and Grandstands*, or are not interior-related. The most recent I-Standard is *ICC 700, National Green Building Standard* (or *NGBS*). Published in 2008, this standard was developed in conjunction with and published by the National Association of Home Builders (NAHB). The *NGBS* was written to coordinate with the I-Codes and was created specifically for residential buildings including single-family and multi-family homes, home remodeling/additions, and hotels/motels—as long as they are not classified as Institutional Occupancies (as explained in Chapter 2).

The *NGBS* is unique in that, in addition to setting minimum requirements, it uses a point system to rate the environmental impact of the design and construction of a building. Similar to LEED or Green Globes green rating systems (see Appendix B), it allows a project to accumulate points as sustainable requirements in different sections of the code are incorporated into the project. These sections include lot preparation and design, resource efficiency, energy efficiency, water efficiency, indoor environmental quality, and operation and maintenance. The standard allows the design to take two different paths, either a prescriptive path or a performance path. In each case, as more sustainable practices are used, more points are attained so that a building can be classified as one of the four threshold levels: Bronze, Silver, Gold, or Emerald. (See also the sections Sustainability Considerations in Appendix C and Appendix D for more information.)

Specific sections of the *NGBS* can be selected by a jurisdiction to establish a minimum level of compliance specific to their needs. For example, a jurisdiction may require all new residential buildings to meet the minimum threshold of Silver. Or, if water conservation was critical in that jurisdiction, the water conservation section of the standard might require a higher Gold rating while the remaining sections may only require a Silver rating. Since the thresholds are part of an enforceable standard, the requirements are reviewed by the code official as part of the code process.

TESTING AGENCIES AND CERTIFICATION

Standards affect the way building materials and other products are made. Many of these standards are required by the building codes. Others are required by the federal government or a code jurisdiction. For example, some jurisdictions are already requiring building products that meet some level of sustainability. In addition, there are optional industry standards that are available for specification. (See also the inset titled *Industry Standards* on page 380.)

Building materials and products for interior projects must meet the required standards and related tests. Manufacturers typically use outside testing agencies to obtain third-party certification of their products. There are a number of independent testing agencies and certification organizations in the United States and throughout the world that have been approved to perform these tests. A manufacturer will either send them a component or a finished product, which is then tested and evaluated.

Tested products are given a permanent label or certificate to prove that they pass a required standard. Depending on the test and the specific standard, the manufacturer will either attach a label to the product or keep a certificate on file. For example, a fire-rated door will typically have a label on the edge of the door or rated glazing might have the details etched into the glass. Other materials, such as carpets or wallcoverings, might not be easily labeled. Instead, these labels may be located on samples or available from the manufacturer upon request.

Often, these testing agencies and certification organizations have their own mark of approval. Underwriters Laboratories (UL) labels are a common example. (See the inset titled *UL Labels* on page 45.) There are also several government-based certifications, such as ENERGY STAR® and WaterSense®, in addition to sustainable-related certifications, such as Green Seal, GREENGUARD, and FSC Certified. Some manufacturers are developing more comprehensive Environmental Product Declarations (EPD) and Life Cycle Assessments (LCA) as well. (See Appendix B.)

The codes, standards, and federal regulations typically require that tested and/or certified products be specified. It is also important to keep records of the specified products. (This is discussed more in the section Documentation and Liability in Chapter 10.)

ASTM International

The American Society for Testing and Materials (ASTM) is a standards-writing organization formed in 1898 as a nonprofit corporation. In 2002, it changed its name to ASTM International to reflect its global reach and participation. ASTM International primarily manages the development of standards and the promotion of related technical knowledge received from over 30,000 members around the world. There are numerous ASTM committees and subcommittees set up to review and manage all this information.

There are more than 12,000 ASTM standards used to specify materials, assure quality, integrate production processes, promote trade, and enhance safety. Developed using the ANS process, they are updated and/or published each year in a multiple-volume *Annual Book of ASTM Standards*. These standards are divided into 15 different categories, 2 of which include construction and textiles. Many of the ASTM standards are referenced in the codes and other reference materials. Copies of these standards can be obtained from ASTM International. In addition, they publish a special grouping of standards for the building construction industry. In 2003, ASTM International worked with the ICC to develop a comprehensive volume that contains all the standards that are referenced in the *IBC*. It is updated every 3 years to coincide with the publication of the *IBC*. Titled *ASTM Standards: As Referenced in the 2009 IBC*, the 2009 edition contains the *IBC* standards as well as numerous others related to code inspection, and so forth. The NFPA codes reference some of these standards as well.

ASTM International is taking an active role in coordinating the development of sustainable standards. The first two available standards, *E2114, Terminology for Sustainability Relative to the Performance of Buildings*, and *E2129, Practice for Data Collection for Sustainability Assessment of Building Products*, establish the basic vocabulary and methodology for the practice of sustainable design. Developed in 2005, *ASTM E2432, Guide for General Principles of Sustainability Relative to Buildings* has been instrumental in setting basic principles from which other sustainable standards can be developed. (See also Appendix B.) Although not referenced by the codes, they are used by manufacturers to evaluate new sustainable products and by standards organization to develop additional sustainable standards. In 2009, ASTM indicated the intent to develop certification programs so that it will be able to provide independent third-party certification for sustainable programs.

NSF International

The National Sanitation Foundation (NSF) formed in 1944. Now known as NSF International, it is a standards organization that focuses on food, water, indoor air, and the environment. Using the ANS process, NSF International has developed

✎Note

The largest international standards-setting organization is the International Organization for Standardization (ISO), with national standards bodies in more than 140 countries. Few ISO standards are referenced in the ICC or NFPA codes. See Appendix B for more information.

more than 50 standards. NSF also tests and certifies a wide variety of products. They have done this for years in the plumbing industry, where the NSF Mark is widely known. More recently, it has been approved to provide third-party certification for a number of sustainability programs, including the Environmental Protection Agency's (EPA's) WaterSense® program. (See the inset titled *Federal Sustainability Certifications* on page 477.)

Some of the standards created by NSF can be found in the ICC and NFPA codes. In 2006, NSF worked with ICC to develop a comprehensive volume that contains all the NSF standards that are referenced in the I-Codes. Titled the *NSF Standards: As Referenced in the 2009 IPC/IRC/UPC*, it is updated every 3 years. It covers the standards referenced in the ICC's *IPC* and the *IRC* as well as the IAPMO's *UPC*. (See the section Plumbing Codes earlier in this chapter.)

More recently, NSF has been creating various sustainability standards. The first interior finish standard, *NSF 140, Sustainable Carpet Assessment Standard*, was published in 2007. It is considered the first multi-attribute sustainable ANSI standard for building materials in the construction industry. NSF has developed and continues to develop other sustainability standards as well, including ones for resilient flooring, wallcovering, and fabric for commercial furnishings. (See the section Sustainability Considerations in Chapter 9 for more information.)

American Society of Heating, Refrigeration, and Air-Conditioning Engineers

The American Society of Heating, Refrigeration, and Air-Conditioning Engineers (ASHRAE) came into existence in 1959 with the merger of two engineering groups. ASHRAE is a worldwide standards organization. It sponsors research projects and develops standards for performance levels of HVAC (heating, ventilating, and air conditioning) and refrigeration systems. ASHRAE standards, developed using the ANS process, include uniform testing methods, design requirements, and recommended standard practices. ASHRAE also produces various guides and other special publications to assist with the implementation of its standards.

In the past, ASHRAE standards were typically used by mechanical engineers and refrigerant specialists and installers. More recently, ASHRAE started developing sustainable-related standards. These include *ASHRAE/IESNA 90.1, Energy Standard for Buildings Except Low-Rise Residential Buildings*, and *ASHRAE/IESNA 90.2, Energy-Efficient Design of New Low-Rise Residential Buildings*, which were developed in conjunction with the Illuminating Engineering Society of North America (IESNA). These standards, now updated on a 3-year cycle, address building elements such as the building envelope, light fixtures and controls, HVAC systems, water heating, and energy management. They are referenced by the ICC and

◤Note

Two federally developed labeling systems include ENERGY STAR® for electrical devices and WaterSense® for plumbing fixtures. (See Chapter 7, Chapter 8, and the inset *Federal Sustainability Certifications* on page 477 for more information.)

◤Note

In addition to the standards it creates, ASHRAE publishes multiple guides including the 2009 *Advanced Energy Design Guidelines (AEDGs)*.

NFPA energy codes and are the basis for most of the energy provisions required in the United States. (See the sections Energy Codes and the Energy Policy Act earlier in this chapter.)

ASHRAE also recently partnered with the U.S. Green Building Council (USGBC) and IESNA to develop another sustainable standard titled *ASHRAE/USGBC/IES 189.1, Standard for the Design of High-Performance Green Buildings Except Low-Rise Residential Buildings*. Completed in 2009, it is a comprehensive sustainability standard that incorporates environmental responsibility, occupant comfort and well-being, and community sensitivity. *ASHRAE 189.1* applies to new commercial buildings and major renovation projects, addressing sustainable sites, water use and energy efficiency, a building's impact on the atmosphere, materials and resources, and indoor environmental quality. It is also intended for buildings that wish to exceed the minimum requirement of the energy standard *ASHRAE/IESNA 90.1*. (See Chapter 7.) *ASHRAE 189.1* can be used by a jurisdiction and/or a building owner that wants to incorporate sustainable practices or apply a green rating system (i.e., LEED, Green Globes). The ICC's *International Green Construction Code (IGCC)* references it as well, providing a jurisdiction with an alternate way to meet the *IGCC* requirements. (See the section Sustainability Codes earlier in this chapter.)

Underwriters Laboratories

Underwriters Laboratories (UL) is primarily a testing agency that approves products. It is the largest and oldest nationally recognized testing laboratory in the United States and has a number of testing laboratories around the world. It tests various devices, systems, and materials to see if they meet specific requirements and to determine their relation to life, fire, casualty hazards, and crime prevention. More recently, UL created a sister company, UL Environment™, to provide third-party certification for a variety of sustainability programs. (See Appendix B.)

UL develops and performs tests in conjunction with other standards organizations. When it tests a new product, if a standard exists, UL will use it. If no standard exists, UL will use its own existing standard or create a new one. All of the more than 1000 different UL safety standards, created using the ANS process, are published in the UL *Catalog of Standards*. In addition, UL offers a comprehensive volume of standards used in the *IBC*. Updated every 3 years, the 2009 edition is titled *UL Standards: As Referenced in the IBC*. It is a single volume that contains 35 UL standards referenced in the *IBC* and the building portions (Chapters 1 to 10) of the *IRC*. UL standards are referenced in the NFPA codes as well.

UL's findings are recognized worldwide. When a product is approved, it receives a permanent label or classification marking that identifies Underwriters

UL LABELS

Underwriters Laboratories (UL) tests a wide variety of products all over the world. The UL label is the most widely recognized mark of compliance with safety requirements. These safety requirements are based on UL standards as well as standards from other organizations. (See the inset titled *Testing Agencies and Certification* on page 41.) Most federal, state, and municipal authorities, as well as architects, designers, contractors, and building owners and users, accept and recognize the UL mark.

UL can test whole products, components, materials, and systems, depending on the standard required. Testing close to 20,000 different types of products, examples related to interior projects include building materials, finishes, upholstered furniture, electrical products, HVAC equipment, safety devices, and the like. Once the initial product passes a test, it is retested at random to make sure that it continues to function properly.

There are four common types of labels or UL marks a product sold in the United States (US) and/or Canada (C) can receive. (Other marks are more specific to other industries and/or other countries.) The UL Web site describes them as follows:

1. *Listing Mark:* The most popular, it indicates that samples of the product have been tested and evaluated and comply with UL requirements. It is found on a wide variety of appliances and equipment including alarm systems, extinguishing systems, and light fixtures. The mark generally includes the UL registered name or symbol, the product name, a control number, and the word *listed*.

2. *Classification Mark:* This label may list a product's properties, limited hazards, and/or suitability for certain uses. It is found on building materials such as fire doors as well as industrial equipment. The label includes the UL name or symbol and a statement indicating the extent of the UL evaluation and a control number.

3. *Recognized Component Mark:* This covers the evaluation of a component only, such as electrical parts. The component is later factory-installed in a complete product or system. The label includes a manufacturer's identification and product model number.

4. *Certificate:* This is used when it is difficult to apply one label to a whole system. The certificate indicates the type of system and the extent of the evaluation. It accompanies the product and is issued to the end user upon installation.

UL has other product-specific marks that include the Plumbing Mark for plumbing fixtures and fittings, the Security Mark for security-related products, and the Signaling Mark for such items as smoke detectors and fire alarms. Marks specific to other countries include the S Mark in Japan, the D Mark in Europe, the UL-MX Mark in Mexico, the AR-UL Mark in Argentina, and the BR-UL Mark in Brazil.

More recently, UL created the Energy Mark for equipment and appliances that meet specific energy-efficiency requirements. And, in 2007, recognizing the demand for third-party verification of sustainable products, UL created a subsidiary known as UL Environment™, which validates environmental claims and certifies sustainable products. (See Appendix B for more information.)

✎Note

UL-labeled products may include country-specific identifiers such as US (United States), C (Canada), S (Japan), and D (Europe) to show that they comply with that country's product safety standards.

Laboratories, the word *classified*, a class rating, and a UL control number. (See the example in Figure 5.14 in Chapter 5 and the inset titled *UL Labels* in this chapter.) UL also lists all approved products and assemblies in a number of product directories. The directories most likely to pertain to interior projects include *Building Materials*, *Fire Protection Equipment*, and *Fire Resistance*. These directories, which are used to find information about UL-certified products, components, and materials, are published yearly. In 2001, the directories were reorganized to make them easier to use with the code publications. An electronic version of the directory, known as the *Online Certifications Directory*, is also available online, where it is updated regularly as new information becomes available.

STATE AND LOCAL CODES

✎Note

State and local jurisdictions can have additional code requirements and government regulations that need to be followed. Consult with the jurisdiction of the project.

✎Note

There are two *national* organizations that can provide valuable information as well. They play a major role in supporting the use of codes or standards. They include National Conference of State on Building Codes and Standards (NCSBCS) and National Institute of Building Sciences (NIBS).

In addition to the codes, standards, and federal regulations already mentioned, there are more specific codes within each jurisdiction. Some of these are regulations required on a state level. A common example is the energy legislation many states have passed (as explained earlier). Others are adopted on a more local level and can include, but are not limited to, local municipal ordinances, health codes, zoning regulations, historic preservation laws, and neighborhood conservation restrictions. For example, health codes must typically be followed when working on projects that involve food preparation, such as restaurants. Many state and local jurisdictions have also created "green building programs" that mandate certain buildings to meet specific sustainability standards and/or LEED certification. (See Chapter 10 and Appendix B.) In addition, other occupancies (e.g., hospitals) have regulations that must be incorporated into the design in order for the facility to obtain a license to operate. These regulations can control the size, location, and use of a building, and are usually set and controlled at a local level.

This book does not cover these state and local codes, since they are specific to each jurisdiction. However, it is important to consult the jurisdiction of a project for these specific regulations so that they can be appropriately researched and referenced. (See the section Code Enforcement in Chapter 10.)

INTERIOR CODES CHECKLIST

When working on a new project, it can be difficult to remember all the applicable code sources that must be referenced. Depending on the type of interior project and the jurisdiction in which it is located, you could be using any number of the codes, regulations, and standards described in this chapter. Figure 1.5 is a

Interior Codes and Standards Checklist

Date: _____

Project Name: _____ Space: _____

PUBLICATIONS REQUIRED	YEAR OF EDITION	YEAR OF AMENDMENT (if required)	RESEARCH DATE
Codes and Regulations			
BUILDING CODE—Circle One: IBC NFPA 5000 OTHER _____	_____	_____	__/__/__
Structural Engineer Required? _____ YES _____ NO			
PERFORMANCE CODE—Circle One: ICCPC NFPA[1] OTHER _____	_____	_____	__/__/__
FIRE CODE—Circle One: IFC NFPA 1 OTHER _____	_____	_____	__/__/__
LIFE SAFETY CODE (NFPA 101)	_____	_____	__/__/__
PLUMBING CODE—Circle One: IPC UPC OTHER _____	_____	_____	__/__/__
Plumbing Engineer Required? _____ YES _____ NO			
MECHANICAL CODE—Circle One: IMC UMC OTHER _____	_____	_____	
Mechanical Engineer Required? _____ YES _____ NO			
ELECTRIC CODE—Circle One: NEC OTHER _____	_____	_____	__/__/__
Electrical Engineer Required? _____ YES _____ NO			
ENERGY CODE/STANDARD— Circle One: IECC NFPA 900 OTHER _____	_____	_____	__/__/__
EPAct: ASHRAE 90.1 OTHER _____	_____	_____	__/__/__
RESIDENTIAL CODE—Circle One: IRC OTHER _____	_____	_____	__/__/__
EXISTING BUILDING CODE—Circle One: IEBC OTHER _____	_____	_____	__/__/__
SUSTAINABILITY CODE/STANDARD—Circle One: IGCC ICC700 OTHER _____	_____	_____	__/__/__
ACCESSIBILITY REGULATIONS/STANDARDS			
ADA-ABA Accessibility Guidelines[2]	_____	_____	__/__/__
ICC/ANSI A117.1 Accessible and Usable Buildings and Facilities	_____	_____	__/__/__
Other: _____	_____	_____	__/__/__
OTHER:[3] _____	_____	_____	__/__/__
_____	_____	_____	__/__/__
Standards[4]			
NATIONAL FIRE PROTECTION ASSOCIATION (NFPA):			
NFPA _____	_____	_____	__/__/__
NFPA _____	_____	_____	__/__/__
INTERNATIONAL CODE COUNCIL (ICC)			
ICC _____	_____	_____	__/__/__
AMERICAN SOCIETY OF TESTING and MATERIALS (ASTM)			
ASTM _____	_____	_____	__/__/__
ASTM _____	_____	_____	__/__/__
UNDERWRITERS LABORATORIES (UL)			
UL _____	_____	_____	__/__/__
OTHER: _____	_____	_____	__/__/__
_____	_____	_____	__/__/__

NOTES:

1. Circle NFPA if you are using another NFPA document and plan to use a performance-based requirement listed in that document.
2. All projects should be reviewed for ADA compatibility with few exceptions (i.e., federal buildings, religious facilities, one/two-family homes).
3. Check for other state and local codes including special ordinances, health codes, zoning regulations, and historic preservation laws. List the specific ones.
4. Refer to the codes as well as local requirements to determine which standards are required. List the specific publications.

Figure 1.5 Interior codes and standards checklist.

✎Note

If an interior project is somehow affecting the structure of a building, the services of a structural engineer may be required.

✎Note

To further document your research, make copies of any sections of the codes that specifically pertain to your project and attach them to the code checklist. (Refer to Chapter 10.)

checklist that provides a comprehensive list of these codes and standards. Use this list, or develop your own, to be sure that you reference the necessary codes and regulations.

Before starting an interior project, refer to this checklist to determine which code, standard, and federal publications must be referenced. Remember that not all of them will apply every time. If you are uncertain, consult the code officials in the jurisdiction of the project. Check off the publications you will need in the "Publications Required" column and enter the edition or year of the required publication in the next column. Remember that not every jurisdiction uses the most current edition of a code and that a jurisdiction may have made amendments to an existing publication. If there are amendments, make a note of this in third column.

Do this for each code, regulation, and standard listed. A reminder for engineering involvement is given under each of the code headings. Blank spaces have been provided for specific state or local codes that must be consulted. Blank spaces have also been provided for you to fill in the specific standards and/or federal regulations to be used. For example, depending on the type of project, you could be required to follow the *ADA Standards*, the *ABA Standards*, or the *FHAG*. Or, you can use this space to include some of the newer sustainable standards.

As you work on the project, continue to refer to the checklist to make sure each of the checked codes, standards, and federal regulations is being used. As the research is completed for each publication, enter the date in the "Research Date" column. You will find that as you research the codes, additional standards may be required. Add these to the checklist in the spaces provided or on a separate piece of paper. When the project is complete, keep this form with the project's files for future reference and proof that each of the code sources was reviewed.

CHAPTER 2

OCCUPANCY CLASSIFICATIONS AND LOADS

The occupancy classification of a building or space is generally determined by the way that building or space is to be used. Occupancy classifications have been developed by the codes to address the different hazardous situations, often referred to as *risk factors*, associated with each type of use. These risk factors consider the typical characteristics of both the activity that will occur in the space and the occupants using the space. Risk factors may include spatial characteristics (low light levels, fixed seating, and high sound levels), fuel loads (amount of finish materials, upholstered furniture, and other flammable contents), concentration of occupants, characteristics of the occupants (mobility, age, alertness), and sometimes the familiarity of the occupants with the building. In some cases, these unique characteristics call for additional code requirements so that buildings are safe. For example, more exits are required in auditoriums (Assembly) due to the large number of people using the space, and alternate exiting methods are required in hospitals (Institutional), where occupants often are not mobile for age, health, or security reasons. The different occupancy classifications in the codes are based on these various characteristics. The codes address these conditions for each occupancy classification so that people can be considered equally safe at work, at a crowded concert, or with any other type of use.

In some cases, the projected occupant load will be the most influential component in determining the occupancy classification. The occupant load is considered to be the number of people that is assumed to safely occupy a space or building. Since occupancy classifications and occupant loads are, in a sense, dependent on each other, both should be considered at the beginning of a project. Once the occupancy classification has been determined, the projected occupant load, or expected number of people, is used to determine a number of other code requirements. The first part of this chapter concentrates on occupancy

◢**Note**

The codes often reference the occupancy classifications by letters or a combination of letters and numbers. For example, "A" represents Assembly occupancies and "R-2" represents a Residential occupancy subclassification. (See Figure 2.2.)

classifications and their relationships; occupant loads are discussed in the last part of the chapter. A checklist for both is provided at the end.

UNDERSTANDING OCCUPANCY CLASSIFICATIONS

An occupancy classification must be assigned to every building or space within a building. Determining the occupancy classification is one of the most important steps in the code process. It should be the first thing determined when designing the interior of a building, since virtually every interior code and regulation is based on the building's occupancy. Many examples are listed in Figure 2.1. The occupancy of a space must also be known in order to effectively use most of the remaining chapters in this book. Once the occupancy is known, it will guide the remaining code research.

For some buildings, the occupancy classification may have already been determined. But for a new or existing building that is intended to have different types of tenants, the occupancy classification for each tenant must be determined separately. These different tenants may, in turn, affect the way the shared public spaces are classified. In existing buildings, determining the occupancy classification may be particularly important if the intended use of the building is changing significantly, such as an old warehouse building being renovated into apartments. The occupancy classification needs to be reexamined whenever changes are made in the use of a building or space. Some of these changes are obvious, such as a change in building type. Other changes may be less noticeable but still require reclassification.

Accessibility Requirements	Fire Extinguishing Systems
Alarm Systems	Furniture Selection/Placement
Egress Capacities	Means of Egress
Electrical Devices	Mechanical Loads
Emergency Lighting	Occupant Loads
Finish Selection/Placement	Plumbing Fixtures
Fire Barriers/Partitions	Smoke Barriers
Fire/Smoke Detection Systems	Smoke Detection Systems

Figure 2.1 Interior codes affected by occupancy.

It may also be important to understand how the occupants will actually be using the space or plan to use it in the future. For example, if a space will be used for an open office plan now but in the future will be used as a conference room for training, both Assembly and Business requirements may need to be considered so that the design will address the most stringent code requirements.

The ICC codes and the NFPA codes divide the occupancy classifications slightly different. However, the 10 most common occupancy classifications used throughout the various building and life safety codes are listed below. Some of them also have subclassifications. The occupancy classifications and their subcategories will be discussed in the first part of this chapter.

Assembly occupancies

Business occupancies

Educational occupancies

Factory or Industrial occupancies

Hazardous occupancies

Institutional occupancies

Mercantile occupancies

Residential occupancies

Storage occupancies

Utility or Miscellaneous occupancies

Many of these classifications seem self-explanatory, especially if a building type is straightforward, but remember that three things must be known before the occupancy classification can be accurately determined: (1) the type of activity occurring, (2) the expected number of occupants, and (3) whether any unusual hazards or risk factors are present. These factors can affect the classification of a building type or spaces within a building.

A boutique that sells clothing, for example, has an *activity* that is straightforward. It is a Mercantile occupancy. However, in some cases, small differences in use can change the occupancy classification. For example, a television studio is a Business occupancy, but if the studio allows audience viewing, it will typically be considered an Assembly occupancy. Knowing the specific type(s) of activities that are occurring is important.

Many of the classifications allow for a specific *number of people*. For example, a space may appear to be an Assembly use, but if a small number of people will be using the space, it may be allowed to be classified as Business. When using the *IBC*, if a day care center has fewer than five children, it may be considered Residential, but if it has more than five, it may be considered Institutional or

Educational. So, if the number of occupants increases or decreases, the occupancy classification may need to be reexamined.

Hazards to occupants can include harmful substances and/or potentially harmful situations. (See the inset titled *Risk Factors and Hazards in Occupancies* on this page.) When either is present, different types of requirements are necessary. The storage or use of flammable, explosive, or toxic materials is considered to be hazardous and can either change an occupancy to a stricter classification or require all or part of a building to be classified as a Hazardous occupancy and be subject to tougher codes. Small levels of certain hazardous materials, however, are allowed in almost every occupancy classification. For example, a small amount of paint can be stored in any occupancy. However, in large amounts it would be considered a Hazardous use. Certain situations within a building or the condition of the occupants themselves can create potential risk factors or hazards as well. Low light levels, low awareness or mental capacity, restricted movement due to

RISK FACTORS AND HAZARDS IN OCCUPANCIES

The types of risk factors or hazards found in a building help to determine its occupancy classification. They can vary dramatically from one building type to the next. Each occupancy was created to handle different types of hazards. Some of the risk factors that are typically considered when determining an occupancy classification are:

- ❑ Number of occupants (a large group versus a small gathering)
- ❑ If occupants are at rest or sleeping
- ❑ Alertness of the occupants (considers mental capabilities and inherent distractions caused by the activities going on in the space)
- ❑ Mobility of the occupants (considers physical abilities, age, and security measures)
- ❑ Familiarity of occupants with the space or building
- ❑ Typical characteristics of the space used for a particular activity (includes fixed seating and aisles, light levels, noise levels, etc.)
- ❑ Potential for spread of fire (due to airborne flammable particles, storage of hazardous materials, combustible finishes, decoration or contents, etc.)

These risk factors were considered by the code organizations in the development of each occupancy classification and their various subcategories. It may also be necessary to consider if any of these factors are specifically known to exist within the proposed space. Both the occupants in the space and the use of the space must be considered to correctly determine the occupancy classification. Similar risk factors must also be considered when working with performance codes.

security, and similar characteristics can create potentially hazardous situations. If hazardous materials or situations are expected to be present in the building or space, it may affect the appropriate choice of occupancy classification.

Consult the local code official early in a project whenever there is uncertainty of the correct occupancy classification. It is always a good idea to have a code official confirm the choice of occupancy. If it is determined later that the choice is incorrect or is not approved by the code official, the rest of the research may be incorrect and the design may not meet the appropriate code requirements.

COMPARING THE CODES

The building codes, such as the *International Building Code (IBC)*, and the *Life Safety Code (LSC)* are used to assign an occupancy classification to the uses of a space or building. Knowing the appropriate occupancy classification and/or subclassification is the most important step to understanding what code and standard requirements apply to a space or building. Most of the requirements and a majority of the exceptions will be based on occupancy. And, since the NFPA codes are organized largely by individual occupancy chapters, the correct occupancy classification is necessary to determine the appropriate chapter to be applied to the project.

Other codes also use the occupancy classifications to call out particular code requirements. This includes the fire codes, such as the *International Fire Code (IFC)*, which provides specific fire-related requirements for each occupancy type within its various chapters. The fire codes provide additional requirements for other special uses as well. This includes unusual buildings and rooms that might not be covered in the building codes. Because these uses have unique activities or hazards associated with them, special requirements are called out by separate chapters or sections within the fire codes. For example, the fire codes typically have chapters on airports, clean rooms in laboratories, and rooms used for dry cleaning. If there is a special use in a particular design, research both the building code and the fire code when it is required by a jurisdiction.

The assigning of occupancy classifications by the codes allows some assumptions to be made as to how people will react and move within a space or building in case of a fire or emergency. The prescriptive requirements then define specifically how safety can be achieved. By contrast, when using performance codes, only general parameters for what should be considered about the activities and the occupants are given by the codes. The design must then describe and/or prove

☞ Note

Most code jurisdictions will require the use of a fire code in addition to a building code. Typically, the fire code will either be the *International Fire Code (IFC)* or the NFPA *Fire Code (NFPA 1)*.

how safety is provided. Therefore, if there is an unusual building type or an occupancy with multiple uses, using performance criteria may need to be considered (if allowed by the jurisdiction).

The *ICC Performance Code (ICCPC)* has a section titled "Use and Occupancy Classification" within the "Design Performance Levels" chapter. Instead of grouping types of activities into occupancy classifications, it states that the objective is to identify the primary use of a space or building and the risk factors associated with that use. The risk factors that must be considered include the type of activity, hazards, number of occupants, length of occupancy, alertness (sleeping or awake), familiarity with the space, vulnerability (lack of mobility or cognitive awareness), and whether occupants are related. The NFPA codes discuss similar issues that should be considered by discussing occupant characteristics and assumptions within the "Performance-based Option" chapter in each code. The design must then take into account the unique characteristics of the use and occupants.

Because accessibility requirements apply to almost every occupancy classification or building use, the necessary accessibility documents need to be referenced. The building codes include an accessibility chapter and refers to the accessibility standard *ICC/ANSI A117.1*. Depending on the building type, the Americans with Disabilities Act (ADA) standards or the *FHA Accessibility Guidelines (FHAG)* maybe required as well. In some cases, specific building types will have additional requirements. For example, the *ADA Standards* have requirements that must be met for certain occupancies, such as Mercantile, Residential, and Health Care. Other building uses may be exempt. (See the section ADA Requirements later in this chapter and Appendix A for more information.)

DESCRIPTION OF OCCUPANCIES

⊟Note

Letters are often used to designate an occupancy classification. For example, "A" stands for Assembly and "E" stands for Educational. (See Figure 2.2.)

Use the following description of each occupancy to help determine the occupancy classification of a space or building. In addition, an occupancy may be subdivided into smaller, more specific categories. For example, the *IBC* divides its Assembly occupancy into five different subclassifications. These subclassifications are explained as well. A wide range of common building types has been provided as examples.

The list is not all-inclusive, and it does not replace the applicable code publications. These must be referenced as well. Each code also classifies its occupancies a little differently. For example, the classifications used in this chapter are based on the ICC's I-Codes. Although many are similar to those used in the NFPA codes, the NFPA may use a different name for a classification or subdivide them differently. Refer to Figure 2.2 for a comparison of how each occupancy classification differs in the *IBC* and the NFPA codes.

Occupancy Classification	ICC International Building Code		NFPA Life Safety Code and NFPA 5000	
ASSEMBLY	A-1	Assembly, Theaters (Fixed Seats)	A-A	Assembly, OL > 1000
	A-2	Assembly, Food and/or Drink Consumption	A-B	Assembly, OL > 300 ≤ 1000
	A-3	Assembly, Worship, Recreation, Amusement	A-C	Assembly, OL ≥ 50 ≤ 300
	A-4	Assembly, Indoor Sporting Events		
	A-5	Assembly, Outdoor Activities		
BUSINESS	B	Business	B	Business
			AHC	Ambulatory Health Care
EDUCATION	E	Educational (includes some Day Care)	E	Educational
FACTORY/INDUSTRIAL	F-1	Factory Industrial, Moderate Hazard	I-A	Industrial, General
	F-2	Factory Industrial, Low Hazard	I-B	Industrial, Special Purpose
			I-C	Industrial, High Hazard
HAZARDOUS	H-1	Hazardous, Detonation Hazard	(included in Group I)	
	H-2	Hazardous, Deflagration Hazard or Accelerated Burning		
	H-3	Hazardous, Physical or Combustible Hazard		
	H-4	Hazardous, Health Hazard		
	H-5	Hazardous, Hazardous Production Materials (HPM)		
INSTITUTIONAL	I-1	Institutional, Supervised Personal Care, OL > 16	D-I	Detentional/Correctional, Free Egress
	I-2	Institutional, Health Care	D-II	Detentional/Correctional, Zoned Egress
	I-3	Institutional, Restrained	D-III	Detentional/Correctional, Zoned Impeded Egress
	I-4	Institutional, Day Care Facilities	D-IV	Detentional/Correctional, Impeded Egress
			D-V	Detentional/Correctional, Contained
			H	Health Care
			DC	Day Care
MERCANTILE	M	Mercantile	M-A	Mercantile, > 3 levels or > 30,000 SF (2800 SM)
			M-B	Mercantile, ≤ 3 stories or > 3000 SF (280 SM) and ≤ 30,000 SF (2800 SM)
			M-C	Mercantile, 1 story ≤ 3000 SF (280 SM)
RESIDENTIAL	R-1	Residential, Transient	R-A	Residential, Hotels, and Dormitories
	R-2	Residential, Multi-Dwelling Unit	R-B	Residential, Apartment Buildings
	R-3	Residential, One and Two Dwelling Units	R-C	Residential, Lodging or Rooming Houses
	R-4	Residential, Care and Assisted Living Facilities OL > 5 ≤ 16	R-D	Residential, One and Two Family Dwellings
			R-E	Residential, Board and Care
STORAGE	S-1	Storage, Moderate Hazard	S	Storage
	S-2	Storage, Low Hazard		
UTILITY/MISCELLANEOUS	U	Utility and Miscellaneous		Special Structures and High-rise Buildings

NOTE: The *Life Safety Code* designates between new and existing, the building codes do not.
OL = occupant load, SF = square feet, SM = square meters

Figure 2.2 Comparison of occupancy classifications. (This chart is a summary of information contained in the 2009 editions of the *International Building Code*®, the *NFPA 5000*®, and the *Life Safety Code*®. Neither the ICC nor the NFPA assumes responsibility for the accuracy or completeness of this chart.)

Assembly (A) Occupancy

⏴Note

A restaurant can be classified as a Business or Mercantile occupancy (if the number of occupants is small enough), as an Assembly, or as an accessory to a larger adjacent occupancy.

A building or part of a building is classified as an Assembly occupancy if people gather for political, social, or religious functions, recreation, entertainment, eating, drinking, or awaiting transportation. The most common characteristic of an Assembly occupancy is that it holds a large number of people (usually more than 50) who are unfamiliar with the space. Other common characteristics include such aspects as low light levels, the occupants' lack of awareness of surroundings, and the potential for panic because of the number of occupants. Because of these multiple risk factors, there are a number of additional codes that apply strictly to Assembly occupancies.

The NFPA codes rely primarily on the number of people to determine the classification of an Assembly. The *IBC* bases its classifications more on the type of activity than on the density of occupants. As a result, NFPA codes have fewer Assembly subclassifications. (See Figure 2.2.) Each code also provides specific requirements for unique uses such as malls, theaters with stages, and other building types that may seem to fit the Assembly use. In the *IBC* this information is in a separate special-use chapter; in the NFPA codes it is included in the Assembly occupancy chapters.

The *IBC* has five subclassifications of Assembly based on the type of activity occurring. They are designated as A-1 through A-5.

A-1

This type is for the viewing of performing arts or movies. The space often includes a stage. (There are many code requirements specifically for stages.) The common characteristics of these types of spaces are low light levels and above-normal sound levels. Seating usually consists of fixed seating with well-defined aisles. Occupants are alert but generally unfamiliar with the building.

Sample Building Types

> Motion picture theaters
>
> Radio and television studios with audiences
>
> Symphony and concert halls
>
> Theaters for stage production

A-2

This type is for the consumption of food and drink. Often these spaces have low light levels, loud music, late operating hours, and ill-defined aisles (e.g., movable tables and chairs). The serving of food and drink is the most defining characteristic.

Sample Building Types

Banquet halls

Dance halls (serving food and drink)

Drinking establishments

Fast-food restaurants

Fellowship halls (serving food and drink)

Nightclubs

Restaurants (can also be classified as Business)

Taverns and bars (can also be classified as Business)

A-3

This type is for the gathering of people for worship, recreation, or amusement. Types of activities that are not classified by other types of Assembly are typically included in this subclassification. The common characteristics of this subclassification are clear or defined egress patterns and moderate to low fuel loads. For example, in a church or an auditorium, aisles used for egress are defined by the placement of pews or chairs. Occupants in an A-3 subclassification are also usually alert and are often more familiar with the space than in other assembly uses.

Sample Building Types

Amusement arcades

Armories

Art galleries

Assembly halls

Auditoriums

Bowling lanes

Churches and religious structures

Community halls

Courtrooms

Dance halls (not including food or drink consumption)

Exhibition halls

Fellowship halls

Funeral homes

Galleries

Gymnasiums (without spectator seating)

Lecture halls (can also be Business)

Libraries

Mortuary chapels

Museums

Passenger stations, terminals, or depots (waiting areas)

Pool and billiard rooms

Public assembly halls

Recreation halls and piers

Tents for assembly

A-4

This type is for the viewing of indoor sporting events and other activities with spectator seating. The spectator seating can consist of a defined area for seating or fixed seats such as bleachers. Although A-3 and A-4 can have similar activities, if a defined area for viewing the activities is provided, then it is an A-4. For example, an indoor pool can be classified as an A-3 Assembly, but if the pool area also includes seating for viewing swim competitions, it is considered an A-4. (Similar activities can also occur between A-4 and A-5 Assemblies.)

Sample Building Types

Arenas

Gymnasiums

Indoor skating rinks

Indoor swimming pools

Indoor tennis courts

A-5

This type is for the participation in or viewing of outdoor activities. This would be similar to A-4, except that it is outdoors.

Sample Building Types

Amusement park structures

Bleachers

Grandstands

Stadiums

⬙ Note

A good rule of thumb is that when the occupant load is 50 or more, the requirements for an Assembly occupancy should be researched.

Typically in Assembly occupancies, there are a large number of occupants. Examples include a theater or large restaurant. However, when a space is used for a small group of people to gather—such as a college classroom, an office conference room, or a small restaurant—the codes often allow these uses to be classified under another occupancy type. The *IBC* and the NFPA codes use an occupancy of 50 people or more as the cutoff point. (Some jurisdictions may use a different limit.) For example, if the *IBC* is used, a small restaurant can be classified as a Business occupancy if its occupant load is less than 50. The NFPA codes would reclassify this as a Mercantile occupancy.

In many cases, the codes will also allow an assembly-type use that is part of another occupancy classification to be considered the same occupancy that it serves. It may depend on the size or the occupant load. For example, the *IBC* allows rooms used for assembly purposes that are less than 750 square feet (70 s m) to be classified either as a Business occupancy or as part of the main occupancy classification. Remember, the way a space is classified can affect many code-related design decisions.

Business (B) Occupancy

A building or part of a building is classified as a Business occupancy if it is used for the transaction of business, such as accounting, record keeping, and other similar functions. It also includes the rendering of professional services. Limited areas that are a natural part of a business setting, such as small storage or supply areas and break rooms, are included as well. The risk factors in a Business occupancy are considered to be relatively low. This is because there is a low concentration of occupants, and they are usually alert and generally familiar with their environment. It is considered one of the lowest-risk occupancies.

This classification can become very broad. For example, a smaller Assembly-like occupancy that has fewer occupants can sometimes be classified as a Business occupancy, such as a small restaurant. Conversely, when the function or size of any of the Business building types expands beyond a typical business, the occupancy needs to be reexamined. Examples might include city halls that include assembly areas or college facilities that include an auditorium classroom. These types of uses may be classified as an Assembly occupancy or a mixed occupancy. (See the section Mixed Occupancies later in this chapter.) In addition, for an occupancy that offers health care services similar to a doctor's office, but where procedures are performed that cause four or more patients to be under sedation or conditions that would prevent them from being able to exit the facility without assistance, the facility may need to be classified as an *ambulatory care facility*. Under the *IBC*, this type of use is still considered a Business occupancy but will have specific code requirements that differ from a typical Business occupancy. The NFPA codes have a separate occupancy classification of Ambulatory Health Care. However, in both cases additional requirements will apply.

Educational-type occupancies can also be confusing. Colleges and universities (educational facilities after the 12th grade) are considered Business occupancies. Yet, business and vocational schools are often considered as the same occupancy as the trade or vocation that is being taught. For instance, general classrooms for a college would be classified as Business, but the classrooms for instruction in automotive repair may be considered Factory/Industrial. In addition, places that offer various types of training or skill-development classes can be classified as Business instead of Educational, regardless of the age of the participants. Examples include places that offer music, dance, or tutoring.

◀Note

A wide variety of building types can fall under the Business occupancy classification. For example, a small Assembly, such as a restaurant with fewer than 50 people, as well as college classrooms and outpatient clinics can be classified as a Business occupancy.

Sample Building Types

Airport traffic control towers

Ambulatory care facilities

Animal hospitals, kennels, and pounds (part of the building could be considered Storage)

Automobile and other motor vehicle showrooms

Automobile service stations (can also be classified as Hazardous)

Banks

Barber shops

Beauty shops

Car washes

City halls

Civic administration buildings

Clinics (outpatient)

College and university classrooms

Dentist's offices

Doctor's offices

Dry-cleaning facilities (can also be classified as Hazardous)

Educational facilities (above 12th grade)

Electronic data processing facilities

Fire stations

Florists and nurseries

Government offices

Greenhouses

Laboratories (nonhazardous)

Laboratories (testing and research)

Laundromats

Libraries (can also be classified as Assembly or Business)

Medical offices (separate from Institutional occupancies)

Motor vehicle showrooms

Office buildings

Outpatient clinics, ambulatory

Police stations

Post offices

Print shops

Professional offices (architect, attorney, dentist, physician, etc.)

Radio and television stations (without audiences)

Repair garages (small, nonhazardous)

Telecommunication equipment buildings

Telephone exchanges

Travel agencies

✎Note

Although it would seem normal for colleges and universities to fall under the Educational occupancy, these building types are typically classified as Business or Assembly occupancies.

Educational (E) Occupancy

A building or part of a building is classified as an Educational occupancy if it is used for educational purposes by a specified number of persons at any one time through the 12th grade. Depending on the code publication, the specified number of persons ranges from six to the minimum number of people required for an Assembly occupancy. (For colleges and universities, see Assembly and Business occupancies.) The NFPA codes also specify a minimum amount of time that a space is used for educational purposes. For example, if there are fewer than 12 hours of instruction per week, the building type could be governed by a different occupancy classification according to the *LSC*.

It is common for a typical school to be considered a mixed occupancy due to the auditoriums, cafeterias, and gymnasiums included in this building type. In most cases, these additional uses will be classified separately under an Assembly occupancy. Vocational shops, laboratories, and similar areas within a school will usually be considered Educational, even though they may require additional fire protection. As mentioned in a previous section, if the entire school is considered vocational, some codes may require that it fall into the same classification as the trade or vocation being taught.

If an Educational occupancy also provides care and sleeping accommodations, it could be classified as an Institutional occupancy or a mixed occupancy. For example, the sleeping area of a boarding school or an extended stay rehabilitation program may be classified as Residential. Day care centers can also be classified as Institutional, depending on the number of children and their age. Verify the proper designation with the local code official when necessary.

Sample Building Types

Academies	Junior high schools
Day care centers (can also be considered Institutional)	Kindergartens
	Nursery schools
Elementary schools	Preschools
High schools	Secondary schools

Factory (F) Occupancy

A building or part of a building is designated as a Factory or Industrial occupancy if it is used for assembling, disassembling, fabricating, finishing, manufacturing, packaging, processing, or repairing. This designation generally refers to a building in which a certain type of product is made. The product that is made or the materials used to make the product must typically be considered a low or moderate hazard. If it is a more hazardous material or product, the building or space where it is made may be considered a Hazardous occupancy. The sample product types listed below are typically considered low to moderate types of hazards by the building codes. However, each code groups them a little differently under the Factory/Industrial occupancy, and there may be different code requirements, depending on which hazardous group the product is in. For example, the *IBC* divides its Factory occupancy into F-1 and F-2. The NFPA uses the term Industrial occupancy and has three subclassifications. (See Figure 2.2. Also see Hazardous Occupancy.) These subclassifications are made for the different levels of hazardous materials or activities that are part of the manufacturing process. Refer to the specific code to determine if a manufactured product is considered moderate or low hazard; if more hazardous materials are used or created in the space or building, it may need to be classified as a Hazardous occupancy.

Sample Building Types

Assembly plants

Factories

Manufacturing plants

Mills

Processing plants

Low and Moderate Hazardous Products

Aircrafts

Appliances

Athletic equipment

Automobiles and other motor vehicles

Bakeries

Beverages (alcoholic)

Beverages (nonalcoholic)

Bicycles

Boats (building)

Boiler works

Brick and masonry

Brooms or brushes

Business machines

Cameras and photo equipment

Canneries

Canvas or similar fabrics

Carpets and rugs (includes cleaning)

Ceramic products

Clothing

Condensed powdered milk manufacturing

Construction and agricultural machinery

Creameries

Disinfectants

Dry cleaning and dyeing

Electric light plants and power houses

Electrolytic—reducing works

Electronics

Engines (includes rebuilding)

Film (photographic)

Food processing

Foundries

Furniture

Glass products

Gypsum products

Hemp products

Ice

Jute products

Laboratories (can also be classified as Business)

Laundries

Leather products

Machinery

Metal products (fabrication and assembly)

Millwork (sash and door)

Motion pictures and television filming

Musical instruments

Optical goods

Paper mills or products

Plastic products

Printing or publishing

Recreational vehicles

Refineries

Refuse incineration

Sawmills

Shoes

Smokehouses

Soaps and detergents

Sugar refineries

Textiles

Tobacco

Trailers

Upholstering

Water pumping plants

Wood (distillation of)

Woodworking (cabinetry)

Hazardous (H) Occupancy

A building or part of a building that involves the generation, manufacturing, processing, storage, or other use of hazardous materials is typically classified as a Hazardous occupancy. These materials can include flammable dust, fibers or liquids, combustible liquids, poisonous gases, explosive agents, corrosive liquids, oxidizing materials, radioactive materials, and carcinogens, among others. In general, this classification is categorized by an unusually high degree of explosive, fire, physical, and/or health hazards.

Hazardous building types require additional precautions. Each code sets different standards and has special sections dedicated to hazardous uses, which list very specific materials. In most cases, a Hazardous occupancy can be subclassified as a low, medium, or high hazard. Each building code categorizes the

> ◀ **Note**
>
> The NFPA codes do not have a separate Hazardous occupancy. Instead, it is a subclassification under the Industrial occupancy.

hazards a little differently. Often the lower hazards are made part of the Factory/Industrial or Storage occupancy classification. Each code also has a different number of subclassifications. The *IBC* has five Hazardous classifications (H-1 through H-5). The NFPA codes, however, include high hazard building types as a subclassification under Industrial. (See Figure 2.2.) They do not have a separate Hazardous occupancy. When using the NFPA codes, be careful to identify how that specific code or standard defines the term *hazardous* as they may vary slightly per code publication and the purpose of the regulation. For example, in the *LSC*, the term hazardous is used to describe the level of hazardous *content* of the space, where as in the *NFPA 13, Installation of Sprinkler Systems*, the term is used to define the *ability* of the sprinkler system to control the fire.

An important factor to consider is the amount of hazardous materials. If the amount is small enough, the space or building may not be considered Hazardous by the codes. A common example is a chemistry lab in a high school. As more performance-type requirements are introduced into code publications, more emphasis will be placed on the types of products or materials used in a space rather than concentrating on the type of building.

If a space or building may contain hazardous materials or conditions, consult the specific codes and work closely with the local code officials. Some buildings may require only part of the building to be classified as Hazardous. (Hazardous buildings and materials are beyond the scope of this book.)

Sample Building Types

Airport hangars or airport repair hangars	Paint and solvent manufacturers
Dry-cleaning plants	Paint shops and spray painting rooms
Explosives manufacturers	Pesticide warehouses
Film storage, combustible	Power plants
Firearm/ammunition warehouses	Pumping/service stations
Gas plants	Tank farms
Laboratories with hazardous chemicals	Warehouses with hazardous materials

Institutional (I) Occupancy

A building or part of a building is classified as an Institutional occupancy if it includes medical treatment or other types of care or contains occupants detained under physical or security measures. The primary distinction of this classification is that the occupants are either limited in their mobility, immobile, or incapable of mobility due to physical or security restraints. In most cases, the occupants must depend on others to help them evacuate the building in case of an emergency. The *IBC* has four Institutional subclassifications (I-1 through I-4). The NFPA, on the other hand, separates these uses into different occupancy classifications. The NFPA codes refer to them as Detentional/Correctional, Health Care, and Day Care occupancies. (See Figure 2.2.)

Using the *IBC* designations, each subclassification is described as follows. The similar NFPA classification is given as well. Note, however, that the specific definition for each NFPA occupancy may vary from those in the *IBC*. The minimum and maximum number of occupants can vary as well. For example, the minimum number for an I-4 classification in the *IBC* is 6 and the minimum number for a Day Care occupancy in the *LSC* is 12 children or 3 adults. Refer to the applicable code to determine the occupancy classification correctly. (Also see the inset titled *Rooms and Spaces* on page 73.)

Because some uses can be determined by subtle differences, a discussion with a code official may be required to confirm whether the jurisdiction will consider the facility Institutional, Residential, or one of the other NFPA classifications. The applicable code requirements can vary significantly between these occupancies.

I-1

This type is for the housing and care of a certain number of occupants on a 24-hour basis. The codes often use 16 occupants as the limit. (This number does not include staff.) These occupants, because of age or mental disability, must be supervised. However, they can typically respond to an emergency without physical assistance from staff. If fewer than 16 people were being cared for with the same characteristics, the occupancy would be reclassified as Residential. The NFPA considers this building type a Residential occupancy (Board and Care), which includes a section for larger and smaller types of facilities.

Sample Building Types

Alcohol and drug centers

Assisted living facilities (can also be classified as Residential)

Congregate care facilities (>16 occupants)

Convalescent facilities

Group homes

Halfway houses

Social rehabilitation facilities

I-2

This type is for medical, surgical, psychiatric, nursing, or other type of care on a 24-hour basis for more than five persons. These occupants are not capable of self-preservation. If fewer than five people were being cared for, the occupancy would typically be reclassified as Residential. The similar NFPA category is under a separate occupancy classification called Health Care.

Sample Building Types

Day care centers (24-hour)	Mental hospitals
Detoxification facilities	Nursing homes (intermediate care and skilled nursing)
Hospitals	
Infirmaries	Sanitariums
Limited care facilities	Treatment or rehabilitation centers

I-3

This type is for the detention of more than five persons. These occupants are incapable of self-preservation due to security measures. There are additional "conditions" based on the level of security provided and the amount of free movement allowed within the building that need to be considered to accurately determine the specific code requirements for this use. (This topic is beyond the scope of this book.) The similar NFPA category is the Detention/Correction occupancy classification, which is divided into five separate subclassifications (see Figure 2.2), depending on the level of security.

The *LSC* has special conditions for *lock-up areas* in facilities other than Detentional/Correctional. These areas are similar to the conditions occurring in typical I-3 facilities as the occupants are incapable of self-preservation due to security measures. However, only one person has to be held in this condition for these requirements to apply. A lock-up area is most typically located in facilities such as immigration centers at border crossings, customs facilities in international airports, prisoner holding at police departments, or security areas at parks, sports stadia, and similar uses.

Sample Building Types

Correctional institutions	Prisons
Detention centers	Reformatories
Jails	Work camps
Prerelease centers	

I-4

This type is for the care of more than five persons for less than 24 hours a day. This includes adults and children under 2 years of age. One typical exception is that if adults in this type of facility are capable of self-preservation without help from staff, it would be reclassified as an R-3. (See Residential occupancy R-3.) Another is when the area where children are cared for opens directly to the exterior; it can then be reclassified as Educational. This is considered a Day Care occupancy in the NFPA codes.

Sample Building Types

Adult day cares

Day care centers—caring for infants (can also be classified as Educational)

Mercantile (M) Occupancy

A building or part of a building is classified as a Mercantile occupancy if it is open to the public and used for the display, sale, or rental of merchandise. This classification includes most stores and showrooms, and in some codes includes large malls. The *IBC* groups these into one main occupancy. Mercantile in the NFPA codes has three subclassifications based on the type and size of the building. (See Figure 2.2.)

A group of retail stores may have additional code requirements. Each store would be considered a separate Mercantile occupancy. However, as a group, the stores may also be considered a *covered mall*. The codes have special requirements for malls because, in addition to the large anchor retail stores and the multiple smaller retail tenants, there can be other uses within the same building. Most typically, these include restaurants and entertainment areas. In some cases, the general mercantile requirements apply, and, in other cases, the requirements for a covered mall may apply to the project. (Usually one or the other will be used.) These mall requirements can be found in the "special occupancy" chapter of the *IBC*. In the NFPA codes, special requirements for malls are called out within the Mercantile chapter. When necessary, review these requirements with the local code official.

Sample Building Types

Auction rooms	Department stores
Automotive service stations	Drug stores
Bakeries	Grocery stores

> **◄Note**
>
> According to the NFPA codes, a small use that would normally be classified as a type of Assembly occupancy can sometimes be classified as Mercantile, such as a small diner. (In the *IBC,* this may be reclassified as Business.)

Markets

Paint stores (without bulk handling)

Rental stores

Retail stores

Salesrooms

Shopping centers

Shops

Showrooms

Specialty stores

Supermarkets

Wholesale stores (other than warehouses)

Residential (R) Occupancy

⬛Note

Certain Residential building types may need to be reclassified as Institutional, depending on the number of occupants and their length of stay. Examples include day care centers and nursing homes.

A building or part of a building that acts as a dwelling and provides sleeping accommodations for normal residential purposes is designated as a Residential occupancy. Most of the codes further categorize this classification based on the probable number of occupants and how familiar they are with their surroundings. For example, a person in a hotel would probably not be familiar with the escape routes, making it more hazardous. Such an occupancy will need stricter codes than an apartment complex, where a tenant should be more familiar with his/her surroundings. In some cases, the number of units in the building may also make a difference. (For other occupancies that provide sleeping accommodations but with additional care, see Institutional occupancy.)

The *IBC* has four Residential subclassifications: R-1 through R-4. The NFPA codes separates these into five subclassifications: Apartment Buildings, Hotels and Dormitories, Lodging or Rooming Houses, One- and Two-Family Dwellings, and Board and Care. (See Figure 2.2.) Although these categories are similar to those in the *IBC*, there are differences. Refer to the applicable code to determine the correct occupancy subclassification. (Also see the inset titled *Rooms and Spaces* on page 73.)

R-1

⬛Note

The term *dwelling unit* is often associated with Residential and Institutional occupancies. (See the inset titled *Rooms and Spaces* on page 73 for more information.)

This type is for occupants who are transient or, in other words, do not stay for an extended period of time. If occupants typically stay more than 30 days, a building type may be required to be reclassified as R-2 or another use. In the NFPA, transient residential building types are addressed separately as hotels in the Hotels and Dormitories subclassification or the Lodging or Rooming Houses subclassification.

Sample Building Types

Boarding houses   Lodging and rooming houses

Hotels   Motels

Inns   Rooming houses

R-2

This type is for buildings that contain more than two dwelling units with occupants who are somewhat permanent. The similar NFPA categories include Apartment Buildings, Lodging or Rooming Houses, and Hotels and Dormitories.

Sample Building Types

Apartments

Boarding houses (depends on
    length of stay)

Congregate care facilities (≤ 16
    occupants)

Convents

Dormitories

Fraternities/sororities

Hotels (depends on length of stay)

Live/work units

Monasteries

Motels (depends on length
    of stay)

Multiple single-family
    dwellings

Vacation timeshare properties

> **Note**
>
> *Congregate living* facilities are most often classified as an R-2. This building type contains sleeping units but shared bathroom and/or kitchen facilities (e.g., a small boarding house). If it is a large facility, it may be classified as I-2.

R-3

This type is for more permanent residences but, unlike R-2, it is most often used for single or duplex units. The typical single-family home falls into this category. Some residential care facilities (see R-4) may also be allowed under this classification if the number of occupants is limited to less than 10 or the length of stay is less than 24 hours. Congregate living facilities for 16 persons or less are typically included in this subclassification as well. If the I-Codes are used, a jurisdiction will typically require the use of the *International Residential Code (IRC)* for the specific code requirements. Each NFPA code references its chapter on one- and two-family dwellings. (See Appendix D for more information on family residences.) Verify with the local code official which code is applicable to residential projects.

> **Note**
>
> The accessibility chapter of the *IBC* requires that the work area and the residential area of a live/work unit be evaluated separately.

> **Note**
>
> Single-family homes and duplex units are classified as an R-3 occupancy by the *IBC* and typically require the use of the *International Residential Code (IRC)*. The NFPA designation is One- and Two-Family Dwellings. (Refer to Appendix B.)

R-4

This type is for small to medium-sized residential care facilities. The allowable size of the facility is based on the number of persons receiving care and does not include staff. The typical number of residents is between 6 and 16. If fewer people are receiving care, it may be considered an R-3. If a larger number of people are receiving care, then it may be considered Institutional. (See I-1.) The similar NFPA category would be Residential Board and Care. It could also be considered a Health Care occupancy by the NFPA, depending on the number of occupants. If these types of facilities are protected by an automatic sprinkler system, they may be able to follow the requirements of the *IRC* instead of the *IBC*.

Sample Building Types

Alcohol and drug abuse centers

Assisted living facilities (can also be classified as Institutional)

Convalescent facilities (can also be classified as Institutional)

Group homes

Halfway houses

Retirement homes

Residential board and care facilities

Social rehabilitation facilities

Storage (S) Occupancy

A building or a predominant part of a building is classified as a Storage occupancy if it is used for storing or sheltering products, merchandise, vehicles, or animals. Minor storage uses, such as smaller storage rooms and supply closets, are typically treated as part of the predominant occupancy.

Similar to the Factory/Industrial occupancies, low or moderate hazard contents are typically allowed in the Storage occupancy, while the storage of high hazard contents may cause the building or space to be classified as Hazardous. The classification depends on the type of hazard and the quantity of material being stored. It is important to check the code to determine the level of hazard of the material being stored. A list of low and moderate hazardous items is shown below, but remember that each code groups them differently and each level will have slightly different requirements. The *IBC* has two storage subclassifications—one for moderate hazards (S-1) and another for low hazards (S-2). The NFPA has only one main storage classification. If unsure about the types of hazardous materials being stored, check with the local code official.

In addition, within Storage building types, it is generally understood that relatively few people will occupy the space. If the number of occupants is large or increases substantially in the future, the building occupancy may need to be reclassified.

Sample Building Types

Aircraft hangars (nonhazardous)	Grain elevators
Cold storage facilities	Repair garages (nonhazardous)
Creameries	Truck and marine terminals
Freight terminals and depots	Warehouses (nonhazardous)

Sample Low and Moderate Hazard Storage Contents

Asbestos	Glass
Beer or wine up to 12 percent alcohol in metal, glass, or ceramic containers	Glass bottles, empty or filled with noncombustible liquids
Cement in bags	Gypsum board
Chalk and crayons	Inert pigments
Cold storage	Ivory
Creameries	Meats
Dairy products in non-wax-coated paper containers	Metal cabinets
Dry cell batteries	Metal desks with plastic tops and trim
Dry insecticides	Metal parts
Electrical coils	Metals
Electrical insulation	Mirrors
Electrical motors	New empty cans
Empty cans	Oil-filed and other types of distribution transformers
Food products	Open parking structures
Foods in noncombustible containers	Porcelain and pottery
Fresh fruits and vegetables in nonplastic trays or containers	Stoves
	Talc and soapstone
Frozen foods	Washers and dryers

Utility (U) Occupancy

A building or part of a building that is not typical and/or cannot be properly classified as any of the other occupancy groups is often classified as a Utility, Special, or Miscellaneous occupancy. The building codes and *LSC* list different items in this category, and they are usually covered as a group in a separate chapter or in multiple chapters within each of the codes.

If one of the other occupancies is being housed in an unusual structure, additional codes are usually required. Examples include underground and windowless buildings. The size of the space or building should be a consideration as well. (High-rise buildings are sometimes included here because of the many additional code requirements they must meet.) If unsure whether a building would be considered a Utility or Miscellaneous occupancy, check with the local code official in the early stages of a project. (Unusual structures are beyond the scope of this book.)

◀ Note

The *IBC* also includes requirements for children's playground structures. This applies to play areas inside malls and possibly other interior spaces.

Sample Building Types

Agricultural buildings (including barns, stables, livestock shelters)

Carports

Grain silos

Greenhouses

Mobile homes

Open structures

Parking garages (can also be classified as Storage)

Private garages

Retaining walls

Sheds

Tall fences (over 6 feet, or 1829 mm)

Tanks

Temporary structures

Towers

Underground structures

Walkways and tunnels (enclosed)

Water-surrounded structures

Windowless buildings

NEW VERSUS EXISTING OCCUPANCIES

Since a majority of code requirements are based on the occupancy classification of the space or building, understanding their differences is important. For many projects, there will be additional occupancy-related items that must be considered. In some cases, for example, different code requirements may apply, depending on whether the project is considered a renovation or a new construction. The relationship between these occupancies will affect how the codes must be applied.

Whether an occupancy is new or existing becomes important when using the *Life Safety Code (LSC)*, because the *LSC* separates its regulations into these

ROOMS AND SPACES

Each building or space must be assigned an occupancy classification so that it can be determined which codes apply. In addition, certain rooms within an occupancy can affect the requirements. This is especially true in Residential and Institutional occupancies. The codes have very distinct definitions for various types of spaces, depending on how they are utilized. The following are commonly referenced in the codes:

❏ *Occupiable space.* A room or enclosed space designed for human occupancy that is equipped with means of egress, light, and ventilation, as required by the codes. This can include the spaces and rooms in most occupancies. It excludes such areas as mechanical and electrical rooms, crawl spaces, and attics. If a space is not considered occupiable, it usually does not need to meet typical accessibility requirements as specified in the building codes, the ICC/ANSI standard, and the *ADA Standards*.

❏ *Dwelling unit.* A single unit providing complete independent living facilities for one or more persons, including permanent provisions for living, sleeping, eating, cooking, and sanitation. Building types that fall into this category include single-family homes, apartment units, townhouses, and certain assisted living units. However, a hotel guest room or dorm room can also be considered a dwelling unit if it has a kitchenette, eating area (i.e., table or bar top), and living area (i.e., upholstered seating area) in addition to the typical sleeping area and bathroom. (The ICC/ANSI standard and the *IBC* divide dwelling units into Type A and Type B types for accessibility reasons. Type B dwellings have requirements similar to those of the *FHA Accessibility Guidelines (FHAG)*. Type A dwellings have additional requirements for accessibility.)

❏ *Live/Work unit.* A dwelling unit or sleeping unit where a significant portion (greater than 10 percent, but less than 50 percent) is used for nonresidential use by the tenant. It has a maximum area of 3000 square feet (279 s m) and must be located on the main floor of the unit. (A typical home office would not be considered a live/work unit).

❏ *Sleeping unit.* A sleeping unit or room is used primarily for sleeping and does not fit the definition of a dwelling unit. The space often includes a bathroom, but it would not include a cooking area (or it could include a kitchen area but no bathroom). Examples include typical guest rooms in hotels and boarding houses, jail cells, dorm rooms, and patient rooms in nursing homes or hospitals.

❏ *Guest room or suite.* Similar to a sleeping room, a guest room (or suite) is a term used by the NFPA codes to describe an accommodation that combines living, sleeping, sanitation, and storage facilities within a compartment or a contiguous group of rooms. Examples include rooms and/or suites in hotels, motels, and dormitories.

❏ *Living area or room.* This is considered any occupiable space in a Residential occupancy, other than sleeping rooms or rooms that are intended for a combination of sleeping and living. It includes spaces such as bathrooms (or toilet compartments), kitchens, closets, halls, and storage/utility spaces, but can also include other rooms such as living rooms, dining rooms, family rooms, and dens.

❏ *Habitable room.* A room in a Residential occupancy that is used for living, sleeping, cooking, and eating, but excludes such things as bathrooms, storage/utility spaces, and hallways.

two different categories for each occupancy classification. An occupancy is considered *new* if it falls into one of the following categories:

1. The occupancy is in a newly constructed building.
2. The occupancy is relocated to an existing building.
3. The occupancy is in a new addition to an existing building.
4. The occupancy is remaining in the same building but changing its size or use to a different subclassification.

This last category is important to remember since it is the least obvious. In some cases a change in size or use will cause the occupancy classification to be considered new. However, in other cases, if the change does not result in an increase in hazards or risk factors, the code official may allow it to change subclassification but still be considered existing. A change in occupancy classification can affect a number of other code regulations, including those found in the building codes, the *International Existing Building Code (IEBC)*, and the *LSC*. (See Appendix C for more information on changes in occupancies in existing buildings.) If the occupancy is considered new then many changes may be required to the entire space. If the occupancy is considered existing, then many of the existing conditions may be allowed to remain the same.

The separation of new and existing occupancies in the *LSC* and other NFPA documents allows the code official to require existing facilities, not just new occupancies, to maintain safe environments for its occupants even if the use does not change. Under the typical building code, including the *IBC*, new code requirements do not become retroactively applicable to an existing occupancy. Only when the space is renovated or a major addition is made can existing space be required to meet the newer codes.

Remember, a change in occupancy classification or subclassification can be subtle. Yet, it can change the requirements for the space. For example, if a restaurant changes to a nightclub or a restaurant changes the size of its tables so that more people can occupy the space, both can result in a change of occupancy classification. Even these slight modifications can change the sprinklering, occupant load, exit requirements, and so forth.

◀ Note

When using the *LSC*, it makes a difference if the project is considered new or existing. The *IEBC* may be required instead of the *IBC* in some jurisdictions.

MORE THAN ONE OCCUPANCY TYPE

Two or more occupancies can occur in the same building. In fact, it is actually more common to see several different occupancies in the same building than to see a single-occupancy building. A common example is a large hotel. Many large hotels have restaurants, indoor pools, conference areas, and spas. The hotel itself would be classified as Residential, but the restaurants, pools, and conference areas would be considered Assembly occupancies and the spa would be classified as a Business occupancy.

A variety of examples are listed below so that different building types can be analyzed and differences between various uses can be distinguished. (There are many other possibilities.) Notice how often the Assembly and Business occupancies occur together. These are occupancies that are common in mixed building types.

📝Note

When more than one occupancy exists in the same building or space, it will be considered an accessory, mixed, or multiple occupancy.

- ❏ Hotels (Residential) with restaurants, ballrooms, or workout rooms (Assembly or Business)
- ❏ Elementary, middle, and high schools (Educational) with gymnasiums, auditoriums, and cafeterias (Assembly)
- ❏ Office buildings (Business) with day care centers (Educational or Institutional)
- ❏ Hospitals (Institutional) with cafeterias (Assembly)
- ❏ Reformatories (Institutional) with recreational rooms (Assembly) and offices (Business)
- ❏ Factories (Industrial) combined with the office headquarters (Business)
- ❏ Malls (Mercantile) with small restaurants (Business) or large food courts (Assembly)

It is important to determine if more than one occupancy is occurring in the same building. If so, it can affect a number of other codes, such as those listed in Figure 2.1. These different occupancies can be adjacent horizontally, as in the Plan in Figure 2.3, or vertically in the case of a multi-story building, as shown in the Section in Figure 2.3. Because each occupancy type has different safety risks, special measures are necessary to make the building safe. In general, the codes require that either the occupancies be separated or all of them are treated as one, using the most stringent requirements. The codes describe the relationship of more than one occupancy differently. The *International Building Code (IBC)* refers to the relationship as accessory, separated mixed, or non-separated mixed. In a similar way, the NFPA codes, including the *Life Safety Code (LSC)*, define different occupancies as either accessory, mixed multiple, or separated multiple occupancies. The requirements for each type of "mixed" occupancy will be described in the next sections. For all of these, the ultimate goal is to provide the safest building possible.

Incidental Accessory Occupancies

Certain uses within a building are determined to be hazardous when they exist within any occupancy type. Previously referred to as *incidental use areas*, they are now referred to as *incidental accessory occupancies* in the IBC. They are simply

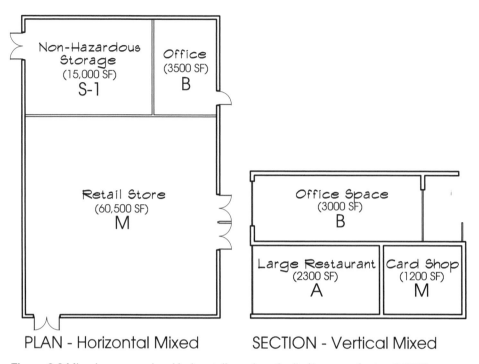

Figure 2.3 Mixed occupancies: Horizontally and vertically (1 square foot = 0.0929 square meter).

referred to as *hazardous areas* in the NFPA codes. However, in both sets of codes, their size is limited and, therefore, they are not considered a separate occupancy. For example, the laundry room within the preschool facility (Educational) shown in Plan A of Figure 2.4 would be considered an incidental accessory occupancy within the other primary-use areas such as classrooms and office areas.

The types of spaces and rooms that are considered incidental accessory occupancies are indicated within the codes either in a table or in the text. These spaces include boiler rooms, furnace rooms, large laundry rooms, and other spaces containing hazardous items or machinery. For example, the *IBC* lists specific incidental accessory occupancies in a table, as shown in Chapter 5 in Figure 5.8. As indicated in this table, additional fire and smoke protection is required for these areas. (This is discussed further in Chapter 5.) When this additional protection is provided, all other code requirements for the incidental accessory occupancies follow the codes required for the main occupancy. If this protection is not provided, the building must be classified as a mixed occupancy. (See the section Mixed Occupancies later in this chapter.) The NFPA codes list these areas within the occupancy chapter in which they are most likely to occur. For example, the requirement to separate soiled linen rooms can be found in the Health Care occupancy chapter.

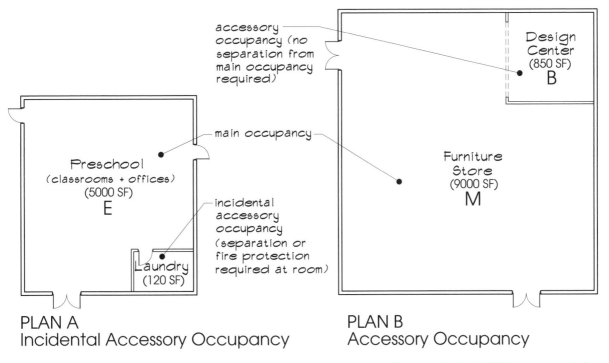

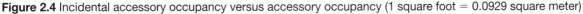

Figure 2.4 Incidental accessory occupancy versus accessory occupancy (1 square foot = 0.0929 square meter)

Accessory Occupancies

Sometimes two or more occupancies exist in a building, but one or more of them is much smaller than the main occupancy type. In this case, the smaller occupancy(ies) may be considered an *accessory* occupancy by the codes. In the *IBC*, for instance, an area can be considered an accessory use if the smaller occupancy classification(s) is less than 10 percent of the total area. (The NFPA codes may allow the accessory use to be a larger percentage of the overall area.) So, using the *IBC*, an example would be a furniture store that offers design services, as shown in Plan B of Figure 2.4. The furniture store is Mercantile (M), but the design center area would be Business (B). However, since the area of the design center is less than 10 percent of the overall area, it can be considered an *accessory* to the main Mercantile occupancy. And, because it can be considered an accessory use, the two areas will not have to be designed under separate occupancy requirements.

Sometimes there are several smaller uses occurring within a larger occupancy classification, and all are located in the same building. An example would be a

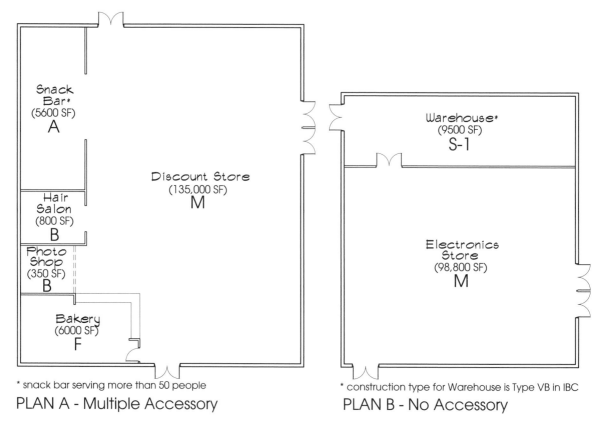

* snack bar serving more than 50 people

PLAN A - Multiple Accessory

* construction type for Warehouse is Type VB in IBC

PLAN B - No Accessory

Figure 2.5 Accessory versus occupancy examples (1 square foot = 0.0929 square meter)

☑**Note**

The NFPA codes allow an accessory occupancy to be a larger percentage of the overall space or building than the *IBC*.

large discount store, like the one shown in Plan A of Figure 2.5. This particular store has a bakery, photo shop, hair salon, and snack bar as part of its space. In this case, all the accessory spaces combined together cannot be more than the allowable percentage of the total area.

In addition to the proportional requirement, an accessory occupancy cannot exceed the allowable area for that occupancy classification in relation to the construction type of the building. For example, Plan B in Figure 2.5 is an electronics store (Mercantile, or M) with its warehouse located in the same building. The warehouse is considered a Storage (S-1) occupancy. It could be considered an accessory occupancy by the *IBC* because it does not exceed 10 percent of the total area of the building. However, because the area of the S-1 occupancy exceeds the allowable area for this particular construction type, the S-1 occupancy cannot be considered an accessory to the Mercantile. In this case, the storage area would be considered a separate storage occupancy and would need to meet the code requirements for an S-1 occupancy classification instead of the requirements for a Mercantile occupancy.

When there are approved accessory occupancies within a space or building, most of the code requirements (including the occupant load calculations and means of egress requirements) are based on the main occupancies. The fire protection requirements, however, are based on the most restrictive use (whether the accessory or main use) and apply to the entire building or space.

In some cases, certain areas are allowed to be accessory regardless of the percentage of area. For example, Assembly areas with an occupant load less than 50 and areas with less than 750 square feet (69.7 s m) can be considered accessory to the main occupancy—a small training room in an office space, for instance. It is useful to a design to determine if an area can be considered accessory to the main area, because it simplifies the code requirements and allows areas to be more open.

However, in both the IBC and the NFPA codes some occupancies cannot be considered incidental or accessory to any other classification. This includes Day Care occupancies (except for religious uses) and certain types of Residential and Educational building types. (Hazardous occupancies can never be considered as accessory to another occupancy.) If the smaller occupancy(cies) cannot be considered accessory, the space or building would need to be designed as a separated or non-separated mixed occupancy regardless of the size. (See the next section.)

Mixed Occupancies

When two or more occupancies in a building or space are relatively the same size or do not meet the requirements to be considered an accessory use, it is a *mixed occupancy*. As a result, the IBC further divides mixed occupancies into separated mixed occupancies and non-separated mixed occupancies. (The NFPA codes also use the term *separated* but it is used in relation to multiple occupancies. This is explained later in the chapter.)

When the different occupancies are divided by the required rated assemblies (e.g., walls, floor, and/or ceiling assemblies), these occupancies are considered by the IBC to be *separated mixed* occupancies. (The requirements for rated assemblies are discussed further in Chapter 5.) Once separated, each occupancy then must meet the requirements of its own occupancy classification. For example, in Plan A in Figure 2.6, the Business (B) occupancy and the Mercantile (M) occupancy are separated by a rated wall. Thus, the code requirements for the Business occupancy would apply to the post office and the Mercantile requirements would apply to the shoe store.

When there is no rated separation between the occupancies, it is considered by the IBC as a *non-separated mixed* occupancy. (This term is not used by

✑Note

Both the *IBC* and the NFPA codes use the term *separated* for when two or more occupancies are divided by rated assemblies—called *separated mixed* by the ICC and *separated multiple* by the NFPA.

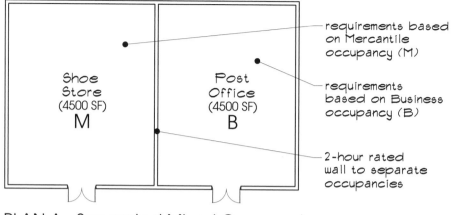

PLAN A - Separated Mixed Occupanices

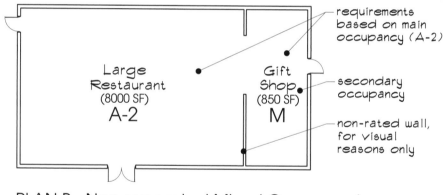

PLAN B - Non-separated Mixed Occupancies

Figure 2.6 Mixed occupancies in the *IBC*: Separated and non-separated (1 square foot = 0.0929 square meter)

the NFPA.) When the occupancies are considered non-separated, each of the occupancies must then meet the requirements of the most stringent occupancy classification, including construction type, allowable area, finishes, fire protection, and exiting requirements. For example, in Plan B of Figure 2.6, the Mercantile (M) and Assembly (A-2) occupancies are separated by a partition only for visual reasons and so are considered non-separated. In this case, the more stringent Assembly requirements for the restaurant would be applied to the entire area of the building, including the gift shop. In buildings where there are both separated and non-separated mixed occupancies, additional requirements apply. For instance, the most stringent fire protection requirements will apply to the entire building.

Many factors can influence the decision to treat a mixed occupancy as separated or non-separated. Constructing rated assemblies for separation can be expensive or undesirable to the design, but having to meet the most stringent exiting requirements, construction type, or area limitations for the whole building or space may limit the design unnecessarily. All these factors must be considered to determine the better choice for a project.

Multiple Occupancies

Multiple occupancies is a term used by the NFPA codes (not the I-Codes). It occurs when two or more occupancies exist in a building or space either horizontally or vertically. Multiple occupancies are designated more specifically as mixed or separated.

The NFPA codes consider a building or space to be a *mixed multiple* occupancy when two or more occupancies exist together and are "intermingled." This can occur if (1) there is no rated separation(s) between the occupancies, (2) the different occupancies use the same exiting components (aisle, corridors, stairs, etc.), or (3) both occur at the same time. For example, refer again to Plan B in Figure 2.6; because there is no rated separation between the Assembly (A-2) and Mercantile (M) occupancies, it is considered a mixed multiple occupancy. In addition, if a portion of the occupants from the restaurant must exit through the gift store as part of the required exiting, that would also make it a mixed occupancy.

A different type of mixed multiple occupancy is shown in Plan A of Figure 2.7. These occupancies are separated by rated walls and may seem to be separated occupancies. However, because the tenants share the corridor when exiting from each space, it would be considered a mixed multiple occupancy by the NFPA. If a multiple occupancy is considered mixed, the construction type, fire protection, and means of egress, as well as other requirements, must follow the most restrictive occupancy requirements. (In this way, it is similar to non-separated mixed occupancies in the *IBC*.)

On the other hand, if the occupancies are separated by rated walls but do not share exiting, then the NFPA considers the area a *separated multiple* occupancy. Like the separated mixed occupancy in the *IBC*, each space must meet the code requirements for its occupancy classification. An example of a separated multiple occupancy can be seen in Plan B of Figure 2.7. Here the multiple occupancy classifications are separated from each other by a rated wall. In addition, each has its own separate means of egress, so they do not share a common corridor. All of these factors make it a separated multiple occupancy.

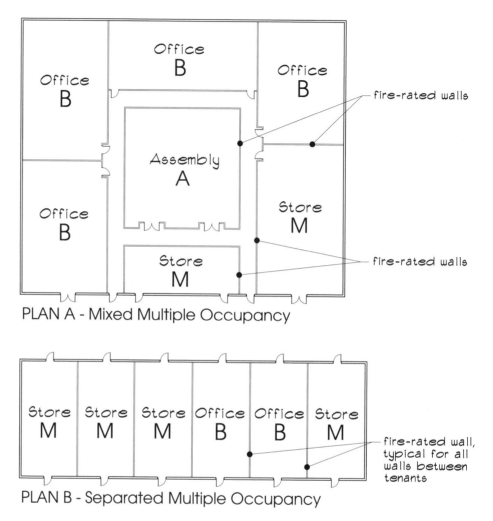

Figure 2.7 Multiple occupancies in the NFPA codes: Mixed and separated.

The NFPA codes designate how a mixed or separated multiple occupancy should be handled. More specific information on multiple occupancies may also be found within each occupancy chapter. These requirements supersede the general requirements for mixed or separated occupancy classifications. These individual occupancy chapters must be reviewed to know when they apply. In addition, a code official may need to be consulted to determine which requirements will apply to the different areas versus the whole building. This is especially important if working in a jurisdiction that requires both the *IBC* and the *LSC*.

ACCESSIBILITY REQUIREMENTS

Almost all occupancy classifications under certain conditions can be considered public accommodations and/or commercial facilities and can be regulated by the *ADA Standards* under the ADA. In addition to the general accessibility requirements described throughout this book, the *ADA Standards* include specific requirements for certain building types within various occupancies. The building codes and the *ICC/ANSI A117.1* accessibility standard also include some similar requirements, although these are not as extensive as those of the *ADA Standards*.

Below is a list of building types found in the *ADA Standards* and the special accessibility requirements required for each. (The type of occupancy classification is indicated as well.) This list is based on the *2010 ADA Standards*. In addition, there are specific storage requirements for any occupancy that requires accessible storage as well as additional requirements specifically for dwelling unites (Residential). When working within these occupancies, the code research should include reviewing the current *ADA Standards* as well as comparing them to the *ICC/ANSI* standard, the accessibility chapter of the *IBC*, and other codes enforced by the local jurisdiction to see if there are contradictory or stricter requirements. Other federal accessibility regulations may also apply (e.g., *FHAG* and *ABA Standards*), as explained in Chapter 1, and additional regulations for certain occupancies may be added in the future. When necessary, consult the local code official or the ADA Access Board for clarification.

Assembly Areas

- ❑ Percentage of accessible wheelchair locations
- ❑ Location and dispersion of wheelchair spaces and companion seats
- ❑ Access to performance areas
- ❑ Types of floor surfaces
- ❑ Possible assistive listening systems
- ❑ Types and placement of listening systems

Businesses and Mercantile

- ❑ Size of checkout counters and worksurfaces
- ❑ Clearance and height of self-service shelves/display units
- ❑ Size of teller windows and information counters
- ❑ Width and quantity of checkout aisles

- ❑ Clearance at security elements
- ❑ Number, size, and types of dressing/fitting rooms
- ❑ Type and clearance of automatic teller machines

Medical and Long-Term Care Facilities (Institutional and Health Care)

- ❑ Size of covered entrances for unloading patients
- ❑ Percentage of accessible toilets
- ❑ Percentage and dispersion of accessible patient bedrooms
- ❑ Dispersion of accessible patient bedrooms
- ❑ Size of maneuvering spaces in patient rooms
- ❑ Clearance area at patient beds
- ❑ Width of accessible doors and aisles

✎Note

The *2010 ADA Standards* has many similar requirements to the ICC/ANSI standard and the accessibility chapter of the *IBC*.

Restaurants and Cafeterias (Business or Assembly)

- ❑ Percentage of accessible fixed tables
- ❑ Access to sunken and raised platforms
- ❑ Width of food service lines
- ❑ Height of counters and self-service shelves
- ❑ Access to controls of vending machines
- ❑ Width of access aisles

Transient Lodgings (Residential)

- ❑ Percentage of accessible sleeping rooms
- ❑ Dispersion of accessible elements in types of rooms
- ❑ Specific requirements within accessible rooms
- ❑ Number and dispersion of rooms for hearing-impaired
- ❑ Dispersion of accessible rooms suitable for disabled with multiple disabilities (mobility, hearing, visual, etc.)
- ❑ Access to rooms and public and common areas
- ❑ Width of door openings
- ❑ Size of maneuvering spaces
- ❑ Percentage of accessible amenities (ice machines, washers and dryers, etc.)
- ❑ Clearance, height, and hardware of storage units

Housing at Places of Education (similar to Transient Lodging and Residential)

- ❏ Percentage of accessible units
- ❏ Dispersion of accessible elements among accessible rooms
- ❏ Specific requirements within accessible rooms
- ❏ Access to rooms and public and common areas
- ❏ Width of door openings
- ❏ Accessible circulation within units
- ❏ Access to kitchen units

Judicial, Legislative, and Regulatory Facilities (Business and Assembly)

- ❏ Access to secured entrances (including an accessible security system)
- ❏ Access to courtroom elements (judge's bench, jury assembly, and deliberation areas, etc.)
- ❏ Access to holding cells (and amenities)
- ❏ Dispersion of accessible cells
- ❏ Accessible security systems
- ❏ Percentage of assistive listening systems

Detention and Correctional Facilities (Institutional)

- ❏ Percentage of holding and housing cells or rooms (and amenities)
- ❏ Dispersion of accessible cells
- ❏ Access to cells and visiting areas

Spaces for Children (Educational and certain Institutional)

- ❏ Access to drinking fountains
- ❏ Access to toilet facilities (including water closets, toilet stalls, lavatories)
- ❏ Access to dining and work surfaces
- ❏ Adjusted reach ranges
- ❏ Height of handrails at ramps and stairs
- ❏ Height of mirrors
- ❏ Height of controls

Transportation Facilities (Assembly or Business)

- ❏ Boarding areas
- ❏ Signs

❏ Accessible routes

❏ Communication elements

Recreational Facilities (Assembly)

❏ Percentage of accessible sauna and steam rooms

❏ Number of accessible means of entry to pool

❏ Number of accessible shooting facilities

Social Service Establishments (Residential)

❏ Access to beds

❏ Access to accessible toilet and roll in showers

DESIGN LOADS

Occupant loads as described in this chapter are not to be confused with two other types of design loads required by the codes—dead loads and live loads. *Dead loads* include all permanent components of a building's structure, such as the walls, floors, and roof. *Live loads,* on the other hand, include any loads that are not the actual weight of the structure itself. They include interior elements such as people, furniture, equipment, appliances, and books. Other loads that are sometimes considered live loads but are separate exterior elements include wind loads, rain and flood loads, snow loads, and earthquake loads. These types of load factors affect the design of the building's structure.

Specific calculations must be made to determine each type of load. These calculations are typically done by engineers during the initial design and construction of a building. Most of the calculations take into consideration that some of the loads will change during the normal use of a building. For example, in an office building it is common for interior walls to change and be relocated as tenants move. The number of people will vary as well.

Some interior projects may require certain live loads to be researched when significant changes are proposed in a project. The most common situations include (1) adding a wall, such as brick or concrete, that is substantially heavier than a standard wall; (2) creating a filing area or library that concentrates the weight at one point; (3) adding a heavy piece of equipment; and (4) adding an assembly seating area in an existing space.

In most cases, a structural engineer is needed to determine if the existing structure will hold the added load/weight. If not, the structural engineer will determine how to add additional support, if possible.

DETERMINING OCCUPANT LOADS

In addition to determining the occupancy classification at the beginning of a project, the occupant load also needs to be determined. The *occupant load* is used to determine how many people can safely use the space. It sets the number of occupants for which adequate exiting must be provided from a space or building. Proper exiting allows people to evacuate safely and quickly. Usually, the occupant load is determined for each space or building either by using a load factor given by the code or by establishing a desired number of occupants. If multiple spaces will be exiting into a common area or *converging* into a common path of travel, the codes require that the occupant load for the shared area be determined by adding the number of occupants who will share a common path to an exit. These methods can be used to determine the number of people that is assumed will be using the corridors, stairs, and exits in the event of a fire.

◿Note

Occupant loads are typically determined using the load factors given by the codes.

Occupant loads are often based on a relationship between the size and use of the space or building. In most cases, this means that a larger space allows more occupants, and the need for more occupants requires a larger space. In some cases, the number of occupants can be increased without increasing the size of the space. However, the building codes, such as the *International Building Code (IBC)*, and the *Life Safety Code (LSC)* do set limits on the allowable concentration of occupants within a building. In addition, the occupant load may be needed to determine the occupancy classification. An example is a restaurant with an occupancy under 50 (Business) and a restaurant with an occupant load over 50 (Assembly).

It is important to determine the occupant load early in the design process because not only will it provide guidance in the correct selection of a building's occupancy classification, but it affects other codes as well. For example, the occupant load is needed to size the means of egress components, such as number of exits and the width of corridors and aisles. (See Chapter 4.) The number of required plumbing fixtures and certain mechanical calculations also depend on the occupant load. (See Chapter 7.) The remainder of this chapter explains occupant loads.

Occupant Load by Load Factor

Because most means of egress requirements will be based on the occupant load, the code must establish a *minimum* level of safety. To do this, each code assigns a predetermined amount of area or square feet (or square meters) required for each occupant based on the occupancy classification and the specific use of the space. This predetermined figure is called the *load factor*. Using the load factor to determine the occupant load typically generates the lowest number or minimum number of occupants for which the space must be designed.

Using the Table

Each code discusses occupant load requirements, including load factors and exiting requirements within the means of egress chapter. The NFPA codes, including the *LSC*, have additional occupant load factors and requirements in each separate occupancy chapter as well. Figure 2.8 is the load factor table from the *IBC*, titled Table 1004.1.1, "Maximum Floor Area Allowances per Occupant." The NFPA codes have similar load factor tables.

The first column in Figure 2.8 is titled "Function of Space." This column lists the different uses for spaces within a building. For example, there is not just one load factor for Assembly occupancies—there are three, including "Assembly with fixed seats" and "Assembly without fixed seats." In addition, under the latter, there is the option of "Concentrated (chairs only—not fixed)," "Standing space," or "Unconcentrated (tables and chairs)." How the space is being used specifically must be considered. The load factors are listed in the next column in square feet per person. (A metric conversion is shown at the bottom of the table.) These areas are given for each of the specific uses or building types within the different occupancy classifications. The load factor indicates the amount of space or area it is assumed each person present will require. Although the square foot figures may seem high for one person, they allow for furniture and equipment and, in some cases, corridors, closets, and other miscellaneous areas.

The area for each load factor refers to the floor area *within* the exterior walls of a building. The load factors are designated as gross or net area. The *gross* area refers to the building as a whole and includes all miscellaneous spaces within the exterior walls. The *net* area refers to actual occupied spaces and does not include ancillary spaces such as corridors, restrooms, utility closets, or other unoccupied areas. The area of fixed items, such as interior walls, columns, and built-in counters and shelving (areas that are not habitable), are also deducted from the overall area.

When net figures are required, it is assumed that the occupants who are using an ancillary area would have left the occupied space to do so and, therefore, would already be taken into account. For example, a person in the corridor of a school would most likely be a student or teacher already accounted for in a classroom.

The Formula

The formula that is used with the load factor tables is

$$\text{Occupant load} = \text{Floor area (sq ft or sq m)} \div \text{Load factor}$$

TABLE 1004.1.1
MAXIMUM FLOOR AREA ALLOWANCES PER OCCUPANT

FUNCTION OF SPACE	FLOOR AREA IN SQ. FT. PER OCCUPANT
Accessory storage areas, mechanical equipment room	300 gross
Agricultural building	300 gross
Aircraft hangars	500 gross

Airport terminal
  Baggage claim
  Baggage handling
  Concourse
  Waiting areas
	
	20 gross
	300 gross
	100 gross
	15 gross

Assembly Gaming floors (keno, slots, etc.)	 11 gross
Assembly with fixed seats	See Section 1004.7

Assembly without fixed seats
  Concentrated (chairs only—not fixed)
  Standing space
  Unconcentrated (tables and chairs)
	
	7 net
	5 net
	15 net

Bowling centers, allow 5 persons for each lane including 15 feet of runway, and for additional areas	 7 net
Business areas	100 gross
Courtrooms—other than fixed seating areas	40 net
Day care	35 net
Dormitories	50 gross

Educational
  Classroom area
  Shops and other vocational room areas
	
	20 net
	50 net

Exercise rooms	50 gross
H-5 Fabrication and manufacturing areas	200 gross
Industrial areas	100 gross

Institutional areas
  Inpatient treatment areas
  Outpatient areas
  Sleeping areas
	
	240 gross
	100 gross
	120 gross

Kitchens, commercial	200 gross

Library
  Reading rooms
  Stack area
	
	50 net
	100 gross

Locker rooms	50 gross

Mercantile
  Areas on other floors
  Basement and grade floor areas
  Storage, stock, shipping areas
	
	60 gross
	30 gross
	300 gross

Parking garages	200 gross
Residential	200 gross

Skating rinks, swimming pools
  Rink and pool
  Decks
	
	50 gross
	15 gross

Stages and platforms	15 net
Warehouses	500 gross

For SI: 1 square foot = 0.0929 m^2.

Figure 2.8 *International Building Code (IBC)* Table 1004.1.1, Maximum Floor Area Allowances per Occupant (*2009 International Building Code*, copyright 2009. Washington, DC: International Code Council. All rights reserved. www.iccsafe.org).

⬗Note

The NFPA codes give load
factors in square feet and
in metric dimensions.
The *IBC* provides a metric
conversion at the bottom of
the load factor table.

⬗Note

Gross area includes all areas
within the exterior walls. *Net
area* consists of all areas
within the exterior walls
minus ancillary spaces such
as corridors, restrooms,
utility closets, and other
unoccupied areas.

To determine the occupant load for a building or space, take the area of the interior space and divide it by the load factor for the appropriate building type and/or use. If the space or building has more than one type of use, the same is done for each area according to its use and added together. This provides the number of occupants that is allowed in the space. If the total results in a fraction over a half of an occupant, round up to the nearest whole number. Depending on the project, calculations for separate areas and separate occupancies may also need to be made and added together. The final occupant load indicates the number of occupants for which the space must designed.

Example 1

To further understand the difference between gross and net area and how to use the load factor table, refer to the floor plan for a library in Figure 2.9. "Library" is listed separately in the *IBC* table in Figure 2.8. This building type is further divided into two separate functions: reading rooms and stack area. A study room, corridor, and utility closet are also noted on the plan. These will have to be addressed as well. The occupant load for each separate function must be determined separately.

The load factor for the stack area of the library is indicated in the table in Figure 2.8 as "100 *gross* square feet (9.3 s m)." So, the area measurement should include the entire stack area with aisles, reference area, checkout counter, and so forth. The occupant load factor for the reading rooms is indicated to be "50 *net* square feet (4.6 s m)," meaning that the area should not include ancillary spaces. Although there is not a specific function listed in the table in Figure 2.8, a study room use is similar to a small conference room. A small conference room may be determined by using the Assembly-Unconcentrated (tables and chairs). The load factor for this use is "15 *net* square feet (1.39 s m)." Both the reading room and the study room areas call for net load factors. Therefore, the corridor or the utility closet adjacent to the reading rooms on the floor plan should not be included when determining the area of the reading room or study room. They are essentially left out of the load factor calculation because they are not considered to contribute additional occupants to the library.

Using the dimensions of the floor plan and the occupant load formula to determine the area for each space, Figure 2.9 shows how to determine the occupant load for the entire library. Rounding up, the total occupant load is 40 people.

Example 2

Sometimes, load factors can be used in a slightly different way. If the area required for a particular occupancy or use needs to be determined, the load factors may help establish the space requirements. This may be helpful in the programming stage of a project. For example, if planning a new office space for a client with

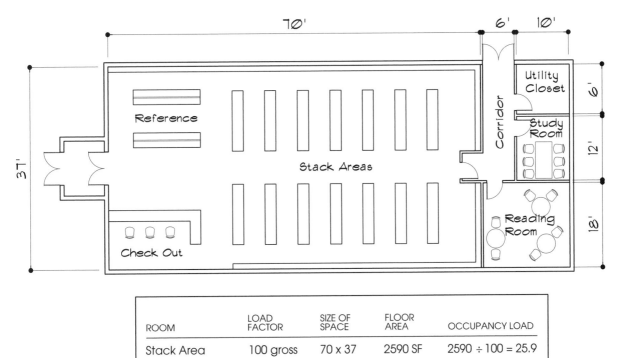

ROOM	LOAD FACTOR	SIZE OF SPACE	FLOOR AREA	OCCUPANCY LOAD
Stack Area	100 gross	70 x 37	2590 SF	2590 ÷ 100 = 25.9
Reading Room	50 net	16 x 18	288 SF	288 ÷ 50 = 5.8
Study Room	15 net	10 x 12	120 SF	120 ÷ 15 = 8
			Total Number of Occupants =	39.7 = 40

Figure 2.9 Occupancy load example: Single occupancy (Library) (1 square foot = 0.0929 square meter).

125 employees, the table can be used to look up the occupant load factor under Business areas (100 gross square feet, or 9.3 s m). Multiply this factor by the number of people intended to occupy the space (125) to determine the minimum size of space needed. In this case, at least 12,500 square feet (1161.3 s m) will be required according to the codes. This can be done for a smaller use such as a breakroom or conference room as well. Although this will provide a good estimate, typically other program requirements must be added to that area to determine the final size of a space or building.

⬥Note

Beginning with the 2006 *IBC,* a new occupant load factor for day care centers was added.

Modifying the Occupant Load

In some cases, it might be desirable to have more people occupy a space than are determined by the load factor. However, if an increased occupant load of a space is allowed, additional exiting for the increased number of occupants must typically be provided. This may require providing additional diagrams showing aisles, exit widths, seating configurations, and/or locations of fixed equipment to the code official for approval. The codes use the term *modified number* because the space is to be designed for an increased number of occupants rather than the number calculated using the load factor.

For example, a client rents a space that is 5000 square feet (464.5 s m) for use as a restaurant (Assembly). Referring to the load factor table in Figure 2.8, the load factor is 15 gross square feet (1.4 s m) for an "Assembly without fixed seats, Unconcentrated (tables and chairs)." By dividing 5000 square feet (464.5 s m) by 15 gross square feet (1.4 s m), the result is an occupant load of 333 occupants. However, if the client wanted to be able to seat 400, then 400 would be considered the desired occupant load—the modified number. The means of egress (i.e., exits, aisles, corridors, and number of doors) would then be designed for an occupant load of 400. That would also be the maximum number allowed within the space at any one time. Making sure that the space or building could handle the increased exiting requirements and other accessible clearances is also necessary. When designing for an increased occupant load, it is advisable to review it with the code official early in the design process.

There may be instances when a *reduced number* is desirable so that a space is designed for a number of occupants less than the calculated load. For example, a storeroom may not typically be occupied by the number of occupants determined by the load factor. In previous codes, designing for a lower number was not generally allowed. Similar to designing for an increased occupant load, designing for a reduced number also must be approved by the code official. Justifying the use and the reduced number may be necessary. In addition, to allow the lower occupant load, the code official can require special conditions and limitations for the use of the space. Remember, designing the space for the lower occupant load can affect the future use of the space because of the lower means of egress capacity.

Occupant Load for Primary and Secondary Spaces

When one or more smaller spaces exits into a larger or primary space before reaching the final exit, the codes usually require that the occupant load of the primary space include the occupant loads of the secondary spaces that exit through it. Two examples are shown in Figure 2.10. The business offices are secondary spaces within the Business occupancy. Occupants must walk through the open office area in order to exit the building. However, the training room would also be considered a secondary space, since it too must empty through the open office area. In this case, the occupant load for the large training room in Figure 2.10 should be calculated separately using an Assembly (A) factor, not the load factor of the main Business (B)

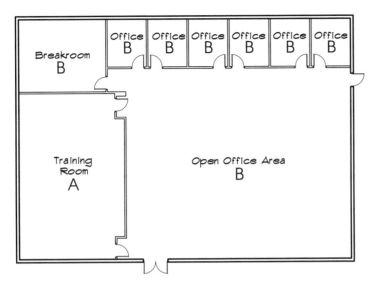

Figure 2.10 Occupant load example: Primary and secondary spaces.

occupancy. When these separate calculations are added together, they provide an occupant load that more accurately addresses the use of the space.

An accessory space can sometimes be considered a secondary space as well. For example, the occupant load for the design center (B) in Figure 2.4B should be added to the occupant load of the Mercantile (M) portion of the furniture store, since the occupants of the design center must walk through the store to exit the building. Each would be calculated separately according to the load factor for its occupancy classification. This total would be used to determine the exiting from the primary space.

Occupant Load for More Than One Occupancy

Whenever there is more than one occupancy in the same space or building, additional calculations are typically required. For example, if two occupancies share the same floor, the occupant load for each occupancy must be determined separately. The exiting requirements for each particular space must then be determined based on each calculated occupant load. However, if these occupancies share common spaces such as exiting corridors or restrooms, the total occupant load of the floor may also need to be determined. This will be used to establish the requirements for the common areas and the exiting requirements for the entire floor. Additional calculations may also be required when mixed or multiple occupancies are found on the same floor or in the same building and when a space used for more than one function. Each of these is explained as follows.

Mixed or Multiple Occupancies

When there is more than one occupancy type on the same floor or in the same building, the occupant load for each occupancy must be calculated separately. These occupant loads are added together to determine the occupant load of the floor. Shared common areas must also be considered. The total occupant load is then used to determine other code requirements, such as exiting and plumbing fixtures. An example is shown in Figure 2.11. In this example, there is a mixture of Mercantile (M) and Business (B) spaces on the first floor and multiple Business (B) spaces on the second floor.

One way to figure the occupant load for the first floor is to calculate the occupant load separately for each tenant space and required common areas and then add them together. Another way (as shown in Figure 2.11) is to combine the areas for all the occupancy classifications that are the same (i.e., all the Business occupancies) and then use the load factor for that use. The same would then be done for the Mercantile occupancies. In this case, because a gross load factor is required, the public areas will also have to be included in the calculations (i.e., lobby, restrooms, main corridor). Typically, this would be proportionally divided among the different occupancy types, as shown in Figure 2.11. (See the note at the bottom of the figure.) Once the occupant load for each occupancy or each tenant is determined, add them together with the common areas to get the total occupant load for the whole floor. The total occupant load on the first floor is 205.

The same process is used for the second floor, as shown in Figure 2.11. However, in this case there is only one occupancy type. The total occupant load for the second floor is 124. The occupant load for each floor (including common areas) will be used for code requirements such as exiting, which affect the entire floor and the stairs. (See Chapter 4.) It will also be used to determine the number of plumbing fixtures in the common toilet facilities on each floor. (See Chapter 7.)

Areas with Multiple Uses

Some buildings or building areas are used for different purposes at different times. For example, a church fellowship hall might be used for a large assembly one night and as a cafeteria the next. The following weekend, it might be used as a gymnasium or exercise room. In other words, any area of a building that has more than one function is considered to have multiple uses. The occupant load is determined by the use that indicates the largest concentration of people. Several calculations may be required to determine which occupancy will provide the largest number.

Occupant Load for Fixed Seats

Fixed seating arrangements are common in some building types, especially in Assembly occupancies. The seats are considered fixed if they are not easily

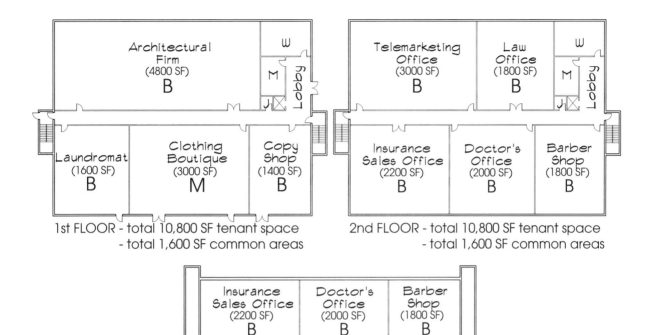

1st FLOOR - total 10,800 SF tenant space
- total 1,600 SF common areas

2nd FLOOR - total 10,800 SF tenant space
- total 1,600 SF common areas

BUILDING SECTION - front side

FIRST FLOOR	LOAD FACTOR	FLOOR AREA	OCCUPANCY LOAD
M (Mercantile) Tenants	30 gross	3000 SF	3000 ÷ 30 = 100
M Common Area*	30 gross	448 SF (1,600 x 28%)	448 ÷ 30 = 15
B (Business) Tenants	100 gross	7800 SF (10,800 - 3000)	7800 ÷ 100 = 78
B Common Areas*	100 gross	1152 SF (1,600 x 72%)	1152 ÷ 100 = 12
		Total Number of Occupants @ 1st FLOOR =	205
SECOND FLOOR			
B (Business) Tenants	100 gross	10,800 SF	10,800 ÷ 100 = 108
B Common Areas	100 gross	1600 SF	1,600 ÷ 100 = 16
		Total Number of Occupants @ 2nd FLOOR =	124
		TOTAL OCCUPANT LOAD FOR BUILDING =	329

*NOTE: Of the total tenant square footage for the 1st floor, the Business tenants occupy 72% of the space (7800 divided by 10,800) and the Mercantile tenant occupies the remaining 28%.

Figure 2.11 Occupant load example: Mixed/multiple occupancy building (1 square foot = 0.0929 square meter).

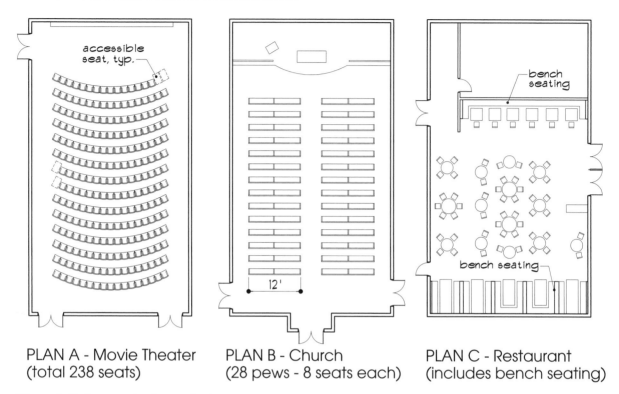

PLAN A - Movie Theater
(total 238 seats)

PLAN B - Church
(28 pews - 8 seats each)

PLAN C - Restaurant
(includes bench seating)

Figure 2.12 Occupant load example: Occupancies with fixed seats.

moved and/or if they are used on a relatively permanent basis. Instead of using the standard formula for calculating the occupant load when separate fixed seats are present, the actual seats are counted. For example, the occupant load in a movie theater, as shown in Plan A of Figure 2.12, would be determined by the number of seats used in the space (including spaces specifically created for wheelchair users).

Counting seats with arms is self-explanatory. However, fixed seating may also consist of continuous seating such as benches, bleachers, and pews. Each of the codes provides a variable (either in the occupant load table or the text) to be used for continuous seating. They typically allow 18 linear inches (457 mm) of seating for each occupant. If, for example, there is a church that has 28 pews and each pew is 12 feet long, as shown in Plan B of Figure 2.12, the 18-inch (457 mm) variable would be used. A 12-foot pew equals 144 inches (3658 mm). Divide the 144 (3658 mm) by the 18-inch (457 mm) variable to get 8 people per pew. Since there are a total of 28 pews, this church has an occupant load of 224 people (28 pews × 8 people/pew).

◢Note

The continuous seating variable will not always evenly divide into the length of the seating. Usually, if the remaining fraction is one-half or greater, round up to include another occupant. Consult the local code official when there is uncertainty.

Booth seating is another type of continuous fixed seating. Booth seating usually has a separate variable provided by the codes. The typical increment is 24 inches (609.6 mm). For example, Plan C in Figure 2.12 shows several types of booth seating. Each should be calculated separately. Measure the length of the bench along the *front* edge (especially at corners) and divide by 24 inches (609.6 mm). Add all the calculations together to determine the occupant load for the bench areas. This would be added to the occupant loads of the other seating areas within the space to determine the total occupant load of the restaurant.

All areas of a building or space need to be included in the occupant count. If the space has different types of seating and different types of activities occurring, each area would be assigned by its specific use. For example, a nightclub might have fixed seating in one area, tables and chairs in another, and a dance floor in another. In this case, calculate the occupant load for all the different areas separately and add them together to get the final count.

☝**Note**

Buildings with fixed seats may require additional occupant load calculations, depending on the amount of adjacent open area. Check with the code official.

Occupant Load for Unusual Uses

There may also be occasions when the building type or the use of a space is not typical. The occupant load factors given in the code table may not be appropriate for a unique use. Or a specific occupancy use may not be listed on the table. On other occasions, a space may not clearly fit into one of the use categories. When this occurs, it is important to meet with a code official for guidance. Typically, only the code official can approve a different or unique load factor. This decision should be made at the beginning of a project, because occupancy classifications and many of the codes depend on the determined occupant load.

USING THE OCCUPANT LOAD

The occupant loads determined at the beginning of a project will be used again later in the code research to determine several aspects of the design. Occupant loads will be used to determine the capacity of the means of egress, such as the number of exits and the width of the exits. It will also be used to determine the number of plumbing fixtures and to size a mechanical system. (This will be discussed later in Chapters 4 and 7.) As the space is being designed, the space should be adequate for the occupant load and the occupant load should be appropriate for the intended use. Also be aware that changes in the occupant load may affect the occupancy classification and many of the applicable code requirements. It should be clear that they have an interactive relationship that can potentially affect several aspects of the design.

⧆ Note

Every assembly room or Assembly occupancy usually requires the approved occupant load to be permanently posted near the main exit from the space. A typical sign might read: "Occupancy by more than 100 persons is dangerous and unlawful."

⧆ Note

Not only can a building have more than one occupancy, but each occupancy can have more than one use for the purpose of determining the occupant load. Therefore, one building or a large tenant space could require a number of calculations.

In all cases, adequate means of egress must be provided for the number of people who will be occupying a space or building. Once the occupant load is set and the means of egress has been designed, the number of people allowed within a space cannot exceed that load or number. For Assembly uses, the approved occupant load is required to be posted for each space. In other spaces, a code official may require the approved occupant load to be posted where a modified occupant load has been used to design the space. Exceeding the posted allowable occupant load is unsafe and unlawful.

CHECKLIST

Figure 2.13 is designed to help you determine the occupancy classification(s) and occupant load(s) for a particular project. It is a basic checklist that is set up to make sure that you address the same typical occupancy questions for each project. The top of the checklist provides spaces to include project information and indicate the code sources used.

The first part of the checklist is used to identify the risk factors and unique conditions that exist within the space or building. For some projects, the occupancy classification may be straightforward or already determined. You can also use the multiple lists in this chapter in conjunction with the codes to help you determine the use of the building or space. However, if special conditions exist or if you are using performance codes, identifying these unique conditions within your project can be important. Check the risk factors you know exist within your space, then compare that to the definitions of each occupancy classification, and/ or subclassification. From what you know about the activities within the space and these risk factors, you should be able to determine the correct occupancy. If hazards are present, note them as well. Each of the code publications lists the types of hazards to look for and whether they are explosive, fire, physical, or health hazards.

Keep in mind that you may have more than one type of occupancy within the space or building. In the next section of the checklist, indicate whether you will need to consider the requirements for incidental uses, accessory uses, mixed occupancies (separated or non-separated), multiple uses (mixed or separated), or fixed seats. Check the ones that apply to your project and use the notes provided in parentheses to assist you in determining the types of occupant load calculations you will require. For example, if you are working on a department store that includes a photography studio as an incidental use, you know that you will have to calculate each area separately. Or you may need to calculate a fixed seating area separate from an open area. (Refer to this chapter for additional information as required.)

Occupancy Checklist

Date: _____

Project Name: _____   Space: _____

Code Source Used (check all that apply): ___ IBC ___ LSC ___ NPFA 5000 ___ OTHER: _____

Occupancy Risk Factors/Hazards (check those that apply):

__ High number of occupants	__ Occupant generally unfamiliar with space
__ Occupants resting or sleeping	__ Unusual characteristics of building/space
__ Alertness of occupants	__ Potential for spread of fire
__ Mobility of occupants	__ Hazardous materials stored or used
__ Age of occupants	Type of hazard: _____
__ Security measures	__ Other: _____

Occupancy Considerations (check those that apply):[1]

__ Single Occupancy (may require more than one calculation based on types of use and/or load factors)

__ Incidental Accessory Occupancies (if separated according to code, include in main occupancy; if not, may need to calculate separately)

__ Accessory Occupancies (occupant load calculated separately from main occupancy; may need to include with main for exiting)

__ Separated Mixed or Multiple Occupancy (calculate occupant load for each occupancy)

__ Non-Separated Mixed Occupancy (*IBC* only) (use strictest occupancy requirements)

__ Mixed Multiple Occupancy (*NFPA* only) (calculate occupant load for each occupancy)

__ Occupancy with Fixed Seats (may need to calculate fixed seats and surrounding open areas)

__ Accessibility Requirements (*ADA Standards*, building codes, ICC/ANSI standards)

Occupant Loads[1]

Calculation 1 - Occupancy Classification: _____
  Building Use (__ NEW __ EXISTING): _____
  __ Load Factor[2] (__ GROSS __ NET): _____
  __ Fixed Seat Variable (__ WITH ARMS __ CONTINUOUS __ BENCH): _____
  Actual Floor Area (__ GROSS __ NET):_____ OR Number/Length of Fixed Seats: _____
  Occupant Load 1 (__ USING LOAD FACTOR FORMULA __ BASED ON FIXED SEATS): _____

Calculation 2 - Occupancy Classification: _____
  Building Use (__ NEW __ EXISTING): _____
  __ Load Factor[2] (__ GROSS __ NET): _____
  __ Fixed Seat Variable (__ WITH ARMS __ CONTINUOUS __ BENCH): _____
  Actual Floor Area (__ GROSS __ NET):_____ OR Number/Length of Fixed Seats: _____
  Occupant Load 2 (__ USING LOAD FACTOR FORMULA __ BASED ON FIXED SEATS): _____

Calculation 3 - Occupancy Classification: _____
  Building Use (__ NEW __ EXISTING): _____
  __ Load Factor[2] (__ GROSS __ NET): _____
  __ Fixed Seat Variable (__ WITH ARMS __ CONTINUOUS __ BENCH): _____
  Actual Floor Area (__ GROSS __ NET):_____ OR Number/Length of Fixed Seats: _____
  Occupant Load 3 (__ USING LOAD FACTOR FORMULA __ BASED ON FIXED SEATS): _____

Total Calculated Occupant Load:_____ (__ SPACE __ FLOOR __ BUILDING)

Modified Occupant Load - Based on Actual Needs: _____

Local Code Approval (when required)
  __ NO __ YES NAME: _____   DATE: _____

NOTES:
1. If there is more than one main occupancy in the same space or building, you may want to use a separate checklist for each.
2. If you are using a gross load factor, you may need to include shared common spaces in addition to the ancillary spaces.

Figure 2.13 Occupancy checklist.

The next part of the checklist is to help you determine the occupant load of the entire space, floor, or building, as necessary for your project. Depending on the types of occupancy considerations you checked, it allows you up to three separate occupant load calculations. You can calculate different parts of the space or building separately and then add them together at the bottom or use one of the calculations to determine the occupant load for any shared common areas. Starting with the first calculation, indicate the occupancy classification and/or subclassification (i.e., Business or Assembly/A-3) and then the building type or use (i.e., Doctor's Office or Library). Also check if space is new or existing. This will be important if you are using the *LSC*. (You may also be required to use the *International Existing Building Code*.)

Continuing with "Calculation 1," the rest of the calculation will depend on whether it is a space with or without fixed seating. More commonly, you will need to use the load factor provided by the codes, so you would check "Load Factor" on the next line and write in the load factor from the code table. Also indicate if it is a gross or net load factor. If, on the other hand, this building use has fixed seats or benches, check "Fixed Seat Variable" on the next line instead, indicate the type of fixed seat, and write in the fixed seat variable provided by the codes. (If the seats are fixed seats with arms, no variable is required.)

The next line is to record the actual floor area to be used for the calculations of the building's use or space. Note whether you determined net or gross square feet (s m). Which measure you use depends on whether the load factor is net or gross. Remember that when net area is required, you do not include the ancillary spaces. (See the definition of net floor area in the Glossary if necessary.) If you indicated that the space has fixed seats, then write in either the total number of fixed seats with arms or the overall length of the continuous seats (i.e., linear length of each bench).

The last part of "Calculation 1" asks you to calculate and record the occupant load for that particular use. Remember, if you are using load factors, divide the actual measured floor area by the load factor you wrote down. If you are using fixed seats, calculate the number of seats using the overall length of fixed seats divided by the fixed seat variable. (Or write in the total number of seats with fixed arms.)

Because you may often have more than one building type or use in the same space, there is a place for you to figure the occupant load for a second and third occupancy or use, if necessary, or for the common areas. Repeat the process for each one. If there are several occupancies, however, you may want to complete a separate checklist for each occupancy or part of a building.

After you have calculated the occupant load for each use, add them together to determine the "Total Calculated Occupant Load" and write this in the space provided. Indicate also the part of the building that was calculated. An additional line is provided in case you have chosen to design the space using a modified number for the occupant load. For example, a special Assembly space may need a slightly higher occupant load because of the anticipated use of the space. Note this adjusted number in the "Modified Occupant Load" space. Use the back of the checklist to write down the reason for the adjustment.

A code approval section has been provided at the bottom of the checklist. It may not always be necessary to get approval from your code official at this point in a project, but each situation is different. (See the section Preliminary Review in Chapter 10.) If the project includes an unusual occupancy or building type or if you need approval on a modified occupant load, you may want to discuss these with the code official early in the programming and design process. Remember, it is important to accurately determine both the occupancy classification(s) and the occupant load(s) at the beginning of a project, since a number of other codes depend on them. Record the name and the date of your discussion in this section.

This checklist allows you to document essential information that will be used in the rest of your code research. As mentioned, most of the code requirements and allowable exceptions will be based on the occupancy classification and the occupant load. Having this information clearly documented may be useful if questions come up during your research.

CHAPTER 3

CONSTRUCTION TYPES AND BUILDING SIZES

Construction types are very important at the time a building is being constructed. Structural engineers and architects must be thoroughly familiar with them to determine the construction systems and materials that can be used throughout a building—both exterior and interior. There are several considerations that go into choosing a structural system and a construction type, including building size and height, intended occupancy classification, affordability, and sustainability.

Construction types become a consideration on interior projects as well. When working on an interior project that requires the reconfiguring of building elements, such as relocating walls, making changes to floor or ceiling conditions, or adding a ramp, it is important to be familiar with the different types of construction to determine what changes can be made to the existing building. Some construction types are stricter than others. Both the existing construction type and the occupancy classification (see Chapter 2) will play a role in what the codes will require.

This chapter includes a basic discussion of construction types, building heights, and floor areas as required by the codes. It includes how they are typically used for new construction and how they can affect an interior project. The first half of this chapter concentrates on construction types, explaining what they are, how to determine them, and how they relate to occupancy classifications. This is followed by a discussion of sustainability as it relates to construction types and certain building materials. The second half of the chapter focuses on building sizes as they relate to interior projects.

UNDERSTANDING CONSTRUCTION TYPES

Every building is made up of a variety of what the codes define as *building elements* and *structural elements*. They can be as simple as four exterior walls and a roof or as complicated as the many parts that make up a high-rise building. For example, columns, floor/ceiling systems, interior walls, and vertical shafts are all considered building elements. Structural elements are building elements that actually support the weight of the building and its contents. For example, a column is both a structural element and a building element, but a vertical shaft is only a building element. Some of these elements are covered in the construction type chapters of the codes. These requirements will be explained in this chapter. Additional elements are discussed in other sections of the codes. (See Chapter 5.)

The codes define the differences in construction types by governing the kinds of materials allowed for construction of each of the structural elements in a building and by establishing minimum hourly fire-resistance ratings for each essential building element. The materials that are allowed in each construction type are most often described as noncombustible, limited combustible, and combustible. Depending on the level of fire resistance required, the codes will specify the type of material allowed. For example, Type I construction, which requires the highest level of fire resistance, must consist almost completely of noncombustible materials; combustible materials are only allowed in limited amounts and specific locations.

Each construction type also assigns a minimum fire rating to building elements. These ratings are based on the number of hours the building element must be fire resistant, meaning that it will not be adversely affected by flame, heat, or hot gases. Note, though, that fire resistant does not mean fireproof. Instead, it is an hourly *fire endurance rating*. By controlling each element, the codes are able to regulate the fire resistance of a whole building. On an interior project, the most critical building element will be interior walls, but a particular project scope may affect a number of other elements as well.

The Code Table

The building codes and the *Life Safety Code (LSC)* have a similar table that lists the requirements for each type of construction. Figure 3.1 is the International *Building Code (IBC)* construction type table, Table 601, "Fire-Resistance Rating Requirements for Building Elements (hours)." Similar tables can be found in the NFPA codes.

In the *IBC* table in Figure 3.1, the construction types are listed across the top of the table in descending order from the most fire resistive (Type I) to the least fire resistive (Type V). The various structural or building elements are listed down the side to the left. The hourly fire endurance ratings are listed under the construction types for each structural element in the body of the table.

Most of the construction types are further divided into subcategories. These subcategories indicate whether the structural elements are required to be

TABLE 601
FIRE-RESISTANCE RATING REQUIREMENTS FOR BUILDING ELEMENTS (hours)

BUILDING ELEMENT	TYPE I		TYPE II		TYPE III		TYPE IV	TYPE V	
	A	B	A[d]	B	A[d]	B	HT	A[d]	B
Primary structural frame[g] (see Section 202)	3[a]	2[a]	1	0	1	0	HT	1	0
Bearing walls Exterior[f, g]	3	2	1	0	2	2	2	1	0
Interior	3[a]	2[a]	1	0	1	0	1/HT	1	0
Nonbearing walls and partitions Exterior	See Table 602								
Nonbearing walls and partitions Interior[e]	0	0	0	0	0	0	See Section 602.4.6	0	0
Floor construction and secondary members (see Section 202)	2	2	1	0	1	0	HT	1	0
Roof construction and secondary members (see Section 202)	$1^{1}/_{2}$[b]	1[b, c]	1[b, c]	0[c]	1[b, c]	0	HT	1[b, c]	0

For SI: 1 foot = 304.8 mm.

a. Roof supports: Fire-resistance ratings of primary structural frame and bearing walls are permitted to be reduced by 1 hour where supporting a roof only.

b. Except in Group F-1, H, M and S-1 occupancies, fire protection of structural members shall not be required, including protection of roof framing and decking where every part of the roof construction is 20 feet or more above any floor immediately below. Fire-retardant-treated wood members shall be allowed to be used for such unprotected members.

c. In all occupancies, heavy timber shall be allowed where a 1-hour or less fire-resistance rating is required.

d. An approved automatic sprinkler system in accordance with Section 903.3.1.1 shall be allowed to be substituted for 1-hour fire-resistance-rated construction, provided such system is not otherwise required by other provisions of the code or used for an allowable area increase in accordance with Section 506.3 or an allowable height increase in accordance with Section 504.2. The 1-hour substitution for the fire resistance of exterior walls shall not be permitted.

e. Not less than the fire-resistance rating required by other sections of this code.

f. Not less than the fire-resistance rating based on fire separation distance (see Table 602).

g. Not less than the fire-resistance rating as referenced in Section 704.10

Figure 3.1 *International Building Code* Table 601, Fire-Resistance Rating Requirements for Building Elements (hours) (*2009 International Building Code*, copyright 2009. Washington, DC: International Code Council. All rights reserved. www.iccsafe.org).

protected or remain *unprotected*. In a construction type where the structure is allowed to be *unprotected*, no additional treatment or materials are required to be added to the natural fire-resistant characteristics of the structural system. In a construction type that is required to be *protected*, structural components must be enclosed or covered in materials that add to the fire resistance of the system. This allows for a wide variety of construction systems and components. (Also see the inset titled *Protected or Unprotected* on page 116.) The *IBC* table generally uses the "A" and "B" designation to indicate protected (A) and unprotected (B). For example, in Figure 3.1, the difference between a protected and an unprotected structural frame can be seen. Type IIIA has a 1-hour rating and Type IIIB has no rating. In the case of a Type I construction, IA is considered highly protected and

ICC International Building Code (2009)	NFPA NFPA 220 Standard (2009)
(no equivalent)	I (442)
TYPE IA Highly Protected	I (332)
TYPE IB Protected	II (222)
TYPE IIA Protected	II (111)
TYPE IIB Unprotected	II (000)
TYPE IIIA Protected	III (211)
TYPE IIIB Unprotected	III (200)
TYPE IV Heavy Timber	IV (2HH) Heavy Timber
TYPE VA Protected	V (111)
TYPE VB Unprotected	V (000)

NOTE: The NFPA 220 table is repeated in the Life Safety Code appendix and the NFPA 5000. As of the 2006 editions, all three NFPA tables are the same.

Figure 3.2 Comparison of construction types. (This chart is a summary of information contained in the *International Building Code* and the *NFPA 220*. Neither the ICC nor the NFPA assumes responsibility for the accuracy or completeness of this chart.)

IB is considered protected. (This is shown in Figure 3.2.) The NFPA documents use a different numbering system to indicate the various hourly ratings. (This can be seen in the comparison in Figure 3.2 and will be discussed below.)

Every building, whether new or existing, must fall under one of the construction types. To be classified, it must meet the minimum requirements for every structure or building element in that type. If it fails to meet even one of the criteria, it will be classified in the next less restrictive type of construction. For example, if a building meets all the requirements of a construction Type I in Figure 3.1 except that the floor construction is rated only 1 hour, the whole building will be classified as a Type IIA.

This becomes important on interior projects. When adding new or modifying existing interior building elements, the construction type of the building needs to be identified to maintain consistency with the existing building materials and maintain the required minimum hourly rating of each building element. If the correct rated materials or assemblies are not specified or the hourly rating of a building element required by the building's construction type is affected, the whole building's classification could be reduced. For example, if part of an existing concrete floor is chipped away to create a slope to the drain for a new tiled shower, this may reduce the fire-resistance rating of the floor/ceiling assembly. Not only would this violate the building codes, but it would also be reducing the safety of the building and affecting such things as building insurance and liability.

COMPARING THE CODES

In some respects, the way that the various codes define construction types is very similar. For example, The *International Building Code (IBC)* and the NFPA codes refer to construction types as Type I through Type V. In addition, a Type I construction is considered noncombustible in both the *IBC* and the NFPA documents. However, the required ratings for specific structural elements within each construction type may vary between codes. (See Chapter 5 for more information on fire-rated interior building elements and assemblies.) Because the rating of the structural elements is one of the main ways that construction types are defined, this could mean that a building's structure may be considered a Type I for one code but a Type II if the building is reviewed under a different code.

The *IBC* uses a written description and Table 601 to describe the different construction types. The NFPA codes, including the *LSC*, define the construction types based on another standard, *NFPA 220, Standard on Types of Building Construction*. A comparison of the construction types in the *IBC* and the NFPA 220 can be seen in Figure 3.2. (If a jurisdiction requires the use of the *IBC* and the NFPA 220 standard, the strictest requirements will apply.)

The *NFPA 220* table, which defines the construction types for the NFPA, is also included in the *LSC* appendix since it does not have a chapter dedicated to construction types. Instead, it refers to the *NFPA 220* and lists the allowable construction type for each occupancy within the text.

In certain cases, the use of performance codes may also be allowed. Both the *ICC Performance Code (ICCPC)* and the NFPA codes provide alternate performance criteria that can be used when dealing with the construction elements of a building. For interior projects, these may be useful when dealing with an older building that is not easily classified within the current construction types or that includes materials or assemblies not addressed by the codes. In the *ICCPC*, for example, the criteria for fire resistance of structural members within a building are not given in hourly ratings, but are required to be "appropriate" for the particular use of the structural member, its potential exposure to fire, the height of the building, and the use of the building.

In an older building, it may be difficult to determine if all the components within the structure consist of noncombustible materials. Or the rating of a particular building element or assemblies may be impossible to determine. Without this clear information, it may be difficult or impossible to classify the construction type of an older building. Similarly, when changes occur to the interiors, matching existing construction methods may not meet current code standards. In these cases, using performance-based codes may provide better solutions for the design of the project. But, as always with performance codes, this will require proving to the code official that the design and specifications meet the criteria set by the performance criteria.

Construction types are not specifically referenced in the newer sustainability codes and standards, such as the *ASHAE 189.1*. However, certain sustainable requirements may affect the materials used in certain building and structural elements. Some of these requirements are discussed in the section Sustainability Considerations later in this chapter.

COMBUSTIBLE VERSUS NONCOMBUSTIBLE

The hourly ratings in a construction type table such as the *IBC* table in Figure 3.1 indicate how fire resistant a material or an assembly of materials must be. The ratings represent the length of time a material or a combination of materials must resist fire. The resistance of these materials is based on how easily they ignite, how long they burn once ignited, how quickly the flames spread, and how much heat the material generates. Most products are differentiated as either noncombustible, fire resistant, limited combustible, or combustible. The higher hourly fire ratings typically indicate that noncombustible materials are required, and the lower ratings indicate that fire-resistant materials or limited combustible materials are allowed. For example, Type I and Type II are usually designated to be constructed of noncombustible materials; Type III is a combination of combustible and noncombustible materials; and Types IV and V are typically allowed to be constructed of fire-resistant and combustible materials. Combustible materials are usually allowed by the codes when no ratings are specified and in limited amounts in construction types considered to be noncombustible.

Noncombustible materials are defined as materials that will not ignite, burn, support combustion, or release flammable vapors when subject to fire or heat. These materials are required to pass *ASTM E136, Standard Test Method for Behavior of Materials in a Vertical Tube Furnace at 750 degrees C.* They are used to prevent substantial fire spread, since they do not contribute fuel to a fire. (See the inset titled

High-Rise Buildings on page 121.) Four basic materials are generally considered noncombustible: steel, iron, concrete, and masonry. Their actual performance in the event of a fire, however, depends on how they are used. Occasionally, they may require additional fire treatment or protection for extra strength and stability. For example, steel has a rapid loss of strength at high temperatures and must be given extra protection if used on its own. To avoid this, steel is often encased in concrete or covered in a protective coating.

On the other side of the spectrum are *combustible materials*. These are materials that will ignite and continue to burn when the flame source is removed. Wood is a common combustible item. However, wood and other construction materials can be chemically treated to achieve some fire resistance. For example, chemically treated wood is called "fire-retardant treated wood" (also commonly known as *FRTW*). These are considered *fire-resistant materials* and are typically tested using *NFPA 703, Standard for Fire Retardant-Treated Wood and Fire-Retardant Coatings for Building Materials*. Once treated, they will delay the spread of a fire by a designated time period and can prevent or retard the passage of heat, hot gases, and flames. The fire-retardant treatment allows the material to be used in more places throughout a building. It can even be substituted for materials required to be noncombustible where specified in the code. For example, some fire-treated wood can be used in most rated walls. (See the inset titled *Combustible Materials* on page 110.) It can also be used as finish materials and trim in even the most stringent construction types.

Wood can also be considered fire resistant if it is large enough in diameter. *Heavy timber* is considered to be fairly fire resistant because of its size. Typically, columns are required to be at least 8 × 8 inches (203 × 203 mm) and beams a minimum of 6 × 10 inches (152 × 254 mm). The bigger the timber, the longer it takes to burn. Heavy timber builds up a layer of char during a fire that helps to protect the rest of the timber.

The NFPA uses an additional term to define certain types of fire-resistant materials. *Limited combustible materials* are defined as materials that do not meet the requirements of noncombustible material because they do have some capacity to burn. Although treated materials typically fall into this category, the material is considered limited combustible only if it passes a specific standard test. The test used to determine if a material or assembly is considered limited combustible is *NFPA 259, Standard Test Method for Potential Heat of Building Materials*. Some materials may also be required to be tested using *ASTM E84, Standard Test Method of Surface Burning Characteristics of Building Materials* or *NFPA 255, Standard Method of Test of Surface Burning Characteristics of Building Materials* (see Chapter 9) to be considered limited combustible.

These fire-resistant and limited combustible materials can also be used in conjunction with other materials to create rated assemblies. The materials work together as an assembly to create higher fire resistance. (See Chapter 5.)

◤Note

Even when a construction type is considered noncombustible, some combustible materials can be used. Refer to the codes for specifics.

◤Note

Noncombustible is different from *fire-resistant*. Additional precautions should be taken when fire-resistant material is used in place of noncombustible materials.

◤Note

Some fire-retardant chemicals may cause wood to absorb more moisture. This can cause loss of strength, rot, decay, corrosion of fasteners, poor paint adhesion, staining, and even loss of the fire-retardant chemical. Therefore, in high-moisture areas, the correct type of fire-treated wood must be specified.

COMBUSTIBLE MATERIALS

Combustible, limited combustible, or treated materials are allowed in all construction types, even in noncombustible Type I and Type II, in limited amounts and uses. The following are some of the allowable uses of combustible materials.

❏ Fire-retardant treated wood (FRTW) in non-load-bearing walls less than 2 hours
❏ Thermal or acoustical insulation with a flame spread not greater than 25
❏ Interior finishes, trim, and millwork for doors, door frames, and window sashes
❏ Blocking required for mounting handrails, millwork, and cabinets
❏ Construction of certain platforms for worship, music, and other entertainment
❏ Foam plastics and other plastics installed according to the code
❏ Plastic glazing and decorative veneers
❏ Nail strips and furring strips (fire blocking may be required)

Some of these items will be described in more detail in Chapters 5 and 9. In each case, there are requirements for the proper installation of these materials and exceptions for situations in which the materials may not be allowed. For example, if a hardwood floor is installed with sleepers (i.e., furring strips) on a noncombustible floor slab, the code specifies how to fire block the space created by the sleepers. Refer to the codes for more information.

For example, wood studs used with gypsum board on both sides can create a 1-hour-rated wall. Other common fire-resistant materials include gypsum concrete, gypsum board, plaster, and mineral fiber products.

When the construction type tables specify a rated structure or building element, this means that the element must be composed of the appropriate rated building materials. Fire-rated products or fire-rated assemblies should be specified when required. All fire-rated products are tested to obtain an hourly fire rating. Manufacturers must label their tested products to ensure that they have passed the tests. Chapter 5 elaborates on fire ratings and how to specify rated materials and assemblies.

DETERMINING CONSTRUCTION TYPES

There may be times when the construction type of a building needs to be determined for an interior project. For example, the scope of some interior projects may affect the building or structural elements of an existing building. Since these elements are essential to maintaining the proper construction type of the building, it is important to be aware of the acceptable building materials that can be used. The next sections will discuss how to determine construction types of existing buildings using the code tables. Buildings with more than one construction type and occupancy-related issues will be discussed as well.

Using the Table

The building codes and the standard *NFPA 220* each give a detailed description of the construction types within their text. The construction type tables, such as the one shown in Figure 3.1, need to be used in conjunction with these descriptions as well as those in the *LSC*. Since each code is slightly different, it is difficult to summarize all the construction types. Instead, some generalities are presented here and are shown in Figure 3.3.

> ◀**Note**
>
> The main difference between Type I and Type II construction is the fire-resistance ratings of the structural members.

Types I and II

These are the strictest construction types. These buildings are typically constructed with steel and concrete and are considered noncombustible. The main difference between these two types is the required hourly ratings of the structural elements, as shown in the *IBC* Table 601. The types of combustible and limited combustible materials and allowable locations are indicated specifically in the text of the code. Wood, for example, is very rarely used, and is highly fire retardant if used at all. High-rise buildings and many large buildings fall into this category.

Type III

> ◀**Note**
>
> Both gypsum board and the new synthetic gypsum board comply with *ASTM C1396, Standard Specification for Gypsum Board.* Both are allowed as noncombustible building materials.

This construction type is considered combustible because it is a mix of noncombustible and combustible elements. The exterior is usually composed of noncombustible materials such as masonry, but the interior structural elements and roof may be wholly or partially constructed with wood. This construction type is typical of small office buildings with wood or metal stud interior partitions and urban buildings where spread of fire from building to building is a concern.

Type IV

This construction type is sometimes referred to as *mill construction* or *heavy timber*. It is typically composed of heavy-timber structural members and wood floors. Although these buildings are predominantly wood, the char created during a fire results in a natural fire resistance to the structure. Modern heavy-timber

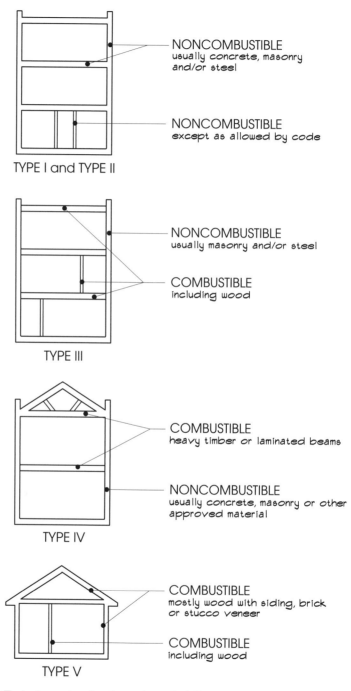

Figure 3.3 Typical construction type characteristics.

construction is usually made of wood-veneer-laminated beams and trusses. Because of the large timber members, these buildings are relatively easy to identify. It is important to note that for interior projects in this type of construction, there can be no concealed spaces such as soffits, plenums, or suspended ceilings.

Type V

This is the most combustible construction type and is basically an all-wood structure. These buildings are usually characterized by wood-framed exterior walls and interior walls. The exterior may have a veneer of brick, siding, or stucco. These buildings are typically small. Common examples include a residential house, a small dentist's office, or a convenience store.

When determining the construction type of an existing building that seems to have a combination of noncombustible and combustible components, almost every building element needs to be examined using a process of elimination. The materials that have been used to construct the building, as well as the materials that have not been used need to be identified. The building will be classified by the lowest-rated element or by the use of the most combustible material. For example, if a building does not meet the bearing wall rating for Type I even though the other structural elements meet the requirements, it will be considered a Type II. Or, if combustible materials are predominantly used, then it cannot be classified as a noncombustible construction type.

Example

When designing an interior project where reconfiguration or addition of building elements is required, the construction type(s) of the building will need to be determined. Although many interior projects involved mostly non-load-bearing walls, other building elements become a factor as well. The ratings of some *interior* building elements will be found in the construction type table, such as the one in Figure 3.1. These elements include load-bearing walls. Although the building codes also include a non-load-bearing wall category in the table, additional information is typically included within the text.

As explained later in Chapter 5, these elements become important when adding walls, finished ceilings and ceiling elements, doors, and interior glazing elements They will also be a factor when penetrating them with items such as sprinkler pipes, ducts, or conduit. Remember, it is important to specify the correct building material for interior elements, because if the rating is too low, the whole building might be reclassified into a lower category.

For example, a client may request the design of office spaces on the first floor of an existing three-story building. Before the correct rating and materials for the interior walls and ceilings can be specified, the building's construction type needs to be identified. To do this, the materials used to construct the building's existing structure must be determined. Questions that should be asked include: Is the frame wood, steel, concrete block, or other masonry? What are the exterior walls? Are the floors wood or concrete? Go through the process of elimination described in the previous section.

As the existing materials are identified, the construction type can most likely be determined. When necessary, try to obtain the original construction documents, consult the original building architect, or review the building with

ATRIUMS AND MEZZANINES

Atriums and mezzanines are common design elements used in the interior of a building. The codes set a number of additional requirements for them, some of which are described here. However, check the codes for the specifics and work closely with the local code officials. (Typically, engineers are required as well.)

Atriums

An atrium is commonly found in building lobbies and shopping malls. It is basically a multi-story space contained within a building, often surrounded by glass or open balconies. Atriums are required to be separated from all adjacent spaces by fire-resistance-rated walls. When glass is used as part of the enclosure, additional requirements may be necessary. The codes also usually limit the number of floors that can open directly into the atrium to three floors, unless additional fire protection is included. New atriums are allowed only in a fully sprinklered building. In addition, a mechanical smoke exhaust system is usually required at the ceiling and is typically tied into other fire-protection systems that would activate the exhaust system should a fire occur.

Mezzanines

A mezzanine is an intermediate floor level placed between the floor and the ceiling of a room or space. It is usually allowed only if it does not exceed more than one-third of the room or area in which it is located. There can be more than one mezzanine in a space, and even some at different levels, but the one-third rule would still apply. (This can be greater in higher fire-resistant construction types and in sprinklered buildings.) The appropriate headroom must also be provided at each level. The construction of a mezzanine is required to be the same as the construction type of the building in which it is located, and it is usually not counted as a story when determining the building height. Typically, the mezzanine must be open to the room in which it is located and requires one or two exits to the room or space below.

a structural engineer. Once the construction type is known, the construction type table and other information in the codes will be used to design the interior elements of a space such as walls, ceilings, and column wraps. Other examples are given in Chapter 5.

Mixed Construction Types

It is unusual for multiple construction types to be located in a single building structure; however, they do occur. Examples would include a medical office building adjacent to a hospital or a factory connected to its business offices. Each of these could be different construction types allowed by the occupancy classification and building size. Typically, different construction types must be separated from each other. If this separation is created by a vertical wall it is called a *fire wall*. A *party wall* is a similar separation wall but is located on a shared lot line between two parcels of land. If the different construction types are on top of each other, it is called a *horizontal assembly*. (These are discussed in more detail in Chapter 5.) Whether the separation is vertical or horizontal, it creates, in effect, two or more separate buildings.

In most cases, a fire wall must extend from the foundation of a building through the roof to a parapet wall and must be constructed so that it will remain stable even if one side of the wall or building collapses during a fire. Likewise, a horizontal separation will have to extend over the entire floor to all of the exterior walls or another vertical fire wall. In previous editions of the building code, ratings for these separation walls were included in the construction type tables. The *IBC* now includes this information elsewhere in the code. (See Chapter 5.)

Occupancy Requirements

Construction types set minimum building requirements. These requirements determine the structural integrity of a building for a required time period in case of a fire. This, in turn, may set certain occupancy requirements. For example, Type I is the strictest construction type, and will result in the most fire-resistant building and allow the most evacuation time. This evacuation time is important for all occupancy classifications, but even more critical for larger buildings with more occupants. (See the inset titled *High-Rise Buildings* on page 121.)

Because some occupancies require more evacuation time than others, they require a stricter construction type. Assembly, Hazardous, and Institutional occupancies are the strictest. In a few cases, the code will not allow an occupancy to be in a particular construction type. For example, according to the *IBC*, Institutional (I-2) occupancies cannot exist in a Type VB construction type. (Occupancy classifications are described in more detail in Chapter 2.)

☐Note

There are special provisions in the codes that allow parking garages to be adjacent to or below different occupancy types and/or construction types.

PROTECTED OR UNPROTECTED

When discussing building limitations in the building code, the issue of *protected* and *unprotected* is often a source of confusion. Whether the construction of a building is considered protected or unprotected has nothing to do with the use of an automatic sprinkler system. Instead, *unprotected* indicates that the structural elements of a building have not been treated in any additional way to increase their fire resistance beyond the natural characteristics of the materials. *Protected* indicates that the structural elements of a building have been treated to increase their fire resistance. This may include the use of noncombustible or limited combustible materials or fireproofing materials to enclose or cover the elements of the structural assembly. Ultimately, a protected construction type provides more resistance to fire than the same construction type that is unprotected.

Note, however, that the inclusion of a sprinkler system within a building does affect the building's limitation in a similar way. A building that has an approved automatic sprinkler system is allowed greater area and often more stories than the same construction that is not sprinklered. Sprinklering a building will often double the allowable area for a particular construction type. (See Chapter 6 for additional sprinkler trade-offs.)

Specific sections of the building codes and each occupancy chapter in the *LSC* specify the minimum construction type requirements for each occupancy. This becomes especially important when the occupancy classification of an existing building is being changed. Since many jurisdictions use both a building code and the *LSC*, it is important to consult both codes and use the strictest construction type requirements. When there are discrepancies, consult the local code official for clarification. (Additional fire-restrictive requirements are described in Chapters 5 and 6.)

SUSTAINABILITY CONSIDERATIONS

✎Note

The Rainforest Alliance has compiled a list of environmentally responsible wood products. Called *SmartGuide to Green Building Sources*, this resource can be downloaded from their Web site, www.rainforest-alliance.org.

For new buildings and additions to existing buildings, the choice of a structural system must first meet the requirements for the occupancy classification of the building or space (see Chapter 2) and the building size and height (as discussed later in this chapter). However, sustainability requirements can also impact the construction type of a building. The *International Green Construction Code (IGCC)*, for example, does not specify construction types for buildings. Instead, it includes requirements for material selection and the management of those materials during the construction process. This can be accomplished in two ways.

The *IGBC* allows a performance analysis of materials which is accomplished by developing a life cycle analysis (LCA) of the various components of the building. (LCAs are described in more detail in Appendix B.) If an LCA is not developed, the *IGCC* provides specific sustainable quantities and characteristics that must be met, such as recycled content of specific materials (post-consumer and pre-consumer), recyclability of materials, use of bio-based materials, and use of indigenous or locally available material.

Steel and concrete are typically part of the structural system and are included in most construction types. Both the composition and the use of these materials are generally considered to have green aspects. For example, steel is often made of 100 percent recyclable content and easily recycled during deconstruction and from scraps. Concrete can be composed of recycled content and is easily recycled for various construction products.

Wood can also be part of the structural system or a part of an interior wall assembly. Wood is generally considered a renewable material; however, there are additional considerations. Sustainable wood products should come from sustainably managed forests. The Forestry Stewardship Council (FSC) is one organization that identifies the forests that are managed based on their standard *FSC Principles and Criteria*. FSC Certified lumber has been certified to meet these criteria and is considered to be more sustainable than wood that has been harvested traditionally. The organizations that certify these products in the United States include Smartwood Program and Scientific Certification Systems. (See the section Sustainable Standards and Certification Programs in Appendix B.) The *IGCC* requires that wood meeting these standards either be labeled or have a certificate of compliance. (LEED and Green Globes recognize these standards and certifications in their point systems as well.)

The *IGBC* also requires a certain proportion of the materials be bio-based materials, meaning they are derived from living matter. The bio content of these materials must be evaluated based on *ASTM D6866 Standard Test Methods for Determining the Biobased Content of Solid, Liquid, and Gaseous Samples Using Radiocarbon Analysis* and the federal standard *7 CFR 2902*.

The sustainable standard *ASHRAE/USGBC/IES 189.1, Standard for the Design of High-Performance Green Buildings Except Low-Rise Residential Buildings* may also be applicable to a specific project. This standard has similar sustainable requirements for the materials used in a building, including the structural components. For example, *ASHRAE 189.1* can require wood components, including structural framing, sheathing, and subflooring found in certain construction types be composed of predominately certified wood. This certified wood must meet the requirements of *ISO/IEC Guide 59* or *WTO Technical Barriers to Trade* guidelines. And, similar to the *IGCC*, *ASHRAE 189.1* allows an LCA to be developed as an alternate way of meeting the specific requirements of these guidelines.

◀Note

Certified wood is considered sustainable. Certifications include FSC Certified and SFI Certified. (California has a separate certification as well.) These certification programs typically consist of fiber sourcing, chain of custody tracking, and certified product labels.

◀Note

United States Congress added the protection of timber to the Lacey Act of 1900. Effective November 2008, timber harvested illegally outside the United Standard cannot be sold legally in the United States.

◀Note

Structural steel and reinforcing steel in many cases can be composed totally of recycled scrap steel.

◀Note

Concrete as a structural and interior element has many green qualities such as durability, thermal mass, resistant to both fire and environmental damage, and local availability. In addition, concrete does not offgas or negatively affect the indoor air quality when the building is occupied.

UNDERSTANDING BUILDING HEIGHT AND AREA

✎Note

If a project entails enlarging a building either horizontally or vertically, consult the codes as well as the appropriate experts—engineers, architects, contractors, and local code officials. Such a project is beyond the scope of this book.

Building height and area are directly related to construction types. Building height and floor area control the overall size of a building. Similar to construction types, a building's size is usually determined at the time the building is originally constructed. Even when additions are made, the overall size of the building must remain within the appropriate height and area limitations.

Although code limitations on building size will not play a major role in interior projects, it is important to be aware of them and know when they apply. Most interior projects will not require an analysis of the size requirements. In most instances, the height and area of a building will be predetermined and will not need to be considered. However, it may necessary to make sure that an occupancy is appropriate for the selected building. (See the Example on page 120.)

Comparing the Codes

Building codes such as the *International Building Code (IBC)* set limitations for the height and area of a building. These limitations are based on occupancy type, construction type, whether the building is sprinklered, and whether there are adjacent buildings. Once the building size is determined, all other code requirements work together to make the building safe for its occupants. (The *Life Safety Code (LSC)* does not regulate a building's size.) Performance codes, such as the *International Code Council Performance Code (ICCPC)*, do not have specific criteria for limiting the size of the building. Rather, they set goals and objectives for structural stability, fire safety, means of egress, and the acceptable level of damage or impact caused by a fire for the building's size and use.

The fire codes do not set limitations on the overall size or height of a building either. They will, however, designate when a building must be divided into separate fire areas (either within a floor or between stories) to control the size of the area that can be directly affected by a fire. (This is discussed in Chapters 5 and 6.) The fire codes will also determine when large areas must be sprinklered. Therefore, the fire codes affect the fire safety of a building regardless of its size or height. They also set limitations on large spaces and potentially hazardous uses within a building. If a fire code is required by a jurisdiction, it should be reviewed to determine when the requirements apply.

The Code Table

The building codes control a building's height and area, and each code has a chart that sets specific parameters. Figure 3.4 is a table taken from the *IBC*, titled Table 503, "Allowable Height and Building Areas."

TABLE 503
ALLOWABLE BUILDING HEIGHTS AND AREAS[a]

Building height limitations shown in feet above grade plane. Story limitations shown as stories above grade plane.
Building area limitations shown in square feet, as determined by the definition of "Area, building," per story

GROUP		TYPE I A	TYPE I B	TYPE II A	TYPE II B	TYPE III A	TYPE III B	TYPE IV HT	TYPE V A	TYPE V B
HEIGHT (feet)		UL	160	65	55	65	55	65	50	40
					STORIES (S) AREA (A)					
A-1	S	UL	5	3	2	3	2	3	2	1
	A	UL	UL	15,500	8,500	14,000	8,500	15,000	11,500	5,500
A-2	S	UL	11	3	2	3	2	3	2	1
	A	UL	UL	15,500	9,500	14,000	9,500	15,000	11,500	6,000
A-3	S	UL	11	3	2	3	2	3	2	1
	A	UL	UL	15,500	9,500	14,000	9,500	15,000	11,500	6,000
A-4	S	UL	11	3	2	3	2	3	2	1
	A	UL	UL	15,500	9,500	14,000	9,500	15,000	11,500	6,000
A-5	S	UL	UL	UL	UL	UL	UL	UL	UL	UL
	A	UL	UL	UL	UL	UL	UL	UL	UL	UL
B	S	UL	11	5	3	5	3	5	3	2
	A	UL	UL	37,500	23,000	28,500	19,000	36,000	18,000	9,000
E	S	UL	5	3	2	3	2	3	1	1
	A	UL	UL	26,500	14,500	23,500	14,500	25,500	18,500	9,500
F-1	S	UL	11	4	2	3	2	4	2	1
	A	UL	UL	25,000	15,500	19,000	12,000	33,500	14,000	8,500
F-2	S	UL	11	5	3	4	3	5	3	2
	A	UL	UL	37,500	23,000	28,500	18,000	50,500	21,000	13,000
H-1	S	1	1	1	1	1	1	1	1	NP
	A	21,000	16,500	11,000	7,000	9,500	7,000	10,500	7,500	NP
H-2[d]	S	UL	3	2	1	2	1	2	1	1
	A	21,000	16,500	11,000	7,000	9,500	7,000	10,500	7,500	3,000
H-3[d]	S	UL	6	4	2	4	2	4	2	1
	A	UL	60,000	26,500	14,000	17,500	13,000	25,500	10,000	5,000
H-4	S	UL	7	5	3	5	3	5	3	2
	A	UL	UL	37,500	17,500	28,500	17,500	36,000	18,000	6,500
H-5	S	4	4	3	3	3	3	3	3	2
	A	UL	UL	37,500	23,000	28,500	19,000	36,000	18,000	9,000
I-1	S	UL	9	4	3	4	3	4	3	2
	A	UL	55,000	19,000	10,000	16,500	10,000	18,000	10,500	4,500
I-2	S	UL	4	2	1	1	NP	1	1	NP
	A	UL	UL	15,000	11,000	12,000	NP	12,000	9,500	NP
I-3	S	UL	4	2	1	2	1	2	2	1
	A	UL	UL	15,000	10,000	10,500	7,500	12,000	7,500	5,000
I-4	S	UL	5	3	2	3	2	3	1	1
	A	UL	60,500	26,500	13,000	23,500	13,000	25,500	18,500	9,000
M	S	UL	11	4	2	4	2	4	3	1
	A	UL	UL	21,500	12,500	18,500	12,500	20,500	14,000	9,000
R-1	S	UL	11	4	4	4	4	4	3	2
	A	UL	UL	24,000	16,000	24,000	16,000	20,500	12,000	7,000
R-2	S	UL	11	4	4	4	4	4	3	2
	A	UL	UL	24,000	16,000	24,000	16,000	20,500	12,000	7,000
R-3	S	UL	11	4	4	4	4	4	3	3
	A	UL	UL	UL	UL	UL	UL	UL	UL	UL
R-4	S	UL	11	4	4	4	4	4	3	2
	A	UL	UL	24,000	16,000	24,000	16,000	20,500	12,000	7,000
S-1	S	UL	11	4	2	3	2	4	3	1
	A	UL	48,000	26,000	17,500	26,000	17,500	25,500	14,000	9,000
S-2[b, c]	S	UL	11	5	3	4	3	5	4	2
	A	UL	79,000	39,000	26,000	39,000	26,000	38,500	21,000	13,500
U[c]	S	UL	5	4	2	3	2	4	2	1
	A	UL	35,500	19,000	8,500	14,000	8,500	18,000	9,000	5,500

For SI: 1 foot = 304.8 mm, 1 square foot = 0.0929 m².

A = building area per story, S = stories above grade plane, UL = Unlimited, NP = Not permitted.

a. See the following sections for general exceptions to Table 503:
    1. Section 504.2, Allowable building height and story increase due to automatic sprinkler system installation.
    2. Section 506.2, Allowable building area increase due to street frontage.
    3. Section 506.3, Allowable building area increase due to automatic sprinkler system installation.
    4. Section 507, Unlimited area buildings.
b. For open parking structures, see Section 406.3.
c. For private garages, see Section 406.1.
d. See Section 415.5 for limitations.

Figure 3.4 *International Building Code (IBC)* Table 503, Allowable height and building areas *(2009 International Building Code,* copyright 2009. Washington, DC: International Code Council. All rights reserved. www.iccsafe.org).

These tables govern the size of a building by setting height and floor area limits by occupancy classification within each type of construction. In Figure 3.4, all of the occupancy classifications used by the *IBC* are listed down the left side of the table. Along the top are the construction types (Type I to Type V). Under each construction type is the letter "A" to designate a *protected* construction type and the letter "B" to designate an *unprotected* construction type. (See the inset titled *Protected or Unprotected* on page 116.) The remainder of the table provides the height and area limitations for these categories.

When the type of construction is cross-referenced with the occupancy classification, the table will indicate two sets of figures. The top figure indicates the maximum allowable number of stories. The bottom figure in the corresponding box indicates the maximum allowable area per floor. (The areas are indicated in square feet; a metric conversion factor is given at the bottom of the chart.) Some classifications allow unlimited (UL) size or number of stories depending on the occupancy and the construction type. Others are not permitted (NP) at all. (Additional notes are given at the bottom of the table.)

Example

If a space is being designed for a particular occupancy classification in a building that was not originally built for that occupancy, the codes may need to be checked to see if it is allowed. An example would be an Ambulatory Health Care facility moving into an existing office building. Even if the previous tenant had the same use, the requirements may have changed. It is important to make sure that the occupancy or use can occupy a building with a particular construction type and that it does not exceed the area or height limitations. It is important to determine this early in the design process to establish if a project is feasible.

For instance, a client may need help selecting a space or building or a client who owns a building may need help looking for a particular tenant. If helping the former, the occupancy classification of the proposed use would need to determined, the approximate number of occupants wound need to be calculated (to determine the approximate area required), and the construction type restrictions for that occupancy would need to be established. Based on this information, the code will either (1) provide restrictions for a specific occupancy to help limit the choice of buildings to the stricter construction types or (2) provide no restrictions so that any type of building is allowed.

In this example, a client is considering an existing two-story building to renovate into a hotel. It has 12,000 square feet (1115 s m) per floor. The construction type of the building has been determined to be a Type VB. Two things need to be confirmed: that a hotel use can be located in the building according to the building code and that the building has the area required by the code for that use. The client has already determined that the total number of occupants (including guests and employees) will be 100 people. According to the *IBC*, hotels are an R-1 occupancy classification. (See Chapter 2.) The occupant load table and formula found in Chapter 2 need to be used to determine how many square feet (or square meters) are required for a 100-person hotel. The occupant load table in Figure 2.8 indicates that the load factor for Residential uses is 200 gross square feet (GSF) (18.58 g s m). By adjusting the formula **Occupant load = Floor area ÷ Load factor** to **Floor area required = Load factor × Occupant load**, the total would be 200 GSF 100 people = 20,000 square feet (1858 s m) of floor area. Since the building is a total of 24,000 square feet (2230 s m), sufficient area is provided in the existing building. However, it still needs to be determined if the occupancy is allowed in this construction type.

HIGH-RISE BUILDINGS

The most common definition of a high-rise building is any building that exceeds 75 feet (23 m) in height. This dimension is based on the fact that the ladders on fire department vehicles typically do not reach past this point. Therefore, the building height is typically measured from the lowest ground level a fire truck can access outside the building to the floor of the highest occupiable story.

The codes apply stricter requirements to high-rise buildings because of additional dangers posed by the increased height and characteristics of a tall building in the event of a fire. One particular danger created by a tall building is that it is often impractical to evacuate all the occupants within a reasonable time. Also, because the fires are often beyond the reach of the fire department equipment, they must be fought in place within the building. Compartmentation (including protected stairwells and areas of refuge), means of egress, and active fire protection systems (including detection and suppression) become very important. (See Chapters 4, 5, and 6.) Smoke control is also critical because tall buildings are affected by the stack effect of smoke during a fire. Additional safeguards include the mandatory use of automatic sprinkler systems and an overlapping of detection and suppression systems.

Since September 11, 2001, there has been much discussion as to whether high-rise buildings can be made safer in the event of fire or other emergencies. Some changes to the codes have been introduced, such as the use of elevators as part of occupant evacuation and the need for a dedicated stair for fire-fighters in the event of a major fire. Other changes are still being discussed and researched to determine their practicality and appropriateness.

With this minimum area of 20,000 square feet (1858 s m), go back to the allowable area table in Figure 3.4. The table indicates that this use cannot be located within this existing building. A Type VB construction type for an R-1 allows only 7000 square feet (650 s m) per floor on two floors, for a total of 14,000 square feet (1301 s m). However, if the various building elements in the structure can be protected and the building can be reclassified as a Type VA, a hotel of this size could be located in this building, because the allowable area per floor is increased to 36,000 square feet (12,000 square feet × floors = 36,000 total square feet, or 1115 s m × floors = 3345 s m). But, adding protection to the structure might not be feasible. Instead, additional area increases allowed by the codes may need to be considered For example, if an automatic sprinkler system is installed, the allowable area could be increased significantly. The existing building could then be renovated into a hotel.

HEIGHT AND AREA LIMITATIONS

⏴Note

Some local jurisdictions may use a shorter dimension to define the height of a high-rise building based on local conditions and fire department equipment.

A building's maximum size is limited by many factors, such as construction type, occupancy classification, and location. In other cases, the regulated size may be exceeded if the building is equipped with features such as automatic sprinklers and fire walls.

Some of the typical rules and most common exceptions when evaluating allowable building heights and floor areas are listed here as reference points to help guide the code research.

1. *Construction type.* Generally, the stricter the construction type and the more noncombustible a building, the larger the allowed building area and height. For example, Type I construction, which is noncombustible and most protected, in many cases has no height limitations and few area limitations.

2. *Occupancy classification.* Certain occupancy classifications will restrict the size of a building as well as the type of construction. For example, in the *IBC* an Assembly (A-1) occupancy in a Type VB construction cannot exceed one story or 5500 square feet (511 s m). Other occupancies need to meet specific requirements to allow an increase in area and/or height. These requirements are stated in other sections of the code, usually by occupancy. For example, an Educational building that has at least two exits per classroom with one opening directly outdoors can increase in size.

3. *Number of occupants.* As the number of occupants increases and the occupants become more immobile, there will be more restrictions on the height and area. Assembly and Institutional occupancies are especially affected. (See Chapter 2 for occupant loads.)

4. *Location.* The location of or distance to adjacent buildings, as well as the amount of street frontage, can affect the allowed area. For example, buildings with permanent surrounding open spaces can increase the amount of floor area from what is indicated in the tables. This exterior space prevents fire spread to or from adjacent buildings.

5. *Sprinklers.* The use of an approved automatic sprinkler system can increase the allowable number of stories or the floor area allowed. Because automatic sprinklers can contain or extinguish a fire before it has the chance to weaken the structure, some buildings are allowed a construction type with more combustible elements or allow a larger area. Other occupancies such as I-2 (hospitals) require sprinklers in buildings of any size. (See Chapter 6 for additional sprinkler trade-offs.)

6. *Fire walls.* Fire walls can subdivide a building so that each area is treated as a separate entity. Each area, which is actually considered a separate building, must stay within its own size limitation for that construction type, allowing the overall building to become larger. (See Chapter 5 for more information.)

7. *Hazardous.* Hazardous occupancies have a number of specific requirements. Projects for Hazardous occupancies will often require additional research.

8. *Single stories.* Single-story buildings are usually allowed greater flexibility in the size of the floor area. Each code sets a limit on the height of the story.

9. *Mezzanines.* Each code treats mezzanines differently. Usually they can be considered part of the story in which they are located but sometimes, because of their size, they must be treated as a separate story. There are a number of other limitations as well. (See the inset titled *Atriums and Mezzanines* on page 114.)

10. *Basements.* Area and height requirements for basements are specific to each code. Whether a basement is counted as a story depends on how much of it is above ground level and the occupancy of the building.

Determining construction types and building sizes may not be a part of every interior project. These variables are usually determined at the initial construction of the building. However, if structural or building elements are added/modified or if the occupancy classification of a building changes, the affects this has on the building and overall project may need to be identified. This needs to be accomplished in the early stages of the design project. It may be determined that the project is not feasible, or certain things (e.g., sprinklers) may need to be included in the design to make it comply with the codes. Work closely with the appropriate professionals when necessary. These include architects, engineers, contractors, and code officials.

CHAPTER 4

MEANS OF EGRESS

A means of egress is most commonly described as a continuous and unobstructed path of travel from any point in a building to its exterior or a public way. A means of egress is comprised of both vertical and horizontal passageways, including such components as doorways, corridors, stairs, ramps, enclosures, and intervening rooms. The design of these components is crucial to the safety of the building occupants in normal use of a building and especially during emergencies.

There are two main strategies for the means of egress: evacuation and "defend in place." *Evacuation* means that the occupants will be provided with a direct path out of the building. In a *defend in place* strategy, occupants will go to a specific area, either on the same floor or on another floor, to wait for assistance and/or be provided with an alternative method to exit the building. Every means of egress has various components. This chapter explains how these components work together. The first half of the chapter concentrates on explaining the components of the means of egress. The rest of the chapter discusses how to determine the required quantities, sizes, and locations of the parts of the means of egress. Accessibility requirements are also discussed throughout the chapter and a means of egress checklist is provided at the end of the chapter.

Although the codes usually separate means of egress codes and accessibility requirements, they should be considered together. In most cases, the means of egress will be required to be accessible or special conditions will have to be provided. This chapter has combined the discussion of these topics wherever possible. (The figures typically show the strictest requirements as well.)

Remember that not every type of means of egress mentioned in this chapter will be used in every interior project. In addition, many existing buildings will already have the correct number of exits. If working with just one occupant or tenant in the building, the exiting within and from that tenant space will only need to be considered. Some projects may require reevaluating the existing exit requirements and making alterations. Other projects will require more extensive calculations. Either way, every interior project must meet specific means of egress requirements.

◁ Note

There are two basic strategies for means of egress: evacuation of occupants and "defend in place."

In this chapter the wide variety of codes, standards, and federal regulations that pertain to the means of egress is discussed. Some of the requirements are based on occupant loads as discussed in Chapter 2. Specific fire ratings are also required for each means of egress. Chapter 5 explains the fire-rating requirements for building materials and assemblies. Chapter 9 explains the different types of finishes allowed in each area of a means of egress.

COMPARING THE CODES

Although the various codes define the parts of the means of egress in similar ways, the specific requirements can vary. For instance, all the codes agree that the means of egress include exit accesses, exits, and exit discharges. However, the required width of exits, allowable length of corridors, and hourly fire-resistance rating of the components and similar requirements may differ between codes.

The building codes and the *Life Safety Code* (LSC) set most of the requirements for the various parts of the means of egress. Each of these code publications has a chapter dedicated to means of egress. In the NFPA codes, specific requirements are also included in the individual occupancy chapters. In the *LSC*, these requirements can be different for new or existing buildings or spaces. If a jurisdiction enforces a building code as well as the *LSC*, their requirements will need to be compared so that the most restrictive ones are used.

The fire codes include requirements that affect the means of egress as well. In the *International Fire Code* (IFC), for example, the chapter titled "Means of Egress" includes several sections that repeat the information found in the means of egress chapter in the *IBC*. However, the *IFC* also includes maintenance requirements so that the means of egress remain usable after the building or space is occupied. These include limitations on the use of decorations, mirrors, and other objects that may obstruct the egress path. In addition, the *IFC* includes special requirements for existing buildings that may allow exceptions to the requirements for new buildings. (See Appendix C.) In the "Emergency Planning and Preparedness" chapter of the *IFC*, the code requires that occupants be made aware of evacuation procedures. This typically includes announcing the location of exits at assembly events and practicing fire drills in schools. The fire code also often requires egress patterns to be posted in certain locations. Although these requirements may not directly affect the design of a space, there may be some cases where developing these diagrams is part of the project.

The *ICC Performance Code* (ICCPC) also has a chapter dedicated to means of egress. Additional information is included in the chapter titled "Pedestrian Circulation." This chapter includes accessibility criteria as well. For performance criteria in the NFPA codes, each code includes a performance chapter.

◢Note

The 9/11 Commission Act of 2007 is a federal legislation that calls for the development of voluntary, private-sector standards for emergency preparedness. The 2009 edition of the *LSC* includes two new appendixes that provide additional emergency evacuation requirements.

◢Note

Many accessibility requirements are similar in the 2003 ICC/ANSI standard and the *2010 ADA Standards*, but these documents are not the same. Both the *ADA Standards* and the ICC/ANSI standard should be checked to make sure the most stringent requirements are used.

Although this chapter does not set specific requirements for the means of egress, it does require that a building and its design allow occupants sufficient time to evacuate, relocate, or have a "defend in place" location. Obviously, this could be achieved in several ways. The chapter also sets several objectives for safety during an emergency that, in turn, affects the means of egress.

Although all the same elements of a means of egress discussed by the prescriptive codes—such as area of refuge, travel distance, and unobstructed path—can be part of a performance design, those specific terms are usually not used by performance codes. Instead, the phrases are more generic, like "safe place," "appropriate to the travel distance," and "adequate lighting." Therefore, it may not matter if a particular area is a corridor or a passageway according to the definition of the prescriptive code. Instead, what matters is how it works within the path to safety.

In addition, performance codes require the designer to consider the characteristics of the occupants, the characteristics of the design, and the hazards that may exist to determine and identify the specific challenges in evacuating a particular space or building. For example, consider if the occupants are capable of moving to an exit independently, are limited in physical mobility, or are confined by certain security measures. Understanding the special conditions that exist within a building and using the performance criteria may allow, when necessary, a unique system of evacuation to be developed. Prescriptive codes may then be used to define other specific elements of the means of egress, such as the location of exit signs and emergency lighting. (Rarely are performance codes used for the design of the entire means of egress.) As always, when using performance criteria, establish the appropriate criteria of the design and then provide supporting evaluations and information to the code official for approval.

Because the means of egress in most cases is required to be accessible, these requirements must also be reviewed in conjunction with the appropriate federal regulation, such as the Americans with Disabilities Act (ADA) standards. The building codes also reference the *ICC/ANSI A117.1* accessibility standard. As discussed throughout this chapter, accessibility requirements will affect the size of many of the means of egress components, as well as the shapes and mounting heights of the various elements that occupants must use as part of the means of egress. Both the *ADA Standards* and the ICC/ANSI standard set minimum requirements that are, in many cases, stricter than the codes. Compare the *ADA Standards* with the ICC/ANSI standard as well as the accessibility chapter in the building codes to confirm the strictest requirements. Some of these differences are explained in this chapter. Others may be found as more research is done for a particular project. Remember, if there is a conflict in the requirements, the strictest requirements must be met—in other words, satisfy the need for both accessibility and safety.

In addition, review the particular occupancy classification(s) of a project. Although most of the regulations are fairly consistent, some occupancies allow

◀ Note

The Access Board, ICC, and NFPA have all created comparison documents of the accessibility requirements found in each of their respective publications. These documents can be found on their Web sites.

certain exceptions or have additional requirements. Some of the exceptions are given in the means of egress chapters, and others are grouped by occupancy classification in different sections of the codes. Assembly occupancies especially must be reviewed, since the use of fixed seats can create unusual egress paths. (See the section Aisles and Aisle Accessways later in this chapter.)

MEANS OF EGRESS COMPONENTS

Means of egress is a broad term that encompasses almost every part of a building interior as well as some exterior elements. Each of the codes divides a means of egress into three main categories: exit access, exit, and exit discharge. In all cases, a public way is the final destination of a means of egress. In some cases, an area of refuge will also be a part of the means of egress, as explained below. All of the means of egress components are defined as follows:

❏ *Exit access:* The portion of a means of egress that leads to the entrance of an exit. It includes any room or space occupied by a person and any doorway, aisle, corridor, stair, or ramp traveled on the way to the exit.

❏ *Exit:* The portion of a means of egress that is fully enclosed and separated from other interior spaces by fire-resistance rated construction, and is between the exit access and the exit discharge or public way. It can be as basic as the exterior exit door or it can include enclosed stairwells and ramps. In some special cases, it can include certain corridors or passageways. The components of an exit are distinguished from the exit accesses by higher fire ratings.

❏ *Area of refuge:* A space or area providing protection from fire and/or smoke where persons who are unable to use a stairway (or elevator) can remain temporarily to await instructions or assistance during an emergency evacuation.

❏ *Exit discharge:* The portion of a means of egress between the termination of an exit and the public way. It can be inside a building such as the main lobby, or outside a building such as an egress court, courtyard, patio, small alley, or other safe passageway.

❏ *Public way:* The area outside a building between the exit discharge and a public street. Examples include an alley or a sidewalk. The area must have a minimum clear width and height of not less than 10 feet (3048 mm) to be considered a public way.

It is important to understand the relationship of these components and when each exists. The simplest relationship is when the exit access leads directly to an exit that takes occupants out of the building. This is shown conceptually in Figures 4.1A and 4.1B. In the first diagram, the exit is simply an exterior door.

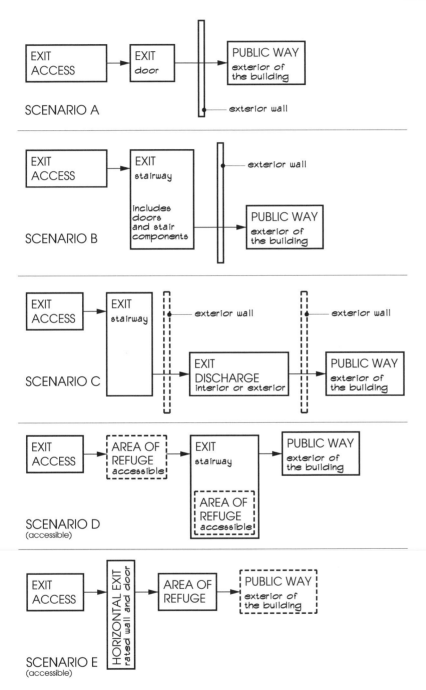

Figure 4.1 Means of egress components.

In the second diagram, the exit is an exit stair that opens at the bottom to the exterior of the building. In some cases, an exit does not end at the exterior of the building or public way but leads into an exit discharge. As shown in Figure 4.1C, the exit discharge connects the exit to the public way. The exit discharge can be either inside or outside the building. In either case, the code will have specific requirements for its use.

The typical means of egress assumes that occupants can exit the building without any special help. The other basic relationship is when an "accessible means of egress" must be provided. This type of egress path is usable by a greater range of occupants including those with mobility limitations who, for example, cannot use the exit stair to exit the building. The codes usually require that at least two of the required exits be accessible. An *accessible means of egress* includes the common components of a means of egress (i.e., exit access, exit, and sometimes exit discharge components). However, it may also include an area of refuge. The area of refuge is not considered the end point for the accessible means of egress but a place where people with disabilities can wait for additional help to reach the public way. As indicated in Figure 4.1D, an area of refuge can occur adjacent to but before entering an exit stairway or within the exit stairway. In this scenario, emergency personnel will eventually assist or carry the occupant down the stairway to the public way. In special cases, an area of refuge can be included in the elevator lobby when the elevator has met special requirements to be used as part of the building's means of escape. (See Figure 4.12.) The disabled occupants will then be escorted by emergency personnel to a public way using the elevator. In some cases, as shown in Figure 4.1E, the exit access leads through a horizontal exit to an area of refuge on the same floor. If necessary, emergency personnel will take disabled occupants down a stairway or elevator from the area of refuge side of the building. (See the sections Areas of Refuge and Horizontal Exits later in this chapter.)

In order to know what requirements apply to a particular space, it is necessary to know whether it is part of the exit access, exit, or exit discharge. For example, different finish classifications will be required for an area that is an exit access than for one that is part of an exit. (See Chapter 9.) Some means of egress components within a space may be easy to identify. For others, the path of the occupants may need to be considered to identify the relationship of a component and its role within the means of egress. This is shown on the floor plan in Figure 4.2.

In the floor plan in Figure 4.2, different shading patterns indicate whether the space is considered an exit access, an exit, an exit discharge, or a public way. For example, exit stairs are always considered exits, however, in some cases, a space such as a corridor may be considered to be more than one part of the means of egress. The location of an occupant can determine what part of the means of egress a particular room or space would be considered and, ultimately, what

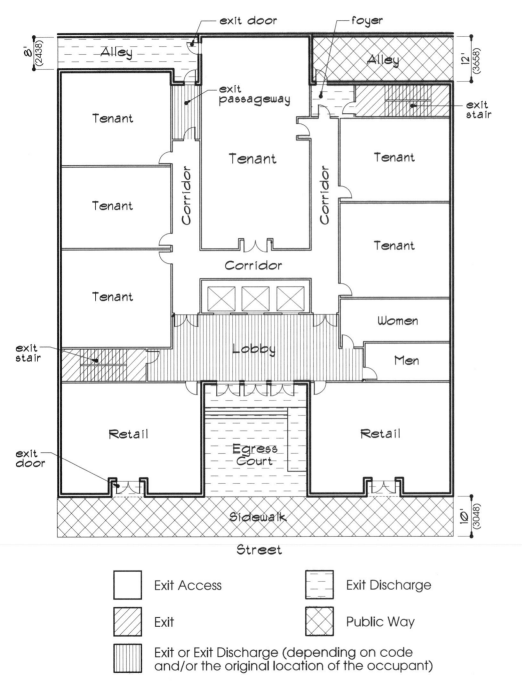

Figure 4.2 Means of egress in a typical building.

◀Note

If a building or space is only required to have one exit, it typically must be an accessible means of egress.

requirements must be applied to it. For example, if a person were standing in the lobby of this diagram, the distance from the person to the exterior door would be the exit access and the exterior door would be the exit. Once through the exterior door, the person would be in an exterior exit discharge (egress court), because, in this case, the sidewalk is the public way. However, for a person coming down the stairway at the left of the plan and emptying into the lobby, the stairway is the initial exit component, the lobby is then part of the exit discharge, and the exterior door is the end of the interior exit discharge because it leads to the exterior of the building. From that point, the egress court continues as an exterior exit discharge until it reaches the sidewalk, as previously discussed. When a space can be considered more than one part of the means of egress, it must meet the requirements of the most restrictive component.

Although the parts of an exit can be defined somewhat differently by the various codes, they all assume that a means of egress will be continuous. This path provides protection to the occupant from the floor of origin to the ground level and public way. And, because an exit has a higher fire rating and provides a better level of protection, the codes also assume that an occupant is relatively safe once he or she reaches an exit. The requirements for the types of means of egress and their components ensure that the level of protection is maintained until the occupant is in the public way.

What follows is a description of the types of means of egress and the various components of each. Exit accesses are described first. These components are elaborated in more detail, since similar components in the other means of egress categories have many of the same requirements. For example, exit access stairs and exit stairs are used for different purposes and require different fire protection, but they both use the same tread and riser dimensions, landing widths, handrail requirements, and so on.

EXIT ACCESSES

◀Note

When determining the path of the means of egress, remember that, except for doors, the typical headroom required from floor to ceiling is a minimum of 90 inches (2286 mm).

An *exit access* is that portion of a means of egress that leads to an exit. It leads an occupant from a room or space to an exit and can include doors, stairs, ramps, corridors, aisles, and intervening rooms. Exit accesses do not necessarily require a fire-resistance rating or need to be fully enclosed. For example, a corridor in a tenant space usually does not need to be rated; however, a main building corridor connecting the tenants and the public spaces may be required to be rated. (See Chapter 5 for information on fire ratings.)

The type and location of an exit access depend on the layout of the building or space and the location of the occupants in the area. For example, in a large, open space or room that has a door as the exit, the exit access is the path of travel to that exit door. In a multi-story building where an enclosed stair is the exit, the exit access can include the enclosed corridor leading to the exit and the rooms and doors leading into the corridor. (See Figure 4.2.)

Each component of an exit access is described in this section. The descriptions include the basic code requirements, as well as many of the necessary accessibility requirements. (The various diagrams typically include the most restrictive code and accessibility requirements.)

Doorways

Doors within the means of egress can be part of the exit access, exit, or exit discharge depending on where they are located. The codes regulate each component of a doorway similarly in each of these conditions. First, the door itself must be of a particular type, size, and swing. In addition, the way that the door can be used by occupants while exiting is also regulated. The various components of a door as regulated by the codes is discussed in this section. (Fire ratings for doors are discussed in Chapter 5.)

Doorway and Door Size

The most common exit access door is used along a corridor and connects the adjacent rooms or spaces to the exit access corridor. In addition, all other doors encountered along the way to the exit are also considered exit access doors. The codes set minimum dimensions for doors within the means of egress. Most doors in the means of egress cannot be less than 80 inches (2032 mm) high. The building codes, the ICC/ANSI standard, and the *ADA Standards* specify that when in an open position, a door must provide 32 inches (813 mm) of clear width. Since this must be the clear inside dimension, as shown in the Plan in Figure 4.3, typically a door that is at least 36 inches (914 mm) in width must be used. However, depending on the number of occupants that have to use the specific doorway, multiple doors and larger widths may be necessary. Determining the required size and number of doors is described in the section Exit Width later in this chapter. In addition, the codes may require larger doors and widths in certain occupancy classifications.

Door Type and Configuration

Usually, the codes require an egress door to be side-hinged and swinging. The direction of the swing depends on its location. In most cases, means of egress doors must swing in the direction of exit travel. However, the door cannot reduce

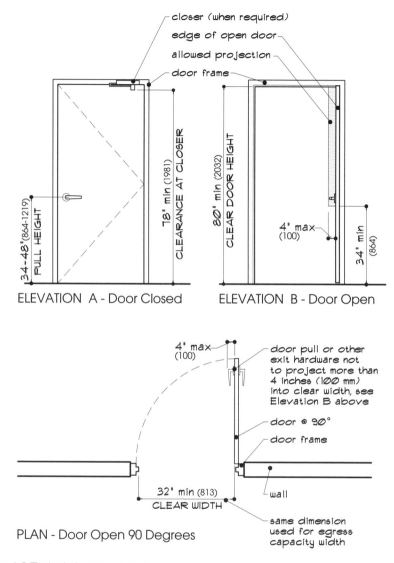

Figure 4.3 Typical clearances at doors.

any required stair landing dimensions or corridor width by more than 7 inches (178 mm) when the door is fully open. (This includes the door hardware, as shown in Plan B of Figure 4.4) The door also cannot reduce the required corridor width by more than half in any open position. Additional accessibility maneuvering clearances are required as well. Depending on whether the approach to the door

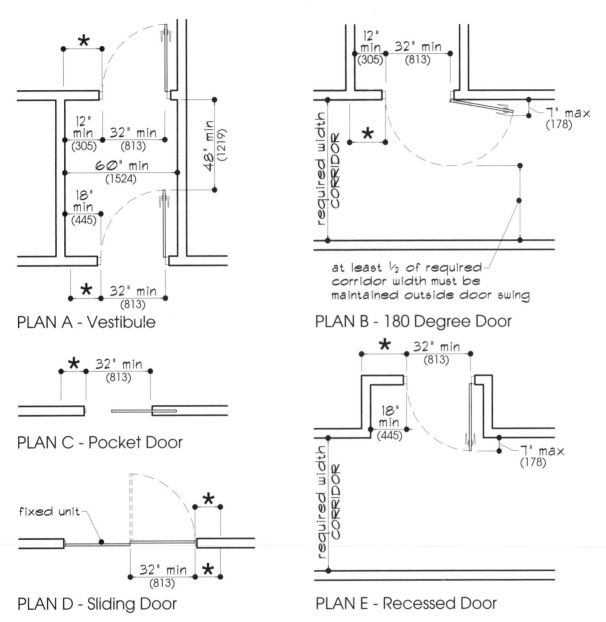

PLAN A - Vestibule

PLAN B - 180 Degree Door

PLAN C - Pocket Door

PLAN D - Sliding Door

PLAN E - Recessed Door

★ minimum clearances at latch side of door will vary from
0 – 42 inches (0 – 1065 mm) depending on approach,
refer to the ADA and ICC/ANSI standards for specifics

Figure 4.4 Typical clearances at doorways.

◪ Note

Most doors are side-hinged and swinging. However, certain occupancies are allowed to use other types of doors under certain conditions. These include sliding doors, balanced doors, overhead doors, revolving doors, security grills, and turnstiles. Check the codes for specific requirements.

◪ Note

In the *IBC*, all doors located in rooms or space that are Assembly or Educational occupancies with an occupant load of 50 or more must use panic or fire hardware.

is from the push or pull side and the hinge or latch side, a minimum clearance of 12, 18, or 24 inches (305, 445, 610 mm) is typically required. (See Figure 4.4.) If an existing condition makes it virtually impossible to obtain the required accessible clearances, an automatic door may be an option.

To avoid obstruction of the required widths, the codes allow some smaller occupancies or rooms to have doors that swing into the space. An example would be an office or a small conference room. (Usually the limit is less than 50 occupants.) However, if an interior project requires a door to swing out toward the path of exit travel, there are several options that can be used to meet the minimum code requirements. The most common ones are listed next. Figure 4.4 indicates these options and highlights the critical dimensions required by the codes and the ADA and ICC/ANSI standards.

1. Increase swing of door. Use a 180-degree swing door instead of a 90-degree door to allow it to open fully against the wall. This can be done only if a corridor is wide enough, as shown in Plan B of Figure 4.4.

2. Create alcove. Recess the door into the room, as shown in Plan E of Figure 4.4, so that the walls create an alcove that the door can swing into. (The alcove must allow maneuvering room.)

3. Enlarge landing. Enlarge the landing at the door, such as by widening a corridor or lengthening a vestibule, to allow enough maneuvering space. Typical vestibule dimensions are shown in Plan A of Figure 4.4.

4. Possible use of sliding door. Use a sliding door in low-traffic areas and when allowed by the codes. (See Plans C and D in Figure 4.4.)

Other types of doors are allowed to be part of the means of egress in certain situations. These types include revolving doors, power-operated swinging doors, and horizontal sliding doors. Because they work differently than a typical swinging door type, the codes impose additional requirements for their use in an emergency. For example, revolving doors are required to collapse to provide the minimum clear width, and power-operated swinging doors are required to be capable of opening manually in case of emergency or loss of electricity. Automatic sliding doors can also be used in some cases, but when pushed with a certain force; they must be capable of swinging into the direction of exit travel. Manual sliding doors are typically allowed only when the occupant load of the space is very low. The *IBC* allows that use of this type of door when the occupant load is 10 or less. For instance, sliding glass doors may be used in a hospital where visual monitoring of patients is critical. The codes will also limit the number of these special doors in certain occupancies, including Institutional and Mercantile occupancies.

Door Hardware

The codes require that the hardware on exit access doors be easily and read-ily used by occupants. This is so that occupants are not delayed in evacuating a building because of difficulty in opening a door in their path. Door handles (levers), pulls, and panic and fire exit hardware can be used on doors in the means of egress. In most cases, the location of the door, the number of occupants using the door, and the occupancy classification will determine what type of hardware can be used. For example, in an elementary school (Educational), the classroom doors are required to have lever-type hardware, but the doors to the exterior must have exit hardware.

Typically, doors within the means of egress path cannot be locked because locks would hinder egress. However, in some cases a lockable or delayed release door may be allowed. This is typically allowed for security purposes. For exam-ple, in some Institutional occupancies (both hospital and detention) areas are allowed to be locked. For the safety and security of the occupant, special condi-tions must exist for this to be allowed such as additional monitoring or an auto-matic release with the onset of the sprinkler system. Electromagnetic locks that will automatically unlock with the loss of power are allowed for special condi-tions and exceptions. (This is explained more in the section Security Systems in Chapter 8.)

The building codes and the ADA and ICC/ANSI standards also require that all door pulls meet the requirements for accessible operating devices. They must be a certain shape and be installed at a specific height, not projecting more than 4 inches (100 mm) into the clear width. (See Elevation A in Figure 4.3.) Any operating device must be capable of operation with one hand and without much effort. For example, lever, push-type, and U-shaped pulls are considered accessible.

> **⊴Note**
>
> In the 2009 *IBC*, panic hardware must comply with *UL 305* and fire exit hardware must be listed by *UL 10C* and *UL 305*.

Opening Force

For each type of door, the building codes set a maximum allowable force that is required to manually open the door. For typical swinging doors, the allowable force is usually between 5 and 15 pounds (22 to 67 N). However, for other special types of doors such as revolving, automatic, or sliding, the allowable force may vary from 30 to 180 pounds (133 to 801 N), depending on their use and loca-tion. The ADA and ICC/ANSI standards also set maximum force allowances for doors that are along the accessible route or are part of an accessible exit. These requirements must be compared to determine which ones apply to the door and its intended use.

Closers may also be required by the codes or accessibility standards so that the door is self-closing. For example, doors within rated walls are required to be self-closing to maintain the fire separation. In some cases, restroom doors are required to be self-closing for privacy and accessibility. Or, for convenience, it may be desirable to have a door to a particular room close after every use. In all cases, the maximum allowable force required to open the door still applies. The closer must also be located on the door and frame so that it does not interfere with head clearance requirements, as indicated in Figure 4.3. In some cases, the time it takes the door to close is also regulated by the codes and the accessibility standards. (For additional information, see the section Security Systems in Chapter 8.)

Stairways

Exit access stairs are not as common as exit stairs. Exit access stairs are typically found within a space when one tenant occupies more than one floor of a building or where there is a mezzanine within a space. For example, a set of stairs between the 16th and 17th floors within a tenant space will allow the occupant to move between the two floors without leaving the tenant space. Usually, these exit access stairs do not need to be enclosed with rated walls unless the same stair connects more than two floors. Most of the requirements for an exit access stair are the same as those for exit stairs. (See also the section Exit Stairs later in this chapter.)

There are a number of different stair types in addition to the straight run stair. These include curved, winder, spiral, scissor, switchback, and alternating tread stairs. Most of these are allowed by the codes as part of the exit access on a limited basis, depending on the occupancy classifications, the number of occupants, the use of the stair, and the dimension of the treads. However, some of them may not be allowed as a means of egress. In addition, the materials used to build the stairway must be consistent with the construction type of the building. (See Chapter 3.)

All stairs are required to meet specific code and accessibility requirements. The most important are the tread and riser dimensions. The most common dimensions are shown in Figure 4.5, with a minimum tread depth of 11 inches (279 mm) and a range of 4 to 7 inches (100 to 178 mm) for riser height. The actual size of the riser will be determined by the overall vertical height of the stairway. Once the riser size is determined, it is not allowed to fluctuate more than a small fraction from step to step. The shape and size of the nosings in relation to the riser are defined as well. Various nosing examples are shown in Figure 4.5.

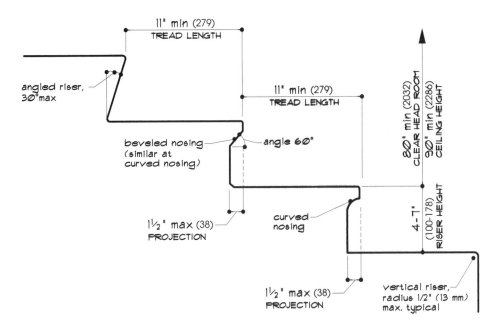

Figure 4.5 Typical stair requirements: Treads and risers.

A flight of stairs is defined by the codes to be the run of stairs from one floor or landing to another. There must be a landing at both the top and bottom of a flight of stairs. In addition, the codes do not usually allow a single flight to rise more than 12 feet (3658 mm). The width of the stair (as determined later in this chapter) determines the minimum dimensions of these required landings or platforms. Other variables must also be considered. For example, when fully open, the door into the stair cannot project into the required clear exit width more than 7 inches (178 mm), and the door cannot reduce the required exit width by more than half at any open position, similar to the door shown in Plan B of Figure 4.4. Additional stair requirements are shown on the Plan in Figure 4.6. Any required areas of refuge may also increase the size of a landing. (See the section Areas of Refuge later in this chapter.)

The ceiling above a stair and its landing must also meet certain requirements. Both a minimum ceiling height and minimum headroom are set by the codes. As shown in the Elevation in Figure 4.6, the minimum ceiling height is typically 90 inches (2286 mm). It is measured vertically from the landing and the front edge of the tread of the stair to the ceiling directly above. Some projections below that height are allowed. These may include structural elements, light fixtures, exit signs, or similar ceiling-mounted items. However, a minimum

✎Note

Open risers are allowed for stairways that are not required to be part of the accessible means of egress as long as a 4-inch (102 mm) sphere cannot pass through. They are also allowed in I-3, F, H, and S occupancies for stairways not used by the public and in some spiral stairways.

✎Note

The requirements for the bottom handrail extension on stairs differ, depending on which accessibility document is used. (See Figure 4.8.) If necessary, consult with a code official and/or another regulatory representative to determine how to satisfy these conflicting requirements.

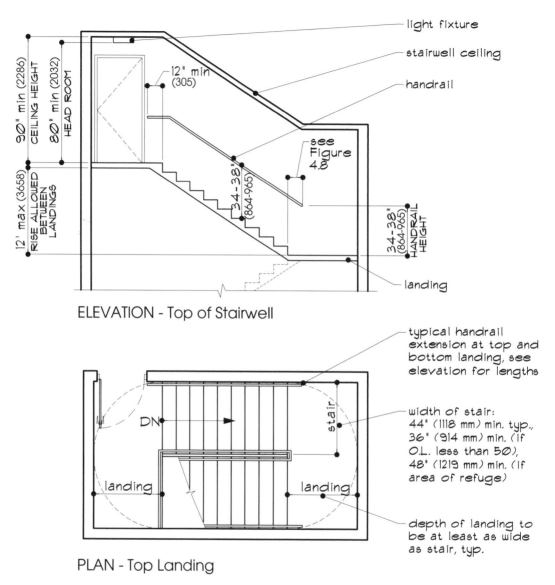

ELEVATION - Top of Stairwell

PLAN - Top Landing

NOTE: If an open stairway, guards at a minimum height of 42 inches (1067 mm) would be required in addition to handrails.

Figure 4.6 Typical stairway requirements: Clearances.

headroom of 80 inches (2032 mm) must be maintained. This height is measured in the same way.

Handrails and guards are regulated as well. Most stairs require a handrail on both sides. (See the codes for exceptions.) When wide stairs are used, additional intermediate handrails may be required. The building codes and accessibility standards require handrails to be certain styles and sizes, to be installed at specific heights and distances from the wall, and to be continuous wherever possible. The *IBC* now indicates two types of handrails. Type I is the typical circular handrail as shown in Figure 4.7. (Type II, which includes additional shapes, is only allowed in certain Residential occupancies.) Figures 4.7 and 4.8 indicate some of these typical handrail dimensions and locations. Handrails must also typically extend a certain distance beyond the top and bottom of the stairway and have an uninterrupted grip. (The bottom extension requirement may vary. See the note in Figure 4.8.)

Guards may also be required in certain locations. Guards are railings that are required by the code to keep people from falling off when there are changes in elevation. They are typically necessary whenever there is a drop over 30 inches (760 mm) where occupants are walking and there is no adjacent wall. The most common example of a guard is at a balcony or a stair when a side of the stair is exposed and not enclosed by a wall, as shown in Figure 4.8. In most instances, the guards must be at least 42 inches (1067 mm) high. Lower heights are allowed in some residential occupancies. Guards at Assembly spaces have special requirements. (Check the code for specifics.) If a handrail is also required, it must be mounted at the required height for a handrail along with the guard, as shown in Figures 4.7 and 4.8.

The guard must typically be designed so that nothing with a diameter of 4 inches (100 mm) can pass through any opening created by the rail configuration. This is shown at the top of Figure 4.8. In addition, 4 3/8 inches (111 mm) is allowed above the handrail and 6 inches (152 mm) is allowed between the bottom rail and the steps. There are additional requirements and exceptions for particular occupancy types. Refer to the codes to determine if these apply. These requirements must be met whether a prefabricated rail system is specified or a custom rail is designed.

Escalators and Moving Walks

Escalators and moving walks are not typically allowed as a means of egress. However, there are some exceptions in existing buildings. Existing escalators may be allowed only if they are fully enclosed within fire-rated walls and doors. Some may also have specific sprinkler requirements.

✎ Note

The width of a *stair* is measured to the outside edges of the steps. The width of a *ramp* is measured to the inside face of the handrails.

✎ Note

The 2009 *IBC* allows additional shapes for handrails used in some Residential occupancies. These are referred to as Type II handrails. The standard shape required by the codes is referred to as Type I.

✎ Note

Handrails are critical during an emergency. When stairs are full of smoke, handrails often are the only guide to an exit.

✎ Note

If glass is used as part of a handrail or guard, it must pass safety glass requirements as required by the codes. (See Chapter 5.)

✎ Note

As of the 2006 *IBC*, certain Residential occupancies may allow a slightly larger rail opening.

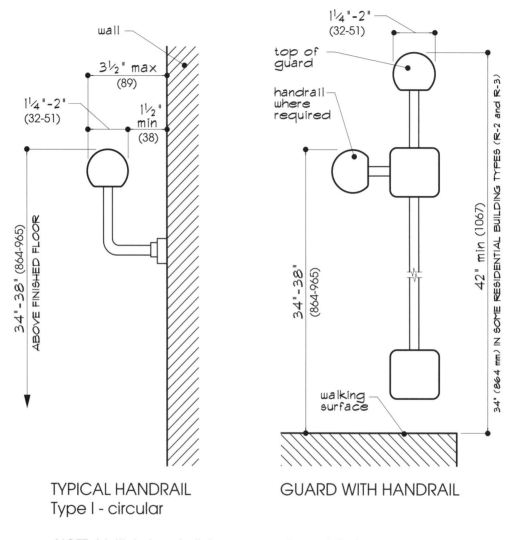

TYPICAL HANDRAIL
Type I - circular

GUARD WITH HANDRAIL

NOTE: Multiple handrail shapes are allowed. Refer to ADA
and ICC/ANSI standards for specific requirements. The
IBC also allows more than one type, allowing the newer
Type II handrials in certain Residential occupancies.

Figure 4.7 Typical handrail (Type I) and guard sections.

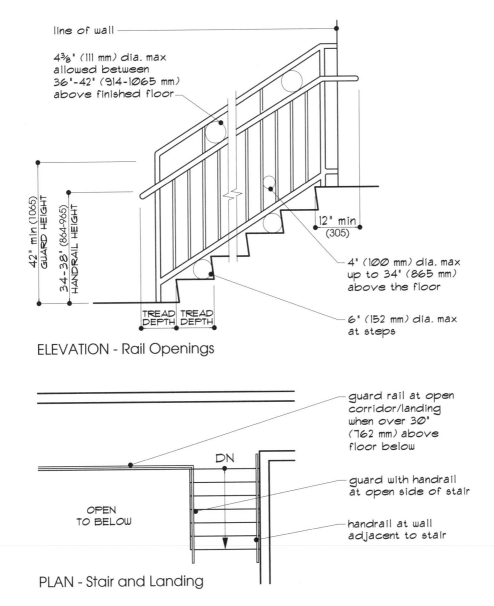

line of wall

4⅜" (111 mm) dia. max
allowed between
36"-42" (914-1065 mm)
above finished floor

42" min (1065) GUARD HEIGHT

34-38" (864-965) HANDRAIL HEIGHT

12" min (305)

4" (100 mm) dia. max
up to 34" (865 mm)
above the floor

6" (152 mm) dia. max
at steps

TREAD DEPTH TREAD DEPTH

ELEVATION - Rail Openings

DN

OPEN
TO BELOW

guard rail at open
corridor/landing
when over 30"
(762 mm) above
floor below

guard with handrail
at open side of stair

handrail at wall
adjacent to stair

PLAN - Stair and Landing

NOTE: Older editions of the ICC/ANSI standard and the original ADAAG
require the bottom rail extension at stairs to equal the depth of one tread plus
12 inches (305 mm). You may need to consult a code official or other regulatory
representative when this conflicts with the new requirements as shown above.

Figure 4.8 Typical handrail and guard requirements.

⬛Note

Elevators, escalators, and moving walks are typically *not* considered means of egress, since the codes do not usually allow them to be used as an exit during an emergency. However, this is changing as more elevators are required as an accessible means of egress. (See the section Elevators later in this chapter.)

⬛Note

A ramp with a lower slope ratio should be used whenever possible. For example, a 1 to 16 ratio is more manageable and safer for persons with disabilities than the 1 to 12 slope allowed by the codes.

⬛Note

There is a distinction between ramps and curb ramps. Curb ramps are typically exterior ramps cut through or leading to a curb. Other ramps can be interior or exterior.

⬛Note

Ramps not specifically designed or intended for the disabled can usually have a slightly steeper slope, as allowed by the codes. This should be verified with the local code official. However, it is advisable to use an accessible slope whenever possible.

Newer escalators and moving walks are usually installed as an additional path of travel or as a convenience to the occupants. Some of the more common occupancy classifications that use escalators and moving walks are Assemblies, large Mercantile, and certain Residential occupancies. According to the *LSC*, new escalators must comply with ASME A17.1/CSA B44, *Safety Code for Elevators and Escalators* and existing escalators must comply with ASME A17.3, *Safety Code for Existing Elevators and Escalators* for safety. In most cases, each space or building must still have the required number of enclosed stairs as specified by the codes.

Ramps

In general, ramps are used wherever there is a change in elevation and accessibility is required. Although changes in elevation should be avoided on a single floor, if steps are provided, then a ramp must be provided as well. In certain building types such as hospitals (I-2) ramps are required for any change in elevation; stairs are not allowed. The most important requirement of a ramp is the slope ratio. Most codes and accessibility standards set the *maximum* ratio at 1 unit vertical to 12 units horizontal. That means that for every vertical rise of 1 inch, the horizontal run of the ramp must extend 12 inches. The same proportion would be required in centimeters: 1 centimeter to 12 centimeters. This is shown at the top of Figure 4.9.

Typically, a ramp must be at least 36 inches (914 mm) wide (measured to the inside of the handrail). The other important requirement is the use of landings. The codes and the ADA and ICC/ANSI standards require landings at certain intervals and of certain dimensions. In most cases, the width of the landing must be the same as the width of the ramp, although a minimum length of 60 inches (1524 mm) is usually required, as shown in Landing A on the Plan in Figure 4.9. When changes in direction are required, the landing must allow a 60-inch (1524 mm) turnaround, as shown in Landing B in Figure 4.9. To limit the length of a ramp, a landing is usually required for every rise of 30 inches (760 mm) or a run of 30 feet (9144 mm). Landings are also required at the top and bottom of every ramp and must take into account any adjacent doors. Both the landings and the ramps may require specific edge details and a rough type of nonslip surface. (Refer to the ADA and ICC/ANSI standards for specifics.)

The construction of the ramp and its handrails is similar to that of stairs. Handrails are typically required when the ramp exceeds a certain length or rise. Similar to stairs, the handrails are required to extend a certain distance beyond the landing. (See the Elevation in Figure 4.9.) Guards are also required when there is no adjacent wall and the overall rise of the ramp is greater than 30 inches (760 mm). Width and clearance requirements for ramps are similar to those for corridors.

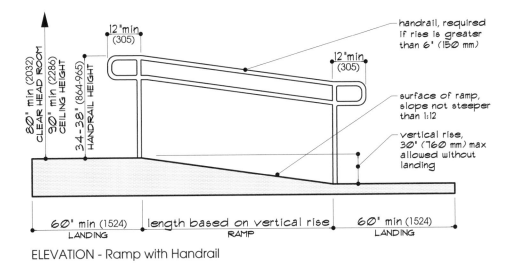

ELEVATION - Ramp with Handrail

PLAN - Landing Options

NOTE: Ramps and landings not adjacent to a wall, must have curb, edge protection, and/or rail to prevent people from slipping off the ramp. See the ADA and ICC/ANSI standards and the building codes for specifics.

Figure 4.9 Typical ramp requirements.

Corridors

As part of a means of egress, a corridor is required by the codes to be enclosed. (This makes it different than an aisle, which will be discussed next.) A corridor can be part of an exit access or an exit. An exit access corridor leads to the exit in a building. Typically, these corridors are either nonrated or have a 1-hour fire rating, depending on their location, the occupant load they are serving, and whether the building is sprinklered. For example, the corridor in a small tenant space leading to a door that empties into the main exit access corridor for the building is not typically required to be rated. By contrast, the main exit access corridor that connects each of these tenant spaces and leads to the exit stairs will typically be required to be rated 1 hour. (In some cases, if sprinklers are used, a rating may not be required.) This rating also determines the fire rating of the doors entering the exit access corridor. (See the section Means of Egress Components in Chapter 5.)

The codes have minimum and maximum requirements for the width and the length (travel distance) of a corridor. The codes require minimum widths for corridors to ensure that there is adequate room for the number of people using the corridor to get to the nearest exit. The travel distance is limited so that occupants will reach an exit within a reasonable amount of time. (Travel distances are described later in this chapter.) The corridor widths required by the codes are indicated in Figure 4.10A. 44 inches (1118 mm) is typically the minimum required width. However, the type of use and the occupant load usually determine the final corridor width. For example, in some occupancies a wider corridor may be required for moving beds or to accommodate the movement of people between spaces. Smaller widths may be allowed in smaller spaces and many Residential building types.

In addition, specific accessibility clearances must be met. These are shown in Figures 4.10B through 4.10F. These include (B) passing room for two wheelchairs in extra-long corridors, (C) minimum clearances for corridors that change direction, (D) turning space in narrow corridors, (E) maximum depth of objects protruding into the corridor, and (F) maneuvering space in a switchback configuration. Although a 60-inch (1524 mm) wide corridor, as shown in Figure 4.10B, is not specifically required by the codes or the accessibility standards, an area along the accessible path that allows a wheelchair to turn around is required. Typically, at least one turning space, as shown in Figure 4.10D, is required if the corridor is not 60 inches (1524 mm) wide. Additional ones might be needed in longer corridors. When doors are recessed or used at the end of a corridor, additional clearances must be added to the width of the corridor to make sure that the access to the door is wide enough. (See the clearances in Figure 4.4 and the example given in the section Exit Widths later in this chapter.)

Aisles and Aisle Accessways

An exit access *aisle* is similar to an exit access corridor in that it is a passageway required to reach an exit. The difference is that a corridor is enclosed by full-height walls, while an aisle is a pathway created by furniture or equipment. A short portion of an aisle that leads to another aisle is called an *aisle accessway*. The codes and the *ADA Standards* set minimum widths for both aisles and/or aisle accessways.

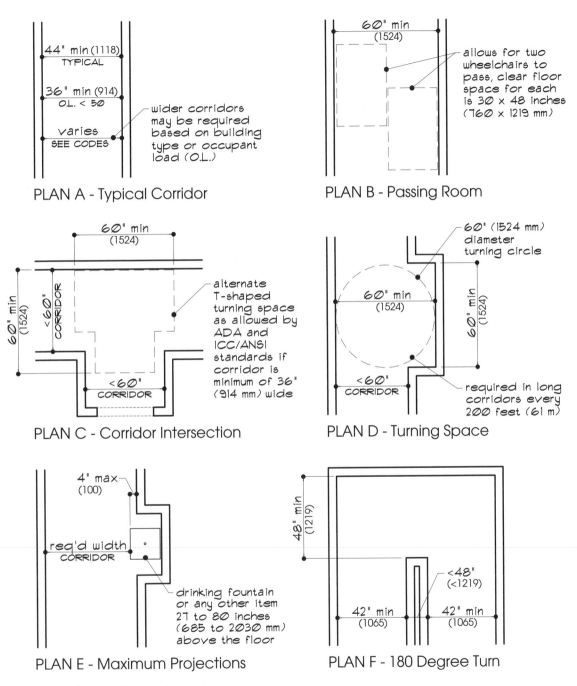

PLAN A - Typical Corridor

44" min (1118)
TYPICAL

36" min (914)
O.L. < 50

varies
SEE CODES

wider corridors may be required based on building type or occupant load (O.L.)

PLAN B - Passing Room

60" min
(1524)

allows for two wheelchairs to pass, clear floor space for each is 30 x 48 inches (760 x 1219 mm)

PLAN C - Corridor Intersection

60" min
(1524)

60" min
(1524)

<60"
CORRIDOR

<60"
CORRIDOR

alternate T-shaped turning space as allowed by ADA and ICC/ANSI standards if corridor is minimum of 36" (914 mm) wide

PLAN D - Turning Space

60" (1524 mm) diameter turning circle

60" min
(1524)

60" min
(1524)

<60"
CORRIDOR

required in long corridors every 200 feet (61 m)

PLAN E - Maximum Projections

4" max
(100)

req'd width
CORRIDOR

drinking fountain or any other item 27 to 80 inches (685 to 2030 mm) above the floor

PLAN F - 180 Degree Turn

48" min
(1219)

<48"
(<1219)

42" min
(1065)

42" min
(1065)

Figure 4.10 Typical corridor requirements.

Note

The widths of aisles and corridors are calculated similarly. Each is based on the occupant load of the space or set by the code minimums.

Note

Aisle accessways have special width requirements and can usually be less than the width of an aisle.

Note

Aisles assume travel in two directions. Aisle accessways assume travel in only one direction.

Aisles can be created by fixed seats or movable furniture. Common building types with fixed seats are theaters and stadiums. When there are no fixed seats, aisles can be created by tables, counters, furnishings, equipment, merchandise, and other similar obstructions. For example, aisles are created between movable panel systems in offices, between tables and chairs in restaurants, and between display racks in retail stores.

Aisles, like corridors and other parts of the exit access, must be sized for the number of people using them. So, in many cases, the width of the aisle will be determined by the same calculation using the occupant load as are other parts of the means of egress. (See the section Exit Widths later in this chapter.) However, the codes set minimum widths of aisles as well. This is different for aisles with fixed seats and movable seating or furnishings.

Aisles and aisle accessways created by *fixed seats* are typically found in Assembly occupancies. Because of the large number of occupants, the codes set strict requirements for the width of these aisles and aisle accessways, depending on the size of the occupancy, the number of seats being served, and whether it is a ramp or a stair. The minimum distances between the seats and the point where the aisles terminate are also regulated. The requirements for these aisles and aisle accessways are located in separate sections of the code that cover Assembly uses. In the NFPA codes, this information is included in the separate Assembly chapters. Because there are several factors that influence these widths, refer to the specific requirements in the codes to determine the required width for aisles at fixed seats.

For *movable seating or furnishings*, such as between tables and chairs in a restaurant, the minimum aisle width is typically 36 inches (914 mm). This is shown in Figure 4.11. However, accessibility requirements for aisle width and the placement of seating must also be considered. Although the codes allow some nonpublic aisles to be less than 36 inches (914 mm) wide, the *ADA Standards* include various width requirements where accessible routes are necessary and have additional requirements for specific uses such as restaurants, cafeterias, and libraries. (Refer to the *ADA Standards* for specifics.) The most common width requirement, however, is a minimum of 36 inches (914 mm).

The codes provide additional width requirements at movable seating for aisle accessways. These are shown in Figure 4.11 as well. These dimensions are much narrower than those of aisles because they are used by fewer occupants and are limited in length. These minimum widths are often determined by the length of the accessway. The length is measured to the centerline of the farthest seat according to the code. If an aisle accessway at a row of tables or chairs is less than 6 feet (1829 mm) and is used by four or less people, the codes do not set a minimum width. However, for an aisle accessway that is between 6 and 12 feet (1829 to 3658 mm) in length, the accessway must be at least 12 inches (305 mm) wide.

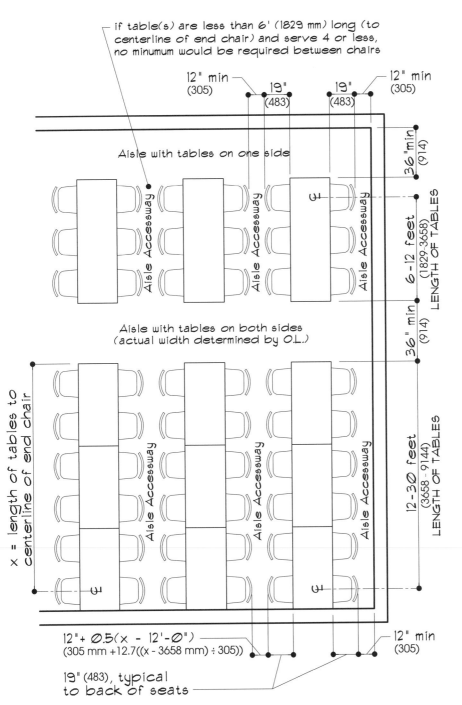

if table(s) are less than 6' (1829 mm) long (to centerline of end chair) and serve 4 or less, no minumum would be required between chairs

12" min (305)   19" (483)   19" (483)   12" min (305)

Aisle with tables on one side

Aisle Accessway   Aisle Accessway   Aisle Accessway

36" min (914)

6-12 feet (1829-3658) LENGTH OF TABLES

36" min (914)

Aisle with tables on both sides (actual width determined by O.L.)

x = length of tables to centerline of end chair

Aisle Accessway   Aisle Accessway   Aisle Accessway

12-30 feet (3658 - 9144) LENGTH OF TABLES

12" + 0.5(x - 12'-0") (305 mm +12.7((x - 3658 mm) ÷ 305))   12" min (305)

19" (483), typical to back of seats

Figure 4.11 Typical aisle and aisle accessway requirements: Tables and chairs.

For a longer aisle accessway between 12 and 30 feet (3658 to 9144 mm) long, a separate calculation is required. This required formula is shown at the bottom of Figure 4.11. (Also see the Example 2—Aisle and Aisle Accessways on page 173.) When tables and movable chairs are used in an aisle accessway, the minimum width is measured from a point 19 inches (483 mm) from the edge of the table to allow for the chair, as indicated in Figure 4.11. If the seat is a fixed stool, however, the width would be measured from the actual back of the seat.

Aisle accessways as defined by the code will not usually meet the clearance requirements of the accessibility standards. Additional clearance is usually required to maneuver a wheelchair. For this reason, accessible seating is typically provided along the main aisles. (This is shown in a restaurant in Figure 4.20 and in a theater in Figure 2.12A.) However, an appropriate amount of accessible seating must be provided. The area served by an aisle accessway may also need to be accessible. Therefore, in some cases, additional width for accessibility may be necessary.

Remember that aisles and aisle accessways can be created by a variety of interior furnishings and elements, including banks of filing cabinets, kiosks, chairs, copiers, and similar elements. In Business and Mercantile occupancies, the codes typically require that aisles be a minimum of 36 inches (914 mm). Aisle accessways created by display units in Mercantile occupancies, however, can be a minimum of 30 inches (760 mm). These minimums may not be wide enough to provide an accessible path. Where an accessible path is required, the aisles and aisle accessways may need to be wider. The codes may also limit the length of the aisle accessway, depending on the occupant load.

Adjoining or Intervening Rooms

Although an exit access should be as direct as possible, some projects may require an access path to pass through an adjoining room or space before reaching a corridor or exit. Most of the codes will allow this as long as the path provides a direct, unobstructed, and obvious means of travel toward an exit. Such a path may be as simple as a route from a doctor's office that requires passing through the waiting room to reach the corridor.

It is this requirement that allows smaller rooms adjoining larger spaces to exit through the large room to access a corridor. For example, a number of private offices might surround an open office area. Some other common adjoining or intervening rooms that are not restricted by the codes include reception areas, lobbies, and foyers. Exit accessways are allowed to pass through these rooms or spaces as long as they meet the specified code requirements.

The codes do place some restrictions on this rule, especially on rooms that tend to be locked some or all of the time. Storage rooms, restrooms, closets, bedrooms, and other similar spaces subject to locking are not allowed to be part of an exit access unless the occupancy is considered a dwelling unit or has a minimum number of occupants. Rooms that are more susceptible to fire hazards, such as kitchens and file rooms, are also restricted. (See the inset titled *Rooms and Spaces* on page 73. Also refer to the building codes and the *LSC* for additional requirements.)

⊴Note

In certain cases, the *IBC* allows the exit access to pass through the back storage area in a Mercantile occupancy.

EXITS

At the end of the exit access is an *exit*. An exit is a portion of the means of egress that is separated from all other spaces of the building. Unlike an exit access, all exits must be *fully enclosed and rated*, with minimal penetrations. A typical example of an enclosed and rated exit is a stairway. Fire-rated walls, rated doors, and other rated through-penetrations are used to make an exit a *protected way of travel* from the exit access to the exit discharge or public way. The typical fire rating for an exit is 1 or 2 hours. All components of the exit must have the same hourly rating. Some stairwells and other exits must be smoke protected as well. (See Chapter 5 for additional fire rating and smoke protection information.)

There are four main types of exits found in an interior project: exterior exit doors, enclosed exit stairways, horizontal exits, and exit passageways. In addition, an exit may include an area of refuge. An elevator is also sometimes used as an exit. These are explained throughout this section. Each must exit into another exit type, into an exit discharge, or directly onto a public way. The codes also have specific quantity, location, and size requirements for all exits. These are explained later in this chapter. Other basic code requirements and accessibility standards are similar to those for exit accesses, as described in the previous section.

⊴Note

The exterior exit door is the only type of exit door that consists of the doorway alone. Other exit doors are found in exit stairs, exit passageways, and horizontal exits, but they are a part of the whole exit enclosure. (See the section Rated Doors Assemblies in Chapter 5 for additional door requirements.)

Exterior Exit Doors

An exterior exit door is an exit that simply consists of a doorway. It is located in the exterior wall of the building and typically leads from the ground floor of the building to the open air of an exit discharge or a public way. For example, it might be a door at the bottom of an exit stair, at the end of an exit access corridor, or out of a building lobby on the ground floor. In older buildings, there may be an exterior door on each floor that leads to a fire escape attached to the exterior of the building. An exterior door is not typically required to be rated unless the exterior wall is rated because of the potential exposure to fire from an adjacent building. (See Figure 4.3 for typical clearance requirements.)

⊴Note

The required width of an exit stair can vary between 36 inches (914 mm) and 56 inches (1420 mm), depending on the occupancy, occupant load, and accessibility requirements.

Exit Stairs

☞ Note

When exit stairs continue past the exit discharge at grade level, an approved barrier must be used. Typically a gate (e.g., a metal gate) is installed at the grade-level landing of the stair to prevent occupants from continuing to the basement or sublevels during an emergency.

An exit stair is the most common type of exit and is composed of a protected enclosure. It includes the stair enclosure, any doors opening into or exiting out of the stairway enclosure, and the stairs and landings inside the enclosure. What makes an exit stair different from other stairs is that its enclosure must be constructed of rated assemblies. (See Chapter 5.)

Exit stair widths are determined in the same manner as the widths of other exits, as explained later in this chapter. The doors of an exit stair must swing in the direction of the exit discharge. In other words, all the doors swing into the stairway except at the ground level, where the door swings toward the exit discharge or public way. (The basic stair requirements are described earlier under Stairways in the section Exit Accesses. Also see Figures 4.5 through 4.8.) Exit stairs may also include an area of refuge if required by the codes. This is explained below.

Horizontal Exits

☞ Note

The codes place certain limitations on a horizontal exit, such as the size and the number of occupants it can serve. Some are mentioned in this chapter. Refer to the codes for the specific limitations.

A horizontal exit is different from the other exits because it does not lead a person to the exterior of a building. Instead, it provides a protected exit to a safe area of refuge. This area of refuge may be another part of the same building or an adjoining building. As the name implies, there is no change in level. This allows the occupants to move into a safe zone where they can either wait for help or use another exit to safely leave the building. A horizontal exit can also be a part of a "defend in place" means of egress strategy for a building.

The components of a horizontal exit consist of the walls that create the enclosure around the areas of refuge and the doors through these walls. Plan A of Figure 4.12 shows an example of a horizontal exit in a one-story building. In this case, a horizontal exit is used for one of the two required exits from Area A and one of the three required exits from Area B. Plan B of Figure 4.12 indicates the horizontal exits between the rated walls of a building core and the exterior wall. In this example, occupants from Area A can exit into Area B, and vice versa, because there are doors that swing in both directions of travel. Thus, each area serves as the area of refuge for the other area. When the horizontal exit leads to another building, such as in Plan C of Figure 4.12, structural features such as balconies and bridges can also be used. In this example, a horizontal exit is used for Building A into Building B, but Building B is not using the horizontal exit into Building A. This can be determined because the doors swing only in the direction of Building B. (Building B, therefore, must have the required number of exits without using the horizontal exit.)

☞ Note

When determining the width for doors, as described later in this chapter, only the doors swinging in the direction of egress may be counted.

The codes specify how to determine the additional area that must be provided in the area of refuge to hold the occupants who come through the horizontal exit.

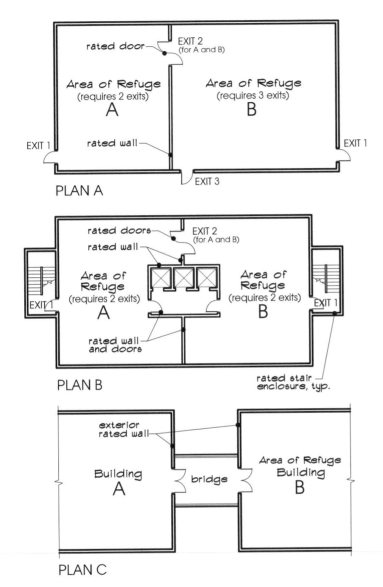

Figure 4.12 Horizontal exit examples.

This additional area varies, depending on the occupancy classification. For example, the typical factor is 3 square feet (0.28 s m) per person for most occupancies, but for occupancies where occupants are confined to beds, 30 square feet (2.8 s m) may be required. It is assumed that this additional area is required for people to wait or to travel through to the exit.

The codes also place strict requirements on the horizontal exit components. Since they are part of an exit, the walls and doors used to make the enclosures must be fire rated. The walls must either be continuous through every floor to the ground or be surrounded by a floor and ceiling that are equally rated. This rated wall usually has a rating of 2 hours. The doors must also be rated (usually 1 1/2 hours) and swing in the direction of an exit. If the horizontal exit has an area of refuge on both sides, two doors must be used together, each swinging in the opposite direction, to serve the occupants on either side. (See Figures 4.12A and 4.12B.) In most cases, horizontal exits can be used for only a portion of the total number of required exits. The number allowed varies according to the occupancy classification. A horizontal exit cannot serve as the only exit in any case.

Horizontal exits can be used in any occupancy classification. They can be considered part of an accessible means of egress required by the codes. The most common use is in Institutional occupancies. Hospitals use horizontal exits to divide a floor into two or more areas of refuge. This allows the employees to roll patients' beds into safe areas should a fire occur. Prisons also use horizontal exits so that a fire can be contained and the entire prison will not have to be evacuated in an emergency. Other common types of buildings that use horizontal exits are large factories, storage facilities, and high-rise buildings.

Exit Passageways

An exit passageway is a type of horizontal passage or corridor that provides the same level of protection as an exit stair. An exit passageway must be a fully enclosed, fire-rated corridor or hallway that consists of the surrounding walls, the floor, the ceiling, and the doors leading into the passageway. It is most commonly used to extend an exit and must typically be the same width as the adjacent exit as well as have the same level of fire protection. For example, an exit passageway can be used to extend an exit to the exterior of the building, as indicated in Plan A of Figure 4.13. In this example, the exit stair empties into a corridor instead of directly to the exterior of the building. Since it has the same rating as the stair, occupants leaving the exit stair are still in a protected enclosure until they reach the exterior of the building.

Another way to use an exit passageway is to bring an exit closer to the occupants in the building, as shown in Plans B and C of Figure 4.13. This is especially useful when needing to shorten a travel distance. (Travel distance is explained later in this chapter.) For example, if the travel distance to the door of an exit stair is 10 feet (3048 mm) longer than allowed, instead of relocating the exit stair an exit passageway can be added leading to the door of the exit stair, as shown in Plan B. The door of this newly created exit passageway is now the endpoint for

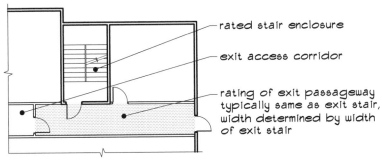

PLAN A - Connecting Exit Stair to Exterior Exit

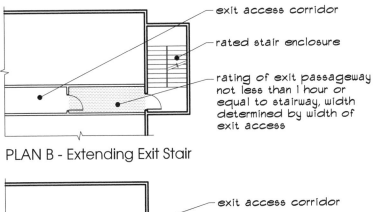

PLAN B - Extending Exit Stair

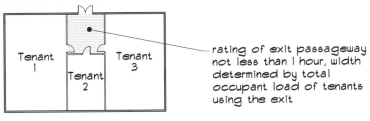

PLAN C - Extending Exterior Exit

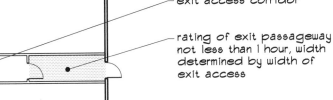

PLAN D - Connecting Tenants to Exterior Exit

Figure 4.13 Exit passageway examples.

measuring the travel distance. This can also be used to bring an exterior exit door closer to the interior of the building, as shown in Plan C of Figure 4.13. In both cases, the travel distance to the exit is reduced.

An exit access such as a door leading out of a tenant space can also exit into an exit passageway, as indicated in Plan D of Figure 4.13. This typically occurs on the ground floor of a building when secondary exits are required. In addition, when the tenants occupy the perimeter of the building, an exit passageway may be created between two of the tenants so that an exterior door can be reached off the common corridor. This is often seen in malls and office buildings with center building cores.

Elevators

◀**Note**

Accessible elevator requirements are different for private dwelling units and other buildings. Check the *ADA Standards*, the *FHAG*, and the *ICC/ANSI A117.1* standard for specifics.

◀**Note**

The 2004 *ADA-ABA Accessibility Guidelines* include many additional requirements for elevators to allow for a greater range of designs and more types of elevators.

◀**Note**

Elevators can be an efficient option to evacuate occupants from the multiple floors of high-rise buildings. This became especially apparent in review of the events of September 11, 2001.

There are typically two types of elevators: freight and passenger elevators. In most cases, elevators are not used as part of the required means of egress for a space or building. That means that typically *they are not counted* when determining the total number of exits provided in a building. Instead, elevators are typically used for convenience by occupants of the building. Elevators are linked to a building's smoke alarm system and when a smoke detector is activated during a fire, the elevators automatically are recalled to an approved location (usually the ground floor). Firefighters can then use the elevators to access the upper floors to fight the fire and assist in the evacuation of disabled occupants. Because they are not used for typical occupant evacuation, directional signage is required in the elevator lobby as well as a diagram that identifies the direction to the nearest exit for occupants.

In certain situations, however, elevators can be used to evacuate occupants. There are two reasons that elevators could be used as part of the means of egress: accessibility and speed of evacuation. In the past, occupants would wait in areas of refuge for assistance from emergency personnel in order to use the elevators. Occupants could also be required to exit through a horizontal exit to another area of the building and then evacuated by elevator. However, under the current *IBC*, elevators can be used as an exit without the use of an area of refuge or horizontal exit if the building is sprinklered.

For an elevator to be considered part of the means of egress, additional code provisions must be met. These requirements affect its location within the building, the construction of the elevator shaft, the type of elevator cab, and the controls of the elevator. The elevator itself must comply with emergency operation and signaling device requirements, as specified in *ANSI/ASME A17.1, Safety Code for Elevators and Escalators*, and be provided with standby power. Other special mechanical and electrical requirements are necessary as well. The elevator may require an adjacent area of refuge, an enclosed fire-rated lobby (as shown in Plan C of Figure 4.14), and two-way communication.

Because of all the specific requirements, the decision to include an elevator as an exit is typically made during the initial design of the building and is not part of a typical interior project or renovation. Retrofitting an existing elevator

ELEVATORS

Although new code requirements allow an increased use of elevators as a means of egress, especially in high-rise buildings, they are typically not used as part of the means of egress during an emergency. However, since they are used on a daily basis during normal operation, elevators must meet specific accessibility requirements as defined in the codes, the *ADA Standards*, and the *ICC/ANSI A117.1* standard. The following list includes some of the more common requirements. (Diagrams are available in the ADA and ICC/ANSI standards.)

1. Automatic operation with self-leveling within a certain range
2. Power-operated sliding doors that open to a minimum width
3. Door delay and automatic reopening device effective for a specific time period
4. Certain size car, depending on the location and size of the sliding door (longer cabs allow for the transport of beds and gurneys should it be required)
5. Hall call buttons and car controls with a specific arrangement, location, and height (including Braille and raised lettering)
6. Minimum distances from hall call button to elevator door
7. Hall lanterns and car position indicators that are visual and audible
8. Specific two-way emergency communication system
9. Handrail on at least one wall of the car
10. Floor surfaces that are firm, stable, and slip resistant
11. Minimum lighting levels
12. Specific door jamb signage at the hoistway entrance on each floor
13. Emergency exit signs located near elevator doors

Although many of the requirements are consistent between the codes and accessibility publications, there are some variations. The requirements listed above may also vary, depending on whether the elevators are intended for general use, for travel to designated floors only, or for more limited use. In addition, in buildings of a certain height, the codes may require at least one of the passenger elevators to be larger for use with an ambulance stretcher. Refer to the building codes, the *ADA Standards*, and the ICC/ANSI standard for specifics.

⬧Note

Platform lifts are a form of elevator. They are usually used in existing buildings when short vertical distances must be covered for accessibility reasons and a ramp is not feasible. Most are not allowed as a means of egress, but the *ADA Standards* do provide exceptions.

and shaft in most cases would be costly. Currently, using elevators as exits even in new buildings is not as common as providing areas of refuge in stairways and at elevator lobbies. However, more consideration is being given to the way elevators can be used for evacuation of occupants. This may become an increasingly important option as high-rise buildings are built to extreme heights.

Even if elevators are not to be used as exits, when they are included in a building, typically at least one is required to be accessible for use by persons with disabilities. (This is an exception for some two-story buildings.) Many new buildings are required to make all passenger elevators accessible. If the elevators are existing, they must be made as accessible as possible. (See the inset titled *Elevators* on the previous page and Appendix A.) New or replacement elevators are usually designed in conjunction with an engineer or an elevator consultant.

AREAS OF REFUGE

⬧Note

Elevators can sometimes be used as a means of egress, especially in high-rise buildings, but many additional code requirements must be met that may make the cost prohibitive.

An *area of refuge* is an area where one or more people can wait safely for assistance during an emergency. It is considered a part of an accessible exit, and it is a typical component of a "defend in place" means of egress strategy. These areas provide safety because they are typically required to be enclosed by fire and/or smoke partitions. Areas of refuge are usually provided adjacent to exit stairwells, in exit stairwells, or at elevator lobbies, as indicated in Figure 4.14.

An area of refuge located adjacent to an exit stair provides room for wheelchairs while maintaining the required exit width to the exit stairway, as shown in Plan A of Figure 4.14. When an area of refuge is located within an exit stairwell, the landings at the doors entering the stair are enlarged so that one or more wheelchairs can comfortably wait for assistance without blocking the means of egress at the landing and stair. This is shown in Plan B of Figure 4.14. The number of wheelchair spaces that must be provided is determined by the occupant load of the floor. The most common requirement is one space for every 200 occupants. (Other accessible means of egress on the same floor level can be considered as well.) Although the egress width of an exit stair is usually determined by the occupant load, a stair with an area of refuge may be required to have a minimum width of 48 inches (1219 mm) to allow the disabled person to be carried down the stair by emergency personnel. An area of refuge can also be located adjacent to the elevator, as shown in Plan C of Figure 4.14. An area of refuge is required if the elevator is serving as an exit. (See the previous section Elevators.)

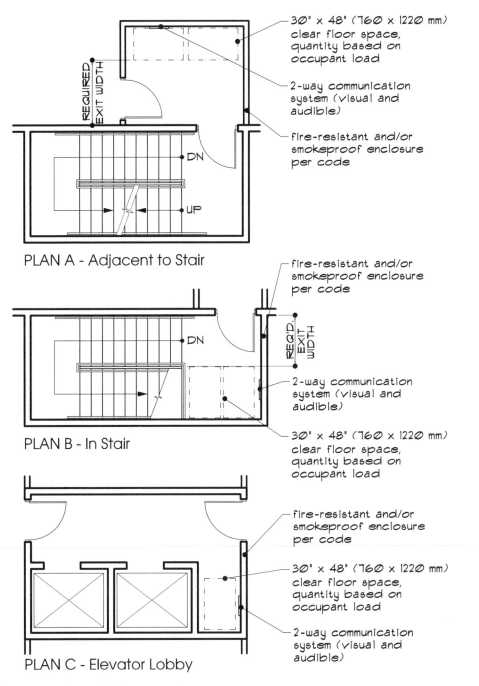

30" x 48" (760 x 1220 mm) clear floor space, quantity based on occupant load

2-way communication system (visual and audible)

fire-resistant and/or smokeproof enclosure per code

PLAN A - Adjacent to Stair

fire-resistant and/or smokeproof enclosure per code

2-way communication system (visual and audible)

30" x 48" (760 x 1220 mm) clear floor space, quantity based on occupant load

PLAN B - In Stair

fire-resistant and/or smokeproof enclosure per code

30" x 48" (760 x 1220 mm) clear floor space, quantity based on occupant load

2-way communication system (visual and audible)

PLAN C - Elevator Lobby

Figure 4.14 Area of refuge examples.

☞Note

When an area of refuge is used in conjunction with an exit stair, the minimum stair width as required by the codes will usually increase.

☞Note

In the 2006 *IBC,* areas of refuge were required in sprinklered as well as nonsprinklered buildings. Previous editions as well as the current 2009 *IBC* do not require them in sprinklered buildings.

Whether or not a building requires areas of refuge will depend on the code and the enforceable edition. For example, the 2006 *IBC* requires all buildings to have an *accessible* means of egress which would typically include an area of refuge. The 2003 *IBC* and the most current 2009 *IBC* both allow an exception to the requirement to provide an area of refuge if the building has an automatic sprinkler system. If both the *IBC* and the *LSC* are required by the jurisdiction of a project, the area of refuge requirements may need to be confirmed with a code official.

A horizontal exit provides another type of area of refuge. It is different in that it does not provide a small separated area but, instead, divides an entire floor of a building into separate areas using a rated wall. When passing through the door, the whole space beyond the door becomes an area of refuge. An occupant can either wait for assistance or use the available exit stairs. (See the section Horizontal Exits earlier in the chapter.)

The codes typically use the term *area of refuge;* the original *ADAAG* uses the term *area of rescue assistance.* The *2010 ADA Standards* rely on the *IBC* to define when an area of refuge is necessary; however, general accessibility requirements still apply to the area. (The typical clear floor space for wheelchairs is 30 inches [760 mm] wide by 48 inches [1219 mm] long.) In addition, the area of refuge is required to be clearly identified with visual and tactile signage directing building occupants and have a two-way emergency communication system. In some cases, both visual and audible communication must be provided. (Check the codes for specifics.)

EXIT DISCHARGES

An *exit discharge* is that part of a means of egress that connects an exit with a public way. It is typically found on the ground floor of a building; however, in older buildings, a fire escape is sometimes described as an exit discharge—connecting the exterior exit door(s) on each level to the sidewalk or alley. The required fire rating of an exit discharge will vary, depending on the type and where it is located. In some types of exit discharge, the enclosure may be allowed to have a lower rating than the exit it serves.

The first three exit discharges described in this section are used on the interior of a building. Others are exterior exit discharges. The width of an exit discharge is typically dictated by the width of the exit it is supporting, but accessibility requirements must be taken into consideration as well. Usually, when more than one exit leads into the exit discharge, the width of the exit discharge is a sum of these exit widths. In existing buildings, an existing exit discharge may dictate the maximum size of an interior means of egress. The key to determining if an exit discharge exists is that it occurs after a protected exit. A few common examples are explained below. Many of these are also shown in Figure 4.2.

Main Lobby

One of the most common interior exit discharges is the ground floor lobby of a building. For example, an exit stair may empty out into the lobby. The distance between the door of the exit stair and the exterior exit door is the exit discharge. An example is shown in Figure 4.2. However, a lobby is not always considered an exit discharge. For example, the lobby shown in Figure 4.13D is not an exit discharge because it connects exit accesses, not exits. An exit discharge occurs only after a protected exit.

Foyer or Vestibule

An interior exit discharge can include an enclosed foyer or vestibule. These are small enclosures on the ground floor of a building between the end of a corridor and an exterior exit door, as labeled and shown in Figure 4.2. In addition, the energy codes (see Chapter 8) often require these to separate conditioned interior spaces from the outside air.

If the size of the enclosure is kept to a minimum, the codes may not require it to have a fire rating. Therefore, it would be considered an exit discharge instead of an exit passageway. Remember that the *ADA Standards* and the ICC/ANSI standard require the size to be large enough to allow adequate maneuvering clearance within the vestibule or foyer and the swing of the doors. (See Plan A in Figure 4.4.)

Discharge Corridor

Occasionally, a corridor is considered an exit discharge. Usually, this occurs in older buildings where an exit stair empties into a ground floor corridor. If there is not a fire-rated exit passageway connecting the exit stairs to the exterior exit door, the corridor becomes an exit discharge. Usually this is not recommended and is allowed only if the entire exit corridor is protected by automatic sprinklers. (See the codes for specifics.)

Egress Court

An egress court is an exterior exit discharge, as shown in Figure 4.2. It can be a courtyard, patio, or other type of partially enclosed exterior area. It is the portion of the exit that connects the exterior exit door to the public way.

Small Alley or Sidewalk

If the width of an alley or sidewalk is less than 10 feet (3048 mm), it is no longer considered a public way. Instead, it becomes an exterior exit discharge that connects the exterior exit door to a larger alley, sidewalk, or street. An example includes the alley shown in Figure 4.2. The sidewalk in this figure would also be considered an exit discharge if it was less than 10 feet (3048 mm) wide.

MEANS OF EGRESS CAPACITY

✎ Note

When determining means of egress, two things may need to be determined: egress capacity, including quantity and exit width, and egress *arrangement*, including locations and travel distances.

✎ Note

When an interior project involves only part of a building or floor, the exit capacity for this new area needs to be determined. However, it is also important to make sure that the other existing building exits can accommodate this new area. In some cases, the existing exits may need to be increased or the size of the new space or occupant load needs to be decreased.

The capacity of the means of egress reflects the number of people that can safely exit a building in an emergency. This part of the chapter concentrates on determining means of egress capacities. It answers the questions How many? How large? and In what locations? The main factors to be determined include the number of exits, exit width, arrangement of exits, and allowable travel distance. These must be determined on any interior project, whether changing a room, a tenant space, one floor, or an entire building. Dead-end corridors and common paths of travel must also be considered. Each is explained in the next few sections.

In most cases, an interior project will not change the exiting capacity of the building itself. Exits for an entire building are determined during the initial building design, and they usually allow for future changes within the building. However, there may be instances in which redesigning an entire floor may increase the occupant load, requiring an exit to be added or enlarged. For example, a new occupant may require the exits to be updated to meet a more current code, or a different occupant type or greater occupant load may require additional exits.

Each aspect of exit capacity is dependent on the others. So, in many cases, it may be necessary to work back and forth in the calculations to determine the final number and widths of exits. For example, exit widths will depend on the required number of exits. But the number and location of required exits depend on the occupant load and maximum travel distances. If any of these change or exceed the maximum requirements, the calculations have to be adjusted. The requirements must be determined using the building codes, such as the *International Building Code (IBC)*, and the *Life Safety code (LSC)* as well as any accessibility requirements, such as those found in the ADA and ICC/ANSI standards. When necessary, have a code official review and approve the calculations early in the design of the project. (See Chapter 10.)

Number of Exits

Typically, the number of exits required by the codes should be established before determining the total width required for each exit. Most of the codes require a minimum of two exits, whether they are for an entire building or a space within the building. However, in each occupancy classification, a single exit from a space or building is sometimes allowed when specific requirements are met.

The number of exits is based on the occupant load of the space or building. Use the occupant load tables in the codes (such as the one shown in Figure 2.8 in Chapter 2) to determine the occupant load of the area requiring exits. If determining the required number of exits for an entire building, the occupant load must be calculated for each floor or story. Each floor is considered separately.

When a floor has mixed occupancies or more than one tenant, the occupant load of each occupant or tenant must be calculated and added together to get the total occupant load for the floor. If determining the number of exits for a particular room, space, or tenant within the building, only the occupant load for that area needs to be calculated. (Refer to Chapter 2 for a more detailed explanation of occupant loads and how to calculate them.)

Once the occupant load for the space or entire floor is established, refer to the building codes and/or the *LSC* to calculate the required number of exit locations. Each code has the same basic breakdown, as shown in the *IBC* Table 1021.1, "Minimum Number of Exits for Occupant Load" shown in Figure 4.15.

It is important to remember when confirming the required number of exits for a multi-story building that the number of exits cannot decrease as one proceeds along the egress path toward the public way. Therefore, the floor with the largest occupant load determines the number of required exits for all lower floors. For example, if the floor with the highest occupant load is in the middle of the building, all the floors below it must have the same number of exits. This is easily accomplished by one or more continuous exit stairwells, each counting as an exit on each floor that opens into it. (See the Example that follows.)

Each of the codes allows exceptions to the total number of exits. The most typical exception allows only one exit in smaller buildings or spaces. This is generally

TABLE 1021.1
MINIMUM NUMBER OF EXITS FOR OCCUPANT LOAD

OCCUPANT LOAD (persons per story)	MINIMUM NUMBER OF EXITS (per story)
1-500	2
501-1,000	3
More than 1,000	4

Figure 4.15 *International Building Code* Table 1021.1, Minimum Number of Exits for Occupant Load (*2009 International Building Code*, copyright 2009. Washington, DC: International Code Council. All rights reserved. www.iccsafe.org).

allowed in an occupancy that has a minimum number of occupants and a minimum travel distance to the exit. (This will be discussed in more detail later.) Figure 4.16 shows two tables from the *IBC*. Table 1021.2, "Stories with One Exit," lists the one-exit requirements for a single floor of a building based on where the story (i.e., floor) is located in the building. (The organization of this table has changed significantly since the previous edition.) Table 1015.1, "Spaces with One Exit or Exit Access Doorway," lists the one-exit requirements for separate tenant spaces or areas. In both tables, the information is listed by occupancy classification (or use group). The NFPA codes provide similar information within their texts.

TABLE 1021.2
STORIES WITH ONE EXIT

STORY	OCCUPANCY	MAXIMUM OCCUPANTS (OR DWELLING UNITS) PER FLOOR AND TRAVEL DISTANCE
First story or basement	A, B[d], E[e], F[d], M, U, S[d]	49 occupants and 75 feet travel distance
	H-2, H-3	3 occupants and 25 feet travel distance
	H-4, H-5, I, R	10 occupants and 75 feet travel distance
	S[a]	29 occupants and 100 feet travel distance
Second story	B[b], F, M, S[a]	29 occupants and 75 feet travel distance
	R-2	4 dwelling units and 50 feet travel distance
Third story	R-2[c]	4 dwelling units and 50 feet travel distance

For SI: 1 foot = 304.8 mm.

a. For the required number of exits for parking structures, see Section 1021.1.2.

b. For the required number of exits for air traffic control towers, see Section 412.3.

c. Buildings classified as Group R-2 equipped throughout with an automatic sprinkler system in accordance with Section 903.3.1.1 or 903.3.1.2 and provided with emergency escape and rescue openings in accordance with Section 1029.

d. Group B, F and S occupancies in buildings equipped throughout with an automatic sprinkler system in accordance with Section 903.3.1.1 shall have a maximum travel distance of 100 feet.

e. Day care occupancies shall have a maximum occupant load of 10.

TABLE 1015.1
SPACES WITH ONE EXIT OR EXIT ACCESS DOORWAY

OCCUPANCY	MAXIMUM OCCUPANT LOAD
A, B, E[a], F, M, U	49
H-1, H-2, H-3	3
H-4, H-5, I-1, I-3, I-4, R	10
S	29

a. Day care maximum occupant load is 10.

Figure 4.16 *International Building Code* Table 1021.2, Stories with One Exit, and Table 1015.1, Spaces with One Exit or Exit Access Doorway (*2009 International Building Code*, copyright 2009. Washington, DC: International Code Council. All rights reserved. www.iccsafe.org).

Each code has additional exceptions as well. Check the specific occupancy section of the required code publications to determine the exceptions, since each occupancy classification addresses unique means of egress issues. Some occupancies may require additional exits, while others may reduce the number of exits, depending on the situation. The occupancy classifications with the most exceptions and special requirements are Assembly, Institutional, and Residential occupancies. The following Example, which describes how to determine the number of exits for an entire building, provides an overall concept for determining exit quantities. (See the next section for additional examples.)

☑Note

It is not uncommon for a multi-story building to have a large Assembly occupancy on the top floor. If it has the largest occupant load, it can dictate the exit requirements for the whole building.

Example

Figure 4.17 is the outlined section of a multi-story building. It indicates the occupant load for each floor and the number of exits based on these occupant loads (using the code table shown in Figure 4.15). The fourth floor has the largest occupant load, with a total of 1020, and, therefore, requires the largest number of exits. The code specifies four exits for any occupant load over 1000. As a result, every floor below it must also have four exits, even though their occupant loads specify fewer exits. Four separate exit stairs that are continuous from the fourth to the first floor would meet the requirement. The first floor would require the exit doors to be located in four separate locations.

Each of the floors above the fourth floor has a lower occupant load than the fourth floor. Since these floors are above the fourth floor, fewer exits can be used. The seventh floor has the largest occupant load (above the fourth floor), so it controls the exit quantity for the seventh, sixth, and fifth floors. Three exits must be provided for these floors. However, the eighth floor has an even lower occupant load, requiring only two exits. So, in this example, at the eighth floor, only two exit stairs are required; at the seventh floor, a third stair is required; and beginning at the fourth floor, a fourth exit stair is required.

In most cases, these decisions will be made in the initial design and construction of a building. However, in some cases, when the use of an existing building changes significantly, an additional exit stairway may be required.

Exit Widths

The building codes and the *LSC* set minimum width requirements for each part of the means of egress. These include exit access and exit doors and the various corridors, aisles, stairs, and ramps that connect these doors. Different components will require different exit widths. Remember, in general, this minimum width

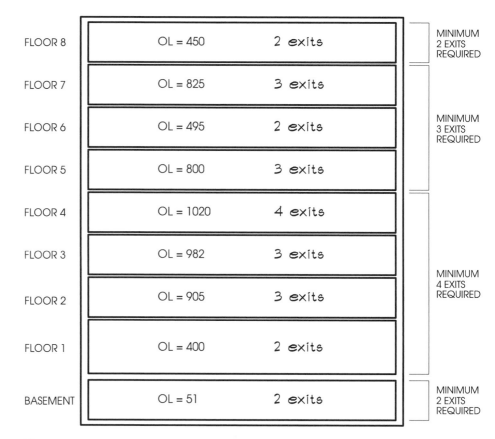

Figure 4.17 Number of exits example (multi-story building).

must be maintained throughout the means of egress. It cannot be reduced anywhere along the path of travel as it moves toward the exit discharge and/or public way. (The exception is at some door locations, which is explained later in this chapter.) Therefore, it is important to determine the exit width of each exit component in question so that the minimum exit width can be obtained.

Like the number of exits, exit widths are based on the occupant load of an area or floor. Each is calculated separately to accommodate a specific area. If determining the exit widths for a multi-story building, the exit sizes are determined by the floor with the largest occupant load. Usually, that means figuring the occupant load of every floor to find the one with the largest occupant load. That floor will require the largest exit widths and dictate the exit widths of every floor below it. For example, in Figure 4.17, the fourth floor would determine the width of the exit stairs from the fourth floor down to the first floor.

Exit widths must also be determined for every enclosed area and separate tenant space. The same basic principles apply. Instead of using the occupant load of the entire floor, use the occupant load for that particular space. If it is a room, the calculation will determine the width of the door. If it is a tenant space, the exit door(s) and any corridor(s) leading up to the door(s) will be determined. On the other hand, the width of the shared exit access corridor leading from each tenant space to the exit stairs is based on the total occupant load for that floor. If there is more than one tenant on a floor, the occupant loads of each must be added together to determine the required exit width for that floor.

Once the occupant load is established for the floor or space, multiply it by the specific width variables supplied by the codes. This results in the total exit width that is required. The *IBC* gives two variables. If determining the required width of a stairway, the occupant load is multiplied by .3 inches (7.62 mm). If determining the width of other egress components such as exit access corridors, aisles, ramps, and exit door widths, multiply the number of occupants using the component by .2 inches (5.08 mm). The difference in the width variables for exit stairs and other level exits is based on the fact that stairs cause a person to decrease speed and, therefore, could result in more people using the stairwell at one time during an emergency. The larger stair variable allows for stairs to be wider than level exits such as corridors and ramps. Therefore, if calculating exit widths for an exit stair and the exit passageway or corridor leading from the stair, the stair should be calculated first, since an exit width must be maintained as it moves toward the public way.

The NFPA codes such as the *LSC* have similar requirements. However, the NFPA codes assign different variables for specific occupancy classifications as shown in Table 7.3.3.1, "Capacity Factors" in Figure 4.18. These additional variables allow for the difference in occupancy classifications where wider exit widths are needed for faster egress times in more hazardous occupancies. Although in the past, a building equipped with an approved automatic sprinkler system was assigned a smaller factor to allow a narrower path, this is no longer allowed.

After determining the total exit width required by the code, compare it to the total number of exits already determined for that space or floor. (See the previous section.) The total width must be equally distributed among the total number of exits serving the area. For example, if calculating the width for an entire floor, the determined width must be divided among all exits leaving the floor. If the determined width is for a room or tenant space, it is divided among the exits leaving the calculated area. If it is a space that contains aisles or aisle accessways, additional calculations may be required. (See Examples 1 and 2 that follow.)

> **◀Note**
>
> The required width of a corridor leading to an exit stair will typically be less than the required width of the stair.

Table 7.3.3.1 Capacity Factors

Area	Stairways (width per person)		Level Components and Ramps (width per person)	
	in.	mm	in.	mm
Board and care	0.4	10	0.2	5
Health care, sprinklered	0.3	7.6	0.2	5
Health care, nonsprinklered	0.6	15	0.5	13
High hazard contents	0.7	18	0.4	10
All others	0.3	7.6	0.2	5

Figure 4.18 *Life Safety Code* Table 7.3.3.1, Capacity Factors (Reprinted with permission from *NFPA 101®*, *Life Safety Code®*, Copyright © 2008, National Fire Protection Association, Quincy, MA. This reprinted material is not the complete and official position of the NFPA on the referenced subject, which is represented only by the standard in its entirety.)

When determining exit widths, make note of the following additional requirements. All of them can affect the final width. (Additional ones may be required for specific occupancies.)

1. *Minimum door widths:* Building codes and accessibility standards require all means of egress doors to provide a minimum clear width of 32 inches (813 mm). In practical terms, a standard 36-inch (914 mm) wide door, when open, will provide 32 inches (813 mm) of clear width. (See Figure 4.3 for a diagram of clear width dimension.) Therefore, if an exit width of 30 inches (760 mm) is calculated, a 36-inch (914 mm) door will still need to be specified.

2. *Maximum door widths:* The building codes do not allow any leaf of a door used as part of the means of egress to be more than 4 feet (1220 mm) wide. Therefore, if 60 inches (1524 mm) of exit width is needed, more than one door will need to be provided. If two separate 36-inch (914 mm) doors are used, this will provide 64 inches (1630 mm) of clear width. This exceeds the required width but is the closest increment. (Remember, each single 36-inch [914 mm] wide door must be considered in increments of 32 inches [813 mm] of clear width, which is the minimum for the codes and the accessibility requirements.) If 40 inches (1015 mm) of exit width are required, a 48-inch (1219 mm) door would provide adequate width, whereas a 36-inch

◈ Note

Each single 36-inch [914 mm] wide door must be considered in increments of 32 inches [813 mm] of clear width, which is the minimum for the codes and the accessibility requirements.

(914 mm) door would not and two 36-inch (914 mm) doors might seem excessive.

3. *More than one exit:* The required width of an exit access (e.g., a corridor) can be affected if it leads to more than one exit on the floor that it serves. In that case, its width can typically be reduced. This is determined by dividing the total occupant load of the floor by the number of exits to which the exit access connects. This is done before making any calculations. (See Example 1, explained next.)

4. *Minimum exit discharge width:* When an exit discharge, such as a corridor, leads from an exit enclosure, its width cannot be less than that of the exit.

5. *Minimum corridor and stair widths:* In no case can a corridor width or stair width be less than 36 inches (914 mm); however, the typical code minimum is 44 inches (1118 mm), and some codes require accessible stairs to be a minimum of 48 inches (1219 mm) wide. The building codes set additional minimums for certain occupancy classifications. The ADA and ICC/ANSI standards also specify certain accessibility and clearance requirements that may affect the width of a means of egress. (See Figures 4.4, 4.6, 4.9, and 4.10, as well as Example 1 that follows.)

6. *Exiting from basement:* If a building has a basement that is occupied, some codes require the occupant load of the level of discharge to be increased. The exit discharge on the ground floor would need to allow for the exiting of the basement level(s) in addition to the upper floors. (Not all of the codes require this cumulative effect.)

7. *Minimum horizontal exit sizes:* Horizontal exits are allowed only if the area of refuge created is large enough to accommodate its own occupants and those from the "fire side." For most occupancies, the codes allow 3 square feet (0.28 s m) of floor space per occupant. Increased area for the area of refuge is required for Institutional occupancies. (See section Horizontal Exits earlier in the chapter.)

8. *Unobstructed paths:* The exit path must be clear and unobstructed. Unless the codes or accessibility requirements specifically state that a projection is permitted, nothing may reduce the determined exit width. The most common exceptions include a handrail that meets accessibility requirements, a nonstructural trim or wall application less than 1/2 inch (13 mm) thick, a wall sconce or other device not deeper than 4 inches (100 mm), or a door that does not project more than 7 inches (178 mm) when open. (See Figures 4.4 and 4.10E.)

9. *50 percent rule:* In some occupancies, the expected loss of any one exit location cannot reduce the total capacity of the exit width by more than 50

⌐Note

The total width of the exits will usually be more than that required by the codes because of all the additional code and accessibility requirements.

percent. For example, in a large Assembly occupancy, if multiple exit doors are required at the main entrance/exit and that location becomes blocked by a fire, the total exit width may be reduced significantly. If additional exit locations do not provide for at least 50 percent of the total exit width required, additional exit locations or additional doors at the other exits must be added.

10. *Aisles and aisle accessways:* The codes set additional requirements for aisles and aisle accessways. Different aisle widths are required, depending on whether the aisles are created by fixed seats or movable furniture. The typical minimum width for an aisle between tables and chairs is 36 inches (914 mm). Although the occupant load determines the actual width, some jurisdictions may require at least 44 inches (1118 mm). Aisle accessways have additional code requirements. (See the section Aisles and Aisle Accessways earlier in the chapter and Example 2 below.)

◤Note

Aisle accessways and horizontal exits have additional variables and specific requirements that must be met. Refer to the codes.

The goal of these and other exit requirements is to balance the flow of the occupants during an emergency. The goal is to make sure that an occupant can reach an exit and then get through it without any delay.

Example 1—Corridor and Doors

Figure 4.19 is the floor plan of the second floor in a two-story, mixed-use building that is nonsprinklered. The client has requested three tenant spaces to be designed in this vacant floor. The final layout must have the correct number and width of exits. Spaces A and C (Business) are typical tenant office spaces, and Space B is a wholesale retail store (Mercantile). The following process would be used:

Space A

Based on the occupant load and using the *IBC* table in Figure 4.15, two means of egress leading out of Space A are required. (Referring to the chart shown earlier in the section Number of Exits, the occupant load of 125 is under 500.) The required width of the exits for Space A now need to be determined to make sure that two 36-inch (914 mm) doors are enough.

This space is considered a Business occupancy. Using the *LSC* table in Figure 4.18, the exit width variable for "Level Components and Ramps" is 0.2 inch (5 mm) for a nonsprinklered building. To determine the width of the exit doors, take the occupant load of 125 and multiply it by the level exit variable of 0.2 inch (5 mm). This equals 25 inches (635 mm). This is the total required width that must be divided between the two doors. Hence, each door must be at least 12.5

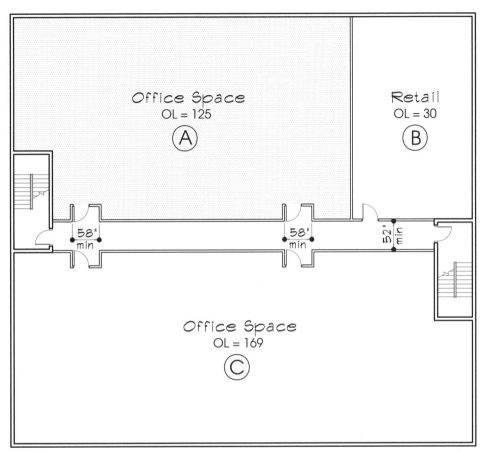

NOTE: Although typical minimum corridor width is 44 inches (1118 mm), additional width is often needed for accessibility clearances. A 60-inch (1524 mm) turning space is usually also required.

Total Occupant Load (OL) = 125 + 30 + 169 = 324

Figure 4.19 Egress width for a mixed occupancy building (nonsprinklered building).

inches (317.5 mm) wide. However, since the code requires all means of egress doors to provide a minimum clear width of 32 inches (813 mm), each door must be specified as a 36-inch (914 mm) wide door. (Note that the 25 inches (635 mm) seems to indicate that only one door or exit is required instead of two. That is why the number of exits required should be determined first.)

The size of the doors will also determine the minimum door alcove into the space and the corridor width within the tenant space. In this case, the corridors must work with a 36-inch (914 mm) door. However, the codes typically specify that a corridor cannot be less than 44 inches (1118 mm). Additional accessibility standards require at least 18 inches (445 mm) to be clear on the latch and pull side of the door. (Refer to Figure 4.4 and the ADA and ICC/ANSI standards.) Therefore, a minimum of 54 inches (36 + 18) (or, 1319 mm [914 + 445]) is needed for the door and pull clearance. On the hinge side of the door, a minimum of 4 inches (100 mm) will also be needed to allow for a hollow metal door frame and the structural framing around the door. Adding these together, a minimum 58-inch (1459 mm) wide alcove is required on the pull side of the door.

Inside the tenant space on the push side of the door, accessibility standards require a clearance of 12 inches (305 mm) (instead of 18 inches [445 mm]). Therefore, the required width on the tenant side can be 52 inches (1319 mm).

Floor

This is a mixed-occupancy floor. That means that before determining the exit widths for the entire floor, it is necessary to make sure that the egress width variables are the same for both Group B and Group M occupancies. Refering to the *LSC* table in Figure 4.18, both fall within the category of "all others" and require 0.3 inch (7.5 mm) for stairs and 0.2 inch (5 mm) for level components. (If they were different for the different occupancies, the higher of the two variables would be used.) The occupant loads for each tenant must also be added together to obtain the total for the floor. This total is 324 occupants.

Since the width variable for the stairs will result in a larger width, it should be determined first. The occupant load of 324 multiplied by the 0.3 (7.5 mm) stair variable equals 97.2, or 97 inches (2464 mm). (Typically, if it is less than 0.5, round down; if it is 0.5 or more, round up.) This total is divided between the two exit stairs, leaving 48.5 inches, or 49 inches (1245 mm). Therefore, each run of both stairs must be at least 49 inches (1245 mm) wide to meet the code requirements. (Note that this 49-inch [1245 mm] width cannot be reduced as the exit moves toward the public way. If the exit stairs empty into a corridor or exit passageway at the ground level, they must be at least 49 inches [1245 mm] wide as well.)

To determine the width of the corridor leading to the exit stairs, the layout of the floor must first be examined. Since there are two exit stairs, each stair needs to serve only one-half of the total occupant load for the floor. Therefore, the corridor width can be reduced as well. Take the total occupant load of 324 and divide it in half to obtain 162 occupants. Then multiply 162 by the level variable of 0.2 inch (5 mm) to obtain a minimum corridor width of 32.4, or 33 inches (838 mm). That means that the doors entering the exit stairs can each be the minimum 36-inch (914 mm) width. However, most codes specify a 44-inch (1118 mm) minimum for the corridor. If using the same 36-inch (914 mm) door,

✎ **Note**

The accessibility clearance required at the latch side of a door can include the width of the door frame adjacent to the latch.

✎ **Note**

As the various examples reveal, all the means of egress requirements must be determined and compared together. Each affects the other.

MEANS OF EGRESS   ❏   173

allow 4 inches (100 mm) on the hinge side of the door (for door frame and wall construction), and allow the 12-inch (305 mm) accessibility requirement on the push side of the door; the total exit width of the corridor for the floor is 52 inches (1319 mm). An additional consideration is that it takes 60 inches (1524 mm) for a person in a wheelchair to turn around. If the corridor is not 60 inches (1524 mm) wide, there are two options: either provide alcoves with sufficient turnaround space or add a turnaround space like the one shown in Plan D in Figure 4.10.

Example 2—Aisles and Aisle Accessways

Figure 4.20 shows the floor plan of a restaurant in a sprinklered building. It has an occupant load of 100. In this example, there are aisles and aisle accessways of different lengths and capacities. Each aisle and aisle accessway width must be determined separately. Some widths will be determined by the minimums set by the codes; others will require calculations. To determine the main aisle widths (indicated as W in the figure), the occupant load of the space and the number of exits must be calculated. Then, the calculated exit width should be compared to the minimum width required by the codes. The larger width should be used in the design. Refer back to the *LSC* table in Figure 4.18 and use the process described in Example 1 to calculate the required exit access width. First, multiply the occupant load of 100 by 0.2 inch (5 mm) to get a total exit width of 20 inches (510 mm). Then, because there are two exits, the total exit access width is divided between the two exits. So, the calculated exit width is 10 inches (254 mm). However, the codes set a minimum width for aisles of 36 inches (914 mm) for this Assembly occupancy situation. The main aisles (W) are therefore required to be at least 36 inches (914 mm) wide.

◀Note

The formula for calculating the width of accessways translates slightly differently when the formula is converted to metric values.

If the occupant load is much greater, however, the calculated aisle width may be larger than the required minimum aisle width. For example, if the occupant load was 300, the calculated width would be 45 inches (1143 mm). The main aisles (W) would then be 60 inches (1524 mm) wide instead of the minimum 36 inches (914 mm).

Next, the widths of the aisle accessways need to be determined. Some are determined by standard widths given by the codes, as discussed earlier in the chapter. (See Figure 4.11.) For example, the codes do not require a minimum width for the aisle accessway A at the lower right of the plan because of its limited length and capacity. The minimum width at the aisle accessway B at the left of the plan is 12 inches (305 mm). This is added to the 19 inches (483 mm) required for the chair (D) to obtain the overall distance between tables. (See the section Aisles and Aisle Accessways earlier in this chapter.) However, since aisle accessway C is longer than 12 feet (3658 mm), the required width must

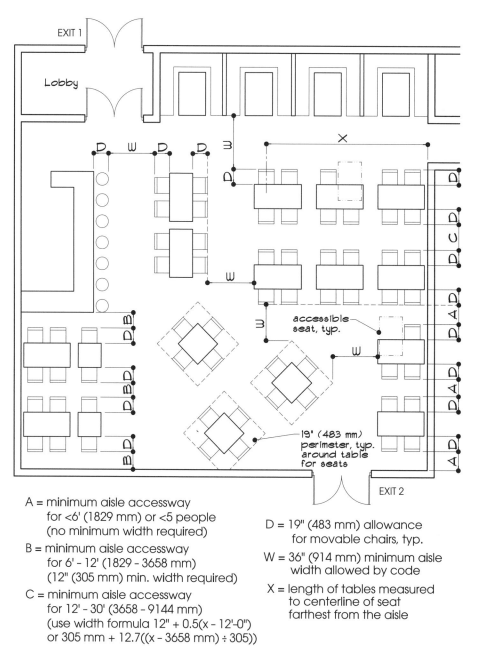

A = minimum aisle accessway
for <6' (1829 mm) or <5 people
(no minimum width required)

B = minimum aisle accessway
for 6' – 12' (1829 – 3658 mm)
(12" (305 mm) min. width required)

C = minimum aisle accessway
for 12' – 30' (3658 – 9144 mm)
(use width formula 12" + 0.5(x – 12'-0")
or 305 mm + 12.7((x – 3658 mm) ÷ 305))

D = 19" (483 mm) allowance
for movable chairs, typ.

W = 36" (914 mm) minimum aisle
width allowed by code

X = length of tables measured
to centerline of seat
farthest from the aisle

Figure 4.20 Egress and aisle widths for moveable tables and chairs (sprinklered building, occupant load [OC] = 100).

be calculated. The building codes and the *LSC* use a similar formula to obtain this calculation. The formula is 12 inches + 0.5 (x—12 feet); when using metrics, the formula is 305 mm + 12.7 ([x—3658 mm] ÷ 305). By using this formula, the calculated width of an aisle accessway will be wider for longer aisle accessways. As shown in Figure 4.20, the variable "x" is the length of the aisle, measured from the end of the last table to the centerline of the seat farthest from the aisle. In this case, the length of aisle accessway C is 17 feet (5182 mm); therefore, 12 inches + 0.5 (17—12 feet) = 12 inches + 0.5(5) = 12 + 2.5 = 14.5. So, a width of 15 inches (381 mm) must be provided in addition to the 19 inches (483 mm) required for the chairs.

◤Note

For Assembly occupancies, the required minimum aisle width varies if the aisle is level or includes steps or a ramp. Consult the codes for specific requirements.

ARRANGEMENT OF EXITS

The arrangement of exits is also specified by the codes. The building codes and the *LSC* require exits to be located as remotely from each other as possible so that if one becomes blocked during an emergency, the other(s) may still be reached. The maximum distance a person can travel before reaching these exits is also specified by the codes. The next sections explain how to locate exits based on using concepts such as the half-diagonal rule, travel distance, dead-end corridors, and common paths of travel.

Half-Diagonal Rule

When two or more exits are required, at least two of the exits must be a certain distance apart. This is referred to as the *half-diagonal rule*. This rule requires that the distance between two exits be at least one-half of the longest diagonal distance within the building or the building area the exits are serving. The easiest way to understand this rule is to review Figure 4.21. These diagrams are representative of open building plans or separate tenant spaces within a building. In a tenant space, the measurement is unaffected by the presence of other surrounding spaces. The shape or size of the area or the building does not matter. The longest possible diagonal in that space must be found. Measure the length of that diagonal in a straight line from one corner of the floor plan to the other corner (as represented by "D" in each case). Then take one-half of that length. The result indicates how far apart the exits must be. This is the *minimum* distance allowed between the two exits. The *IBC* requires the distance to be measured to the centerline of each door; the NFPA codes allow it to be measured to the edge of the door.

◤Note

When there are two or more exits, two of the exits must be located at a distance equal to at least half of the longest diagonal within the space or building. This is referred to as the *half-diagonal rule*.

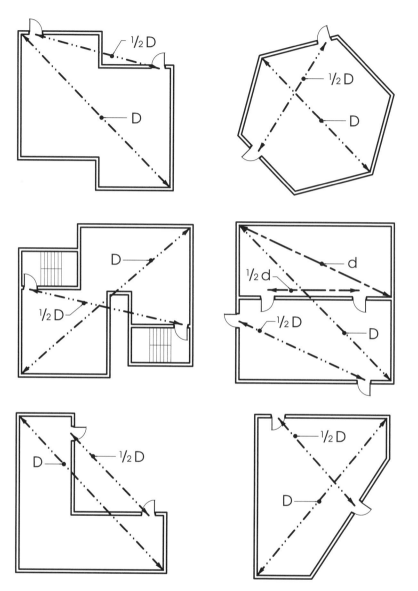

D = Diagonal or Maximum Distance

½ D = Half of Diagonal or Minimum Distance

NOTE: Some codes allow the minimum distance to be 1/3 the overall diagonal in lieu of 1/2 if the building has an automatic sprinkler system.

Figure 4.21 Half-diagonal rule example: Building.

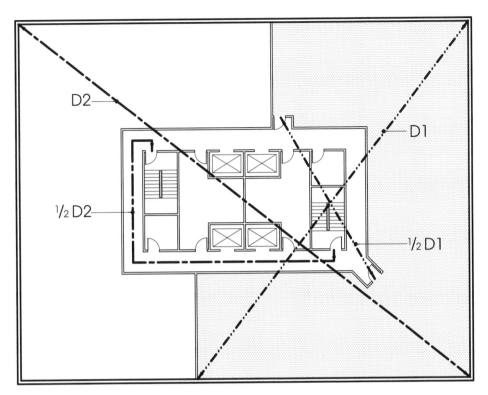

D1 = Diagonal Distance for Tenant Space

D2 = Diagonal Distance for Entire Floor

NOTE: Some codes allow the minimum distance to be 1/3 the overall diagonal in lieu of 1/2 if the building has an automatic sprinkler system.

Figure 4.22 Half-diagonal rule example: Tenant and floor.

When a building has exit enclosures, such as exit stairs that are interconnected by a fire-rated corridor, some of the codes, including the *IBC*, require the exit distance to be measured differently. Figure 4.22 illustrates this point for an entire floor in relation to a tenant space. The overall diagonal length (D2) is also measured using a straight line across the top of the floor plan. On the other hand, when placing the two exits at the stairwells, the half-diagonal distance between the exits (HF D2) is measured along the path of travel within the rated corridor. (The tenant space exit access doors are located using a straight line.)

When more than two exits are required, at least two of the exits must be placed using the half-diagonal rule. The remaining exits should be placed as

◀ Note

Typically, when a building is sprinklered, the two exits can be located at a distance equal to at least one-third of the overall diagonal of the space or building.

remotely as possible so that if one exit becomes blocked in an emergency, the others will still be usable. Most of the codes also allow an exception to the half-diagonal rule if the entire building is equipped with an automatic sprinkler system. In some cases, the one-half measurement can be reduced to one-third. (Refer to the codes.)

Travel Distance

In general, travel distance is the measurement of an exit access. It is the measurement of the distance between the most remote, occupiable point of an area, room, or space to the exit that serves it. Two types of travel distance are regulated by the codes. First, the codes limit the length of travel distance from within a single space to the exit access corridor. This is known as a common path of travel, because all the occupants of that space will have to travel in approximately the same direction before they come to two options for exiting. (See the section Common Path of Travel later in this chapter.) The codes also regulate the length of travel distance from anywhere in a building to the exit of the building or floor. These are separate travel distance calculations, and the information is located in different areas of the codes.

Travel distance from within a *single space* is basically determined the same way by the building codes and the *LSC*. Travel distance within a single space is especially important when the occupant load requires only one exit. Typically, if the travel distance within a tenant space exceeds 75 feet (22,860 mm), then an additional exit is necessary even if the occupant load does not require it. There are exceptions. For example, in many occupancies, if there is an automatic sprinkler system within the building, the travel distance in the space usually can be increased from 100 feet (30,480 mm). Other exceptions may require shorter travel distances, such as in some Hazardous occupancies. (Refer to the specific codes for more information.)

Likewise, travel distance to the exit for the *entire building or individual floor* is basically determined the same way by the building codes and the *LSC*. The difference in each code is the standard distance allowed and the format of the information. The *IBC* uses Table 1016.1, "Exit Access Travel Distance," as shown in Figure 4.23. The NFPA codes include the regulations in each occupancy chapter. In addition, the *LSC* has a chart in its appendix that includes all common path limits, dead-end corridor limits, and travel distance limits.

Travel distance is not measured in a straight line; instead, it is measured on the floor along the centerline of the natural path of travel. The measurement starts 1 foot (305 mm) from the wall at the most remote point (usually the corner of a room) and moves in a direct path toward the nearest exit, curving around

TABLE 1016.1
EXIT ACCESS TRAVEL DISTANCE[a]

OCCUPANCY	WITHOUT SPRINKLER SYSTEM (feet)	WITH SPRINKLER SYSTEM (feet)
A, E, F-1, M, R, S-1	200	250[b]
I-1	Not Permitted	250[c]
B	200	300[c]
F-2, S-2, U	300	400[c]
H-1	Not Permitted	75[c]
H-2	Not Permitted	100[c]
H-3	Not Permitted	150[c]
H-4	Not Permitted	175[c]
H-5	Not Permitted	200[c]
I-2, I-3, I-4	Not Permitted	200[c]

For SI: 1 foot = 304.8 mm.

a. See the following sections for modifications to exit access travel distance requirements:
    Section 402.4: For the distance limitation in malls.
    Section 404.9: For the distance limitation through an atrium space.
    Section 407.4: For the distance limitation in Group I-2.
    Sections 408.6.1 and 408.8.1: For the distance limitations in Group I-3.
    Section 411.4: For the distance limitation in special amusement buildings.
    Section 1014.2.2: For the distance limitation in Group I-2 hospital suites.
    Section 1015.4: For the distance limitation in refrigeration machinery rooms.
    Section 1015.5: For the distance limitation in refrigerated rooms and spaces.
    Section 1021.2: For buildings with one exit.
    Section 1028.7: For increased limitation in assembly seating.
    Section 1028.7: For increased limitation for assembly open-air seating.
    Section 3103.4: For temporary structures.
    Section 3104.9: For pedestrian walkways.
b. Buildings equipped throughout with an automatic sprinkler system in accordance with Section 903.3.1.1 or 903.3.1.2. See Section 903 for occupancies where automatic sprinkler systems are permitted in accordance with Section 903.3.1.2.
c. Buildings equipped throughout with an automatic sprinkler system in accordance with Section 903.3.1.1.

Figure 4.23 *International Building Code* Table 1016.1, Exit Access Travel Distance (*2009 International Building Code*, copyright 2009. Washington, DC: International Code Council. All rights reserved. www.iccsafe.org).

any obstructions such as walls, furniture and equipment, or corners with a clearance of 1 foot (305 mm). The measurement ends at the exit. Typically, this will be a door. Common examples include the following:

1. The exterior exit door

2. The door to an enclosed exit stair

3. The door of a horizontal exit

4. The door to an enclosed exit passageway

5. The door to an enclosed area of refuge

6. The door to the exit access corridor (for a common path of travel)

✐Note

Whenever a jurisdiction requires both a building code and the *LSC,* compare the maximum travel distances between the two. In most cases, the shortest required distance applies. Also check the sprinkler requirements and individual occupancies for any exceptions to the allowable travel distances.

⬛ Note

If an occupancy has an open stairway within its space that is part of an exit access, it must be included in the travel distance. It is measured up to the centerline of the nosing of the top tread. Then take the measurement of the stair on the angle of the stairway in the plane of the tread nosing. Measure from the top tread nosing to the bottom tread nosing to get the stair travel length. To continue the overall travel distance, start at the bottom edge of the last riser to the exit.

⬛ Note

Typically, if the longest travel distance within a space to the entry door exceeds 75 feet (22,680 mm), the space would require two exits.

⬛ Note

If designing a number of different tenant spaces in the same building, the travel distance must be measured for each tenant. It does not matter if the tenants are all the same occupancy. If they are separated from each other by a demising wall, they must be treated separately.

Maximum travel distances for an individual floor can increase in length in certain occupancies when additional requirements are met. (Refer to the specific codes.) This can be seen in the *IBC* table in Figure 4.23. The use of an automatic sprinkler system typically increases the allowed travel distance from 50 to 100 feet (15,240 to 30,480 mm). For example, in a Business occupancy in a nonsprinklered building the 200-foot (60,960 mm) travel distance can be increased to 300 feet (91,440 mm) if sprinklers are added.

Example

The floor plan in Figure 4.24 gives an example of measuring travel distances in a space that requires only one means of egress. The floor plan is that of an accounting firm that occupies part of one floor in a four-story sprinklered building. It is considered a Business occupancy. Since it is a new occupancy and separate from the other tenants in the building, it must have a travel distance acceptable to the current code requirements.

The dashed line on the floor plan indicates the path of travel distance. The travel distance measurement starts at the most remote point—in other words, the farthest point from the exit. It is indicated by the "X" on the floor plan. The first calculation is to determine if this tenant space will require a second exit. (Only one is required by the occupant load.) In this case, the exit is the door leading from the tenant space to the exit access corridor, as indicated by "A." Therefore, the travel distance measurement ends at the center of this door. Since the tenant has two points that seem to be about the same distance from the exit, both must be measured. The measurement starts 1 foot (305 mm) from the wall at the farthest corner and moves toward the exit using the most direct path and staying 1 foot (305 mm) away from any obstacles. Obstacles can include walls, corners, furniture, fixtures, equipment, and machinery.

Once the travel distance line is drawn as directly as possible, measure the line to get the travel distance measurement. In the example in Figure 4.24, the longest travel distance to "A" is 57 feet (17,374 mm). Since it does not exceed the minimum 75 feet (22,860 mm) required by the code, a second exit is not required.

The next calculation is to determine the travel distance to the exit for the building floor. In this case, the exit is the door leading into the exit stair, as shown by "B." Therefore, the travel distance measurement begins at the same point as before but ends at the center of this exit stair door. The distance is measured along the longest path and extends to the stairwell. In this example, the longest travel distance to "B" is 81 feet (24,689 mm). Compare this to the maximum travel distances allowed by the codes. Using Figure 4.23, the *IBC* table indicates

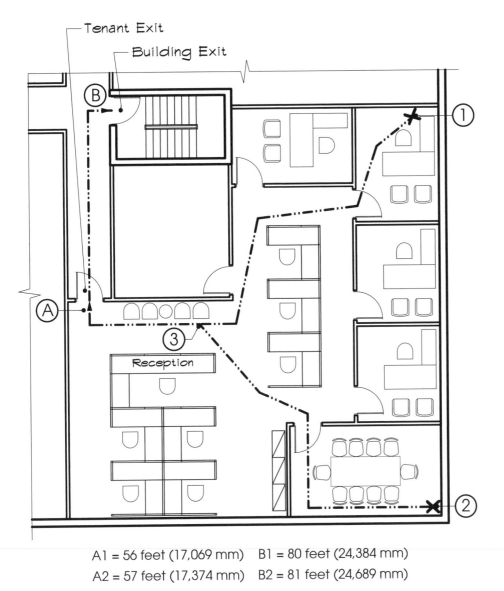

Tenant Exit

Building Exit

A1 = 56 feet (17,069 mm)   B1 = 80 feet (24,384 mm)
A2 = 57 feet (17,374 mm)   B2 = 81 feet (24,689 mm)

Figure 4.24 Travel distance example: Tenant space (sprinklered building).

that for Business occupancies the travel distance limit is 300 feet (91,440 mm) for sprinklered buildings. The design of the accounting firm's floor plan meets the codes, since both measurements are below the maximum travel distance allowed. (If this had been a nonsprinklered building, the travel distance would have still met the code.)

TRAVEL DISTANCE FACTORS

Travel distance measurement is not based on a code formula. Rather, it is based on the space or building as a whole. *The Life Safety Code Handbook (2003)* lists the factors on which the required code travel distances are based:

The estimated number, age, and physical condition of building occupants and the rate at which they can be expected to move

The type and number of expected obstructions, such as display cases, seating, and heavy machinery that must be negotiated

The estimated number of people in any room or space and the distance from the farthest point in that room to the door

The amount and nature of combustibles expected in a particular occupancy

The rapidity with which a fire might spread, which is a function of the type of construction, the materials used, the degree of compartmentation, and the presence or absence of automatic fire detection and extinguishing systems

Obviously, travel distance will vary with the type and size of an occupancy and the degree of hazards present.

◢Note

In some jurisdictions, the placement of freestanding furniture and moveable panel systems does not create dead-end corridors. It is assumed that in an emergency this furniture can be moved or climbed over.

Dead-End Corridors

A dead-end corridor is a corridor with only one direction of exit. In other words, if a person turns down a corridor with a dead end, there is no way out except to retrace his or her path. An example of a dead-end corridor has been indicated on the floor plan in Figure 4.25.

The codes set maximum lengths for dead-end corridors because they can be deadly in an emergency. When a corridor is filled with smoke, it is difficult to read exit signs. Occupants could waste valuable time going down a dead-end corridor, only to find out that they have gone the wrong way and must turn back. If a dead-end corridor is long, a person can easily get trapped by fire and/or smoke.

The building codes and the *LSC* describe the limits of a dead end within the text. (In the *LSC*, they are also listed in a table within its appendix.) The most common dead-end length is a maximum of 20 feet (6096 mm). It is measured 1 foot (305 mm) from the end of a corridor, following the natural path of travel, to the centerline of the corridor that provides the choice of two means of egress. In some codes, when an automatic sprinkler system is installed, a dead-end corridor

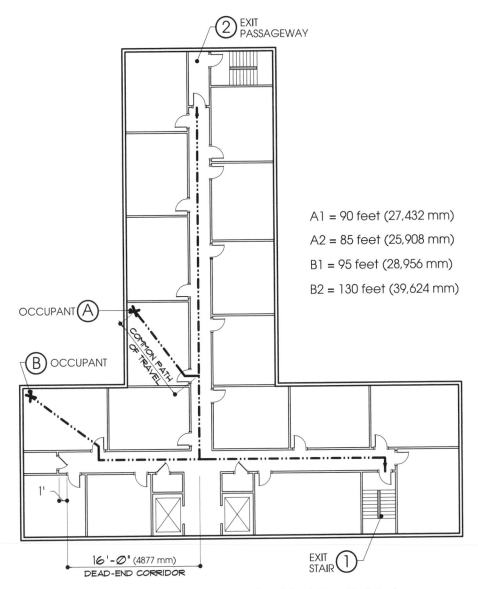

② EXIT PASSAGEWAY

A1 = 90 feet (27,432 mm)

A2 = 85 feet (25,908 mm)

B1 = 95 feet (28,956 mm)

B2 = 130 feet (39,624 mm)

OCCUPANT Ⓐ

COMMON PATH OF TRAVEL

Ⓑ OCCUPANT

1'

16'-0" (4877 mm)
DEAD-END CORRIDOR

EXIT STAIR ①

Figure 4.25 Travel distance example: Building (hotel) (sprinklered building).

can be longer. For example, in the *IBC*, a dead-end corridor in a sprinklered building in Business, Factory, Storage and some Educational, Institutional, Mercantile, Residential, occupancies is allowed to be up to 50 feet (15,240 mm) in length. There may be other conditions that would allow longer dead-end corridors. (Refer to the codes for specifics.)

◀Note

Some of the codes allow a dead-end corridor longer than 20 feet (6096 mm) when sprinklers are present. It depends on the type of occupancy.

Although it would be best to eliminate dead-end corridors altogether, it is not always possible—especially in older existing buildings. If one becomes necessary, locate the rooms or spaces that are least used at the end of the corridor. When a dead-end corridor longer than 20 feet (6096 mm) is unavoidable, which can sometimes happen in older buildings, contact the code officials in that jurisdiction.

Example

A second travel distance example is an entire third floor of a hotel in a sprinklered building. The floor plan in Figure 4.25 indicates that there are two exits. Both are enclosed stairways. (In this example, it is assumed that the elevators do not constitute an exit in an emergency.) Refer back to the *IBC* table in Figure 4.23. Under the Residential (R) occupancy for hotels, the maximum travel distance allowed is 250 feet (76,200 mm) for a sprinklered building. (The bottom of the table gives the metric conversion unit.) This means that an occupant located anywhere on the floor of this hotel cannot travel more than 250 feet (76,200 mm) to reach the closest exit.

In this example, several measurements must be made. Point A, as indicated on the floor plan, is midway between the two exits. An occupant in this location must be able to reach at least one exit within 250 feet (76,200 mm). In both cases (A1 and A2), the total distance is less than this.

Point B must also be within 250 feet (76,200 mm) from the enclosed exit stairs. Note, however, that the point is located in a dead-end corridor. The length of the dead end can not be longer than 20 feet (6096 mm). Since the dead-end length is 16 feet (4877 mm), proceed to measure the travel distance. As shown in Figure 4.24, the travel distance to both exits (B1 and B2) is less than the 250-foot (76,200 mm) maximum distance.

Common Path of Travel

Some of the codes set maximum lengths for common paths of travel. The specified length depends on the occupancy and in some cases whether the building is sprinklered. These restrictions in length can apply to either of the following types of common paths of travel. The first type occurs when a person can travel in only *one direction* to reach the point where there is a choice of two exits. For example, a dead-end corridor can be considered a common path of travel. Both paths B1 and B2 in Figure 4.24 are also common paths of travel. In addition, any room that has only one exit door also has a common path of travel, as indicated at "A" in Figure 4.25. The common path is measured similarly to travel distance, starting 1 foot from the wall at the most remote location. It is the distance from this point measured along the natural path of travel to the centerline of the first corridor or aisle that provides a choice of two paths of travel to remote exits.

The second definition of a common path of travel is an exit access where two paths merge to become one. The *merged* path becomes the common path of travel. For example, a reception area in a tenant space typically becomes a common path of travel. Two corridors or aisles accessing the various rooms and/or offices would merge together at the reception area to arrive at the door exiting the space. This is shown in Figure 4.24 beginning at point "3" and leading to "B." Most exit discharges can be considered a common path of travel, such as a lobby or vestibule, where other means of egress must converge to leave the building.

SIGNAGE

A variety of signs are required by the codes in a means of egress. These include exit signs and other exiting and location-related signs. Some signs will be required by the codes; others may be requested by the client. Various types of signs are discussed below. (Restroom signs are discussed in Chapter 7.) It is important to specify the signage products that meet the requirements of the jurisdiction as well as accessibility standards, including the *ADA Standards*.

Exit Signs

Exit signs are typically required whenever a floor or space has two or more exits. They must be installed at the doors of all stair enclosures, exit passageways, and horizontal exits on every floor. They must also be installed at all exterior exit doors and any door exiting a space or area when the direction of egress is unclear. For example, a sign is often required when a corridor changes direction or provides an option for more than one direction. The purpose of the exit sign is to lead occupants to the nearest exit or to an alternate exit if necessary. Although codes provide some specific requirements about the placement of exit signs, additional signs may be necessary to clearly designate a path or location within a space or series of corridors. (See the following section, Other Signs.)

The building codes and the *LSC* specify the placement, graphics, and illumination of exit signs. The 2009 *IBC* requires certain exit signs to be tactile as well. Exit signs are allowed to be externally or internally lit. Internally illuminated signs are allowed to be electrically powered, self-luminous, or photoluminescent. However, according to the *IBC*, all types of internally illuminated exit signs are required to be listed and labeled according to *UL 924, Standard for*

Safety of Emergency Lighting and Power Equipment. The codes may also refer to *NFPA 170, Standard for Fire Safety Symbols.* The *ADA Standards* and ICC/ANSI standard have specific regulations that address accessibility as well. For example, a tactile sign is required at an area of refuge, stairwell, exit ramp, and other exit components.

Exit signs located directly over an exit door are usually required only to say "EXIT." Signs that lead occupants to the exit doors often are required to have directional arrows. (Some jurisdictions may allow the use of other languages where a majority of the occupants may speak a language other than English. And in some cases, graphic signs without words may be used.) Confirm the specific requirements with the jurisdiction. For example, contrast letters on exit signs are usually available in green and red; some jurisdictions, however, allow only red.

When placing exit signs, the most common requirement is that no point within the exit access can be more than 100 feet (30,480 mm) from the nearest visible sign. Therefore, if there is a long corridor or a large space, additional exit signs are often required. Figure 4.26 indicates typical locations of exit signs within a building and within a tenant space. The general rule is to use a regular exit sign at an exit or exit access door and directional exit signs at all other locations (i.e., corridors, open areas). Although exit signs are usually ceiling mounted or wall mounted, some jurisdictions may also require exit signs to be located near the ground so that they can be seen when smoke gathers at the ceiling. The *LSC* also requires floor-proximity egress path markings in some new occupancies.

Other Signs

In addition to exit signs, other exit-related signs may be required, especially when a means of egress is confusing. For example, if a regular door or stairway can be mistaken for an exit, the codes typically require that a "NO EXIT" sign be posted on the door. (Supplemental lettering such as "STOREROOM" or "TO BASEMENT" can be used to indicate the name of the area as well.) Exiting signage can also include signs that help orient the occupants to their location in the building (e.g., floor levels, stair numbers, and floor numbers at stairs and elevator banks).

An area of refuge has multiple signage requirements including tactile signage and directional signage as well as posted instructions. (See codes for specifics.) Other code-required signage typically includes labeling entrance and exit doors, indicating locked doors, and so on. An example would include a fire exit sign mounted on the corridor side of a stairwell door that also says "KEEP DOOR CLOSED." (Other signs may be requested by the client, such as room names and/or room numbers.)

When a sign is required by codes, the building code may include specific requirements for its placement, size, letter type and size and specific message.

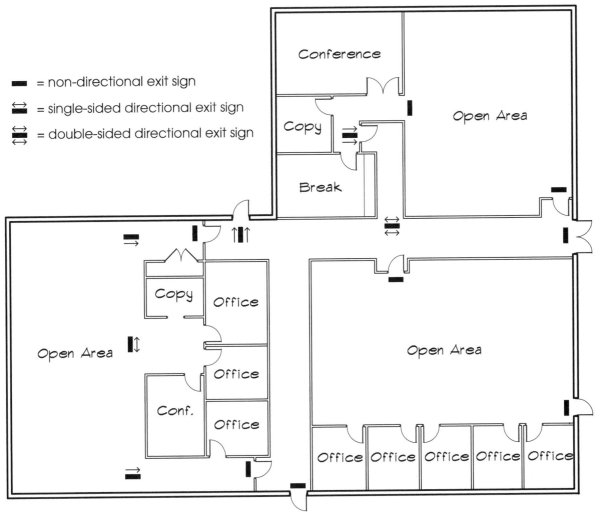

Figure 4.26 Exit sign location example.

The codes may also refer to the ICC/ANSI standard for other specific accessibility requirements. Similar regulations are required by the *ADA Standards* whenever a sign is permanent and must be followed even when the sign is not required by codes. For example, a room number sign would need to meet accessibility requirements. Specifics include lettering heights, mounting locations, lettering contrast, and, in certain cases, the use of Braille. Mounting locations in relation to the door are specified as well. Most commonly, a sign must be mounted 48 to

60 inches (1219 to 1524 mm) above the floor. Typically, this height is measured to the baselines of the lettering on the sign. The sign must also be mounted on the latch side of the door. If it is a double door, the sign should be mounted to the right of the door. Clear floor space in front of the sign may also be required. (See Figure 7.11 in Chapter 7 for other information.)

EMERGENCY LIGHTING AND COMMUNICATION

Like exit signage, emergency lighting is typically required whenever two or more exits are present. Sometimes referred to as exit lighting, emergency lighting must be connected to a backup system in case of power failure during an emergency. This could mean connection to a backup generator in the building or battery packs located within the light fixture. Generally, the codes require emergency lighting to be provided at all exits and any aisles, corridors, passageways, ramps, and lobbies leading to an exit. Both general exit lighting and exit and area of refuge signs must be lit at all times when a building is in use. The codes specify minimum lighting illumination levels. Lower levels might be allowed for certain building types, such as theaters, concert halls, and auditoriums. (Chapter 8 describes emergency lighting in more detail.)

Beginning in 2009, the *IBC* and *IFC* require that the path within the exit stair and other exit enclosures and exit passageways in high-rise buildings to have luminous markings that define the path. (The *LSC* includes similar requirements.) These exit path markings can be photoluminescent or self-illuminating. The codes require that the steps, landings, handrails, perimeters, doors, door frames, and door hardware be marked. In addition obstacles along that path that project more than 4 inches (102 mm) must be marked as well. The codes have specific requirements how to properly mark each element. (Check the codes for specifics.)

In addition to emergency lighting, the codes use other devices and ways to help occupants find the exits and areas of refuge in case of an emergency or fire. Many of the components of the fire alarm systems within a building, for example, help notify occupants that there is a fire and in some cases where the fire is located. (These systems are discussed further in Chapter 6.) It is important not to rely on just one type of signal or directional system. For example, thick smoke can make exit signs difficult to see, or an occupant who is hearing impaired may not hear an audible alarm. A more complete exiting system will use a mix of audible sounds, voice communication, and specific visual signals to communicate to the occupants. The codes will specify when each of these is required by the occupancy or size of the space. However, an additional level of communication may be more appropriate for a particular project. (See also the section Emergency Voice/Alarm Communication Systems in Chapter 6 and the inset titled *Integrated Alarms* on page 257.)

CHECKLIST

Although a means of egress has a number of components, the ultimate goal is to provide a direct route or exit to the exterior of a building. The checklist in Figure 4.27 has been prepared to help you design the means of egress for your project. It helps you to determine which components must be researched, reminds you of the required calculations, and provides a form for documentation of your research.

The top of the checklist is used to identify the use and size of the project. You should indicate the name of the project and/or the space that you are currently researching. The checklist also asks for the occupancy classification of that project as well as the occupant load. (See Chapter 2.) Next, you are asked to indicate the scope of the project. For example, if you check "Floor," that means you are designing an entire floor of a building. You must calculate the egress capacities for everything on that floor, including the exit stairs leaving the floor. If you are designing a portion of a floor, such as a "Space/Tenant" space on a multi-tenant floor, your main concern will be that tenant.

The first section addresses requirements for exit access portions of the means of egress. First, you are asked to identify components of the exit access that will be included in your project. For example, if you are laying out a space for a single tenant with an open office plan, you may need to research aisle requirements. However, if you are laying out an entire floor area, you may have to consider corridor requirements as well as aisle requirements. By checking which ones apply to your project, you will know which codes and accessibility requirements must be researched. Use the section called Exit Access 1 for the first component and Exit Access 2 for the second component. For example, Exit Access 1 may be used to document the corridor requirements and Exit Access 2 may be used to document the door requirements. If you have multiple exit access components, you may need additional sheets.

You will ultimately need to determine the required width for each component and note it in these sections. Note also which variable and method you used. (See the section Exit Widths to help you with this calculation.) As you lay out your design, it is important to examine the egress path that you are creating and keep maximum travel distances in mind. The checklist includes a place to record

> **✎Note**
>
> Particular attention should be given to the type of occupancy when determining means of egress requirements, since the codes may allow exceptions or require more stringent regulations, depending on the occupancy.

Means of Egress Checklist

Date: _____

Project Name: _____ Space: _____

Main Occupancy (new or existing): _____Occupant Load: _____

Type of Space (check one): _____ Building _____ Floor _____ Space/Tenant _____ Room

---

Exit Access Requirements: (if more than 2, attach additional calculations)

Exit Access 1 (check/research those that apply and fill in the corresponding information)

Type of Component(s): __ DOOR __STAIR __ RAMP __CORRIDOR __ AISLE __ INTERVENING ROOMS

Required Width: _____ Using: __ LEVEL VARIABLE __STAIR VARIABLE __OTHER VARIABLE

Exit Access 2 (check/research those that apply and fill in the corresponding information)

Type of Component(s): __ DOOR __STAIR __ RAMP __CORRIDOR __ AISLE __ INTERVENING ROOMS

Required Width: _____ Using: __ LEVEL VARIABLE __STAIR VARIABLE __OTHER VARIABLE

Travel Distance (check those that apply and indicate lengths where required)

__ Common Path of Travel: _____   __ Max. allowed travel distance for space: _____

__ Dead-End Corridor: _____   __ Max. allowed travel distance for floor/building: _____

Exit Requirements: (may require up to 4 exits; if more than 2, attach additional calculations)

Required Number of Exits (check those that apply and indicate quantity where shown)

__ One Exit Exception   __ Required Number of Exits: _____

__ Minimum of Two Exits   __ Number of Exits Provided: _____

Location of Exits Determined By (check one)

__ 1/2 Diagonal Rule   __ Other Remoteness Requirement

__ 1/3 Diagonal Rule (if allowed)   Explain: _____

Exit 1 (Check/research those that apply and fill in the corresponding information)

Type: __ EXTERIOR DOOR __EXIT STAIR __EXIT PASSAGEWAY __HORIZONTAL EXIT __AREA OF REFUGE

Required Width: _____ Using: __LEVEL VARIABLE __STAIR VARIABLE __MINIMUM REQUIRED

Number of Doors: _____ Distributed: __EVENLY AMONG EXITS __ASSEMBLY EXCEPTION

Exit 2 (Check/research those that apply and fill in the corresponding information)

Type: __EXTERIOR DOOR __EXIT STAIR __EXIT PASSAGEWAY __HORIZONTAL EXIT __AREA OF REFUGE

Required Width: _____ Using: __LEVEL VARIABLE __STAIR VARIABLE __MINIMUM REQUIRED

Number of Doors: _____ Distributed: __EVENLY AMONG EXITS __ASSEMBLY EXCEPTION

Exit Discharge Components: (check those that apply and research if required)

__ MAIN LOBBY __ FOYER __VESTIBULE(S) __DISCHARGE CORRIDOR(S) __EXIT COURT(S)

Other Code and Accessibility Requirements to Consider: (check/research those that apply)

__ Doors: Type, Swing, Size, Hardware, Threshold, Clearances, Fire Rating

__ Stairs: Type, Riser Height, Tread Depth, Nosing, Width, Handrail, Guard, Fire Rating

__ Ramps: Slope, Rise, Landings, Width, Edge Detail, Finish, Handrail, Guard

__ Corridors: Length, Width, Protruding Objects, Fire Rating

__ Aisles: Fixed Seats, No Fixed Seats, Ramp(s), Steps, Handrails

__ Intervening Rooms: Type, Size, Obstructions, Fire Rating

__Signage and Lighting: Exit signs, photoluminescent markings, emergency lighting, evacuation maps

---

NOTES:

1. Refer to codes and standards for specific information as well as ADA and ICC/ANSI standards for additional requirements.
2. Attach any floor plans indicating locations of components and other paperwork required for calculations.
3. Check specific occupancy classifications and/or building types for special requirements that may apply.

Figure 4.27 Means of egress checklist.

the allowable dead-end corridors as well as the overall maximum travel distance for both a space and/or the entire floor. You should also research and note the limitations for common paths of travel. These may affect the location of exits as well as the most appropriate layout of various rooms and furniture.

Next, you must determine how many exits are required from each space, the overall space, or the entire floor. Although two exits are almost always required, in some cases you may be allowed to have only one exit. In other cases, you will be required to have multiple exits. Note which requirement applies to your project. If you are working with an existing space, note how many exits are already provided. You can check this against how many are required.

If two or more exits are required, the codes set various requirements so that all of the exits are not easily blocked by a single fire. Note in the next section which requirement you used to locate the exits. For example, did you verify that two exits meet the half-diagonal rule, or is the building sprinklered and you are allowed to use the one-third diagonal rule? If you are evaluating an existing layout and location of exits, note which rule the existing exits meet. You may want to attach a reduced copy of the floor plan to show your measurements.

Once you know the number of exits and their location, you must determine the required width for the exits. The following section of the checklist gives you a place to document two separate exit locations. (Attach additional calculations as required.) First, indicate what type of exit is used. For example, one exit may be a door and the second exit may be a horizontal exit. These different exit types will require separate calculations. Then research the requirements for each exit and record the calculated or minimum width required. Depending on the type of exit, also note the variable that was used in your calculations or note that you used the minimum width required by the codes. Finally, indicate the number of actual doors that will be or are provided at each exit location. Remember that although exit width is typically distributed equally between exits, a large Assembly use may require a different distribution. (See the section Exit Widths earlier in this chapter.)

If your project includes an exit discharge, indicate the type in the next section and research the requirements for that particular situation. You may need to attach documentation of your research to this checklist for your records.

The last section of the checklist indicates the main means of egress components and typical characteristics that must be researched. Many of these will require additional calculations. Check any that apply, and use the codes and the accessibility standards as well as this book to determine what is required for your project. All of the required calculations and special code information should be attached to the checklist and kept with the project records. Check the building code and/or the *LSC*, the *ADA Standards*, and the ICC/ANSI standard. In addition, note any exceptions that are allowed.

◀ Note

Once a building occupant moves into the protected portion of a means of egress, as he/she exits the building, the level of protection cannot be reduced or eliminated unless an exception is allowed by the jurisdiction of the project.

CHAPTER 5

FIRE AND SMOKE RESISTANT ASSEMBLIES

Approximately 75 percent of all codes deal with fire and life safety. Their enforcement affects virtually every part of a building, focusing first on prevention and then on early detection, control and suppression as the primary means of providing safe buildings. Interior fire-related codes focus on protecting the occupants of the building, allowing time to evacuate during a fire as well as access for firefighters and equipment. The ultimate goal of fire-related codes is to confine a fire to the room of origin, and therefore limit the spread of the fire and prevent flashover. All this gives occupants time to exit the building safely and firefighters time to address the control and suppression of the fire.

The codes include provisions for both fire protection and smoke *protection*. In the past, most regulations were directed to controlling fire within a building. Yet smoke can be just as deadly as fire, if not more so, because of how fast it can travel. The toxicity of the smoke is a large factor as well. Whether a fire is full-blown or just smoldering, the smoke it produces can travel quickly and cause harm to the occupants of the building before the fire ever reaches them. The smoke causes asphyxiation, obstruction of sight, and disorientation, making evacuation difficult.

Because the control of fire and smoke is such a serious life safety issue, the prevention of fire and smoke spread is addressed in the codes in several ways. The codes and standards place strict requirements on the *materials* that are used to construct a building. The construction type of a building, as discussed in Chapter 3, assigns an hourly fire-resistance rating to almost every structural element in a building, including walls and floor assemblies. Other parts of the codes place restrictions on the building materials used inside the building. These materials include everything from interior walls, windows, and doors to ductwork, wiring, and plumbing pipes. Interior finishes and furniture, as discussed in Chapter 9, are regulated by codes and standards as well. All of these materials and components are considered combustible materials that can feed and sustain

⬣Note

More people die from asphyxiation due to smoke than from burns due to fire. Toxicity from burning or smoldering items also causes a large number of deaths.

⌐Note

A balance of active and passive fire protection systems is necessary for a safe building.

a fire within a building. Also known as *fuel loads*, they are restricted and managed by the codes.

In addition to regulating the materials that go into a building or space, the codes require various *systems* that are intended to promote fire safety. Generally, the systems can be defined as passive fire-protection systems, active fire-protection systems, and exiting systems. The specific issues in each category are listed below.

Passive Systems

Passive systems focus on prohibiting and containing fires. They are sometimes referred to as *prevention systems*. These elements are considered *passive* because, once in place, nothing else has to occur for them to be part of the control of a fire. Most parts of a passive or prevention system are discussed in this chapter:

⌐Note

Passive fire protection systems may also be referred to as *prevention systems*.

- ❏ Fire and smoke barriers and partitions (e.g., walls)
- ❏ Horizontal assemblies (e.g., floors, ceilings)
- ❏ Opening protectives (e.g., windows, doors)
- ❏ Through-penetration protectives (e.g., firestops, draftstops, dampers)
- ❏ Finishes and furniture (e.g., wall coverings, finish floor materials, upholstered pieces, mattresses, and similar elements) (These are discussed in Chapter 9.)

Active Systems

These systems are considered *active* because they have to be *activated* in order to work against the fire.

- ❏ Detection systems (e.g., detectors, fire alarms, communication systems) (These systems are discussed in Chapter 6.)
- ❏ Extinguishing and suppression systems (e.g., fire extinguishers, fire hoses, sprinkler systems) (These systems are discussed in Chapter 6.)
- ❏ Emergency lighting (These systems are discussed in Chapters 4 and 8.)

Exiting Systems

Exiting systems are the elements of a space or building that assist and direct occupants to a place of safety.

- ❏ Means of egress (e.g., corridors, exits, stairs, ramps, and similar components) (These components are discussed in Chapter 4.)
- ❏ Exit communication systems (e.g., signage, audible, visual communication) (These are discussed in Chapters 4 and 6.)

Each system plays an important part in making a building safe. In recent code development, emphasis on the use of active systems such as automatic sprinkler systems has changed many requirements. However, most experts agree that a balance of active and passive systems is necessary for the safest building. In other words, components of each system should be included in the overall fire protection design.

This chapter discusses how compartmentation in interior projects works as part of the passive fire protection system by using assemblies that resist the spread of fire or smoke. These assemblies include fire walls, fire barriers and partitions, horizontal assemblies, smoke barriers and partitions, opening protectives, and through-penetration protectives. Each type is explained in this chapter. A discussion of sustainable-related requirements is provided at the end of the chapter along with a fire- and smoke-resistance checklist. (Detection and suppression systems will be discussed in the following chapter.)

COMPARING THE CODES

The building codes typically have several chapters pertaining to passive and active fire protection systems within a building. In most cases, the codes discuss passive and active systems separately. For example, each building code has a chapter that addresses the *passive* fire protection elements of a building. The *International Building Code* (IBC) refers to it as "Fire and Smoke Protection Features." The *Life Safety Code* (LSC) has a chapter entitled "Features of Fire Protection." A number of requirements for fire-resistance-rated partitions can also be found in the means of egress chapter as well as the occupancy-related chapters within each code. Together these chapters define the use of compartmentation for a space or building. Other chapters and sections within these codes contain information on active fire protection systems. (These systems are discussed in more detail in Chapter 6.)

The building codes set additional regulations by specifying the types of materials and assemblies and where they should be used. These requirements are included in the building codes in the chapters on construction types, as well as in the fire protection chapters. When specific testing and installation methods are required, the building codes and the LSC refer to various standards. Many of these are NFPA standards. The NFPA standards that are more interior-related are listed in Figure 5.1. These and other standards are discussed throughout this chapter.

The fire codes also give requirements for the different types of fire-resistance-rated construction. For example, the *International Fire Code* (IFC) has separate

◆ Note

A number of cities and some states have adopted their own fire codes including California, Boston, Massachusetts, and New York City. Others have created their own code based on the *IFC* such as Florida, New Jersey, and New York State.

NFPA 80	Standard for Fire Doors and Other Opening Protectives
NFPA 92A	Standard for Smoke-Control Systems Utilizing Barriers and Pressure Differences
NFPA 92B	Standard for Smoke Management Systems in Malls, Atria, and Large Spaces
NFPA 105	Standard for Installation of Smoke Door Assemblies and Other Opening Protectives
NFPA 204	Standard for Smoke and Heat Venting
NFPA 221	Standard for High Challenge Fire Walls, Fire Walls, and Fire Barrier Walls
NFPA 251	Standard Methods of Tests of Fire Resistance of Building Construction and Materials
NFPA 252	Standard Methods of Fire Tests of Door Assemblies
NPFA 255	Standard Method of Test of Surface Burning Characteristics of Burning Materials
NFPA 257	Standard on Fire Test for Window and Glass Block Assemblies
NFPA 259	Standard Test Method for Potential Heat of Building Materials
NFPA 270	Standard Test Method for Measurement of Smoke Obscuration Using a Conical Radiant Source in a Single Closed Chamber
NFPA 288	Standard Methods of Fire Tests of Floor Fire Door Assemblies Installed Horizontally in Fire-Resistance-Rated Floor Systems
NFPA 555	Guide on Methods for Evaluating Potential for Room Flashover
NFPA 703	Standard for Fire-Retardant Treated Wood and Fire-Retardant Coatings for Building Materials

NOTE: There are other standards organizations with similar standards as those shown above. These include ASTM and UL standards. See other figures in this chapter for more detail.

Figure 5.1 Common NFPA standards for building materials and assemblies.

chapters titled "Fire-Resistance Rated Construction." However, this *IFC* chapter concentrates on the maintenance required once the assemblies are installed so that their integrity is maintained. In some cases, the requirements of the fire code are repeated within the building codes so that the related documents are consistent. When a fire code is required by a jurisdiction, the applicable building code and fire code need to be compared to know all the requirements that apply to a project.

In addition, performance codes and criteria may be very useful when designing a passive fire-protection system, especially in an existing building. Sometimes the best balance for a particular building may require innovative engineering not represented in the prescriptive codes. And because even new buildings or spaces do not always fit the configurations assumed by the codes, broader ideas about compartmentation sometimes need to be explored. In these situations, the use of a performance code, such as the *ICC Performance Code (ICCPC)*, may be helpful if allowed by a jurisdiction. In addition, the *IBC* allows for alternative methods and materials. For fire and smoke protection, the *IBC* includes *Section 715.3, Alternative Methods for Determining Fire protection Ratings*, which provides performance criteria to establish the fire-resistance rating of an untested assembly. These methods have to be reviewed and approved by a code official similar to the performance codes.

Although the *ICCPC* does not have a specific section or chapter on the use of rated walls, it does set objectives for overall building safety during a fire, including the protection of occupants. The *ICCPC* also sets criteria for preventing a fire, limiting the impact of a fire, the exposure to hazards because of burning materials, and the overall fuel load. The performance-based chapters in the NFPA codes also include design criteria and fire scenarios to be considered in the performance design.

The performance codes and alternate methods criteria within each building and fire code may also allow the use of new materials and assemblies. However, confirm that these methods will be allowed by the jurisdiction. As in most cases, even when performance codes are used to design an overall fire-protection plan, many of the related prescriptive requirements would be used as part of the design as well.

Sustainability codes and standards, such as the *International Green Construction Code (IGCC)*, do not include information on fire-rated construction. However, because these codes and standards require certain construction materials to be sustainable, careful attention must be given to the materials used in rated walls and other assemblies. (This is discussed more in the section Sustainability Considerations later in this chapter.)

The Americans with Disabilities Act (ADA) standards and other accessibility standards such as *ICC/ANSI A117.1* do not play a major role in passive fire-prevention requirements. However, many of the fire-resistant components such as fire doors and enclosed stairwells are still required to meet the accessibility requirements. Since Chapter 4 has already discussed the accessibility requirements related to doors, stairs, and other means of egress, this chapter will mention the *2010 ADA Standards* and the ICC/ANSI standard only a few times.

COMPARTMENTATION IN A BUILDING

The overall concept of a passive fire-protection system is *compartmentation*. Compartmentation is the separation of areas in a building to control fire and smoke by the use of wall, floor, and ceiling assemblies. The codes specify when certain areas must be separated from another area and when the spread of fire or smoke must be limited. Some of these assemblies will be required to be fire rated; others will need to be smoke rated or a combination of both. (These are discussed later in this chapter.)

Compartments are created by fire-resistance-rated assemblies, which include fire walls, fire barriers, horizontal assemblies, and fire partitions. These assemblies create separate, self-contained areas within a building and sometimes separate "buildings" in a single structure. As a result, the fire can spread to only a limited area before meeting resistance from the rated assemblies. These areas are required by the code at certain intervals, between different uses and where different levels of hazard may exist. In certain situations, a designer may chose to create separate fire areas for better fire protection. (The requirements for the doors, windows, and other penetrations within the fire-rated walls are discussed later in this chapter.)

The control of smoke can be just as important or more important than the control of fire. And because assemblies that have fire-resistance ratings do not necessarily resist the spread of smoke, the codes also require the use of smoke barriers and smoke partitions in some cases. When required, these assemblies become part of the compartmentation of the space or building. When assemblies are required to be both fire resistant and smoke resistant, they are referred to as fire barriers and smoke barriers (as discussed later in this chapter).

The use of an automatic sprinkler system within a building will affect the requirements for compartmentation as well. For example, if a building is equipped with a fully automatic sprinkler system, some fire-rating requirements may be reduced or eliminated. This will be discussed in more detail in the next chapter. (See the section Sprinkler Systems in Chapter 6.) However, during a project, it is important to know if an automatic sprinkler system will be provided or if an approved one exists within the building so that the appropriate compartmentation requirements can be researched.

Each type of separation wall or assembly used to create a rated compartment has specific requirements, depending on its use and location. The various uses of fire-resistance-rated walls and smoke-tight walls as part of compartmentation are discussed in the next several sections.

FIRE WALLS

Note

Fire walls are not usually added to existing buildings. They are very costly because the wall must extend continuously from the foundation of the building up to or through the roof.

Fire walls are used by the codes either within a building structure or between buildings to create two or more separate buildings according to the code. The main purpose of a fire wall is to provide complete vertical separation between areas in a building. A fire wall has a separate foundation from the rest of the building structure and extends to the roof. Within a building, it must extend at least from exterior wall to exterior wall. In some cases, the wall is required to extend beyond the exterior walls and project through the roof (i.e., a parapet wall). When the fire wall is located on a lot line and shared between two build-ings, it is referred to as a *party wall.*

Fire walls can be used to subdivide a building with two separate types of construction or to create building divisions within the same construction type for the purpose of allowing larger building areas. (See Chapter 3.) For example, if a medical office building and a hospital were built of different construction types but were built so that they were connected, a fire wall might be necessary to separate the different uses and construction types. Another example would be the design for a factory that exceeded its allowable area; fire walls could be used to divide the total area into two or more smaller areas that fall within the allowable area limitations.

Fire walls are built so that if the construction on one side of the wall fell during an emergency, the fire wall and the construction on the other side would remain standing. They are typically tested using *NFPA 221, Standard for High Challenge Fire Walls, Fire Walls, and Fire Barrier Walls.* A fire wall can be rated a mini-mum of 2 hours, but the most common required rating is 3 or 4 hours. Which rat-ing is required is usually determined by the occupancy classification within the building, as shown in the *IBC* Table 706.4, "Fire Wall Fire-Resistance Ratings" in Figure 5.2. The rating of the fire walls are listed by the occupancy classification. If the two areas of the building were different occupancies, the highest rating would be required. Although the NFPA codes set a minimum rating of 2 hours for a fire wall, other specific requirements are listed within the text and in the occupancy chapters. Within a fire wall, openings and penetrations are very lim-ited. In some cases, certain penetrations are not allowed. Check the codes for the specific requirements for each fire wall location.

Because fire walls are usually planned and built during the initial construc-tion of the building, they may not be part of a typical interior project. However, if the fire wall needs to be penetrated for any reason (e.g., adding a door),

◀Note

For certain occupancies, the codes allow horizontal separations (between floors) that work like fire walls to separate a single structure into different construction types or buildings. (See Chapter 3.)

TABLE 706.4
FIRE WALL FIRE-RESISTANCE RATINGS

GROUP	FIRE-RESISTANCE RATING (hours)
A, B, E, H-4, I, R-1, R-2, U	3[a]
F-1, H-3[b], H-5, M, S-1	3
H-1, H-2	4[b]
F-2, S-2, R-3, R-4	2

a. In Type II or V construction, walls shall be permitted to have a 2-hour fire-resistance rating.
b. For Group H-1, H-2 or H-3 buildings, also see Sections 415.4 and 415.5.

Figure 5.2 *International Building Code* Table 706.4, Fire Wall Fire-Resistance Ratings (*2009 International Building Code*, copyright 2009. Washington, DC: International Code Council. All rights reserved. www.iccsafe.org).

additional research is necessary to make sure that the fire-resistance rating is maintained. To determine the fire-resistance rating of an existing fire wall, it may be necessary to refer to the original construction documents or contact the original architect to obtain the actual rating.

FIRE BARRIERS, HORIZONTAL ASSEMBLIES, AND FIRE PARTITIONS

Fire-rated assemblies are used by the codes to create compartments within a building or space. By separating the different areas of a building (sometimes both horizontally and vertically), the spread of a single fire and transfer of the heat generated by that fire can be limited. There are three basic types of rated assemblies: fire barriers, fire partitions, and horizontal assemblies. Fire barriers and fire partitions are vertical building elements such as walls and shaft enclosures that have a fire-resistance rating. Horizontal assemblies are floor/ceiling or ceiling/roof assemblies that have a fire-resistance rating. The codes determine when each type is required to provide the appropriate level of compartmentation within the building or space.

Fire barriers are walls that have a fire-resistant rating and in most cases must be continuous and extend vertically from the top of a floor assembly to the bottom of a floor/ceiling assembly. For example, a fire barrier would extend through a suspended ceiling to the slab above. When a fire barrier intersects another fire-resistance-rated assembly—either another wall or a horizontal assembly (i.e., floor/ceiling assembly)—additional fire blocking is required at the joint. In addition, the number of openings in a fire barrier, including doors and windows, is limited. The doors, windows, and other penetrations in the rated assemblies must be rated as well. (Opening protectives and through-protectives are discussed later in this chapter.)

Floor/ceiling or ceiling/roof assemblies that are required by the codes to be rated are referred to as *horizontal assemblies*. They serve the same function as fire barriers but are horizontal instead of vertical building elements. In most cases, horizontal assemblies must meet requirements similar to those of fire barriers. Horizontal assemblies extend horizontally from one rated wall or exterior wall to another. Where fire barriers and horizontal assemblies meet, the joints must be sealed. Openings and penetrations are limited and must be protected as well.

In most cases, when the codes require the separation of a specific area, both fire barriers and horizontal assemblies are required. (These separation requirements will be discussed in more detail throughout this section.) When the walls, floors, and ceiling assemblies surrounding an area have the same fire-resistance rating, it creates a complete compartmentation or enclosure (both vertically and

◁**Note**

A fire barrier provides more protection than a fire partition. (Refer to Figure 5.3.)

◁**Note**

Keep in mind that fire and smoke barriers are important components of a means of egress. A safe means of egress, as required by the codes, is a combination of the requirements discussed in Chapters 4, 5, 6, and 9 of this book.

horizontally)—like a four-sided box with a top and bottom. An example would be the enclosure of an exit stairway where all four walls, the floor, and the ceiling/roof have a 2-hour rating. Depending on the codes, fire barriers and horizontal assemblies are tested using *ASTM E119, Standard Test Methods for Fire Tests of Building Construction and Materials, NFPA 251, Standard Methods of Tests of Fire Resistance of Building Construction and Materials,* or *UL 263, Standard for Fire Tests of Building Construction and Materials,* depending on the code. They may also be required to pass *NFPA 221, Standard for High Challenge Fire Walls, Fire Walls, and Fire Barrier Walls.*

Keep in mind that an assembly may need to meet more than one code requirement. This is especially true for structural components such as a floor/ceiling assembly that must also meet construction-type requirements. (See Chapter 3.) For example, if a space or room requires a 1-hour rated floor horizontal assembly, but the construction type requires the floor assembly to be rated 2 hours for that construction type, the floor assembly must provide the 2-hour rating. The highest required rating must be provided. If a horizontal separation is required and the existing floor/ceiling assembly does not provide an adequate fire-resistance rating, then a rated ceiling assembly may need to be installed below the existing ceiling structure.

Fire partitions are similar to fire barriers, but in most cases have less restrictive requirements. In the *IBC,* the term fire partition is used in addition to *fire barrier* to mean a *vertical* rated partition that separates certain uses within a building. (This term is not used by the NFPA.) Fire partitions are most often used to separate exit access corridors, tenant spaces in malls, dwelling and/or sleeping units, and elevator lobbies from the rest of the floor. (Refer to the inset titled *Rooms and Spaces* on page 73.) However, according to the *IBC,* fire partitions do not provide the same level of protection as fire barriers. For example, although fire partitions can extend from structure to structure in a building, they are also allowed to stop at a rated ceiling system; fire barriers cannot. This difference is shown in Figure 5.3.

A fire partition separates one area from another but is not always required to be a full enclosure. In other words, the floor and ceiling assemblies typically have to have the same rating; but when used to separate tenant spaces in malls, dwelling units, sleeping areas, and corridors or certain construction types, they do not. A fire partition usually has a rating of at least 1 hour. In certain situations, corridor walls and walls between dwelling and sleeping units are allowed to have a lower rating. Often an automatic sprinkler system is required for the lower rating. Yet, like a fire barrier, openings in a fire partition are required to be protected, although the number of openings is not limited. The NFPA codes do not differentiate between fire barriers and fire partitions. However, by allowing exceptions to the requirements for fire barriers (in cases where the *IBC* calls for the use of fire partitions) and by adding requirements where a higher level of separation is necessary, the fire-rating requirements of the codes are similar.

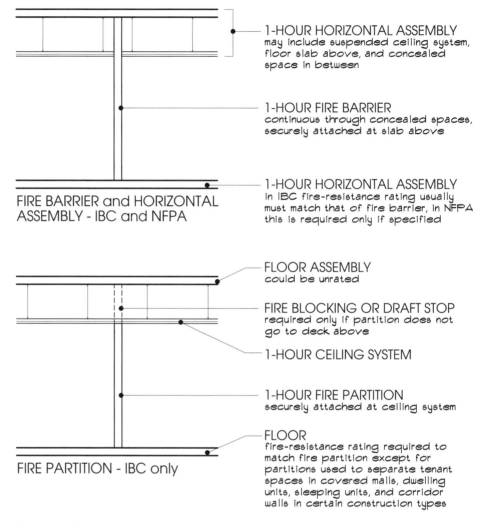

Figure 5.3 Fire barriers, horizontal assemblies, and fire partitions.

◀**Note**

The 2009 *IBC* requires the hourly rating for rated wall assemblies to be indicated on the wall above the finished ceiling at specific intervals along the wall.

The codes now require that fire walls, fire barriers and partitions, and smoke barriers and partitions be marked in the field. The marking must indicate the type of use (i.e., fire barrier or fire partition) and the hourly rating it provides. This mark can be above the finish ceiling but it must be accessible. The information has to be repeated at approximately 30-foot intervals along the length of the wall and be of a legible size lettering. This is not required in certain Residential uses with drywall ceilings. However, this is very useful when working on a project in an existing building since it is a quick way to determine the location of existing rated walls.

It is very common for a rated wall to be added or modified during an interior project. Whether the project includes a new layout, new finishes, or the addition of wiring and cabling, work done may affect a rated wall. Therefore, determine the correct use and rating of the fire barrier, horizontal assembly, or fire partition if adding a new one or make any changes to an existing one. Also, keep in mind that for all three, the presence of an automatic sprinkler system may allow for lower fire-resistance ratings. Therefore, the rating depends on the purpose of the fire barrier, horizontal assembly, or fire partition, the occupancy classification, and if the space or building has sprinklers. (The sprinkler system must meet the current code requirements.) The most common uses of fire barriers, horizontal assemblies, and fire partitions for compartmentation are described next. (Smoke Assemblies are explained in the next section.)

◢Note

When walls are added to an existing structure, it may be necessary to determine if the existing design load of the building will support these walls. See the inset titled *Design Loads* on page 86.

Fire Areas

Fire barriers and exterior walls are used within a building to separate one area from another, creating two or more *fire areas*. (When a fire wall is used to create separate buildings, the buildings are considered separate fire areas as well). Fire areas are most often required within a single-occupancy type to provide compartmentation. For example, fire areas can be used to divide a large factory building into separate areas. The separate fire areas may allow one area of a building to be sprinklered and another to remain nonsprinklered, as shown in the plan in Figure 5.4. (This is different from using a fire wall to divide a large factory into separate buildings, as explained in the section Fire Walls earlier in this chapter.) In some cases, the codes require separate fire areas within a building. For example, a fire area is almost always required to separate a Hazardous use from another occupancy type. An example would be a small area of hazardous materials being stored within a large Storage occupancy. (This is different from incidental accessory occupancies, as described later.) It may also be desirable to split a large floor into two or more fire areas if sprinklers are required in one area to manage fire protection and because of hazardous conditions.

In addition, a horizontal assembly can be used to create individual fire areas between each floor of a multi-story building. For example, in the building shown in the Section in Figure 5.4, the Business and Factory uses are separate fire areas. As in the previous example, this may allow one floor to be sprinklered and another to be nonsprinklered. A fire area can also include more than one floor. This is determined by the codes. For example, high-rise buildings are usually divided into separate fire areas every couple of floor levels.

◢Note

Fire ratings for floor/ceiling assemblies are first controlled by the construction type of the building. However, other sections of the codes will affect the rating of these assemblies as well.

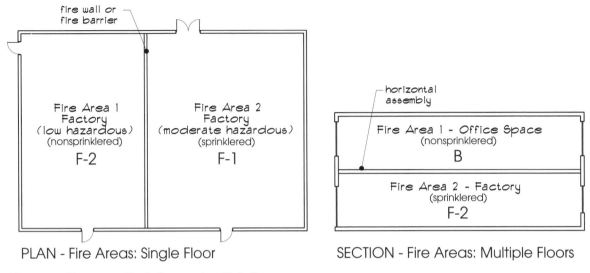

Figure 5.4 Fire areas: Single floor and multiple floors.

The required fire-resistance rating of the fire barrier or horizontal assembly separating each fire area is determined by the code. Each building code has a table similar to *IBC* Table 707.3.9, "Fire-Resistance Rating Requirements for Fire Barrier Assemblies or Horizontal Assemblies Between Fire Areas," as shown in Figure 5.5. Other sections of the code will indicate when a fire area is required and then reference the table to indicate the appropriate hourly rating. The Plan in Figure 5.4 is an example of separate fire areas being created within a Factory occupancy. One area of the factory is considered F-2 because it contains materials that are considered low hazard. The other part of the factory contains more hazardous materials and is considered F-1. Knowing this and using the *IBC* table

Figure 5.5 *International Building Code* Table 707.3.9, Fire-Resistance Rating Requirements for Fire Barrier Assemblies or Horizontal Assemblies Between Fire Areas (*2009 International Building Code*, copyright 2009. Washington, DC: International Code Council. All rights reserved. www.iccsafe.org).

TABLE 707.3.9
FIRE-RESISTANCE RATING REQUIREMENTS FOR FIRE BARRIER ASSEMBLIES OR HORIZONTAL ASSEMBLIES BETWEEN FIRE AREAS

OCCUPANCY GROUP	FIRE-RESISTANCE RATING (hours)
H-1, H-2	4
F-1, H-3, S-1	3
A, B, E, F-2, H-4, H-5, I, M, R, S-2	2
U	1

in Figure 5.5, the rating of the fire barrier between the fire areas can be determined. It is 3 hours. (The strictest requirement applies.) This may allow one area to be sprinklered and the other to be nonsprinklered. It can also be seen from the table that certain occupancies, such as Hazardous ones, can require ratings as high as 4 hours.

Occupancy Separation

When more than one type of occupancy exists within a building or space, it is considered a mixed occupancy or a multiple occupancy, depending on which code is being used. It can be treated as a separated or non-separated mixed occupancy or as a separated or mixed multiple occupancy. (See the discussion of mixed and multiple occupancies in Chapter 2.) In order for it to be considered separated, each occupancy must be separated from the other by a fire barrier or horizontal assembly.

Occupancy separation may be required in various situations. The most obvious one is when multiple tenants of different occupancy types are located in one building. An example might be a building that has a restaurant, retail stores, and offices, each operated by different tenants. Another case is when a single user or owner operates more than one use (e.g., occupancy) within a single structure—for example, a sports center that includes a gymnasium (Assembly) and an exercise apparel store (Mercantile) in the same building. (The store might also be considered an accessory. See the section Accessory Occupancies in Chapter 2.)

In the past, all occupancies were typically required to be separated by at least a 1-hour fire rating. However, beginning in 2006, the *IBC* code requires only occupancies that have dissimilar risk factors to be separated by a fire barrier or horizontal assembly. This allows many occupancies that previously were required to be separated by fire-resistance-rated construction to be have unrated walls separating them. (These unrated walls typically still have to be smoke tight, however, as described later.)

Each building code and the *LSC* use a table similar to *IBC* Table 508.4, "Required Separation of Occupancies (Hours)," shown in Figure 5.6, to indicate when separation is required. In this table, the occupancies that are considered to have similar risk factors have been grouped together along the top of the chart and similarly down the left side. For example, B, F-1, M, and S-1 occupancies are grouped together. To determine if a rated separation is required, cross-reference the occupancy classifications along the top and the left side of the table. For example, in Plan A of Figure 5.7 there is an Assembly occupancy adjacent to a Business occupancy. Using the table in Figure 5.6, locate the group including Business (B) along the top and then locate Assembly (A) at the left side. Where the (B) column and the (A) row meet, a rating of 1 hour for a sprinklered (S)

TABLE 508.4
REQUIRED SEPARATION OF OCCUPANCIES (hours)

OCCUPANCY	A[d], E		I-1, I-3, I-4		I-2		R		F-2, S-2[b], U		B, F-1, M, S-1		H-1		H-2		H-3, H-4, H-5	
	S	NS	S	NS	S	NS	S	NS	S	NS	S	NS	S	NS	S	NS	S	NS
A[d], E	N	N	1	2	2	NP	1	2	N	1	1	2	NP	NP	3	4	2	3[a]
I-1, I-3, I-4	—	—	N	N	2	NP	1	NP	1	2	1	2	NP	NP	3	NP	2	NP
I-2	—	—	—	—	N	N	2	NP	2	NP	2	NP	NP	NP	3	NP	2	NP
R	—	—	—	—	—	—	N	N	1[c]	2[c]	1	2	NP	NP	3	NP	2	NP
F-2, S-2[b], U	—	—	—	—	—	—	—	—	N	N	1	2	NP	NP	3	4	2	3[a]
B, F-1, M, S-1	—	—	—	—	—	—	—	—	—	—	N	N	NP	NP	2	3	1	2[a]
H-1	—	—	—	—	—	—	—	—	—	—	—	—	N	NP	NP	NP	NP	NP
H-2	—	—	—	—	—	—	—	—	—	—	—	—	—	—	N	NP	1	NP
H-3, H-4, H-5	—	—	—	—	—	—	—	—	—	—	—	—	—	—	—	—	1[e, f]	NP

S   = Buildings equipped throughout with an automatic sprinkler system installed in accordance with Section 903.3.1.1.

NS = Buildings not equipped throughout with an automatic sprinkler system installed in accordance with Section 903.3.1.1.

N   = No separation requirement.

NP = Not permitted.

a. For Group H-5 occupancies, see Section 903.2.5.2.
b. The required separation from areas used only for private or pleasure vehicles shall be reduced by 1 hour but to not less than 1 hour.
c. See Section 406.1.4.
d. Commercial kitchens need not be separated from the restaurant seating areas that they serve.
e. Separation is not required between occupancies of the same classification.
f. For H-5 occupancies, see Section 415.8.2.2.

Figure 5.6 *International Building Code* Table 508.4, Required Separation of Occupancies (Hours) (*2009 International Building Code*, copyright 2009. Washington, DC: International Code Council. All rights reserved. www.iccsafe.org).

◄**Note**

A fire barrier typically must extend from the top of the floor/ceiling assembly to the underside of the floor, slab, or roof deck above. It must pass through concealed spaces such as the plenum space above a suspended ceiling.

building and a rating of 2 hours for a nonsprinklered (NS) building are indicated. Since the building in this example is nonsprinklered, the wall that separates the two occupancy classifications must have a fire-resistance rating of 2 hours. (Notes at the bottom of the table clarify the abbreviations used in the table and offer exceptions based on specific circumstances.) If the same table was used to determine the fire rating between the Business (B) and Mercantile (M) occupancies in Figure 5.7, no rated separation would be required because they are grouped together in the table.

Occupancy separation can be required vertically as well. For example, if a Storage (S-2) use was located on the floor below the Business (B) occupancies in Figure 5.7, the table would be used again to determine that a 2-hour fire-resistance separation is required between these occupancies in a nonsprinklered building. The horizontal assembly then would need to provide the required rating. Since floor/ceiling assemblies can also be regulated by construction types,

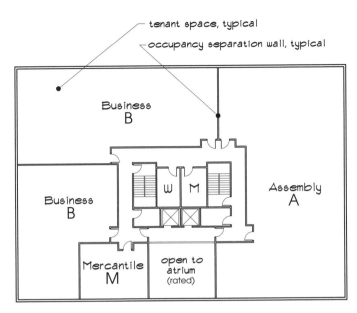

PLAN A - Multi-Tenant Building

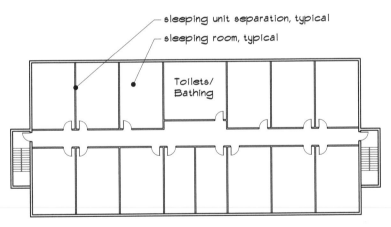

PLAN B - Multiple Residential Units (Dormitory - 2nd Floor)

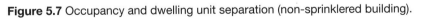

Figure 5.7 Occupancy and dwelling unit separation (non-sprinklered building).

this rating should be checked as well and the strictest requirement should be used. For example, if working on a project in an existing building requiring a 3-hour-rated floor assembly between occupancies, the rating of the floor assembly would need to be checked based on the construction type of the building. If the existing floor assembly provides only a 1-hour rating, for example, additional rated materials would be necessary to increase the fire resistance to 3 hours, as required by the codes. If the floor assembly meets or exceeds the required occupancy separation requirement, no additional materials are necessary.

Tenant Separation

In past codes, all tenants in a multi-tenant building were required to be separated by some level of fire-resistance-rated construction. This was typically referred to as a *tenant separation* wall (also known as a *demising* wall). However, most recent building codes treat adjacent tenants as an occupancy separation issue. In other words, the codes no longer require a rated separation between tenants of the same occupancy, such as a law office next to an accounting office, which are both Business occupancies. In addition, because of recent changes in the way that the *IBC* determines the need for rated partitions between different occupancies, in some cases even tenants that are different occupancy classifications may not be required to be rated. (See Occupancy Separation above.)

However, there is an exception. Tenant separation still applies to tenants within a covered mall. In most cases, tenants within a mall (e.g., stores, restaurants) are required to be separated by a fire partition. The walls open to the mall are not required to be rated. A covered mall has many specific code requirements because of its unique organization and use. If designing a covered mall, additional research would need to be done on these unique code requirements.

Dwelling and Sleeping Unit Separation

Dwelling units and sleeping units within most Residential occupancies are required by the codes to be separated by fire partitions. Examples include different units in a hotel, dormitory, or apartment building. (See also the inset titled *Rooms and Spaces* on page 73.) These must also be separated from other adjacent occupancy classifications by a fire partition. However, a dwelling or sleeping unit adjacent to another use but of the same occupancy classification, such as the lobby of a hotel, would not have to be separated by a fire partition.

Fire partitions separating dwelling and sleeping units are typically rated 1 hour. In some cases, the walls in a sprinklered building will be allowed a lower rating. For example, a 1-hour separation is required between sleeping units in a dormitory, as shown in Plan B of Figure 5.7, but the floor/ceiling assembly between the first and second floors would only require a rating of 1 hour if there were additional sleeping or dwelling units on the floor below. These walls often need to meet sound transmission requirements as well. (See the inset titled *Sound Transmission* on page 209.)

◀**Note**

Even though walls separating tenants may not be required to be rated, they are usually required to resist the passage of smoke.

◀**Note**

Walls that divide living units, such as sleeping units in hotels and dormitories and dwelling units in apartment buildings, must also meet sound transition code requirements. (See inset titled *Sound Transmission* on page 209.)

SOUND TRANSMISSION

Sound can be transferred between spaces by reverberation (i.e., echoes) and/or by the lack of absorption of the sound by the structure or content of the space. Noise can be caused by equipment, telephones, HVAC systems, conversations, and may other sources. All of these can contribute to the need to control sound transmission. The goal of sound transmission requirements in the codes and standards is to lessen the affect of this transfer. Sound traveling from one space to another can be both a privacy issue as well as considered "noise pollution" affecting the indoor environmental quality (IEQ) of a building. Therefore, sound attenuation issues are regulated by the building codes and sustainability codes and standards. (In some cases, these codes will need to be used in conjunction with requirements for fire-rated assemblies.)

The two most common measurements used are Sound Transmission Coefficient (STC) and Noise Reduction Coefficient (NRC). STC indicates approximately how much sound a wall, ceiling, floor, or window will stop from transferring through to the adjacent space. The NRC of a room rates the noise level of an interior space. Acoustical type ceilings, carpet, sound attenuation panels, laminated gypsum board, upholstered furniture, and office panel systems can all contribute to the control of reverberation and decrease the noise level, thus reducing the potential sound transmission between spaces.

Many of the building codes and standards concentrate on the prevention of air-borne sound transmission between specific types of spaces such as hotel and dormitory rooms or apartment units. Specific STC levels for partitions and assemblies are required. For example, the codes and standards require the separation between residences on multiple floors to have a minimum STC rating of 50. (Federal housing units may require a higher STC separation.) The *International Building Code (IBC)* also requires walls, partitions, and floor/ceiling assemblies that separate dwelling units and dwelling units from public areas (e.g., corridors, stairs, service areas) to limit sound transmission. These elements must maintain a STC of not less than 45 to 50 when tested under the standard *ASTM E90, Standard Test Method for Laboratory Measurement of Airborne Sound Transmission Loss of Building Partitions and Elements.* This may also affect the types of sealants and insulation used to close pipes, electrical outlets, recessed cabinets, bathtubs, and similar elements in the walls.

Another sound transmission measurement used by the codes is the Impact Insulation Class (IIC), which is used to determine the sound being transmitted through the structure and building elements (not airborne sounds). The *IBC* requires floor/ceiling assemblies to meet certain IIC requirements as tested by *ASTM E49, Standard Test Method for Laboratory Measurement of Impact Sound Transmission Through Floor-Ceiling Assemblies Using the Tapping Machine.* For example, the floor/ceiling assemblies between dwelling units and public areas must have an IIC that is not less than 45 to 50.

Sustainability requirements are mainly intended to prevent the negative effects of long-term exposure to noise. However, the green aspects of materials that are used to achieve sound

(Continued)

attenuation are also important. For example, specifying batt insulation made from recycled cotton fibers instead of fiberglass would be more desirable. Many energy efficient mechanical systems are quieter than previous models and thus add to the green and sustainable quality of the building both by conserving energy and providing a quieter environment.

The *International Green Construction Code* (IGCC) requires walls and floor/ceiling assemblies that separate Assembly, Factory and Mercantile occupancies from Business, Institutional or Residential occupancies to have a maximum STC of 50 as tested by *ASTM E90*. Noise generated by mechanical equipment or emergency generators cannot have an STC over 6. Background noise created by the mechanical system is also regulated by the *IGCC* according to the specific use of the space. Types of spaces regulated include open-offices, corridors, and lecture halls. In addition, the NRC must be between 25 to 45. This level of sound control must be measured and met for over half of the rooms within the building not including closets, storerooms, or toilet facilities. The *IGCC* requires a report to be generated by a third-party and submitted to the jurisdiction to document compliance with the code.

Accessibility codes and standards do not dictate sound transmission. They are mostly concerned that verbal communication is clear to the occupants. This can include voice communication that is part of the fire alarm or emergency warning system and the ability to hear instruction in a learning situation. However, the *2010 ADA Standards* references *ANSI S12.60-2002, Acoustical Performance Criteria, Design Requirements and Guidelines for Schools* which applies to classrooms, gymnasiums, conference rooms, and offices.

◀ Note

Noise can be caused by equipment, telephones, HVAC systems, conversations, and may other sources. All of these can contribute to the need to control sound transmission.

In addition, the construction type of the building may require a rated floor/ceiling assembly. For instance, a hotel that is built using a Type I or Type II construction type will require a floor/ceiling assembly with a higher rating than 1 hour. An apartment building with a Type VB construction type would have a floor/ceiling assembly with no rating.

Incidental Accessory Occupancies

The codes require that certain rooms within a building, such as machine rooms and laundry rooms, be separated from the other parts of the building. These are called *incidental accessory occupancies*. (See the discussion of incidental accessory occupancies in Chapter 2.) The codes require these rooms to be enclosed by fire barriers. The required ratings are given in the text and by tables within the codes. The *IBC* Table 508.2.5, "Incidental Accessory Occupancies," in Figure 5.8 lists the types of rooms or areas that are considered incidental within the *IBC*.

If one of these rooms is located in a building or particular occupancy, additional fire protection might be necessary. For example, the waste collection room shown in the nonsprinklered building in Figure 5.9 is 180 square feet (16.7 s m).

TABLE 508.2.5
INCIDENTAL ACCESSORY OCCUPANCIES

ROOM OR AREA	SEPARATION AND/OR PROTECTION
Furnace room where any piece of equipment is over 400,000 Btu per hour input	1 hour or provide automatic fire-extinguishing system
Rooms with boilers where the largest piece of equipment is over 15 psi and 10 horsepower	1 hour or provide automatic fire-extinguishing system
Refrigerant machinery room	1 hour or provide automatic sprinkler system
Hydrogen cutoff rooms, not classified as Group H	1 hour in Group B, F, M, S and U occupancies; 2 hours in Group A, E, I and R occupancies.
Incinerator rooms	2 hours and automatic sprinkler system
Paint shops, not classified as Group H, located in occupancies other than Group F	2 hours; or 1 hour and provide automatic fire-extinguishing system
Laboratories and vocational shops, not classified as Group H, located in a Group E or I-2 occupancy	1 hour or provide automatic fire-extinguishing system
Laundry rooms over 100 square feet	1 hour or provide automatic fire-extinguishing system
Group I-3 cells equipped with padded surfaces	1 hour
Group I-2 waste and linen collection rooms	1 hour
Waste and linen collection rooms over 100 square feet	1 hour or provide automatic fire-extinguishing system
Stationary storage battery systems having a liquid electrolyte capacity of more than 50 gallons, or a lithium-ion capacity of 1,000 pounds used for facility standby power, emergency power or uninterrupted power supplies	1 hour in Group B, F, M, S and U occupancies; 2 hours in Group A, E, I and R occupancies.
Rooms containing fire pumps in nonhigh-rise buildings	2 hours; or 1 hour and provide automatic sprinkler system throughout the building
Rooms containing fire pumps in high-rise buildings	2 hours

For SI: 1 square foot = 0.0929 m², 1 pound per square inch (psi) = 6.9 kPa, 1 British thermal unit (Btu) per hour = 0.293 watts, 1 horsepower = 746 watts, 1 gallon = 3.785 L.

Figure 5.8 *International Building Code* Table 508.2.5, Incidental Accessory Occupancies (*2009 International Building Code*, copyright 2009. Washington, DC: International Code Council. All rights reserved. www.iccsafe.org).

The *IBC* table in Figure 5.8 indicates that waste and linen collection rooms over "100 square feet (9.3 s m)" are required to be separated by a fire barrier with a rating of 1 hour or to be sprinklered. Because this building is nonsprinklered, this room would require fire protection to keep it separate from the rest of the space. For many of the incidental accessory areas listed in the table, an automatic sprinkler system can be provided instead of the fire barrier, and in some cases both a fire barrier and an automatic sprinkler system are required. The NFPA codes list similar information within each occupancy chapter.

◁Note

The number and cost of fire-resistance-rated walls are reduced by designing rooms with like fire ratings adjacent to each other—for example, a linen collection room and a laundry room.

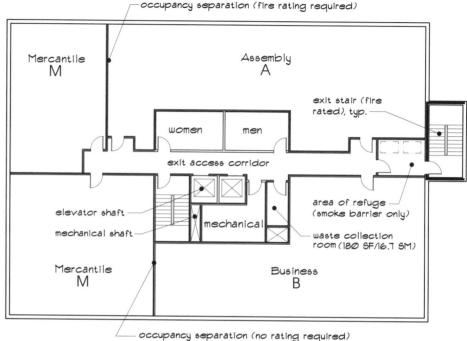

Figure 5.9 Rated building components (nonsprinklered building).

Vertical Shaft Enclosures

⊴Note

Shafts used for refuse
and laundry chutes have
additional requirements.
Refer to the building codes.

Fire barriers are used to create vertical shaft enclosures for such things as elevators, dumbwaiters, and building systems such as mechanical chases. Examples of these are shown in Figure 5.9. A stairwell can be considered a vertical shaft as well. The fire ratings for vertical shaft enclosures are primarily determined by the number of floors that they penetrate. Typically, a 1-hour or 2-hour separation is required. These walls are usually continuous from the bottom of the building to the underside of the roof deck. When a shaft terminates at a floor level, the top and bottom of the shaft may also require a horizontal assembly.

⊴Note

Atriums also have additional
fire protection requirements.
See the inset titled *Atriums
and Mezzanines* on
page 114 and the codes
for specifics.

For elevators, the codes limit the number of elevator cars in a single shaft or hoistway enclosure to usually no more than two to four. If more elevators are used, additional rated walls will be required to separate them. In addition, each shaft often requires specific venting, smoke detection, and standby power. (See the section Elevators in Chapter 4.) The rating of an elevator shaft is also determined by the number of floors that it penetrates. (See the sections Smokeproof Vertical Shafts and Stairs later in this chapter.)

Means of Egress Components

In many cases, parts of the means of egress, as discussed in Chapter 4, are required to be separated by fire barriers. (Smoke barriers, as explained in the next section, may also be required.) These can include stairwells, exit passageways, horizontal exits, and other exit enclosures. In most cases, the fire-resistance rating must be provided both vertically and horizontally. The ratings typically get stricter as an occupant moves toward the exit. For example, an exit access may require a 1-hour rating, and the exit may require a 2-hour rating. As the different means of egress are discussed, refer to Figure 5.10 for examples of the components that require fire-resistance ratings. Within the building codes and the *LSC*, these requirements are given in tables and within the chapters that discuss fire-resistance ratings and occupancy requirements.

Stairways

Typically, the walls that enclose *exit stairs* must meet the same requirements as a vertical shaft. Usually these stairs must have a 1-hour rating if the stairs are three stories or less and a 2-hour rating if they are four or more stories. Protection from smoke may also be required. (See Chapter 4 for additional information on stairs.) An *exit access stair* may also require a fire-rated enclosure if it connects more than two floors.

The walls surrounding a rated stairwell would be considered fire barriers and must be vertically continuous through each floor and fully enclose the stair. In most cases, the floor and ceiling of an exit access stair must also consist of rated horizontal assemblies. To protect the fire ratings of these assemblies, only limited penetrations are allowed. In addition, in a high-rise building the stairwells are required to be smokeproof to serve as an area of refuge. (See the section Areas of Refuge below.)

> **▣ Note**
>
> When dead space below a fire-rated stairway is used for storage, it cannot block the means of egress in any way. That means the door into the storage must be outside the stair enclosure. And the storage compartment must be totally surrounded by fire-rated assemblies that have the same rating as the stair enclosure.

Horizontal Exits

A horizontal exit is used to provide an alternate exiting method within a building. It uses a fire barrier to provide an exit from one space into another on the same floor of a building. (This is discussed in more detail in Chapter 4.) Although a horizontal exit in effect creates separate areas within a building in a manner similar to that of fire areas, the intent of the separation is different. A fire area is created to limit the spread of fire. A horizontal exit, on the other hand, provides an exit away from the fire. A horizontal exit also usually includes smoke protection. Typically, the wall requires a rating of 2 hours and must extend to the exterior walls.

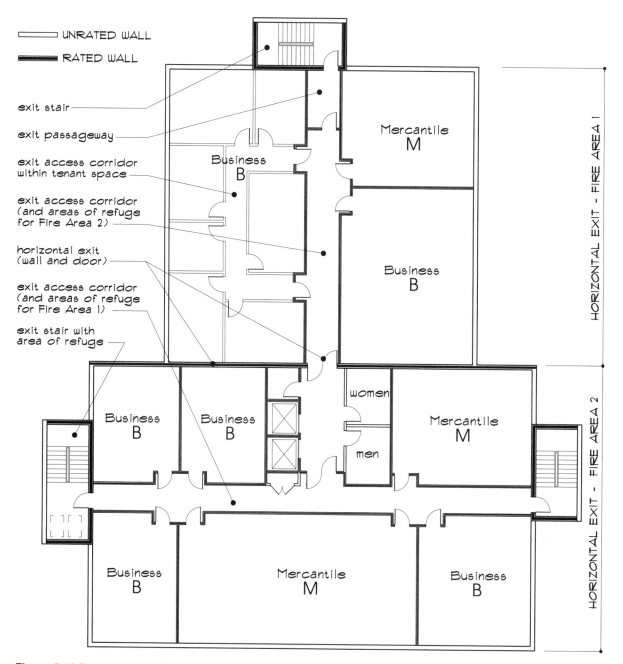

Figure 5.10 Rated means of egress components (nonsprinklered building).

Areas of Refuge

Areas of refuge are often required as part of an accessible exit. Because these areas are meant to provide a place for people with disabilities to wait for further assistance in exiting the building, the codes require that they be separated by a smoke barrier. Smoke barriers provide a minimum fire-resistance rating of 1 hour and prevent the intrusion of smoke. (Smoke barriers are explained in more detail next.) Sometimes an area of refuge can be located within other parts of the means of egress, including an exit stair, an elevator lobby, or on the other side of a horizontal exit. The separation requirements of the other means of egress components will often be higher than just a smoke barrier. In these cases, the separation of the area of refuge must meet the more restrictive requirements.

Corridors

Exit access corridors are corridors that lead to an exit or an exit stairwell. The rating of exit access corridors ranges from ½ hour to 1 hour. Each of the codes provides this information differently. The *IBC* uses Table 1018.1, "Corridor Fire-Resistance Rating," in Figure 5.11. To determine the rating of the corridor using this table, three things are required: the occupancy classification, the occupant load served by the corridor, and whether the building is sprinklered. (See Chapter 2 for occupant load information.) For example, for an exit access corridor in a Business (B) occupancy that has an occupant load greater than 30 and is nonsprinklered, the table indicates that a rating of 1 hour is required. If the building was sprinklered, then the corridor would not be required to be rated. If the same Business

⊲Note

Within a single tenant space, rated corridors are often not required. The rating of a corridor within a building depends on whether the building is sprinklered.

TABLE 1018.1
CORRIDOR FIRE-RESISTANCE RATING

OCCUPANCY	OCCUPANT LOAD SERVED BY CORRIDOR	REQUIRED FIRE-RESISTANCE RATING (hours)	
		Without sprinkler system	With sprinkler system[c]
H-1, H-2, H-3	All	Not Permitted	1
H-4, H-5	Greater than 30	Not Permitted	1
A, B, E, F, M, S, U	Greater than 30	1	0
R	Greater than 10	Not Permitted	0.5
I-2[a], I-4	All	Not Permitted	0
I-1, I-3	All	Not Permitted	1[b]

a. For requirements for occupancies in Group I-2, see Sections 407.2 and 407.3.
b. For a reduction in the fire-resistance rating for occupancies in Group I-3, see Section 408.8.
c. Buildings equipped throughout with an automatic sprinkler system in accordance with Section 903.3.1.1 or 903.3.1.2 where allowed.

Figure 5.11 *International Building Code* Table 1018.1, Corridor Fire-Resistance Rating (*2009 International Building Code,* copyright 2009. Washington, DC: International Code Council. All rights reserved. www.iccsafe.org).

occupancy had an occupant load less than 30, the exit access corridor would not be required to be rated. Typically, corridors within a small tenant space do not require a rating. However, exit access corridors that serve an entire floor are usually required to be rated, especially in nonsprinklered buildings.

The *IBC* considers the walls in an exit access corridor to be a type of fire partition. Therefore, the rating of the floor/ceiling assembly is required to have the same fire-resistance rating as the partition except in certain construction types.

Corridors used as exits, however, such as *exit passageways*, usually must have a 2-hour fire rating. In this case, both the *IBC* and the NFPA codes require that a fire barrier be used and that the horizontal assembly at the floor and ceiling provide the same fire resistance rating as the walls. For example, if a stairwell with a rating of 2 hours emptied into a lobby, then the lobby would be considered an exit discharge component and would have to maintain the 2-hour rating. Refer to the specific requirements of each exit component to determine the required rating.

SMOKE BARRIERS AND SMOKE PARTITIONS

Smoke barriers and smoke partitions are another part of the passive fire-protection system. Smoke barriers typically provide a higher level of protection than smoke partitions and are often used to create compartments. Smoke barriers *restrict* the movement or passage of smoke and fire gases and are often required to have a fire-resistance rating. Smoke partitions only *limit* the passage of smoke and fire gases and are typically not required to have a fire-resistance rating. The idea of smoke partitions was developed by the ICC and the NFPA to take the place of numerous exceptions that had allowed smoke barriers to be nonrated.

Smoke barriers must be continuous and sealed completely where there are joints and where they meet other smoke barriers, smoke/fire barriers, and exterior walls. A smoke barrier can consist of either a *wall assembly* or a *full enclosure*. A full enclosure consists of vertical walls and horizontal ceiling and floor assemblies that create a continuous smokeproof compartment. Vertically, smoke barriers must extend from the floor below to the ceiling assembly above. When used horizontally as a floor/ceiling assembly, they must extend to a smoke barrier wall or an exterior wall.

Smoke barriers are required by the code to separate and protect different types of situations. Although they often require a fire-resistance rating, walls with a rating do not necessarily resist smoke. Therefore, the codes also limit the penetrations allowed in the smoke barrier. If a penetration is allowed, additional requirements are specified. For example, the building codes include requirements for the use of doors, including the type of door, the use of automatic release door closers, and the operation of the door. Smoke dampers are often required at mechanical ducts.

A *smoke partition*, on the other hand, may be allowed by the codes when a lesser degree of protection from smoke is acceptable for life safety. Unlike smoke barriers, smoke partitions can terminate at suspended ceiling systems and some solid ceilings, as described by the codes (similar to fire partitions, as shown in Figure 5.3). The ceilings are also allowed to be penetrated by certain items, such as speakers, recessed lighting, diffusers, and similar ceiling elements not typically allowed in smoke barriers. Other requirements also tend to be less restrictive. For example, in some cases a duct passing through a smoke partition may not require a smoke damper; however, other penetrations are regulated. These will be discussed in the section Opening Protectives later in this chapter.

Additional requirements for smoke barriers and smoke partitions depend on their specific use. Many of these requirements are specified in the building codes, the fire codes, and the LSC. The mechanical codes include requirements as

SMOKE AND HOW IT TRAVELS

To gain a better understanding of smoke control systems and how they work, it is important to know how smoke moves. The Council on Tall Buildings and Urban Habitat, in the book *Fire Safety in Tall Buildings,* describes five major driving forces that cause smoke movement:

1. *Buoyancy.* As the temperature of smoke increases during a fire, it becomes buoyant due to its reduced density. As the buoyancy increases, pressure builds and the smoke is forced up through any available leakage paths to the floor above and to adjacent areas.

2. *Expansion:* As a fire develops, it emits gases. These gases expand and create pressure, causing smoke to be forced out of an enclosed fire compartment.

3. *HVAC:* As a fire progresses, the HVAC system can transport smoke to every area it serves. The system can also supply air to a fire, increasing its intensity.

4. *Stack effect:* The stack effect is a result of exterior air temperature. Generally, if it is cold outside, there is usually an upward movement of air within the building shafts, such as stairwells, elevators, and mechanical shafts. When the outside air is warmer than the building air, the airflow moves downward. This air movement can move smoke a considerable distance from a fire.

5. *Wind:* Windows frequently break during a fire, causing outside wind to force smoke through doors into adjacent spaces and other floors.

In a fire situation, smoke movement can be caused by one or more of these driving forces. That is why the correct use and placement of smoke barriers can be critical. (The three stages of a fire are explained in the inset titled *Fire Development Stages* on page 373.)

well. (See Chapter 7.) Additional requirements are specified in standards such as *NFPA 92A, Standard for Smoke-Control Systems Utilizing Barriers and Pressure Differences; NFPA 92B, Standard for Smoke Management Systems in Malls, Atria, and Large Spaces;* and *NFPA 105, Standard for the Installation of Smoke Door Assemblies and Other Opening Protectives.* The various uses of smoke barriers and smoke partitions, as walls and full enclosures, are discussed next.

Smoke Compartments

Smoke compartments are sometimes created within a building where protection from smoke is required. These compartments are created by smoke barriers. Although smoke barrier walls typically extend from outside wall to outside wall and from floor to floor, they do not necessarily have a fire-resistance rating. To create a smoke compartment, wall, floor, and ceiling assemblies are used to construct the full smoke enclosure. An example would be a stairwell with an area of refuge.

To make them smoke resistant, only limited openings are allowed in the smoke barrier. In full enclosures, additional mechanical functions are required for ventilation and air circulation. A smoke detector typically activates the ventilation system and automatically closes all doors with a closing device.

Smoke compartments are also typically used in Institutional occupancies to subdivide floors used by patients for sleeping or treatment. More recently, the *IBC* requires large ambulatory health care facilities to be separated into multiple smoke compartments requiring the use of smoke barriers as well. (See the discussion of this building type in Chapter 2.) Each compartment created by the smoke barrier provides a temporary area of refuge from the adjacent compartment. These are different from horizontal exits and are not usually considered exits. Horizontal exits require a fire barrier and a smoke barrier, which provides another way to protect the occupants in the event of a fire. (See the section Horizontal Exits in this chapter and Chapter 4.) In most cases, occupancies that call for smoke compartments are required to be sprinklered.

Smokeproof Vertical Shafts

Vertical shaft enclosures for stairs, elevators, and waste and linen chutes in some cases, must be smokeproof, especially if a building is over a certain height. As mentioned earlier, the walls and openings of all vertical shafts must be fire rated. To make them smokeproof, the walls need to meet the requirements of smoke barriers and all openings into the shaft must automatically close upon detection of smoke. A *smokestop door* is usually also required. This is a door specially designed to close tightly and inhibit the passage of smoke. (See the section Rated Door Assemblies later in this chapter.) This door is typically connected to the smoke detection and standby power systems in the building.

To create the necessary smoke protection, smokeproof shafts also typically need to be pressurized. Certain mechanical components are used so that, should a fire occur, the smoke does not get sucked into the vertical shaft.

Vestibules

Any vestibule adjacent to a smokeproof stairwell or elevator hoistway that is located between the shaft and the exterior exit door must also be smokeproof. The walls of the vestibule typically consist of smoke barriers and sometimes the floor/ceiling assemblies as well. The codes require the vestibule to be a certain size. The doors must also be fire rated, have self-closing devices, and have a drop sill to minimize air leakage.

The ceiling of the vestibule must be high enough so that it serves as a smoke and heat trap and allows an upward-moving airflow. Ventilation is required as well. It might be as simple as an opening in an exterior wall for *natural* ventilation. The most common is *mechanical* ventilation with vents opening to the outside air. The codes regulate a number of items, such as the type of system used, the amount of supply and exhaust air, and the location of duct openings. (See Chapter 7.)

OPENING PROTECTIVES

The codes regulate when an opening can be used in a rated assembly. For rated assemblies in certain situations, no openings may be allowed. In others, there may be size limitations. The sizes are typically limited to a percentage of the total size or area of a wall. In many cases, additional and/or larger openings are allowed in a sprinklered building. When an opening is allowed in a rated assembly, an *opening protective* is usually required. An opening protective is a rated assembly that prevents the spread of fire or smoke through an opening in a rated wall. An opening protective is usually a door or a view window. Unlike wall and floor/ceiling assemblies that are assigned a fire-resistance rating, door assemblies are assigned a *fire-protection rating*. The required rating of the opening protective component is determined by the rating of the wall in which it is located. Not only are the ratings important to the integrity of the entire wall during a fire to stop the spread of fire and smoke, but they are also crucial for the evacuation of the occupants during a fire. Opening protectives can also be considered a type of through-penetration system, which is discussed later in the chapter. Through-penetration components control openings required by wiring, ducts, pipes, and similar penetrations in a building. Both are components that are intended to maintain the integrity of a rated wall or floor/ceiling assembly.

The fire-protection ratings for opening protectives are determined by the building codes and the *LSC*, the same codes that determine construction assemblies. Depending on the code, the information is found in tables or within the text. For example, the *IBC* has two tables that must be referenced. These are shown in Figure 5.12. They include Table 715.4, "Fire Door and Fire Shutter Fire Protection Ratings," and Table 715.5, "Fire Window Assembly Fire Protection Ratings." These

TABLE 715.4
FIRE DOOR AND FIRE SHUTTER FIRE PROTECTION RATINGS

TYPE OF ASSEMBLY	REQUIRED ASSEMBLY RATING (hours)	MINIMUM FIRE DOOR AND FIRE SHUTTER ASSEMBLY RATING (hours)
Fire walls and fire barriers having a required fire-resistance rating greater than 1 hour	4 3 2 $1^1/_2$	3 3[a] $1^1/_2$ $1^1/_2$

Fire barriers having a required fire-resistance rating of 1 hour:
    Shaft, exit enclosure and exit passageway walls
    Other fire barriers
	
	1
	1
		
		1
		$^3/_4$

Fire partitions:
    Corridor walls
 	
    Other fire partitions
	
	1
	0.5
	1
	0.5
		
		$^1/_3$ [b]
		$^1/_3$ [b]
		$^3/_4$
		$^1/_3$

Exterior walls	3 2 1	$1^1/_2$ $1^1/_2$ $^3/_4$
Smoke barriers	1	$^1/_3$ [b]

a. Two doors, each with a fire protection rating of $1^1/_2$ hours, installed on opposite sides of the same opening in a fire wall, shall be deemed equivalent in fire protection rating to one 3-hour fire door.
b. For testing requirements, see Section 715.4.3.

TABLE 715.5
FIRE WINDOW ASSEMBLY FIRE PROTECTION RATINGS

TYPE OF ASSEMBLY		REQUIRED ASSEMBLY RATING (hours)	MINIMUM FIRE WINDOW ASSEMBLY RATING (hours)
Interior walls:	Fire walls	All	NP[a]
	Fire barriers	> 1 1	NP[a] $^3/_4$
	Smoke barriers	1	$^3/_4$
	Fire partitions	1 $^1/_2$	$^3/_4$ $^1/_3$
Exterior walls		> 1 1	$1^1/_2$ $^3/_4$
Party wall		All	NP

NP = Not Permitted.
a. Not permitted except as specified in Section 715.2.

Figure 5.12 *International Building Code* Table 715.4, Fire Door and Fire Shutter Fire Protection Ratings, and Table 715.5, Fire Window Assembly Fire Protection Ratings (*2009 International Building Code,* copyright 2009. Washington, DC: International Code Council. All rights reserved. www.iccsafe.org).

tables indicate where a rated opening protective is required in each type of rated construction assembly. Based on the fire-resistance rating of the wall or partition, the fire-protection rating of the fire door assembly or fire window assembly can be determined. (Smoke barriers are included on the tables as well.) To use this table, two things are needed: the type of vertical assembly and its required rating. For example, if a door is being added in an existing 2-hour fire barrier, the first table indicates that it would require a 1½-hour-rated fire door assembly. However, if a window is being added, the second table indicates that it would not be allowed—or not permitted (NP). The building codes and the *LSC* also reference a number of standards for additional information. For example, *NFPA 80, Standard for Fire Doors and Other Opening Protectives*, is specified for the installation of fire doors and windows. Others, as explained later, are specifically for fire and smoke testing.

The intent of the codes and other standards is to regulate openings in rated walls, floors, and ceilings so that the required rated construction does not lose its effectiveness. The most common opening protectives are described next.

Rated Door Assemblies

As mentioned in Chapter 4, the codes actually describe doors as door assemblies. A typical door assembly consists of three main components: door, frame, and hardware. The doorway (or wall opening) can also be considered part of the door assembly—including the lintel above and the threshold below. Other doors, such as the rated doors listed in Figure 5.13, may consist of even more parts. If the door is a fire door, the whole assembly must be tested and rated as one unit. Each of the following door components has certain characteristics that make it fire rated.

RATED DOORS	RATED WINDOWS	RATED GLAZING
Access Doors	Casement Windows	Clear Ceramics
Accordion/Folding Doors	Double-Hung Windows	Glass Block
Bi-Parting Doors	Hinged Windows	Insulated Glass
Conveying System Doors	Pivot Windows	Laminated Glass
Chute Doors	Service Counter Windows	Light Diffusing Plastic
Floor Fire Door	Side Lights	Light-Transmitting Plastic
Hoistway Doors	Stationary Windows	Fire-Rated Glazing
Horizontal Doors	Tilting Windows	Tempered Glass
Overhead Doors	Transom Windows	Transparent Ceramics
Swinging Doors	View Panels	Wire Glass

Figure 5.13 Types of regulated opening protectives.

✎Note

Fire-rated doors and windows are designed to protect the opening under normal conditions with clear space on both sides. When combustible materials are stored against them, the protection is not guaranteed.

✎Note

The rating of the opening protective is typically lower than that of the construction assembly.

✎Note

Typically, no openings except for a limited number of doors are allowed in fire walls that require a 3-hour to 4-hour rating.

Doors and Frames

If the wall is fire rated, the door and frame must be rated as well. Because a protection rating is assigned to the entire door assembly, fire doors are typically specified and sold by the manufacturer as a whole unit. To obtain a rating, the door and frame must undergo a fire test as specified in *NFPA 252, Standard Methods of Fire Tests of Door Assemblies.* Alternate tests include *UL 10B, Standard for Fire Test of Door Assemblies,* and *UL 10C, Standard for Positive Pressure Fire Tests of Door Assemblies.* Rated doors used horizontally in fire-resistance-rated floor/ceiling assemblies may also need to pass *NFPA 288, Standard Methods of Fire Tests of Floor Fire Door Assemblies Installed Horizontally in Fire Resistance-Rated Floor Systems.* Both the *IBC* and the NFPA codes require fire-rated doors to be tested by a positive-pressure test that better resembles actual fire conditions than previous tests.

When smokestop doors are used in smoke barriers, they must undergo additional testing as required in *NFPA 105, Standard for the Installation of Smoke Door Assemblies and other Opening Protectives,* or *UL 1784, Standard for Air Leakage Tests of Door Assemblies.* Any door that passes the required tests is assigned a fire protection rating, varying from 3 hours to 1/3 hour (20 minutes), and receives a permanent label, which indicates the manufacturer's name and/or logo, the name of the testing agency, and the rating it received. An example of this label is shown in Figure 5.14.

Certain doors may also require a rated sill as part of the frame. For example, smokestop doors usually require a sill to maintain a continuous seal around the door. The construction of the sill can vary, depending on the type of door and the construction of the floor on either side of the door. If a door requires a sill, the profile of the threshold will need to be considered. In most cases, it must meet accessibility requirements based on the *ADA Standards* and the ICC/ANSI standard. (See Figure 9.17 in Chapter 9.) (Chapter 4 discusses doors in relation to size, swing, accessibility, and the means of egress concerns.)

Figure 5.14 Typical label for a fire-rated door assembly. Reprinted with permission from Ceco Door Products.

Since doors usually undergo more stringent testing, make up only a portion of an entire wall, and are not generally exposed to the same level of fire as walls, their ratings are not as strict as those of the walls in which they are located. However, properly specified door assemblies maintain the integrity of the fire barrier. In the past, doors that had a fire-protection rating were typically flush and were either solid core wood or hollow metal. And even currently, very few panel doors meet the fire-protection requirements, although some are available. Recent developments in materials, including glazing, are allowing more options in configurations and finishes for rated doors. Fire-rated frames can be wood, steel (i.e., hollow metal), or aluminum, depending on the rating required. The most commonly specified rated frame is hollow metal. The glazing used in fire-rated doors must also meet certain requirements. (This is discussed later in this chapter.)

> **✎ Note**
>
> Oversize doors cannot be labeled because of their size. Instead, their approval is based on a certificate of inspection furnished by an approved testing agency.

Door Hardware

The most common door *hardware* includes hinges, latches and locksets, pulls, and closers. Hinges, latch sets, and closing devices are the most stringently regulated on fire-rated doors. For example, fire-rated hinges must be steel or stainless steel, and a specific number are required for each door. Both the hinges and the latch set are important to hold a fire door securely closed during a fire. To be effective, they must be able to withstand the pressure and heat that are generated during a fire.

Fire-rated exit doors also require a specific type of latch or pull. The most common is called *fire exit hardware*. Fire exit hardware is tested and rated. A similar type of hardware is called *panic hardware*. Both consist of a panel or bar that must be pushed to release the door latch. However, panic hardware is not tested and should not be used on fire-rated doors. The most common occupancy classifications that require fire exit hardware are Assembly and Educational. Although the codes do not require it in every occupancy, it is often used on exit doors. In occupancies that are not required to use fire exit hardware, approved lever hardware can be used.

Other issues can affect the choice of hardware on a door, including locking methods for security. (See the section Security Systems in Chapter 8.) In addition, *NFPA 80* places restrictions on the height at which kickplates or other protection devices can be installed on fire doors. The requirements of the *ADA Standards* and other accessibility standards should also be considered in the final selection of hardware. (See Chapter 4.) However, providing the proper means of egress and maintaining the fire rating of the doors are most important for the safety of the occupants.

The codes also require that fire-rated doors be *self-closing*. This means that the door must have a device called a *closer* that closes the door after each use.

> **✎ Note**
>
> When selecting fire-rated door hardware, it is important to meet the additional requirements set in the ADA and the ICC/ANSI standards, such as the shape of the item and the height of installation. (See Chapter 4.)

> **✎ Note**
>
> If a building is fully sprinklered, the codes may allow an exit door to have an automatic closure with a longer than standard time delay.

Closers, in general, can be surface mounted or concealed within the door, frame, or floor. Verify that the closer application does not violate the rating of the door assembly in each case. A closer may be tested as part of the door assembly with numerous test standards including *UL 10B, Standard for Fire Tests of Door Assemblies; UL 10C, Standard for Positive Pressure Fire Tests of Door Assembly;* and *UL 228, Standard for Door Closers-Holders, With or Without Integral Smoke Detectors.* Another standard, *ANSI/BHMA A156.4, Door Controls-Closers,* tests the door closer for adjustable closing speed, closing force, cycle time, pivot performance, and finish grade. The closing speed and force can be an important element as to the door's ability to meet the requirements in the *ADA Standards.*

If it is desirable that certain rated doors be open all the time, an electromagnetic or pneumatic hold-open device can be used. This device holds the door in an open position until an emergency occurs. Either a fusible link is triggered by heat or the activation of a smoke detector causes the door to close. This type of door is considered *automatic-closing* and is allowed in many occupancies within the code. Doors on electromagnetic or pneumatic hold-open devices are tested using standard *UL 228.* (For additional hardware standards, see the section Security Systems in Chapter 8.)

Fire Window Assemblies

A fire window assembly is considered an opening protective. It is an assembly that typically consists of a frame and an approved rated glazing material. It can be part of a door assembly, such as a transom, sidelight, or vision panel, or can be a completely separate entity. These and other types of rated windows are listed in Figure 5.13. The most common interior applications for a fire-rated window assembly are view panels within corridor walls, room partitions, and smoke barriers.

Fire window assemblies are given a fire-protection rating similar to that of doors and are usually classified by hourly designations. Like doors, they must be tested as a complete assembly. The established testing requirements are typically specified in *NFPA 257, Standard on Fire Test for Window and Glass Block Assemblies.* The required rating of a window depends on the location within the building. Generally, such fire-protection ratings are not greater than 1 hour. However, when referring back to the *IBC* code Table 715.4 in Figure 5.12, it also indicates that in some fire barriers, fire windows are not permitted at all (as indicated by NP). When the codes require a rated window assembly, the assembly must have a permanent label applied by the manufacturer guaranteeing its fire-protection rating. On the other hand, when a window is used in a smoke partition that is not fire rated, the codes do not typically require the window to have a fire-protection rating. Instead, it must be sealed to prevent the passage of smoke.

Rated Glazing and Frames

Like rated walls, rated glazing helps to protect occupants from various aspects of a fire, including flame, smoke, and radiant heat. The codes set specific requirements for the size, thickness, location, and types of glazing materials that can be used in opening protectives such as fire doors and fire windows. This information is found in the building codes and the *LSC* in tables or within the text. Size limitations may be given as a maximum height and width or a maximum area. Typically, the rated glazing can be any shape or configuration as long as it doesn't exceed the maximum sizes.

Glazing products used in fire-rated assemblies are assessed by their ability to stay in place in the event of a fire, resistance to thermal shock in a hose stream test, strength against human contact, and resistance to heat transfer to the unexposed side. As part of an opening protective, most glazing is given a *fire-protection* rating. In some cases, glazing can also meet the standards to receive a *fire-resistance* rating similar to that of a rated wall. (This is described later in this section.) When glazing is used in a rated window, it must meet the requirements of *NFPA 257, Standard on Fire Test for Window and Glass Block Assemblies* or *UL 9, Standard for Fire Test of Window Assemblies*. When it is used in a rated door or fire barrier, it must meet the requirements of *NFPA 252, Standard Methods of Fire Tests of Door Assemblies*. Based on the results of these tests, the glazing assembly is given a fire-protection rating. In most cases, the glazing in a rated assembly will also be required to be tested by *NFPA 80, Standard for Fire Doors and Other Opening Protectives*. Check the codes for the tests necessary based on the specific use of the glazing in the rated assembly.

Beginning in 2006, the codes require all new fire-protection-rated glazing to be labeled with a special mark to indicate the manufacturer, the test standard used, and the results of the test. In the past, glazing required a similar mark but did not include as much information. The special mark indicates the result of the appropriate test and how the glass can be expected to work within the fire barrier. For glazing used in a fire window, the mark should indicate that the glazing has met the fire-resistance and hose-stream requirements of *NFPA 257* and provide the fire-protection rating of the glazing in minutes. For glazing used in a fire door or directly in a fire barrier, additional information is given to indicate whether the glazing meets the requirement of the fire-resistance rating, the hose stream, and/or the temperature rise parts of *NFPA 252* (or *UL 10C*). The fire-protection rating in minutes is also given. These permanent markings become important during the life of the building so that, in the future, designers, owners, and code officials know what rating is provided and needs to be maintained.

When used in certain locations, both rated and unrated glazing products must also meet safety requirements. These safety tests are used to determine the

Note

If a window is large enough to be mistaken for a door, the codes require a rail to be installed across the window at a specific height.

Note

Labels required on rated glazing are added by a third-party agency during the manufacturing process to ensure reliability.

Note

The new labels required on rated glazing include more information that indicates clearly what standards the glazing meets and its expected performance during a fire. This is helpful to know so that the level of protection can be maintained.

◀Note

CPSC CFR 1201 is used to test the impact rating of glazing located in hazardous locations as defined by the *IBC. ANSI Z97.1* is used when glazing is not located in a door or near water elements but impact is still a concern.

◀Note

In addition to fire resistance, heat transfer must be considered when using large amounts of glass.

resistance to impact. For example, all glazing in locations that could be subject to impact are required to pass the federal standard *16 CFR 1201, Safety Standard for Architectural Glazing Materials.* The glazing receives a rating of Category I or II. Category I represents glazing that will resist the equivalent impact of a small child or young teenager. Category II represents glazing that will resist the equivalent impact of a full-grown adult. Therefore, a Category II glazing is more impact-resistant. Glazing not located in doors or saunas, showers and other bathing elements may be tested under *ANSI Z97.1, Safety Glazing Materials Used in Buildings—Safety Performance Specifications and Method of Test.* In this test, the glazing is given a rating of A, B, or C. Class A material is equivalent to Category II glazing material; Class B is comparable to Category I. A Class C is for use for fire-resistant materials that are not required to be impact resistant.

In the past, there were very few options for glazing products that could obtain a fire-protection rating, fire-resistance rating, or resist impact rating. Now there are more options, and new products continue to be developed. Each has unique characteristics to consider when selecting them for a project. This section will briefly discuss each of the general types of glazing that are currently available.

Wired Glass

There are two types of wired glass: nonsafety and safety. The traditional type of wired glass, *nonsafety wired glass*, consists of wire mesh sandwiched between two layers of glass. The steel wire helps to distribute heat and increase the strength of the glass should a fire occur. Wired glass can obtain a fire-protection rating of up to 45 minutes. In most cases, the codes set limits on the sizes of wired glass allowed in rated assemblies specific to the type of rated wall and its location. For example, the *IBC* uses the table shown in Figure 5.15, Table 715.5.4, "Limiting Sizes of Wired Glass Panels." This is for wired glass used in rated doors or as fire windows in rated walls. In the left column, the table lists the various opening fire-protection ratings that are allowed. The first five fire ratings are specifically for rated doors. The table indicates the maximum square inches and the height and width of the glazing that can be used in the assembly based on the rating of the door. Fire windows are indicated separately at the bottom of the table. (Note that the higher ratings do not allow any glazing.) Additional information is found in the text both in the fire-protection chapter and in the glazing chapter of the building code.

Nonsafety wired glass does not resist impact well and does not pass *CFR 1201* for Category I or II. In the past, the building codes allowed wired glass to meet a lower standard for use in certain applications. However, they also limited the size of the glass. Since it does not pass *CFR 1201*, nonsafety wired glass may be

TABLE 715.5.4
LIMITING SIZES OF WIRED GLASS PANELS

OPENING FIRE PROTECTION RATING	MAXIMUM AREA (square inches)	MAXIMUM HEIGHT (inches)	MAXIMUM WIDTH (inches)
3 hours	0	0	0
1½-hour doors in exterior walls	0	0	0
1 and 1½ hours	100	33	10
¾ hour	1,296	54	54
20 minutes	Not Limited	Not Limited	Not Limited
Fire window assemblies	1,296	54	54

For SI: 1 inch = 25.4 mm, 1 square inch = 645.2 mm².

Figure 5.15 *International Building Code* Table 715.5.4, Limiting Sizes of Wired Glass Panels *(2009 International Building Code,* copyright 2009. Washington, DC: International Code Council. All rights reserved. www.iccsafe.org).

allowed in some fire-rated walls but is not allowed in doors or any hazardous locations.

Safety wired glass provides additional options. It looks like traditional wired glass but is either laminated or uses a film to give it a higher level of impact resistance. Laminated wired glass can achieve a Category I impact resistance standard; however, filmed wired glass can meet both the Category I and II standards. As a result, laminated wired glass may not be suitable or allowed in high-traffic locations in certain occupancy classifications, such as Educational, but filmed wired glass may be used in larger openings and in doors. Both nonsafety and safety wired glass are still affordable and dependable materials; however, they might not be an appropriate choice, especially in certain locations.

Specially Tempered Glass

Not all tempered glass can be used in a rated wall. If the glass has been specially tempered, it can usually receive a 20- or 30-minute fire-protection rating, allowing it to be used in 1-hour-rated walls. Tempered glass can be used in fairly large sizes. And, because it is typically six times stronger than wire glazing, it also meets the requirements for a Category II for impact loads. However, because it cannot pass the hose stream test, it should not be used near sprinkler heads. This may limit the use of specially tempered glass in certain locations.

Glass Block

Glass block is typically given a fire-protection rating of 45 minutes or less and is usually allowed in a wall with a maximum 1-hour rating. There are new types of

✑Note

Most glazing that is rated
more than 45 minutes is
also required to protect
against radiant heat transfer.

glass block that have ratings of 60 to 90 minutes, but glass block with this type of fire-resistance rating may not be addressed in the codes. Where glass block is allowed, there are often restrictions on the area of glass block used as an interior wall. The codes also set limits when glass block is used as a view panel in a rated wall and may require the block to be installed in steel channels.

Clear Ceramics

Clear ceramics, also known as transparent ceramics, have very high resistance to heat and can resist the thermal shock of the hose stream test. Because of this, they can be rated from 20 minutes to 3 hours and can typically be used in much larger sizes than wired glass, sometimes up to 23 square feet (2.1 s m) if approved by a code official. In addition, they can have up to four times the impact resistance of safety wired glass, usually achieving a Category II classification.

Although clear ceramics are considered transparent, they may have slightly more distortion and tint than some other glazing products. Clear ceramics can also be installed as insulated glass units (IGU). These units are made with two layers of glass with an air space between them. In this configuration they not only provide fire protection but help to reduce sound transmission as well. For use in interior applications, ceramic glazing can be sandblasted with decorative designs to enhance the aesthetics of the design. As part of an IGU, the ceramic layers can be tinted, mirrored, or clear to provide additional design elements. These characteristics make the use of clear ceramic products desirable in areas such as lobbies and offices, where aesthetics and safety are key.

✑Note

Check with the codes
and standards and the
jurisdiction for the specifics
on these new types of
glazing. They may not be
allowed in every situation.

Laminated Glass

Laminated glass typically consists of two pieces of glass laminated together, which can have various types of material sandwiched between them. Laminated glazing has traditionally been desirable for its impact resistance. Sometimes called insulated or multilayered, laminated glazing can be up to 10 times stronger than traditional, nonsafety wired glass and can have a Category I or II rating, so it can be used in multiple locations where safety is a concern. Although it typically has a limited rating of 20 minutes when used in a door, laminated glazing can obtain a rating of 45 to 90 minutes as an interior window. This allows its use as a window or sidelight in a rated wall in sizes larger than typical wired glass. In addition, laminated glass can be sandblasted to make it opaque or create a decorative pattern.

Transparent Wall Units

As previously mentioned, openings in walls are typically assigned fire-protection ratings and walls are given fire-resistance ratings. So, when glazing is used in a wall, it typically is only required to have a fire-protection rating. However, newer products have made it possible for some glazing assemblies to meet requirements similar to those of a wall and be given a fire-resistance rating. These "wall units" are an assembly of different materials, including glazing products, to create a unit that is transparent, fire resistant, and, in some cases, self-supporting. Often, these products use an inert material between two glazing components that, when exposed to heat, turns into foam and creates the fire-resistant quality. These transparent wall units can typically be used for larger or unlimited openings or even in place of a conventional solid rated wall.

Because of the possibility of someone walking toward or adjacent to these walls, these transparent walls must pass high-impact safety tests for Category I and Category II glazing. And they must be tested according to *ASTM E119, Standard Test Methods for Fire Tests of Building Construction and Materials*. They can be rated up to 2 hours and must pass the fire hose stream test. A unique characteristic of these units is that they do not allow the transfer of heat from the fire side of the "wall" to the opposite side, like typical glazing. This allows them to be used as a "full glass" barrier wall, such as at a stairwell, when approved by a code official. Like other rated glazing, these units are required by the codes to have a label. This label indicates the manufacturer and whether the glazing meets the fire-resistance, hose stream, and temperature rise requirements of *ASTM E119*. The fire-resistance rating of the glazing unit in minutes is also given.

Frames for Rated Glazing

Most glazing materials, especially rated glazing, must be fixed within a frame. Similar to door frames, fire window frames must be rated to create the required fire-protection rating. Most rated glazing is installed in hollow steel frames. The rating of the frame typically matches the rating of the glazing. Rated frames are also used around the windows installed in fire-rated doors and other fire-window assemblies. Even glass block is required to be installed in a steel frame in certain applications.

Like the newer glazing products, new framing products are becoming available. These framing systems are much thinner than traditional rated frames. Although some systems can be rated for only 20 to 45 minutes, others may reach a rating of 1 to 2 hours. Some products also have resistance to the transfer of heat. The design and performance requirements of a specific installation will need to be determined to correctly choose a framing system.

THROUGH-PENETRATION PROTECTIVES

A through-penetration is defined as an opening that pierces the entire thickness of a construction assembly, such as a wall or floor/ceiling assembly. When these construction assemblies are fire rated, the codes require the penetrations to be protected with rated assemblies such as firestops, draftstops, fireblocking, and fire dampers. (The codes also include shutters as a common opening protective.) These rated assemblies act as prevention systems and are referred to as through-penetration protection systems. Through-penetration protection systems are required to have a *fire-protection* rating. Not only are the ratings important to the integrity of the entire fire barrier or horizontal assembly during a fire to stop the spread of fire and smoke, they are also crucial for the evacuation of the occupants. The most common through-penetration protectives are described in this section.

Firestops and Smokestops

Firestops are a type of through-penetration protection system that is required in fire and smoke barriers and horizontal assemblies. Their purpose is to restrict the movement of fire and hot gases through openings made in the fire-resistance-rated walls and floor/ceiling or roof/ceiling assemblies. In some cases, they are required to limit the transfer of heat as well. They seal and protect any opening created by penetrations, such as plumbing pipes, electrical conduit and wire, HVAC ducts, communication cables, and similar types of building service equipment that pass through walls, floors, and ceilings. They may also be required at the intersection of walls and ceilings and at seams in gypsum board in rated walls.

The building codes, the *Life Safety Code (LSC)*, and the *National Electrical Code* (NEC) require the use of listed and approved firestops in fire and smoke barriers and horizontal assemblies. They are rated under *ASTM E814, Standard Test Method for Fire Tests of Through-Penetration Fire Stops*, or UL 1479, *Standard for Fire Tests of Through-Penetration Firestops*. These tests established two ratings. An *F-rating* is based on the number of hours the firestop resists flame and hot gases, its hose stream performance, and whether it remains in the opening. The *T-rating* is stricter and includes the *F-rating* criteria plus a maximum temperature riser. In order to specify a firestop, either the rating or the specific listed device needs to be identified. Each code has slightly different criteria.

A number of noncombustible materials can be used to create firestops. These include fire-rated caulk, silicone foam, mortar, mineral wool, fire-resistive board, wire mesh, collars, and clamp bands. They can be divided into two groups: systems and devices. A *firestop system* is typically constructed in the field and added after the through-penetration has been installed. The most common way to create a firestop is to fill the open space between the penetrating item and the fire barrier with fire-rated material and finish it with an approved sealant. However, when the openings are close to the size of the item penetrating the assembly, only the rated caulk or other sealant is required. This can be seen in Figure 8.2 in Chapter 8. The amount of damming materials and/or noncombustible sealant is specific to the location of the penetration, the dimension of the opening, the type of smoke or fire barrier, and the type and size of the penetrating item.

A *firestop device* is factory built and is typically installed as part of the through-penetration. For example, it may be a sleeve installed within the wall or floor assembly to allow a pipe to pass through, such as the one shown at the plumbing pipe in Figure 7.12 in Chapter 7. There are two types of devices that prevent the spread of flame and smoke while retarding the rise in temperature, as required by a T-rating. Endothermic firestops release water when exposed to heat. This causes a cooling effect that enables the installation to meet the fire rating required by the code. An intumescent firestop expands in volume under fire conditions, forming a strong char. This expansive caulk seals the gaps created as the penetrating items melt away.

When a firestop is used in a smoke barrier, it must act as a *smokestop* as well. However, not all firestops are rated to stop smoke. To be used in a smoke barrier, a firestop must pass an additional test for air leakage using *UL 1479*. This portion of the test provides the firestop with another rating, called an *L-rating*. Typically, if the L-rating is 5 or less, the firestop can be used as a smokestop.

Some devices and construction elements penetrate only one side of a wall, such as an electrical outlet or sprinkler head. These are called *membrane penetrations*. (Refer again to Figure 8.2 in Chapter 8.) Although similar, they are not technically a through-penetration. However, in a rated wall, these too must be protected. The codes define the allowable placement and size of these items within a rated wall. For example, the codes limit the size of an opening cut for an outlet box. They also require adequate filling of the area around the penetration and may require additional fireblocking, depending on the location. (See Electrical Boxes in Chapter 8 for more information.)

Fireblocks and Draftstops

Fireblocks (or fireblocking) and draftstops are used to restrict the spread of smoke and fire through concealed spaces should a fire occur. *Fireblocking* uses building materials to prevent the movement of air, flame, and gases through *small* concealed areas. In interior projects these could occur in several conditions, such as:

❏ *Dropped or coved ceilings:* If a wall stops at the underside edge of a dropped or coved ceiling, fireblocking may be required at the top of the wall to break the continuous air space.

❑ *Double stud walls:* When a deeper wall assembly is necessary to accommo-date large pipes and mechanical ducts or for acoustical separation, a double stud wall system may be used. In a long double stud wall, fireblocking may be required at certain intervals to limit the continuous air space.

❑ *Stairs:* Blocking may be required at the openings at the top and bottom of a run of stairs to block the open space created between the steps and the ceiling below.

❑ *Concealed floor spaces:* When hardwood floors or other finishes are installed on furring strips (i.e., sleepers), fireblocking may be required at certain intervals to limit the continuous space between the sleepers.

Draftstops use building materials to prevent the movement of air, smoke, gases, and flame through *large* concealed spaces. Typically, these spaces include certain floor/ceiling spaces, attics, and concealed roof spaces in Residential type uses. The codes specify where draftstops are required and the allowable size of the spaces they divide. For example, the attic space in a row of townhouses might require a draftstop to be constructed above each tenant separation wall. Typically required in combustible construction types, draftstops can be required in noncombustible construction as well. However, in either type of construction, draftstopping may not be required if the building has an automatic sprinkler system.

Although there are no specific tests for materials that can be used as fire-blocks and draftstops, each code lists acceptable materials within its text. They tend to be noncombustible types of materials. Some examples include gyp-sum board and certain sheathing and plywood materials. The material must be properly supported so that it remains in place during an initial fire.

Damper Systems

A damper is another type of opening protective. (See the inset titled *Smoke and How It Travels* on page 217.) It is used specifically in HVAC systems, either where a duct passes through a rated assembly or where an air transfer opening is cut into a rated assembly. It is typically specified by the mechanical engineer. It is a device arranged to automatically interrupt the flow of air during an emergency so that it restricts the passage of smoke, fire, and heat.

There are two kinds of fire or smoke damper systems: static and dynamic. A *static damper system* automatically shuts down during a fire, whereas a *dynamic damper system* remains in operation even during a fire. Dynamic dampers can be used in either static or dynamic HVAC systems, but static dampers can be used only in static systems. Depending on their installation, fire and smoke dampers may also be used to control the volume of air for the heating and cooling system during normal use. The energy codes also require dampers to control outside air.

◈Note

In addition to fire dampers, smoke dampers, and ceiling dampers, some jurisdictions may require the use of a corridor damper.

When a fire occurs, the dampers stop or regulate the potential flow of heated air, smoke, or flame through the duct system. Three main types of dampers are used in HVAC systems: fire dampers, smoke dampers, and ceiling dampers. If required, combination fire and smoke dampers also are available. Each type of damper has a specific test standard it must meet. These are mentioned as the various dampers are explained next.

Fire Dampers

Fire dampers are required by the codes in several locations. They are typically required in ducts that penetrate rated wall assemblies, at air transfer openings in rated partitions, and similar penetrations in rated horizontal assemblies. One can be installed within the duct or on the outside as a collar fastened to the wall or ceiling. The most common fire damper includes a fusible link on either side of the assembly the duct is penetrating. This fusible link melts during a fire when the area reaches a certain temperature, causing the fire damper to close and seal the duct. A similar system would be used on either side of an air transfer opening.

The rating of a fire damper can range from 1½ to 3 hours. The length of the rating is determined by the codes and depends on the rating of the fire-rated construction assembly that the duct passes through. Each building code has a table similar to *IBC* Table 716.3.2.1, "Fire Damper Rating," as shown in Figure 5.16. This table indicates the required damper ratings based on the type of penetration. Once the rating of the assembly is known, it is easy to determine the required fire damper rating. The required fire test for fire dampers is *UL 555, Standard for Fire Dampers*. It is used to determine the hourly fire rating of a fire damper.

TABLE 716.3.2.1
FIRE DAMPER RATING

TYPE OF PENETRATION	MINIMUM DAMPER RATING (hours)
Less than 3-hour fire-resistance-rated assemblies	1.5
3-hour or greater fire-resistance-rated assemblies	3

Figure 5.16 *International Building Code* Table 716.3.2.1, Fire Damper Rating (*2009 International Building Code,* copyright 2009. Washington, DC: International Code Council. All rights reserved. www.iccsafe.org).

Smoke Dampers

Smoke dampers are similar to fire dampers, but they are activated by smoke rather than heat. They are typically required when ducts penetrate a smoke barrier. Since smoke barriers are not required by the codes as often as fire-rated partitions and assemblies, smoke dampers are not used as often as fire dampers. When the smoke damper is required, it is installed with a smoke detector. The smoke detector is typically located inside the duct, so that when it detects smoke it causes the smoke damper to close off the duct. Sometimes a smoke damper will be part of a smoke evacuation system. In the event of a fire, the action of the smoke dampers would be controlled by the system. *UL 555S, Standard for Smoke Dampers*, is the test standard for smoke dampers. The test assigns a smoke damper one of four classes (Class I, Class II, Class III, and Class IV), with Class I being the most effective. Combination fire/smoke dampers must comply with *UL 555* and *UL 555S*.

Ceiling Dampers

Ceiling dampers, referred to in the codes as *ceiling radiation dampers*, are used in suspended ceilings that are part of the rated horizontal assembly, such as a floor/ceiling or roof/ceiling assembly. The damper can be located in the duct or can be part of the air diffuser that supplies air to the space. In case of fire, ceiling dampers prevent heat from entering the space between the ceiling and the floor or roof above. They also prevent the heat from traveling through the duct system. The ceiling damper closes when the heated air tries to move up through the damper. Ceiling dampers are regulated by *UL 555C, Standard for Ceiling Dampers*.

TEST RATINGS

Various standard tests have been mentioned throughout this chapter. The National Fire Protection Association (NFPA), ASTM International, and Underwriters Laboratories (UL), in conjunction with the American National Standards Institute (ANSI), have established a wide variety of standard fire tests. These tests are performed by third-party testing agencies. Manufacturers use these agencies to ensure reliability and confirm that their products meet specific requirements.

Different tests are used for wall, ceiling, and floor assemblies and the items that penetrate these assemblies. These are explained below and are summarized in Figure 5.17.

RATED ASSEMBLIES AND MATERIALS	REQUIRED TESTS[1]
FIRE WALLS	NFPA 221
RATED WALL AND FLOOR/CEILING ASSEMBLIES	
(fire-rated)	ASTM E119 UL 263 NFPA 251 (or NFPA 221)
(smoke-control)	NFPA 92A NFPA 92B
RATED DOOR CLOSERS	UL 228 UL 10B UL 10C ANSI/BHMA A156.4
RATED DOOR ASSEMBLIES[2] (fire doors)	NFPA 252 UL 10B and UL 10C ASTM E2074 (withdrawn 2007)
(smoke doors)	NFPA 105 UL 1784
FLOOR FIRE DOORS CEILING ACCESS DOORS	NFPA 288 (or ASTM E119)
FIRE WINDOWS AND SHUTTERS WIRED GLASS GLASS BLOCK[3]	UL 9 NFPA 257 ASTM E2010 (withdrawn 2007)
FIRE-RATED GLAZING[3]	NFPA 257 (or ASTM E119)
FIRESTOPS	ASTM E814 UL 1479
RATED DAMPERS (fire damper) (smoke damper) (ceiling damper)	 UL 555 UL 555S UL 555C

NOTES:
1. NFPA 80 is not a fire test but should also be referenced since it regulates the installation of an assembly and therefore can affect the final rating.
2. A 20-minute (1/3-hour) door does not require a hose stream test.
3. If large amounts of glass are used, it could be considered a fire barrier rather than a window and the radiant heat should be tested using ASTM E119 or NFPA 251.

Figure 5.17 Summary of tests for rated assemblies and materials.

Tests for Wall and Floor/Ceiling Assemblies

Standardized tests are developed to determine the reaction of materials and assemblies to fire in specific uses within a building. There are two basic groups of tests for wall and floor/ceiling assemblies. One group of tests evaluates the fire resistance of a material or assembly; the other evaluates how a material reacts to fire. These tests apply to the rated wall, floor, and ceiling assemblies required by the codes, as well as the building and structural elements used in the various construction types (see Chapter 3) required by the codes.

The fire-resistance tests generally evaluate how long an assembly will contain a fire, retain its own structural integrity, or both. The tests measure the performance of construction assemblies in three areas: (1) the temperature rise on the protected side of the assembly; (2) the smoke, gas, or flames that pass through the assembly; and (3) the structural performance during exposure to the fire. If the assembly being tested is a load-bearing assembly, the test measures the load-carrying ability during exposure to fire. In addition, if a wall or partition obtains a rating of 1 hour or more, it is subject to a hose stream test to see if it will resist disintegration. (Other components, such as certain doors, may have to pass a pressure test as well.)

Based on their performance in these tests, the assemblies are assigned fire-resistance ratings according to the time elapsed when the test is terminated, based on hourly increments. Some tests are used to determine how the assembly will restrict or limit smoke. All of these tests were discussed earlier in the chapter as each assembly was explained and are summarized in Figure 5.17.

The other group of tests evaluate how a material or product reacts to fire. These tests specifically measure the extent to which a material contributes to the dangerous elements of a fire, including heat, smoke and combustion products, and flame spread. Whether a material is considered combustible, limited combustible, or noncombustible is also determined by these types of tests. Some of these tests were discussed in Chapter 3. Others by NFPA are shown in Figure 5.1. (ASTM has a number of comparable tests.) The codes will specify when each test is required. Others may be required by a jurisdiction.

Tests for Opening and Through-Penetration Protectives

Opening protectives and through-penetration protective systems must also pass specific tests. These tests were mentioned earlier as each system was explained. For example, fire doors must conform to the test requirements of *NFPA 252*, and fire windows and shutters must meet the requirements of *NFPA 257*. The various fire tests are summarized in Figure 5.17. *NFPA 80, Standard for Fire Doors and Other Opening Protectives*, is also important for opening protective requirements and is

> **✎Note**
>
> *ISO 834,* the standard used by European countries, is similar to *NFPA 251.*

> **✎Note**
>
> In the past, fire-door tests were conducted in furnaces under neutral pressure. Now most tests require a positive-pressure test.

and maintained properly. Keep the following factors in mind when specifying rated assemblies:

1. *If a product is not used the way a manufactured specifies or if the contractor does not use the correct materials, its rating becomes void.* It must be retested the way it is built or have fire protection added to create the rating.

2. *If the construction of the joints between the assemblies, such as wall-to-wall, wall-to-ceiling, or wall-to-floor, is substandard, fire and smoke can penetrate no matter how good each assembly is.* Specifying the correct installation standard is just as important as specifying the right assembly.

3. *Conventional openings, such as electrical switches and outlets in wall assemblies and electrical raceways and pull boxes in floor/ceiling assemblies, can affect the fire endurance of an assembly.* Some assemblies are tested with these penetrations; others are not. (See more in Chapter 8.)

4. *A fire can impair the stability of a structural assembly or building element.* If a fire occurs and the assembly is exposed to flame and heat, this exposure can affect the strength and structural integrity of the building materials. After a fire, the original fire rating may no longer be valid.

When a rated assembly is required, the codes will often reference one or more of the 3 publications mentioned above. The codes may also allow other ways to determine the appropriate construction assembly. For example, some codes specify construction assemblies and their ratings in their text. The *IBC* includes a table that lists and describes the installation of various structural elements, walls and partitions, and floors and roofs and their ratings. In addition, the *IBC* includes a section that allows "alternative methods for determining fire protection ratings" that may be used when standard testing methods do not work well for a specific design. (See the section Comparing the Codes.) Depending on the jurisdiction, it may be possible to reference these *IBC* details or use the alternate method rather than using one of the three publications.

The codes already have provisions for allowing calculations or an engineering analysis of a proposed or existing construction assembly to determine the rating of the assembly. These calculations may be based on information given by the codes concerning the fire resistance of certain materials or they may be performance based. For most projects, referring to the tested assemblies represented by the publications listed above will be appropriate. For existing construction or for innovative design elements that are required to be rated, the calculated or performance criteria may be required. If using special calculations or criteria in the performance codes, it is necessary to meet with the code official to discuss the design early in the process and then be prepared to provide the requested documentation to support the design. In many cases, this will require the assistance of other design professionals and engineers.

In either case, it is important to document accurately the rated assemblies and the compartmentation created by these assemblies. Construction drawings should indicate which walls or partitions are required to be rated and their required fire-resistance rating. In addition, when providing details for their construction, reference the required testing and installation standards and the assigned number of the tested assembly if possible. All rated opening protectives and through-penetration protectives must be properly noted as well. In addition, everything should be verified during construction to confirm that they are installed correctly. If they are not, they will not provide the required compartmentation and may fail in the event of a fire. (See the section Documentation and Liability in Chapter 10.)

SUSTAINABILITY CONSIDERATIONS

The building code, fire code, and/or *Life Safety Code (LSC)* will determine when the rated assemblies are required; however, different construction materials can be used. For example, a rated assembly could be composed of wood or metal studs with gypsum board or concrete and concrete block. These are common materials used for rated assemblies, yet they can also have significant recycled content and recyclable characteristics. Although the sustainability codes and standards do not place direct requirements on rated assemblies, they do have requirements that can affect the materials choices. These choices cannot negate the fire-resistance rating of a wall. Both the *International Green Construction Code (IGCC)* and the sustainability standard *ASHRAE/USGBC/IES 189.1, Standard for the Design of High-Performance Green Buildings Except Low-Rise Residential Buildings* have requirements for the use of green building materials, many of which impact the composition of rated walls and construction within an interior project.

Both sustainability documents require efficient use of materials during the construction process, management of the construction waste by proper disposal, and recycling of left over materials. Materials produce different levels of waste and have unique recycling characteristics. For example, the *IGCC* sets percentages for use of previously used, recycled, recyclable, regionally available, and bio-based materials. In many cases wood and concrete are both regionally available and are considered bio-based. All of these characteristics contribute to the level of sustainability in a project.

Materials and products can be evaluated by the various sustainable standards and certification programs that have been developed, some of which are referenced by the sustainability codes and standards. For example, a certain percentage of the wood used throughout a project must typically be certified and follow a chain of custody process. This includes the certification process by the Forestry Stewardship Council (FSC) as discussed in Chapter 3.

A sustainability standard commonly referenced includes the state of California's *Section 01350, Standard Practice for the Testing of Volatile Organic Emissions from Various Sources Using Small-Scale Environmental Chambers* (also known as *CA/DHS/EHLB/R-174 Standard Practice*). It includes procedures to measure the volatile organic compound (VOC) emissions of building products, among other things. *Section 01350* is required by the state of California and referenced in the *IGCC* and *ASHRAE 189.1* to test building products such as gypsum board, wood structural panels, particle board, insulation products, and the like. Certain building products, such as wood subflooring, may also need to meet specific urea-formaldehyde requirements. (See the section Sustainability Considerations in Chapter 9.)

Other industry sustainability standards are more comprehensive. For example, The Institute for Market Transformation to Sustainability (MTS) developed the standard, *MTS 2006:4, SMART Sustainable Building Product Standard*, which can be used to test any building product, except carpet and textiles. A product tested using this standard is evaluated over its entire supply chain for multiple environmental benefits and impacts, not just for VOC emissions. (See Appendix B.) Another available standard is Green Seal's *Standard GS-36, Environmental Standard for Commercial Adhesives*. This and other standards may be required for adhesives and sealants used in building interiors. (See also Chapter 9.)

Everything that is included inside or placed on a wall needs to be considered— both for its contribution to green design and how it potentially affects the rating of the wall. This can include insulation, sound attenuation, caulking, and so forth. For example, both the building codes and *ASHRAE 189.1* set various levels of sound transmission levels for wall and floor-ceiling assemblies. However, the products that are used in the assembly to achieve the desired sound transmission characteristics cannot reduce or compromise the require rating of the assembly. (See the inset titled *Sound Transmission* on page 209.)

> **☑ Note**
>
> SMART standards rate the products tested similar to a green rating system. Products are tested and classified in three categories based on the number of points received: Silver, Gold, and Platinum. All SMART standards include the use of a Life Cycle Assessment (LCA) as explained in Appendix B.

> **☑ Note**
>
> When choosing a product to minimize sound transmission for environmental quality and for sustainability, the affect on the fire-protection rating of a rated wall must be considered.

CHECKLIST

Figure 5.19 is a fire-resistance checklist that can be used on your interior projects or as a guideline to make your own checklist. It indicates each type of fire-rated assembly, smoke-rated assembly, opening protective, and through-penetration protective typically regulated by the codes. The checklist can be used to remind you of what to look for and research on a project, as well as to give you a place to record the necessary code information for future reference. Not every type of fire-resistant component is included in every project. The checklist, however, must be used in conjunction with the codes and standards based on the occupancy classification of the project and the construction type of the building.

Fire and Smoke Resistance Checklist

Date: _____

Project Name: _____ Space: _____

Occupancy (new or existing):_____

Type of Construction: _____

REQUIRED FIRE PROTECTION (CHECK THOSE THAT APPLY)	EXT'G (YES/NO)	LOCATION IN BUILDING	TYPE OF MATERIAL OR ASSEMBLY REQUIRED (LIST INFORMATION)	HOURLY RATING OR FIRE TEST REQUIRED (LIST TYPE)

Fire Barriers, Horizontal Assemblies, and Fire Partitions[1]
__ Fire Wall(s)
__ Fire Area(s)
__ Occupancy Separation(s)
__ Dwelling or Sleeping Unit(s)
__ Incidental Accessory Occupancy(ies)
__ Vertical Shaft Enclosure(s)
__ Means of Egress Component(s)
  __ Exit Stairway(s)
  __ Exit Access Stairway(s)
  __ Horizontal Exit(s)
  __ Area(s) of Refuge
  __ Exit Corridor/ Passageway(s)
  __ Exit Access Corridor(s)
__ Floor/Ceiling Assembly(ies)
__ Other: _____				

Smoke Barriers and Partitions[1] __ Smoke Compartment(s) __ Vertical Shaft(s) __ Vestibule(s) __ Other: _____				
Opening Protectives __ Rated Door Assembly(ies) __ Fire Door(s) __ Smoke Door(s) __ Fire Window Assembly(ies) __ Rated Glazing and Frame(s) __ Special Hardware __ Other: _____				
Through-Penetration Protectives Engineer Required? __ YES __ NO — Firestop(s) __ Fireblocks(s) __ Draftstop(s) __ Damper System(s) __ Fire Damper(s) __ Smoke Damper(s) __ Other: _____				

NOTES:

1. Remember that fire and smoke assemblies need to be considered both vertically and horizontally.
2. Refer to codes and standards for specific information, including sustainability codes and standards when required.
3. Attach all testing verification, including copies of manufacturer labels and/or copies of rated assembly details.

Figure 5.19 Fire-resistance checklist.

The checklist begins with the standard blanks for the project and space name, the occupancy classification of the project, and the construction type of the building. (If necessary, refer to Chapters 2 and 3 to determine these.) The remainder of the checklist indicates the various types of interior assemblies and protectives. To the left of each component is a blank space so that you can check off each of the components used in your project.

Then, for each assembly that you checked off, fill in the necessary information. If the assembly or component already exists in the building, make a note in the "Existing" column. This will be helpful when you need to match existing conditions. Use the next column to indicate the location of the system. For example, indicate where vertical shafts are located on the floor plan. It may be helpful to attach a reduced-scale floor plan and locate these components graphically.

The next two columns are used to indicate the specific types of systems or material used and the types of tests and/or ratings required by the codes and standards. This information will help you to select the correct products as you are specifying for the project and/or when you are working with an engineer. For example, you can indicate the type of firestop to be used and the rating it must provide, or indicate the size and type of rated glazing that will be used and the specific tests it must pass. For each type of assembly affected, you may want to indicate whether it is a fire and/or smoke barrier, a fire and/or smoke partition, or a horizontal assembly.

As you are filling out the checklist, you may have to consult engineers or other professionals to determine exact requirements. Use this form throughout the project as a guideline and a reminder of the items to be researched and completed. When the checklist is completed, file it and any other pertinent testing and code information required with the project paperwork for future reference. (See Chapter 10.)

CHAPTER 6

FIRE PROTECTION SYSTEMS

As mentioned in the previous chapter, fire and smoke are the primary threats to the safety of the occupants in a building. Fire and smoke can travel quickly both horizontally and vertically unless special efforts are made to prevent this from happening. Compartmentation of fire areas was discussed in Chapter 5. The use of rated assemblies in this *passive* system of fire protection is considered the first step in controlling the spread of smoke and fire. In addition to compartmentation, an *active* system that reacts when a fire is detected within a building or space can be used to provide another level of fire protection. This chapter will discuss the active fire-protection system and its components, which include detection, alarm, and extinguishing systems, providing a fire-protection checklist at the end of the chapter.

The overall aim of the fire-protection system is to detect a fire in a building or space, warn the occupants, and suppress the fire until the fire department arrives. (In some cases, the system will extinguish the fire.) If that fire can be detected quickly, occupants have more time to exit the building safely and with less panic. Also, if the fire can be suppressed or extinguished early in its development, less damage to the building and its contents may occur. Although the main concern of the codes is occupant safety and not necessarily the contents of the building, a fire that is allowed to develop uncontrolled can cause severe structural damage to the building. This can lead to loss of life of the occupants who have not yet exited the building or the firefighters attempting to deal with the fire.

In some cases, the owner's concerns for the contents of a building or space may make fire protection desirable even when not required by the codes. For example, it may be important for a small museum area that contains valuable historic letters to be protected or a service-based business to maintain its customer records. Other building owners are starting to add more redundancy as threats other than fire are becoming more prevalent. In most cases, these systems should be installed using the same standards required by the code.

◁Note

In the past, fire-protection systems such as fire extinguishers and sprinkler systems were known as *suppression systems*. The codes now refer to these as *extinguishing systems*.

◁Note

In the future, fire-protection systems will be combined more often with other building systems designed to protect the occupants from emergencies other than fire. See the inset titled *Integrated Alarms* on page 257.

245

◀**Note**

Some jurisdictions
are moving toward
performance-based fire and
life safety codes, allowing
for more flexibility in the
design of a fire-protection
system.

Depending on the system and the specific code requirements, the fire-protection system may be completely automatic, manual, or a combination of both. The codes determine which aspects of the system must be automatic and which are allowed to be under the control of the occupants. For example, some occupancies do not require automatic detection and notification of fire and instead rely on manual fire alarms. In a fully automatic system, however, once a detector indicates that there is a fire, it sets off an alarm to warn the occupants to evacuate and then initiates the extinguishing system.

All of the systems discussed in this chapter are directly tied to the plumbing, mechanical, or electrical system of a building. For this reason, an engineer is typically involved in this portion of a project. (This was also the case with dampers, as discussed in Chapter 5.) However, as the designer, collaboration is typically necessary to designate preferred locations of devices, to coordinate the locations of various design elements, and be involved in other decisions that may affect a design project. Some examples may include locating fire extinguishers and fire alarms, selecting the type of sprinkler heads in decorative ceilings, and coordinating the location of sprinkler heads with the location of the light fixtures.

COMPARING THE CODES

Although a complete fire-protection system includes detectors, alarms, and suppression or extinguishing systems, not all of these will be required in all buildings or spaces. The building codes and the *Life Safety Code (LSC)* determine the level of fire protection required according to the type of occupancy, the use of the space, and the size and height of the building. In some cases, such as a mixed occupancy, a detection and fire alarm system may be required in only one area of the building. The codes also specifically address requirements for the use of fire dampers and other devices that are used in conjunction with fire-protection systems. (See Chapter 5.) When certain systems are used, the codes often allow for greater flexibility in other areas of the codes such as construction types, rating of interior walls, and overall area and building heights.

Many jurisdictions also require the use of a fire code, which provides additional requirements. Some of the information overlaps between the building codes and the fire codes. Other chapters in the fire codes are unique and indicate when specific active fire-protection systems are required beyond their requirement in the building codes, the proper installation of automatic sprinkler systems, and additional requirements including maintenance for the use of active systems. (The fire codes typically include prescriptive requirements as well as performance criteria for the development of active protection systems.)

◀**Note**

The *International Building
Code (IBC)* includes
several sections which
are taken directly from the
International Fire Code (IFC).
These sections include a
"[F]" in the title, indicating
it comes from the *IFC*. If
information from the *IBC* is
duplicated in the *IFC*, a [B] is
included in the section.

When specific testing and installation methods are required, the building codes, the fire codes, and the *LSC* refer to a number of the standards published by the National Fire Protection Association (NFPA). The NFPA standards specify locations, design details, and installation requirements, as well as testing standards that must be followed. Some of the standards deal with fire prevention. Others concentrate on detection and suppression systems. The standards most often used for interior projects are listed in Figure 6.1. Although these codes and standards are most often used by a mechanical or electrical engineer, understanding the scope of these codes is important in the development of the design. They will be included in the discussion of each type of system.

In the past, almost all fire-protection systems were designed based on the prescriptive code requirements. These technical requirements were based on criteria established by the industry (often as a result of a devastating fire) and were determined by typical engineering calculations. Now performance design is an increasingly acceptable way to design a fire-protection system that can address the special needs of a design or building. It is most often used with multi-level atriums and one-of-a-kind facilities. It can also be helpful for buildings that do not meet the current codes, such as an historic building with an open stairwell, or a space with an unusual design, such as a unique ceiling pattern. In other cases, special needs of the occupants or unique kinds of fire hazards may need to be considered.

With performance design, the design team defines the level of safety that must be provided. This can include how quickly a fire needs to be detected, how soon the suppression system activates, who will be notified of the fire, the safest egress patterns, and other criteria. The unique characteristics of the space or building are also considered. Then specific engineering calculations and computer fire modeling are used to analyze and create a system that responds best for that design. For example, one model determines the burn rate and heat-release rate of various construction materials in order to calculate potential fire sizes. Computer models can also calculate how fast a fire is likely to burn and the amount of smoke and carbon monoxide it may produce. In most cases, the design will use the performance criteria for selected parts of the building, but the rest of the fire-protection system will be specified according to the prescriptive code requirements.

Fire detection and suppression systems are not typically part of sustainability codes and standards. However, there are some things to consider. These are discussed in the section Sustainability Consideration later in this chapter.

Accessibility standards such as the Americans with Disabilities Act (ADA) and the *ICC/ANSI A117.1* do not play heavily in the development of fire protection systems. The main accessibility requirement for fire prevention has to do with fire alarms and accessible warning systems. Also keep in mind that any device

NFPA 10	Standard for Portable Fire Extinguishers
NFPA 11	Standard for Low-, Medium-, and High-Expansion Foam
NFPA 12	Standard for Carbon Dioxide Extinguishing Systems
NFPA 12A	Standard on Halon 1301 Fire Extinguishing Systems
NFPA 13	Standard for the Installation of Sprinkler Systems
NFPA 13D	Standard for the Installation of Sprinkler Systems in One- and Two-Family Dwellings and Manufactured Homes
NFPA 13R	Standard for the Installation of Sprinkler Systems in Residential Occupancies up to and Including Four Stories in Height
NFPA 14	Standard for the Installation of Standpipes and Hose Systems
NFPA 15	Standard for Water Spray Fixed Systems for Fire Protection
NFPA 16	Standard for the Installation of Foam-Water Sprinkler and Foam-Water Spray Systems
NFPA 17	Standard for Dry Chemical Extinguishing Systems
NFPA 17A	Standard for Wet Chemical Extinguishing Systems
NFPA 20	Standard for the Installation of Stationary Pumps for Fire Protection
NFPA 70	National Electric Code
NFPA 70A	National Electric Code Requirements for One- and Two-Family Dwellings
NFPA 72	National Fire Alarm Code
NFPA 110	Standard for Emergency and Standby Power Systems
NFPA 111	Standard on Stored Electrical Energy Emergency and Standby Power Systems
NFPA 170	Standard for Fire Safety and Emergency Symbols
NFPA 720	Standard for the Installation of Carbon Monoxide (CO) Detection and Warning Equipment
NFPA 750	Standard on Water Mist Fire Protection Systems
NFPA 2001	Standard on Clean Agent Fire Extinguishing Systems

NOTE: There may be other NFPA standards not listed above that are specific to an occupancy, especially certain hazardous occupancies. Other standards, such as *NFPA 25*, may pertain to the inspection and maintenance of a system.

Figure 6.1 Common NFPA standards for fire-protection systems.

that is part of the fire-protection system and meant for occupant use must be placed at accessible reaching heights and locations and cannot be located so that it becomes a projection into the accessible path. Signage, as well as the type and location of the operational mechanisms, is also important. These items will be discussed throughout the chapter.

DETECTION SYSTEMS

The best way to protect the occupants in a building from the dangers of a fire is to know that there is a fire as early as possible. This, of course, allows more time to contain the fire and remove the occupants, if necessary, before the danger escalates. Detection systems are meant to recognize the first signs of a fire. For this reason, detectors are also known as *initiating devices*, because their activation initiates the rest of the fire-protection system. Although there are several different types of detection systems, the most common systems rely on the detection of heat or smoke. (See also the inset titled *Carbon Monoxide Detection* on page 250.)

In most cases, the requirements in the codes will determine if a detection system is required throughout the building or in certain fire areas or zones. These specific fire zones can be large areas of a building, an entire floor, or selected rooms. If more protection is not required by the codes, the building owner may ask that the fire protection of certain areas be supplimented. In all cases, the type of detection should be appropriate for the anticipated type of fire. For example, most fires will release heat and smoke, but a liquid fire causes a drop in temperature instead. In addition, smoke detectors are better for a smoldering fire but heat detectors are better for large flaming fires in large spaces.

Fire detection systems have changed dramatically over the last several decades due to technological advances. Today, these systems can employ everything from programmable computers to video detection and remote controls. Detectors can be programmed to require that more than one aspect of a fire be detected before signaling the alarm system to prevent unnecessary false alarms. Other programs will require additional types of alarm verification. (See the inset titled *Fire Technology* on page 252.)

These modern advances in detection systems have resulted in better-protected buildings. They have also resulted in continuous updates to the codes and standards. The *NFPA 72, National Fire Alarm Code* provides the minimum performance, location, installation, and maintenance requirements for detection systems. The building codes, the fire codes, and the *LSC* will indicate when a detection system is required and reference the *NFPA 72* for more specific information. The codes typically specify the use of smoke detectors. In some cases, a heat detection device may also be required. Both of these detectors, as well as fire alarm pull boxes, are discussed next.

Most of the time, collaboration with an electrical engineer or fire-protection designer is necessary to coordinate these systems with the rest of the design. Detection systems must also be integrated into other systems within the building, including the electrical system. Detection systems rely on electricity as their main power source, and in most cases require an emergency source of power as well. (See Chapter 8.)

Note

Newer types of detectors can recognize various fire *signatures.* Examples include the amount of smoke and the change in temperature. New video smoke detectors and video flame detectors are also available.

Note

Never paint over smoke detectors, sprinkler heads, or other fire safety equipment. It can hamper their effectiveness. Many detectors operate by fusible links. Paint may keep the fusible links from melting.

Note

Some jurisdictions may already require carbon monoxide detectors in certain Residential occupancies. Check with the jurisdiction.

CARBON MONOXIDE DETECTION

Carbon monoxide is produced by incomplete combustion of organic materials. It accumulates in the body over time and prolonged exposure to carbon monoxide can be fatal. The first sign of a problem is often occupants' experiencing flu-like symptoms. Continued and prolonged exposure will cause drowsiness to the point of unconsciousness and ultimately death.

Exposure to this gas occurs most frequently from appliances or engines powered by gas, such as automobiles, lawnmowers, stoves, and hot water heaters. These items are often used in and around Residential occupancies. In 2009, the *International Residential Code* started requiring carbon monoxide alarms in one- and two-family dwellings if the home includes a fuel-fired appliance or an attached garage. (See Appendix D.) Typically, an alarm must be located outside of or adjacent to bedrooms. The most recognized industry standard is *UL 2034, Standard of Safety for Single and Multiple Station Carbon Monoxide Alarms.* However, if a jurisdiction requires the standard *NFPA 720, Standard for the Installation of Carbon Monoxide (CO) Detection and Warning Equipment,* additional alarms may be required on every level of a home. This NFPA standard also includes alarm requirements for other occupancy classifications.

The reliability of carbon monoxide alarms has improved. High levels of carbon monoxide will trigger the alarm more quickly while lower levels must be present for a period of time before the alarm will trigger. Once sounded, the alarm relies on the occupants to report to authorities, usually the fire department, so that the problem can be resolved. Carbon monoxide detection may be required in other occupancies in the future.

Smoke Detection

◨ Note

Smoke detectors will increase in importance as more finishes and furnishings become flame resistant. (See Chapter 9.) Such materials will be more likely to smolder for long periods of time without a flame at temperatures too low for sprinklers to respond.

Since smoke and toxic gases are the main killers in a building fire, smoke detection systems are important in every design. Smoke detectors are especially effective in detecting smoldering fires that do not produce enough heat for sprinkler activation. For this reason, smoke detectors are the most widely used initiating device.

Smoke detectors can be used in two ways. They can be wired to act individually (e.g., single-station) or as a group (e.g., multi-station). Based on the type of detector, the type of alarm it has, and how it is wired, it can signal one area (or zone) or a whole building. (See the section Alarm Systems later in this chapter.) They are often used in conjunction with a smoke damper. (See Chapter 5.) Other smoke detectors may be required to recall elevators or activate automatic doors when smoke is present. For example, the detector acts as a releasing device so that the door will automatically close. Both multiple- and single-station detectors must be tied into the building's power source.

The codes specify when smoke detection is required based on the evacuation needs of the occupants and/or if the building type includes sleeping accommodations. Examples include Institutional, High Hazard, and most Residential occupancies as well as high-rise buildings and ambulatory health care facilities. However, the codes do not typically specify where to locate them within a space or building. Instead, *NFPA 72* includes some requirements. For example, in larger spaces, detectors should be spaced 30 feet (9.1 m) apart to protect 900 square feet (84 s m) where ceilings are smooth, with no obstructions. A detector can be ceiling mounted or wall mounted. Typically, it should be mounted 4 inches (102 mm) from the wall/ceiling intersection so that air currents do not cause smoke and heat to bypass the smoke detector.

The standard *NFPA 90* specifies the location of smoke detectors in the ductwork of air distribution systems. (See the section Damper Systems in Chapter 5.) The placement of other smoke detectors is typically based on the design and layout of a space or building. For example, in a cooking area, the smoke detector should not be placed where standard cooking procedures may activate the alarm. Instead, they are typically required in an exhaust hood. When unusual design situations occur or include unique elements, such as coffered ceilings, work with the manufacturer and the local code officials to locate the detectors.

Heat Detection

Next to the smoke detector, the heat detector is the most common type of detection system. Heat detectors are sensitive to any change in temperature. This can be especially important in liquid fires, where a drop in temperature occurs. Heat detectors can monitor temperatures at a specific spot or monitor the temperature range within a designated area. For example, they might be placed along an assembly line in a factory. Often, heat detectors are used with smoke detectors to avoid false alarms. In these systems, more than one sign of fire is needed before an alarm is signaled. A combination may also be used in highly sensitive areas so that the detection of either smoke or heat will active the fire-protection system.

Manual Fire Alarms

The codes consider a manual fire alarm to be part of the detection system. In this case, however, it is the occupant who detects the fire. He or she then sets off the manual alarm by the use of a *pull station* or *alarm box*. If an automatic smoke detection system or sprinkler system is not provided in a building, a manual fire alarm is typically required by the codes. However, certain occupancies require a manual fire alarm even if a smoke detection system or sprinkler system is provided. It will depend on the number of occupants, the capabilities of the occupants, and

FIRE TECHNOLOGY

For more complex or large projects, expanding technology is allowing for additional ways to recognize the presence of fire because fire creates more than smoke and heat. Fire produces various types of symptoms. These include molecular gases (smoke that includes carbon dioxide), aerosols, heat conduction, thermal radiation (heat), and acoustic waves. New technology that includes combination, multi-criteria, and multi-sensor detectors allows for the detection of these multiple symptoms to determine if a fire really exists. This allows for better detection of a fire and reduces the number of false alarms.

For example, the presence of smoke does not necessarily mean that there is a fire. Someone with a cigarette standing directly below a smoke detector could cause it to alarm. More sophisticated detection systems will then compare that input with the presence of other symptoms of fire or whether another smoke detector nearby indicates that there is smoke. If no other symptoms of fire exist, the detection system may delay setting off the fire alarm until another symptom is present or the smoke continues.

Technology, especially the use of computers, has created advances not only in the individual detectors but in the detection systems as well. Now systems can monitor and check each detector individually to see if it is working properly. In the event of a fire, a detection system can determine the exact location of the fire, not just the floor on which the fire originated, and notify certain areas or zones in the facility rather than the entire building. The sensitivity of a particular zone of detectors can also be modified to allow for different levels of heat, or other symptoms that might be present in normal conditions.

Newer tools, such as remote fire command stations and graphic annunciation panels, which indicate exact locations within a building using imported CAD drawings, provide valuable information to local authorities responding to an emergency. Another technology currently being developed involves the use of video systems that can detect and analyze a fire. (See also the inset titled *Integrated Alarms* on page 257.)

◁ Note

Some building types may require the use of a protective cover over the pull box to deter vandalism. This is usually determined by a code official.

the height of the building as well as other specific requirements. Common examples include Educational occupancies and large Assembly and Business occupancies. Although the alarm does not usually activate the extinguishing system, it will notify the occupants of a problem.

When manual fire alarms are provided, the codes typically require the box to be located adjacent to the entrance of each exit doorway. The alarm box should be easily seen and located on the latch side of the door no farther than 5 feet (1524 mm) from the doorway. Some occupancies may require a more unique location. For example, alarm boxes in hospitals are typically located at control rooms or nurses' stations for use by staff. In addition, on any given floor, the travel distance

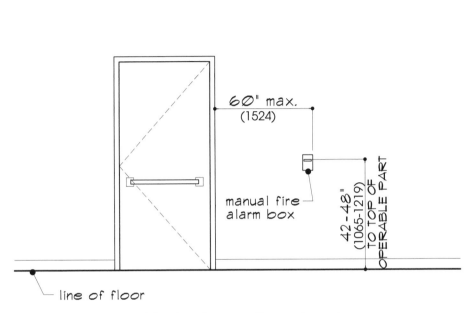

line of ceiling

60" max.
(1524)

manual fire
alarm box

42-48"
(1065-1219)
TO TOP OF
OPERABLE PART

line of floor

Figure 6.2 Typical manual fire alarm box mounting requirements.

to an alarm box must typically be within 200 feet (60 m), so additional boxes may be required. The codes also specify their color, signage, and power supply.

Since the device is meant to be used by building occupants, accessibility requirements for the mounting of the alarm box will apply. The height of the box must be within the accessible reach range (for side or forward approach) and typically have a clear floor space of 30 inches (760 mm) by 48 inches (1220 mm) in front of it. In addition, new types of manual alarms have been developed to be more easily used by persons with disabilities. These include devices that are more easily grasped and do not require complex movement to activate. Figure 6.2 indicates the typical location of an alarm box according to code and accessibility requirements.

✎Note

Instead of listing all the alarm requirements within its text, the 2004 *ADA-ABA Accessibility Guidelines* references the 1999 and 2002 editions of the *NFPA 72, National Fire Alarm Code.*

ALARM SYSTEMS

Alarm systems within a building or space make occupants aware that something unusual is occurring. In most cases, they are used to warn occupants that a fire has been detected and that they should evacuate. Alarm systems also can be used

✎Note

The 2009 codes reference the 2007 edition of *NFPA 72*. The 2010 *NFPA 72* was renamed *National Fire Alarm and Signaling Code* since it includes more information on emergency voice/alarm communication systems (EVACSs) and mass notification systems (MNSs).

✎Note

Multiple codes must be reviewed for alarm requirements. These include the fire codes, building codes, *LSC,* and *NFPA 72.* The *National Electrical Code (NEC)* must also be referenced for the design and installation of the system. (See Chapter 8.)

✎Note

Visual alarms can be referred to in a number of ways. Depending on the publication and the manufacturer, they can be called visual alarm signals, visible signal devices, visual signaling appliances, or visual notification appliances.

to notify occupants of other types of emergencies, such as toxic spills, severe weather conditions, or a possible bomb threat. (See the section Emergency Voice/ Alarm Communication Systems later in this chapter.) The fire codes, the fire-protection chapters of the building codes, and the *Life Safety Code (LSC)* specify the type of alarm, its location, and the wiring required. For installation of the alarms and other details, the codes also refer to the standard *NFPA 72, National Fire Alarm Code.* Certain accessibility requirements also apply. These requirements are found in the ICC/ANSI standard and the *ADA Standards.*

The devices that make up the different types of alarm systems are sometimes referred to as notification appliances. An alarm system can be activated either *manually* by the use of a pull device or *automatically* by a detection system or automatic sprinkler system. The codes will specify which type of system is required for a particular occupancy classification. Some occupancies may require both types of activation.

There is also a difference between single-station and multiple-station alarms. A *single-station* alarm will sound only within the area where the fire is detected to warn the occupants in the immediate area. A *multiple-station* alarm system is a system of fire alarms that is interconnected so that the indication of fire anywhere in the building will sound all the alarms within the building so that total evacuation can begin. In larger occupancies, the alarms may be interconnected to create specific zones so that evacuation can be controlled in stages or by floor. In other occupancies, such as hospitals or nursing homes, the signal will only annunciate at a controlled station, such as a nurses' station, so that only staff is alerted. The alarm can also go to a remote control room where someone decides what action should be taken. Often, the fire alarm will notify the local fire department as well.

Like the detection system described in the previous section, the alarm system is tied to the electrical system of a building and may be tied to other similar systems. For example, a building may be required to have a control panel at the fire department entrance to the building so that firefighters can quickly determine the location of the problem. (See also the inset titled *Integrated Alarms* on page 257.) An electrical engineer will typically design the alarm system and reference the appropriate codes. Collaboration will be necessary to coordinate the location of devices with other design elements and confirm that the system meets the intent of the design. The various types of alarm systems are described next.

Visual and Audible Alarm Systems

Alarms are required to use both audible and visual signals. This ensures that the majority of people within a building will be notified that a fire or emergency is occurring. An *audible* alarm signals an emergency by a loud sound. The sound can be a steady hornlike sound, a pattern of sound, or bell sounds. A *visual* alarm signals using a strobe light or rotating beacon. The strobe usually emits a pulsing light that cannot easily be ignored or is intended to awaken occupants who are sleeping. Where different types of warnings are required, each would have a different pattern or intensity. For example, the fire alarm may make a single loud blast, but the emergency alarm may be a pattern of short blasts. There are also alarm devices that have both audible and visible notification in one unit. (When a combination device is used, it must be located according to the requirements for visual alarms.)

An *audible alarm* must be set within a certain decibel and pressure range so that it exceeds the prevailing sound level in the room or space where it is used. For example, an audible alarm in a factory where machines are working may require a louder sound than one in an office building. In most cases, the alarm must be able to be heard throughout the building and must be located accordingly. The alarms must also be placed in a natural path of escape and at each required exit from a building (within approximately 5 feet [1524 mm] of the exit) because the noise from the alarm helps the occupants to locate the exits during a fire. Audible alarms must meet certain accessibility requirements that affect the type, sound level, and pulse rate. Although locations for audible alarms are not specified, if they are more than 4 inches (100 mm) deep, they must be mounted high enough on the wall not to create a protrusion into a path of travel.

Visual alarms are basically white or clear flashing lights used as an alarm signal and are sometimes referred to as *strobes*. Visual alarms were first required because of the ADA. Similar requirements are now included in the codes and the ICC/ANSI standard as well as the *ADA Standards*. The color, intensity, flash rate, and pulse duration of a visual alarm are regulated by the codes and standards. In addition, they must be placed in specific locations—certain heights above the floor and certain distances apart. (See the *ADA Standards* and the ICC/ANSI standard for details.) When required, they must be provided in all public use areas such as restrooms, corridors, and lobbies in addition to any common use areas such as meeting rooms, breakrooms, examination rooms, and classrooms. In occupancies with multiple sleeping units, a certain percentage of the units must be equipped with a visual alarm as well. (Devices located in sleeping units have additional mounting requirements.)

It may be necessary coordinate the placement of the audible and visual alarm systems with an engineer based on the design of the space to ensure that the alarms can be seen and heard. In particular, the distance of occupied spaces from the origin of the alarm and any doors that would reduce the level of sound should be considered. In addition, the placement of the devices must meet accessibility requirements.

Note

A *public mode* alarm notifies all occupants. A *private mode* alarm notifies only control staff.

Note

Visual alarms must typically be installed in more locations than audible alarms, since a visual alarm can be observed only in the space in which it is installed.

Note

Visible alarms are not required in exits such as stairwells because of the distraction and/or tripping hazards they may create.

Emergency Voice/Alarm Communication Systems

Note

An emergency voice/alarm communication system can use prerecorded or live announcements or both. A jurisdiction may require one over another and often requires approval of the message(s).

Some occupancies and building types are required by the codes to have an emergency voice/alarm communication system (EVACS) tied into the fire alarm system. These include factories, some Institutional occupancies such as hospitals and assisted living facilities, large storage facilities, occupancies in high-rise buildings, and other Assembly and Hazardous occupancies. An EVACS is similar to a public address system and provides direction to the occupants during an emergency. The codes will specify speaker locations for each occupancy based on *paging zones* created within the building and, at a minimum, required paging zones at each floor, elevator group, exit stairway, and areas of refuge. It is also required to be tied to an emergency power source (see Chapter 8).

Typically activated by an automatic fire detector, a sprinkler waterflow device, or a manual fire alarm box, the EVACS will sound an alert tone followed by voice instructions. The codes allow the system to be used for other announcements as long as the fire alarm use takes precedence. The emergency message may vary. For example, occupants may be told to evacuate, relocate to another part of the building, or remain in place. Some systems may also indicate the location of the emergency. *NFPA 72* includes standards that regulate the message as well as the location of speakers so that it is clear and easily understood by the occupants.

Note

Although the building and fire codes currently reference the 2007 edition of *NFPA 72*, some jurisdictions may require the 2010 edition since it includes more information on EVACSs and MNSs.

Newer to the codes is the use of a mass notification system (MNS). Part of an emergency voice/alarm communication system, an MNS is becoming more common in large facilities with multiple buildings. Examples include college campuses and industrial complexes. Recognizing that there are other dangers (weather emergencies, terrorist threats, etc.) that building occupants must be warned about, *NFPA 72* now allows mass notification events to take priority over fire alarm signals. An MNS is unique because a wide array of technology is used to notify occupants of an emergency. A system is often integrated with other building systems and can consist of visible and tactile signals, video imaging, graphics, and text. (See the inset titled *Integrated Alarms* on page 257.) If working with an occupancy that requires an EVACS and/or an MNS, check for specific code requirements and include the necessary accessibility requirements as well. (See previous section.)

Accessible Warning Systems

Note

Some jurisdictions may allow the use of *directional sound* devices in a building to assist occupants in locating exits. These devices provide intuitively audible cues for easier egress.

As already mentioned, visual alarms were first required by the ADA for accessibility. Now, both audible and visual alarms are required by the building codes, the fire codes, and the *LSC*, as well as the *ADA Standards*. Although not currently required by the codes, additional accessible warning systems are available. The ADA does not specifically require these other types either; however, it does require that an appropriate system be provided for occupants with disabilities. The safety of the occupants using the space or building must be considered and a special type of system may be required. For example, tactile notification

INTEGRATED ALARMS

Fire safety systems and alarms can be integrated with other building controls, such as mechanical and security systems. When alarm systems are connected to a mechanical system, they can shut down the air distribution system that would spread smoke to other parts of the building. When they are connected to the security system, they can signal the unlocking of doors that are normally required for security. When they are connected to the communication system, they can initiate audible direction to the building occupants. With the use of new technology, computers, motion detectors, and closed-circuit cameras can be used to tie multiple systems together to monitor and control evacuation and monitor a fire in a more comprehensive way.

As technology changes and improves, the *NFPA 72, National Fire Alarm Code* continues to evolve to allow more options for alarm systems to become part of other building systems. (See the inset titled *Building Automation Systems* on page 356 for more information.) It also requires several safety measures to be incorporated into the integrated network. Some jurisdictions, however, may limit full integration if local fire departments are not equipped to work with the new technology.

Newer mass notification systems may also be integrated with a building's alarm system. (Requirements can be found in the 2007 and 2010 *NFPA 72*.) Designed to be more secure than the typical emergency alarm system, they are used to provide early warning to building occupants and to communicate how to behave during a variety of emergency situations. MNSs are already being used in some government and military buildings, college campuses, and other large multi-building facilities. They incorporate traditional alarm and voice-delivery systems as well as a wide variety of other technologies that can be used separately or in conjunction with each other depending on the emergency. Examples include scrolling electronic signs in more public areas, indoor paging systems, outdoor speaker systems, "pop-up" messages on computer networks, and distributed text messaging.

The development of software and products to work within an integrated system is ongoing. However, this type of system is complex and most suitable for complex projects. If designing an extensive project, collaboration with a fire-protection system designer and other engineers is typically required.

appliances that produce a vibrating sensation could be specified where a large number of occupants are seeing impaired and hearing impaired, such as those in a special school or dormitory. A visible text messaging system could also be used to assist persons with other types of disabilities. In these cases, the *ADA Standards* would be referenced for the placement and visual characteristics of audible and visual alarms. In some building types, such as hotels, the *ADA Standards* specify the percentage and distribution of rooms or units that require these systems.

With the growing influence of the ADA on safety and accessibility concerns for the disabled, new types of accessible warning systems will continue to be developed. There can sometimes be conflicts within the technical requirements between the accessibility standards and the codes. However, the greatest degree of accessibility should be provided.

EXTINGUISHING SYSTEMS

Extinguishing systems were also referred to as suppression systems in older editions of the codes. These systems provide for the control and extinguishment of fires once they occur. Like detection and alarm systems, their design and installation often need to be coordinated with other trades and professionals. Since most of them use water, a mechanical engineer usually needs to be involved as well. Typically, a fire-protection designer or an engineer will design the system and reference the appropriate codes. (See Chapter 7.)

The most common extinguishing systems include fire extinguishers, standpipes, fire hoses, and sprinkler systems. These are explained in more detail throughout this section.

Fire Extinguishers

Portable fire extinguishers are one means of fire suppression meant for use by the building occupant. Since they are movable and do not require access to plumbing lines, they are often specified by the designer on interior projects. They can be surface mounted where space allows or recessed within a wall using a special cabinet. The cabinet must either have a vision panel or be clearly marked with a sign because the fire extinguisher must be visible at all times. The fire extinguisher must also be tested and have an approved label.

Typically, it is the fire codes and the *LSC* that specify the occupancies and types of building uses that require fire extinguishers. (Beginning in 2009, the *IBC* duplicates the fire extinguisher information from the *IFC*.) The codes also refer to *NFPA 10, Standard for Portable Fire Extinguishers*, which provides more detailed

◀Note

Some fire alarm and/or emergency voice/alarm communication systems may require the use of up to 2-hour-rated cable assemblies. See Chapter 7 for additional information on low-voltage cabling.

◀Note

Both the building codes and the fire codes should be referenced when determining extinguishing systems. The fire codes often include additional requirements.

◀Note

When surface mounting a hand-held fire extinguisher, review both code and accessibility heights and projection requirements.

information, including specific numbers, sizes, and extinguisher types. Most occupancies require an extinguisher. Specific areas or rooms within a building require them as well. For example, most commercial kitchens, as well as smaller kitchens and breakrooms, require a fire extinguisher. (Other NFPA publications provide fire extinguisher requirements for special occupancies.) Some specific location requirements include the following:

- ❑ Within 30 feet (9145 mm) of commercial cooking equipment
- ❑ In areas where flammable or combustible liquids are stored, used, or dispensed
- ❑ In buildings under construction
- ❑ Where open flames are present
- ❑ In laboratories, computer rooms, generator rooms, and other special hazard areas

Fire extinguishers are available in various sizes and contain an array of substances. The type of extinguisher required will depend on the occupancy and/or contents of the space. The fire codes will typically classify a space or building as either a Class A, B, or C fire hazard. Class A is the least hazardous and the most common. In a Class A space, no occupant can be more than 75 feet (22,860 mm) from a fire extinguisher when fire extinguishers are required. (Other classes require shorter distances.) This distance as well as the overall size of the space or building will determine the final quantity and size of the extinguishers selected. (Annex E of *NFPA 10* explains how to calculate.) Ideally, extinguishers should be located along normal paths of travel. Figure 6.3 is an example of a large office space, indicating typical fire extinguisher locations in the overall space as well as in the breakroom.

The codes typically specify the maximum height of the extinguisher based on its weight, as shown in Figure 6.4. However, because a fire extinguisher is meant to be used by an occupant, it must also be accessible. It must be mounted at an accessible height and be located within accessible reach from a front or side approach, as required by the *ADA Standards* and the ICC/ANSI standard. The top of Figure 6.4 indicates the required code and accessibility heights in relation to the fire extinguisher cabinet. In addition, the extinguisher cannot protrude more than 4 inches (100 mm) into a path of travel. This may eliminate the use of bracket-mounted fire extinguishers in certain areas. Often a fire extinguisher cabinet is recessed either partially or fully into a wall. The bottom of Figure 6.4 shows two types of partially recessed cabinets. Even the pull on the cabinet needs to be within the 4 inches (100 mm).

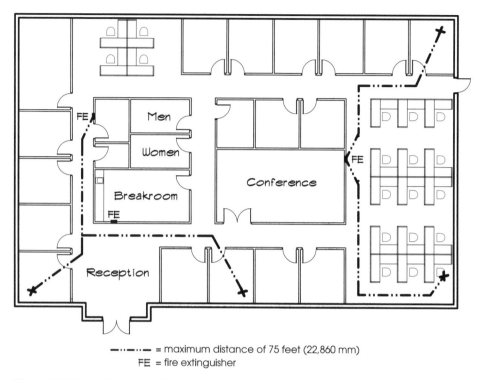

——··—··— = maximum distance of 75 feet (22,860 mm)
FE = fire extinguisher

Figure 6.3 Travel distance to fire extinguishers example.

Standpipes and Fire Hoses

Standpipes and fire hoses are typically installed during the initial construction of a building. However, they may also need to be upgraded when new work is done in an existing building. They are a manual, fixed fire system. Some are easily recognized by the glass-enclosed cabinet and the folded fire hose. Others are simply large-diameter pipes that extend vertically through a building with connections for fire hose hookup. The system supplies water for extinguishing fires and can be used by firefighters or building occupants, depending on the class and type of system.

Classes of Standpipes

Three classes of standpipes are classified by the codes. The classes are based on the purpose and intended use of the system.

1. *Class I.* Designed for fire department use or use by limited building personnel trained in its operation, Class I standpipes consist of pipes with high-pressure 2 1/2-inch (64 mm) outlets for hookup to fire department hoses.

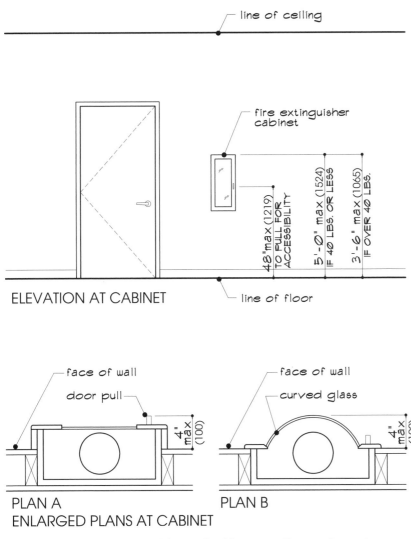

line of ceiling

fire extinguisher
cabinet

48" max (1219)
TO PULL FOR
ACCESSIBILITY

5'-0" max (1524)
IF 40 LBS. OR LESS

3'-6" max (1065)
IF OVER 40 LBS.

ELEVATION AT CABINET

line of floor

face of wall

door pull

4" max
(100)

PLAN A

face of wall

curved glass

4" max
(100)

PLAN B

ENLARGED PLANS AT CABINET

Figure 6.4 Typical fire extinguisher and cabinet-mounting requirements.

2. *Class II.* Primarily designed for building occupants, Class II standpipes have hoses attached that are usually limited to 1 1/2 inches (38 mm) in diameter or less. They are designed for small-scale fire protection and are mostly used in buildings that do not have a sprinkler system.

3. *Class III.* Class III is a combination of Class I and Class II standpipes. It is designed for use by the building occupants or the fire department. It includes both a 2 1/2-inch (64 mm) outlet for fire department hookup and a 1 1/2-inch (38 mm) outlet with a 1 1/2-inch (38 mm) hose and nozzle.

◁**Note**

A standpipe riser (e.g., pipe) may also serve as a sprinkler system riser if specific codes requirements are met.

Types of Standpipes

There are also five different types of standpipe systems:

1. *Automatic wet system.* An automatic wet system has a water supply within the piping system that is ready upon demand. It is considered the most effective and most reliable system.

2. *Automatic dry system.* An automatic dry system is normally filled with pressured air and is allowed where freezing may occur. The use of a hose valve is required to admit water into the system.

3. *Manual wet system.* A manual wet system does not have water in the pipes themselves but is connected to a water supply that must be pumped into the pipes by the fire department.

4. *Manual dry system.* A manual dry system does not have water within the pipes or in an attached supply. The water must be pumped in from a source from the fire department. It is commonly used in parking garages.

5. *Semiautomatic dry system.* A semiautomatic dry system is similar to an automatic dry system, but a remote control located at the hose connection is required to activate the valve to admit water into the system.

The type and class of a required standpipe depend on the code, the type of occupancy, the height of the building, and the presence of an automatic sprinkler system. The types of buildings that may require standpipes include multi-story buildings with or without sprinklers, high-rise buildings (see the inset titled *High-Rise Buildings* on page 121), storage buildings, and certain other spaces. Also, large stages within any building type must have a standpipe.

Each code sets slightly different requirements for standpipes. These requirements are included in the building codes and fire codes. The codes also refer to the standard *NFPA 14, Installation of Standpipes and Hose Systems,* which further specifies the number, type, and locations of standpipes. When required, a standpipe is typically located at each floor level in an exit stair enclosure, on each side of a wall adjacent to the opening of a horizontal exit, and at the entrance of an exit passageway. Not only does this provide easy access, it also provides fire protection for 1 to 2 hours. Class II standpipes may require additional locations for accurate coverage with the fire hose. Since Class II and Class III standpipes are meant for use by building occupants, placing the fire hose cabinet so that it is accessible also becomes important. Both the pull to the cabinet and the operable parts in the cabinet should be at accessible heights and reach ranges.

Sprinkler Systems

Automatic sprinkler systems are invaluable in the containment of a fire. Research shows that the number of lives lost during a fire is greatly reduced when automatic sprinklers are present. As a result, more occupancies and use groups are required to install automatic sprinkler systems where previously these systems were optional. In fact, both the ICC codes and the NFPA codes now require sprinkler systems in one- and two-family homes. (See Appendix D.) In addition, when an automatic sprinkler system is installed, the codes allow trade-offs in other aspects of a design. For example, when an automatic sprinkler system is provided within an incidental use room, the 1-hour separation is often not required. (Refer to the section Sprinkler Design Issues later in this chapter for additional trade-offs.)

Automatic sprinklers are devices that are sensitive to heat. Most commonly, only the sprinkler heads directly exposed to the heat will activate and release water. (In some cases, especially with older systems, all the sprinklers in the system may release water.) Other sprinkler systems may be wired to and activated by a smoke or fire alarm. In fact, most sprinkler systems are required to be tied into an alarm system so that the occupants, the appropriate building personnel, and the fire department are notified of the emergency should a sprinkler activate. Although water damage may occur from the release of water by the sprinkler system (5 to 25 gallons or 19 to 95 liters/minute, depending on the type of sprinkler), it will be considerably less than the damage that would occur if the fire department had to extinguish the fire with a fire hose (200 to 250 gallons or 757 to 946 liters/minute).

The NFPA is the main source for sprinkler requirements. *NFPA 13, Standard for Installation of Sprinkler Systems,* is the standard most often referenced by the codes and is used throughout the country. It lists detailed design and installation requirements, and references a number of other NFPA standards. (Other sprinkler standards are shown in Figure 6.1.) However, it is the building codes, the fire codes, and the *LSC* that specify when an automatic sprinkler system is required. Each code specifies the types of occupancies, types of buildings, and special rooms that generally require sprinklers. The type of construction may also make a difference. In buildings with more than one occupancy, the codes will specify the fire-rated construction required between each occupancy.

Uses and Occupancies Requiring Sprinkler Systems

When certain conditions exist, almost any occupancy can be required to have an automatic sprinkler system. However, each occupancy also has exceptions for

◁ **Note**

Since automatic sprinklers have been in use since the beginning of the twentieth century, some older buildings may have systems that are considered antiquated. Ultimately, a code official must decide whether an old system needs to be replaced to meet current code requirements.

◁ **Note**

Depending on the occupancy, the amount of hazards, and the type of system, most sprinkler systems require each sprinkler head to cover and protect 90 to 200 square feet (8.4 to 18.6 s m). The typical distance between the sprinkler heads ranges from 12 to 15 feet (3658 to 4572 mm). It is usually up to the sprinkler designer or engineer to determine the exact requirements.

◀ Note

In recent years, some existing building types have been required to add a sprinkler system. These include hospitals, nursing homes, and high-rise buildings.

when an automatic sprinkler system is not required. The size of the space, the number of occupants, the mobility of the occupants, the height and area of the overall building, the types of hazards present, and sometimes the capacity of the local fire department all factor into when the fire and building codes require sprinklers.

Occupancies that typically require sprinkler systems include Assembly, Health Care, and Hazardous occupancies, as well as other occupancies with large square footages (s m). The codes now require them in many Residential occupancies as well. (See Appendix D.) Certain building types are also required to have sprinkler systems. These are shown below. In addition, incidental accessory occupancies, as discussed in Chapter 5 (see Figure 5.8), are often allowed to use an automatic sprinkler system in place of fire-resistance-rated construction. Many of these are listed below as well. In each case, refer to the code for the specific requirements.

Building Types
- ❑ Aircraft hangars
- ❑ Amusement buildings
- ❑ Parking garages
- ❑ Covered malls
- ❑ High-rise buildings
- ❑ Underground structures
- ❑ Unlimited area buildings
- ❑ Windowless story

Special Rooms and Areas
- ❑ Atriums
- ❑ Commercial kitchen exhaust hood and duct systems
- ❑ Drying rooms
- ❑ Duct systems exhausting hazardous materials
- ❑ Furnace and boiler rooms
- ❑ Laboratories and vocational shops
- ❑ Laundry rooms over 100 square feet (9.29 s m)
- ❑ Incinerator rooms
- ❑ Rooms with hazardous materials
- ❑ Smoke-protected assembly seating
- ❑ Spray-painting shops or booths

❏ Stages

❏ Tops of rubbish and linen chutes (additional if three or more floors)

❏ Unenclosed vertical openings

❏ Waste and linen collection rooms over 100 square feet (9.29 s m)

Other common locations for sprinklers depend on the design. Unique situations often call for additional sprinkler locations. For example, if a continuous glass assembly is used as a rated wall, additional sprinkler heads may be required on both sides of the wall. Even using some finishes, such as light-transmitting plastic (see Chapter 9), may require the use of additional sprinkler heads.

Types of Sprinkler Systems

An engineer typically determines which type of sprinkler system to use. Using the codes and the NFPA standards, the engineer also determines the size and number of pipes and the spacing of the sprinkler heads. Although *NFPA 13* recognizes seven types of automatic sprinkler systems, most systems are one of these four types:

1. *Wet pipe system*: A wet pipe system is the most common system. It uses water to extinguish a fire and consists of pipes that are water filled at all times. When a fire occurs, the heat from the fire activates the sprinkler. The heat melts the fuse link, causing water to discharge immediately. This type is typically considered the most effective and is used most often.

2. *Dry pipe system*: A dry pipe system is used in unheated building types such as storage facilities and parking garages as well as other areas such as attics and freezers. They are used to prevent freezing. Instead of water, the pipes are filled with pressurized air or nitrogen. When activated by the heat of a fire, the air is released and water floods the pipes to extinguish the fire.

3. *Deluge system*: A deluge system is an open-head water system. It is usually activated by a separate detection system (sometimes a controlled system) and is used in hazardous situations. The deluge system discharges large quantities of water to control severe fires. In areas where large quantities of water are not desirable (e.g., electrical situations), it can be used in conjunction with other agents.

4. *Preaction system*: A preaction system is a combination of wet and dry systems to allow delayed reaction and warning signals. Like the deluge system, it is activated by a detection system. The delayed reaction allows the system to be manually intercepted and turned off if the sprinklers are not necessary. It is used primarily in areas where property is susceptible to water damage (e.g., museums) or where sprinkler pipes are likely to get damaged.

Both wet and dry systems require the same piping. The risers supply the water from the building's incoming water supply to the cross mains at each floor. The cross mains supply the branch lines. Sprinkler heads are located at the end of each branch line.

Types of Sprinkler Heads

Sprinkler heads vary by how quickly they respond to a fire, the size of the orifice, and the distribution of water, as well as other special features. The orientation of the head also makes a difference in its effect. The most common orientations include pendant, upright, sidewall, recessed, and concealed. Figure 6.5 explains these orientation styles and their uses. The orientation of the head is typically determined by the design or construction requirements, the location of the head, and the area it is meant to cover. For example, a finished ceiling will require a sprinkler head with a different orientation than an exposed or open ceiling. In some cases, a wall-mounted head will allow better coverage. Following are the most common types of sprinkler heads. (New types of sprinklers are constantly being developed to address the specific needs of building uses and design ideas.)

1. *Standard spray head*: This is the most common type of sprinkler head. It can be used in most occupancies and building uses. Each head can typically cover approximately 225 square feet (20.9 s m).

2. *Fast-response sprinkler head*: This type is activated by a low level of heat. The name is somewhat misleading since it does not mean that this system will respond more quickly than other systems. Response time is affected by ceiling height, spacing, ambient room temperature, and distance below the ceiling. However, it may activate earlier because it requires less heat. Sprinkler systems described as early-suppression and quick-response types typically use fast-response sprinkler heads.

3. *Residential sprinkler head*: This type is not typically intended to extinguish the fire. Instead, it minimizes the heat buildup and the production of carbon monoxide, which reduces the toxicity of the space while the occupants are exiting. They have a unique spray pattern different from that of standard or quick-response sprinklers and are often recessed when used in Residential occupancies. Although designed for *NFPA 13D* systems, they can also be used in *NFPA 13R* and *NFPA 13* systems as allowed by code. (See Figure 6.1.)

4. *Quick-response sprinkler head*: Sometimes residential and quick-response sprinklers are thought to be the same type. However, they have different uses, spray patterns, and designs. Quick-response heads can be used in Residential and Commercial occupancies as allowed by the codes.

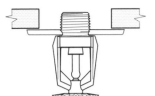

PENDANT
the head is surface mounted and
extends below the finished ceiling,
most commonly used in finished
ceilings and suspended ceiling tiles

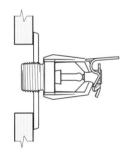

UPRIGHT
the head is fully exposed and sits
above the branch 'feed lines' that
supply the water, typically used in
spaces with high or unfinished ceilings

SIDEWALL
the head is surface mounted to a
finished wall, commonly used in corridors
and small rooms where one head or one
row will adequately cover the area
(also available to be mounted recessed)

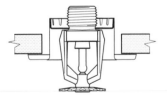

RECESSED
the head is partially recessed into
the ceiling, the depth of the recess
can vary but the lower portion of the
head is always exposed, often used
in residential occupancies

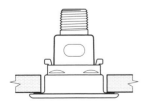

CONCEALED
the head is fully recessed and includes
a cover that hides the fusible element
so that you cannot see it, the cover falls
off when a fire occurs to allow the head
to activate and disperse water, often
used in decorative ceilings

Figure 6.5 Orientation of sprinkler heads (Line drawings reprinted with permission
from Viking Group [www.vikingcorp.com]).

⬛ Note

A more recent development in fire suppression is a water mist system that produces a fine spray that leaves little residual water.

⬛ Note

Some manufacturers now offer flexible sprinkler head connections that attach to the end of a cross main or branch pipe. Designed for use in suspended ceilings, they are easier to relocate when the layout of a space changes.

⬛ Note

When ceiling finishes consist of combustible materials such as light-transmitting plastic or fabric panels, the codes typically require sprinkler heads to be installed in the ceiling as well as in the deck above the ceiling finish.

5. *Extended coverage sprinkler head*: These heads have a spray pattern that can cover up to 400 square feet (37.2 s m), requiring fewer heads but higher water pressure and water flow rate. These are often used in large open areas. Some can be considered quick response.

6. *Large-drop sprinkler head*: These heads deliver water in large droplets and are often used in occupancies where a fire may be difficult to suppress, such as a large storage facility.

7. *Open sprinkler head*: These heads are used in deluge systems. The heads remain open and are not activated by their own heat detector but by a separate detector. These systems are often monitored or controlled. When activated, the heads release large amounts of water. They are used in areas where a severe fire could occur.

8. *Specialty sprinkler head*: Specialty sprinklers are available for other needs of a space, such as tamper-resistant or corrosion-resistant sprinklers. In addition, many new types of sprinkler heads are available for specific design criteria to meet both functional requirements and aesthetic needs. Decorative sprinkler heads with custom colors, flush or low profiles, and other similar features are available. Different types of cover plates can also be used to conceal recessed sprinkler heads. These may be especially desirable in lobbies, conference rooms, and living areas where other types would distract from the design of the space.

Sprinkler Design Issues

Although adding a sprinkler system is expensive, it usually saves money in other areas of construction. The codes allow automatic sprinkler systems as a trade-off for other code requirements. It may be a major trade-off, such as constructing a larger building, or a smaller trade-off, such as not having to rate a wall. For example, in some occupancies, the corridor walls are not required to be rated if the building is sprinklered. Other common sprinkler trade-offs are listed in Figure 6.6. Before using one of these trade-offs, refer to the specific codes and confirm it is allowed by the local jurisdiction. Also, remember that an existing sprinkler system must typically meet the current code requirements of an automatic sprinkler system before any of the sprinkler trade-offs can be used.

For interior projects, the most significant design issues include the selection of the type(s) of sprinkler system and sprinkler heads and the layout of the sprinkler heads. These decisions are based on the actual situation, as well as the code requirements. For instance, the configuration of the space and the desired coverage determine the layout of the sprinkler heads. The ceiling

BUILDING AREA
May allow some buildings to increase in size horizontally, resulting in more square feet per building.

BUILDING HEIGHT
May allow one story to be added to the height of a building.

CONSTRUCTION TYPES
May allow a less fire-resistant construction type.

MEANS OF EGRESS
May allow an increase in the distance of travel from the most remote point to the exit; allow certain escalators not to be enclosed; allow certain exit stairs and accessible elevators not to have an area of refuge; allow longer dead-end corridors.

FIRE AND SMOKE SEPARATION
May allow up to three floor levels of stairways and other openings between floors not to be fully enclosed; eliminate separate means of venting smoke in elevators; omit fire dampers; reduce number of draftstops; allow larger areas of glazing; lower fire-ratings of assemblies; lower rating of opening protectives; allow less compartmentation in high-rise buildings.

FIRE PROTECTION
May reduce number of fire and/or smoke alarms; reduce number of fire extinguishers; eliminate or reduce number of standpipes.

INTERIOR FINISHES AND FURNISHING
May allow a lower class rating of a finish; eliminate firestops behind raised finishes; allow additional foam plastic insulation; allow additional decorative trim; allow lower furniture ratings.

NOTE: An existing sprinkler system must typically meet the most current code requirements of an automatic sprinkler system before any of the sprinkler trade-offs listed above can be used. Consult with a code official when necessary.

Figure 6.6 Common sprinkler trade-offs.

◀ **Note**

Before using any of the allowed sprinkler trade-offs, confirm that the building or space has an approved automatic sprinkler system, as defined by the code used in the local jurisdiction

height and type of ceiling may also affect the layout, as will the type of desired head and head orientation. For example, different types will be used if the ceiling is sloped, horizontal, smooth, or coffered. An exposed ceiling versus a finish ceiling also makes a difference. For many projects, these will be determined in conjunction with an engineer or fire-protection (sprinkler) designer as they design the overall sprinkler system based on the layout and design of the space. Specialty sprinkler heads in certain areas, such as lobbies or conference rooms, may also be used for aesthetic reasons.

◀ **Note**

In a multi-story building, it is possible to have a sprinkler system installed in one story and not another.

Note

A project may have more than one type of sprinkler head, such as a concealed head in a decorative ceiling and an exposed pendant in less public areas.

Familiarity with common sprinkler layout parameters is important so that other aspects of the design, such as lighting, ceiling grids, decorative ceiling elements, and furr downs, can be coordinated. It is a good idea to coordinate these items with the sprinkler designer early in a project. For example, a sprinkler head typically requires a clearance of 18 inches (457 mm) below the deflector. The location of partial-height walls, tall furniture, shelving, or cabinetry can block the coverage of some sprinkler heads. In addition, any obstruction that exceeds 4 feet (1219 mm) in width may require an additional sprinkler head to be installed in or under the obstruction. This can include such things as a large air duct in an exposed ceiling, a decorative ceiling panel, or a kiosk or specialty display. The use of specialty sprinklers may require additional clearances. (See the codes and *NFPA 13* for more information.)

Changes to an existing space can also affect the proper layout of the sprinkler heads. If the occupancy classification in a space has changed, the existing layout of sprinklers may not be adequate. The addition or removal of walls may affect the required sprinkler head locations needed for proper coverage, or the addition of a suspended ceiling may require a change in the type of sprinkler head. In addition, if making changes to an existing space, the existing sprinkler system or layout may not be compliant with the most current codes for that occupancy classification or space. The effect of modifications to a sprinklered space should always be considered in the design. Collaborate with a system designer to coordinate these issues, or for small projects work closely with a licensed contractor.

Note

In some locations, drapes and blinds on windows and glass walls may affect the performance of a sprinkler system.

Alternative Extinguishing Systems

Sprinklers may not be appropriate in every situation. Fires can begin in enclosed spaces or in locations where they are shielded from the sprinkler head. Other fires ignite and travel too quickly. In some cases, the fire should not be extinguished with water. For example, restaurant kitchens and other rooms with the potential for a grease fire should limit the use of water as an extinguisher. It is also best not to use sprinklers close to large electrical equipment such as the computer and telephone equipment found in telecommunication rooms. Other buildings that contain extremely valuable items, such as libraries and museums, will want to limit water damage and may eliminate sprinklers, limit their use, or use an alternative extinguishing system.

When a sprinkler system does not use water, the system is often referred to as *non-water-based fire extinguishing.* Alternate systems include wet-chemical, dry-chemical, foam, carbon dioxide, halon, and clean-agent extinguishing materials. Each agent may have a separate standard it must meet, many of which are listed in Figure 6.1. The codes generally allow the code official to approve the appropriate

Note

If working on a project in which a sprinkler system may be inappropriate, research other fire-extinguishing systems, as well as automatic fire-detection systems.

alternative agent. This allows the designer and the client to propose the best agent for the situation.

In the past, systems that discharged halon were widely used in situations where a water-based system was not desirable. But since halon has been determined to contribute to the erosion of the ozone layer, it is no longer produced. Halon systems that are properly maintained in existing buildings may remain in use. However, a space that undergoes significant changes is typically required to replace the halon with a clean-agent alternative such as halocarbon or inert gas.

SUSTAINABILITY CONSIDERATIONS

Fire detection and suppression systems are critical to life safety and their requirements are comprehensively covered by other codes and standards. These systems are not typically part of the sustainability codes and standards. It could be argued, however, that an automatic sprinkler system benefits the environment. When used to suppress a fire, a sprinkler system minimizes toxic gases created by the fire, saves existing building materials so that less waste enters landfills, and uses much less water than conventional firefighting.

Currently, the *International Green Construction Code (IGCC)* offers a compliance elective that allows an automatic sprinkler system to be supplied with non-potable water from an on-site rainwater collection system. A code jurisdiction can require this elective for certain types of projects in their jurisdiction, or, depending on the jurisdiction, a project designer may be able to select this elective for a specific project. If selected, the sprinkler system would also require emergency power for the pump and controls at the collection system as well as a device that monitors the volume of water.

The fire protection industry is also starting to incorporate sustainable practices. For example, many sprinkler manufacturers now indicate how much recycled content is used in their sprinklers, valves, and fittings. And, newer systems are being developed that use less water and more earth-friendly alternate agents (e.g., biodegradable foam).

CHECKLIST

Figure 6.7 is a fire-protection checklist that can be used on your interior projects or as a guideline to make your own checklist. It indicates each main type of detection, alarm, and extinguishing system required by the codes. The checklist can be used to remind you of what to look for and research on a project, as well as

◢Note

If a building or space is required by the codes to have sprinklers, sprinklers are also typically required in the electrical room and the communications room. It is usually the local code official that decides if an alternative extinguishing system can be used.

◢Note

When testing a sprinkler system, sustainable practices can be put into place to recycle or reuse the water that is flushed through the system.

Fire Protection Checklist

Date: _____

Project Name: _____   Space: _____

Main Occupancy (new or existing): _____

Type of Construction: _____

REQUIRED FIRE PROTECTION (check those that apply)	EXT'G (yes/no)	LOCATION(S) IN BUILDING	TYPE OF SYSTEM/ITEM REQUIRED (list information)	QUANTITIES REQUIRED (new or add'l)
Detection Systems Engineer Required? ___ YES ___ NO __ Smoke Detectors(s) __ Heat Detector(s) __ Manual Fire Alarm(s) __ Other: _____				

Alarm Systems
 	
Engineer Required? ___ YES ___ NO
__ Visual/Audible Alarm(s)
    __ Audible only
    __ Visual only
__ Emergency Voice/Alarm Communication System(s) (EVACS)
__ Accessible Warning System(s)
__ Other: _____				

Extinguishing Systems
 	
Engineer Required? ___ YES ___ NO
__ Fire Extinguisher(s)
__ Fire Extinguisher Cabinet(s)
__ Standpipe(s)
__ Fire Hose(s)
__ Sprinkler System(s)
    __ Types of Head(s)
    __ Orientation of Head(s)
__ Alternative Extinguishing System(s)
__ Other: _____				

NOTES:

1. Refer to codes and standards for specific information as well as *ADA Standards* and ICC/ANSI standard for additional requirements.
2. If an automatic sprinkler system is used, make sure it is approved and check for possible code trade-offs.
3. Consult and coordinate detection/alarm systems with electrical engineers and extinguishing systems with mechanical engineers.
4. Note on floor plans the location of fire-rated walls and floor/ceilings for placement of required fire dampers and firestops.

Figure 6.7 Fire-protection checklist.

to give you a place to record the necessary code information for future reference. Remember, however, that it must be used in conjunction with the codes and standards required in your jurisdiction, as well as the *ADA Standards* and other accessibility requirements.

The checklist begins with the standard blanks for the project and space name, the occupancy classification, and the construction type of the building. (If necessary, refer to Chapters 2 and 3 to determine these.) The remainder of the checklist lists the types of detection, alarm, and extinguishing systems. To the left of each component is a blank space so that you can check off the systems required in your project. For example, if you are using alarms, some may need to be both visual and audible. Others may need to be only visual. Check only those that apply.

Then, for each component that is required, fill in the necessary information. If the system or component already exists in the building, make a note in the "Existing" column. This will be helpful when you need to match existing conditions. Use the next column to indicate the location of the system. For example, indicate which areas of the building or space require a sprinkler system. You may want to use a separate checklist for different areas of a building or attach a copy of a floor plan locating the devices.

The next two columns are for you to indicate the specific types of systems or components and quantities that may be required. Use the lists and figures in the text to help you. For example, for sprinkler systems you might list a wet pipe system with standard spray as the type of head and pendant/concealed as the orientation of the head. If an emergency voice/alarm communication system (EVACS) or other integrated system is being used, you can list the predominant components such as loud speakers, scrolling signs, and computer pop-ups. You can also note any specific accessibility requirements in this column or on the back of the checklist.

As you are filling out the checklist, consult with the appropriate engineer or other experts to determine the exact requirements necessary for your project. Other protection-related systems and/or devices may be required as well, especially with the trend toward more building security and the importance of Homeland Security. A code jurisdiction or building owner may request additional items such as multi-sensor detectors, a mass notification system (MNS), tactile notification appliances, or multi-colored light strobes. In the future, the codes will address more of these issues, but in the meantime, additional efforts may be required for the protection of a building's occupants.

CHAPTER 7

PLUMBING AND MECHANICAL REQUIREMENTS

This chapter covers two separate code items—plumbing codes and mechanical codes. Unlike most of the codes already discussed in the previous chapters, the mechanical and plumbing codes address issues that concentrate on health and welfare concerns instead of life safety.

Interior projects that include major plumbing or mechanical work will usually require collaboration with a professional engineer who should know and incorporate these codes. (Whether an engineer is involved depends on the amount of work that needs to be done and the code jurisdiction's rules regarding the use of a licensed engineer.) On smaller projects that do not require the services of an engineer, such as adding a breakroom sink or moving a supply vent, a licensed plumbing or mechanical contractor will know the requirements that apply. However, when designing an interior project, it is important to know certain requirements in each code. Examples include knowing how to determine the quantity of plumbing fixtures required in a project and how to correctly locate them in a space, and being aware of how a design affects various components of a mechanical system.

The codes, standards, and federal requirements for plumbing and mechanical systems will be discussed throughout this chapter. The first part of the chapter is dedicated to the plumbing codes required for interior projects. It covers the quantities and types of plumbing fixtures and plumbing facilities required by the codes and discusses the accessibility standards for each. It concludes with a discussion of plumbing-related sustainability requirements. The second part of the chapter discusses the main types of mechanical systems and the codes and standards that affect the various components, followed by a section that covers mechanical-related sustainability issues. The last part of the chapter introduces

Note

Life safety is becoming more of an issue for plumbing and mechanical systems with the possibility of chemical, biological, or radiological threats to a building.

Note

Requirements for other plumbing-related items such as sprinklers and standpipes (as discussed in Chapter 6) are found in the building codes and other standards.

Note

Whether an engineer is required depends on the jurisdiction of the project. Each jurisdiction has specific requirements for professional services and stamped drawings. (See Chapter 10.)

a checklist that incorporates the various plumbing and mechanical requirements discussed throughout the chapter.

COMPARING PLUMBING CODES

There are two main plumbing codes. The *International Plumbing Code (IPC)*, published by the International Code Council (ICC), is the most widely used plumbing code. The National Fire Protection Association (NFPA) collaborates with the International Association of Plumbing and Mechanical Officials (IAPMO) to publish the *Uniform Plumbing Code (UPC)*. (This is not to be confused with the legacy code with the same title.) In addition, the Plumbing-Heating-Cooling Contractors Association continues to publish its *National Standard Plumbing Code (NSPC)*, which may be in use in some jurisdictions. Verify which plumbing code a jurisdiction enforces.

The plumbing codes cover all parts of a plumbing system and include requirements for such things as water supply and distribution, water heaters, and sanitary and storm drainage, as well as vent, trap, and interceptor requirements. (See the inset titled *Plumbing Systems* on page 278.) The codes also reference multiple industry standards. The chapter most often referenced in the *IPC* when designing an interior space is the chapter on plumbing fixtures. In the *IPC* this chapter is titled "Fixtures, Faucets and Fixture Fittings." It describes the types of fixtures and their requirements and supplies a table that indicates the number and types of plumbing fixtures required for each occupancy classification or building type. This table is discussed later in this chapter. (Water consumption requirements are in a separate chapter.)

The plumbing codes are not the only resource for plumbing requirements. The building codes also have a chapter dedicated to plumbing-related requirements. For example, the *International Building Code (IBC)* has a chapter titled "Plumbing Systems." For the most part, these short chapters refer to their respective plumbing codes and other standards for additional requirements. The *IBC* also duplicates the minimum toilet facility requirements and the plumbing fixture table found in the *IPC*. In addition, the "Interior Environment" chapter of the *IBC* includes a short section on materials for toilet and bathing facilities. Other plumbing-related items such as sprinkler systems, standpipes, fire hoses, and fire extinguishers (as discussed in Chapter 6) are covered in other sections of the building codes specific to fire protection. These sections often refer to various standards as well.

Additional plumbing requirements will be found in the energy codes and the newer sustainability codes. The energy requirements are mandated by the

---

◀Note

On projects that require minimal plumbing work, such as adding a small toilet facility, the mechanical contractor may be able to work directly from the construction drawings or supply plumbing "shop" drawings.

◀Note

In 2007, Underwriters Laboratories (UL) introduced a new UL Plumbing Mark for plumbing fixtures. Products bearing this mark demonstrate compliance with the *IPC* and the *IBC*.

federal government. (See Chapter 1.) The use of a sustainability code or standard will depend on the jurisdiction of the project. Some clients may also want sustainability addressed in the design of their building or space. These codes can affect the fixtures selected as well as the overall design of the plumbing system and will be described in more detail in the section Plumbing Sustainability Considerations later in this chapter.

Depending on the project, the performance codes may also need to be referenced. When using the *IPC* and other corresponding I-Codes, plumbing-related performance criteria will be found in the *ICC Performance Code* (*ICCPC*), which has a chapter dedicated to plumbing. Its sections include personal hygiene, laundering, domestic water supplies, and wastewater. The *UPC*, on the other hand, has some alternate materials and methods provisions within the code but does not include a performance chapter. Instead, the performance chapter in other applicable NFPA codes should be referenced for related performance criteria.

Specific accessibility requirements must be followed when selecting and locating plumbing fixtures. Both the Americans with Disabilities Act (ADA) standards and the ICC/ANSI accessibility standard *ICC/ANSI A117.1* provide similar requirements. Accessibility requirements are also found in the accessibility chapter of the building codes. The building codes then reference the ICC/ANSI standard for specifics. When used together, they include such things as minimum clearances, location requirements, ease of control use, and other accessibility standards. These accessibility requirements are discussed in this chapter as they apply to various plumbing fixtures, plumbing facilities, and other related items. Note, however, that the accessibility requirements in each document are not always the same. (Some of the differences will be described throughout this chapter, with the most stringent requirements used in each diagram. Consult original sources when required.)

NUMBER OF PLUMBING FIXTURES

Determining the number of plumbing fixtures is the first step when designing an interior project that requires them. The number of plumbing fixtures required by the codes must be calculated when there is new construction, when a building addition is made, and when an occupancy classification changes. The number of water closets, urinals, lavatories, sinks, drinking fountains, bathtubs, showers, and other required plumbing fixtures will affect the types of toileting and/or bathing facilities required in each project. Typically, the number of *fixtures* needs to be known before the type or number of *facilities* can be determined. The total number of fixtures will also affect how many are required to be accessible.

All these factors will affect the design. For example, the number of standard and accessible water closets will affect the size of a restroom or toilet facility, and the type of drinking fountain may affect the width or shape of a corridor. The plumbing code table is explained first, followed by a discussion of other code and accessibility requirements. Requirements for each fixture and how to use them together for the necessary toileting and bathing facilities will be discussed in the next sections.

PLUMBING SYSTEMS

Most plumbing systems can be broken down into three main components:

1. *Drainage system:* This part of the plumbing system is usually referred to as the *drain-waste-vent (DWV)* system. It consists of wide pipes, since it operates on gravity, starting at the plumbing fixture and ending at the public sewage system. It consists of three parts. *Traps* are used at the discharge of each fixture to prevent odors, gases, and insects from entering the building. Branch and stack *pipes* are required to transport the used water from the trap to the sewer. (It is a *soil stack* if it carries solid human waste and *a waste stack* if it carries other wastes.) And vertical stack *vents* penetrate the roof of a building and allow harmful gases to escape as water is discharged.

2. *Water supply system:* This system consists of small-diameter pipes that use pressure to convey hot and cold water. First is the *main water line,* which brings water into the building from the public water system. Once in the building, it splits into two *distribution lines*. One leads cold water directly to the plumbing fixtures, and the other leads to a water heating system before it is distributed to a fixture. The water supply system is controlled by valves located both at the entry into the building and at each fixture.

3. *Plumbing fixtures:* The fixtures are the beginning of the drainage system and the end source for the water supply system. They consist of water closets, lavatories, urinals, sinks, drinking fountains, bathtubs, showers, dishwashers, clothes washers, and other miscellaneous fixtures.

With the development of newer sustainable plumbing systems, some of these components may vary. For example, a building may include a graywater system, which consists of waste flows from lavatories and hand-washing sinks, bathtubs and showers, and clothes-washing machines. These systems use separate drainage pipes to collect this reclaimed water (and sometimes rainwater as well) for reuse in water closets, urinals, and subsurface irrigation; it will use public water for these functions only if additional water is needed. A waterless urinal is another example. Instead if a traditional trap which requires water, this plumbing fixture uses a special cartridge or liquid to contain sewer gases.

The Code Table

The number and type of plumbing fixtures required are determined by a table in the plumbing code. Each plumbing code has a table similar to the *IPC* Table 403.1, "Minimum Number of Required Plumbing Fixtures," shown in Figure 7.1. (The same table is also repeated in the *IBC* as Table 2902.1.) For each occupancy classification, the table lists the number of water closets, lavatories, bathtubs or showers, drinking fountains, and other miscellaneous fixtures, such as service sinks and washing machines, required by the codes. The number of required fixtures per person is based on the occupant load within the building or space. Typically, every floor in a building will require at least one toilet or restroom, but the actual number of fixtures and facilities depends on the type of occupancy and the number of occupants. In addition, some tenant spaces may want their own toilet facilities even if they are not required by the code. For example, an executive might want a private bathroom. In other cases, the code may require an additional facility to be added if a tenant or occupant does not have access to the common building facilities. For example, a guard station separate from the main building may need its own restroom.

The calculated occupant load depends on the occupancy classification of the space or building and is determined using the building code. (See Chapter 2 for more information on occupant loads.) Once the occupant load for the space or building is known, the plumbing fixture table is used to determine the number and type of plumbing fixtures required. Before calculating, however, the 2009 *IPC* specifies that the total number of occupants be divided in half, so that 50 percent represents the male occupants and 50 percent represents the female occupants. (Previous editions did not specify this so the fixture count could be obtained in more than one way, resulting in various counts.) Once the occupant load it divided in half, the fixture ratios in the table are used to do the calculations. If the calculated fixture total results in a fraction, *round up* to the nearest whole number.

For example, if designing a school that will have 680 occupants, the first step is to divide this total number in half to represent 340 males and 340 females. Then, refer to the Educational (E) occupancy section of the table in Figure 7.1. It requires one water closet for every 50 people. By dividing 340 by 50 and rounding up, the fixtures require include a minimum of 7 water closets for men and 7 water closets for women. Continuing across the *IPC* table, the school in this example would require the same number of lavatories for each sex, 7 drinking fountains, and 1 service sink. These numbers would then be used to design the appropriate plumbing facilities for the school.

The plumbing fixture table should be used in conjunction with the other plumbing and fixture requirements specified in the plumbing code chapter. For

◀ Note

Remember that the plumbing fixture tables specify *minimum* requirements. It may be practical to include more fixtures, especially in Assembly occupancies, where it is normal for large groups of people to use the restrooms all at the same time, such as during intermissions.

◀ Note

In previous editions of the code, the total occupant load was used to determine the number of plumbing fixtures. This total was then divided between males and females and rounded up when necessary. The 2009 *IPC* clarifies that the total occupant load be divided in half before doing the calculations, which, because of rounding up, can cause a slightly different result.

NO.	CLASSIFICATION	OCCUPANCY	DESCRIPTION	WATER CLOSETS (URINALS SEE SECTION 419.2)		LAVATORIES		BATHTUBS/ SHOWERS	DRINKING FOUNTAIN[e,f] (SEE SECTION 410.1)	OTHER
				MALE	FEMALE	MALE	FEMALE			
1	Assembly	A-1[d]	Theaters and other buildings for the performing arts and motion pictures	1 per 125	1 per 65	1 per 200		—	1 per 500	1 service sink
		A-2[d]	Nightclubs, bars, taverns, dance halls and buildings for similar purposes	1 per 40	1 per 40	1 per 75		—	1 per 500	1 service sink
			Restaurants, banquet halls and food courts	1 per 75	1 per 75	1 per 200		—	1 per 500	1 service sink
		A-3[d]	Auditoriums without permanent seating, art galleries, exhibition halls, museums, lecture halls, libraries, arcades and gymnasiums	1 per 125	1 per 65	1 per 200		—	1 per 500	1 service sink
			Passenger terminals and transportation facilities	1 per 500	1 per 500	1 per 750		—	1 per 1,000	1 service sink
			Places of worship and other religious services.	1 per 150	1 per 75	1 per 200		—	1 per 1,000	1 service sink
		A-4	Coliseums, arenas, skating rinks, pools and tennis courts for indoor sporting events and activities	1 per 75 for the first 1,500 and 1 per 120 for the remainder exceeding 1,500	1 per 40 for the first 1,520 and 1 per 60 for the remainder exceeding 1,520	1 per 200	1 per 150	—	1 per 1,000	1 service sink
		A-5	Stadiums, amusement parks, bleachers and grandstands for outdoor sporting events and activities	1 per 75 for the first 1,500 and 1 per 120 for the remainder exceeding 1,500	1 per 40 for the first 1,520 and 1 per 60 for the remainder exceeding 1,520	1 per 200	1 per 150	—	1 per 1,000	1 service sink
2	Business	B	Buildings for the transaction of business, professional services, other services involving merchandise, office buildings, banks, light industrial and similar uses	1 per 25 for the first 50 and 1 per 50 for the remainder exceeding 50		1 per 40 for the first 80 and 1 per 80 for the remainder exceeding 80		—	1 per 100	1 service sink
3	Educational	E	Educational facilities	1 per 50		1 per 50		—	1 per 100	1 service sink
4	Factory and industrial	F-1 and F-2	Structures in which occupants are engaged in work fabricating, assembly or processing of products or materials	1 per 100		1 per 100		(see Section 411)	1 per 400	1 service sink
5	Institutional	I-1	Residential care	1 per 10		1 per 10		1 per 8	1 per 100	1 service sink
			Hospitals, ambulatory nursing home patients[b]	1 per room[c]		1 per room[c]		1 per 15	1 per 100	1 service sink per floor

Figure 7.1 *International Plumbing Code® (IPC®)* Table 403.1, Minimum Number of Required Plumbing Fixtures (*2009 International Plumbing Code*, copyright 2009. Washington, DC: International Code Council. All rights reserved. www.iccsafe.org).

| NO. | CLASSIFICATION | OCCUPANCY | DESCRIPTION | WATER CLOSETS (URINALS SEE SECTION 419.2) | | LAVATORIES | | BATHTUBS/ SHOWERS | DRINKING FOUNTAIN[e,f] (SEE SECTION 410.1) | OTHER |
				MALE	FEMALE	MALE	FEMALE			
		I-2	Employees, other than residential care[b]	1 per 25		1 per 35		—	1 per 100	—
			Visitors, other than residential care	1 per 75		1 per 100		—	1 per 500	—
		I-3	Prisons[b]	1 per cell		1 per cell		1 per 15	1 per 100	1 service sink
			Reformitories, detention centers, and correctional centers[b]	1 per 15		1 per 15		1 per 15	1 per 100	1 service sink
			Employees[b]	1 per 25		1 per 35		—	1 per 100	—
		I-4	Adult day care and child care	1 per 15		1 per 15		—	1 per 100	1 service sink
6	Mercantile	M	Retail stores, service stations, shops, salesrooms, markets and shopping centers	1 per 500		1 per 750		—	1 per 1,000	1 service sink
7	Residential	R-1	Hotels, motels, boarding houses (transient)	1 per sleeping unit		1 per sleeping unit		1 per sleeping unit	—	1 service sink
		R-2	Dormitories, fraternities, sororities and boarding houses (not transient)	1 per 10		1 per 10		1 per 8	1 per 100	1 service sink
		R-2	Apartment house	1 per dwelling unit		1 per dwelling unit		1 per dwelling unit	—	1 kitchen sink per dwelling unit; 1 automatic clothes washer connection per 20 dwelling units
		R-3	One- and two-family dwellings	1 per dwelling unit		1 per dwelling unit		1 per dwelling unit	—	1 kitchen sink per dwelling unit; 1 automatic clothes washer connection per dwelling unit
		R-3	Congregate living facilities with 16 or fewer persons	1 per 10		1 per 10		1 per 8	1 per 100	1 service sink
		R-4	Residential care/assisted living facilities	1 per 10		1 per 10		1 per 8	1 per 100	1 service sink
8	Storage	S-1 S-2	Structures for the storage of goods, warehouses, storehouse and freight depots. Low and Moderate Hazard.	1 per 100		1 per 100		See Section 411	1 per 1,000	1 service sink

a. The fixtures shown are based on one fixture being the minimum required for the number of persons indicated or any fraction of the number of persons indicated. The number of occupants shall be determined by the *International Building Code.*

b. Toilet facilities for employees shall be separate from facilities for inmates or patients.

c. A single-occupant toilet room with one water closet and one lavatory serving not more than two adjacent patient sleeping units shall be permitted where such room is provided with direct access from each patient sleeping unit and with provisions for privacy.

d. The occupant load for seasonal outdoor seating and entertainment areas shall be included when determining the minimum number of facilities required.

e. The minimum number of required drinking fountains shall comply with Table 403.1 and Chapter 11 of the *International Building Code.*

f. Drinking fountains are not required for an occupant load of 15 or fewer.

example, the text will specify when urinals are allowed. The table also has multiple footnotes. When determining the number of plumbing fixtures and how to arrange them within a project, be aware of the following important aspects of the code:

1. *Male/female ratios:* In most cases, the plumbing fixture table will require the same number of fixtures for male and female toilet facilities. However, under the Assembly occupancies, some of the ratios are different for male and female water closets. The code has taken into account the expected male/female ratio and the typical rate at which the facilities will be used. (Also see item 8.) If any calculation results in a fraction, round up for the required number of fixtures. If plumbing fixtures need to be calculated for multiple occupancies on the same floor, each would be calculated separately for male and female and then added together for the results for each sex before rounding up.

2. *Grouping fixtures:* The required number of plumbing fixtures for toilet facilities can be combined into one common restroom (separate for males and females) if all applicable building occupants have access to them. For example, if five female water closets are required on a floor, they can be combined into one women's restroom. However, in a large building, maximum travel distances might limit the number of fixtures that can be grouped together. (See item 6.) In addition, a certain percentage of the fixtures on each floor will need to be accessible. (See the next section.)

3. *Family/Assisted-use facilities:* Typically, separate facilities are required for each sex. However, certain circumstances allow or require the use of a family or assisted-use facility (also known as a unisex facility). First, the codes will *allow* certain smaller occupancies, with limited square footage and minimal occupants, to use a single facility with one lavatory and one water closet. Common examples include small office spaces and restaurants, individual retail stores, laundries, and beauty shops. In these cases, the plumbing codes give some parameters, but the final decision is usually made by the code official. The codes also *require* some occupancies to have a separate family/assisted-use toilet or bathing facility in addition to the main facilities. They are intended to allow someone who is elderly or disabled, or even a child, to be assisted by someone of the opposite sex. These family or assisted-use toilet facilities are usually required when six or more water closets are provided. This includes many Assemblies and large Mercantile occupancies (e.g., malls). In addition, recreational facilities (e.g., gyms or health spas) that provide separate-sex bathing facilities will also require a family or assisted-use bathing room. These unisex facilities are counted in the total number of plumbing fixtures required, not in addition to the

required number, and are usually noted by a sign such as "Family" or "Unisex." In each case, this facility must be fully accessible. (See the section Single-Toilet Facilities later in this chapter.)

4. *Private facilities:* A separate toilet facility provided for private use by a tenant or individual cannot be deducted from the total common facilities required for general use on the floor or in the building. For example, an executive suite might have a private toilet within the suite. These private facilities are not typically required to be accessible, just adaptable. (See the section Single Toilet Facilities later in this chapter.)

5. *Public and employee facilities:* Typically, toilet facilities must be provided for the customers, patrons, and visitors of the space as well as the employees who work in the space. In most occupancies, either separate public and employee facilities can be provided or they can be combine into one facility. Typically, a combined facility must be located within the employee working area. However, if the location is not accessible to the public, separate toilet facilities are typically required. An example may be a toilet facility located in a manufacturing area that might not be safe for a customer to walk through. Toilet facilities in Mercantile and Assembly occupancies such as restaurants, nightclubs, retail stores, and malls are allowed to be shared as well, but if shared, the public facility cannot be accessed through certain spaces. (See also item 6 below.) Some jurisdictions may require larger restaurants to have separate employee and customer facilities. In addition, Detentional/Correctional and Health Care occupancies must typically keep their employee toilet facilities separate from those of the inmates and patients.

6. *Access to facilities:* The codes limit the travel distances to public and employee toilet facilities. Typically, no path of travel to the toilet facility can be longer than 500 feet (152 m). (Travel distance in covered malls usually cannot exceed 300 feet [91.4 m].) In addition, public toilets cannot be accessed through kitchens, storage rooms, or closets. For example, public toilet facilities cannot be located within a restaurant kitchen or a retail store storage room. However, public facilities can be accessed from the exterior (e.g., gas service station) or the interior of a building. All routes should also meet the accessibility requirements of the *IBC* as well as the *ADA Standards*. (See Chapter 4.)

7. *Unusual use group:* If a particular occupancy or use group is not covered by the plumbing fixture table, a local code official should be consulted for the specific requirements. (To get an estimate, use the type of occupancy most similar to the project; however, remember that the code official makes the final decision.)

◢**Note**

The plumbing codes limit the travel distance to toilet facilities within a building.

8. *Unusual male/female ratios:* An adjustment may be made to the total number of fixtures or to the ratio of male to female facilities in certain cases. The codes typically allow this option in special circumstances if coordinated with the local code official. The performance codes also allow for flexibility based on the intended use of the space or building. In addition, some jurisdictions have *potty parity* regulations that allow modification to the values provided within the code tables. These regulations often apply to Assembly occupancies. Modifications take into account factors like the probable division of the male and female populations using the facilities, the frequency of use by each gender, and the difference in time it takes each gender to utilize the facilities. An example would be a sports stadium. With approval from the code official, the allocation of fixtures in facilities that are used predominantly by one gender, such as an all-female health club or an all-male dorm, may also be able to be modified. In each case, satisfactory data must be provided to the code official.

Accessibility Percentages

After establishing the number and type of plumbing fixtures required by the codes, the accessibility of these fixtures must be determined. These requirements are found in the accessibility chapter of the building codes, the ICC/ANSI standard, and the *ADA Standards*. Typically, all the fixtures used in a family/assisted-use or single-toilet facility must be accessible. Other requirements will be based on the number of fixtures within each facility. For example, in multi-toilet facilities (as discussed later in this chapter), the number of water closets used in one room will determine the number of stalls that need to be accessible in that room. Other accessible facilities are based on the type of occupancy. For example, when an occupancy has a number of individual dwelling or sleeping units, such as hotels and apartment buildings in Residential occupancies and hospitals in Institutional occupancies, the percentage of units that are required to be fully accessible is also given. (See Chapter 2 for more information on occupancy classifications.)

In some existing buildings, it may be necessary to add a single-toilet or single-bathing facility that is accessible when it is not possible to adapt an existing facility. For example, more than one existing water closet may need to be removed to make room for an accessible one requiring a larger stall; this, in turn, may reduce the total number of fixtures to below what is required by the plumbing code. In some cases, adding a separate accessible single-toilet facility instead may satisfy the requirement for an accessible toilet when allowed in a jurisdiction. Sometimes a unisex facility that covers male and female requirements is

Note
Assembly occupancies that have seasonal outdoor seating and/or entertainment must include the occupant load for these areas when determining the number of required plumbing fixtures.

Note
When several single-toilet or single-bathing facilities are clustered together, such as those found in health care facilities, the 2006 *IBC* requires 50 percent of them to be accessible.

Note
The 2003 ICC/ANSI standard and *2010 ADA Standards* provide alternate requirements for plumbing fixtures used primarily by children. When designing a building or space for children 12 years of age or younger, consult these documents.

allowed. Also note, as mentioned earlier, that the plumbing code requires some building types to have a separate family or assisted-use toilet facility in addition to and separate from the other required accessible facilities. This facility should follow the *ADA Standards* and other accessibility requirements, since its primary intention is for elderly or disabled individuals. (See the section Toileting and Bathing Facilities later in this chapter.)

PLUMBING FIXTURE REQUIREMENTS

Once the number and types of fixtures required by the plumbing code table and the number of fixtures that have to be accessible is determined, the next step is researching the specific requirements for each fixture. The most common plumbing fixtures are listed on the plumbing code table and are discussed here. These include water closets, urinals, lavatories, sinks, drinking fountains, bathtubs, and showers. Requirements for other types of fixtures are discussed in the plumbing code as well. Examples include bidets, food waste grinders, and laundry trays. In most cases, the codes simply reference industry standards for the installation of these fixtures, so they will not be discussed. However, if using more specialized fixtures such as baptisteries, aquariums, ornamental and lily ponds, ornamental fountain basins, and swimming pools, check for other code requirements. The *IPC* also includes requirements for Health Care fixtures. Fixtures in certain building types, such as restaurants and hospitals, may need to meet local health code requirements as well. A jurisdiction may have other special requirements. For example, certain jurisdictions now require the use of automatic faucets in public toilet facilities.

The one code requirement that all plumbing fixtures have in common is that each fixture must be durable and finished with a smooth, impervious material. Although most fixtures are fabricated by the manufacturer this way, it might become an issue when specifying or designing custom plumbing fixtures. (See the section Finish Requirements later in this chapter.) Many fixtures must also meet certain water consumption standards as required for water conservation. (This will be discussed in more detail in the later section Plumbing Sustainability Considerations.)

Typically, the *ADA Standards* and the accessibility chapter in the building codes will specify when a fixture is required to be accessible. If a fixture is to be accessible, the codes refer to the ICC/ANSI standard. Specific dimension and location requirements are located in both the *ADA Standards* and the ICC/ANSI standard. Although all fixtures must meet the basic code requirements, if a fixture is required to be accessible, different dimension and clearance criteria

📝Note

Except for water closets and bathtubs, the clear floor space required for accessibility at most plumbing fixtures is 30 by 48 inches (760 by 1220 mm).

📝Note

The clear floor space at an accessible water closet varies depending on if the water closet is located in a room or stall, if the stall is wheelchair-accessible or ambulatory-accessible, and if the toilet is wall hung or floor mounted within the stall.

📝Note

In the *2010 ADA Standard*, the wheelchair accessible stall and single toilet facilities must provide for a side transfer at the water closet. The clear floor space specified in the standard allows for this.

📝Note

The 2003 ICC/ANSI standard requires vertical grab bars at the side wall of water closets, showers, and bathtubs. The *ADA Standards* do not.

must usually be met. This section will discuss the various code and accessibility requirements for each fixture. The next section will explain additional requirements necessary when using these fixtures together in a toilet or bathing facility. (Refer to the plumbing and building codes, the *ADA Standards*, and the ICC/ANSI standard for the specific requirements.)

Water Closets

The codes typically require every floor in a building to have at least one water closet (i.e., toilet). The plumbing code requirements for water closets include the types allowed and the clearances for installation. The most common requirement is that all water closets specified for public or employee use must have an elongated bowl and a hinged seat with an open front. The codes also specify the maximum flow and water consumption allowed per flush. (See the section Plumbing Sustainability Considerations later in this chapter.) Clearances for installation include specific dimensions at each side and in front of the bowl. For example, the *IPC* requires a typical water closet to have a minimum of 15 inches (381 mm) from the center of the bowl to any side wall, partition, or vanity and at least 21 inches (533 mm) clear in front of the bowl. If enclosed, the compartment cannot be less than 30 inches (762 mm) wide by 60 inches (1524 mm) deep and it must have a privacy lock.

Accessible water closets must meet other requirements. For example, instead of a 15-inch (381 mm) minimum to the centerline of the bowl, 16 to 18 inches (405-455 mm) is typically required. (The original *ADAAG* requires 18 inches [455 mm].) The height of the toilet seat must be between 17 and 19 inches (430 to 485 mm), as shown in Figure 7.2. Additional requirements are specified in the *ADA* and ICC/ANSI standards. These include a variety of required floor clearances, depending on how the water closet is used. It matters whether the water closet is the only one in the room or in a toilet compartment (i.e., stall). It can also depend on the type of stall and whether the water closet is wall hung or floor mounted. (See the section Toilet and Bathing Facilities for additional options.) The most common accessible clear floor space for a single water closet is 60 by 56 inches (1525 by 1420 mm). This extra clearance allows for the maneuverability of a wheelchair and access to grab bars.

Accessible water closets can have an automatic flushing mechanism or a manual control. If a manual flush control is used, it must be located on the "open side" of the toilet at a certain height (reach range) above the floor (see Figure 7.2) and must meet certain operable conditions. For example, it must be operable with one hand, and it cannot take more than 5 pounds (22.2 N) of force to operate. Additional requirements for accessories such as grab bars and toilet paper dispensers are described later in the chapter.

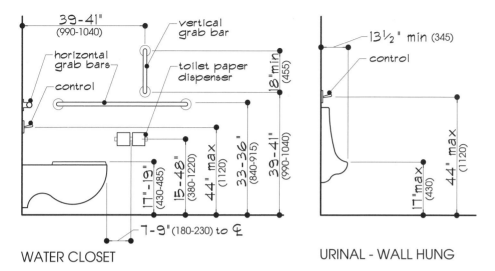

WATER CLOSET

URINAL - WALL HUNG

NOTE: The vertical grab bar is required by the 2003 ICC/ANSI standard. Refer to the ICC/ANSI and ADA standards for additional grab bar and toilet paper dispenser information. A privacy panel may be required; refer to the codes and standards.

Figure 7.2 Typical accessible plumbing fixture dimensions: water closets and urinals.

Urinals

Urinals are not required by the plumbing codes in all occupancies. They are typically found in the male restrooms of schools, restaurants, clubs, lounges, transportation terminals, auditoriums, theaters, and churches. If they are required, they are usually substituted for one or more of the required water closets but only up to a certain quantity. (Trough urinals are not allowed.) The *IPC* does not allow the number of urinals to be substituted for more than 67 percent of the required number of male water closets in Assembly or Educational occupancies and 50 percent in all other occupancies. Like water closets, urinals must meet a maximum water consumption requirement when flushed. Waterless urinals are an option as well. In addition, the codes specify the type and location of the finish material surrounding the urinal for ease of cleaning and sanitation. (See the section Finish Requirements later in this chapter.)

When urinals are provided, the plumbing codes require minimum clearances for installation similar to those for water closets. If only one is provided, the *IBC* does not require it to be accessible; however, the *ADA Standards* does. Therefore, if urinals are provided, at least one must comply with accessibility requirements. It must be either a stall-type or a wall-hung fixture with an elongated rim at a maximum height of 17 inches (430 mm) above the floor, as shown in Figure 7.2. The *2010 ADA Standards* also requires the rim to be a minimum depth of 13 1/2

◀ **Note**

Review urinal privacy screen requirements in both the *IPC* and the accessibility publications. Requirements vary.

◪Note

Although not required by the *ADA Standards*, the use of automatic water and flushing controls that activate upon movement are also considered accessible. They may be required by the sustainability codes and/or some jurisdictions in certain occupancies.

◪Note

Although not required by the codes, installing waterless, antiseptic hand-sanitizer dispensers can also reduce water usage since some occupants will use it in place of a lavatory. When installed, however, the *LSC* does place restrictions on the location of the dispenser since the alcohol-based liquid is considered flammable.

◪Note

When determining the clear floor space at a fixture, the clearances are dictated by the clear kneespace and toespace, not necessarily the location of the wall supporting the fixture.

inches (345 mm). Clear floor space allowing a front approach must be provided as well. This is typically 30 by 48 inches (760 by 1220 mm). Urinals used by the public or by employees require walls and/or partitions (i.e., privacy panels) to create privacy. When a privacy panel is used, it can be located either inside or outside the clear floor space. If it is located inside the required clear floor space, it cannot extend past the front edge of the urinal rim. The accessible flush control requirements are similar to those for water closets.

Lavatories

Anywhere a water closet is used, a lavatory (i.e., hand-washing sink) must also be installed. However, the same ratio is not always used by the codes. When multiple fixtures are needed, the codes typically require fewer lavatories than water closets/urinals. The plumbing codes set minimum clearances for installation similar to those for water closets and urinals. Therefore, when placed next to a water closet, the centerline of a lavatory is required to be a minimum of 30 inches (762 mm) from the centerline of the water closet. When there are multiple lavatories in a continuous counter, there must be a minimum of 30 inches (762 mm) from centerline to centerline of each lavatory. In addition, the *IPC* limits the amount of hot water delivered by the faucet in the lavatory, especially in public facilities, to prevent scalding, and it must conform to specific water consumption requirements. Some jurisdictions may set additional water use limits, especially in certain building types, requiring the faucet to be automatic (i.e., sensor-operated) or metered so that it is self-closing.

When the lavatory is required to be accessible, the faucet must meet additional requirements. The faucet must be within accessible reach ranges and have controls that are easy to operate. Lever handles, push types, and automatic faucets are often used. Accessibility requirements call for at least one lavatory on each floor (or at least 5 percent if multiple lavatories) to be fully accessible. This includes the depth and height of the fixture as shown in Figure 7.3. Where a continuous counter or vanity is provided, the entire run of lavatories is often made accessible for consistency of design. A washfountain that has multiple sprayheads and can accommodate multiple users at once is another option. (Per the *IPC*, every 20 inches [508 mm] of rim space is considered one lavatory.) These are found in building types such as schools, athletic facilities, industrial plants, movie theaters, and large retail facilities. (See the section Multiple Toilet Facilities for additional requirements.)

An accessible lavatory or washfountain must meet specific clearances as well. Most important is the clear floor space leading up to the lavatory and the kneespace and toespace underneath. The typical clear floor space required is 30 by 48 inches (760 by 1220 mm) that extends a certain distance under the sink to allow for a forward approach. (See Figure 7.6.) The distance it can extend under

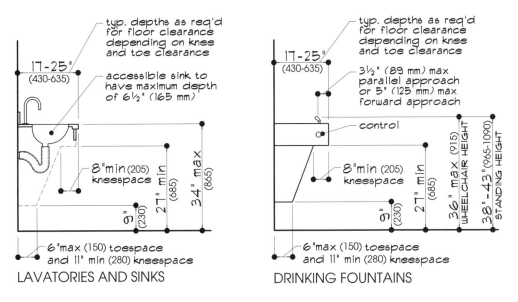

NOTE: The original ADAAG also specifies a clearance between the floor and apron at the sink/lavatory of 29" min (735 mm). If drinking fountain is located on an accessible path, you may need to create an alcove so that the drinking fountain does not project into the corridor more than 4" (100 mm).

Figure 7.3 Typical accessible plumbing fixture dimensions: lavatories, sinks, and drinking fountains.

the lavatory can range from 17 to 25 inches (430-635 mm) depending on the clearances provided for kneespace and toespace as shown in Figure 7.3. Because kneespace is required, all hot water and drain pipes must be covered to prevent contact. A cover can be as simple as insulated pipe wrapping, or it can be part of the countertop design, as shown in Figure 7.3; however, the cover must be removable to allow access to the pipes when necessary. (Insulated covers must meet flammability finish requirements. See Chapter 9.)

Sinks

Sinks required by the codes are usually considered miscellaneous fixtures on the plumbing fixture table. They can include service sinks, utility sinks, kitchen sinks, and laundry basins. Some are required by the code, depending on the occupancy. For example, most occupancies require a utility sink (i.e., janitor or mop sink), although certain Residential occupancies are exempt. Other sinks are installed even when they are not required by the plumbing code. For example, kitchen or bar sinks in breakrooms are fairly common additions to an interior project. Utility sinks are not generally required to be accessible. However, in most non-Residential occupancies, at least one sink (and at least 5 percent

✐**Note**

There are at least three different ways to prevent contact with hot water and drain pipes under a lavatory or sink: (1) wrap them with insulated materials, (2) create an enclosure around the pipes, or (3) reconfigure the location of the pipes.

✐**Note**

Installing lavatories and sinks with drains located toward the rear of the bowl can help save kneespace. Some pipes can be installed inside the wall if planned in advance.

☞ Note

The 2003 ICC/ANSI standard and *2010 ADA Standards* allow for some parallel approaches to lavatories, sinks, and drinking fountains. However, a clear floor space positioned for a forward approach is preferred.

☞ Note

Additional sink requirements for some occupancies or building types, such as restaurants and hospitals, are set by the local health department within a jurisdiction.

☞ Note

When plumbing pipes under an accessible sink are wrapped with insulation, the insulation must meet Class A requirements of the *Steiner Tunnel Test*. (See Chapter 9.)

when multiple sinks are used) is usually required by the codes to be accessible. A breakroom sink, for instance, must be accessible. Similar to lavatories, sinks must have faucets that meet water consumption requirements.

Most of the accessibility requirements are for kitchen-type sinks. The mounting requirements are similar to those for lavatories, as shown in Figure 7.3. The height is especially important when designing pantry areas in a breakroom or kitchenettes in a hotel room, where the counter height is typically 36 inches (915 mm) above the floor. An accessible counter has a maximum height of 34 inches (865 mm) at the sink, which means that either a bilevel counter is needed or the entire counter is lowered to 34 inches (865 mm) above the floor. The depth of a kitchen counter should also be limited to 25 inches (635 mm) so that any reach ranges for items installed above the sink are not obstructed.

Typically, the design of the counter with the sink must allow for a front approach. Similar to a lavatory, the typical clear floor space is 30 by 48 inches (760 by 1220 mm) that extends between 17 and 25 inches (430-635 mm) under the sink depending on the clearances at the toespace and kneespace. Clearances can be provided by leaving it open below the sink and covering the pipes accordingly or by installing specially designed doors that, when open, provide full clearance below. It is also best to use a sink that is not too deep. A common depth of an accessible sink is 6½ inches (165 mm).

Drinking Fountains

Drinking fountains are required in most occupancies except certain Residential occupancies. If a building has more than one floor, the codes require that each floor have its own drinking fountain. However, restaurants that serve water are typically exempt from supplying a drinking fountain. More recently, the plumbing codes and some local code jurisdictions have also started to make allowances for spaces that provide bottled water dispensers and/or water coolers in common areas. According to the *IPC*, water dispensers or coolers cannot be substituted for more than 50 percent of the required drinking fountains. Therefore, if a space requires one drinking fountain, a drinking fountain must be installed. However, the 2009 *IPC* also allows an exception for occupancies with an occupant load of 15 or less. (See footnote "f" on the table shown in Figure 7.1.) Examples include a small office space or day care, where other sources of drinking water can be used instead.

The codes restrict the location of drinking fountains, bottled water dispensers, and water coolers. They cannot be installed in public toilet rooms or the vestibules leading to the toilet room. One of the most common locations for a drinking fountain is the corridor outside the restroom area. This typically provides a central location for the user and easy access to the plumbing pipes. If the drinking fountain is located in a corridor or other accessible path of travel, it must be located so that it will not be considered a "protruding object." In many cases, this will require an alcove or recessed area along the corridor. (An example is shown in Figure 7.6.) A protruding object is considered to be any object between 27 inches (685 mm) and 80 inches (2030 mm) above the floor that protrudes more than 4 inches (100 mm) into an accessible path of travel.

The *IBC* requires a minimum of two drinking fountains on each floor of a building and within "a secured area" (e.g., tenant space, employee area of a retail store): one that is wheelchair-accessible and one that is at standing height for people who find it difficult to bend low. The wheelchair-accessible drinking fountain, like the one shown in Figure 7.3, requires the spout to be no higher than 36 inches (915 mm) above the floor and to have a front or side control that is easy to operate. A standing-height drinking fountain should be mounted so that the spout is between 38 and 43 inches (965 and 1090 mm) above the floor. Therefore, when the *IPC* requires one drinking fountain, the space will actually require either two separate water fountains or one "hi-low" drinking fountain that combines the two types. When more than one fixture is required, 50 percent must be standing height and 50 percent must be wheelchair-accessible.

Wheelchair-accessible drinking fountains must have a clear floor space of 30 by 48 inches (760 by 1220 mm) that allows for a front approach. This will typically require a cantilever-type drinking fountain that is wall mounted. The position of the clear floor space in relation to the wall will depend on the kneespace and toespace clearances provided as shown in Figure 7.3. If the unit is built into an alcove, the alcove must be a minimum of 36 inches (915 mm) wide to allow for the forward approach. (See Figure 7.6.) (Parallel approach drinking fountains were allowed in the original *ADAAG*. Some exceptions are still allowed in the new ADA and ICC/ANSI standards.) Accessible floor clearances are not required at standing-height drinking fountains.

Bathtubs

Bathtubs are most commonly found in Residential occupancies such as hotels, dormitories, and apartment buildings as well as single-family homes. When a bathtub is required, typically a shower can be used in its place. (Many Institutional occupancies require a tub or shower as well, but showers are typically used.)

Although the plumbing codes do not regulate the size or type of bathtub, they do have requirements for certain accessory components, including the faucet, enclosure, and mechanical equipment. The faucet must be able to regulate the mix of hot and cold water to prevent scalding and meet water consumption requirements. If the tub is enclosed by glass and/or glass doors, safety glass must be used, as specified in the building codes. In addition, if a whirlpool or spa-type bathtub that includes a motor is used, the codes require that access be provided

> **Note**
>
> The *IPC* indicates the number of drinking fountains required, not requiring them in certain smaller occupancies. The *IBC* requires two different types of drinking fountains and does not allow for these exceptions. The final decision will be up to the local code official.

> **Note**
>
> When locating a drinking fountain in a corridor or other path of travel, remember that it cannot project more than 4 inches (100 mm) into the path, according to the ADA ICC/ANSI standards.

> **Note**
>
> One of the best types of accessible bathtub seats is one that extends from outside the tub into the head of the tub. It allows a person to do the maneuvering outside the tub before sliding in.

to the pump. Often this requires preplanning in the arrangement of the room and/or how certain finishes, such as ceramic tile, are being used.

If a bathtub is required in an accessible bathing room, it must meet specific requirements. As shown in Figure 7.4, there are certain height and location requirements for the tub itself, as well as for the faucet controls. In addition, the shower spray unit must be able to convert from a fixed to a hand-held unit and have a hose that is at least 59 inches (1500 mm) long. If there is a tub enclosure, it cannot hinder any of the accessible requirements and no tracks can be mounted to the top of the tub rim. (Glass doors are not recommended at accessible bathtubs.)

All accessible tubs must also have a seat. This can include either a removable in-tub seat that spans the width of the bathtub that is 15 to 16 inches (380 to 405 mm) deep, or a permanent fixed seat a minimum of 15 inches (380 mm) deep at the head of the tub. The grab bar locations at the walls and the clear floor space required at the side of the tub will depend on the type of seat used and the accessibility publication referenced. For example, the back wall of a bathtub requires two horizontal grab bars. These grab bars must be longer when a fixed seat at the end of the tub is used. The typical clear floor space at a bathtub with a removable seat is 30 inches (760 mm) by the length of the tub. When a fixed seat is used, the clear floor space should extend a minimum of 12 inches (305 mm) past the seat end of the tub. (Also refer to the section Bathing Facilities later in this chapter and Figure 7.7.)

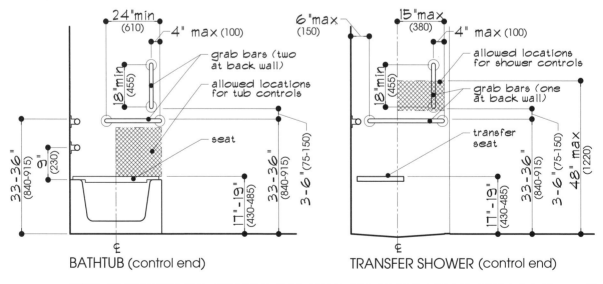

NOTE: An accessible shower head must be able to convert from a handheld to a fixed type with a hose at least 59" (1500 mm) long. Vertical grab bars are required by 2003 ICC/ANSI standard.

Figure 7.4 Typical accessible plumbing fixture dimensions: bathtubs and showers.

Showers

Like bathtubs, showers are typically required by the plumbing code in Residential and Institutional occupancies. (In many cases, they are allowed to replace the bathtub.) Some Assembly occupancies, such as gymnasiums and health clubs, require showers as well. In addition, manufacturing plants, warehouses, foundries, and other similar establishments may require showers if employees are apt to be exposed to excessive heat or skin contamination. The plumbing fixture table shown in Figure 7.1 will indicate when they are required.

The plumbing code specifies the type of shower pan and drain that must be used. If a glass enclosure is used it must meet safety glazing requirements (see Bathtubs) and have an access door that is at least 22 inches (559 mm) wide. The code also requires faucets to meet maximum flow rates for water consumption and maximum hot water temperatures to prevent scalding. When prefabricated showers and shower compartments are not used, the codes specify the types of finish materials allowed. (See the section Finish Requirements later in this chapter.) The size of a shower is regulated by the code as well. Overall, the typical shower cannot be less than 900 square inches (0.58 s m), with the minimum size in either direction typically being at least 30 inches (762 mm). The minimum shower wall height is 70 inches (1778 mm) above the shower drain.

If a shower is required to be accessible, two types of showers are usually allowed: transfer showers and roll-in showers. *Transfer showers* are smaller and are typically required to have an inside clear dimension of 36 by 36 inches (915 by 915 mm) and a clear floor space in front of the shower of 36 by 48 inches (915 by 1220 mm). They must also include a fixed or folding seat of a specific size and shape. *Roll-in showers* are more elongated and are typically 30 by 60 inches (760 by 1525 mm) in size with a larger adjacent clear floor space of 36 by 60 inches (915 by 1525 mm). An alternate roll-in shower is also an option in the 2003 ICC/ANSI standard and *2010 ADA Standards*. Grab bar sizes and locations are different for each type of shower. (See Figure 7.8.)

Accessible controls and shower spray unit requirements are similar to those for an accessible bathtub. Allowed locations are shown in Figure 7.4. If a curb or threshold is used, it can only be 0.5 inch (13 mm) high. (If it is more than 0.25 inch [6.4 mm], the edges must be beveled. See Figure 9.19 and the section Accessible Finishes in Chapter 9.) This is especially important in roll-in showers so that the curb does not hinder the wheelchair user. In addition, if an enclosure is used (i.e., a shower stall or door), it cannot obstruct the transfer of the person into the shower or any use of the controls in the shower. (Also see the section Bathing Facilities later in this chapter.)

✍Note

When safety showers are required, also refer to ANSI Z58.1, Emergency Eyewash and Shower Equipment.

✍Note

Seats are required in transfer showers. They are optional in roll-in showers but must be a folding type if it extends into the minimum clearances.

✍Note

The 2003 ICC/ANSI standard and *2010 ADA Standards* allow the clear floor space at roll-in showers to be 30 inches (760 mm) deep instead of 36 inches (915 mm) deep.

Dishwashers and Clothes Washers

There are very few code requirements for dishwashers and clothes washers. Dishwashers are typically not required. Clothes washers are required only in certain Residential occupancies. For example, a clothes washer connection is typically required in a one- or two-family dwelling. In buildings with multiple Residential units, one clothes washer is usually required for every 20 units. These are usually combined together in a shared laundry room. The plumbing codes will indicate when they are required and provide installation standards. However, if multiple clothes washers are used in a laundry-type facility, a floor drain is usually required as well.

When multiple clothes washers and/or clothes dryers are provided in a laundry facility, typically at least one of each needs to be accessible. If it is top loading, the top of the machine should be no higher than 36 inches (915 mm) above the floor. If it is a front-loading machine, the bottom of the opening must be between 15 and 34 inches (380-865 mm) above the floor. All operable parts should be within accessible reach ranges and typically accessible floor clearances positioned for a parallel approach and turning space should also be provided to allow approach to and use of the appliance.

⬛ Note

Accessible requirements for washers and dryers are included in newer editions of the ICC/ANSI standard and the *2010 ADA Standards.*

TOILET AND BATHING FACILITIES

After establishing the required number and type of plumbing fixtures for a project, they need to be located properly within the space or building. The requirements for each plumbing fixture were discussed in the previous section. Each fixture must meet certain code and accessibility requirements. However, plumbing fixtures are often used in a group to create a toilet facility or a bathing facility. Not only do the fixtures need to be grouped together so that the individual requirements of each fixture are still met, but when the fixtures are grouped together, additional code and accessibility requirements must also be met in the construction and layout of these facilities.

The codes require that all toilet and bathing rooms have privacy. This includes privacy at the entrance to the restroom and within the room when there are multiple water closets and bathing fixtures. When a restroom is connected to a public area or passageway, it must be screened so that no one can look directly into the toilet or bathing facility. This is usually accomplished with either a vestibule leading into the room or a deliberate arrangement of walls in front of or beyond the doorway. When a door is used at the entrance, the codes typically require a closer on the door so that it self-closes with each use.

⬛ Note

In occupancies where multiple single-toilet rooms or bathing rooms are clustered in a single location, at least 50 percent of them must be accessible.

In addition, the *ADA Standards* and the ICC/ANSI standard require all restrooms, whether they are fully or partially accessible, to be directly accessible to the public. This includes minimum door clearance into the room and an unobstructed turning space within the room, as well as accessible corridors leading to the facility. The *ADA Standards* and the accessibility chapter in the building codes typically indicate when an accessible facility is required. The ADA and ICC/ANSI standards then specify requirements for the use of stalls, grab bars, and accessories. (See Chapter 4 for additional information on corridor and door clearances.)

Various types of toilet and bathing facilities and their requirements are described next, followed by a discussion of the appropriate use of finishes, grab bars, accessories, and signage.

Single-Toilet Facilities

Single-toilet facilities consist of one lavatory and one water closet. They are used in a building or space for a number of reasons. Most commonly, they are used in smaller spaces or occupancies where only one female and one male single-toilet facility is required. Single-toilet facilities are also used as a unisex facility. As described earlier in this chapter, these may be allowed as a shared facility in a smaller occupancy or required as a family or assisted-use toilet facility in an Assembly and Mercantile occupancy. A unisex toilet facility may also have to be added during the renovation of an existing building if new accessible plumbing fixtures are required but the size of an existing multi-toilet facility cannot be modified to accommodate them.

Most single-toilet facilities must be accessible. However, there are exceptions in Institutional (e.g., hospital) and Residential (e.g., hotel) building types where there are multiple dwelling units. Accessibility requirements also do not apply to a facility added for private use, such as an executive toilet room. Instead, the *IBC* requires that the private facility be adaptable, so that it could easily be converted to an accessible room if it becomes necessary. For example, the room should be sized accordingly and blocking should be included in the walls so that grab bars can be added and fixtures may be adjusted for later conversion.

In a fully accessible single-toilet facility, all fixtures, accessories, and grab bars must be mounted at accessible heights and specific floor clearances must be provided. Figure 7.5 indicates the requirements of a typical accessible single-toilet facility. (Two floor plan options are provided.) A similar facility could be used for a unisex toilet room. However, if designing a family or assisted-use toilet room such as those required in certain Mercantile or Assembly occupancies, additional space can be added to allow for someone to assist in the room or to

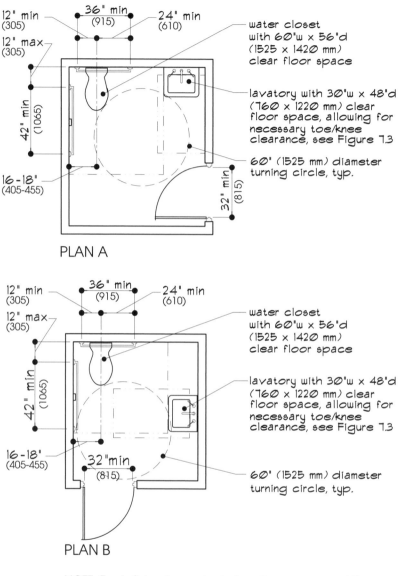

PLAN A

PLAN B

NOTE: Each fixture's required clear floor space and the room's required turning space can overlap, but the door cannot swing over the clear floor space. The existing ADAAG requires 18" (455 mm) to centerline of toilet.

Figure 7.5 Accessible single-toilet facility examples. (See also Figures 7.2, 7.3, and 7.9 for accessible fixture and accessory heights and Figure 7.2 for vertical grab bar location.)

allow for amenities not typically required by the codes, such as a fold-up changing table or a wall-mounted baby seat. (See Figure 7.9.)

The fixtures in single-toilet facilities must be arranged so that the required clear floor space for each fixture is unobstructed. However, as shown in Figure 7.5, the clear floor spaces for different fixtures can overlap each other. In addition, all accessible toilet facilities require an unobstructed turning space that is 60 inches (1525 mm) in diameter. This circle can overlap the clear floor space and the space under the fixtures where kneespace and toespace is provided. (It is helpful for the clear floor spaces and the turning circle to be drawn directly on the floor plan in the construction drawings to indicate compliance.) The door into the room is not allowed to open over the clear floor space required at any fixture. However, both the *2010 ADA Standards* and the 2003 ICC/ANSI standard do allow the door to swing over the required turning space. (Older edition did not always allow this.)

Multiple-Toilet Facilities

When multiple plumbing fixtures are required for males and/or females in the same space or floor, a multiple-toilet facility is used—one for males and one for females. In a multiple-toilet facility, the water closets must be separated from each other and from the rest of the room by water closet compartments (i.e., toilet stalls). There are many ways to design the layout of a multi-toilet facility. Figure 7.6 shows one type of layout. The plumbing codes require minimum clearance dimensions to the side of each fixture and in front of each fixture as well as a minimum water closet compartment size. These dimensions were explained for each fixture in the section Plumbing Fixture Requirements and are included in Figure 7.6. The figure also includes the minimum dimensions required for a standard toilet stall, as shown by "C." Urinals must be separated by a partition (i.e., privacy panel) as well, but no doors are required. (See the section on Urinals earlier in the chapter for more information on privacy panels.)

When there are multiple fixtures located in a toilet facility, typically at least one of each is required to be accessible and additional regulations must be met. These requirements are found in the *IBC*, the ICC/ANSI standard, and the *ADA Standards*. For example, a multi-toilet facility must have at least one accessible lavatory. However, when six or more lavatories are provided in one room, one lavatory must include "enhanced reach ranges" where all faucet and soap dispenser controls are a maximum of 11 inches (280 mm) from the front edge of the lavatory. (See the ICC/ANSI standard for more information.) In addition, at least one water closet in each multi-toilet facility must be accessible. However, if there is a combined total of six or more water closets and urinals, the codes require that two of the water closets be accessible.

◢Note

Doors swinging into accessible restrooms or toilet stalls cannot reduce the clear floor space required for each fixture. However, depending on the standard and the jurisdiction, the door is sometimes permitted to swing into the 60-inch (1525 mm) turning space.

◢Note

The clear floor spaces required at each plumbing fixture can overlap each other. The 60-inch (1525 mm) turning circle can overlap the clear floor space; it can overlap part of the fixture too, but only if there is appropriate kneespace and toespace.

◢Note

Partitions used to create toilet stalls must allow specific toe clearances. (See Figure 7.9.)

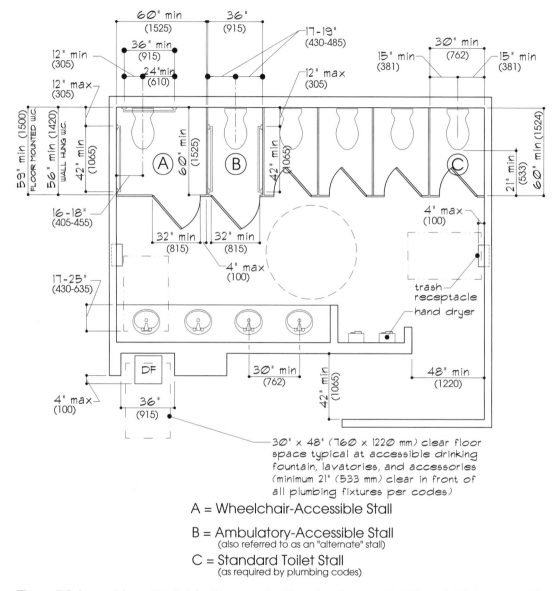

A = Wheelchair-Accessible Stall

B = Ambulatory-Accessible Stall
(also referred to as an "alternate" stall)

C = Standard Toilet Stall
(as required by plumbing codes)

Figure 7.6 Accessible multi-toilet facility example. (See also Figures 7.2, 7.3, and 7.9 for accessible fixture and accessory heights and Figure 7.2 for vertical grab bar location.)

There are two types of accessible stalls. When one accessible stall is required, it must allow for use by a person in a wheelchair, often called a *wheelchair-accessible* stall or compartment, as shown by "A" in Figure 7.6. If the door swings out, the typical size of this stall is 56 by 60 inches (1420 by 1525 mm) if it is a wall-hung water closet and 59 by 60 inches (1500 by 1525 mm) if it is a floor-mounted water closet. If the door swings in, it cannot overlap these clear floor spaces. Toespace clearances and specific grab bar locations are important as well. If a second accessible stall is required, the "alternate stall" described in the *ADA* and ICC/ANSI standards can be provided. This alternate stall is also called an *ambulatory-accessible* stall or compartment. Shown as stall "B" in Figure 7.6, it is not as wide and the arrangement of grab bars is different, requiring the watercloset to be centered in the stall. The alternate stall configuration provides for a person who has a mobility disability but who does not necessarily use a wheelchair.

In addition to the clear floor space required in each accessible stall, a clear floor space must be provided at each accessible urinal, lavatory, and accessory in the facility. At least one area in the room must also allow a 60-inch (1525 mm) diameter turning space. (See the sections Grab Bars and Accessories later in this chapter.)

Note

The plumbing codes typically require a floor drain in multiple-toilet facilities.

Note

A standard accessible stall and the "alternate" stall are shown in Figure 7.6. However, the use of the alternate stall is not typically required unless six or more stalls are provided.

Bathing Facilities

Unlike toilet facilities, bathing facilities include a shower or bathtub. The shower or tub can be used either in conjunction with the lavatory and water closet or separately in its own room. Most Residential occupancies and dwelling units will require a bathroom that includes a water closet, lavatory, and bathtub or shower. Sleeping rooms in some occupancies might require this as well. (See the inset titled *Rooms and Spaces* on page 73.) Examples include residential houses, apartments, hotel guest rooms, and guest rooms in assisted living facilities. Other building types, including many Institutional occupancies, will have either separate bathing rooms or group bathing facilities. For example, a nursing home room may have toilet facilities in the patient rooms, but have a separate bathing room on each floor that is shared by the patients and allows the staff to assist with the bathing. Other building types, such as schools, dormitories, health spas, and even prisons, are more likely to have group bathing facilities where there are multiple showers in one room.

When a building has multiple bathing fixtures or facilities, a percentage of the units will be required to be accessible. (Specific requirements are found in the codes, *ADA Standards*, and the ICC/ANSI standard.) For example, a certain number of guest rooms in a hotel must be accessible. That means that the room and the adjoining bathroom must be accessible. If multiple bathing fixtures (i.e., shower

Note

In certain Institutional building types, such as rehabilitation centers, all bathing facilities are required to be accessible. Other Health Care facilities may only require a percentage of them to be accessible.

stalls) are used in the same room, at least one of them must be accessible. In some cases, a separate accessible unisex bathing facility may be *allowed* instead. A family or assisted-use bathing facility is also *required* by the codes in recreational facilities where separate-sex bathing rooms are provided. The unisex bathing facility would then include a lavatory and a water closet in addition to the bathtub or shower. The purpose of the accessible bathing or bathroom is to allow someone in a wheelchair or with another disability to have full access to all fixtures. It also allows that person to be assisted by another person. (A family/assisted-use bathing facility could also count as a family/assisted-use toilet facility if both are required.)

At each accessible plumbing fixture, the grab bars and controls must be mounted at accessible heights and specific floor clearances must be provided. Figures 7.7 and 7.8 give several examples of single-bathing facilities. Specific floor clearances are designated for each type of bathing fixture. For example, as shown in Figure 7.7, a bathtub with a removable seat in the tub will require less floor space than one with a fixed seat at the end of the tub. In Figure 7.8, a roll-in shower is larger and will require more clear floor spaces than a transfer shower. In addition, the 60-inch (1525 mm) diameter turning space must be included in each accessible facility. Lavatories are typically allowed to overlap the larger clear floor spaces required at tubs and roll-in showers (not transfer showers). A variety of layouts are possible, depending on the type of bathing fixture. However, when designing the space, it is important to also know how the space is to be used. Additional space may be necessary to allow for assisted help. Additional grab bars might also be useful or be required by a jurisdiction. If it is a multi-fixture bathing facility, at least one of each type of accessory (soap dispenser, paper towel dispenser, and so forth) in the space must be accessible as well. (See Accessories and Grab Bars section later in this chapter.)

Finish Requirements

Both the plumbing codes and the "Interior Environment" chapter of the *IBC* specify that public toilet and bathing rooms must have smooth, hard, nonabsorbent surfaces. This limits the spread of germs and allows for easy cleaning. It applies to all floor finishes, the intersections of the floor and wall, and the wall base. For example, the *IBC* typically requires the floor finish throughout the room to extend upward onto the wall at least 4 inches (102 mm) to allow for wet mopping without damaging the wall. (Previous editions of the codes required 6 inches [152 mm].) Ceramic tile is often used to meet these requirements. Walls must also have smooth, hard, nonabsorbent finishes at certain distances around urinals and water closets and surrounding shower and tub compartments. This can be accomplished with ceramic tile as well as other applied vinyl or plastic coverings.

✎ Note

When the *IGCC* requires a building or tenant space to provide long-term bicycle parking and storage, it also typically requires at least one on-site changing room and shower facility.

✎ Note

Finish requirements for toilet and bathing facilities are found in the plumbing codes and the building codes.

Some jurisdictions will also allow epoxy paint. In addition, any accessories such as grab bars and soap dishes installed on or within the walls must be properly sealed to protect the wall beyond. (See also the section Accessible Finishes in Chapter 9.)

The codes require that stall panels and privacy screens be made of impervious materials as well. A variety of materials can be used, including laminate, stainless steel, stone, solid surface, and painted metal. Finish requirements are also important when custom fixtures are designed and used. For example, a custom counter with an integral sink must be impervious and free of unnecessary concealed spaces. Both the *IPC* and the *UPC* list allowable alternate fixture materials that include soapstone, chemical stoneware or plastic, and stainless steel and other corrosion-resistant metals. In addition, the plumbing chapter in the *ICC Performance Code* more generally states that all plumbing fixtures shall be constructed "to avoid food contamination and accumulation of dirt or bacteria and permit effective cleaning." This may allow finishes such as wood and concrete to be used as long as they are sealed properly. Many options are possible, but ultimately, the code official in the jurisdiction of the project will have the final approval.

Grab Bars

The *ADA Standards* and the ICC/ANSI standard include requirements for grab bars. They are required at accessible water closets, showers, and tubs. They must be located beside and/or behind the water closet and within various reach ranges for bathing fixtures. Grab bars must also be mounted at specific heights. Most commonly, a horizontal grab bar must be mounted at 33 to 36 inches (840 to 915 mm) above the finished floor at water closets, bathtubs, and showers. This height is measured to the top of the gripping surface, as shown in Figures 7.2 and 7.4. The 2003 ICC/ANSI standard requires a vertical grab bar at certain water closet, bathtub, and shower locations as well.

The specific length, spacing, and orientation (horizontally or vertically) depend on the location of the grab bar in relation to the type of fixture. Locations have been shown in the various toilet and bathing facility floor plans used in this chapter. The size and strength requirements of the grab bar are also regulated. The typical diameter allowed is 1¼ to 1½ inches (32 to 38 mm), which must be mounted with a clearance of 1½ inches (38 mm) between the grab bar and the wall. In addition, some jurisdictions or local agencies (e.g., health department) may require grab bars in locations other than those specified by the ADA or ICC/ANSI standards. For example, a diagonal bar may be required over a tub to assist in getting in and out of the tub. A *swing-up* grab bar at certain toilet locations, as described in the 2003 ICC/ANSI standard, is another option. It can be used as

◀Note

Toilet and bathing facilities must also be mechanically ventilated. See the Exhaust Requirements section later in this chapter.

◀Note

The 2003 ICC/ANSI standard requires vertical grab bars at water closet, bathtub, and shower locations. Additional grab bars may be required by certain code jurisdictions over and above what is required by the *ADA Standards* and the ICC/ANSI standard.

◀Note

The height of a grab bar is measured to the top of the gripping surface, not the centerline.

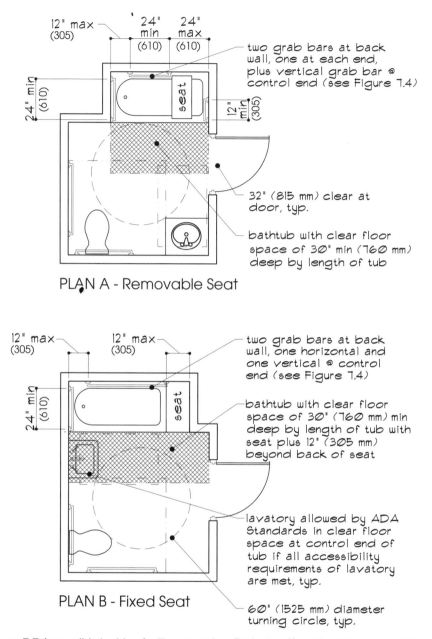

PLAN A - Removable Seat

12" max (305)

24" min (610)

24" min (610)

24" max (610)

12" min (305)

two grab bars at back wall, one at each end, plus vertical grab bar @ control end (see Figure 7.4)

32" (815 mm) clear at door, typ.

bathtub with clear floor space of 30" min (760 mm) deep by length of tub

PLAN B - Fixed Seat

12" max (305)

12" max (305)

24" min (610)

two grab bars at back wall, one horizontal and one vertical @ control end (see Figure 7.4)

bathtub with clear floor space of 30" (760 mm) min deep by length of tub with seat plus 12" (305 mm) beyond back of seat

lavatory allowed by ADA Standards in clear floor space at control end of tub if all accessibility requirements of lavatory are met, typ.

60" (1525 mm) diameter turning circle, typ.

Figure 7.7 Accessible bathing facility examples: Bathtubs. (See also Figures 7.2, 7.3, 7.4, and 7.9 for accessible fixture and accessory heights and vertical grab bar locations. See Figure 7.5 for additional information on water closets and lavatories.)

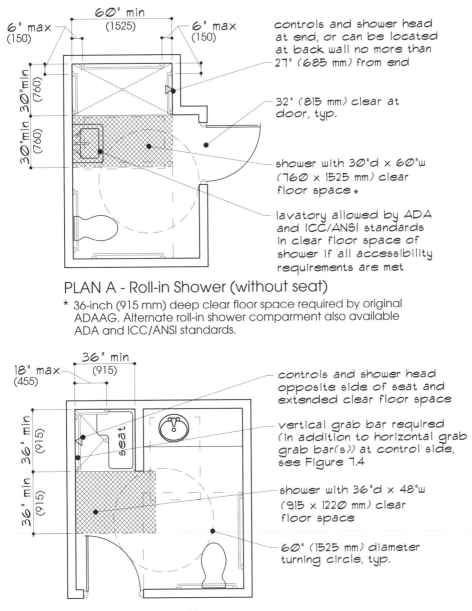

6" max (150)

60" min (1525)

6" max (150)

30" min (760) 30" min (760) 30" min (760)

controls and shower head at end, or can be located at back wall no more than 27" (685 mm) from end

32" (815 mm) clear at door, typ.

shower with 30"d x 60"w (760 x 1525 mm) clear floor space *

lavatory allowed by ADA and ICC/ANSI standards in clear floor space of shower if all accessibility requirements are met

PLAN A - Roll-in Shower (without seat)

* 36-inch (915 mm) deep clear floor space required by original ADAAG. Alternate roll-in shower comparment also available ADA and ICC/ANSI standards.

18" max (455)

36" min (915)

36" min (915) 36" min (915)

seat

controls and shower head opposite side of seat and extended clear floor space

vertical grab bar required (in addition to horizontal grab grab bar(s)) at control side, see Figure 7.4

shower with 36"d x 48"w (915 x 1220 mm) clear floor space

60" (1525 mm) diameter turning circle, typ.

PLAN B - Transfer Shower

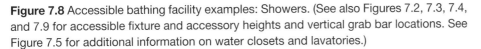

Figure 7.8 Accessible bathing facility examples: Showers. (See also Figures 7.2, 7.3, 7.4, and 7.9 for accessible fixture and accessory heights and vertical grab bar locations. See Figure 7.5 for additional information on water closets and lavatories.)

support by a disabled person when in position, or it can be moved out of the way to allow another person to assist. (Refer to the ADA and ICC/ANSI standards for additional grab bar options.)

Accessories

Restroom accessories are also regulated by the *ADA Standards* and the ICC/ANSI standard. Accessories include but are not limited to mirrors and medicine cabinets, dispensers, receptacles, disposal units, air hand dryers, and vending machines. The type or number of accessories is not typically specified by the codes. However, a certain number of accessories are required to be accessible. In single-toilet and bathing facilities, where one of each type of accessory is used, all accessories must be accessible. In multi-fixture facilities, at least one of each type of accessory must be accessible.

A wide variety of accessory styles are available. For example, both a hand dryer and a paper towel dispenser are available in accessible styles. However, the appropriate choice is usually dependent on the type of space, the traffic pattern of the occupants, and the client's preference. A client may prefer a hand dryer instead of a paper towel dispenser to eliminate the continual cost of towels as well as limit the amount of trash and maintenance of the facility. (In some cases, a jurisdiction will require specific accessories for certain building types.)

When selecting an accessible accessory, the controls on the device must be easy to operate using one hand, with minimal turning and pressure. Devices that are automatic or use levers or push buttons are typical choices. In addition, it is important that the location of a device does not create a projection of more than 4 inches (100 mm) into the accessible circulation path. In order to accommodate this, many accessories are available that recess fully or partially into a wall. To avoid unnecessary projections and allow for required floor clearances within a toilet or bathing facility, it is a good idea to recess fixtures whenever possible. When a recessed fixture cannot be used, walls can be built to provide an alcove so that the fixture is not in a direct path. For example, in Figure 7.6, an alcove was created to allow the deeper hand dryers to be surface mounted on the wall. (The trash receptacles are shown partially recessed into the wall in the same figure.)

In addition, accessories that are accessible must be installed so that they are within certain reach ranges. Typically, they are required to be installed so that the operating part of the device is between 15 inches (380 mm) and 48 inches (1220 mm) above the floor. For example, a fold-down changing table, an amenity often supplied in public restrooms, must be installed so that when folded down, the top is no higher than 34 inches (865 mm) above the floor—similar to an accessible counter height. Other accessories such as toilet paper holders have minimum and maximum placement; they must be located a certain distance from the front edge of the water closet while allowing for the adjacent grab bar. (See Figure 7.2 and the ADA and ICC/ANSI standards for specific requirements.) For most accessories, a maximum of 48 inches (1220 mm) above the floor is required, as shown in Figure 7.9. The actual height will usually be lower than this and depends on the accessory, how it operates, and the design of the space. Clear floor space in front of the accessory is also required. Typically, at each accessible accessory, a clearance of 30 by 48 inches (760 by 1220 mm) should be allowed. This does not include the accessories located within a toilet stall. (See Figure 7.6.)

Signage

Requirements for signage are found in the *IPC*, the *IBC*, and the accessibility documents. Most toilet and bathing facilities will require at least one sign. The type of sign will depend on the type of facility and the types of other facilities located in the same building. For example, if a building contains both accessible and nonaccessible facilities, the nonaccessible facilities must have a sign indicating the location of the accessible ones. Each multi-toilet or multi-bathing facility must also indicate the location of the nearest family or assisted-use facility. Then each accessible facility must have a sign that includes the International Symbol of Accessibility (the wheelchair symbol).

These signs are similar to the women's toilet facility sign, the family toilet facility sign, and the bathing facility sign shown in Figure 7.10. (If all the facilities in the building are fully accessible, the International Symbol of Accessibility may not be needed on any of the facility signs.) Each accessible stall in a multi-toilet or multi-bathing facility must also post a sign of the International Symbol of Accessibility on the accessible stall door (see Figure 7.10). In addition, the 2009 *IPC* requires directional signage to be posted at the entrance of a building or space which indicates the route to a public toilet facility (as required for customers, patrons, and visitors).

Typically, signage located at toilet and bathing facilities must be accessible. The signs must be both visual and tactile and allow for lettering and symbols in a specified size and proportion. Contrast between the sign and the lettering, as well as raised lettering and the use of Braille, is also important. (See the ADA and ICC/ANSI standards for specifics.) Accessible signs must also meet certain mounting requirements. As shown in Figure 7.11, the sign must be located on the latch side of the door entering the facility (not the hinged side). In most cases, it must also be located between 48 and 60 inches (1220 to 1525 mm) above the floor. This height is typically measured to the baseline of the lettering on the sign. (The

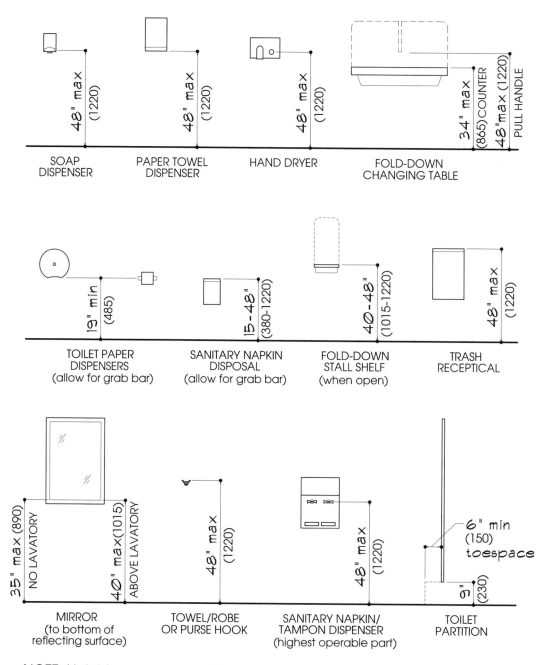

NOTE: Heights are measured to control part of accessory. If accessory is in path of travel, it cannot protrude from wall more than 4 inches (100 mm).

Figure 7.9 Typical accessible toilet accessory heights.

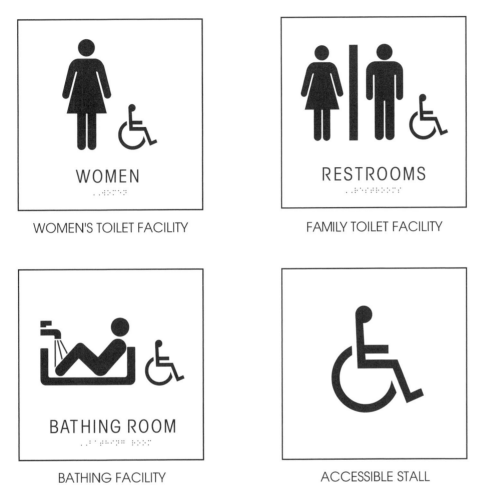

Figure 7.10 Types of accessible signs for toilet and bathing facilities. (Illustrations by APCO Graphics, Inc. [www.apcosigns.com].)

original *ADAAG* measures this to the centerline of the sign.) If a vestibule is used and there is no door, the sign should be located on the right side of the opening. If there is no wall space on the correct side of the door, it should be located on the nearest adjacent wall. Although the sign is not required to be a certain distance from the door frame or opening, it must be located far enough from the door so that the door swing does not overlap the required clear floor space of 18 by 18 inches (455 by 455 mm) below the sign. This is shown in Figure 7.11. The overall goal is to allow a person to get close enough to the sign to read the raised letters or Braille without any obstructions.

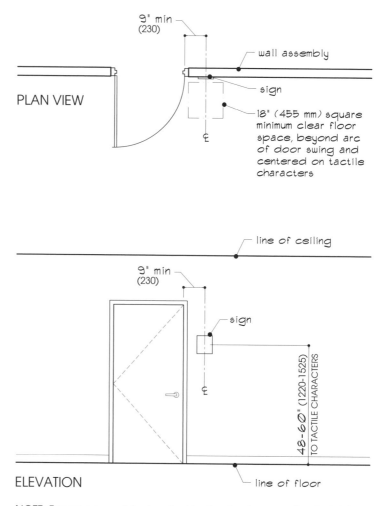

NOTE: For an accessible sign that is visual only, mounting height may vary. See ADA and ICC/ANSI standards for additional requirements.

Figure 7.11 Typical accessible tactile sign locations.

PLUMBING SUSTAINABILITY CONSIDERATIONS

Various codes, standards, and federal laws continue to be created and passed in an effort to make buildings more sustainable and more energy efficient. Water conservation is part of this effort as well, because when less water is used, less energy is used by the utility companies supplying the water and less energy is used inside the building to heat and distribute the water.

The plumbing codes include some sustainable-related requirements. For example, as mentioned earlier in the chapter, various plumbing fixtures must meet minimum water consumption requirements. Most plumbing fixtures and faucets currently made in the United States are built to meet or exceed these standards. Other more restrictive low-flow and low-consumption requirements are found in the energy codes, such as the *International Energy Conservation Code (IECC)*, and the standard *ASHRAE/IESNA 90.1, Energy Standard for Buildings Except Low-Rise Residential Buildings* as required by the Energy Policy Act.

The *International Green Construction Code (IGCC)* includes additional requirements for fixtures and faucets (i.e., fixture fittings). Various tables provide the maximum allowed flow rate for each type of fixture as well as the estimated daily use per occupant and the average duration of each use for each type of fixture. Using these numbers, along with the expected number of occupants, the total expected water consumption for the building can be calculated. This information can be used to help specify "low-flow" plumbing fixtures so that the building's overall water consumption falls within certain thresholds as required by the code. In some cases, the fixture or fitting must also meet the requirements of the Environmental Protection Agency's (EPA's) WaterSense® program, which certifies products that meet minimum water consumption standards set by the EPA. (See the inset titled *Federal Sustainability Certifications* on page 477.) Plumbing fixtures that are considered low-flow include high-efficiency fixtures, dual-flush toilets (which provide a full flush mode for solids and light flush mode for liquids), and waterless urinals, among others.

Rather than concentrate on the efficiency of individual plumbing fixtures, the energy codes focus their requirements on the water heating system. The *IGCC* also references the *IECC* for this information and includes requirements for waste water heat recovery systems. These systems use the heat recaptured from warm outgoing drain water to preheat incoming main water on its way to the water heater. It is required in certain Assembly, Factory, Institutional, and Residential occupancies and building types. Other sustainable techniques include recirculating systems for centralized hot water distribution and point-of-use water heating systems to reduce the need to transport hot water long distances.

Other plumbing-related requirements covered by the *IGCC* include water metering and measuring building water sources (e.g., potable, reclaimed, on-site) and use of alternate on-site sources such as rainwater and graywater (i.e., waste flows from bathing, lavatories, and wash machines) for certain water-related functions. Similar requirements are included in *ASHRAE/USGBC/IES 189.1, Standard for the Design of High-Performance Green Buildings Except Low-Rise Residential Buildings*. Both the *IGCC* and *ASHRAE 189.1* also include performance criteria so alternate sustainable fixtures and systems may be allowed by a jurisdiction as well. For example, composting toilets (using foam-flush or no-flush) may be an

Note

The newest technology in efficient plumbing fixtures includes low-flow faucets, dual-flush toilets, water-free urinals, and solar powered faucets. Some jurisdictions require certain types of fixtures in new construction. Others are required by the energy and sustainability codes.

Note

ASHRAE 189.1 includes requirements for special water features, such as ornamental fountains. When alternate on-site sources or reclaimed water cannot be used, the standard limits the size of the water feature.

Note

Some form of a building automation system (BAS) is typically required when following sustainability codes and standards so that water and energy efficiencies can be measured and monitored. See the inset on page 356 for more information.

Note

Even though allowed by the sustainability codes and standards, some jurisdictions may not allow the use of reclaimed or graywater systems inside a building.

option in certain facilities such as universities, offices park visitor centers, and other recreational areas.

Some of these water conservation and energy-efficiency items are incorporated into the plumbing system design by the mechanical engineer. However, others affect the selection of fixtures and appliances used in the space. Since older fixtures may not meet the most current water consumption standards, this may limit the reuse of existing fixtures in renovation projects. In addition, if specifing fixtures manufactured in other countries, confirm that they will meet the necessary requirements. These requirements must also be considered when custom fixtures are designed and used; research the specific requirements. (See Appendix B for more sustainability information.)

Note

A mechanical engineer typically designs the mechanical system. It will depend on the size and jurisdiction of the project. Each jurisdiction has specific requirements for professional services and stamped drawings. (See Chapter 10.)

COMPARING MECHANICAL CODES

When working on an interior project, collaboration with a mechanical engineer may be required since various parts of a design can affect the mechanical system, such as the location of walls and ceilings and the selection of light fixtures and other electrical equipment. It may also be necessary to coordinate the preliminary design with the engineer to make sure that enough clearance for mechanical appliances and equipment is allowed, especially as it affects ducts and ceiling heights. Coordination of supply diffuser and return grill locations may be necessary as well. (Also see the inset titled *Mechanical Systems* on page 311.)

Note

On projects that require minimal mechanical work, such as adding or relocating a few supply diffusers and return grilles to an existing system, the mechanical contractor may be able to work directly from the drawings or supply the required "shop" drawings.

Although each of the building codes has a chapter on mechanical systems, they simply refer to the mechanical codes and other standards where most of the actual requirements are found. There are two main mechanical codes: the *International Mechanical Code (IMC)* published by the International Code Council (ICC), which is the most widely used, and the *Uniform Mechanical Code (UMC)* published by the International Association of Plumbing and Mechanical Officials (IAPMO) in partnership with the National Fire Protection Association (NFPA). The mechanical engineer should know which code is required.

The mechanical codes contain the requirements for the installation and maintenance of heating, ventilation, cooling, and refrigeration systems. Chapters in the mechanical code include requirements for ventilation and exhaust systems, duct systems, chimneys and vents, boilers and water heaters, refrigeration, hydronic piping, and solar systems, among others. Numerous standards are referenced as well. These include those from the NFPA, the American National Standards Institute (ANSI), and the American Society of Heating, Refrigeration, and Air-Conditioning Engineers (ASHRAE).

Note

Depending on the project, the ICC or NFPA fuel gas code may also be required, as well as some requirements from the corresponding fire code.

The mechanical codes reference the energy codes and standards. In addition, the federal government mandates the use of the *ASHRAE/IESNA 90.1, Energy*

Standard for Buildings Except Low-Rise Residential Buildings as part of the Energy Policy Act (EPAct) (See Chapter 1.) These energy requirements as well as the newer sustainability codes will also affect the design and use of a mechanical system. (These requirements are discussed more in the section Mechanical Sustainability Considerations later in this chapter.) As a result, some engineers are designing HVAC systems using performance-based requirements and specifications.

The allowable performance criteria for the *IMC* are found in a mechanical chapter of the *ICC Performance Code (ICCPC)*. The *ICCPC* generally states that the installation of mechanical equipment must "safeguard maintenance personnel and building

MECHANICAL SYSTEMS

Mechanical systems are often referred to as *HVAC systems*. (This acronym stands for heating, ventilation, and air conditioning.) They can be separate or combined into one system. A wide variety of HVAC systems are available. Various components can be used to customize a system as well. The system that is selected and used in a particular building depends on a number of factors, including the size and use of the building, the number of occupants, the cost, and the maintenance. The three main types of mechanical systems are described as follows:

1. *All-air systems:* This system uses centrally located fans to circulate hot and cold air to and from a space through long runs of ductwork. All-air systems are the most widely used mechanical systems in large buildings. They include the variable air volume system (VAV), which is more popular, and the constant air volume system (CAV).

2. *All-water systems:* This system uses pipes to transport hot and cold water to and from each space where the air is locally circulated by a convector or fan to create the hot and cold air. The most common all-water system is the electric baseboard convector system found in private residences. Other systems include fan-coil terminals, closed loop heat pumps, and hydronic convectors (i.e., "chilled beams").

3. *Air and water systems:* This is a combination system that uses a central fan to circulate fresh air to a space where it is heated or cooled by water before entering the space. The most common combination system is the air-water induction system.

Newer systems are continually being developed to meet the energy requirements in the codes and standards. One of these new systems combines heat and power. Also known as "cogeneration," the system collects the heat generated from producing electricity and uses it to heat (or cool) the water or air for the HVAC system.

Most mechanical systems will require some type of ductwork to supply the air, registers to distribute the air, and/or grilles to retrieve the return air. Some buildings use ductwork to return air as well. This is called a *duct system*. Other buildings use a *plenum system*, whereby the open space above the suspended ceiling and/or the enclosed vertical shafts are used to collect the return air. A raised floor system may also be used to create a floor plenum.

occupants from injury and deliver air at the appropriate temperature for health and comfort." This allows flexibility for the engineer if a building requires a custom mechanical system to be designed. Other performance requirements are given in the *ICCPC* for refrigeration and piped services. If using the *UMC*, the performance chapter in other NFPA codes would need to be referenced for performance criteria. The energy and sustainability codes have some performance-based criteria as well.

Very few accessibility issues affect mechanical code requirements. However, they do become important when locating devices, such as thermostats, that are used by the occupants of the building. These accessibility-related items are mentioned in the sections that follow.

MECHANICAL REQUIREMENTS

All types of mechanical systems will need to meet certain code requirements. Some of these are a part of the building codes. For example, Chapters 5 and 6 of this book discussed ventilation of vertical shafts and fire/smoke dampers. The building codes also have a chapter on interior environments that includes mechanical-related items such as ventilation and temperature control. In addition, some parts of a system may need to meet the sound transmission requirements. (See the inset titled *Sound Transmission* on page 209.) Other provisions are found in the mechanical codes and the standards they reference as well as the energy codes. The main mechanical-related requirements to be aware of as a designer are discussed below. (Other mechanical code items are more specific to an engineer and are not discussed.) Sustainability codes and standards are discussed later.

Mechanical Rooms

Mechanical rooms can include furnace or boiler rooms, fan rooms, and refrigeration rooms. (They are also sometimes called appliance rooms.) Depending on the size of the building and the type of mechanical system used, these rooms can be separate or combined into one. It is the size and location of the mechanical room(s) that are important. The codes specify that each room must have a minimum door width and an unobstructed passageway so that appliances and equipment can be easily replaced. In addition, minimum working space along the control side of each appliance is required. If a mechanical room needs to be located in an interior project, work closely with the mechanical engineer to size the room correctly. In addition, these rooms often need to have fire-rated walls. (See Chapter 5 for fire-rating requirements.) Mechanical rooms are not typically required to be handicap accessible.

Cooling Loads

The cooling load refers to how much energy is required to cool a space. It is one of the main factors in determining the size and type of a mechanical system. (Heating loads are also a determining factor.) Although the number and size of exterior windows and the type of glazing are usually already determined on an interior project, many other interior aspects affect the cooling load. These include the overall size of the space, how the space is divided, and the number of people (occupant load) expected to use the space. Even the types of window treatments used in a space can affect the temperature of a building. For example, certain window shades can reflect the sun's heat.

The number of light fixtures and other equipment is also a large contributing factor. The location of equipment such as computers, printers, copiers, fax machines, and various appliances in specific areas of the design may affect the necessary distribution of cooling. In addition, audio/visual, communication, security, and other special systems must be considered. Therefore, it is important to work closely with the client, the engineers, and other consultants to accurately determine all the requirements for the space or building.

The mechanical engineer uses the specification of each light fixture and every electronic piece of equipment to determine how much heat will be generated within the space. This is measured in BTUs (British thermal units). The total expected number of electrical BTUs is factored in with the other loads of the space to correctly determine the required load of the HVAC system. All of these factors are used by the mechanical engineer in conjunction with the codes and standards to determine the size of the main unit, the size of the ducts, and the number of supply diffusers and return grilles required. These loads are also critical to determine efficient energy utilization as required by the energy codes. (See also the section Electrical Sustainability Considerations in Chapter 8.)

Zoning and Thermostat Locations

Different areas of a building may be zoned separately to provide different levels of comfort. Typically, parts of a floor or building with similar temperature requirements are grouped into the same zone. For example, perimeter rooms that have exterior windows are typically zoned separately from interior spaces. Other rooms may have particular requirements and need to have a separate zone. Print, copy, and janitorial rooms, for instance, may be "isolated" for better indoor air quality throughout the rest of the building. Some spaces may even have a separate supplemental system because of their special needs. Examples include a kitchen in a restaurant, a locker room in a sports complex, a computer room in a school, and a conference room in an office space.

Each mechanical zone has a separate sensor and thermostat. The mechanical codes do not specify the location of a thermostat. Instead, the environmental chapter in the building codes gives a few guidelines; the energy and sustainability codes include additional requirements. For example, the sustainability codes include information on "thermal comfort" and typically require occupants to have an increased access to thermostat controls. This may require more sensors or thermostats located throughout a space. (Wireless thermostats are another option.) Sustainable buildings also require programmable thermostats so that temperatures can be adjusted when the building is not in use. Ultimately, the number of zones and the location of each thermostat are determined by the engineer and depend on the type of system and the surrounding heat sources.

When a thermostat is located for occupant use, the *ADA Standards* and other accessibility standards require that the thermostat be within accessible reaching heights similar to those of an electrical switch. (See Figure 8.4 in Chapter 8.) Clear floor space in front of the thermostat that allows either a side or front approach may also be required.

> **✎Note**
>
> The building codes, energy codes, and sustainability codes specify minimum and maximum temperature control ranges and other requirements for thermostats.

Exhaust Requirements

Whenever *air is removed* from a building or space, the process is considered exhaust. An exhaust system is usually required by the codes in specific types of rooms and in certain occupancies. An exhaust system can remove air that contains smoke, germs, chemicals, odors, or other unhealthy or contaminated components. This is especially important in more hazardous types of occupancies in order to maintain proper indoor air quality. Exhaust systems are typically required in toilet and bathing facilities, designated smoking areas, and kitchens with cooking appliances. Clothes dryers are also required to be exhausted (see Appendix D). Some Hazardous occupancies require larger exhaust systems that change the air in the space a certain number of times per hour and/or create a specified air flow. Certain areas requiring smoke control, such as atriums or malls, may use an exhaust method as well.

> **✎Note**
>
> *Make-up air* is the air provided in a space to replace the air being exhausted.

The rate at which air must be removed from an area is set by the codes and is generally based on the activity or type of air that is being exhausted. When a pipe or duct is connected to the exhaust fan, it must typically be routed to the exterior of a building. Consideration must be given to its route and how it affects other elements in the building, such as floor/ceiling assemblies or vertical shafts. The mechanical codes also may limit the length of the exhaust pipe or duct, including the number of 45- or 90-degree bends it can make. In some cases, locating rooms that require exhaust close to an exterior wall may be required.

Ventilation Requirements

Whenever outside *air is added* to a building or space, the process is considered ventilation. It can be brought in by natural air flow through operable windows, vents, or louvers (known as *natural ventilation*) or by a mechanical system (known as *mechanical ventilation*). The mechanical codes regulate both. They regulate the size of the window, vent, or louver and the amount of required outside air according to the floor area of the space that is being ventilated and the estimated maximum occupant load. If natural ventilation is not possible, then the space is typically required to be ventilated mechanically.

The mechanical code has a table that lists various occupancy classifications and types of occupied rooms within each classification that require outdoor air. In the past, this table based the ventilation requirements solely on the expected number of occupants in the space. However, more current codes take into consideration other building contents, such as building materials and furnishings, which can also affect the quality of air. Measured in cubic feet per minute (CFM), multiple calculations are needed by an engineer to determine the amount of outside air required in the "breathing zones" of the building. Some specialty rooms, such as a computer or telephone room, may have more specific ventilation requirements. It may be advisable to locate these rooms at or near an exterior wall for easier ventilation. Other areas requiring ventilation include atriums and vestibules.

The mechanical codes now allow more flexibility in the design of a ventilation system. Part of this is due to the energy and sustainability codes and standards. Bringing in outside air with mechanical ventilation uses electricity. And, the more outside air brought into a space, the more the HVAC system has to work to condition the new air. The 2009 *IMC* requires less outdoor air for these reasons. However, this also needs to be balanced with the need for indoor air quality as required by the building codes and the sustainability codes. (See the section Mechanical Sustainability Considerations later in this chapter.) A newer ventilation option includes demand control ventilation (or dedicated outdoor air), which uses zoned sensors to monitor carbon monoxide and adjust the amount of outdoor air as required. This is especially useful in spaces where the number of occupants varies greatly, such as conference rooms and theaters. The energy codes also include requirements for energy recovery systems, which uses the ventilation air being expelled from the building to condition the air coming back in, and air economizers (or "free cooling"), which monitors the outdoor air temperature and humidity levels so that outdoor air can be used to ventilate the building without the need for mechanical conditioning.

◤**Note**

Good ventilation is critical for a building's indoor air quality and can help control such things as the carbon monoxide created by building occupants and naturally occurring gasses such as radon.

◤**Note**

The amount of carbon monoxide in a building is a good indicator of the indoor air quality. Typically, as the levels of carbon dioxide rise, so do levels of other contaminants.

◤**Note**

Plenum ceiling and/or plenum floor returns can continue through structurally created vertical shaft enclosures. Both of these spaces must be isolated from other spaces so that debris in these areas will not be drawn into the return air intake.

Plenum Requirements

Most air-type HVAC systems use either a duct or a plenum for return air. (See the inset titled *Mechanical Systems* on page 311.) When there are no ducts attached to the return grilles, the open space between the ceiling and the floor above creates a ceiling plenum that acts as the duct and collects the return air. (If a raised floor system is used, the plenum space may be at the floor level.) When a plenum system is used, it must be limited to specific fire areas within the building. For example, a plenum cannot pass through a stairwell.

In multi-tenant buildings, the plenum must typically be limited to a particular tenant. This could be accomplished by using a separate HVAC system for each tenant. The other option would be to provide rated dampers where openings allow air to pass through the tenant's demising wall. However, if an opening is cut in a rated assembly to allow the return air to continue across the ceiling (or floor) cavity (i.e., air transfer opening), a rated damper must be added to that opening. This includes fire-resistance-rated partitions or barriers, horizontal assemblies, and smoke barriers. (See Chapter 5.) The building codes also prohibit the use of combustible materials in the plenum space. For example, only certain types of rated electrical and communication cables are allowed (see Chapter 8) and any foam plastic used as a ceiling or wall finish must meet certain standards (see Chapter 9).

⊟Note

Existing ductwork can hinder the placement of fire rated walls. A mechanical engineer or contractor may be needed to reroute the ducts or add dampers.

Duct Requirements

If the mechanical system uses ducts to retrieve the air as well as to supply conditioned air to a space, the codes place fewer restrictions on the types of materials allowed in the ceiling space (or floor space). Instead, the codes place restrictions on the ducts themselves. The building codes set some requirements, such as the use of firestops and fire dampers when a duct passes through a fire-resistance-rated wall and other assembly. Smokestops and smoke dampers may also be required when a wall is considered a smoke barrier. (See Chapter 5.) Figure 7.12 indicates the use of a fire damper on a duct that is passing through a fire-resistance-rated wall assembly. The firestop in this case is fire-rated caulk or sealant used continuously around the fire damper on each side where it passes through the wall. The building codes also specify when a damper or shaft enclosure is required around a duct that penetrates a floor/ceiling assembly.

The mechanical codes specify such things as the size of the ducts, types of rated materials allowed, and mounting and clearance requirements. For example, flexible ducts are typically not allowed to penetrate a rated wall; only rigid ducts are allowed. The codes also prohibit the use of mechanical ducts in certain locations and specify when smoke detectors are required in a duct system. When activated, a duct smoke detector can interrupt the power to the fan distributing

⊟Note

Newer codes include stricter requirements for the bracing of piping and ductwork to allow for seismic support.

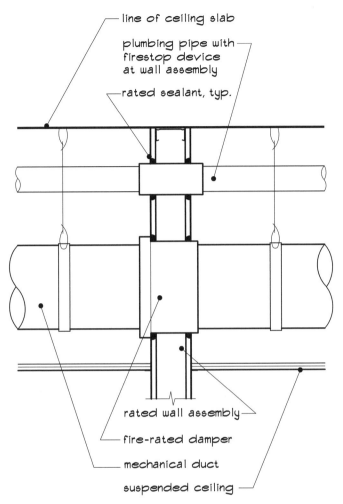

line of ceiling slab

plumbing pipe with
firestop device
at wall assembly

rated sealant, typ.

rated wall assembly

fire-rated damper

mechanical duct

suspended ceiling

Figure 7.12 Mechanical/plumbing penetrations in a rated wall assembly.

the air and close specific dampers. (See the section Smoke Detection in Chapter 6.) Energy codes include additional requirements for the insulation of ducts which include more stringent insulation and sealing requirements. They also typically require motorized dampers in ducts that supply or exhaust outdoor air so that they can be closed when a space is not in use.

Access Requirements

In addition to the appliances in the mechanical room, other equipment and components of a mechanical system, including ductwork and specific duct connections, must allow adequate access for maintenance and inspection. Replacement of major components cannot disable the function of a fire-resistance-rated assembly or remove permanent construction. Suspended ceiling grids, for example, allow easy access to ductwork. When solid ceilings such as gypsum board are used, an access door may be required at specific locations. Some of these accesses might also be required in walls. For example, access must usually be provided at all fire dampers located in the ductwork, at air volume boxes located in the ceiling, and at any shut-off valves used on water type systems. If the assembly is rated, a rated access door is required.

MECHANICAL SUSTAINABILITY CONSIDERATIONS

A large part of a building's energy use comes from the HVAC system. Therefore, the sustainability codes and standards, including the energy codes, provide a number of requirements for mechanical equipment and systems including water-heating systems. In addition, energy requirements mandated by the Energy Policy Act can be found in the standard *ASHRAE/IESNA 90.1, Energy Standard for Buildings Except Low-Rise Residential Buildings* as well as the *International Energy Conservation Code (IECC)*.

Some of the energy requirements were mentioned earlier. The energy codes and standards also require the use of certified equipment that meets minimum efficiency requirements, in addition to the sealing of ducts and building penetrations, specific insulation R-values around ductwork and pipes, types and location of temperature and humidity control devices (including thermostats), automatic shutdown requirements, and types of balancing devices. Requirements for water-heating systems, such as water heaters, storage tanks, boilers, and those used in swimming pools, are included as well. Although many of these items are covered in the mechanical codes, the energy codes provide additional efficiency parameters that must be followed.

The sustainability codes and standards such as the *International Green Construction Code (IGCC)* and *ASHRAE/USGBC/IES 189.1, Standard for the Design of High-Performance Green Buildings Except Low-Rise Residential Buildings* include many similar requirements for mechanical systems. In fact, the *IGCC* often references the *IECC*. However, the *IGCC* and *ASHRAE 189.1* include additional requirements as well, some of which supersede the requirements in *ASHRAE/IESNA 90.1*. Examples include requirements for installing demand control ventilation in densely occupied spaces (see the section Ventilation Requirements earlier in this chapter), air economizers that maximize the use of outside air for conditioning a building, nonpotable water (e.g., graywater, rain water) piping in water-based

✒Note

Newer wireless technology can bring added control and efficiencies to a mechanical system. Temperature sensors, for example, can be easily relocated.

✒Note

Improving the energy efficiency of a mechanical system typically consists of considering both equipment efficiencies and control strategies. Even recessed light fixtures must be properly sealed to eliminate leakage between conditioned and unconditioned spaces.

HVAC systems, and methods for containing pollutants for improved indoor air quality. An HVAC system must also typically be connected to a building automation system (BAS) (see inset on page 356) so that energy and water consumption data can be collected on an hourly basis and monitored remotely.

Sustainable mechanical appliances and equipment are usually required to meet minimum federal certifications for ENERGY STAR, as well as WaterSense when water-based systems are used. (See the inset titled *Federal Sustainability Certification* on page 477.) In some cases these federal certifications are required by the codes too. For example, the *IGCC* requires programmable thermostats to comply with the ENERGY STAR program.

The sustainability codes and standards and the energy codes also include performance criteria that may allow the use of newer sustainable products not yet allowed by the prescriptive codes. For example, the energy codes provide allowances for renewable energy sources such as solar radiation, wind, plant by-products, and geothermal sources. (See Appendix B for more sustainability information.)

◀**Note**

ASHRAE 189.1 also requires the use of the mechanical system to "flush-out" a building with outside air after construction is complete and before it is occupied to help improve the indoor air quality before occupancy.

CHECKLIST

The checklist in Figure 7.13 combines a number of plumbing and mechanical code requirements. The checklist begins by asking you the project and space name, occupancy classification, building type, and occupant load of the space or building you are designing. (These are all explained in Chapter 2.)

The first part of the checklist concentrates on plumbing requirements. It asks you if an engineer is required. This will depend on the size of the project, the amount of plumbing work, and the jurisdiction of the project. (See Chapter 10.) After that, the initial two plumbing sections need to be used together. Sometimes you will already know the type of toilet and/or bathing facilities required in your project. In other cases, you will first need to determine the number of fixtures. For example, the number of required water closets will determine whether you can use "Single (Separate M/F)" toilet facilities or if you need to use "Multi-Toilet" facilities.

The main types of plumbing fixtures are listed in the first column. Use the plumbing code table and the occupant load of the space or floor to determine what fixtures are required and mark these on the list. (See Chapter 2 for information on occupant loads.) You may need to refer to other sections of the code as well. If a fixture is required, write in the total number of fixtures in the next column, separating by male (M) and female (F) where required. This total will be used to fill in the adjacent "Standard Fixtures" column and the "Accessible

◀**Note**

It is often necessary to meet with an engineer in the preliminary stages of a design project so that your design can be coordinated with new and existing plumbing, mechanical, and electrical systems.

Plumbing and Mechanical Checklist

Date: _____

Project Name: _____ Space: _____

Occupancy (new or existing): _____ Occupant Load: _____

Building Type: _____

Plumbing Requirements[2]   Engineer Required ____ YES ____ NO

Type and Quantity of Plumbing Fixtures (check those that apply and insert quantities)

Fixture	TOTAL FIXTURES Required	ACCESSIBLE FIXTURES New	Existing	STANDARD FIXTURES New	Existing
____ Water Closet	M____/F____	M____/F____	M____/F____	M____/F____	M____/F____
____ Urinal	M____/F____	M____/F____	M____/F____	M____/F____	M____/F____
____ Lavatory	M____/F____	M____/F____	M____/F____	M____/F____	M____/F____
____ Sink	M____/F____	M____/F____	M____/F____	M____/F____	M____/F____
____ Drinking Fountain	M____/F____	M____/F____	M____/F____	M____/F____	M____/F____
____ Bathtub	M____/F____	M____/F____	M____/F____	M____/F____	M____/F____
____ Shower	M____/F____	M____/F____	M____/F____	M____/F____	M____/F____
____ Other _____	M____/F____	M____/F____	M____/F____	M____/F____	M____/F____

Type of Facility Required (check those that apply)

Toilet Facilities: ____ Single (Separate M/F) ____ Single (Shared Unisex) ____ Single (Family/Assisted Use)

____ Multi-Toilet: quantity (if more than one each M/F) _____

Bathing Facilities   ____ Single (Separate M/F) ____ Single (Shared Unisex) ____ Single (Family/Assisted Use)

____ Multi-Bath: quantity (if more than one each M/F) _____

Other Plumbing Code/Sustainability/Accessibility Requirements (check/research those that apply)

____ Fixtures: Mounting Heights, Clear Floor Space, Faucet/Control Location, Projections, Water Consumption

____ Faucet/Controls: Ease of Operation (i.e., lever, automatic, etc.), Water Consumption, Water Temperature

____ Grab Bars: Location, Lengths, Heights, Orientation, Additional for Special Situation

____ Accessories: Mounting Heights, Control Locations, Projections, Clear Floor Space

____ Finishes: Smooth/Nonabsorbent, Slip Resistant, Thresholds, Special Locations

____ Room: Turning Space, Overlapping Clear Floor Spaces, Privacy Signage, Stall Size, Door Swing

Mechanical Requirements[2]   Engineer Required? ____ YES ____ NO

Type(s) of Mechanical System(s): _____

Mechanical Room (Size and Location): _____

Air Circulation (Type - Duct, Plenum): _____

Ventilation Required (Type and Locations): _____

Exhaust System Required (Type and Locations): _____

Ceiling Heights Required (Minimums and Clearances): _____

Access Panels Required (Size and Locations): _____

Supply Diffusers Required (Type and Locations - Ceiling, Wall, Floor): _____

Return Grills Required (Type and Locations - Ceiling, Wall, Floor): _____

Thermostats/Zones (Type and Locations): _____

NOTES:

1. Refer to codes and standards for specifics, including energy and sustainability codes and standards as required. Also check the accessibility documents for accessible mounting locations.

2. See Chapter 6 checklist for additional plumbing and mechanical related requirements such as automatic sprinkler system, dampers, etc.

3. Be sure to note on floor plans the location of fire rated walls/ceilings for placement of required fire/smoke stops and dampers.

Figure 7.13 Plumbing and mechanical checklist.

Fixtures" column. Refer to the building codes, the ICC/ANSI standard, and the *ADA Standards* to determine the number that must be accessible. List these required numbers in the "Accessible Fixtures" columns on the checklist, indicating the totals for male and female (where required) and whether they are new or existing. Deduct these accessible fixtures from the total to obtain the number of each standard fixture required. Indicate in the "Standard Fixtures" column how many will be male or female (where required) and whether they will be new or existing. Refer to these numbers as you are locating the fixtures in your design and to determine the types of plumbing facilities.

The next section of the checklist gets into the specifics of toilet and bathing facilities. It provides options to check. Certain types of facilities will be required by the code. For example, if you are designing a smaller space that requires two single-toilet rooms, one for males and one for females, you would check the item "Single (Separate M/F)." A large Assembly or Mercantile occupancy would require a "Single (Family/Assisted-use)" toilet facility in addition to one or more multi-toilet facilities, so you would check both of these and fill in the total number of fixtures. If you are designing an occupancy with an occupant load under 15, you may be allowed to use one single-toilet facility as a "Single (Shared Unisex)." Similar categories are provided for bathing facilities.

The third section under plumbing requirements is a checklist of the various components that are included in a typical toilet and bathing facility. The various requirements that should be researched are listed for each component. You can use this list to verify that you have included the necessary components in each facility and as a reminder to check both the codes and accessibility requirements for each.

The last section of the checklist concentrates on the mechanical system of a project. Again, it asks you whether an engineer is required. It then lists the main mechanical items you should look for in an existing building or be aware of if a new building or space is being designed. Fill in the information as required and refer to it as you plan your design. If necessary, work with an engineer to determine these items. You may also want to attach a reduced copy of the floor plan indicating the location of rated walls and other assemblies so that the location of dampers and other items can be noted.

CHAPTER 8

ELECTRICAL AND COMMUNICATION REQUIREMENTS

This chapter covers the codes, standards, and federal requirements for electrical systems and communication systems. When working on an interior project, knowledge of certain electrical codes and standards is necessary, especially when determining the location and types of outlets, fixtures, equipment, and appliances. Specifying communication systems will also require familiarity with these requirements. However, when a project requires substantial electrical work, an electrical engineer is required to design the electrical system. Larger communication systems will require an engineer or a special consultant. On smaller projects, such as some residential projects or minimal changes to a tenant space, that do not require collaboration with an engineer, a licensed electrical contractor will know the requirements that apply.

✎Note

The *NFPA 70, National Electrical Code* is the most commonly used electric code in the United States.

The electrical and communication requirements are discussed separately in this chapter. The first half of the chapter concentrates on electrical requirements. It begins with a discussion of the various codes and standards that affect electrical systems and then discusses the requirements for the various components of the electrical systems. It also includes a section on sustainability, which highlights energy efficiency in relation to the codes and standards. The second half of the chapter discusses different communication systems and how they are affected by the codes and standards. These systems include telephones, computers, security, background music, and television systems, among others. The sustainability of communication systems is discussed as well.

Throughout the chapter, accessibility-related requirements are also mentioned. These include relevant regulations in the Americans with Disabilities Act (ADA) standards and comparable *ICC/ANSI A117.1* accessibility standard requirements. The last part of the chapter contains an electrical and communication checklist.

COMPARING ELECTRICAL CODES

Traditionally, the *National Electrical Code* (*NEC* or *NFPA 70*), published by the National Fire Protection Association (NFPA), has been the code used by electrical engineers and electrical contractors to design and install a building's electrical system. It is the main electrical code used in the United States. Many of the code requirements found in the *NEC* pertain to the wiring of the electrical room/closets and the many types of cables, connections, and devices used to create the electrical systems in a space or building. (See the following inset titled *Electrical Systems.*) However, the *NEC* also includes information on types and locations of outlets, locations of light fixtures in wet areas, and other requirements

ELECTRICAL SYSTEMS

An electrical system consists of a distribution system (also known as a transmission system) and a premises wiring system. The *distribution system* is controlled by the electrical utility company and originates in huge generators. From these generators, high-voltage wires transport the electricity to transformers. The utility transformers convert the electricity to lower voltages before it enters a building. The utility distribution system ends at the service entrance connection point to the building and usually includes the utility meter.

The *premises wiring system* is the electrical system within the building. Premises wiring begins where the utility service connection is made and extends to the building's main electrical panel and to the outlets used throughout the building for fixtures, appliances, and equipment. In larger buildings, where the utility company provides higher voltages, additional interior transformers may be used before or after the electricity reaches the panel board. This panel board is typically contained in an electrical room and may consist of a main disconnect switch, secondary switches, fuses, and circuit breakers. Sustainable buildings using renewable on-site energy may have additional electrical equipment.

Cables and wires run from this electrical panel to various locations throughout a building. In smaller buildings, these cables or branch circuits are directly connected to the electrical outlets. In larger buildings, feeder conductors are used to distribute the electricity horizontally and vertically to a number of smaller panel boards. These panel boards supply electricity to separate areas within the building. Branch circuits are then used to connect the smaller panel boards to the various electrical outlets. (Newer wireless control systems may also be incorporated.)

The *National Electrical Code* regulates only the portion of the electrical system that is controlled by the building. It does not typically include any part controlled by the electrical utility company. However, as more buildings incorporate some form of on-site renewable energy and start supplying some of their own utilities, this may change.

specific to an interior project. Certain occupancies and building types have additional electrical requirements as well. These include Assembly occupancies, Health Care facilities, and those with dwelling units, and certain facilities with high electrical needs, such as theaters and television studios. There may be instances in which the *NEC* needs to be referenced in addition to other codes and standards that include electrical requirements.

The building codes include a chapter on electrical systems, but these chapters typically reference the *NEC*. For example, the *International Building Code (IBC)* "Electrical" chapter references the *NEC*. The chapter also includes a section on emergency and standby power systems that refers to various other parts of the *IBC*, such as the "Means of Egress" chapter for exit signs and egress illumination and the "Fire Protection Systems" chapter for smoke control systems. These and other requirements need to be coordinated with those found in the *NEC*. The *Life Safety Code (LSC)* also references the *NEC*.

The *NEC* references a number of standards throughout its text. Many of them are NFPA standards, such as those found in Figure 8.1. Other standards organizations with electrical standards include the National Electrical

☑**Note**

The 2006 *ICC Electrical Code—Administrative Provisions (ICCEC)* is the last edition that will be printed by the ICC. This publication has been incorporated into the appendix of the *IBC*. The "Electrical" chapter of the *IBC* now directly references the *NEC*.

NFPA 70	National Electric Code
NFPA 70A	National Electrical Code Requirements for One- and Two-Family Dwellings
NFPA 70B	Recommended Practice for Electrical Equipment Maintenance
NFPA 70E	Standard for Electrical Safety in the Workplace
NFPA 72	National Fire Alarm and Signaling Code
NFPA 75	Standard for the Protection of Information Technology Equipment
NFPA 76	Standard for the Fire Protection of Telecommunication Facilities
NFPA 77	Recommended Practice for Static Electricity
NFPA 110	Standard for Emergency and Standby Power Systems
NFPA 111	Standard on Stored Electrical Energy Emergency and Standby Power Systems
NFPA 262	Standard Method of Test for Flame Travel and Smoke of Wires and Cables for Use in Air-Handling Spaces
NFPA 269	Standard Test Method for Developing Toxic Potency Data for Use in Fire Hazard Modeling

NOTE: There may be other NFPA standards not listed above that are specific to an occupancy, especially hazardous occupancies. Additional standards are available from UL and ASTM as well as ISA and IEEE.

Figure 8.1 Common NFPA standards for electrical and communication systems.

Manufacturers Association (NEMA) and Underwriters Laboratories (UL). In addition to providing supplemental design and installation procedures, these organizations develop standards for the fixtures themselves, as well as provide specific testing and labeling procedures for electrical and communication equipment.

☜**Note**

As of 2009, the *NFPA 900, Building Energy Code (BEC)* is no longer in print as a stand-alone document. (It is still part of the National Fire Code Set.) Instead, the *NFPA 5000* references the standard *ASHRAE/IESNA 90.1.*

The energy codes also include requirements that affect electrical components. The most widely used is the *International Energy Conservation Code (IECC)* by the International Code Council (ICC). It establishes minimum regulations for the design of energy-efficient buildings and references the standard *ASHRAE/ IESNA 90.1.* Some of the same requirements have also been made mandatory by the federal government. (See the sections Energy Codes and Energy Policy Act in Chapter 1.) Additional energy-efficient requirements are included in the newer sustainable documents, including *ASHRAE 189.1.* (See the section ASHRAE in Chapter 1.) Energy-related requirements will be discussed later in this chapter in the section Electrical Sustainability Considerations. (See Chapter 7 for mechanical and water-heating energy requirements.)

The *NEC* does not include performance code requirements for electrical systems, although some performance-related codes are mentioned in the *IECC* as well as the newer sustainability codes and standards. If using other NFPA codes, their performance-related chapters can be referenced for certain performance criteria. In addition, if the *ICC Performance Code (ICCPC)* is allowed by the jurisdiction, it includes electrical-related performance criteria. For example, it includes a chapter on electricity as well as a few electrical-related items in the fire safety chapter. Most of the criteria concentrate on the safe isolation of electrical equipment, devices, and appliances, as well as protection of the building occupants from live parts. In addition, when using the *IBC*, the alternative materials and methods *IBC Section 104.11* is another option. (See Chapter 1.)

Accessibility issues related to electrical systems mostly apply to the mounting height of the outlets and fixtures. In some cases, the projection of light fixtures must also be considered. These and other accessibility requirements from the Americans with Disabilities Act (ADA) standards and the *ICC/ANSI A117.1* accessibility standard, as they apply to electrical systems, will be discussed throughout the chapter.

ELECTRICAL COMPONENTS AND DEVICES

Below is an explanation of the various components and devices of an electrical system in relation to the codes and standards that apply to them. (Energy efficiency will be explained later in the chapter in the section Electrical

Sustainability Considerations.) The *NEC* applies to all types of occupancies and building types. However, there are often separate or additional electrical requirements for Residential occupancies, dwelling units, guest rooms, and/or sleeping units (as discussed below). Dwelling and sleeping units, and sometimes guest rooms, can be found in many Residential occupancies as well as in some Institutional building types. To better understand the definitions of a dwelling and a sleeping unit, refer to the inset titled *Rooms and Spaces* on page 73.

In addition to the various requirements described below, all parts and devices of an electrical system must be tested and approved in order to be used. Most must be labeled as well. (See the inset titled *Testing Agencies and Certification* on page 41.) This includes the electrical panel, cabling, and other components used to create the system, as well as the receptacles, switches, and other devices used by the occupants of the building. Light fixtures, as explained below, must also pass certain tests.

Electrical Panels and Rooms

Three types of electrical panels can be used in a building. The first and largest is the service entrance *switchboard*. It is the main electrical panel that distributes the electricity from the utility service connection to the rest of the building. The *NEC* regulates the size of the room that contains this panel based on the equipment used in the room. For example, one of the most typical requirements is that there must be a clear working space at least 3-feet (914 mm) deep by 30-inches (762 mm) wide in front of the panel and clear space above the panel. (Larger panels may need more clearance.) When the switching panel is two-sided, the code requires enough working space on both sides of the panel. Other equipment in the room, including transformers, will require clearances as well. (See the inset *Electrical Systems* on page 324.) These rooms are typically required to be fire rated (see Chapter 5), and, depending on the size of the room and/or equipment, the door(s) must meet certain egress requirements to include location, direction of swing, and hardware used. The switchboard room must also be ventilated (see Chapter 7) to control heat buildup from the equipment. If it is located on an outside wall, ventilation can be done directly to the outside. If not, ducts and fans must be used to provide outside air ventilation. (Refer to *NEC* for duct location restrictions.)

Power panel boards are used throughout a building to distribute electricity to each floor and/or tenant or dwelling space. They are one-sided electrical panels that are typically housed in electrical closets or in cabinets that are placed in or against a wall. In multi-story buildings, the electrical closets should be stacked directly above each other on each floor so that the electrical systems can be vertically

◢Note

An electrical panel is a common place for a fire to start. When designing interiors, be careful not to locate electrical panels next to stairwells or other main means of egress.

◢Note

There is often a conflict between sprinklers required in an electrical equipment room and/or a communications room and the safety of the equipment due to water damage. Although *NFPA 13* allows sprinklers to be eliminated if certain requirements are met, a dry sprinkler system or an alternate extinguishing system may also need to be considered. (See Chapter 6.)

distributed. Each floor may also have one or more smaller *branch panel boards* that supply electricity to a particular area or tenant. Typically, closets that contain only panel boards do not have to be rated. Closets that contain large transformers and panel boards are required to be rated.

All these requirements are important to know, especially if creating a layout for a new space or building and one or more electrical closets must be located. Work closely with an engineer to make sure that the closets are located as required for distribution and that the room sizes allow electrical panels and other equipment to have the correct clearances. In addition, these rooms typically require a visible sign clearly stating "Electrical Room" or similar approved wording.

Electrical Cabling and Conduit

⬛Note

If a cable is run continuously from the electrical panel to the device, without any intermediate connections, it is considered *a home run*.

To distribute electricity to all areas where it is needed, electrical wiring must pass through many building elements. When electrical wiring is installed, the diameter of any hole created for the passage of the cable cannot be more than 1/8 inch (3 mm) larger than the diameter of the cable, conduit, or other device passing through the hole. When these wires pass through a rated floor, ceiling, or wall assembly, the building codes require the use of a rated firestop and/or smokestop. (See Chapter 5 for more information.)

In some cases, an electrical cable may be allowed to run on its own, while others will require the use of a protected enclosure such as a conduit or raceway. This typically depends on the type of cable and the construction type of the building (see Chapter 3), but it can also depend on the location of the cable within a building. For example, if a cable is run within a rated assembly, it typically must be within a conduit. Certain jurisdictions have special requirements or restrictions as well. Various cables, conduits, and raceways are explained next.

Cabling

⬛Note

Plenum spaces created by suspended ceilings or access (i.e., raised) floor systems require the use of specially rated electrical and low-voltage plenum cables.

The *NEC* specifies the types of electrical wiring or cables that can be used. There are many different types of cables available and each cable must go through testing in order to be classified for its specific use. A variety of testing standards are used in order to determine performance and safety. Other tests are used to evaluate the flammability of the cable and determine its flame spread and smoke density (similar to the *Steiner Tunnel Test* described in Chapter 9). Since the protective sleeve of the cable can be highly toxic when exposed to a fire, certain cables must also undergo a toxicity test. (See the section *Toxicity Test* in Chapter 9.) Once tested, the cable is labeled with its appropriate classification.

The types of electrical cables used on a project are typically specified by the electrical engineer or contractor using the requirements of the *NEC*. Although noncombustible cable is required in many occupancies and most building conditions, certain areas within a building may require other types of cables. For example, special rules apply for wiring in ducts, plenums, and other air handling spaces as well as shafts used for elevators in order to limit the use of materials that would contribute smoke and products of combustion during a fire. (See Chapter 6.) The most common types of cables are listed here:

❏ *Romex*: Romex is the trade name that is commonly used to refer to *nonmetallic-sheathed cable* (Type NM, NMC, or NMS). It consists of two or more insulated conductors and should include a ground wire surrounded by a moisture-resistant plastic material. The *NEC* limits this cable mostly to Residential one- and two-family dwellings and multi-unit dwellings not exceeding three floors.

❏ *Armored cable*: Armored cable (Type AC) sometimes referred to as *BX* or *flex cable*, is a flexible cable that consists of two or more conductors wrapped in heavy paper or plastic and encased in a continuous spiral-wound metal jacket. It is commonly used in commercial applications. In new installations, the *NEC* requires BX to be secured in intervals, but in older installations the cable might have just been fished through walls, floors, and ceilings. In addition, BX is often used to connect light fixtures in suspended ceiling grids to allow relocation flexibility. In most instances, the *NEC* will limit the length of an unsecured flex cable to 6 feet (1.8 m); however, other jurisdictions may be stricter. It is not allowed in damp or wet locations.

❏ *Metal-clad cable*: Metal-clad cable (Type MC) is often used when BX cable is restricted. It looks similar to BX cable, but MC cable has an additional green ground wire that provides extra grounding. As a result, it can be used in more applications than BX cable.

❏ *Flat wire*: Flat wire is the common name for *flat conductor cable* (Type FCC). It is a small cable in a flat housing that allows it to be used under carpet tiles without protruding. (The *NEC* specifies that carpet tiles covering flat wire cannot be larger than 36 inches [914 mm] square.) Flat wire can be used in many applications, and it is often used to rework obsolete wiring systems in existing buildings. The *NEC* prohibits the use of flat wire in wet and hazardous areas and in residential, hospital, and school buildings.

◤**Note**

Some jurisdictions restrict the use of BX cable in buildings even if the *NEC* allows it.

❏ *Fiber optic cable:* In the past, fiber optic cable was used mostly in low-voltage applications. However, it can also be used as a conductor for electrical components such as lighting. In addition, an optical fiber can be run in a cable that contains an electrical wire. When this occurs it is called a composite cable and is classified as an electrical cable according to the type of electrical conductor or wire used with it. (More information on fiber optic and composite cables can be found in the section Low-Voltage Cabling later in this chapter and in Figure 8.8.)

Conduit

◀Note

Empty flexible metal conduit is also known as *green field.*

Another option often used when wiring large residential and most commercial buildings is *conduit.* Also known as *tubing* in the *NEC,* conduit is a hollow piping used to house and protect plastic conductors or cables. More than one wire or cable can be fished through the conduit; however, the code may limit the types of cables that can be used together. For example, electrical cables often are not allowed to be used in the same conduit as communication cables. The conduit may also act as a system ground (see the section Grounding and Circuit Interrupters later in this chapter) and may protect surrounding building materials should a wire overheat.

There are a number of different types of conduit, including rigid and flexible metal conduit and rigid and flexible nonmetallic conduit. (Nonmetallic conduit can be made of plastic, PVC, resin, or fiberglass.) Conduits can also be referred to as *conduit bodies.* This term is used to describe larger raceways that have removable covers for access to the wires inside them. (See the following section Raceways and Cable Trays.) The type of conduit required depends on where it will be used and the types of hazards present. For example, nonmetallic conduit is often used underground to bring the power into a building; however, its use inside a building is usually restricted, especially in fire-rated assemblies. Instead, rigid and flexible metal conduits are most often used in a building interior. Rigid metal conduit is allowed by the *NEC* in all occupancies and in almost any condition. Flexible metal conduit has some limitations. For example, it cannot be used in certain hazardous areas, and its length may be limited.

Other code requirements apply more to the installation of the conduit. This includes the requirements for the diameter of the conduit allowed, as well as the types of connections and the number of bends allowed in each run. In addition, the building codes will require a firestop or smokestop (see Chapter 5) when conduit is installed through a rated wall or ceiling assembly. This is shown as sealant in Figure 8.2. Additional restrictions might be enforced on a local level by a code jurisdiction.

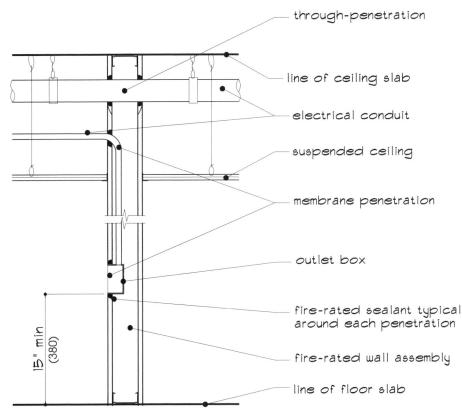

Figure 8.2 Electrical penetrations in a fire-resistance-rated wall assembly.

Raceways and Cable Trays

Like conduit, *raceways* (or *wireways*) can also be used to house and protect electrical cables. The *NEC* may limit their use in some applications, but most of the code requirements are geared instead to the cable connections made within the raceways. Raceways may be used in place of a conduit or in conjunction with other conduits. For example, some types of buildings are constructed with concrete or metal floor raceways that are part of the structural floor system. Often referred to as cells, these raceways come in different shapes and sizes and are often laid out in a grid-type system, allowing cables to be run from one area of a building to another. As a building's needs change, the cabling can be changed and redirected. Other underfloor raceways may be added after the initial construction of a building as part of the finished floor assembly (e.g., a raised floor system).

◄Note

Cable trays are an effective way to distribute cables in existing or historic buildings especially in areas where the existing structure cannot be disturbed.

Raceways may also be mounted on walls for easy access. For example, wireways that are enclosed with removable covers can be installed around the perimeter of a factory to allow access to the cables as locations of equipment change. Openings (e.g., knockouts) in the wireways allow the cabling to be directed to different locations when needed. Other types of raceways can be used to cover a cable run on the surface of the wall. (Certain codes may restrict the use of raceways when used with fire-rated assemblies.)

Historically, *cable trays* have been used in industrial building types to distribute cables across a ceiling. They are also commonly used in commercial applications to run communication-type cables either exposed in an open ceiling or above a suspended ceiling. Cable trays allowed by the *NEC* include the following types: ladder, ventilated trough, ventilated channel, and solid bottom. The *NEC* specifies the width of the tray based on the number of cables, the allowed locations, and the type of electrical cables allowed in the tray, among other things.

Circuitry

◄Note

If an outlet has special power requirements, a dedicated circuit can be specified so that it will be wired separately. This will prevent electrical disturbances from other nearby electrical equipment.

The distribution of electricity is managed and organized by creating different circuits. Separate circuits are created by wiring (or cable) that branches from the main electrical source to different areas of the building or space. Each circuit feeds electricity to a series of light fixtures, outlets, equipment, and/or appliances before it returns to the branch panel or power panel board. Each circuit may be carrying a different voltage and amperage of power. For example, a washing machine will require a 220-volt circuit, which must be separate from the 120-volt circuit required for the lights in the room.

The *NEC* limits the number of volts or amperage that is allowed on a single circuit. Therefore, it is important to supply the electrical engineer with the correct number and types of lighting, equipment, and appliances that will be used in a space or building so that the circuitry can be designed correctly. The engineer uses the specifications of the items to determine the electrical loads of the space and how many circuits are needed to meet the requirements of the code. This can affect the number of light fixtures that can be switched together and the number of fixtures that can be controlled by dimmers. In addition, certain pieces of equipment that require more power may need a circuit that serves only a single outlet. This is called a *dedicated circuit*. It is also known as clean power. The outlet that it serves is referred to as a dedicated outlet. For example, dedicated circuits are often used for large equipment such as copiers and for many appliances such as refrigerators, electric ranges, and clothes dryers. Most mechanical equipment and the main equipment for many communication systems will require a dedicated outlet as well.

Electrical Boxes

There are three main types of electrical boxes: outlet boxes, switch boxes, and junction boxes. Unlike electrical conduit that often penetrates the entire wall or ceiling assembly, electrical boxes usually penetrate only the outer membrane of the wall, as shown in Figure 8.2. (See Chapter 5 for more information on membrane penetrations.)

When electrical boxes are located in fire-resistance-rated walls, floors, or floor/ceiling assemblies, the building codes set additional requirements. These are listed below. (If an electrical box is located in a smoke assembly, additional requirements must be met.)

❑ *Type:* The box must be metal. If not, it must be tested for use in fire-resistance-rated assemblies. In addition, one box typically cannot exceed 16 square inches (0.0103 s m).

❑ *Quantity:* The total number of boxes in one wall or ceiling is limited. The total number of openings in a rated wall or ceiling surface measuring 100 square feet (9.29 s m) cannot exceed 100 square inches (0.0645 s m).

❑ *Location:* When boxes are used on opposite sides of the same wall, the boxes must be separated horizontally by 24 inches (610 mm) unless the boxes are listed for closer spacing or have some type of barrier or fireblocking between them. (See the section Fireblocks and Draftstops in Chapter 5.)

❑ *Firestopping:* Fire-rated caulking or other type of firestop (or smokestop) must be used around the box where it penetrates the membrane to seal the space between the box and the wall. (See Figure 8.2 and the section Firestops and Smokestops in Chapter 5.)

This will apply to any type of electrical box (or communication box) that penetrates a rated assembly or membrane and might affect the design of a room or space. For example, if a breakroom is adjacent to a fire-rated wall, it may be best not to locate the counter with all its required electrical appliances along that wall, due to the number of outlets required. Also be aware of accessibility requirements as they apply to electrical outlets. Similar requirements are given in the *ADA Standards* and the ICC/ANSI standard, as well as in the accessibility section of the building codes. The *NEC* and accessibility requirements are described here for each type of box. Energy efficiency–related issues are included as well.

Outlet Boxes

Outlet boxes can be wall and/or floor mounted for electrical receptacles or wall and/or ceiling mounted for light fixtures. If the box allows for the connection of a

◀Note

If an existing electrical box is not being used, it must either (1) have a cover plate or (2) be totally removed (including the box and all wiring) with the wall opening properly patched.

◀Note

Since the installation of electrical boxes creates a membrane penetration rather than a through-penetration, as described in Chapter 5, firestopping is not always required.

⬛Note

A *pull box* is another type of electrical box that is used during installation as an intermediate box for pulling through long runs of cable.

plug-in appliance or equipment, it is typically called a *receptacle outlet*. When used for a light fixture, the box is often referred to as a *fixture outlet* or a *lighting outlet*. Most outlet boxes are either 2 × 4 inches (50 × 100 mm), such as those used for duplex receptacle outlets or wall sconces, or 4 × 4 inches (100 × 100 mm) for a quadraplex receptacle outlet and certain ceiling fixture outlets. However, other sizes and different depths are available and will depend on the type or number of devices wired to the one box. For example, boxes used for hanging light fixtures are often octagonal.

Outlet boxes are usually mounted within a wall by fastening the box to a stud. For example, in a metal stud and gypsum board wall, the outlet box is mounted to the metal stud and a hole is cut around the gypsum board to allow access to the box. (Surface-mounted boxes are more common on masonry walls.) In the ceiling, the box can be mounted to a joist or directly to the underside of the ceiling slab. The *NEC* specifies that the opening in the wall or ceiling cannot exceed a 1/8-inch (3.1 mm) clearance between the box and the gypsum board. In a rated wall, this gap must be sealed to create a firestop or smokestop. (See the section Light Fixtures later in this chapter for additional box requirements.)

Because the needs of residences are somewhat consistent, the codes provide more specific outlet requirements for Residential occupancies such as homes, apartments, dormitories, and even certain guest rooms in hotels. (They may also include some Institutional building types. See the inset titled *Rooms and Spaces* on page 73.) If a building or space is considered a dwelling unit, the *NEC* specifies the minimum number of electrical boxes to be provided. In each room of the dwelling unit, receptacle outlet boxes must be installed so that no point measured horizontally along the floor line at any wall space is more than 6 feet (1.8 m) from an outlet. (A wall space is generally defined as any fixed wall that is at least 2 feet [600 mm] wide.) An example of how to place the outlets is shown in Figure 8.3. Hallways that connect the rooms within the dwelling unit that are more than 10 feet (3 m) in length also require at least one receptacle outlet. (This does not apply to common hallways or corridors that connect multiple dwelling units to each other.) Of course, additional outlets can always be added based on the needs of the space, but the minimums need to be met. In addition, the *NEC* (and the *IRC*) requires specific location of outlets in bathrooms, kitchens, laundry areas, basements, and garages. (See also the section Grounding and Circuit Interrupters later in this chapter.) And, new in 2008, the *NEC* requires all 15- and 20-ampere receptacle outlets in all types of dwelling units to be tamper resistant.

Since the needs and requirements in non-Residential facilities vary with the activities and equipment needs of a particular tenant or user, the codes do not provide as many specific requirements as for dwelling units. The *NEC* does not specify the frequency of receptacle or lighting outlet boxes in these occupancies.

⬛Note

In Residential occupancies, when a wall is broken by a doorway, fireplace, or similar opening, each continuous wall space of 2 feet (600 mm) or more must be considered separately for the placement of a receptacle outlet.

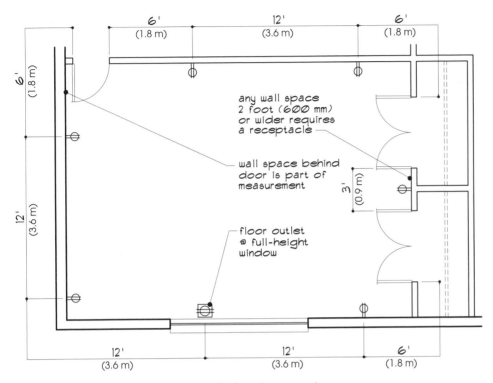

Figure 8.3 Dwelling unit receptacle outlet location example.

Instead, their placement is determined by specific equipment requirements and convenience considerations. For example, the location of a copier or fax machine will determine the location of the receptacle, or the typical length of a cord on a vacuum cleaner may be a good guideline for placement of receptacle outlets within a long corridor. There are some building types, however, that will require special types of receptacle outlets—for example, hospital-grade receptacles at certain patient bed locations.

Certain outlet boxes are required to be accessible. This will depend on the location and use of the outlet, the type of equipment connected to it, and if it is meant for use by employees and/or visitors. An example of a nonaccessible outlet is an outlet in a janitor's closet or an outlet behind a permanent copier where it serves a dedicated use. Consider if there is a possibility that the employee who will use the outlet could be disabled and need the outlet within the accessible reach ranges. Other outlets that are meant to be used by clients, visitors, or the general public should be accessible as well, such as an outlet meant for plugging in a laptop computer. (Certain locations may need to be reviewed with the building owner.) However, when specifying the typical location of wall outlets

◢Note

When placing receptacle outlets, the *NEC* includes additional requirements specific to guest rooms, guest suites, dormitories, and similar spaces, which provide additional safety as well as convenience to the users.

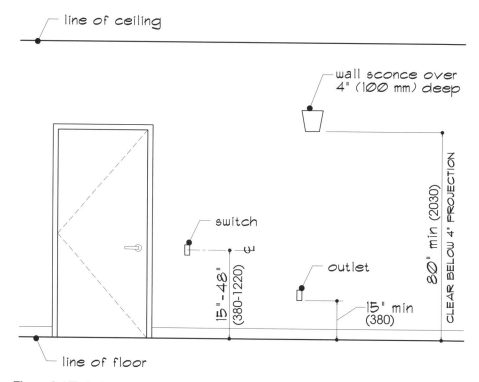

Figure 8.4 Typical accessible electrical device and fixture locations.

in a project, it is a good idea to use a height that meets accessibility requirements whenever possible. Should the function of a room or space change in the future, the outlets will already be accessible.

When the outlet box is mounted on a wall, the typical accessible requirement is that it be located at least 15 inches (380 mm) above the floor, as shown in Figures 8.2 and 8.4. In addition, when designing accessible work areas, such as study carrels in public libraries and workstations in offices, any outlets must be located within the appropriate reach ranges. Whenever possible, locate the outlets directly above the worksurface or counter. For example, many workstation panel systems now come with electrical raceways at counter height rather than the traditional floor location. A special outlet could also be mounted toward the front edge under the worksurface. (Floor outlets are not typically considered accessible, but if they are used, they should not be located within the clear floor space necessary at an accessible counter, table, or desk.)

Switch Boxes

Switch boxes are typically wall mounted and control the lighting (or fixture) outlet. The cable connection between the light fixture and the switch device or control is made at the switch box. This control can be in the form of a toggle, dimmer, sensor, or remote. Many of the code requirements for switch boxes are similar to those for outlet boxes. For example, the switch box must be mounted to a stud or other blocking and the hole cut for the box cannot be larger than 1/8 inch (3.1 mm) around the box.

The *NEC* has requirements specifically for dwelling units. The main requirement is that each habitable room, as well as hallways and stairs that lead up to these rooms, must have a switch outlet that controls the lighting in that room. In addition, a stairway must typically have lighting that is controlled at both the top and bottom of the stair. The energy codes and standards provide additional requirements. For example, the *IECC* requires that sleeping units, such as hotel rooms, have at least one master switch at the room entrance that controls all light fixtures in the space (except the bathroom).

In occupancies and building types that do not include dwelling units, the *NEC* does not specify the frequency of a switch outlet. It allows multiple switches to be ganged together and conveniently located in larger open areas. However, the energy codes and standards require at least one "manual control" (i.e., switch) for each area or room of a commercial building. (This does not include means of egress components.) These same areas must also typically include *dual switching*. Also known as bi-level or split switching, dual switching means that the light fixtures in a space are evenly distributed to two adjacent switches, allowing an occupant to use one of the switches to uniformly reduce the level of illumination by 50 percent. Typically required by the *IECC*, exceptions include sleeping units, storerooms, restrooms, and public lobbies. (Sleeping units have separate requirements.)

When multiple fixtures are ganged together, the *NEC* limits the number of light fixtures that can be circuited to one switch. This number is based on the voltage of the fixtures used. The total voltages are determined by the electrical engineer based on the cut sheets of the selected light fixtures. (See the section Circuitry earlier in this chapter.) In addition, the energy codes and standards typically require automatic lighting shutoff devices in all commercial buildings over 5000 square feet (464.5 s m). This can be accomplished with time-scheduling devices, occupant sensors, daylight sensors, or other similar signals used in open and enclosed spaces. For large open areas, depending on the total square feet, the code or standard may require the space to be split into different switching zones. For example, the *IECC* requires that spaces adjacent to skylights and vertical fenestrations (i.e., windows), known as daylight zones, be switched separately from the general lighting controls. In any location, if an automatic switch sensor is used, the *NEC* requires that the lights be controlled by a manual switch as well. (See also the section Sustainability Considerations later in this chapter.)

Switch boxes must be located within the accessible reaching height above the floor. They must be between 15 and 48 inches (380 and 1220 mm) above the floor, as shown in Figure 8.4, measured to the centerline of the box. Switches that are not required to be accessible are those in areas used only by service or maintenance personnel, such as janitor closets and mechanical rooms. If there are multiple switches to the same fixture, not all of them are required to be accessible.

Junction Boxes

Unlike the other electrical boxes already explained, a junction box is not used to connect an outlet or fixture. Instead, it is used to tie (or splice) several wires together. For example, a main cable run that leaves the electrical panel will, at some point, need to branch off to electrify several light fixtures. At the point where these wires come together, a junction box is typically used to protect the various cable connections and to allow for future access. It is also used as an intermediary *pull box* when there are long conduit runs. The size of the box used will depend on the number of connections that need to be made.

Junction boxes are usually specified by an electrical engineer as part of the design and installation of the electrical wiring. However there may be times when a junction box needs to be specified in a particular location. For example, if a client plans to add a future light fixture in a certain location, a junction box wired for future use would be specified.

The *NEC* requires that a junction box be accessible to the electrician at all times. For example, junction boxes are often located on or near the ceiling. If using a suspended ceiling grid with removable tiles, access becomes very easy. However, if a junction box is located in an area where there will be a drywall ceiling, an access panel must be added. The size of the panel depends on how easily the box can be reached from the underside of the ceiling. If the junction box is located flush with the surface of a wall or ceiling, a blank cover plate can be used as the access panel. If a project includes a number of decorative ceilings, it may be best to coordinate the locations of any necessary junction boxes with the electrical engineer.

GROUNDING AND CIRCUIT INTERRUPTERS

The electrical code requires that all electrical systems be *grounded*. This is accomplished by a third wire that typically accompanies an electrical cable. In general, this ground wire redirects live currents into the earth to prevent a person from getting shocked when there is a short circuit. Because a grounding wire is not always 100 percent effective, in certain cases additional measures must be taken to protect the electrical outlet and the person using it. There are two types of *circuit interrupters* that the *NEC* requires, depending on the location of a receptacle outlet. Both are described below.

Ground Fault Circuit Interrupters

The presence of water makes it easier for an electrical current to flow. If the circuit or outlet is wet or if the person touching the outlet or adjacent appliance is wet or standing in water, there is a much higher chance of getting shocked despite the fact that the circuit is already grounded. As a result, the *NEC* requires special grounded circuits in rooms where water will be present.

These circuits are called *ground-fault circuit interrupters*, also commonly known as *GFCI* (or sometimes *GFI*). The GFCI is a device that is able to detect small current leaks. If a current leak occurs, the GFCI disconnects the power to the circuit or appliance and thus prevents an electrical shock from occurring. The GFCI can be installed in the electrical panel as part of a circuit breaker, or it can be installed as a special type of receptacle at the electrical outlet.

The *NEC* requires that exterior receptacle outlets be GFCIs. On interior projects, typically all standard 125-volt, 15-amp, and 20-amp receptacle outlets located in areas where there is water should be specified as GFCIs. These areas include restrooms, bathrooms, kitchens, breakrooms, bar areas, laundry rooms, and even pools or spas. (Residential garages, crawl spaces, and unfinished basements usually require them as well.) The *NEC* divides these requirements into those for dwelling units (including guest rooms and dorm rooms with provisions for cooking) and those for more commercial applications. (See the inset titled *Rooms and Spaces* on page 73.) Some of the more common *NEC* requirements for GFCIs in building interiors include the following:

❑ *Bathrooms in dwelling units:* The *NEC* requires a receptacle outlet to be located within 3 feet (900 mm) of each bathroom lavatory used in a dwelling unit such as private homes, assisted living facilities, apartments, and hotels. These outlets as well as any other outlet in a dwelling unit bathroom must be GFCI-protected. An example of a hotel bathroom with a GFCI outlet is shown in Plan A of Figure 8.5.

✑Note

A GFCI outlet is not typically required at water coolers unless the water cooler is located in an area where GFCIs are already required.

✑Note

All vending machines (which dispense a product or merchandise) and electrically-powered drinking fountains must be GFCI-protected. Water cooler dispensers do not.

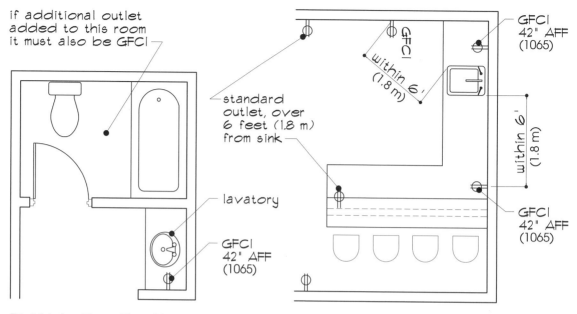

Figure 8.5 Required GFCI outlet location examples.

❏ *Kitchens in dwelling units:* All receptacle outlets that serve the countertop of a kitchen in a dwelling unit, no matter where the sink is located, must be GFCI-protected. This includes outlets in the walls above the counter, outlets in the side of a base cabinet, and outlets required at island and peninsular counters. It does not include standard-height wall outlets (e.g., 15 inches, or 380 mm, above the floor) adjacent to the counter or outlets installed for built-in appliances such as a garbage disposal, refrigerator, or range.

❏ *Laundry, utility, and wet bar sinks in dwelling units:* If there is a laundry, utility, or wet bar sink located in a dwelling unit, any receptacle outlet within 6 feet (1.8 m) of the edge of the sink (or water source) must be a GFCI-protected outlet. This is measured by the shortest distance, as shown in Plan B of Figure 8.5, not by the distance along the wall line. It affects all general outlets as well as those required for appliances. Any outlet outside the 6-foot (1.8 m) perimeter of the sink is not required to be a GFCI.

❏ *Public and/or employee restrooms:* All receptacle outlets provided in public and/or employee restrooms found in nondwelling building types must be GFCI-protected. This includes any outlet near the lavatory as well as any

◀ Note

A GFCI is also available as a device that plugs into an existing outlet. It should be used only on a temporary basis and is often used on a construction site before the permanent wiring has been installed.

other outlet in the room. Examples include restrooms in commercial build-ings, airports, and industrial facilities.

❏ *Commercial and institutional kitchens:* All receptacle outlets located in com-mercial and institutional kitchens used for food preparation and cooking (e.g., includes permanent cooking appliances) must be GFCI-protected. (This does not include a breakroom or kitchenette that provides only a plug-in microwave and/or coffee maker.) The GFCI requirement covers all receptacle outlets in the room or space, not just those that serve the coun-tertop. Examples include kitchens in restaurants, hotels, schools, churches, and similar facilities.

❏ *Sinks in other occupancies:* New in 2008, all receptacle outlets within 6 feet (1.8 m) of the edge of any sink in a nondwelling situation must be GFCI-protected. (See Plan B of Figure 8.5.) Therefore, the typical breakroom or kitchenette (without permanent cooking appliances) now requires GFCIs in certain locations. This also applies to sinks in janitor closets, class-rooms, and the like. (There are some exceptions for sinks in industrial laboratories and health care facilities.)

Additional GFCIs may be required by the *NEC* or by a jurisdiction in certain building types. For example, additional GFCI outlets are required by the *NEC* in certain Health Care occupancies and other GFCI requirements apply to hot tubs, Jacuzzis, pools, and so forth.

Arc-Fault Circuit Interrupters

Sometimes an electrical wire will discharge an unexpected electrical current across the insulation meant to protect it, causing what is known as an *arc-fault*. There are a number of reasons this can happen, but it is usually due to a defect in the cable that shows up after extended use or as a result of unseen damage dur-ing installation or renovation. An arc-fault gets very hot. When it occurs, it cre-ates pressure that will spread hot gases and molten metal to surrounding areas. It has the potential to ignite surrounding combustibles, such as wall insulation, and start a fire. As a safety precaution, the *NEC* requires protection of certain outlets.

Since 1999, the *NEC* has required the use of *arc-fault circuit interrupters*, or *AFCIs*, in the sleeping rooms of all dwelling units. This includes each bedroom in a residential home or apartment building as well as sleeping rooms in other building types such as hotels and nursing homes that are classified as dwell-ing units or are considered guest rooms or suites. (See the inset titled *Rooms and Spaces* on page 73.) In the 2008 *NEC*, the requirement expanded to include most other living areas in a dwelling unit such as family rooms, dining and living rooms, libraries and dens, recreation rooms, and sunrooms as well as

◄Note

Although all electrical outlets in kitchenettes and breakrooms without permanent cooking appliances (e.g., stove or oven) are not required to be GFCI-protected, if the outlet is located within 6 feet (1.8 m) of the edge of the sink it must be GFCI-protected.

◄Note

Fire alarm systems should not be connected to GFCI or AFCI circuits. Single or multiple-station smoke alarms that are not connected to a fi re alarm system (with a control panel), should be connected to AFCI circuits.

◄Note

All approved AFCIs are tested using the standard *UL 1699, Standard for Arc-Fault Circuit-Interrupters.* This standard recognizes five types of AFCIs: branch/feeder, combination, cord, outlet, and portable. The combination-type is what is typically required by the code.

closets and hallways. Not included are bathrooms, kitchens and other areas typically protected by GFCIs.

Every 125-volt, 15-amp, and 20-amp outlet in these rooms must be connected to a circuit that is AFCI-protected. This includes receptacles, light fixture and ceiling fan connections, switches, and even smoke detectors unless they are part of a fire alarm system. (Fire alarms should not be connected.) Unlike GFCIs, where a single device can be replaced to make a receptacle outlet GFCI-protected, AFCI requirements do not allow this. Instead, the entire circuit within the room or space must have AFCI protection so that all devices attached to the circuit are AFCI-protected. This is typically accomplished by installing an AFCI circuit breaker at the electrical panel board. If an arc-fault is detected anywhere along the circuit, the AFCI will essentially disconnect the power to (i.e., de-energize) the entire circuit, thereby making the arc harmless.

Note

The 2008 edition of the *NEC* greatly expanded the use of AFCI protection in a dwelling unit beyond the sleeping room to cover other living areas.

LIGHT FIXTURES

Light fixtures, also called *luminaires* by the *NEC*, have some additional code and standard requirements. The *NEC* requirements are based on the type of light fixture and where it is installed. The building codes specify minimum light levels allowed, while the energy codes and standards concentrate on the energy efficiency of the light fixture. In addition, the location of the fixture may be affected by accessibility requirements and the *ADA Standards*. Many of these requirements are discussed in this section.

Note

UL standards for light fixtures also specify the maximum wattage of the lamp to be used in the fixture. Using a higher wattage can result in overheating and damage to the wiring.

Types of Light Fixtures

Only fire-tested and labeled light fixtures should be used on interior projects. The most widely accepted standards are those created by Underwriters Laboratories (UL). Each light fixture manufactured in the United States is tested to be used in a specific environment or location and is then assigned a UL rating or seal of approval. (See the inset titled *UL Labels* on page 45.) For example, a fixture installed in a damp location, like the ceiling of an enclosed shower unit, must be marked "Suitable for Damp Locations." (Other bathroom fixtures typically do not need this rating.) Other light fixtures are specifically marked for wall mounting, undercabinet mounting, ceiling mounting, and suspended ceiling mounting. Certain fixtures will also note when they are allowed in noncombustible, non-fire-rated, or fire-resistant construction. Selection of the fixture must be appropriate to the location in which it will be used.

Note

A light fixture or other electronic device listed for a wet location can also typically be used in a damp location.

The codes and standards require only UL-approved fixtures on a project. However, not every light fixture is UL approved. When specifying fixtures supplied by countries outside the United States and fixtures made by custom fabricators, additional research may be required. And, because of stricter federal requirements, older fixtures may need to be replaced (not reused) when renovating an existing space. Energy codes and standards limit the overall wattage of a space or building, which in turn affects the types of light fixtures selected for a project. This is explained in more detail in the section Electrical Sustainability Considerations later in this chapter.

In the past, the *NEC* allowed the light fixture to dictate the type of outlet box used to mount the fixture. The 2008 *NEC* requires all ceiling fixtures to be installed in a box rated for 50 pounds (23 kg) regardless of the weight of the fixture. The only exception is for utilization equipment, such as smoke detectors, that do not weigh more than 6 pounds (3 kg). This is not required for wall sconces; instead, these boxes must be marked with the maximum weight permitted. Heavier fixtures, such as ceiling fans and larger pendants or chandeliers, must either be supported independently of the box or be attached to a box made specifically for heavier fixtures. UL standards for light fixtures also specify the maximum wattage of the lamp to be used in the fixture. Using a higher wattage can result in overheating and damage to the wiring as well as affect its efficiency.

Location of Light Fixtures

The *NEC* places strict requirements on the access to the various electrical components that are part of the light fixture. In addition to an accessible electrical box, all light fixtures must be placed so that both the lamp (i.e., light bulb) and the fixture can be replaced when needed. This becomes especially important when light fixtures are used within architectural elements such as ceiling coves, custom light boxes, and specially designed millwork. The custom unit must be designed so that easy access is provided to the fixture. In addition, fixtures used in special applications must be carefully located so that they do not cause the fixture or other adjacent materials to overheat. The performance codes are also very clear on this. For example, the *ICCPC* specifically states that "building elements shall be protected from thermal damage due to heat transfer or electrical arc from electrical power installations." If the light fixture is used in an enclosed space, ventilation might be required to prevent heat buildup, especially when using low-voltage fixtures that tend to get very hot. In addition, if the fixture is used in conjunction with light-transmitting plastics, the "Plastics" chapter of the building codes has additional restrictions

◢Note

Solid-state lighting (SSL) includes light-emitting diodes (LEDs), organic LEDs (OLEDs), and polymer LEDs (PLEDs). Because this technology is so unique, the typical standards used to test and compare lamps do not accurately test SSLs. This makes it difficult to directly compare SSLs with other types of lamps. The Department of Energy is working on standardization through its CALiPER program.

◢Note

Light fixtures that include air handling as part of the mechanical system can typically be used as long as provisions are made to stop the movement of air through the fixtures at the start of a fire.

and may even require additional sprinkler heads to be provided. (Also see the inset titled *Plastic Finishes* on page 419.)

In rated ceiling and wall assemblies, only certain types of light fixtures are allowed. For example, when light fixtures (i.e., recessed cans) are recessed into a ceiling that has a 1-hour fire rating, the mechanical part of the fixture must be rated. If not, a fully enclosed rated box must be built around the housing to maintain the 1-hour rating of the ceiling assembly. In other instances, noncombustible material must also be sandwiched between the fixture and the finished surface. In all cases, specify a fixture meant for the application so that the appropriate air circulation is maintained.

The *NEC* also places restrictions on certain light fixtures installed over bathtubs and shower areas (in any occupancy). It includes all light fixtures except surface-mounted and recessed fixtures. For example, no part of a hanging luminaire, pendant fixture, track fixture, or ceiling fan can be within 8 feet (2.5 m) above the top of the bathtub rim or within 8 feet (2.5 m) above a shower threshold up to 3 feet (900 mm) away from the plumbing fixture. (This is to make sure that they stay out of the reach of a person standing on the tub rim.) This is shown in Figure 8.6. (If the shower has no threshold, the measurement is taken from the floor.) This same requirement applies to hot tubs and similar types of bathing fixtures. Other specific dimensions are given by the *NEC* for light fixtures installed in clothes closets, in show windows, and over combustible materials. For example, a light fixture in a clothes closet must typically be installed so that there is a minimum clearance of 6 to 12 inches (150 to 300 mm) between the fixture and the nearest storage item (e.g., edge of shelf or hanging rod), depending on the type of light fixture. (LED fixtures are now allowed as well.) Similar clearances, although not specified, should be considered in other types of storage spaces where tall shelving may become an issue.

Earlier in the chapter, it was mentioned that the *NEC* requires lighting outlets in certain locations within a dwelling unit. Although it does not restrict the number or location of light fixtures in most non-Residential occupancies, the building codes do set minimum light levels that must be met in all habitable spaces. (See the inset titled *Rooms and Spaces* on page 73.) This is found in the "Interior Environment" chapter of the building code. This chapter specifies the amount of glazing that must be used during the construction of a building to provide natural light in a habitable space. It also specifies the amount of artificial light that must be used in a habitable space when enough natural light is not provided. This often applies to interior rooms and spaces that are not along the perimeter of the building and includes stairways in dwelling units. In these spaces, the lighting must typically provide an average illumination of 10 footcandles (107 lux) over the area of the room at a height of 30 inches (762 mm) above the floor. (Certain occupancies, such as Educational occupancies, may have

Note

Light fixtures placed over tubs and showers require luminaires listed for damp locations (or listed for wet locations when subject to shower spray). Other fixtures in a bathing facility typically do not require this rating. It will depend on the jurisdiction.

Note

Certain types of lighting have additional code requirements. These include high-intensity discharge (HID) lighting, consisting of metal halide (MH), mercury vapor (MV), and high-pressure sodium (HPS), low-voltage lighting, and neon lighting. (Energy regulations are phasing out mercury vapor lamps.)

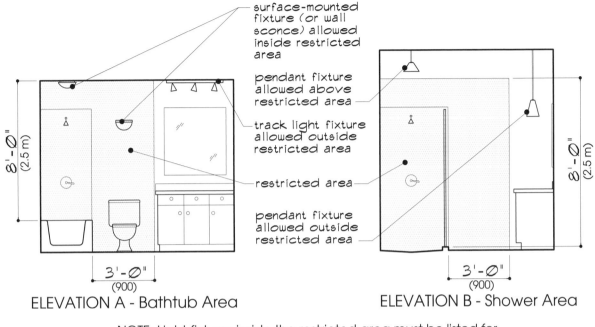

surface-mounted
fixture (or wall
sconce) allowed
inside restricted
area

pendant fixture
allowed above
restricted area

track light fixture
allowed outside
restricted area

restricted area

pendant fixture
allowed outside
restricted area

8'-0"
(2.5 m)

3'-0"
(900)

ELEVATION A - Bathtub Area

8'-0"
(2.5 m)

3'-0"
(900)

ELEVATION B - Shower Area

NOTE: Light fixtures inside the restricted area must be listed for
damp locations (or wet locations if subject to shower spray)

Figure 8.6 Typical lighting restrictions at bathtubs and showers.

additional requirements.) As long as these minimum light levels are met, the number, types, and locations of the light fixtures do not matter, according to the *NEC*. (See the next section for light levels in means of egress.) However, depending on the type of building or space, certain energy-efficiency requirements may also be required. This is explained in the section Electrical Sustainability Considerations later in this chapter.

If the space is required to meet accessibility regulations, then light fixtures must meet certain height requirements. These are found in the *ADA Standards* and the ICC/ANSI standard. Fixtures used as wall sconces must be mounted at least 80 inches (2030 mm) above the floor if they protrude from the wall more than 4 inches (100 mm). This is measured to the bottom of the fixture, as shown in Figure 8.4. This becomes especially important in circulation paths such as corridors and other spaces used by the public. If a light fixture is less than 4 inches (100 mm) deep, then it can be mounted at any height. If the sconce is used in a private room or office, this requirement does not necessarily need to be met. Other fixtures not in a circulation path, such as fixtures mounted above a permanently fixed counter or other millwork, do not need to meet the requirement. This minimum height applies to pendant fixtures as well. When hung from the ceiling, the fixture cannot hang any lower than 80 inches (2030 mm) above the floor unless it is mounted directly over a piece of furniture. (The furniture will prevent anyone from knocking into the light fixture; and if the furniture is moved, the height of the pendant can be changed more easily than that of a wall sconce.)

REQUIRED ELECTRICAL SYSTEMS

The building codes, the fire codes, and the *Life Safety Code (LSC)* have additional requirements for electrical systems. These include emergency power systems and standby power systems. When they are required and to what extent they are required typically depend on the type of occupancy and the building type. (A building owner may want to add these types of systems for other reasons as well.) The building codes and/or the *LSC* will specify when a system is required and refer to the *NEC* for the specifics of the system and how it is installed. The *NEC* also references the standards *NFPA 110, Standard for Emergency and Standby Power Systems* and *NFPA 111, Standard on Stored Electrical Energy Emergency and Standby Power Systems.* Typically, an electrical engineer would design this type of system, but it is important to be aware of both systems because they affect the selection of fixtures and other interior elements.

Emergency Power Systems

Emergency power systems (EPSs) are required by the codes in most buildings to maintain a specific degree of illumination. They are also required in certain building types to provide power for essential equipment, such as fire pumps in high-rise buildings and life-support equipment in hospitals. They are used to back up the normal electrical system in case of an emergency. The goal is to allow the occupants of a building to stay safe or to evacuate safely. The typical EPS must have the capacity to operate such equipment as means of egress lighting, exit signs, automatic door locks, certain fire protection systems, and other emergency equipment.

The building codes and the *LSC* specify emergency lighting requirements. The requirements are found in the "Means of Egress" chapters of the codes. (See also the section Emergency Lighting and Communication in Chapter 4.) Each code specifically states the following basic requirements:

❑ *Illumination level*: Artificial lighting must be present in the means of egress when a building is in use. (There are exceptions for Residential occupancies.) The intensity of the emergency lighting must typically be 1 footcandle (11 lux) at the floor level on the path of egress. (These numbers can

> **✎ Note**
>
> Important sources for emergency and standby power systems are *NFPA 110, Standard for Emergency and Standby Power Systems* and *NFPA 111, Standard on Stored Electrical Energy Emergency and Standby Power Systems.*

be reduced at times of performance in some Assembly occupancies.) More recently, the NFPA codes added that new stairways be illuminated by at least 10 footcandles (108 lux).

❏ *Exit signs*: Exit signs must be located and illuminated in such a way that they can direct occupants safely out of the building. (See the section Signage in Chapter 4.) Exit signs can be externally illuminated, internally lit, or self-luminous. Typically, they must be illuminated by at least 5 footcandles (54 lux) at the illuminated surface and have a contrast level of not less than 0.5. (Some jurisdictions may require similar light levels for area of refuge signs and for signs at elevators used as a means of egress.)

❏ *Emergency power*: Provisions must be made so that in case of power loss, emergency or exit lighting will be available for a certain period of time. Most codes require that exit lighting be connected to an emergency power source that will ensure illumination for at least 1 1/2 hours in case of power failure. For example, in Business occupancies, a battery pack can usually be used as the emergency source of power. In some occupancies, such as Assembly, Institutional, or Hazardous occupancies, a separate source of emergency power, or EPS, must be provided for the exit signs. In all cases, the codes specify how to periodically test emergency lighting equipment to make sure it will work in an emergency.

When allowed, the easiest method of creating emergency lighting in a design project is to add the typical twin-headed emergency light with a battery pack in the appropriate locations. An alternate solution would be to include some of the general lighting fixtures on a separate circuit designated for emergency lighting. This allows the separate circuit to be connected to the main power source as well as the backup power source. And, if one light fixture burns out, it will not leave an area in darkness. Some ways to ensure this are to use dual-lamp light fixtures or to design an overlapping light pattern. In addition, if there are switches connected to the emergency light fixtures, the *NEC* specifies that the switches be located so that it is convenient for authorized persons who will be responsible for their activation. Automatic, motion sensor–type light switches may also be allowed.

The *NEC* provides other requirements for EPSs as well. The main requirement is that when the power changes from the main power source to the emergency system, the delay cannot be longer than 10 seconds. It also gives the specifics for the types of backup systems that can be used. These usually include a generator, a storage battery system, or a totally separate (or redundant) electrical service into the building. Uninterruptible power supplies (UPS) are also sometimes used. Which system to use is typically determined by the electrical engineer and the code official.

⌦Note

Newer energy codes and standards also limit the power of an exit sign to 5 watts in an effort to provide additional energy efficiency in a building.

⌦Note

In some building types, such as hospitals and businesses with critical computer systems, the 10-second power delay may not be acceptable. It may be necessary to add an uninterrupted power supply (UPS) that keeps the electricity flowing during the 10-second transition time.

Standby Power Systems

Standby power systems are similar to emergency power systems. They are used to supply power when the normal power source fails in an emergency. However, instead of operating the emergency systems essential for life safety, standby power is used for other building systems such as the fire pumps, mechanical system, general lighting, communication systems, elevators, and other standby equipment. The *NEC* divides these into two categories: legally required standby systems and optional standby systems.

Legally required standby systems are those that are required by the building codes, the fire codes, the *LSC*, or a code jurisdiction. For example, standby power systems are typically required in some building types, such as certain Assembly, Institutional, and Hazardous occupancies, as well as high-rise buildings. These systems are intended to provide electrical power to aid in firefighting, rescue operations, control of health hazards, and similar operations. They are also mandatory when a building has a smoke control system and may be required for other parts of a building's mechanical ventilation system. (See Chapters 5 and 7.) Many of the requirements for a legally required standby system are similar to those of an EPS. One difference is that the standby system has up to 60 seconds to operate after the failure of the normal power supply.

In other cases, the building owner or tenant may decide to include certain building systems on standby power. These would be considered *optional standby systems*. The decision to provide an optional standby system is usually based on the concern for physical discomfort, serious interruption to a business, or damage to certain equipment. Examples include telecommunication systems, refrigeration equipment, elevators not required on emergency systems, and building automation systems.

The specifics of both types of standby power systems are found in the *NEC* and the standard *NFPA 110*. Often the same system supplying the emergency electrical system will also be used for the standby power system, but it could be a totally separate system. More recently, the *NEC* includes "selective coordination" requirements for legally required standby systems as well as EPSs. Similar to the circuit interrupters described earlier in the chapter, they are protective devices installed to detect overcurrent problems throughout an electrical system. These overcurrent protective devices (OCPDs) are located by the engineer in a manner that causes the least interruption to the system. Should a power surge occur, the service interruption is limited to the circuit experiencing the problem, not the whole facility, which minimizes the extent of the power disruption.

ELECTRICAL SUSTAINABILITY CONSIDERATIONS

The electrical codes and standards concentrate on the safety of an electrical system. The energy codes as well as the newer sustainability codes and standards focus on making an electrical system more energy efficient so that a building is considered more sustainable. Although some of the requirements are similar between these various documents, there are differences. For example, in the energy codes, energy-efficiency requirements first concentrate on the exterior shell of the building. Several factors, including the number and types of windows, affect the amount of electricity needed to condition the interior air and to light the interior spaces over time. The sustainability codes and standards take a different approach. Their goal is to make a building self-sustainable so that ultimately all of its energy is renewable on-site (i.e., net-zero energy). Although the technology to accomplish this is not yet commonly available and/or cost effective, these codes concentrate on setting up systems to monitor the building's electrical system. (This is also required by the 2005 Energy Policy Act. See Chapter 1.) As the requirements get more stringent, these monitoring systems should allow the building owner to analyze the existing conditions and make improvements accordingly.

Inside the building, the energy codes concentrate on efficiency of the equipment. Some of the energy requirements of mechanical and water heating systems were explained in Chapter 7. The goal of many of these requirements is to limit the amount of electricity required to run the systems. Lighting is also a large part of a building's electrical load. The energy codes and required standards can affect the selections of light fixtures as well as their controls (e.g., switches). For example, where daylight is provided, the energy codes require switching to be zoned separate from the areas without daylight exposure. Equipment and appliances, such as copiers, dishwashers, and clothes dryers, are typically not regulated by the codes since they already must meet certain federal energy requirements in order to be sold in the United States. (See Energy Policy Act in Chapter 1.)

Although the energy codes and standards required for electrical systems will typically be incorporated into the design by a electrical engineer, the choice of light fixtures, appliances, and distribution of electrical outlets by the designer can affect the building's efficiency. For example, the *International Energy Conservation Code (IECC)* and the standard *ASHRAE/IESNA 90.1* both include a similar interior lighting power density (LPD) table such as Table 505.5.2, "Interior Lighting Power Allowances," shown in Figure 8.7. The table sets the maximum wattage per square foot (square meter) allowed in various spaces and building types. The total wattage allowed is determined by multiplying the square footage of

✎ Note

Depending on the edition of the *IECC* or ASHRAE standard required by a jurisdiction and that required by the federal government, energy efficiency requirements will vary. Use the most restrictive requirements when necessary.

✎ Note

After considering the building envelope, the three largest components of a building's energy consumption are typically the HVAC system, the lighting system, and the appliances and devices plugged into the electrical system (i.e., plug load).

✎ Note

The *IECC* and *ASHRAE/IESNA 90.1* require lighting power density (LPD) calculations and both include tables with LPD values for a *whole building method* (based on building areas). However, the ASHRAE standard also includes LPD values for a space-by-space method (based on specific functions of the space).

TABLE 505.5.2
INTERIOR LIGHTING POWER ALLOWANCES

LIGHTING POWER DENSITY	
Building Area Type[a]	(W/ft^2)
Automotive Facility	0.9
Convention Center	1.2
Court House	1.2
Dining: Bar Lounge/Leisure	1.3
Dining: Cafeteria/Fast Food	1.4
Dining: Family	1.6
Dormitory	1.0
Exercise Center	1.0
Gymnasium	1.1
Healthcare—clinic	1.0
Hospital	1.2
Hotel	1.0
Library	1.3
Manufacturing Facility	1.3
Motel	1.0
Motion Picture Theater	1.2
Multifamily	0.7
Museum	1.1
Office	1.0
Parking Garage	0.3
Penitentiary	1.0
Performing Arts Theater	1.6
Police/Fire Station	1.0
Post Office	1.1
Religious Building	1.3
Retail[b]	1.5
School/University	1.2
Sports Arena	1.1
Town Hall	1.1
Transportation	1.0
Warehouse	0.8
Workshop	1.4

For SI: 1 foot = 304.8 mm, 1 watt per square foot = W/0.0929 m^2.

a. In cases where both a general building area type and a more specific building area type are listed, the more specific building area type shall apply.

b. Where lighting equipment is specified to be installed to highlight specific merchandise in addition to lighting equipment specified for general lighting and is switched or dimmed on circuits different from the circuits for general lighting, the smaller of the actual wattage of the lighting equipment installed specifically for merchandise, or additional lighting power as determined below shall be added to the interior lighting power determined in accordance with this line item.
Calculate the additional lighting power as follows:
Additional Interior Lighting Power Allowance = 1000 watts + (Retail Area 1 × 0.6 W/ft^2) + (Retail Area 2 × 0.6W/ft^2) + (Retail Area 3 × 1.4 W/ft^2) + (Retail Area 4 × 2.5 W/ft^2).
where:

Retail Area 1 = The floor area for all products not listed in Retail Area 2, 3 or 4.

Retail Area 2 = The floor area used for the sale of vehicles, sporting goods and small electronics.

Retail Area 3 = The floor area used for the sale of furniture, clothing, cosmetics and artwork.

Retail Area 4 = The floor area used for the sale of jewelry, crystal and china.

Exception: Other merchandise categories are permitted to be included in Retail Areas 2 through 4 above, provided that justification documenting the need for additional lighting power based on visual inspection, contrast, or other critical display is *approved* by the authority having jurisdiction.

Figure 8.7 *International Energy Conservation Code®* Table 505.5.2, Interior Lighting Power Allowances (*2009 International Energy Conservation Code*, copyright 2009. Washington, DC: International Code Council. All rights reserved. www.iccsafe.org).

the conditioned spaces in the building by the LPD value on the table. If using the *IECC*, the *whole building method* based on the various "Building Area Types" listed in the table must be used. If using the ASHRAE standard, it includes the same table as well as a second more detailed table that provides LPD values for "Common Space Types." This gives the option of dividing the building into more specific functions and using a *space-by-space method*. (The space-by-space method typically allows for more flexibility.) To meet the code, the sum of all interior lighting power cannot exceed the determined wattage allowance. This can affect the type and quantity of light fixtures included in the design. (Retail spaces have additional calculations as shown in the table footnotes.)

When using the LPD table, allowances are provided for special lighting needs, such as decorative, display, or accent lighting, as well as other safety-required lighting, such as exit signs and emergency lights. Typically, these are not included in the calculation. For example, if calculating the total wattage allowed by the *IECC* for an educational facility with an adjacent office space, the square footage of the spaces for each building type would be determined separately. Then the LPD table in Figure 8.8 would be used to determine how many watts are allowed per square foot: The "Office" building type allows 1.0 watts per square foot and the "School/University" building type allows 1.2 watts per square foot. Multiply the square footage for each building type by the respective LPDs and add the results to determine the maximum wattage allowance for the facility. In this example, when adding up the total wattage of all the specified light fixtures, the following would not be included: emergency lighting, exit and directional signage, specialty lighting in a class room, furniture-mounted task lighting, maintenance task lighting. (See the code and/or standard for specifics.)

The overall goal is to reduce the electrical load required in a building by specifying more energy-efficient fixtures and equipment and/or reducing the number of fixtures. Examples of more energy-efficient light fixtures include high-performance T8 fluorescent fixtures, T5 fluorescent fixtures, or light-emitting diodes (LEDs). The type of lamp will make a difference as well. Some options include using high-output (HO) lamps, high-intensity discharge (HID) lamps, or compact fluorescent lamps in place of incandescent lamps. (See also the section Types of Light Fixtures earlier in this chapter.) The lighting layout also makes a difference. For example, using more indirect lighting combined with task lighting can often help to reduce the overall number of light fixtures. The energy codes and standards will specify additional requirements, such as dual switching and automatic lighting shutoff devices, as explained in the section Switch Boxes earlier in this chapter. Specifying dimmers can also help reduce the power used for a fixture as well as lengthen the life of the lamp in the fixture.

Additional energy-efficient requirements are included in the newer sustainability documents such as the *International Green Construction Code (IGCC)* and *ASHRAE/USGBC/IES 189.1, Standard for the Design of High-Performance Green Buildings*

Note

Newer editions of the *IECC* and *ASHRAE/IESNA 90.1* encourage the use of automatic shutoff task lights. When automatic shutoffs are used, these lights do not need to be calculated as part of the interior lighting allowance.

Note

The Green Seal standard, *GC-12, Environmental Criteria for Occupancy Sensors*, tests motion sensors and switching devices used in small, confined spaces as well as in large, open areas.

Note

The U.S. Department of Energy's Building Energy Codes Program offers COMcheck software and other resources on their Web site to assist with energy code and standard compliance. (See www .energycodes.gov.)

Note

Some jurisdictions have passed "benchmarking" legislation, which requires certain building types to disclose their energy use. Many state and federal buildings require this as well. The EPA's Portfolio Manager, which is part of the ENERGY STAR program, is the software typically used to track energy and water consumption.

⬛Note

Some of the newer energy and sustainability requirements may be in conflict with requirements in the *NEC*. A project may need to be closely coordinated with a local code official.

⬛Note

Emerging lighting technology includes *hybrid lighting,* which uses sunlight-based solar energy to supplement the electrical energy to the fixture.

Except Low-Rise Residential Buildings. For example, the *IGCC* requires the use the *IECC* plus provides additional requirements and benchmarks that must be met. The *ASHRAE 189.1* references *ASHRAE/IESNA 90.1* in many cases; but also includes additional and sometimes stricter requirements. For example, the LPD allowances in *ASHRAE 189.1* are more stringent and supersede those in the other standard (and the *IECC*). Both documents include information on how to manage the energy consumption of a building with details for data collection, data storage, and the like. In addition, *ASHRAE 189.1* requires calculations to determine how much space needs to be allocated for future on-site renewable energy systems. Space will be required on the exterior as well as the interior of a building to allow for equipment, pathways for installation, and associated infrastructure and may affect the layout of an interior space. *ASHRAE 189.1* also includes more details for things such as occupancy sensor controls and ENERGY STAR equipment and appliances. (See the inset titled *Federal Sustainability Certification* on page 477.)

Balancing the requirements of sustainability and energy efficiency with the occupants' safety and visual needs, as well as the aesthetics of the space, is one of the new challenges of design. Both upfront and long-term costs need to be considered as well. For example, facility-wide dimming, although more costly on the front end, can save money long term because of the longer lamp life at each fixture. (Also refer to Appendix B for more information on sustainable design.) In some cases, the requirements in these additional codes and standards may not easily be coordinated with those in the *NEC*. Coordinate closely with an electrical engineer and the local code official when required.

LOW-VOLTAGE CABLING SYSTEMS

The type of cabling system used within a building to support such things as voice, data, video, and security systems is called *structured cabling*. It is also known as integrated cabling or universal cabling. The system is made up of backbone cabling and horizontal cabling. *Backbone cabling* carries the signals to the main distribution areas of the building or space. It begins where the public utility enters the building. This location, where the utility wiring is connected to the building wiring, is called the *demark*. From there it goes to the main equipment room and then to the local communication closet(s). In large commercial projects, fiber cabling is often used for backbone cabling.

The cables that are pulled to each workstation or outlet are known as *horizontal cabling*. Connections to the individual desktops or outlets are typically made through the horizontal cabling system using fiber optic or copper cabling. Because copper is less expensive for individual connections, it is more widely used in horizontal cabling. However, where complex systems must be supported, fiber optics should be considered. A wireless system is another option, especially as technology continues to improve security and transmission rates (i.e., bandwidth). (See the section Low-Voltage Cabling later in this chapter.)

COMPARING COMMUNICATION CODES

A building's communication system can consist of a number of different systems. These include telephones, computers, security, intercoms, audiovisual, and television systems such as surveillance equipment, cable services, and satellite hookups, as well as assistive listening systems. Often many of these systems are closely connected. And, in some cases, fire alarms are integrated into the building's communication system. (See the inset titled *Building Automation Systems* on page 356.)

It may seem that the *National Electric Code* sets few requirements for communication systems compared to the number of requirements for electrical codes. This is partially due to the fact that much of the wiring for communication systems is so low in voltage that it poses fewer safety problems. In addition, it is difficult to create codes for systems that tend to change rapidly. As a result, the communication industry relies more on industry standards to meet certain performance and safety criteria, standards that can be modified more quickly as technology evolves. There are several standards organizations specific to the communication industry. These include the Telecommunications Industries Association (TIA) and the Electronics Industries Alliance (EIA). Even the Builders Hardware Manufacturers Association (BHMA) is involved in creating standards for security devices. Several of these standards will be described below.

The communication systems that are covered by the *NEC* include network-powered communication systems and fire alarm systems as well as certain audio, radio, and television equipment. As with the electrical system, the *NEC* does not regulate the transmission of signals or the connection of communication services to the building. It regulates only the parts of these systems that are inside the building or controlled by the building. The primary concern is the fire hazard caused by the spread of fire along the cables or circuits. Many of the rules for these systems include the type of cable or wiring used, the clearance for power conductors, and the proper grounding procedures. Other codes may also affect certain communication systems. For example, the means of egress requirements in the building codes and the *Life Safety Code (LSC)* must be consulted when a security system is added because of the way the system affects the building's exits. The sustainability codes and standards do not currently affect communication system, however, other industry standards might. (See the section Communication Sustainability Considerations later in this chapter.)

Accessibility requirements that affect communication systems mostly control the mounting height of the outlets. Certain operable equipment can also be a factor. For example, the location of devices such as phones and computer terminals provided for use by the public will typically need to be accessible. Other requirements may be more specific to an occupancy or building type.

⌐**Note**

The sections in the *NEC* that concern communication equipment and systems continue to evolve as these systems become more complex and are used more widely.

For example, in some Assembly occupancies, the building codes and the *ADA Standards* require the use of an assistive listening system. This and other accessibility requirements will be mentioned throughout the rest of the chapter.

COMMUNICATION COMPONENTS AND DEVICES

◄ Note

Various communication systems now operate by computer. These computers may be separate or part of the building's main information technology (IT) system. If separate, they are often also located in the communication room.

This section explains the various components and devices of communication systems as they are affected by the codes and standards. Many projects now require one or more communication consultants to adequately plan the overall system. Consultants can include information technology (IT) specialists, sound engineers, certified low-voltage system designers, and vendor representatives, among others.

It is important to understand the current and future needs of the client and to coordinate the design of the space with the consultants doing the design and installation of the communication system(s). For example, if working on an auditorium project, interior aspects will need to be coordinated with the audiovisual system. Or, if specifying workstations for an open office, the power and voice/data needs will need to be coordinated. In addition, some projects and certain jurisdictions may require the involvement of an electrical engineer during the design of the system and/or a licensed electrician to install the system.

Communication Equipment and Rooms

Every building requires a central area where the incoming communication services are connected to the building's communication systems. Depending on the size of the building, there can be various types of rooms or closets. The *main communication room* is typically located in the basement or on the ground floor as close as possible to the entrance of communication services. (In small buildings, only a small panel located in the electrical room or a closet may be required.) The size of the room depends on the quantity and size of the equipment required and the communication connections that must be serviced. When determining the size of the room, the various consultants and vendors installing the communication systems (e.g., telephone, computer, security) should be consulted.

◄ Note

The main communication room with all its related equipment is the key focus for conservation and improved energy efficiency.

Typically, the main communication room will contain computer equipment for the computer system itself as well as other communication systems, such as telephone and security systems. The *NEC* has specific requirements for the communication rooms that house this equipment, also referred to as information technology equipment (ITE). For example, the room must be separated from the rest of the building by fire-rated walls, floor and ceiling assemblies, and fire-rated doors. The *NEC* also includes requirements on how to condition the space and how to penetrate the rated assemblies enclosing the room. This is especially important because of the heat generated by the equipment. If a raised floor is used, special cable and ventilation requirements must be followed. For the remaining requirements, the *NEC* refers to the standard *NFPA 75, Standard for the Protection of Information Technology Equipment.* (Also see the section Telecommunication Systems later in this chapter.)

In buildings with multiple floors, each floor typically has its own *communication closet* that feeds off the main communication room. There may be separate closets, such as those for telephone and computer equipment, or one room that combines the equipment. Like electrical closets, these communication closets or rooms are usually stacked on top of each other to allow for continuous vertical wiring. The closet provides a central location to distribute cabling throughout the floor or space, either directly to equipment such as telephones and computers or to one or more satellite closets. These intermediate closets also help to limit the length of a cable, since some cable runs are limited to maximum lengths. When there are multiple tenants on the same floor, another closet, known as a *satellite closet,* is often used for each tenant space to allow the separation of utilities. It also allows easier distribution of cables in large buildings. These more remote closets typically do not need to meet the requirements of the main communication room unless they become more than just a remote data terminal.

Low-Voltage Cabling

Cables used for communication systems are different from electrical cables, because of the lower voltages required for communication systems. They are typically referred to as low-voltage cabling. Many are listed in the *NEC;* the more common types are shown in Figure 8.8. (Many have subcategories as well.) There are different cables for different applications. Each type of cable is divided into plenum, riser, general-purpose, and limited-use categories for use in different parts of a building. For example, if a cable is used horizontally in a mechanical plenum space (see Chapter 7), it must be marked as a plenum cable (unless it is in an approved conduit or raceway). A riser cable would be used in vertical shafts. General-purpose cables are typically used in commercial applications with limited-use cables being allowed in dwelling units. Similar to electrical wiring, each of these communication cables must go through various industry standard tests before it can be labeled for its appropriate use. These tests include the fire, smoke, and toxicity tests mentioned earlier in the section Electrical Cabling and

✎Note

In the past, all communication rooms were required to have sprinkler heads. Newer standards that provide alternate options for protection are now available and may be allowed by a jurisdiction.

✎Note

If a low-voltage cable is run continuously in conduit through a fire-rated area or assembly, the cable may not need to be rated.

BUILDING AUTOMATION SYSTEMS

A building automation system (BAS) is sometimes referred to as an integrated building system, a building information network, or an intelligent building system. It consists of various building systems connected into one automated system so that they can communicate with each other and be managed through one source.

The building systems and the various components that can be supported by a BAS include but are not limited to the following:

❏ Mechanical systems: HVAC equipment, dampers, zone/thermostat controls, indoor air quality

❏ Electrical systems: Equipment, lighting systems, energy management, zone/switch controls

❏ Plumbing systems: Water usages, leak detection, sprinkler activation

❏ Security systems: Video, surveillance, access control devices, paging systems

❏ Voice/data systems: Local area networks, cable/satellite TV, telephone systems, wireless devices, audiovisual systems, sound masking systems

❏ Fire safety systems: Alarms, smoke detectors, voice communication systems, mass notification systems, sprinklers

❏ People transport systems: Elevators, escalators

In a BAS, the various systems are linked together so that they can be controlled from a single source. There are a number of propriety software packages, such as BACnet and LonWorks, which can be used to run the BAS. Custom programs can also be used in place of these or as a means of enhancing them. Since each system becomes interconnected to the others, the key is to make sure that various components are correctly prioritized. For example, a fire detection system usually has a higher priority than a security program. The facility manager can then monitor the various systems from one point and use the software to operate and maintain the equipment. The BAS can also be used to identify performance criteria, such as energy use and reliability, and identify potential problems when they arise.

Many new buildings today are incorporating a BAS in the initial design and construction. Adding one to an existing building can be a little more difficult because of the new wiring that may be required. However, recent advances in wireless technology may allow other options. Industry standards available to help integrate these systems include *TIA/EIA 776-5, TIA/EIA 862, and NFPA 731.*

As a designer, it is important to be aware of BASs and be involved in the planning process, since it may affect the design of the space. Once connected, each of the systems must individually meet the necessary code requirements. The interconnected systems can also be used to help meet performance code criteria. For example, a BAS can be used to add life safety features to a building by programming office lights to flash when a fire alarm is activated. Other combined features can enhance energy efficiency, such as integrating lighting with access control systems. Many combinations of system components can be created. Note, however, that a code jurisdiction may restrict the connection of some fire safety systems to a BAS. (See also the inset titled *Integrated Alarms* on page 257.)

COMMUNICATION CABLES		MULTI-PURPOSE CABLES	
TYPE CMP	Communications Plenum Cable	**TYPE MPP**	Multi-Purpose Plenum Cable
TYPE CMR	Communications Riser Cable	**TYPE MPR**	Multi-Purpose Riser Cable
TYPE CM or CMG	Communications General-Purpose Cable	**TYPE MP or MPG**	Multi-Purpose General-Purpose Cable
TYPE CMX	Communications Cable, Limited Use	**COAXIAL CABLE**	
TYPE CMUC	Undercarpet Communications Wire and Cable	**TYPE CATVP**	CATV Plenum Cable
FIBER OPTIC CABLES		**TYPE CATVR**	CATV Riser Cable
TYPE OFNP	Nonconductive Optical Fiber Plenum Cable	**TYPE CATV**	CATV Cable
TYPE OFCP	Conductive Optical Fiber Plenum Cable	**TYPE CATVX**	CATV Cable, Limited Use
TYPE OFNR	Nonconductive Optical Fiber Riser Cable	**FIRE ALARM CABLES**	
TYPE OFCR	Conductive Optical Fiber Riser Cable	**TYPE FPLP**	Power-Limited Fire Alarm Plenum Cable
TYPE OFN or OFNG	Nonconductive Optical Fiber General-Purpose Cable	**TYPE FPLR**	Power-Limited Fire Alarm Riser Cable
TYPE OFC or OFCG	Conductive Optical Fiber General-Purpose Cable	**TYPE FPL**	Power-Limited Fire Alarm Cable

NOTE: Other types and/or subcategories of cables may also be available.

Figure 8.8 Common types of communication cables.

Conduit. Since the speed at which information travels is such a factor, communication cables also go through additional performance testing to determine their bandwidth and capacity levels.

It is typically the communication consultants or vendors that specify the type of communication cable. Below are the main types of cables and/or connections used today.

❏ *Fiber optic cable*: A fiber optic cable transmits light along ultra-thin glass or plastic strands. Each strand is composed of layers of fibers protected by a cabling jacket and a plastic coating. Fiber optic cables provide higher bandwidth than other types of cable, which yields higher speed and capacity. And, because they are smaller and lighter and can withstand greater pulling tension, they are easier to use than copper. In addition, since optical fibers use light waves instead of an electrical current to transmit information, they are not affected by electromagnetic and radio frequency interference. Fiber can also be used over much longer distances before the signal must be amplified, and additional fibers can easily be included in the initial installation for future expansion of a data or communication system. Multi-mode (OM1 – OM3), single-mode (OS1 and OS2), and hybrid fiber optic cables are available. (See also Composite cable further down on this list.)

◢Note

When using copper cabling for telecommunication systems, the industry standards often limit the length of the cable run to 300 feet (91 m).

◢Note

Since cables like CAT 6 and composite cables have multiple pairs, one cable can be used to connect multiple devices (phone, computer, etc.).

◢Note

Some buildings may require 2-hour-rated cables for added protection of certain communication systems. These are called *circuit integrity (CI)* cables. (Type MI electrical cables would be an alternative.)

❑ *Twisted-pair cable*: Twisted-pair cabling, sometimes referred to as *copper cabling*, uses a copper conductor to transmit data using an electrical current. It provides less capacity and speed than fiber optics, but it is still the most common type of low-voltage cabling used today. It is less expensive than fiber optics. The copper wire is twisted into pairs, encased in a protective sheathing, and available shielded and unshielded. The twisting helps reduce the amount of outside interference. Typically used for voice (i.e., telephone) and data (i.e., computer) connections, it is rated by *category*, which indicates its bandwidth performance. Manufacturers are continually developing copper cabling with more capacity. Most installations now use at least Category 5e (CAT 5e) or CAT 6, and in some cases CAT 7/Class F. (As higher categories become available, the cable should go through the appropriate testing before using it in a building.)

❑ *Coaxial cable*: Coaxial cable (*coax* for short) is the standard cable used for video and cable-based transmissions. For example, it is used for cable TV and cable-based Internet connections, closed-circuit television connections, and TV antenna connections. Like twisted-pair cable, it uses conductive metal to transmit data using an electrical current, but instead it has a single central conductor. It has the capacity to carry great quantities of information. Different types include RG-6 cable for cable TV connections, RG-59 for video surveillance systems, and RG-60 for high-definition TV and high-speed Internet.

❑ *Composite cable*: Composite cabling, also known as *hybrid cabling*, bundles various types of cables into one jacket or sleeve. For example, one composite cable containing CAT 5, coaxial, and audio wiring could be run so that multiple communication connections to various systems can be made. This is often used in Residential-type occupancies to eliminate the need to run multiple cables to the same location. A multimedia conference room might also use a cable like this. A variety of composite cables are available—in a variety of qualities. If they consist strictly of communication cables, they are not typically regulated by the *NEC*. A composite cable can also consist of a combination of optical fibers and current-carrying electrical wires. This is called a "conductive" optical fiber by the *NEC* because it can also carry electricity. The *NEC* has separate requirements for these types of composite cables, and they may not always be allowed. (Their use might also be limited by the manufacturer of the equipment being connected to the cable for warrantee reasons.)

❑ *Circuit integrity (CI) cable*: CI cables are a cable assembly that provides a 2-hour fire rating. Cables must pass additional testing requirements to obtain this rating and are labeled with the suffix "–CI." They are used to wire building systems that are essential to the safety of the occupants. Examples include wiring to smoke dampers in ductwork (see Chapter 5) and fire alarm control stations (see Chapter 6).

❏ *Wireless:* Wireless systems use cable to connect the main transmitter to the communication service. Receivers are then used instead of cabling to allow individuals to connect to the system. They use infrared or radio transmission. Sometimes microwave and laser signals are used between facilities, similar to microwave signals used to provide communication links to cell phones. Wireless systems are gaining popularity for all types of buildings and a wide variety of communication systems. Newer technology allows networks to be interconnected, where each device can send/receive data from a number of other devices, so there is less down time and more security. Additional security is created because networks are constantly changing channels, making it more difficult to access information.

> **◢Note**
>
> Certain building materials can be used to provide a radio frequency barrier to minimize signal leakage and electromagnetic interference of wireless systems. Examples include foiled-back drywall and certain window films.

Certain communication cables, especially when used in conjunction with larger network-powered systems, are required by the *NEC* to be grounded. (See the section Grounding and Circuit Interrupters earlier in this chapter.) In addition, when communication cables are installed throughout a building, the codes typically require that they be kept separate from electrical cabling. In most cases, communication cables cannot be placed in any raceway, compartment, conduit, outlet box, or junction box used for electric light or power. (There are exceptions, depending on the type of cable used.) When communication cables are run horizontally across a ceiling, they can usually remain exposed. However, the codes specify that the cables must be run in a "neat and workmanlike manner," and they cannot block access when used above suspended ceiling systems. This is accomplished by using hangers, straps, and cable ties to keep the cables together. They are often secured at the ceiling using cable tray or J-hooks. (In some cases, a listed raceway will be required.) Since the *NEC* allows many types of communication cables to be run together, the various communication vendors will typically share this common path until they reach their respective outlet locations. (Some cables, such as coaxial, must be separated from other communication cables.)

> **◢Note**
>
> A building or space may also use a raised floor system so that all cabling can be installed underneath. The outlet can then be installed flush with the floor.

When communication cables are run down a wall to a particular outlet, many jurisdictions (especially in certain occupancies) require the low-voltage cable(s) to be run in a conduit. (See the section Conduit earlier in this chapter.) Conduit is also required in rated walls. Since the cable must be separate from the electrical cable/conduit, it will require a separate conduit. For example, in a typical office, a computer and/or telephone outlet is often located next to an electrical outlet. Two conduits would be installed in the wall: one for the electrical wiring and one for the low-voltage wiring. The cutouts for the conduit and the box would be similar to those required for the electrical components. In addition, if the conduit or box penetrates a rated assembly or membrane, it must meet the same rating requirements as electrical boxes. (See the section Electrical Boxes earlier in this chapter.)

It is not uncommon for communication systems to be rewired as new types of cabling become available. This is especially true for computer systems that may require a cable upgrade in order to increase the speed of the individual computers. These old cables create unnecessary fire loads and toxic gases should a fire occur and could restrict the air flow in a plenum space. Since the 2002 edition, the *NEC* has required all accessible portions of abandoned low-voltage cables to be removed. (Some jurisdictions may require removal of all abandoned cables.)

TYPES OF COMMUNICATION SYSTEMS

Various types of communication systems are discussed below. The low-voltage cabling used for most of these systems must meet the requirements found in the *NEC* as discussed in the previous section. There are very few other electrical code requirements for communication systems. Instead, some systems have other requirements that need to be met, such as building code or accessibility requirements. Others should meet available industry standards. However, the line between various communication systems is not always clear. For example, certain systems can share the infrastructure of another system. In addition, more systems are using computers as their means of control. If they are connected to the main network computer, not only do they become more dependent on one another, but a particular system might also be required to meet additional requirements. (See the inset titled *Building Automation Systems* on page 356.)

Telecommunication Systems

Telecommunications is a term that includes both voice and data communication. (Radio communication is sometimes included as well.) It is used here to include telephone and computer systems. As already discussed, the *NEC* has specific requirements for the main equipment room that houses the telecommunication system. It also includes specific requirements for the installation of cables with separate sections for information technology (data) cabling and communication (voice) cabling. Most other requirements for telecommunication

---

✑Note

The plastic sleeves covering communication cables can be very toxic if exposed to a fire. The *NEC* requires old, abandoned cables that are accessible to be removed from a building.

✑Note

In addition to providing clear floor space at an accessible public telephone, the telephone must be located on an accessible route within the building.

systems are found in standards developed by the NFPA or by the Telecommunications Industries Association (TIA), in conjunction with the Electronics Industries Alliance (EIA). The standards cover everything from the testing and fabrication of components to the design and installation of an entire system. Some of the NFPA standards are specifically for large data facilities; however, for smaller telecommunication rooms, the standard *NFPA 75, Protection of Information Technology Equipment* can be used. Industry standards not referenced by the codes include *TIA/EIA-568-B, Commercial Building Telecommunications Cabling Standard,* which includes multiple sections that can be used depending on the type of cabling, and *TIA/EIA-569-A, Commercial Building Standard for Telecommunications Pathways and Spaces.* TIA offers other standards for residential and wireless systems as well.

These standards provide specifications and guidance for the installation and maintenance of the telecommunication system. Some of the requirements will affect the design and location of the communication room, as well as the overall design of a space or building. For example, the standards typically limit the length of a copper cable run going from the communication room to a data outlet to about 300 feet (91.4 m). In addition, the standard *TIA/EIA-589-B* incorporates the concept of *zone cabling* (also called zone distribution) for open office areas. This consists of dividing the ceiling into sections or zones and then running communication cables to the center of each zone. An intermediate multi-user outlet or terminal is installed in the ceiling within each zone so that separate cables can be run from the terminal to the outlets in a wall or in a run of workstations. Then, when the layout of an area changes, the cabling needs to be changed only in that particular zone up to the point in the ceiling, not all the way back to the main panel. This avoids having to abandon and remove old cables every time there is a change. (The terminals installed in the ceiling must have the same rating required of the ceiling cable.)

The *NEC* allows low-voltage cables for telephone (voice) outlets and computer (data) outlets to be "terminated" together so that they run through the same conduit to one box. The number of outlets or jacks will determine the size of the box. It is not unusual to have an outlet with four jacks, two for voice and two for data, or even more. Neither the *NEC* nor the standards specify the location of these voice and data outlets. Instead, they are located based on the layout and function requirements of the space. However, voice and data outlet locations must stay within the reach ranges of the *ADA Standards* and the ICC/ANSI standard. This is shown in Figure 8.9. Outlets must be mounted on the wall at least 15 inches (380 mm) above the floor—similar to electrical outlets. Even if an area is not required to be accessible, this height is recommended in case the function of the space changes. (See the section Outlet Boxes earlier in this chapter for more accessibility requirements.) If locating an accessible

Note

Required text telephones are based on the number of interior and exterior telephones. See the *ADA Standards* for additional information.

Note

Although codes do not require public telephones, some projects, such as hotels, may require phones for customer use. These would need to meet accessibility requirements.

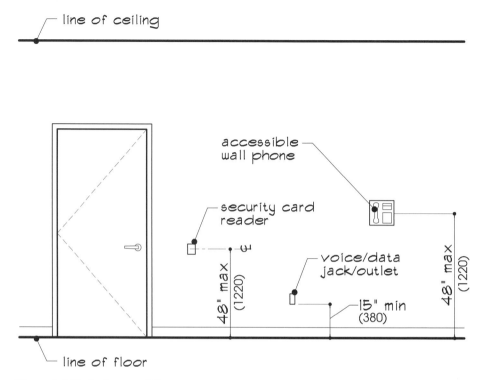

Figure 8.9 Typical accessible communication device locations.

wall-mounted telephone, it must be within 48 inches (1220 mm) above the floor, as shown in Figure 8.9.

Television and Radio Systems

The *NEC* includes some requirements for the installation of television and radio systems. Most of these requirements pertain to the exterior antennae usually located on top of the building to which the interior cabling is attached. Other requirements are geared to the interior coaxial cable that connects the devices to the radio and television receiving equipment, including the separation from certain other types of communication cables and the use of fire-rated cables. If raceways are used to run the cabling, these must be rated as well. (See the section Low-Voltage Cabling earlier in this chapter.) This equipment is used to operate such things as cable television, closed-circuit television, and security television cameras.

Alarm and Voice Communication Systems

Alarm and voice communication systems include such things as fire and smoke alarms, emergency voice/alarm communication systems (EVACSs), intercom systems, and assistive listening systems. Some of these systems are used together or for multiple functions, while others are stand-alone systems. For example, a fire alarm system might also include an EVACS so that the occupants in the building can be given direction during an emergency. This is required by the codes in some occupancies such as Factories. In some cases, a jurisdiction may require a building or facility to use a mass notification system (MNS). (See Chapter 6.) These systems are more sophisticated than a building's general public address system and require connection to an emergency power source. (See also the section Audiovisual Systems next.)

The requirements for fire and smoke alarm systems are given in the fire codes and the building codes. The codes will indicate when they are required and reference standards for additional information. Certain accessibility requirements may also apply. (See the section Alarm Systems in Chapter 6.) These systems typically use low-voltage wiring that must meet additional requirements in the *NEC*. When the alarm system is connected to a building automation system (BAS), the alarm system usually takes precedence over other connected systems because it is critical to the safety of the building occupants. That is why some jurisdictions do not allow its connection to a BAS. However, if it is connected to the other building systems, it can provide added features and often better response times. (See the inset titled *Building Automation Systems* on page 356.)

Another type of voice communication system that is required by the building codes and the *ADA Standards* is an assistive listening system. It is required in Assembly occupancies where audible communication is integral to the use of the space. Examples include a movie theater, a performing arts center, and a courtroom; however, it may be required in other building types as well. The assistive listening system is installed in conjunction with the main sound system and consists of accessible receivers. These receivers amplify the sound and are made available to those with hearing disabilities. The building codes specify the number and types of receivers required within a space or building based on the capacity of seating in the assembly area. The *ADA Standards* and the ICC/ANSI standard provide additional requirements.

Audiovisual Systems

Audio and video systems include everything from the basic stereo system used in a small conference room to a highly complex audiovisual (AV) or multimedia room. The AV system can include a wide variety of components. The *NEC*

◄ Note

Unlike a standard public address system, an emergency voice/alarm communication system is required by the codes in certain occupancies and is tied to the fire alarm system.

◄ Note

The *NEC* limits the types of low-voltage cables that can be installed with fire alarm circuits due to possible interference.

◄ Note

The 2004 *ADA-ABA Accessibility Guidelines* and newer ICC/ANSI standards include new assistive listening performance standards not required in previous editions.

covers equipment and wiring requirements for *audio* equipment and includes public address systems, intercommunication systems, and electronic instruments in this category. The code separates these requirements into permanent audio systems, portable/temporary audio systems, and audio systems near bodies of water (e.g., pools). For permanent audio systems, the *NEC* requirements cover the use of flexible cables, the grounding of equipment racks, the number of cables allowed in a conduit, and the installation of speakers in rated walls.

The *visual* part of an AV system could include television equipment that requires coaxial cable connections (see the previous section) or a variety of other equipment, such as projectors and DVD players, which require additional types of low-voltage cabling. Connection to other communication systems in the building may also be required. For example, the television in a conference center may include video conferencing capabilities, which requires connection to the telecommunication system in order for it to operate, or a computer PowerPoint presentation that may need to be connected to both a projector and the computer network. In addition, many AV systems incorporate computers as part of the main control of the overall system. Although there are multiple standards for the components that make up an AV system, few if any are available for the overall design and installation. Instead, the industry has created multiple reference manuals to assist with this.

For more complicated AV systems or where electrical interference may cause a problem, the *NEC* allows a separately derived electrical system called *technical power*. Previously permitted in motion picture and television studios, it is now allowed in any commercial or industrial building where there is concern that electrical noise may affect audio and video signals. Electrical noise is often caused by the grounds used with electrical wiring. (See the section Grounding and Circuit Interrupters earlier in this chapter.) Technical power systems allow alternate grounding options. However, additional precautions must be taken, which include using GFCI-protected receptacles and certain types of light fixtures if used as part of the system.

Security Systems

Security systems used inside a building typically concentrate on protecting the building from unauthorized entry. However, other systems may be used to contain the occupants. Examples of protecting unauthorized entry include intrusion detection and alarms, access control systems such as card readers and biometric identifiers (e.g., fingerprint scanners and voice recognition), closed-circuit television (CCTV), digital video recording (DVR), and locking systems. These security components can be used individually and in unlimited combinations and typically require space in a building's communication room. It is also more common for these systems to be monitored and controlled remotely through

Note

The *NEC* allows for a unique type of electrical system, called *technical power*, for commercial and industrial buildings where electrical noise may affect audio and video signals.

Note

UL has created three approval marks specifically for the security industry to include security equipment, signaling equipment, and commercial security equipment. (See the inset titled *UL Labels* on page 45.)

e-mail and other electronic devices. In addition, a security system may be tied to other building systems such as a fire alarm system or a mass notification system. (See the inset titled *Building Automation Systems* on page 356.) In each case, the goal is to keep occupants safe.

Although security systems are not required by the code, some aspects of their use and installation are controlled by the codes. In fact, some security components can be in conflict with fire protection requirements, which require occupants to exit a building quickly during an emergency. Because it is an issue of life safety, the *LSC* and the building codes regulate security systems when they affect exiting. For example, the *IBC* includes requirements specific to access-controlled egress doors. The *NEC* covers cabling and installation requirements for certain security systems. And, in 2006, the NFPA introduced the standard *NFPA 731, Installation of Electronic Premises Security Systems,* which includes information on intrusion detection systems, electronic access control systems, and CCTV. Numerous other industry and manufacturing standards are available as well, including ones from Underwriters Laboratories and the Security Industry Association (SIA). Most door hardware and locking-related standards are created by the Builders Hardware Manufacturers Association (BHMA), including newer standards geared to high-security doors.

One of the most significant code concerns is that the locking of doors for security reasons does not interfere with the required means of egress. However, whether part of a standard security system or special security system (e.g., in psychiatric hospitals or prisons), certain doors within the means of egress may require locks. Various locking systems are available that will provide security while not endangering the occupants. Whether the lock should be fail safe or fail secure, determines many of the other characteristics of the locking system. The lock is considered to be *fail safe* if the door automatically unlocks when power goes out, such as in the event of a fire. If the lock is *fail secure*, the door will remain locked even in the event of the loss of power. This type of lock may interfere with exiting if additional precautions are not provided, such as constant monitoring by personnel.

Three types of locks are typically used for security:

1. *Mechanical locks:* Mechanical locks are opened either with a key or by a code entered into a push-button mechanism. These types of locks are not usually allowed on an exit door unless there is constant supervision of the door. However, if it is an exterior door, a push bar or other type of panic hardware can be installed on the interior to allow exiting without a key.

2. *Electrical locks:* Electrical locks can be electromechanical or electromagnetic. Two of the more common types of *electromechanical* locks include delayed egress or alarmed doors. Since they can be fail safe or fail secure, the proper action must be specified if the door is required for exiting. Standards that apply to electromechanical locks include *ANSI/BHMA 156.5, Auxiliary Locks*

and Associated Products and *ANSI/BHMA 156.25, Electrified Locking Devices*, as well as *ANSI/UL 1034, Burglary-Resistant Electric Locking Mechanisms*. Electromagnetic locks, often referred to as *maglocks*, use a magnetic field to hold the metal plate on the door or jamb in place. (These locks are similar to electromagnetic door holders, which are used to hold open fire-rated doors and release them to close when the fire alarm is activated. See the section Rated Door Assemblies in Chapter 5.) Since they have no mechanical parts and depend on electricity, they are considered fail safe and can be safely connected to the fire alarm system and the security system. Standards that apply to electromagnetic locks include *ANSI/BHMA A156.23, Electromagnetic Locks* and *ANSI/BHMA A156.24, Delayed Egress Locks*. Because these doors do not rely on a mechanical latch for closure, additional hardware may be needed on a rated door to properly latch the door as required by the code.

3. *Pneumatic locks:* Pneumatic locks use electromechanical devices and pneumatic air pressure. They are used largely in Institutional occupancies such as hospital and prison facilities. These locks can be locked and released electronically and manually.

✎Note

When deciding on hardware for egress doors, the appropriate combination of locks, latches, exit devices, and alarms must be determined.

The need for a security system should be considered when designing a means of egress. Each type of door should be reviewed both separately and as part of the whole exiting plan. In some cases, the plan may need to be reviewed with a code official. In addition, when a security system is installed as part of a BAS, it cannot disrupt other systems that affect life safety. If the fire alarm is connected to the BAS, the BAS must be programmed to establish the proper priority. The fire alarm typically must take precedence over the security issues. For instance, if a fire activates the fire alarm, certain security doors that are locked must be allowed to open for proper egress. If the power fails, the security doors should unlock as well (depending on the occupancy). This may be good in an emergency to help evacuate a building, but it can also leave a building exposed. It is always a good idea to include manual locks on security doors so that they can be locked after a building is evacuated.

If a space is required to be accessible, even in a high-security area, the security devices that are used by the occupants (or visitors) must be accessible. The requirements are found in the *ADA Standards* and the ICC/ANSI standard. Not only must door handles be accessible (see Chapter 4), but also all security devices must be within accessible reach ranges and must have controls or buttons that are easy to use. The acceptable range is shown at the security card reader in Figure 8.9; however, the actual location will depend on the type of device and how it is used. For example, a card reader will require someone to pass a security card in front of it, while a key pad will need to be viewed by the person punching in the numbers. Both a standing person and someone in a wheelchair need to be considered when determining the height. (In some cases, two devices may be needed—one high and one low.) In addition, the clear floor space in front of the device should be considered and might affect the location of the door. There should typically be at least a 30- by 48-inch (760 by 1220 mm) floor clearance in front of the device. If a turnstile is used, a means must be provided for a person in a wheelchair to get through. (Refer to the *ADA Standards* for specifics.)

COMMUNICATION SUSTAINABILITY CONSIDERATIONS

Communication systems are considered low-voltage and require less electricity to run then other electrical systems. However, when evaluating a building's energy efficiency, all systems should be considered. The key area of focus for sustainable communication systems is typically the main communication room. Not only does it contain large equipment that is energy-consuming, but this equipment needs to be kept cool as well.

Although current sustainability codes do not include provisions for communication systems, there are several things to consider. For example, if using the sustainability standard *ASHRAE 189.1*, it requires the energy-consumption management system to be monitored remotely. (See the section Electrical Sustainability Considerations earlier in this chapter.) This will require the integration of the electrical system with the telecommunication system. Computers will be used to collect and compile the information as well as send the information as required through e-mail, cell phones, and the like. Using a building automation system (BAS) to tie these systems together helps make this possible. (See the inset titled *Building Automation Systems* on page 356.)

There are also a number of sustainability standards being developed by the communications industry. For example, in 2009, the Alliance for Telecommunication Industry Solutions (ATIS) published three standards used to determine telecommunication equipment's energy efficiency. These standards introduce a standard of measurement known as Telecommunications Energy Efficiency Ratio (TEER), which can be used to measure and report energy consumption of telecommunication equipment. Other standards using this system are being developed as well.

CHECKLIST

The checklist in Figure 8.10 combines a number of code and standard requirements for electrical and communication systems. Although an engineer (or other consultant) might determine specific requirements, you should at least note the

Electrical and Communication Checklist   Date:_____

Project Name: _____ Space: _____
Occupancy (new or existing):_____

Electrical Requirements: Engineer Required? ___ YES ___ NO

Types of Electrical Panels (check those that apply and note locations, sizes, etc.)
__ Switchboard: _____
__ Panel Board(s): _____
__ Branch Panel Board(s): _____
Special Cabling Conditions: _____ Conduit Required: __YES __NO
Location of Receptacle Outlets: _____
__ EXISTING __ NEW (Rating of wall(s): _____)
Location of Switches: _____
__ EXISTING __ NEW (Rating of wall(s): _____)
Special Types of Outlets and/or Circuits (check those that apply and note locations)
__ Dedicated Outlets: _____
__ Ground-Fault Circuit Interrupters (GFCI): _____
__ Arc-Fault Circuit Interrupters (AFCI): _____
__ Tamper Resistant Outlets (dwellings): _____
__ Other: _____
Types of Required Equipment (check those that apply, list new and existing, specify if over 120V)
__ Light Fixtures: _____
__ Appliances: _____
__ Equipment: _____
Types of Electrical Systems (check those that apply, list new and existing, etc.)
__ Emergency Electrical System: _____
__ Required Standby System: _____
__ Optional Standby System: _____
__ Uninterrupted Power Supply System (UPS): _____
__ Technical Power System (A/V): _____

Communication Requirements: Engineer Required? ___ YES ___ NO
Type of Communication Systems[4] (check those that apply and insert information)

SYSTEM	VENDOR OR CONSULTANT	CENTRAL LOCATION OF SYSTEM	TYPE OF CABLING OR SPECIAL NOTES
___ Telephone System	_____	_____	_____
___ Information Technology System	_____	_____	_____
___ Cable TV Services	_____	_____	_____
___ Closed Circuit TV System	_____	_____	_____
___ Satellite TV System	_____	_____	_____
___ Voice Notification System	_____	_____	_____
___ Intercom System	_____	_____	_____
___ Assistive Listening System	_____	_____	_____
___ Audio/Visual System	_____	_____	_____
___ Security System	_____	_____	_____
___ Other	_____	_____	_____

NOTES:
1. Refer to codes and standards for specifics, including energy and sustainability codes and standards as required.
2. Check also the *ADA Standards* and ICC/ANSI standard for accessible mounting locations.
3. Note on floor plans the location of fire-rated walls for placement of required fire dampers and firestops (see Chapter 5).
4. See also Chapter 6 for information on various alarm and other notification type systems as required by the codes.

Figure 8.10 Electrical and communication checklist.

items listed. The checklist begins by asking you the project and space name and its occupancy classification. (See Chapter 2 for more information on occupancy classifications.) When using this checklist, you might want to use a floor plan of the space to mark the locations rather than filling in the blanks. The floor plan can then be attached to the checklist as backup. It will also be useful for coordination with the engineer. For each project, the checklist asks you if an engineer is required. This will depend on the size of the project, the amount of electrical or communication work, and the jurisdiction of the project. (See Chapter 10.)

The first part of the checklist concentrates on the electrical requirements. It notes the main electrical items you should determine in your project. You should know where the electrical panels are and their sizes, especially if you need to coordinate the size of a new electrical room or closet with the engineer. Use the "Special Cabling Conditions" to note such things as the use of a plenum mechanical system or the types of rated walls that will affect the type of cabling used. Also note if conduit will be required.

The next several items pertain to the types of outlets located in the project. In some cases, you may be reusing all existing receptacles and/or switches. If you are adding new ones, determine if any will be located in a rated wall and note this in the space provided or on the floor plan. Indicate any special types of outlets as well. The last two electrical categories pertain to types of light fixtures, equipment, appliances, or special systems that may be included in the project. Check those that apply and include any specifics that are required. Use this checklist to remind you of the types of outlets and equipment that should be labeled or noted on your drawings. It is also a good idea to attach the cut sheets of any items that are specified. For example, you may specify the light fixtures and appliances, the client might specify certain equipment being used in the space, and the electrical engineer will specify other electrical devices.

The second half of the checklist pertains to communication systems. Check off the systems that apply to this project and write in additional ones as required. Since most of the details are determined by a consultant, the communication vendor, or an engineer, this part of the checklist will help you keep these systems organized. Spaces are provided for you to fill in the names of the companies installing the system, as well as where the main part of the system will be located. For example, certain items will be included in the communication room. Other items, such as the surveillance monitors for the security system, will be located in other spaces. Any other system considerations should also be noted, including any special cabling required. As the design of these systems develops, you can add the necessary information, as well as equipment and outlet locations, to your floor plans.

CHAPTER 9

FINISH AND FURNITURE SELECTION

Over the years there have been many fatal fires in the United States due to flammable finishes and upholstery. One of the most noted incidents was the 1942 fire in Boston's Cocoanut Grove nightclub, which claimed the lives of 492 people. In response to that deadly fire, Boston established regulations dealing with interior finishes, known as the *Boston Fire Code*. Fatal fires continue to occur in which finishes and furniture are a contributing factor. In 2003 alone, there were several nightclub and nursing home fires in the United States that claimed multiple lives. Whether or not the interior finishes and upholstered furniture are the *cause* of the fire, they are likely to contribute to its spread. A wallcovering, for example, that is *not* flame resistant can spread a fire down the length of an entire corridor in a matter of seconds, setting other flammable items, such as draperies and upholstery, on fire and creating deadly smoke, heat, and toxic fumes.

Building codes and standards include strict instructions on the selection and use of interior finishes, furnishings, and furniture. Chapter 5 discussed fire prevention through the use of rated interior building materials and assemblies (e.g., wall, floor, and ceiling systems). This chapter concentrates on the products that are either placed on top of the building materials (e.g., finishes) or set within the compartments created by the building materials and structural elements (e.g., furniture). These items are considered part of the fuel load and can contribute to the ignition and spread of a fire. As a result, finishes and furniture must undergo testing as well.

The ratings given to finishes and furniture, however, are different from those given to building materials and assemblies. Tested building materials are typically given hourly ratings, which represent the amount of time the material can resist a *fire*. The tests for finishes and furniture concentrate on the potential of a material to contribute to overall fire and smoke growth and spread. Typically, the fire source used is a *flame* (or lighted cigarette) or small fire. Some of the tests are considered small-scale and only use a small portion of the finish or furnishing being tested. Other finish and furniture tests are larger in scale, using not only a larger sample of the finish but also the full assembly consisting of the finish, substrate, adhesive, fasteners, and any other parts. In some cases, an entire room or piece of furniture is simulated.

This chapter begins by explaining the various types of finishes and furnishings as defined by the codes. After comparing the different code documents, the chapter describes the various finish and furniture standards and tests and their results. This information will be helpful when selecting products in conjunction with the requirements found in the codes. (See the section Obtaining Test Results.) Other code requirements, as well as the sustainability and accessibility requirements related to finishes and furniture, are explained later in this chapter. The chapter also discusses requirements not specified in the codes that should be used for both safety and liability reasons. A checklist is provided at the end.

> **◥ Note**
>
> The terminology used to describe products that are more resistant to fire has changed over the years. *Flameproof* is a common term that is usually incorrect, since very few products are totally unaffected by fire. The correct terms are *flame retardant* and *flame resistant*.

TYPES OF FINISHES AND FURNISHINGS

Interior finishes and furnishings covered by the codes and standards include a variety of materials and products and can be divided into seven categories. They are listed and defined as follows and are discussed throughout this chapter.

> **◥ Note**
>
> Most interior finishes and furnishings are considered combustible. The codes typically require that they have some degree of flame spread and smoke development restrictions in order for them to be used in many building interiors.

❑ *Ceiling finishes:* Exposed interior surfaces of a building, including suspended ceiling systems and coverings that can be applied to fixed and movable ceilings, soffits, beams, space frames, and other similar elements.

❑ *Wall finishes:* Exposed interior surfaces of a building, including coverings that may be applied over fixed or movable walls and partitions, toilet privacy partitions, columns, and other similar elements. Examples include vinyl and textile wallcovering, wood paneling or wainscoting, and applied acoustical finishes.

❑ *Floor finishes:* Exposed interior surfaces of a building, including coverings that may be applied over a finished or unfinished floor, stair (including risers), ramp, and other similar elements. Examples include hardwood, ceramic tile, vinyl, linoleum, carpets, and rugs. (Some types of wall base may also be included.)

> **◥ Note**
>
> Works of art such as paintings and photographs are typically not regulated by the code if they do not exceed 20 percent of the wall area. Requirements in certain jurisdictions may vary.

❑ *Window treatments:* Decorative elements that control the amount of light and/or solar heat from a window area. These can include draperies, liners, blinds, and shutters as well plastic films applied to the glass. Curtains used in a space for privacy may also be included. These elements can be made of textiles, wood, vinyl, and other similar materials.

❏ *Trim and decorative materials:* Exposed decorative elements or protective materials attached to the interior wall or ceiling. These include decorative moldings, baseboards, chair rails, picture rails, handrails, and door and window moldings.

❏ *Furnishing finishes:* Exposed finishes found in case goods furniture, systems furniture, and soft seating, such as fabrics, wood veneers, and laminates. This category also includes nonexposed finishes, such as the foam in seating, liners in drapery, and other similar elements.

❏ *Furniture:* Whole pieces of furniture rather than separate parts and finishes. This category usually includes upholstered products, such as seating and moveable panel systems. Also included are mattresses, which consist of the whole mattress composition, including fabric, padding, coils, and similar bedding assemblies.

✐Note

Movable partitions or panel systems are typically classified as furniture. However, if they exceed a certain height, a jurisdiction may consider them to be walls, in which case they would need to meet fire separation requirements. (See Chapter 5.)

FIRE DEVELOPMENT STAGES

To gain a better understanding of how a fire can harm a human being and why fire codes are necessary, it is important to review the different stages in the development of a fire. They can be divided into three stages:

Stage 1: Known as the time of ignition, this first stage is the *initial growth* of a fire. Smoke produced during this stage can travel many feet from the room of origin and pose a threat to humans.

Stage 2: This is the *growth stage*, when the fire begins to ignite material in the immediate area, including finishes and furniture. As a fire starts to consume a large part of a building, the heat generated may cause *flashover*. This occurs when the thermal radiation from the fire causes all the surfaces in an area or room to become heated to their ignition temperature, causing the materials in that area to ignite simultaneously. This explosion usually occurs when a fire reaches the 1200-degree range and will cause the fire to spread rapidly. It also can greatly increase the rate of toxic smoke production.

Stage 3: In this stage the fire is *fully developed,* causing the entire building to quickly become dangerous. Smoke, heat, toxic gases, and possible structural collapse can harm those who remain within range.

The rate at which these stages of fire development can progress varies tremendously with the construction of a building and the finishes and furniture used within. However, the first 5 to 10 minutes of a fire are the most critical. The materials and finishes selected can either contribute to the growth or prevent the spread of a fire—and can play a large role in the beginning stages of a fire. They can also contribute to the amount of toxic fumes. The goal is to lengthen the amount of time during which the occupants can safely evacuate a building.

Until recently, codes often regulated only the first four categories. However, this situation is changing as requirements are getting stricter and more standards are being developed, including those that are considered more sustainable in nature. The codes are referencing more of these standards. Some states may also require the use of finish and/or furniture standards not yet mentioned in the codes, so check with the local jurisdiction.

COMPARING THE CODES

✎Note

NFPA 705 is a standard test that can be used in the field by a code official to assess finishes already installed.

The two main sources for interior finish regulations are the building codes and the *Life Safety Code (LSC)*. The *International Building Code (IBC)* and the NFPA codes each have a chapter dedicated to interior finishes and furnishings. Although the chapters in the codes are organized differently, much of the information is the same. Each chapter includes restrictions on wall and ceiling finishes, floor finishes, decorations and trim, and other special finishes, such as expanded wall-covering and cellular or foam plastics. The *LSC* chapter also includes requirements for furniture.

In some cases, other sections of the codes will need to be referenced. For example, the building codes include a chapter on glass and glazing that has information on the use of safety glass (as discussed in Chapter 5). Finishes for plumbing fixtures and restrooms are found in the plumbing codes as well as the environmental chapter of the *IBC*. (See Chapter 7.) In addition, each separate occupancy chapter in the NFPA codes and special occupancy sections in the I-Codes may list additional finish and/or furniture requirements. (See the section Determining Finish Classifications later in this chapter.)

If a fire code is required by a jurisdiction, it may need to be referenced for additional information. For example, the *International Fire Code (IFC)* has a chapter titled "Interior Finish, Decorative Materials and Furnishings." Although it is similar to the *IBC* finish chapter, it also includes information on upholstered furniture and mattresses for specific occupancies and a section on decorative vegetation (e.g., natural cut trees and artificial vegetation) used indoors. Performance codes, however, do not specifically mention finishes and furniture. But, if a performance code such as the *ICC Performance Code (ICCPC)* were to be used for another portion of a project, finish or furniture selection may become part of the process. For example, if performance criteria were used to design the fire protection system in a building, the fire loads of the selected finishes and/or furniture may need to be incorporated into the computer fire model or engineering calculations. (See the sections Comparing the Codes in Chapters 5 and 6 for more information.)

NFPA 253	Standard Method of Test for Critical Radiant Flux of Floor Covering Systems Using Radiant Heat Energy Source
NFPA 255	Standard Method of Test of Surface Burning Characteristics of Building Materials (withdrawn in 2009)
NFPA 258	Recommended Practice for Determining Smoke Generation of Solid Materials (withdrawn in 2006)
NFPA 260	Standard Methods of Tests and Classification System for Cigarette Ignition Resistance of Components of Upholstered Furniture
NFPA 261	Standard Method of Test for Determining Resistance of Mock-Up Upholstered Furniture Material Assemblies to Ignition by Smoldering Cigarettes
NFPA 265	Standard Methods of Fire Tests for Evaluating Room Fire Growth Contribution of Textile Coverings on Full Height Panels and Walls
NFPA 269	Standard Test Method for Developing Toxic Potency Data for Use in Fire Hazard Modeling
NFPA 270	Standard Test Method for Measurement of Smoke Obscuration Using a Conical Radiant Source in a Single Closed Chamber
NFPA 271	Standard Method of Test for Heat and Visible Smoke Release Rates for Materials and Products Using an Oxygen Consumption Calorimeter
NFPA 272	Standard Method of Test for Heat and Visible Smoke Release Rates for Upholstered Furniture Components or Composites and Mattresses Using an Oxygen Consumption Calorimeter (withdrawn in 2007)
NFPA 286	Standard Methods of Fire Tests for Evaluating Contribution of Wall and Ceiling Interior Finish to Room Fire Growth
NFPA 701	Standard Methods of Fire Tests for Flame Propagation of Textiles and Films
NFPA 703	Standard for Fire Retardant-Treated Wood and Fire-Retardant Coatings for Building Materials

NOTE: There are other standards organizations with standards similar to those shown above. These include ASTM and UL standards. See other figures in this chapter for more detail.

Figure 9.1 Common NFPA standards for finishes and furniture.

◀**Note**

Some jurisdictions have their own finish and furniture regulations. Some of the most stringent ones include those of the city of Boston and the state of California.

Similar to codes for construction materials as discussed in Chapter 5, the code requirements for interior finishes and furniture often refer to various standards. They include standards from the National Fire Protection Association (NFPA), Underwriters Laboratories (UL), and ASTM International (ASTM). Figure 9.1 is an example of the finish- and furniture-related standards from NFPA.

In addition to the standards referenced in the codes, there are other industry standards that may need to be followed. Some standards have been developed and are required by the federal government. Certain cities and states have their own finish and/or furniture regulations as well, some of which are more stringent. This includes the state of California which develops many of its own standards. The newer sustainability codes include standards that concentrate on the indoor air quality (IAQ) of a building, among other things. Since finishes and furniture can greatly affect the IAQ of a building, these standards, when required, must be used in conjunction with the finish and furniture standards that focus on fire safety. This is discussed in more detail in the section Sustainability Considerations later in this chapter.

Accessibility requirements must also be addressed when specifying certain finishes. This is especially important when specifying floor finishes—both for slip resistance and floor level changes. These requirements are found in the Americans with Disabilities Act (ADA) standards and the *ICC/ANSI A117.1* accessibility standard. In addition, both documents provide information on accessible furniture. All of these requirements are discussed later in the chapter in the section Accessibility Requirements.

⬥ Note

The state of California has developed some of its own finish and furniture standards through its California Bureau of Home Furnishings and Thermal Insulation Department. They are known as *technical bulletins*; several are discussed in this chapter as they relate to other required standards.

STANDARDS AND TESTING

⬥ Note

Finish and furniture testing is constantly changing. Older tests are being improved (or phased out) and new tests are being developed. It is critical to keep abreast of the changes so that the appropriate tests are reviewed and referenced when specifying finishes and furniture.

Rather than listing all the specific requirements for finishes, furnishings, and furniture, the codes reference a number of standards. However, the codes set minimum requirements. In some cases, it may be wise to select finishes and furniture that meet more stringent standards than those required by the codes. (See the section Documentation and Liability in Chapter 10.) This section describes the various standards and related tests referred by the codes and/or required by certain jurisdictions. The standards are referenced by the building codes, the fire codes, and the *Life Safety Code (LSC)*.

Each finish and furniture test has a particular purpose. As shown in Figure 9.2, a finish will need a different test, depending on whether it is used as a wallcovering, a drapery, an upholstery, or the like. The application of the finish determines the appropriate test. For example, the *Radiant Panel Test* is required for carpeting applied to floors. If the same carpet is used on a wall, a different test is required. In other situations, a certain test may better represent the proposed use of a finish. For example, the *Room Corner Test* is a more realistic test than the *Steiner Tunnel Test* since its testing apparatus more closely simulates an actual room. Furniture items have their own tests and the type of test required is often dependent on where it will be used in a building. For example, mattresses used in a hotel must

FINISH CATEGORY	FINISH EXAMPLES	TYPICAL TEST REQUIRED
CEILING TREATMENTS[1]	Ceiling Tiles Fabric Coverings Vinyl Coverings Special Finishes	Steiner Tunnel Test Room Corner Test
WALLCOVERINGS[1]	Vinyl Wallcoverings Fabric Wallcoverings Expanded Vinyl Wallcoverings Wood Paneling Wood Veneers	Steiner Tunnel Test Room Corner Test
FLOOR COVERINGS[2]	Carpets Rugs Carpet Padding Hard Surface Flooring Resilient Flooring	Pill Test Radiant Panel Test
WALL BASE	All types 6 inches or less	Radiant Panel Test
WINDOW TREATMENTS AND VERTICAL HANGINGS [2]	Draperies Liners Blinds Wood Shutters Wall Hangings Acoustical Fabrics Panel Fabrics	Vertical Flame Test
TRIM AND DECORATIVE MATERIALS[3]	Decorative Moldings Wainscoting Chair Rails Picture Rails Baseboards	Steiner Tunnel Test Room Corner Test
UPHOLSTERIES	Fabrics Vinyls Battings Welt Cords Foams Interliners Fillings	Steiner Tunnel Test Smolder Resistance Test Smoke Density Test
FURNITURE	Seating Panel Systems Mattresses	Smolder Resistance Test Upholstered Seating Test Mattress Test

NOTES:

1. If the wall or ceiling finish is a site-fabricated stretch fabric system, it may also need to pass *ASTM E2573*.
2. Some finish applications may require an additional test as required by a jurisdiction.
3. If all or part of a finish consists of plastic, it might also need to pass UL 1975 for foam plastics or ASTM D2843 for light transmitting plastics.
4. Any of the finish or furniture applications listed above may also require a toxicity test.

Figure 9.2 Typical regulated finishes/furniture and required tests.

pass a more stringent test than the *16 CFR 1632*, which is required for all mattresses. It is important to know the intent of the test and recognize the meaning of the test results.

In addition, each test or standard provides as specific result. Some of the tests are pass/fail, while others determine and assign a specific class or ranked rating. For example, the *CAL 133* and *NFPA 701* tests are pass/fail tests. If a finish passes, it is allowed; if it fails, it cannot be used. Other tests, such as the *Steiner Tunnel Test* and the *Radiant Panel Test*, assign class ratings to the tested finishes. Still others, such as *LC-50*, provide a ranked number rating. The manufacturer must supply either the letter or number rating for these tests. For example, a tunnel test will result in an A, B, or C rating. The codes will indicate which rating is required. (The type of result for each test is described in this section.)

There are many additional industry standards being used that are not referenced by the codes. These are described by the inset titled *Industry Standards* on page 380 and are not discussed in this book. In addition, there are many newer sustainability standards which are explained in the section Sustainability Considerations later in this chapter.

The standard tests described in this section have been grouped by the common test name. They are also summarized in Figure 9.3. Within each category, specific test names are listed, depending on the standards organization that provides the test. Often ASTM, NFPA, and UL have their own written standard for the same test. The federal government and the state of California have similar tests as well. In most cases, these tests are very similar; however, some differences do occur and are noted as well.

Steiner Tunnel Test

The *Steiner Tunnel Test* is the principal test used to determine both the flame spread and smoke development ratings in the classification of interior finishes applied to walls, ceilings, and other structural elements, such as columns. As one of the first interior finish tests, its name comes from the fact that finishes are tested in a tunnel-like apparatus that is 25 feet (7.62 m) in length. Although the procedure of the test has been refined over the years, the overall test has not changed much since its inception. The same test is used under these names:

❏ *ASTM E84, Standard Test Method for Surface Burning Characteristics of Building Materials*

❏ *NFPA 255, Standard Method of Test of Surface Burning Characteristics of Building Materials* (withdrawn in 2009 but NFPA codes may reference an older version)

❏ *UL 723, Standard for Test for Surface Burning Characteristics of Building Materials*

◄Note

The codes do not necessarily mention or require every finish and furniture test discussed in this chapter. Some are required locally, while others should be incorporated into a project as a matter of practice.

◄Note

Since there is often more than one standard for the same test, it is important to know which tests are comparable. The building codes, fire codes, and *LSC* may reference different standard names for a particular test.

◄Note

The position of the finish sample in the *Steiner Tunnel Test* makes it difficult for some finishes (e.g., plastics) to be tested without a screen for support. Because of this, the codes sometimes recommend other standards.

COMMON TEST NAMES	STANDARD NAME/NUMBER	TYPE OF RATING
STEINER TUNNEL TEST	ASTM E84 UL 723 NFPA 255 (withdrawn 2009)	Class Rating (A, B, or C)
RADIANT PANEL TEST	ASTM E648 NFPA 253	Class Rating (I or II)
PILL TEST	16 CFR 1630 (DOC FF1 - 70) 16 CFR 1631 (DOC FF2 - 70) ASTM D2859	Pass or Fail
VERTICAL FLAME TEST	NFPA 701 ASTM D6413 UL 214 (withdrawn 2005)	Pass or Fail
ROOM CORNER TEST (textile materials)	NFPA 265 UL 1715	Pass or Fail
(nontextile materials)	NFPA 286 ASTM E2257 (similar)	Pass or Fail
SMOLDER RESISTANCE TEST (component)	NFPA 260 ASTM E1353 CAL 117 (similar)	Class Rating (I or II)
(mock-up)	NFPA 261 ASTM E1352 CAL 116 (similar)	Pass or Fail
TOXICITY TEST LC - 50 (or Pitts Test)	NFPA 269 ASTM E1678	Ranked
UPHOLSTERED SEATING TEST (full-scale)	ASTM E1537 CAL 133 UL 1056 (withdrawn 2005)	Pass or Fail
(small-scale)	ASTM E1474 NFPA 272 (withdrawn 2007)	Ranked
MATTRESS TEST (commercial applications)	ASTM E1590 CAL 129	Pass or Fail
(all applications)	16 CFR 1632 (DOC FF4 - 72) 16 CFR 1633 CAL 603	Pass or Fail

NOTE: Any number of the above tests may be required by a jurisdiction depending on the occupancy and its location within a building. In addition, there may be other tests and/or test names not listed above that are more specific to a jurisdiction.

Figure 9.3 Summary of tests for finishes and furniture.

INDUSTRY STANDARDS

Many of the standards required by the codes or mandated by the federal government pertain to interior building materials and products with the intention of protecting the health, safety, and welfare of the building occupant. For example, many of the standards explained throughout this book concentrate on the type of building material and how it is installed. For finishes and furniture, the codes typically reference standards that pertain to the flame resistance, smoke density, and toxicity of the materials.

However, there are numerous other types of industry standards not included in the codes that are available for finishes and furniture, as well as for the many building materials and products used in a space. Some of these standards provide additional safety to the building occupant. Others have to do with the physical properties of the materials and their durability. There are finish standards, for instance, that address the colorfastness, lightfastness, breaking strength, and abrasion resistance of the material. This may not be important for life safety, but because of the industry standards and testing, they guarantee consistency of manufacturing. It allows a comparison of test results between various finishes and/or products so that the appropriate material can be chosen for the project requirements. (See also the inset titled *Testing Agencies and Certification* on page 41.)

There are also industry standards that manufacturers follow in the production of their products so that consistency is maintained during production. For example, resilient flooring manufacturers might use standard *ASTM F1914, Standard Test Methods for Short-Term Indentation and Residual Indentation of Resilient Floor Covering*, which measures the amount of initial and residual indentation that can occur in the material; systems furniture manufacturers typically use *UL 1286, Standard for Office Furnishings* to confirm the electrical and structural integrity of the components of the system, among other things. Other standards may be useful to include in the project specifications for consistency of installation, such as the standard *CRI 102, Standard for Installation of Commercial Carpet*.

New standards are continually being developed. For example, numerous performance-based standards have been developed to provide consistency in the computer modeling and engineer calculations needed when using performance codes. More recently, the industry is concentrating on standards that relate to sustainability. (See Chapter 1 and the section Sustainability Considerations included in each chapter.) These green standards can also be used when specifying to compare and select various sustainable products.

Using the tunnel apparatus, a finish is tested in a horizontal position attached to the entire length of the tunnel ceiling, as shown in Figure 9.4. The sample consists of the finish and any required substrate and/or adhesive (or other securing method) that would be used in the actual installation of the finish. For example, if a wallcovering is intended to be used on gypsum board, the sample

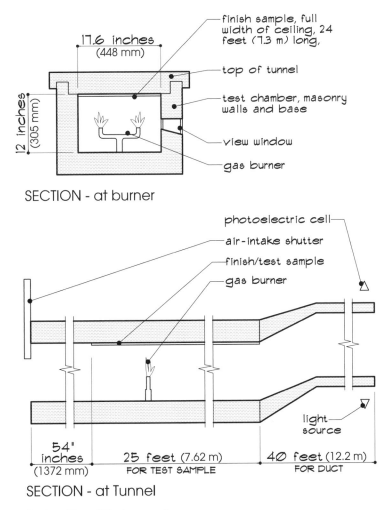

Figure 9.4 *Steiner Tunnel Test* apparatus.

will consist of the wallcovering applied to one layer of gypsum board using the adhesive recommended by the manufacturer. Once the sample is secured, a flame is started at one end and a regulated draft is applied through the tunnel. The time that it takes the flame to travel down the length of the tunnel is measured and is used to create the flame spread index (FSI). The density of the smoke in relation to a light source is measured at the opposite end of the tunnel. This determines the smoke development index (SDI). These two indexes are used to assign a classification to the finish.

✎Note

Some woods that have been treated with a fire retardant can qualify as a Class A interior finish. Most untreated wood will either have a Class C flame spread rating or no rating at all.

In the codes, these classifications are grouped into three categories for interior wall and ceiling finishes, with Class A being the most restrictive and Class C being the least. (Floor finishes have a different test and rating system, as described next.) The classifications consist of the following:

- ❏ Class A: Flame spread index 0–25, smoke development index 0–450
- ❏ Class B: Flame spread index 26–75, smoke development index 0–450
- ❏ Class C: Flame spread index 76–200, smoke development index 0–450

⊴Note

The *Steiner Tunnel Test* is used for a wide range of materials in addition to wall and ceiling finishes. Examples include fire retardant-treated wood, fire-retardant coatings, and pipe and duct insulation (including pipe covers used under lavatories).

The *flame spread index* (FSI) indicates the speed at which a fire may spread across the surface of a material. The lower the number, the slower the fire will spread, which allows more time to evacuate the space or building. The index is determined by comparing the results of the test to the burning characteristics of two known materials, glass-reinforced cement board and red oak flooring. Arbitrarily, the cement board is given a flame spread of 0 and red oak flooring is assigned a flame spread of 100. All other materials are assigned FSI values based on their test results. Both interior finishes and building materials can be required by the codes to pass this test. Figure 9.5 shows the flame spread ratings for a variety of materials. It provides a wide range of possible results, depending on the type of material.

The *smoke development index* (SDI) determines how much visibility there is in a given access route when a material is on fire and creating smoke. The maximum

Material	Flame spread
Glass-fiber sound-absorbing planks	15 to 30
Mineral-fiber sound-absorbing panels	10 to 25
Shredded wood fiberboard (treated)	20 to 25
Sprayed cellulose fibers (treated)	20
Aluminum (with baked enamel finish on one side)	5 to 10
Asbestos-cement board	0
Brick or concrete block	0
Cork	175
Gypsum board (with paper surface on both sides)	10 to 25
Northern pine (treated)	20
Southern pine (untreated)	130 to 190
Plywood paneling (untreated)	75 to 275
Plywood paneling (treated)	100
Carpeting	10 to 600
Concrete	0

Figure 9.5 Typical flame spread of common materials (*2009 International Building Code*, copyright 2009. Washington, DC: International Code Council. All rights reserved. www.iccsafe.org).

SDI of 450 was determined by Underwriters Laboratories and is based solely on the level of visibility through the smoke created by the test. This would affect an occupant's ability to see exit signs while evacuating a building. The smoke development rating actually remains the same in each classification. Any finish with an SDI over 450 would create too much smoke and, therefore, would typically not be allowed by the codes.

Since the smoke development requirement does not change, it is the FSI number that distinguishes the difference in each class. Note, however, that there is no direct relationship between the FSI and the SDI. One finish can have low ratings on both, while another can have a low flame spread but a high smoke development rating. Any tested finish that results in an FSI or SDI above what is allowed by the codes would be considered a nonrated finish.

Radiant Panel Test

The *Radiant Panel Test* is used to rate interior floor finishes such as carpet, resilient flooring, and hardwood floor assemblies as well as wall base. Two standard tests are available:

❑ *NFPA 253, Standard Method of Test for Critical Radiant Flux of Floor Covering Systems Using a Radiant Heat Energy Source*

❑ *ASTM E648, Standard Test Method for Critical Radiant Flux of Floor Covering Systems Using a Radiant Heat Energy Source*

Originally developed to simulate the type of fire that develops in corridors and exitways, the test measures the floor covering's tendency to spread a fire. Although flooring is not considered a major cause of fire spread, the flooring material in exit access corridors can be of concern because it can add to fire growth when flame and hot gases radiate through the walls from a fire in an adjacent room.

The test determines the minimum energy required to sustain flame on a floor covering. In this test, a finish sample is secured to a substrate and then placed at the bottom of the test chamber, as shown in Figure 9.6. The finish sample consists of the entire floor covering system, which includes the floor covering, any required padding, adhesive (or other securing method), and the substrate. The sample is preheated by a radiant heat source mounted at a 30-degree angle from the sample and then exposed to a gas burner. If the sample begins to burn, two things are measured as soon as the flame goes out: the length of the burn marks and the amount of radiant heat energy at the farthest part of the burned area. Both of these measurements are compared to existing data (e.g., a flux profile graph) in order to determine the *critical radiant flux* (CRF).

✎Note

The *Radiant Panel Test* was originally created by the National Institute of Standards and Technology (NIST) and was known as *NBS IRS75-950*. (NIST was previously known as the National Bureau of Standards.)

✎Note

The NFPA notes that most fire deaths due to smoke inhalation in the United States occur in areas other than the room of fire origin and are caused by fires that have spread beyond the room of origin.

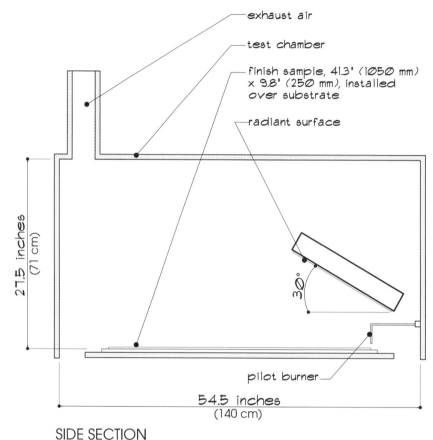

SIDE SECTION

Figure 9.6 *Radiant Panel Test* apparatus.

The CRF is measured in watts per square centimeter. The higher the value, the more heat energy it takes to ignite the finish, making it more resistant to flame spread. Test results determine whether a floor finish will be considered a Class I or a Class II. Class I is more flame resistant. (Floor coverings that do not fall within one of these two categories are considered nonrated or nonclassed.) The CRF for each is as follows:

❏ *Class I:* CRF, minimum of 0.45 watts per square centimeter
❏ *Class II:* CRF, minimum of 0.22 watts per square centimeter

These two classes are referenced by the codes. Not all occupancies require a floor finish that has been tested by the *Radiant Panel Test.* If it is required, only exits and exit access corridors are typically regulated. (See the section Determining Finish Classifications later in this chapter.) Although this test is often associated with the testing of carpet, these ratings will also apply to other floor finishes. These include resilient floors such as VCT, as well as hardwood flooring installed over a combustible substrate such as plywood. (Hardwood floors applied directly to concrete are typically not required to be rated.) When furring strips are used under a floor covering, such as hardwood floors, other code restrictions may apply, as discussed later in this chapter. (See the section Other Restrictions toward the end of the chapter.)

The fire codes and the *LSC* also now require all wall base that is 6 inches (152 mm) or less to meet the requirements of this test. The base must at least meet the requirements of a Class II. If it is installed where Class I flooring is required, then the base must be a Class I as well.

Pill Test

In addition to the *Radiant Panel Test*, all carpets and certain rugs manufactured for sale in the United States have been required, since 1971, to meet federal flammability standards. Also known as the *Pill Test*, it uses a methenamine tablet (or pill) to ignite the sample during the test. This pill replicates a small ignition source such as a slow-burning cigarette or a glowing ember from a fireplace.

The test places a pill in the center of a carpet (or rug) sample, as shown in Figure 9.7. The pill is ignited and once the flame or glow has gone out, the distance that the carpet has burned beyond the original ignition point is measured. If the charred portion extends to more than 3 inches (76 mm), the sample fails.

This pass/fail test indicates the ease of surface ignition and surface flammability of a material. There are two versions of this test produced by the federal government: one regulates large rugs and wall-to-wall carpeting and the other is for area rugs. ASTM has a standard for these tests as well. The three tests are:

❑   *16 CFR 1630* (or *DOC FFI-70*), *Standard for the Surface Flammability of Carpets and Rugs*

❑   *16 CFR 1631* (or *DOC FF2-70*), *Standard for the Surface Flammability of Small Carpets and Rugs*

❑   *ASTM D2859, Standard Test Method for Ignition Characteristics of Finishes Textile Floor Covering Materials* (includes testing procedures for carpets and rugs)

The federal government requires that all carpets and rugs sold in the United States be tested using *16 CFR 1630* and *16 CFR 1631*. Carpets must pass the test to be sold in the United States. All rugs must be tested; however, a small rug (less than

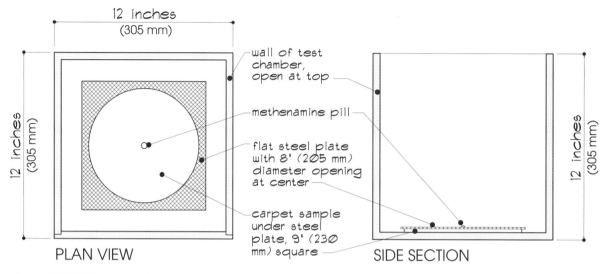

Figure 9.7 *Pill Test* apparatus.

24 square feet) is not required to pass the *Pill Test*. If the rug does not pass, it must be labeled as flammable. The building codes typically require all carpets and large rugs (e.g., those tested by *16 CFR 1630* or *ASTM D2859*) to pass this *Pill Test* no matter what occupancy they are used in. Smaller rugs are not covered by the building code, but their use should be limited, especially in commercial applications, if they have not passed the *Pill Test*. (Their use may need to be confirmed with a code official.) Although this test is considered standard protocol, and is referenced by the codes, other flooring finish regulations are required for occupancies that warrant more careful restrictions or where a codes official deems it necessary for a particular situation. (See *Radiant Panel Test* in the previous section.)

Vertical Flame Tests

Vertical Flame Tests are generally required for *vertical treatments* such as curtains, draperies, window shades, large wall hangings or tapestries, and plastic films used for decorative purposes. Any vertical finish that is exposed to air on both sides is considered a vertical treatment. This includes wall hangings because air can get between the wall and the hanging. However, if a fabric or tapestry is fully secured to a wall using adhesive, it will usually need to meet the requirements of a *Steiner Tunnel Test*—or a *Room Corner Test*, as described next.

The *Vertical Flame Tests* include the following:

❑ *NFPA 701, Standard Methods of Fire Tests for Flame Propagation of Textiles and Films*
❑ *ASTM D6413, Standard Test Method for Flame Resistance of Textiles (Vertical Test)*

> ◢ **Note**
>
> A third *Vertical Flame Test*, *UL 214*, was withdrawn by Underwriters Laboratory in 2005. Instead, *NFPA 701* is the most commonly referenced standard.

These tests are more realistic than the *Steiner Tunnel Test* because a flame source is used to create a vertical burning of the finish rather than the horizontal burning used in the tunnel test. *NFPA 701* is the oldest version of the test and the most commonly referenced by the building codes and the *LSC*. It is divided into two separate pass/fail tests known as *Test Method 1* and *Test Method 2*.

In both test methods, the sample must be exposed to conditions similar to those in which the fabric will be used. For example, fabrics for table linens must be laundered and drapery fabrics should be dry-cleaned. This gives the most realistic test results. It also indicates how important it is for clients to know how to clean and maintain the items specified and installed. If they do not follow the manufacturer's recommendations, the fabric's performance in a fire will be affected. The two test methods are described next.

Test Method 1

Test Method 1 is a small-scale test and is required for lighter-weight fabrics that are either single-layered or multi-layered. These include window curtains and drapes and other treatments such as swags, vertical folding shades, roll-type window shades, and fabric blinds (vertical and horizontal). These also include stage or theater curtains, hospital privacy curtains, display booth separators, table skirts, and linens, as well as textile wall hangings. (The maximum weight of the fabric is typically set at 700 grams per square meter—or approximately 20.5 ounces per square yard.)

The test consists of hanging a fabric sample vertically on a bar in a test cabinet, as shown in Figure 9.8. A gas burner is applied to the lower edge of the sample. Once the flame source is removed, the sample is allowed to burn until it extinguishes itself. If any part of the sample falls to the floor, it must self-extinguish within 2 seconds. In addition, the remaining sample is weighed and cannot be less than 40 percent of its original weight. Both requirements must be met for the fabric to pass the test.

Test Method 2

Test Method 2 is a similar test done on a larger scale. It is used for heavier fabrics and fabrics that have vinyl coatings, such as blackout blinds and lined draperies using a vinyl-coated blackout lining. It also includes plastic films, awnings, tarps, and banners. In addition, this test might be used for larger drapery assemblies that have multiple layers and folds, which takes into account the effect of air trapped between fabric layers.

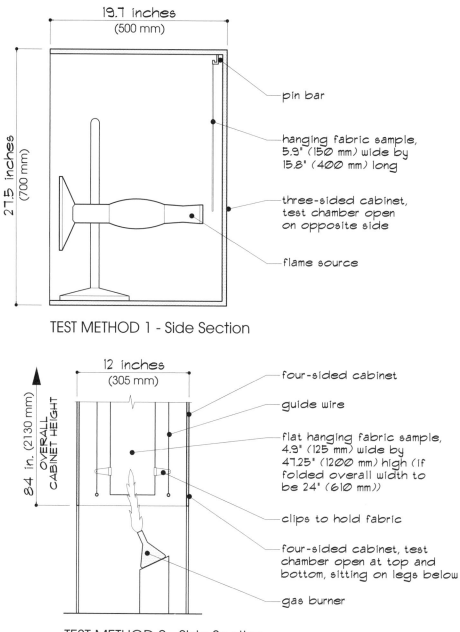

19.7 inches
(500 mm)

27.5 inches
(700 mm)

pin bar

hanging fabric sample,
5.9" (150 mm) wide by
15.8" (400 mm) long

three-sided cabinet,
test chamber open
on opposite side

flame source

TEST METHOD 1 - Side Section

12 inches
(305 mm)

84 in. (2130 mm)
OVERALL
CABINET HEIGHT

four-sided cabinet

guide wire

flat hanging fabric sample,
4.9" (125 mm) wide by
47.25" (1200 mm) high (if
folded overall width to
be 24" (610 mm))

clips to hold fabric

four-sided cabinet, test
chamber open at top and
bottom, sitting on legs below

gas burner

TEST METHOD 2 - Side Section

Figure 9.8 *Vertical Flame Test* apparatus.

This test uses a larger cabinet and a longer fabric sample as shown in Figure 9.8. The sample is hung from a rod at the top of the cabinet (either folded or flat) and exposed to a flame source at the bottom for 2 minutes. When the flame source is removed, the sample must self-extinguish within 2 seconds in order to pass the test. In addition, the burn marks left on the sample cannot exceed a certain char length. If the char remaining from the burn exceeds certain limits, the fabric will fail even if it extinguished itself within 2 seconds.

Room Corner Tests

Another standard test must be used when napped, tufted, or looped textiles are used as "wallcoverings" on walls and ceilings. These typically include carpets and carpet-like textiles. Currently there are two versions of the test—one for *textile* wallcoverings and the other for *nontextile* wall and ceiling finishes such as expanded vinyl wallcovering. All of these tests are generally referred to as *Room Corner Tests*. As the name implies, an entire room is used in these tests and the flame source is located in one corner of the room.

A *Room Corner Test* is a more accurate representation of actual building conditions because of the full room simulation. The test determines how an interior finish material will add to fire growth (including heat and smoke) and create combustion products such as gases. It also determines whether the finish will cause flashover or fire spread beyond the initial fire location. And, since it is considered a more stringent test than the *Steiner Tunnel Test*, the codes will usually allow one of these tests in lieu of meeting the requirements of the tunnel test. (See building codes for specifics.) The two versions of the tests are described separately below.

Textile Wallcoverings

The most current *Room Corner Test* standards for textile wallcoverings include:

❏ *NFPA 265, Standard Methods of Fire Tests for Evaluating Room Fire Growth Contribution of Textile Coverings on Full Height Panels and Walls*

❏ *UL 1715, Fire Test of Interior Finish Material*

These are pass/fail tests that simulate a fire within a full-size room, as shown in Figure 9.9. Finish samples are secured to the walls in the room using the adhesive intended for actual use. The test allows for two options. *Method A* requires the finish sample to be mounted partially on two walls of a compartment like that shown in Figure 9.9. *Method B* requires the finish sample to be mounted fully on the one rear wall and two long side walls.

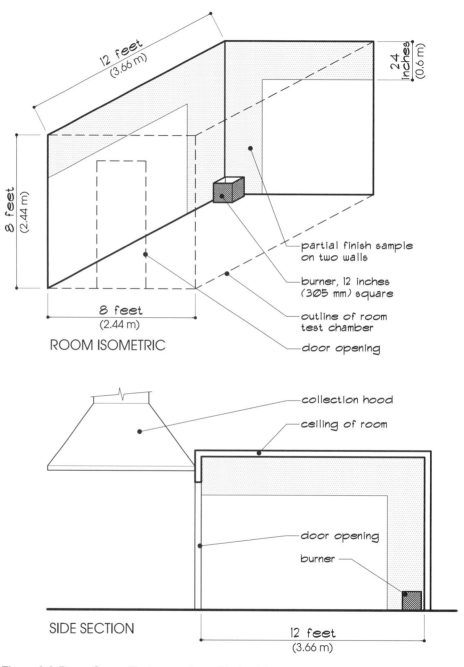

Figure 9.9 *Room Corner Test* apparatus—Method A.

Once the finish sample is secured to the walls, the rest of the test is the same. A fire source is started in the corner of the room. A square box located 2 inches (51mm) from the back corner of the room is ignited. (See Figure 9.9.) It is first ignited at a heat level of approximately 40 kilowatts for 5 minutes and then increased to approximately 150 kilowatts for an additional 10 minutes. A duct system located outside the open doorway of the room collects the gases created by the fire and measures the gas velocity, temperature, and concentrations of gases. A finish passes the test if certain criteria listed in the standard are met. For example, the flame cannot extend to the ceiling during the first heat exposure, and flashover cannot occur during the second heat exposure. The codes typically reference both standards shown above but limit their use to test Method B. Regardless of whether Method A or Method B is used, if all listed criteria are not met, the finish fails.

✎Note

The *International Fire Code* still allows the use of test Method A in *NFPA 265,* but this is for existing buildings only. Other codes allow only Method B.

Nontextile Wallcoverings

There are two other standards that are also considered *Room Corner Tests*. However, they test nontextile wallcoverings that can be used on walls as well as ceilings. Expanded vinyl wallcoverings are typically tested using these standards. The standards are similar:

✎Note

In addition to the *Room Corner Test*, the 2009 ICC codes allow expanded vinyl wall and ceiling coverings to be tested using the *Steiner Tunnel Test* as long as an additional standard (*ASTM E2404*) is used for the preparation and mounting of the test sample.

❑ NFPA 286, *Standard Methods of Fire Tests for Evaluating Contribution of Wall and Ceiling Interior Finish to Room Fire Growth*
❑ ASTM E2257, *Standard Test Method for Room Fire Test of Wall and Ceiling Materials and Assemblies* (similar)

The basis for these tests and the *Room Corner Tests* described above is similar. For example, the same simulated room shown in Figure 9.9 is used—same size, same instruments, same burning source, and so on. The finish samples are even applied to the room in the same way as in Method B described above. However, for this test, the finish sample must also be secured to the ceiling of the room as well as the walls. (If it is exclusively a ceiling finish, then the finish sample can be applied only on the ceiling.) Additionally, the flame source is placed closer to the corner of the room so that it is in direct contact with the walls. The first ignition heat level and exposure length is also the same as in the test for the textile wallcovering, but the second exposure increases to approximately 160 kilowatts for 10 minutes. In addition to the criteria used for textile wallcoverings, tested finishes are given a smoke release value. If the nontextile finish does not pass all the required criteria or exceed the smoke release value (which is similar to the 450 SDI set by the *Steiner Tunnel Test*), it will fail.

✎Note

The *IBC, IFC,* and *LSC* consider finishes that pass *NFPA 286* equivalent to Class A of the *Steiner Tunnel Test.*

The *ASTM E2257* test is similar to the NFPA test, except that different heat levels and time frames are used during the test. *NFPA 286* is the test most referenced by the codes. A textile finish must typically pass this test to be used on a ceiling.

Smolder Resistance Tests

The *Smolder Resistance Test* is also known as the *Cigarette Ignition Test*. It is a non-flame test that uses an actual smoldering cigarette as the ignition source to see how a product will smolder before either flaming or extinguishing. The test consists of putting a lighted cigarette on a sample and then covering it with a layer of sheeting material. The cigarette is allowed to burn its full length unless ignition occurs. (If ignition occurs, the sample automatically fails.) Once the cigarette burns its full length, the char length is measured in all directions. If the char is longer than allowed by the test, the sample does not pass.

This test is required by the *LSC* and the fire codes. Most commonly it is required for most new upholstered furniture in board and care facilities, nursing homes, hospitals, detention and correction facilities, and college and university dormitories. Although the methods used are virtually the same, there are two types of this test. One version of the test evaluates the individual *components* that make up a piece of furniture, while the other version evaluates a combination of components or a partial *mock-up* of the piece of furniture. The codes will typically require one or the other, not both. Each is explained below.

Components

One type of *Smolder Resistance Test* is used to test an individual finish or textile. It is a pass/fail test and includes the following similar tests.

❑ *NFPA 260, Standard Methods of Tests and Classification System for Cigarette Ignition Resistance of Components of Upholstered Furniture*

❑ *ASTM E1353, Standard Test Methods for Cigarette Ignition Resistance of Components of Upholstered Furniture*

❑ *CAL 117, Requirements, Test Procedures and Apparatus for Testing the Flame Retardance of Resilient Filling Materials Used in Upholstered Furniture* (similar)

This test applies to a wide variety of furniture components and includes cover fabrics, interior fabrics, welt cords, decking materials, and barrier materials, as well as filling or padding materials. These filling/batting materials can be natural or man-made fibers, foamed or cellular materials, resilient pads of

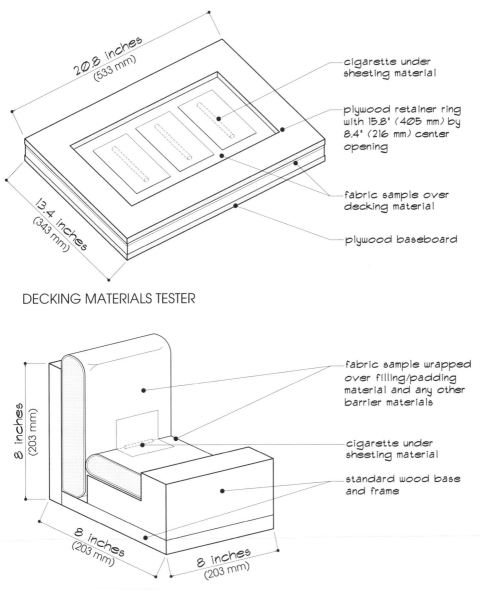

cigarette under
sheeting material

plywood retainer ring
with 15.8" (405 mm) by
8.4" (216 mm) center
opening

fabric sample over
decking material

plywood baseboard

DECKING MATERIALS TESTER

20.8 inches
(533 mm)

13.4 inches
(343 mm)

fabric sample wrapped
over filling/padding
material and any other
barrier materials

cigarette under
sheeting material

standard wood base
and frame

8 inches
(203 mm)

8 inches
(203 mm)

8 inches
(203 mm)

MINI-MOCK-UP TESTER

Figure 9.10 *Smolder Resistance Test:* Tester options.

natural or man-made fibers, or loose particulate filling materials such as shredded polyurethane or feathers and down.

Depending on the component, the finish sample could be tested on one of two types of test apparatus: a "decking materials tester" or a "mini-mock-up tester." Both of these are shown in Figure 9.10. For example, samples that consist of decking material are typically tested horizontally using the decking material tester. Other components, such as fabrics, welt cords, filling or padding, and barrier materials, are assembled individually or in combination to fit on the standard base unit of the mini-mock-up tester. The mini-mock-up allows these materials to be tested with the cigarette in a crevice.

Although the test provides a cigarette resistance classification, Class I or Class II, it is essentially a pass/fail test. If the material resists ignition from the cigarette and does not exceed the maximum char length, it passes the test and is classified as Class I. Any material that does not pass the test is classified as Class II.

◄Note

The *CAL 117* test is slightly different than other *Smolder Resistance Tests* for components, using a burner instead of a cigarette for some component types.

Mock-ups

Another *Smolder Resistance Test* was developed specifically for furniture mock-ups. This test is more realistic because the mock-up consists of multiple components used in realistic combinations. The most common tests include:

❏ NFPA 261, *Standard Method of Test for Determining Resistance of Mock-up Upholstered Furniture Material Assemblies to Ignition by Smoldering Cigarettes*

❏ ASTM E1352, *Standard Test Method for Cigarette Ignition Resistance of Mock-up Upholstered Furniture Assemblies*

❏ CAL 116, *Requirements, Test Procedure and Apparatus for Testing the Flame Retardance of Upholstered Furniture* (similar)

All the materials that are to be used in the actual upholstered furniture are included in the mock-up, similar to the actual piece of furniture. The mock-up is shaped similarly to the mini-mock-up in Figure 9.10 except that two sides (perpendicular to each other) are required instead of one; one side represents the back and the other represents the arm of the upholstered piece. The mock-up is also larger overall than the one in the previous test.

The test is essentially the same as the component mini-mock-up test previously described, except that multiple cigarettes are lit at the same time during the test instead of just one. For example, cigarettes are put in the crevices of the seat cushion and armrest, on the cushion edge, in the center of the cushion, on top of armrests, and so on. As a result, the test gives a better indication of how a whole piece of furniture will react rather than just one layer. At the end of the test, the char length is measured and the mock-up sample is given a pass or fail rating. It passes if ignition did not occur and the char falls within the designated length.

◄Note

The *CAL 116* test is slightly different than other *Smolder Resistance Tests* for mock-ups.

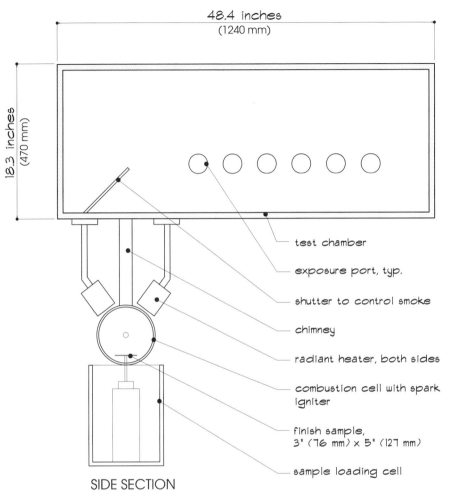

48.4 inches
(1240 mm)

18.3 inches
(470 mm)

test chamber

exposure port, typ.

shutter to control smoke

chimney

radiant heater, both sides

combustion cell with spark
igniter

finish sample,
3" (76 mm) x 5" (127 mm)

sample loading cell

SIDE SECTION

Figure 9.11 *Toxicity Test* apparatus.

Toxicity Test

Toxicity testing is one of the newer types of finish and furnishing tests. The first *Toxicity Test* was developed by the University of Pittsburgh and was known as the *Pitts Test* or *LC-50*. More recent versions of the test are:

❏ *NFPA 269, Standard Test Method for Developing Toxic Potency Data for Use in Fire Hazard Modeling*

❏ *ASTM E1678, Standard Test Method for Measuring Smoke Toxicity for Use in Fire Hazard Analysis*

◀ Note

Some states, such as California, ban certain fire retardants and other additives used in plastics, foam, and upholstered furniture due to the toxins they emit.

The test measures the amount of toxicity a material emits when it is burned. The testing covers a wide range of materials in addition to finishes and furniture. Included are wall, ceiling, and floor finishes, furniture upholstery, mattresses, and bed pads, as well as electrical wire and conduit, mechanical ductwork, thermal insulation, and plumbing pipes. The degree of toxicity is reported as an LC$_{50}$ value.

The test consists of subjecting a small finish sample (or other material) to an ignition source and then exposing it to radiant heat lamps. (See Figure 9.11.) The concentration of gaseous toxicants are monitored. The data collected, along with the measured mass loss of the test sample, is used to predict the LC-50 rating of the test sample. The same procedure is then repeated using six live mice in order to confirm the predicted LC-50 rating, and adjustments are made as required based on the reaction of the mice.

Although it is a rated test, at this time there are no set standard ratings. However, more manufacturers are testing their products and listing the LC-50 ratings on them. Therefore, when selecting a finish or furnishing with an LC-50 rating, two or more products should be compared. The higher the test score the better, since higher ratings are less toxic. Some jurisdictions require a rating to remain within or above the natural wood ratings of LC-16 through LC-25.

Although the tests are not currently required by the ICC or NFPA codes, this situation may change in the future. Some jurisdictions will require the test. The state of New York, for example, was one of the first to enforce the test. Check with the local code jurisdiction for specific requirements.

Upholstered Seating Tests

Most of the standard tests described so far test individual finishes and components. Other tests are available for upholstered seating and mattresses. These test more of the full assembly. There are two basic types: full-scale tests and small-scale tests. A *full-scale test* can use an actual piece of furniture or a large mock-up of that piece of furniture, whereas a *small-scale test* uses smaller mock-ups that consist of multiple parts or components of a piece of furniture.

Full-Scale Tests

The full-scale test is a pass/fail test of a *whole* piece of furniture rather than of an individual finish or material. It was first developed by the state of California and titled *California Technical Bulletin 133*, also referred to as either *CAL 133* or *TB 133*. Since then, other standards organizations have developed similar tests. Tests that are considered full-scale furniture tests are shown below.

❑ *ASTM E1537, Standard Test Method for Fire Testing of Upholstered Furniture*

❑ *CAL 133, Flammability Test Procedure for Seating Furniture for Use in Public Occupancies*

The aim of the test is to eliminate the flashover that occurs in the second phase of a fire. (See the inset titled *Fire Development Stages* on page 373.) It is a flame-resistance test that measures the carbon monoxide, heat generation, smoke, temperature, and weight loss of an entire piece of furniture. The test sample is either an actual upholstered piece of furniture or a full-scale mock-up that simulates the construction of the furniture item. There are three options of the test (A, B, or C), two of which are done with the test sample in the corner of an enclosed room. Similar to a *Room Corner Test*, the exhaust collection hood is located outside the room. In the third option (Option C), shown in Figure 9.12, the collection hood is directly above the test sample. In each case, a burner is held just above the upholstered seat, ignited, and then turned off. The exhaust hood collects all the products of combustion. The furniture sample passes the test if the peak heat release and the total energy release do not exceed a predetermined level.

The California test was originally developed for furniture used in public buildings in any area or room that contains 10 or more pieces of seating. This applies to prisons, health care facilities, nursing homes, day care facilities, stadiums, auditoriums, and public assembly areas in hotels and motels. Newer editions of the *LSC* and *IFC* require upholstered furniture that passes *CAL 133* and/or *ASTM E1537* in certain occupancies where sprinklers are not used. If it is not required by the local jurisdiction, *CAL 133* products can still be specified to provide better protection to the occupants in certain projects. (See also the inset titled *CAL 133–Tested Products* on page 400.)

Small-Scale Tests

The small-scale tests listed below were often required for upholstered furniture and mattresses in commercial, institutional, and high-risk building types. However, these tests are not referenced by more current codes. The tests measure how quickly upholstered furniture and mattresses will ignite. They also measure the rate of heat release.

❑ *ASTM E1474, Standard Test Method for Determining the Heat Release Rate of Upholstered Furniture and Mattress Components or Composites Using a Bench Scale Oxygen Consumption Calorimeter*

❑ *NFPA 272, Standard Method of Test for Heat and Visible Smoke Release Rates for Upholstered Furniture Components or Composites and Mattresses Using an Oxygen Consumption Calorimeter* (withdrawn in 2007)

⬛Note

Two other full-scale upholstered seating tests are no longer in use: *NFPA 266*, withdrawn by NFPA in 2003, and *UL 1056*, withdrawn by UL in 2005. The *IFC* and the *LSC* now reference standard *ASTM E1537*.

⬛Note

Many furniture manufacturers offer *CAL 133*–compliant seating. Work closely with the manufacturer to specify correctly.

⬛Note

The *CAL 133* test is essentially the same as *ASTM E1537*, but it uses an alternate size test room and has a few stricter requirements.

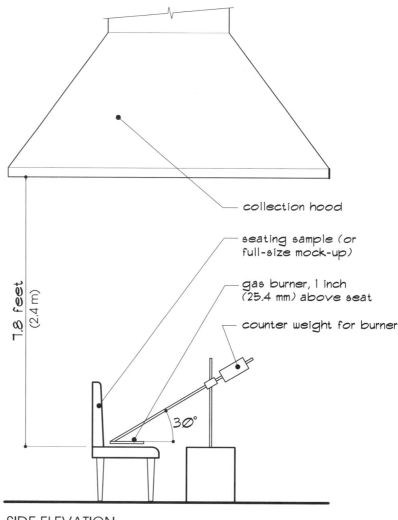

7.8 feet (2.4 m)

collection hood

seating sample (or full-size mock-up)

gas burner, 1 inch (25.4 mm) above seat

counter weight for burner

30°

SIDE ELEVATION

Figure 9.12 *Upholstered Seating Test* apparatus: Full-scale.

The sample used in this test consists of various components, including the fabric and padding material of the proposed upholstered item plus any layers in between, such as liners, polyester fiber, and other fillers. The assembled finish sample is in the shape of a small block 2 inches (100 mm) square. Although it is small, the test results are still useful in predicting the performance of a full piece of furniture.

Mattress Tests

Although mattresses can be tested using the small-scale tests mentioned in the previous section, there are other tests that apply only to mattresses, some of which are required by the federal government. These are all considered full-scale tests and include the following:

❏ *ASTM E1590, Standard Test Method for Fire Testing of Mattresses*

❏ *CAL 129, Flammability Test Procedure for Mattresses Used in Public Buildings*

❏ *16 CFR 1632 (or DOC FF4-72), Standard for Flammability of Mattresses and Mattress Pads*

❏ *CAL 603, Requirements and Test Procedure for Resistance of a Mattress/Box Spring Set to a Large Open Flame*

❏ *16 CFR 1633, Standard for the Flammability (Open Flame) of Mattresses and Mattress/ Foundation Sets*

The first two tests are the most stringent and are required by the fire codes and the *LSC* for new mattresses in certain occupancies such as board and care facilities, nursing homes, hospitals, detention and correction facilities, and college and university dormitories. (It is not intended for use in the evaluation of residential mattresses.) These tests determine the heat release, smoke density, generation of toxic gases (carbon monoxide), and weight loss that occur when an individual mattress or a mattress with its foundation (i.e., box spring) is exposed to a flame.

To conduct the *ASTM E1590* test, the mattress or mattress set is placed on a frame with an exhaust hood above, similar to Figure 9.12. A T-shaped gas burner is positioned to the side of the test sample and the exhaust hood collects all the products of combustion for up to 30 minutes after the flame is removed. The results of the pass/fail test is based on the peak heat and energy release. (The *CAL 129* test has slightly different requirements.)

The third mattress test listed above, *16 CFR 1632*, is required by the federal government and is applicable to mattresses used in single-family dwellings as well as commercial projects. It is a pass/fail test that measures the char size created when exposed to a lit cigarette, similar to the *Smolder Resistance Test* discussed earlier in this chapter. It is required for most types of mattresses as well as mattress pads sold in the United States. The codes also require this test, requiring a maximum char length of 2 inches (51 mm) in certain occupancies. (California has a similar test known as *CAL 106*.)

The last two mattress tests are more recent. *16 CFR 1633* is a federally required test based on California's newer mattress test, *CAL 603*. These tests use a dual-burning gas flame device to apply flames to the sides and top of a mattress or mattress set, simulating a fire caused by bed linens rather than a smoldering cigarette. Effective July 2007, all mattresses sold in the United States must comply with both federal mattress tests *16 CFR 1633* and *16 CFR 1632*.

◁Note

All mattresses sold and used in the United States must pass the federal tests *16 CFR 1632* and *16 CFR 1633*. Mattresses used in certain commercial facilities must pass additional stricter tests.

CAL 133-TESTED PRODUCTS

Even if *CAL 133* or one of the other related standards is not required by a jurisdiction, *CAL 133*–tested products can still be specified to provide additional safety to the building occupants. More seating that is *CAL 133*–compliant is now available. In addition, manufacturers can usually explain how to combine various fabrics and components in order to meet *CAL 133* requirements. Furniture testing continues to be more accepted and enforced throughout the country. As laws and standards are getting stricter, there are more areas of liability for the designer. (Refer to the section Documentation and Liability in Chapter 10.) Here are some other issues to consider:

❑ Selecting a special fabric or "COM" (customer's own material) may change the *CAL 133* test results for a piece of furniture if it has not been pretested by the manufacturer. Additional testing costs may apply. The lead time or length of production may also be extended.

❑ Specifying a fireblock liner may make a piece of furniture *CAL 133* compliant. Fireblock liners are often used between the foam and upholstery instead of using a flame-retardant foam. Other items such as fire-retardant thread might also need to be considered. Work with the manufacturer and within the requirements of the test standards.

❑ Buildings with sprinklers are not always required to have *CAL 133*–tested furniture. However, should a fire occur, the lack of tested furniture can become an issue.

❑ Be aware that specifying custom furniture, as well as having furniture reupholstered, can be a problem. Unless a mock-up is built and tested, there is no way a one-of-a-kind piece of furniture can be tested under *CAL 133*. It ruins the piece being tested.

❑ As with all other tested finishes and furniture, the way a piece of furniture is cleaned and maintained affects its rating. As the designer, the appropriate maintenance information should be given to the client so that furniture is maintained to the manufacturer's specifications.

DETERMINING FINISH CLASSIFICATIONS

◤ Note

The *ICCPC* does not specifically discuss alternate options for finishes and furniture.

As mentioned earlier, the building codes, the fire codes, and the *LSC* all have a chapter on interior finishes. Many of the standards and tests described in the previous section are required by one or more of the codes. These will be listed within the text of each code either in the finish chapters, the various occupancy chapters, or in other areas. For example, the *IBC* also has chapters on glazing and plastics that may need to be referenced. (Also see the inset titled *Plastic Finishes* on page 419.) The NFPA codes will have additional requirements in their occupancy chapters. Stricter requirements may be required for certain occupancies or building types. If working in a jurisdiction that requires more than one of these code publications, compare the requirements to make sure that the most restrictive ones are being used, especially since many jurisdictions use both a building code and the *LSC*.

Each finish chapter in the building code and the *LSC* also includes an interior finish table that specifies required finishes for certain means of egress and types of buildings. The table is described in more detail below and is followed by an example of how to use it.

The Code Table

The interior finish table in the building codes and the *LSC* provides the allowable ratings for various finishes. Figure 9.13 shows a copy of the *LSC* Table A.10.2.2, "Interior Finish Classification Limitations." It includes information on wall, ceiling, and floor finishes. The table in the *IBC* is Table 803.5, "Interior Wall and Ceiling Finish Requirements by Occupancy." (It is also repeated in the *IFC*.) Unlike the NFPA tables, the table in the *IBC* does not specify floor finishes, since this information is included within its text. In addition, the *IBC* divides the table into sprinklered and nonsprinklered buildings, while the *LSC* table is based on nonsprinklered buildings and uses a footnote in the table to cover requirements for sprinklered buildings.

Five different finishes classes need to be understood to use the finish tables correctly. There are three classes for wall and ceiling finishes (Classes A, B, and C), which are obtained using the *Steiner Tunnel Tests*, and two separate classes for interior floor finishes (Classes I and II), which are obtained using the *Radiant Panel Tests*. (Refer to the section Standards and Testing earlier in this chapter.) These different classes recognize that all parts of the means of egress must be safe. However, it is especially important for exits to be free of fire and smoke for safety and visibility.

Before using the *LSC* table shown in Figure 9.13, the occupancy classification of the building (or space) needs to be determined and whether it is considered new or existing. (This is described in Chapter 2.) Once the occupancy is known, the table lists the finish classes allowed in each area of the building. Each of the codes divides these areas similarly. They consist of exits, exit access corridors, and other rooms or spaces. (Refer to the section Means of Egress Components in Chapter 4 for a description of each.) For clarification, the *IBC* lists the exit category as "exit enclosures and exit passageways."

Reading across the table in Figure 9.13 for a particular occupancy, it indicates which class of finishes is allowed in each of these areas. Generally, the closer to the exterior of a building or exit discharge, the stricter class rating and fire resistance of the finish. Spaces that are not separated from a corridor, such as

✎Note

If a jurisdiction requires the use of a sustainability code or standard or a green building program (see Chapter 10), these include requirements for finishes and/or furniture as well. The requirements must be coordinated with the building and life safety codes. (See the section Sustainability Considerations later in this chapter.)

✎Note

If working on a building in one of the cities or states with its own code, check with that jurisdiction for further requirements. (Other states are beginning to increase their requirements for finishes and furniture as well.)

✎Note

The codes have different requirements for sprinklers and how they affect the use and placement of interior finishes and furniture. See the section Sprinkler Design Issues in Chapter 6 and the codes for more information.

Table A.10.2.2 Interior Finish Classification Limitations

Occupancy	Exits	Exit Access Corridors	Other Spaces
Assembly — New			
>300 occupant load	A	A or B	A or B
	I or II	I or II	NA
≤300 occupant load	A	A or B	A, B, or C
	I or II	I or II	NA
Assembly — Existing			
>300 occupant load	A	A or B	A or B
≤300 occupant load	A	A or B	A, B, or C
Educational — New	A	A or B	A or B; C on low partitions†
	I or II	I or II	NA
Educational — Existing	A	A or B	A, B, or C
Day-Care Centers — New	A	A	A or B
	I or II	I or II	NA
Day-Care Centers — Existing	A or B	A or B	A or B
Day-Care Homes — New	A or B	A or B	A, B, or C
	I or II		NA
Day-Care Homes — Existing	A or B	A, B, or C	A, B, or C
Health Care — New	A	A	A
	NA	B on lower portion of corridor wall†	B in small individual rooms†
	I or II	I or II	NA
Health Care — Existing	A or B	A or B	A or B
Detention and Correctional — New	A or B	A or B	A, B, or C
(sprinklers mandatory)	I or II	I or II	NA
Detention and Correctional — Existing	A or B	A or B	A, B, or C
	I or II	I or II	NA
One- and Two-Family Dwellings and Lodging or Rooming Houses	A, B, or C	A, B, or C	A, B, or C
Hotels and Dormitories — New	A	A or B	A, B, or C
	I or II	I or II	NA
Hotels and Dormitories — Existing	A or B	A or B	A, B, or C
	I or II†	I or II†	NA
Apartment Buildings — New	A	A or B	A, B, or C
	I or II	I or II	NA
Apartment Buildings — Existing	A or B	A or B	A, B, or C
	I or II†	I or II†	NA
Residential Board and Care — (See Chapters 32 and 33.)			
Mercantile — New	A or B	A or B	A or B
	I or II		NA
Mercantile — Existing			
Class A or Class B stores	A or B	A or B	Ceilings — A or B; walls — A, B, or C
Class C stores	A, B, or C	A, B, or C	A, B, or C
Business and Ambulatory Health Care — New	A or B	A or B	A, B, or C
	I or II		NA
Business and Ambulatory Health Care — Existing	A or B	A or B	A, B, or C
Industrial	A or B	A, B, or C	A, B, or C
	I or II	I or II	NA
Storage	A or B	A, B, or C	A, B, or C
	I or II		NA

NA: Not applicable.

Notes:

(1) Class A interior wall and ceiling finish — flame spread, 0–25 (new applications), smoke developed, 0–450.

(2) Class B interior wall and ceiling finish — flame spread, 26–75 (new applications), smoke developed, 0–450.

(3) Class C interior wall and ceiling finish — flame spread, 76–200 (new applications), smoke developed, 0–450.

(4) Class I interior floor finish — critical radiant flux, not less than 0.45 W/cm².

(5) Class II interior floor finish — critical radiant flux, not more than 0.22 W/cm², but less than 0.45 W/cm².

(6) Automatic sprinklers — where a complete standard system of automatic sprinklers is installed, interior wall and ceiling finish with a flame spread rating not exceeding Class C is permitted to be used in any location where Class B is required and with a rating of Class B in any location where Class A is required; similarly, Class II interior floor finish is permitted to be used in any location where Class I is required, and no critical radiant flux rating is required where Class II is required. These provisions do not apply to new detention and correctional occupancies.

(7) Exposed portions of structural members complying with the requirements for heavy timber construction are permitted.

†See corresponding chapters for details.

Figure 9.13 *Life Safety Code* Table A.10.2.2, Interior Finish Classification Limitations (Reprinted with permission from *NFPA 101*®, *Life Safety Code*®, Copyright © 2008, National Fire Protection Association, Quincy, MA. This reprinted material is not the complete and official position of the NFPA on the referenced subject, which is represented only by the standard in its entirety.)

reception areas in Business occupancies and waiting areas in Health Care occupancies, would be considered part of the exit access corridor.

Some occupancies in the table have a symbol or footnote following the recorded class. This indicates that the occupancy has further finish restrictions or requirements. Further research will be required in the *LSC* or the building codes under the specified occupancy. The fire codes may also have requirements specific to a certain occupancy. Occupancies and building types that most often have additional finish-related requirements follow, with examples of each.

❑ *Assembly*: Fabric of stage curtains, motion picture screens, stage scenery, specifics for assembly seating, storage of personal effects and clothing versus metal lockers, exhibit booths

❑ *Educational (and Day Care)*: Percentage of bulletin boards, posters, and/or artwork/teaching materials attached to walls, storage of personal effects and clothing versus metal lockers

❑ *Health Care*: Allowances for finishes below 48 inches (1.2 m) in corridors, fabrics for cubicle curtains, allowable wall decorations, upholstered furniture and mattresses

❑ *Detentional/Correctional*: Fabric of privacy curtains, allowable wall decorations, waste container specifications, upholstered furniture and mattresses (also with regard to vandalism)

❑ *Mercantile*: Plastic signage, temporary kiosks, ceiling-supported fabric partitions, display window allowances

❑ *Hotels and Dormitories*: Draperies, wall hangings, and mattresses

❑ *Board and Care/Nursing Homes*: upholstered furniture and mattresses, allowable wall decorations

❑ *Unusual Structures*: Water-resistant finishes in buildings located in flood zones, finish restrictions in atriums

❑ *Hazardous*: Limited use of combustible finishes

The general rule of thumb is that stricter finishes are required in occupancies where the occupants are immobile or have security measures imposed on them that restrict freedom of movement. This includes Institutional occupancies, such as Health Care and Detentional/Correctional facilities, or where occupants are provided with overnight accommodations, such as hotels and dormitories. In contrast, more relaxed requirements are found in Industrial and Storage occupancies where occupants are assumed to be alert, mobile, and fewer in number. Certain buildings that have fewer stories and lower occupant loads may also allow fewer restrictions.

✎Note

Decorative vegetation such as natural cut trees and artificial plants is also regulated by the codes. The *International Fire Code (IFC)* includes requirements for these in its "Interior Finish" chapter.

✎Note

Most finish and furniture standards do not apply to one- and two-family dwellings. For example, wall and ceiling finishes only need to meet the requirements of Class C finishes. Other exceptions are the *Pill Test* for carpets and rugs and some mattress tests. (Refer to Appendix D.)

The bottom of the table also includes a note that automatic sprinklers used throughout a building can change the required finish class ratings. The *LSC* uses this note to allow a required finish class to be reduced by one rating if there is an approved automatic sprinkler system in a building. For example, if a space in an nonsprinklered building normally requires a *Steiner Tunnel Test* Class B finish, the same space in a sprinklered building would require a Class C finish. As noted above, the *IBC* specifies this information more clearly within the table itself. Therefore, it is important to know if the building has an *approved* automatic sprinkler system before reducing a finish class. (Confirm with a local code official if necessary.)

Example

Figure 9.14 is a floor plan of a high school without a sprinkler system. To design the interiors of this existing school, a code table such as the table in Figure 9.13 must be referenced. Under "Educational—Existing" in the occupancy column of this table it indicates the following:

❑ Class A wall and ceiling finishes must be used in all exit areas, such as stairwells.

❑ Class A or B finishes are allowed in exit access areas, such as corridors.

❑ Any of the three classes (A, B, or C) is allowed in all the remaining spaces, such as classrooms, offices, and so on.

However, many high schools are considered multiple occupancies by the codes because of the gymnasiums, auditoriums, and/or cafeterias typically built with them. If the auditorium in this high school, for example, was designed for 325 people, the finish requirements for this area would be found in the occupancy column of the table under "Assembly—Existing" in the subcategory "≥300 occupant load." The required finish classes are almost the same except that, in this case, Class C finishes will not be allowed in the general areas of this assembly space.

In the previous example, the table did not specify a particular class of floor finish anywhere in the school. However, if designing the interior of a new day care center, the table indicates that a Type I or II floor finish is required in exits and exit access corridors. Therefore, a floor covering that passes a *Radiant Panel Test* must be used. (See Figure 9.3.) Newer code requirements also require that certain wall bases pass the same test. (See the section Radiant Panel Test for details.)

When specifying finishes, also consider if the building or space is used for multiple functions. For example, it is common for day care centers to be located

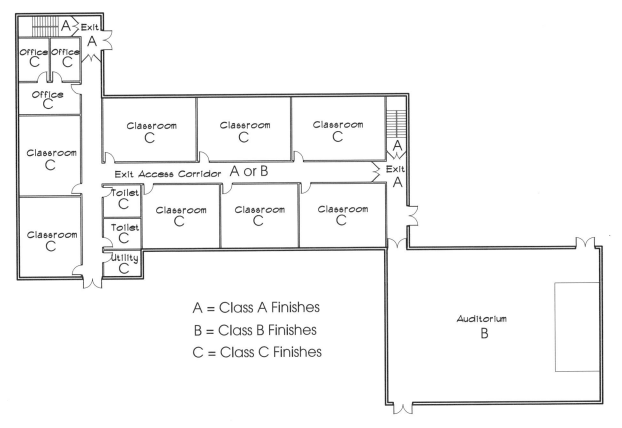

Figure 9.14 Finish selection example (high school) (nonsprinklered building).

in buildings that share other functions, such as churches or residential homes. Meet the requirements of the most restrictive use.

OBTAINING TEST RESULTS

Some of the standards and tests described earlier in this chapter are specifically referenced and are therefore required by the code or a specific jurisdiction. Others are industry standards that should be referenced when necessary. For each test standard used, it is important to know if the test results in a pass/fail, a specific class rating, or a ranking. Refering back to Figure 9.3, this information is shown for each type of test. For example, the *Radiant Panel Test* is a rated test that results in a Class I or a Class II rating. The manufacturer tests its products using these standards and provides the appropriate test results for each item. By comparing these ratings by what is required by the codes, the appropriate finish and/or furniture can be selected. (Request the information from the manufacturer, if it is not provided.)

Manufacturers typically test their products before putting them on the market. Manufacturers realize that their finishes and furniture must meet code requirements in order for them to be readily specified for a project. How to find and obtain the required test results is explained below.

Pretested Finishes and Furniture

Many manufacturers either list the test results on their samples and products or provide the information upon request. (See the inset titled *Testing Agencies and Certification* on page 41.) Some examples include the written information on the back of carpet books and on cards attached to fabric samples. Many manufacturers also provide sample specifications on their Web sites. Similar labels and/or specifications can be found for most wallcoverings, floor coverings, ceiling coverings, and other finishes. Even rated upholstered furniture must be labeled with the required tests.

Figure 9.15 shows the finish specifications for a Maharam upholstery fabric. Along with other necessary information, the specification indicates the standard

Coincide009 Caribbean

Design: Maharam Design Studio
Style: 465808
Application: Seating
Content: 100% Polyester
Finish: Stain Resistant
Backing: Acrylic
Width: 54" (137cm)
Repeat: 1 1/8" H / 2.9cm H
Abrasion: 100,000+ double rubs ▣
Flammability: This textile meets all appropriate flammability requirements, including California Bulletin #117 and NFPA 260, and is compatible with California Bulletin #133. ♦
Lightfastness: 60+ Hours ☀
Maintenance: W/S-Clean with water-based cleanser or mild, water-free dry cleaning solvent.
Reduced Environmental Impact: Environmentally Improved Manufacturing Process: heavy metal free dyes with high exhaustion rates
ISO 14001 Environmental Management System: Manufactured at an ISO 14001 certified facility.
Reduced Emissions: Greenguard and Greenguard for Children and Schools certified for indoor air quality.
US Contract Net: $26.00
Canadian Contract Net: C$27.50
© 2010 Maharam

Figure 9.15 Typical specifications for an upholstery finish sample.

tests the fabric has passed under "Flammability." (Also notice the sustainable-related information listed; see the section Sustainability Considerations later in this chapter.) The flammability heading indicates that the fabric has passed *CAL 117* and *NFPA 260* and that it is compatible with *CAL 133*. There is also a flame symbol at the end of the flammability information. This symbol, or certification mark, indicates that the fabric has passed certain industry tests.

This symbol was created by the Association for Contract Textiles (ACT). ACT was founded in 1985 to provide the design industry with information to help designers choose the right products for their projects. Concentrating on the contract interiors market, ACT sets standards for upholstery, wallcoverings, panels and upholstered walls, and drapery. A total of five ACT certification marks are voluntarily used by a large number of textile manufacturers on their products; each mark indicates the test(s) or standard(s) that the material must meet in order to bear the symbol.

Although there are five different marks, the main certification mark that relates directly to the codes is the flammability symbol. This symbol is shown in Figure 9.16, along with the type of application for the interior finish and the standards that it meets. Depending on the intended use of the finish, the flame symbol indicates that a fabric has acheived Class A of the *Steiner Tunnel Test (ASTM E 84)*, passed test Method 1 of the *Vertical Flame Test (NFPA 701)*, or passed the *Smolder Resistance Test (CAL TB 117)*. So, if a fabric's specification or tag indicates the flame mark, it means that the material meets the requirements of at least

> **✎ Note**
>
> The five ACT certification marks indicate a material's characteristics in terms of flammability, colorfastness, physical properties (such as pilling, breaking, and seam slippage), and abrasion. (See the inset titled *Industry Standards* on page 380.)

> **✎ Note**
>
> Some finishes will list multiple test results on their sample information. This indicates that the finish can be used in more than one type of application.

Flammability

The measurement of a fabric's performance when it is exposed to specific sources of ignition.

Upholstery
California Technical Bulletin #117 Section E – Class 1 (Pass)

Direct Glue Wallcoverings and Adhered Panels
ASTM E 84-07 (Adhered Mounting Method) – Class A or Class 1

Wrapped Panels and Upholstered Walls
ASTM E 84-07 (Unadhered Mounting Method) – Class A or Class 1

Drapery
NFPA 701-2004 Method 1 – Pass

Note: The above guidelines, which are subject to change without notice, represent minimum requirements only and may not reflect requirements and laws in all locations.

Figure 9.16 Flammability portion of *ACT Textile Performance Guidelines* (Reprinted with permission from the Association for Contract Textiles, Inc. [ACT]. The flame mark is a Registered Certification Mark and owned by ACT, Inc. See ACT Web site for the entire guidelines and the most current edition, www.contracttextiles.org.).

one of the tests. (Class 1 under *ASTM E84* was referenced by some of the legacy codes.) Referring back to Figure 9.15, since this fabric sample is intended for use as upholstery, the flame symbol indicates the fabric passes *CAL 117*. (This information is also repeated in the text of the label.)

Upholstered furniture also has an industry system for flammability labeling. One, developed by the Upholstered Furniture Action Council (UFAC), is a voluntary industry standard originally created in 1978 to increase the cigarette-ignition resistance of prefabricated furniture. Typically used for residential furniture, a manufacturer is able to attach an approved UFAC hangtag if the upholstered furniture meets testing requirements similar to NFPA 260, the *Smolder Resistance Test* for components. Similarly, in the contract furniture industry, the BIFMA International requests that its manufacturer members produce upholstered furniture that at least meets the standard NFPA 261—the *Smolder Resistance Test* for mock-ups.

For most interior projects, upholstered furniture is manufactured specifically for the project. In these cases, the UFAC label will not apply. Instead, textiles and furniture will meet other code and industry standards as required for a specific project. If rated upholstered furniture (or mattress) is specified to meet certain testing requirements, the delivered piece should include a label by an approved agency confirming it meets the appropriate requirements. This is required by the codes for certain occupancies.

Nontested Finishes and Furniture

There will be situations in which testing information is not available. For example, a smaller finish manufacturer that makes specialty items may not be able to afford to test all of its finishes and/or furniture. Or, a certain finish may need additional testing before it can be used in a particular occupancy or jurisdiction. In these cases, the finish will either have to be tested or be properly treated.

The standards organizations such as UL, ASTM, and NFPA can help determine where to get a finish tested. There are a number of third-party *testing agencies* throughout the country that will perform the tests necessary to classify a material. (Some agencies also act as treatment companies as well.)

However, these flame tests can be costly, because they need to be performed under conditions simulating actual installations. For example, a wallcovering should be tested on the appropriate wall surface with the adhesive that will be used to secure it to the wall, or a carpet with the padding that will be used underneath it. The alternative is to have the finish treated. This is often much more cost effective. Before doing so, though, it is suggested to confirm that the local jurisdiction will allow an added fire-retardant coating as a way to meet finish code requirements.

There are several *treatment companies* that will add fire-retardant coatings, also known as flame-resistant finishes, to materials that have not initially passed the required tests. (Ask the manufacturer for locations.) The retardant can be either a surface treatment or a fire-resistant coating applied as a backing. It will delay ignition of a material and slow flame spread, usually without changing the basic nature of the material. (See the inset titled *Flame-Retardant Treatments* on page 410.) It can also lower the smoke development value.

The typical procedure requires sending the fabric (or other finish) to the treatment company, indicating which tests the finish must comply with. The treatment company will add the appropriate fire-retardant coating. For example, if a fabric wallcovering needs to have a Class B rating, tell the company it must meet the *Steiner Tunnel Test*'s Class B rating. If working in one of the stricter jurisdictions, such as the city of Boston, tell the testing company that the fabric needs to pass the *Boston Fire Code* or any of the other required codes. In addition, if specifying sustainable finishes, request that low-emission treatments be used.

When wood is used as an interior finish, it may need to be treated as well. For example, if wood veneer is being used as a wallcovering or a large area of wood paneling in a commercial space, it may need to meet the appropriate class rating of the *Steiner Tunnel Test* as required by the codes. Very few woods qualify as Class A or B. Most are considered Class C or below. (Some wood species are shown in Figure 9.5.) It depends on the species of wood and the thickness of the wood being used. Typically, thinner woods and veneers have lower ratings than thicker ones. However, some new types of intumescent paints and coatings may be applied to the wood to improve its performance and obtain a better rating. These coatings expand and char when exposed to heat, which protects the wood underneath, and must typically meet the standard *NFPA 703, Standard for Fire Retardant-Treated Wood and Fire-Retardant Coatings for Building Materials.* However, check with the local code official to confirm this type of finish will be accepted.

The fire-retardant treatments and coatings can usually upgrade nonclassed finishes and can even raise the performance of some rated materials to a higher class. Upon completion of the work, a finish treatment company should be able to provide a Certificate of Flame Resistance indicating which tests the finish will pass. If completed in the field, the appropriate information should be obtained from the manufacturer and the company that applied the coating.

Similar steps must be taken for any finish or furnishing when the necessary test results are not given by the manufacturer. This can include, but is not limited to, any of the ones listed in Figure 9.2. In some cases, it may be too costly to have an item tested and/or treated. For example, having a piece of furniture tested may only make sense if a large quantity of the same item is ordered. Many

⬛Note

Whenever concentrated amounts of furniture are used in a project, check the design load of the building or space. (See the inset titled *Design Loads* on page 86.) Some examples include library areas, file rooms, and assembly seating.

⬛Note

When specifying office systems furniture using a customer's own material (COM), the UL Recognized Components directory can be used to find preapproved rated fabrics. (Go to www.ul.com, click on Certifications, and search for "office panel fabrics.")

FLAME-RETARDANT TREATMENTS

A flame-retardant treatment may be necessary for certain items in a project; however, be aware that the treatment can sometimes alter the finish or piece of furniture. For example, in some cases they are immersed in a chemical bath. Below are a number of problems that can occur when a fire retardant is added to a fabric.

The fabric may shrink.

The hand or feel of the fabric may change, perhaps resulting in stiffening of the fabric.

The strength of the fabric may decrease, causing it to tear more easily.

If a fabric has a texture, the texture may flatten or become distorted.

The treated fabric may give off toxic fumes, especially in the presence of fire.

A wet treatment may cause the dye in the fabric to bleed or possibly change or fade in the future.

A treated fabric may no longer meet the low-emitting standards required for indoor air quality in sustainable buildings.

If concerned about any of these issues, consult the company treating the fabric and, when necessary, submit a sample for testing prior to purchasing or treating the entire amount. The results are often based on the content of the fabric and the type of treatment used. It is also better to have a fabric treated prior to applying it to a surface or piece of furniture in case there are any problems.

manufacturers can also suggest how to add or substitute certain materials to a piece of furniture to obtain the test results required. For example, a fire block liner added to a sofa may allow it to comply with *CAL 133.*

ACCESSIBILITY REQUIREMENTS

The accessibility chapter of the building codes, the *ADA Standards*, and the ICC/ANSI standard put very few accessibility restrictions on finishes and furniture. The pertinent regulations can be broken down into three main categories: floor finishes, seating, and surfaces. However, also consider any operable parts that are part of a finish or furnishing system. Each of these is described below. Check the codes, the ADA regulations, and any other required accessibility standards for specifics and to determine the most stringent requirements. (Also see Accessibility Requirements in Chapter 2.)

Accessible Finishes

Currently, floor coverings are the main type of finish that must meet accessibility requirements. Both the ADA and the ICC/ANSI standards require that the floor surface along accessible routes and in accessible rooms be stable, firm, and slip-resistant. Floor finishes, such as carpet and padding, cannot be too thick or too loose and must be securely fastened at the edges. This is often accomplished in commercial projects by using carpet that is glued directly to the floor (without padding) or by using carpet tiles. The accessibility standards specify that the carpet pile cannot be more than 0.5 inch (13 mm) high and, whether it is cut pile, loop, or a combination, the pile must be level. Any exposed edges must also have trim.

Slip-resistant finishes are especially important at ramps and steps. They also become critical when using hard surface flooring such as polished marble, concrete, ceramic tile, VCT, rubber, or hardwood. These products must meet a specific static coefficient of friction (SCOF) for both wet and dry conditions. Since high-gloss finishes can be a problem, some manufacturers have products that provide a rougher finish coat. Therefore, in addition to specifying the correct finishes, the correct way to clean or seal the finished product may also need to be specified.

Accessible floor finish requirements also include beveled transitions or ramps for even slight changes in elevation that can occur between different floor surfaces. For example, as shown in Figure 9.17, there may be a change in floor level where stone or marble is adjacent to another type of flooring. Floor changes can also occur at the threshold of a door. The goal is to make sure that wheelchairs have easy access. Typically, the change in vertical height cannot be more than 0.5 inch (13 mm). If the overall height is between 0.25 inch (6.4 mm) and 0.5 inch (13 mm), a bevel must be added with a slope not steeper than a ratio of 1 to 2. This is shown in Sections A and B in Figure 9.17. If the distance is 0.25 inch (6.4 mm) or less, no bevel is required, as shown in Section C. When a change in elevation is more than 0.5 inch (13 mm), as shown in Section D, the requirements for an accessible ramp must be met. (See the section Ramps in Chapter 4.)

Flooring surfaces that create detectable warnings may be required in certain occupancies as well. A detectable warning consists of a change in floor finish to alert someone with poor vision of an approaching obstacle or change in level. The warnings typically consist of contrasting textures, such as alternate smooth and rough stone, grooved concrete, or rubber flooring with a raised pattern. (Although not required, contrasting colors can also be beneficial.) They are mostly required at building exteriors and transportation platforms, but they can apply to interiors as well—for example, at an entrance to a hazardous area or at

Note

Directly gluing a carpet to the floor instead of using a pad will help to eliminate thickness problems, as well as future warping or binding of the carpet from wheelchair use.

Note

Since floors in accessible paths of travel must be slip-resistant, polished floor finishes such as marble and VCT can become a problem. Special slip-resistant sealers may be needed.

Note

When floor surfaces, such as entry mats and floor grills, are used, the ADA and ICC/ANSI standards include specific requirements. The openings must be small enough so that a 0.5 inches (13 mm) sphere cannot pass through and any elongated openings must be perpendicular to the path of travel.

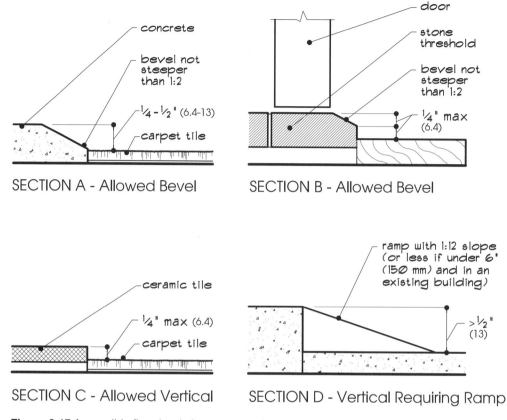

Figure 9.17 Accessible floor level change examples.

the top of an escalator or exposed stairway. (Refer to both the ICC/ANSI standard and the *2010 ADA Standards* for specifics.)

Accessible reach ranges must be considered for certain finishes or decorative elements when they are located in spaces required to be accessible. For example, the controls to a window blind or drape must be at accessible heights and easy to operate. They must be located between 15 and 48 inches (380 to 1220 mm) above the floor to allow either a front approach or a side approach. (Clear floor space in front of the controls should also be provided.)

Other finishes are not regulated by the ADA or ICC/ANSI standards, however, there are benefits of using certain finishes for accessibility reasons. For example, using handrails along corridors in Health Care occupancies that contrast with the wall finish makes them easier for people with visual impairments to see. Contrasting baseboards also help. Using finishes this way can be especially helpful in public spaces and occupancies where a wide variety of people use the space.

Accessible Furniture

Accessibility regulations for furniture can be divided into seating and work-surface-related items. Requirements for these can be found in the accessibility chapter of the building codes, the *ADA Standards*, and the ICC/ANSI standard, depending on the item used and the type of space. Often, the codes will indicate when an item is required to be accessible and then refer to the ICC/ANSI standard for the specifics. The code requirement is usually based on the building type or occupancy. For example, in a restaurant, the building code typically requires that at least 5 percent of the dining tables be accessible. The ICC/ANSI standard is then referenced to determine what makes a table accessible. Many of these requirements are also found in the *ADA Standards*.

In other projects, it may not always be clear when a piece of furniture needs to be accessible. Spaces designed specifically for public use must meet the requirements of the *ADA Standards*, but other areas of a space, such as certain employee work areas, are not necessarily required to be accessible. For example, the furniture in every employee office or workstation is not required to be accessible. In some cases, these items only need to be adjustable and/or replaceable to meet changing needs. Yet, shared spaces in an employee work area (e.g., breakrooms and conference rooms) are usually designed to be accessible to allow for a variety of current and future employee needs.

In addition, when placing furniture, consider any other required accessibility clearances. For example, a bookcase located across from a desk in an office should not block the clearance required at the door. (See Figure 4.4 in Chapter 4.) Any minimum paths of travel must also be maintained. This includes corridors, aisles, and aisle accessways. This is explained in more detail in Chapter 4. Seating and furniture requirements are discussed below.

Seating

The type of seat is not typically regulated, but rather the number and location that are provided for wheelchairs. The *ADA Standards* generally require seating to be accessible in all public and common use areas. This can be as simple as providing enough clear floor space among the other seating in a waiting area to allow a person in a wheelchair to wait. Other public-use areas like restaurants may be required to provide wheelchair access to all their tables.

◄**Note**

The 2003 ICC/ANSI standard and *2010 ADA Standards* include requirements for accessible fixed benches. Specific dimensions and clearances allow for ease of transferring from a wheelchair to a bench.

In addition, the placement of surrounding furniture must allow the required maneuvering areas, even though the furniture may seem movable. (Usually, only a certain percentage of the dining surfaces or tables is required to be accessible.)

When there are fixed seats, the building codes and the *ADA Standards* also require a certain number of the seating spaces to be provided for wheelchairs. This is especially important in Assembly occupancies, where the number of wheelchair locations is based on the total number of seats provided. For example, a movie theater with fixed stadium seating must allow for special wheelchair locations that are equally dispersed with the other seating and meet a variety of requirements. (See Figure 2.12A in Chapter 2.) Even study carrels in libraries must meet certain accessibility percentage requirements to allow wheelchair access. (Refer to the *ADA Standards*, the building codes, and the ICC/ANSI standard for specifics. If a fixed bench is supplied, the standards include additional requirements.)

In nonpublic or employee work areas, the *ADA Standards* require that accessible seating be provided when required for special needs. For example, a person may need a desk chair with special features. In these cases, work closely with the client to determine what type of seating is required.

Counters, Tables, and Worksurfaces

Accessible counters, tables, and worksurfaces cover a wide variety of uses. Counters can include hotel reception desks, hospital check-in desks, security check desks, teller windows, ticketing counters, service counters, food-service lines, and check-out aisles in retail stores. The ADA and ICC/ANSI standards further delineate other surfaces into dining surfaces and worksurfaces. Dining surfaces include bars, tables, lunch counters, and booths. Worksurfaces include writing surfaces (e.g., conference tables), study carrels, student laboratory stations, and baby changing tables. The building codes and the *ADA Standards* will specify when counters, dining surfaces, and worksurfaces in public spaces must be accessible. For example, the *IBC* requires a sales counter in a retail store to be accessible. If there is more than one, a percentage of the total must be accessible. Similarly, the *ADA Standards* require reception desks in public areas (or at least one of them, if there is more than one) to be accessible to the public. In each case the ADA and ICC/ANSI standards both specify that a portion of the counter at least 36 inches (915 mm) in length must be no higher than 36 inches (915 mm) above the floor, with clear floor space in front so that the public can access the desk. An example is shown at the top of Figure 9.18.

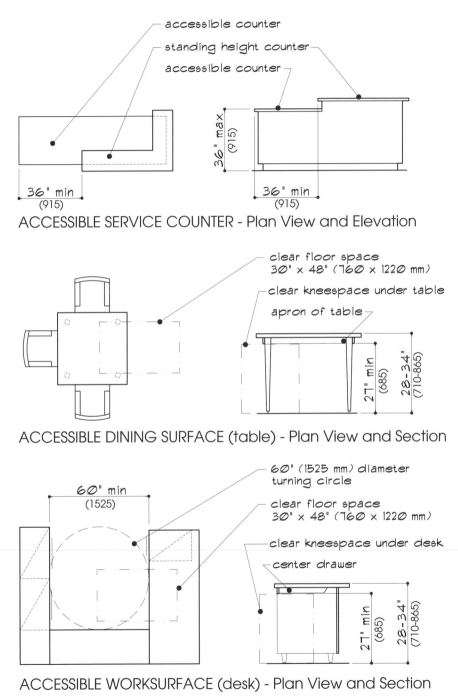

accessible counter

standing height counter

accessible counter

36" max (915)

36" min (915)

36" min (915)

ACCESSIBLE SERVICE COUNTER - Plan View and Elevation

clear floor space
30" x 48" (760 x 1220 mm)

clear kneespace under table

apron of table

27" min (685)

28-34" (710-865)

ACCESSIBLE DINING SURFACE (table) - Plan View and Section

60" min (1525)

60" (1525 mm) diameter turning circle

clear floor space
30" x 48" (760 x 1220 mm)

clear kneespace under desk

center drawer

27" min (685)

28-34" (710-865)

ACCESSIBLE WORKSURFACE (desk) - Plan View and Section

Figure 9.18 Accessible worksurface and furniture examples.

Note, however, that the employee side of the desk does not necessarily need to meet accessibility requirements such as reach ranges, clear access spaces, and location of equipment. That decision should be based on a variety of factors and is usually up to the owner of the building and/or space. For example, if there is only one reception desk in a space, the entire desk is typically made accessible should an employee with special needs be hired in the future. The desk could also be designed so that the employee side is adjustable. On the other hand, if there are multiple reception desks in the same space, not all of them are required to be fully accessible. The final decision is usually made by the client. Instead, they may need to be made accessible for employees in the future. (Document these decisions; see Responsibility for Compliance in Appendix A.)

To make the employee side of the desk accessible, follow the additional requirements found in the ADA and the ICC/ANSI standards. The same requirements apply to other tables and worksurfaces that are required to be accessible. Typically, the top of the surface must be between 28 and 34 inches (710 and 865 mm) above the floor. There must also be at least a 27-inch (685 mm) high by 30-inch (760 mm) wide kneespace plus specific toespace below the worksurface and a certain amount of clear floor space leading up to the worksurface. (A 60-inch [1525 mm] turning space may also be required.) The requirements can be seen in Figure 9.18. Examples are shown for a table and desk, but similar requirements would apply to other types of accessible surfaces as mentioned above. (Similar requirements also apply to breakroom and kitchen counters, as explained in Chapter 7.)

OTHER CODE RESTRICTIONS

In addition to the many standards discussed earlier in the chapter, there are a number of other common code restrictions used by the building codes and the *Life Safety Code*. These are explained below. However, there will always be exceptions and unusual circumstances. For these, consult the local code official when necessary. (Sustainability-related code requirements are discussed in the next section.)

1. *10 percent rule:* When trim and decorative materials are kept to a maximum of 10 percent of the particular wall or ceiling area to which it is attached, they can usually have a lower rating than what is required. For example, door and window trim is typically required to meet or exceed Class C of the *Steiner Tunnel Test*. This trim is allowed in spaces that required Class A and B finishes if the trim does not exceed 10 percent of the area. In other

spaces, if the trim does not exceed 10 percent, combustible materials may be allowed. These materials must be evenly distributed. If concentrated in a specific area, such as a paneled wall in a law office or a large banner in a college facility, it is considered an interior finish and must meet typical finish requirements. Noncombustible trims and decorative materials are not limited. (Some occupancies, such as certain Assembly types, may allow a higher percentage before this rule applies.)

2. *Thickness rule:* Any wall or ceiling covering that is more than 0.036 inch (0.90 mm) thick is to be treated as an interior finish. Therefore, thermally thin finishes such as paint and most wallpapers (not vinyl wallcoverings), when applied to noncombustible building materials, do not have to be rated. Various tests have proven that thermally thin finishes do not significantly contribute to the fuel of a fire when they are applied to noncombustible building materials such as gypsum board, brick, and concrete. (This rule does not apply when finishes are continually applied on top of each other.)

3. *Furring strips:* When interior finishes are applied to furring strips instead of directly to fire-rated or noncombustible building materials, the furring strips cannot exceed a thickness of 1.75 inches (44 mm). In addition, the intervening spaces between the strips must be filled with a fire-rated material or fire blocked at specific intervals. Examples include wood flooring or wall paneling installed over furring strips. These code requirements reduce the chance of fire spread between the finish and the construction assembly behind it. (Note that furring strips may not be allowed behind certain thicker finishes. Wood flooring cemented directly to a noncombustible floor assembly is typically allowed.)

4. *Sprinkler rule:* When a building has an automatic sprinkler system, the codes may allow a lower finish class rating, and finishes without ratings may sometimes replace rated finishes. (Check with the local jurisdiction. An existing sprinkler system may not meet the most code current requirements and thus would not allow a lower-rated finish.)

5. *Means of egress:* All exits and paths of travel to and from the exits must be clear of furnishings, decorations, or other objects. This includes no draperies on or obscuring exit doors and no mirrors on or adjacent to exit doors. In addition, attention must not be drawn away from the exit sign.

6. *Foam plastics:* Cellular or foam plastic materials typically cannot be used as wall or ceiling finishes unless they comply with the 10 percent rule. In addition, they must pass multiple tests as specified in both the finish chapter and the plastic chapter of the building codes. Typically, if foam plastics are used as a finish, they must not only meet the flame spread requirements of the *Steiner Tunnel Test,* but also those of a large-scale test such as the

◢Note

In the more current codes, interior wall base is considered separate from other trims and decorative materials. All wall base 6 inches (152 mm) or less must now be tested using the *Radiant Panel Test.* (Refer to that test section earlier in this chapter.)

◢Note

Vinyl wallcovering is regulated in all thicknesses because of its burning characteristics. It has a high smoke density. Expanded vinyl wallcovering must meet additional testing requirements due to its woven textile backing.

◢Note

When renovating an existing space, existing finishes (e.g., wallcovering) should always be removed before installing new ones.

Room Corner Test, and be of a certain thickness and density. In addition, the codes may specify that certain foam furnishings or contents be tested using *UL 1975, Standard for Fire Test for Foamed Plastics Used for Decorative Purposes.* (Foam plastics that do not pass a large-scale test are typically allowed only when the foam plastic is covered by a noncombustible material that acts as a thermal barrier. The *LSC* includes additional requirements.)

✎Note

Light-transmitting plastics used as interior finishes, for light fixture diffusers, or as interior signage must pass specific flame and/or fire tests and be labeled.

7. *Light-transmitting plastics:* Light-transmitting plastics include items such as Plexiglas and resin panels that can be used in a variety of applications, such as wall panels, light-diffusing panels, and signage. These are also available with fabrics sandwiched between two layers. Specific requirements for these plastics are found in the plastics chapter of the building codes and include large-scale test requirements as well as size, fastening, and sprinkler requirements. (Plastic veneers must comply with the finish chapter in each code. See also the inset titled *Plastic Finishes* on page 419.)

8. *Insulation:* Various types of insulation can be used on an interior project. Those used within an assembly, such as a wall assembly, for sound insulation must meet the requirements of the assembly especially as they apply to fire codes. (See Chapter 5 and the inset titled *Sound Transmission* on page 209.) Materials categorized as Class A in the *Steiner Tunnel Test* are often required. Similar requirements apply to the insulation materials used to wrap pipes and ducts, including those used to cover plumbing pipes under accessible sinks. (See Chapter 7.)

9. *Site-fabricated stretch systems:* Site-fabricated stretch systems typically consist of a track system (or frame), fabric (or vinyl), and infill core material. The systems can be used for acoustical, decorative, or tackable purposes. The ICC codes now recognize this unusual application and require the stretched fabric system to be tested as an assembly using either (1) the *Room Corner Test* or (2) the *Steiner Tunnel Test* in conjunction with the standard *ASTM E2573, Standard Practice for Specimen Preparation and Mounting of Site-fabricated Stretch Systems.*

10. *Safety glass:* The requirements for glass are covered by the "Glass and Glazing" chapter in the building codes. In addition to fire-rated glazing, glass can be used in a number of other interior applications. Examples include a glass panel in a stair railing, a shower enclosure, a decorative glass sign or feature, and a table top. Based on the location and the thickness and size of the glass, the codes will require the glazing to pass certain tests to meet safety glass requirements. For example, tempered glass is often required. (See the section Rated Glazing and Frames in Chapter 5.)

PLASTIC FINISHES

In the past, plastic-related codes were geared to plastics (e.g., insulation) used on the exterior of a building. However, it has become more common for plastics to be used as decorative elements in interior projects, and some code requirements apply to these as well. Essentially, there are two main types of plastics. The first is *thermosetting plastic* that cannot be softened again after being cured. This includes materials such as polyurethane, melamine, epoxy, and silicone. When exposed to fire, they typically decompose rather than burn and have the potential for creating toxic gases. The second is the type of plastic that can be recycled. It is called *thermoplastic* and is capable of being repeatedly softened by heating and hardened by cooling. It consists of polyvinyl chloride (PVC), acrylics (Lucite and Plexiglas), acetates, polycarbonate (Lexan), polyester (Mylar), polyethylene, polypropylene, and certain resins, as well as nylon. During a building fire, these typically melt.

The codes divide these various plastics into several different categories for the purpose of providing restrictions:

Foam or cellular plastics—such as those used for trim and moldings

Pyroxylin plastics (consisting of imitation leather or other materials coated with pyroxylin)—such as those used as upholstery on furniture or wall panels

Light-transmitting plastics—such as those attached to fluorescent light fixtures or used as decorative panels with back lighting

Plastic veneers—such as those used on millwork or as decorative panels

Fiber reinforced polymers or fiberglass reinforced polymers—such as those used as decorative trim and/or light-transmitting material

High-density polyethylene (HDPE) —such as that used for specialty finishes

Plastic signage—larger signs such as those used in covered malls or possibly large rear-projection television screens

The building codes provide requirements for these plastics in both the finish chapter and the plastics chapter. When using plastics, both chapters will need to be referenced—as well as the occupancy chapters and the fire codes in some cases. Depending on the application and the type of plastic, different tests will be required. Some are finish-related tests such as the *Room Corner Test*. Other tests are those used for building materials. The use of plastics may also affect the location of sprinkler heads. For example, additional sprinkler heads are often required where large light-transmitting plastic panels are used.

Interior finishes may be further restricted by the occupancy classification of a building. Certain building occupancies have stricter codes and more specific requirements. For example, pyroxylin plastic such as imitation leather is not allowed in Assembly occupancies. These additional requirements are addressed by the building codes, the fire codes, the *LSC*, the *ADA Standards*, and the ICC/ANSI standard in specific occupancy sections. (See also the list in the section Determining Finish Classifications earlier in this chapter.)

Generally, occupancies where the occupants have mobility difficulties have stricter requirements than occupancies with fully mobile occupants. The occupancies that allow overnight provision for multiple occupants are usually the strictest. These include Institutional occupancies, such as Health Care and Detentional/Correctional facilities, and most Residential occupancies (except single-family homes). For example, hotels must use additionally rated finishes and furnishings such as bedding and draperies.

SUSTAINABILITY CONSIDERATIONS

Note

The VOCs typically found in many finishes and furniture vaporize at room temperature. This contributes to the creation of ozone and other toxins inside the building which can lead to unhealthy indoor air quality.

The code and standards requirements for sustainable finishes and furniture are different from the standards discussed earlier in this chapter. Traditionally, the codes have concentrated on the characteristics of materials and products that could contribute to the ignition and spread of a fire, focusing on the life safety of the building occupants. However, more recent findings have shown that the toxicity of these finishes and furniture can affect the health, safety, and welfare of the people that use these spaces every day, as well as the environment. For example, the *Toxicity Test*, as explained earlier in the chapter, tests the toxicity of finishes and other building material when they burn. Other toxicity-based tests, as required by the sustainability codes and standards, determine the level of volatile organic compounds (VOCs) that can offgas and possibly affect indoor air quality (IAQ). This, in turn, affects the overall indoor environmental quality (IEQ) of a space or building.

Note

A green rating system, such as LEED or Green Globes (as explained in Appendix B), can also require the use of a sustainability standard or product certification.

The state of California was one of the first jurisdictions to require sustainable finishes and/or furnishings, requiring low-emission finishes in schools. California also introduced the first sustainability code in 2008 (see Chapter 1). Now other sustainability documents are available for adoption by a jurisdiction. These include the *International Green Construction Code (IGCC)* and the standard *ASHRAE/USGBC/IES 189.1, Standard for the Design of High-Performance Green Buildings Except Low-Rise Residential Buildings*. All of these documents include sustainable requirements for finishes and furniture. Some requirements have specific conditions that need to be met; other requirements reference a sustainable product standard or product certification program for compliance. These are explained below.

Sustainable Product Standards

Some sustainable product standards (SPS) test a wide variety of building products, including interior finishes and furniture. For example, the state of California's *Section 01350, Standard Practice for the Testing of Volatile Organic Emissions from Various Sources Using Small-Scale Environmental Chambers* (also known as *CA/DHS/EHLB/R-174 Standard Practice*) provides an overview of special environmental requirements such as energy guidelines, water efficiency, and IAQ. However, some of its key elements are procedures to measure the VOC emissions of building products and office furniture. The Institute for Market Transformation to Sustainability's (MTS) standard *MTS 2006:4, SMART Sustainable Building Product Standard* is another standard that can be used to analyze a wide variety of building products. (See the section Sustainability Considerations in Chapter 5 for more information on sustainable building products and construction materials.) Other more product-specific SPS are described below.

⬕Note

The SMART standards program by MTS tests and classifies building products in three categories based on the number of points received: Silver, Gold, and Platinum. All SMART standards also include the use of a Life Cycle Assessment (LCA). (See Appendix B.)

Finish Standards

Some SPSs are more specific to a particular type of finish. For example, the most common green standard for carpeting is *NSF/ANSI 140, Sustainable Carpet Assessment.* (This standard is the same as the *California Gold Sustainable Carpet Standard.*) Developed by NSF International in conjunction with the Carpet and Rug Institute (CRI) and MTS, the standard is based on life cycle assessment (LCA) principles (see Appendix B) and offers three levels of achievement for attaining various stages of reduced environmental impact—Silver, Gold, and Platinum. These performance requirements address the economic value throughout the supply chain and the sustainable attributes required for specification. It also encourages carpet manufacturers to develop manufacturing processes that are more environmentally friendly.

For all other flooring, the standard typically used is *MTS 2006:1, SMART Sustainable Flooring Standard 2.0.* The flooring products it analyzes include resilient, wood, tile, and laminate, among others. However, in 2010, NSF International released a new standard specifically for resilient floor coverings titled *NSF/ANSI 332, Sustainability Assessment for Resilient Floor Coverings.* This new standard may be increasingly used in the future.

Another SPS developed by MTS is specifically for fabrics. *MTS 2004:1, SMART Sustainable Textile Standard 2.0* tests and classifies fabrics used for building interiors

⬕Note

Two additional SPSs by NSF International are expected to be released in 2011. Developed for other finish categories, these standards include: *NSF/ANSI 336, Sustainable Commercial Furnishings Fabric Assessment* and *NSF/ANSI 342, Sustainability Assessment for Wallcovering Products.*

(including upholstery) as well as apparel. The standard analyzes all components of the textile, including the filaments and fibers used in the preparation of the fabrics (including woven, knitted, tufted, nonwoven fabrics), the materials used in the production of these fabrics (including backings and coatings), and the various end products (including fabrics, binders, fillers, and apparel).

Furniture Standards

There are several furniture-related SPSs as well. Two standards developed by BIFMA International concentrate on the measurement of VOCs: *ANSI/BIFMA M7.1, Standard Test Method for Determining VOC Emissions from Office Furniture Systems, Components and Seating* and *ANSI/BIFMA X7.1, Standard for Formaldehyde and VOC Emissions of Low-Emitting Office Furniture Systems and Seating.* They can be used to measure VOC concentrations in built-in cabinets, shelves, and worksurfaces (i.e., millwork) as well as office furniture systems and seating. BIFMA also collaborated with NSF to develop *BIFMA e3, Furniture Sustainability Standard.* This SPS addresses many other sustainability criteria that must be followed by the manufacturer including material utilization, energy and atmosphere impacts, human and ecosystem health, and social responsibility; it is directly connected to BIFMA's new product certification program called level™ (see next section).

Millwork Standards

In addition to the two BIFMA standards mentioned above, there are other SPSs that can be used to specify built-in millwork (i.e., cabinetry) components so that it meets sustainable criteria. For example, millwork must typically consist of products that do not contain added urea-formaldeyde. This includes composite wood and agrifiber products such as particleboard, medium density fiberboard (MDF), wheatboard, and strawboard. These must typically meet the California standard *Section 93120, Airborne Toxic Control Measure to Reduce Formaldehyde Emissions from Composite Wood Products.* In addition, any adhesives and sealants used in the millwork, or for securing other finishes used in an interior space, must meet specific VOC levels. Examples include adhesives used to secure plastic laminate and veneers to the substrate. (or secure wallcovering or carpet to a surface). One SPS that can be used is *GS-36, Environmental Standard for Commercial Adhesives.* Others are specified in the codes and standards.

Product Certifications

The standards mentioned above can be directly referenced in the sustainability codes and standards. In other cases, the codes reference a product certification

⬙Note

Finishes that do not have a specific SPS are commonly tested using California's standard *Section 01350.* For example, wallcoverings and ceiling coverings are often required to be tested using the *Section 01350* to measure specific emission requirements and VOC content. Paints and coatings can also be tested using this standard.

⬙Note

Two additional Green Seal SPSs include: *GS-11, Environmental Standard for Paints and Coatings* and *GS-47, Environmental Standard for Stains and Finishes.*

program which in turn will use one of the SPSs as a benchmark within the certification process. (See Appendix B for more information on product certification programs.) For example, two product certifications typically referenced by the sustainability documents include *Green Label* and *Green Label Plus*. Developed by the Carpet and Rug Institute (CRI), both programs use *NSF/ANSI 140* (see previous section) to test carpet, cushions, and adhesives. The Green Label program identifies products with very low emissions of VOCs. The Green Label Plus program is similar but sets higher benchmarks for IAQ and identifies the lowest emitting products using an additional SPS titled *ASTM D5116, Standard Guide for Small-Scale Environmental Chamber Determinations of Organic Emissions from Indoor Materials/Products.*

Another flooring product certification is called *FloorScore*®. Developed by the Resilient Floor Covering Institute (RFCI) in conjunction with Scientific Certification Systems (SCS), it certifies a wide variety of hard surface flooring for compliance with indoor air quality emission requirements. Products tested include vinyl, linoleum, rubber, ceramic, laminate flooring, and engineered hardwood flooring as well as wall base and stair treads. The standard used to verify the VOC emissions criteria is California's *Section 01350.*

Two other commonly referenced product certification programs were developed by GREENGUARD Environmental Institute (GEI). *GREENGUARD Indoor Air Quality Certified* is a program for low-emitting interior building materials, furnishings, and finish systems. The program *GREENGUARD Children & Schools*^{SM} is similar but the tested products must meet even more rigorous emissions criteria.

Level is a certification program developed specifically for furniture and is based on the standard *BIFMA e3* (see previous section). It is applicable to all types of furniture, components, and materials. The products are evaluated for conformance to the standard. The production processes and the manufacturer are audited and verified as well. The certification is modeled after LEED with specific prerequisites, optional credits, and three conformance levels. Products that are certified receive a *level* conformance mark, with *level* 3 being the highest level awarded. The *Indoor Advantage*™ certification program reviews furniture as well. It uses the standard *ANSI/BIFMA X7.1* as well as other requirements (such as those found in LEED) to test products for VOCs. Developed by SCS, it is composed of two programs: *Indoor Advantage*, which certifies office furniture, and *Indoor Advantage Gold*, which certifies paints and coatings, adhesives and sealants, insulation, wall coverings, and furnishings.

Whether selecting or designing new finishes, furniture, or built-ins for a project, there are many additional sustainability requirements, standards, and certification programs that need to be considered. Although not all of them are required by a particular sustainable code or standard at this time, they will

⬛ Note

A third program offered by GEI is GREENGUARD Building Construction^{SM} which certifies the design, construction, and ongoing operations of newly constructed buildings specifically to minimize the risk of mold.

⬛ Note

SCS, GEI, and NSF also act as the third-party certifier for many of these programs. Each has a database listing approved products on their Web sites.

⬛ Note

There are several product certifications for wood including FSC Certified and SFI Certified. (See Chapter 3.)

⬛ Note

For a current list of sustainable finishes and furniture product certification programs and life cycle assessments listed by manufacturer, go to www.interiorsandsources .com. (See also Appendix B.)

provide health benefits to the building occupants and possible cost savings to the client or building owner. Many manufacturers are listing these SPSs and/or certifications on the products they sell (see an example in Figure 9.15) or have it available upon request. (See also Appendix B.)

CHECKLIST

The checklist in Figure 9.19 has been designed to help you with any project that requires finish and/or furniture selection. It can be used for one particular project, or a separate checklist can be used for each space or room within the project. This is helpful if you have a variety of rooms or spaces, each with its own finishes and furniture. It is also helpful when some rooms or areas have stricter requirements than others. For example, requirements for public areas are often stricter, and typically require finishes and furniture that are different from those of other areas within the project.

The top of the checklist asks you for the project and space name, the occupancy classification of the project (and whether it is new or existing), and the building type. It is important to determine the occupancy and the building type at the beginning, since both are needed to determine which tests are required by the codes. (See Chapter 2 for more information on occupancy classifications.)

The rest of the checklist assists you with product selection and testing research. The first column lists the most common wall finishes, ceiling finishes, floor coverings, window treatments, and furnishings/furniture. Check the ones that will be used in the space or project so that you can narrow down the number of finishes and furniture that must be researched, tested, and/or treated. Blank spaces have been left to fill in items not listed on the checklist.

Once you know the types of finishes and furniture you will need to specify, use the charts in Figures 9.2 and 9.3 and refer to the codes to determine which tests are required. For example, if you are using direct-glue carpet on the floor, you may need only to verify that it passes the *Pill Test*. In other types of spaces, it may require a Class I or Class II rating; if it is being used as a wall finish, the *Room Corner Test* must be passed as well. Use the second column to write down the name of the test required for each finish and furnishing you checked off in the first column. If it is a rated test, include the rating required by the code. (See Figure 9.3 for test names and specific standard numbers.)

You should not start selecting finishes or furniture until you have determined the tests required for each area. Then, as you select and research each finish or piece of furniture, you can compare the product information and labels

Finishes and Furniture Checklist

Date: _____

Project Name: _____ Space: _____

Occupancy (new or existing): _____

Type of Space (check one): _____ Exit _____ Exit Access _____ Other Space

REGULATED FINISHES, FURNISHINGS, AND FURNITURE (CHECK THOSE THAT APPLY)	TEST METHOD REQUIRED (FILL IN TEST NAME)	MANUFACTURER AND CATALOG #	MANUFACTURER TESTED (YES OR NO)	FINISH TREATMENT (YES OR NO)	DATE COMPLETED
Wallcoverings __Vinyl Wallcovering __Textile Wallcovering __Expanded Vinyl Wallcovering __Carpet Wallcovering __Stretch Fabric System __Light-Transmitting Plastics __Wood Paneling/Veneers __Decorative Molding/Trim __Other: _____					
Wall Base Type: _____					
Ceiling Finishes __Suspended Ceiling Grid __Textile Ceiling Finish __Stretch Fabric System __Plastic Light-Diffusing Panels __Decorative Ceiling __Decorative Molding/Trim __Other: _____					
Floor Coverings __Carpet (Broadloom) __Carpet Tile __Rugs __Carpet Padding __Resilient Flooring __Hardwood Flooring __Other: _____					
Window Treatments __Draperies __Liners __Blinds __Wood Shutters __Other: _____					
Furnishings/Furniture __Fabric __Vinyl/Leather __Batting/Filling __Welt Cord __Interliners __Upholstered Seating __Mattresses __Plastic Laminates/Veneers __Other: _____					

NOTES:
1. Refer to codes and standards for specific information, including the sustainability codes and standards when required.
2. Check also the *ADA Standards* and ICC/ANSI standard for accessibility-related finish and furniture requirements.
3. Attach all testing verification including copies of manufacturer labels and treatment certificates.

Figure 9.19 Finishes and Furniture Checklist.

to the checklist to see if they meet the testing requirements. Indicate the manufacturer and the catalog number of the finish or piece of furniture you select in the third column of the checklist. Use the remaining part of the checklist to indicate either the test results verified by the manufacturer or the name of the treatment company that will treat the finish.

For each finish or furnishing listed, be sure that any necessary tests are completed. If required tests are listed on the manufacturer's label or finish book, make a copy of the information. If the manufacturer cannot verify that a finish has passed a required test, you will need to have the finish treated (if allowed by the jurisdiction) and make sure that the treatment company sends you a certificate verifying its compliance with the test.

After you have gathered all the testing information and have the required documentation, you should attach it to the checklist and file it with your project files in case this information is required in the future. In addition, check the *ADA Standards* and any other required accessibility codes or standards to determine if any special regulations must be met, and document these as well.

CHAPTER 10

CODE OFFICIALS AND THE CODE PROCESS

Each chapter in this book discusses a specific step in the code process, beginning in Chapter 1 with determining the publications required by a code jurisdiction, moving on to Chapter 2 with determining occupancy classifications, and ending in Chapter 9 with finish and furniture requirements. Throughout each chapter, references are made to code officials, jurisdictions, and the code approval process. This chapter concentrates on the code process as a whole. It introduces the different types of code officials and the various steps that should be taken for a smooth approval of a design. It also discusses how to document the code information effectively and how performance and sustainability requirements need to be incorporated from the beginning of a project.

While reading this chapter, the important thing to remember is that the interior of a building must be designed in conjunction with the codes, standards, and federal regulations required in that jurisdiction. All research of these regulations must be thorough and properly recorded in the project drawings and specifications. It is the designer's responsibility to make sure the design meets the intent of the codes. It is the code official's job to review the project drawings and verify their code compliance. Although the code official is there to guide and answer questions, it is not the official's responsibility to design the space or to do the research for the designer. The designer must apply the various code requirements properly and work in conjunction with the code official.

> **◢Note**
>
> There are various types of code consultants who can be used to provide added expertise during code research, especially on large projects.

AUTHORITY HAVING JURISDICTION

The codes refer to the *Authority Having Jurisdiction,* or *AHJ.* This term is used to indicate the entity that has the authority to decide whether the design and construction are compliant with the required codes and to enforce code compliance. In general, it can mean a legally defined area, a specific code department, or an

> **◢Note**
>
> The *Authority Having Jurisdiction,* or *AHJ,* can be a legally defined area, a code department, or an individual code official.

individual code official who has the right to review and approve construction. Together, these entities decide which codes are being enforced, manage the review and approval of the design and construction, and monitor construction within their area to ensure that buildings are safe. As the designer, it is important to know the roles and responsibilities of the AHJ and know how and when to work with it to ensure that a project meets the code requirements. Each type of AHJ is described in more detail in this section.

Code Jurisdiction

The code jurisdiction of a project is determined by the location of the building. A jurisdiction is defined as a geographical area that uses the same codes, standards, and regulations. The specific authority that enforces the code can vary from state to state. Most often, the codes are regulated on a local level, such as a county or city municipality. When a local jurisdiction chooses a code, the code becomes a local law and is enforced by the local code department. (See the section Code Enforcement later in this chapter.)

In other cases, the state mandates a statewide code that must be followed by each jurisdiction within the state. Sometimes this state code is used in conjunction with other locally adopted codes, or it might apply to buildings in more rural areas that do not have a local code. Typically, the state will at least enforce regulations on state-owned buildings.

Just as each jurisdiction decides which codes are being enforced, it also decides when to change or update the codes. The newest edition of the code may not be the one being enforced. Each jurisdiction can also make amendments to a code that can change the original code requirements. These modifications may remove a particular requirement, call for a more stringent requirement, and/or modify a requirement so that it is more relevant to that jurisdiction. (See the section Code Publications in Chapter 1 for more information.)

It is important to check with the jurisdiction of a project to determine which edition of the codes and standards is being enforced and if there are any addendums that should be included. In addition, which jurisdiction governs a project should also be confirmed. A project may fall under the authority of more than one jurisdiction. For example, a building within the city limits may need to follow the requirements of both the city and the state. On the other hand, a rural project might not have a local governing code, so the requirements of the state would need to be met.

Code Department

The code department, or building department, is the local government agency that administers and enforces the codes within a jurisdiction. Some small jurisdictions may have a code department that consists of only one person or code official, while larger jurisdictions may consist of many different agencies and departments. The administration chapters in the building codes and the *Life Safety Code (LSC)* give basic requirements for the code review and administrative process. However, each code department can modify these requirements to suit its own organization. For example, a large code department may require multiple sets of drawings to be submitted, whereas a small code department may require only one set. These modifications are often included in the local amendments to the enforced code. (See the inset titled *Administration Chapter* on page 431.)

Most code departments utilize digital technology to simplify and expedite the code submission process. Examples include:

❏ *Online permit applications and processing:* Allows permit applications to be filed online. (Some jurisdictions may also allow the construction documents to be submitted electronically.)

❏ *Electronic plan submission and review:* It allows plans to remain in the electronic format from design to permit review, allowing for markups to be done electronically. (See also the section Future Technology at end of this chapter.)

❏ *Scheduling and conducting inspections:* Site inspections can be posted in the field using wireless devices, allowing for quicker turnaround times. (See the section Construction and Inspection later in this chapter.)

It is important to contact the code department that will be reviewing a project to understand how that department works. The role of the code officials can vary in different jurdictions and may affect the best way to work with them.

Code Official

A code official, also known as a building official, is someone who has the authority to administer, interpret, and enforce the provisions of the adopted and/or amended code within a particular jurisdiction. The code official is also included when the codes refer to the AHJ. However, the term "code official" has been used throughout this book as a general term to describe a number of different people and functions.

In reality, the role of a code official can be filled by a variety of people, each with a different job title. The number of code officials will vary by jurisdiction. In smaller jurisdictions, one person may have several responsibilities. For example, there may be one person who does multiple types of inspections. In larger jurisdictions, there may be several people with the same title grouped into a department, each with his or her area of expertise. Some jurisdictions may also hire a

❧Note

The International Accreditation Service (IAS), a subsidiary of the International Code Council (ICC), offers an accreditation process for code departments. It is used to evaluate a code department in 13 categories including customer service, code interpretation and enforcement, and fiscal strength. A number of departments have either received or are pursuing this accreditation.

private agency to handle some of the responsibilities. The most common types of code officials are described as follows:

- *Plans examiner:* A code official who checks the construction drawings (including floor plans), specifications, and other documents both in the preliminary stages and in the final permit review stage of a project. The plans examiner checks for code and standards compliance. Designers typically work most closely with the plans examiner.

- *Building inspector:* A code official who visits the project job site after a permit is issued to make sure that all construction complies with the codes as specified in the construction documents and in the code publications. (See the section Construction and Inspection Process later in this chapter.)

- *Fire marshal:* A code official who typically represents the local fire department. A fire marshal checks the drawings in conjunction with the plans examiner during both the preliminary stages and the final permit plan review, checking the construction documents for fire code and means of egress compliance. The fire marshal also typically reviews the project job site upon completion of construction, and, depending on the type of project, may perform periodic reviews during the life of the building.

With the growing complexity of the building industry, the role of the code official has increased in scope. Most jurisdictions require code officials to have specific levels of experience in the design or construction industry. The administration chapter in each building code sets experience standards, but each jurisdiction can modify them based on the qualifications considered important. Code officials must understand how the building's structural system, means of egress, detection and suppression systems, and similar aspects work together to conform to the code requirements to protect the occupants of the space or building. They must also understand the actual building process. (See the inset titled *Administration Chapter* on the next page.)

The International Code Council (ICC) has developed a certification process for code officials. This process requires knowledge of specific areas of construction and code compliance in order to qualify for assigned titles. A "Certified Building Official" (CBO) has passed examinations on technology, legal issues, and code enforcement management. CBOs must also have experience doing plan reviews for various types of projects. Other specialty certificates are available depending on the type of code official and the level of expertise they want to develop. For example, there are various certifications for inspectors and plan examiners. Other certifications are available for building, electrical, plumbing, mechanical, housing, accessibility, and even green areas of construction, which requires the CBO to be experienced with inspections in their specific area of expertise. NFPA has set up certification programs to coordinate with their codes as well. In some jurisdictions, this type of certification has become mandatory to be employed as a code official.

With the introduction of new materials and new types of integrated systems, the job of the building official now requires a new level of design knowledge. Like other professionals involved with the design and construction industry, building officials attend continuing education seminars to keep up with changes in the codes and technology. It is becoming more and more important for the code official to be involved early in the design process in order to develop the best design. This will become increasingly true as more projects are designed using sustainable concepts, alternative methods and materials, and performance codes. The code official will have to agree that the design and/or building materials satisfy the intent of the code. There will be situations in which neither the designer nor the code official will be able to rely on the straightforward approach of the prescriptive code for a particular design solution. (See the inset titled *Performance Codes* on page 452 and *ICC Evaluation Services* on page 20.)

◢Note

The ICC is in the process of creating a certification exam titled Inspector of Green Building Technologies. A code official who passes this exam will be familiar with the most current sustainable code requirements as well as green building rating systems such as LEED and Green Globes. (See Appendix B.)

ADMINISTRATION CHAPTER

The first chapter in most of the codes is the "Administration" chapter. (The 2009 edition of the *IBC* uses the chapter title "Scope and Administration.") This chapter discusses the qualifications and responsibilities of the code official and the code process. It also includes requirements that the designer needs to meet. Here is a list of typical information included in an administrative chapter based on the *International Building Code (IBC)*:

❏ Intent of the code and others referenced within

❏ Scope of work requiring code compliance

❏ Duties and powers of the code official and the code department

❏ Permit requirements and related fees

❏ Submittal requirements for construction documents

❏ Types of required inspections

❏ Requirements for certificates of occupancy

❏ Connection of service utilities

❏ Means of appeals

❏ Types of violations

❏ Issuance of stop work orders

Other codes, such as performance codes and sustainability codes, will have additional information pertinent to the use of the code. The "Administration" chapter of the building codes is the one that is most often modified by the local jurisdictions. Check for local amendments to confirm any revisions.

CODE ENFORCEMENT

As discussed in the previous section, each jurisdiction adopts its own set of codes and standards. (See Chapter 1 for a more detailed description of each.) However, there are other requirements that need to be followed when work-ing on an interior project. These can include requirements from other regulatory agencies within the state, from sustainable programs instituted by a jurisdiction, and from laws mandated by the federal government. Some or all of the following may need to be incorporated depending on the type of project and where it is located.

Local and State Agencies

In addition to the codes required by the jurisdiction, certain projects may be under the authority of another agency, which develops and enforces its own regulations. Examples include schools, day care centers, restaurants, and hospitals. These regulations may be enforced on a state, county, or city level. For example, the local health department will usually have specific requirements that must be met for restaurants. Other building types, such as hospitals, may need to com-ply with other state and local regulations. Some zoning and historical ordinances can also affect an interior project. Depending on the project, the requirements of these agencies may need to be incorporated in addition to the codes and stand-ards. Check with the local jurisdiction. It may be helpful to have a review with a representative from the required agency(ies) before finalizing a design. And in some cases, a site visit after construction is required for approval.

> **⬛Note**
>
> Certain occupancy classifications and/or building types must meet additional regulations enforced by state or local agencies. Examples include hospitals, restaurants, day care centers, and schools.

Sustainability Programs

There are some sustainable provisions in the existing codes, especially in the energy codes, plumbing codes, and mechanical codes; however, more comprehen-sive sustainability codes and standards are either in the process of being devel-oped or are waiting to be adopted. (See Chapter 1.) With the growing interest in sustainable design and green construction processes, many jurisdictions have instituted their own sustainability programs. Until a more standardized code is adopted nationwide, these jurisdictions are using a variety of ways to institute and enforce sustainable practices.

Many cities and some states, for example, now require the use of a green rating system such as LEED or Green Globes (see Appendix B) for certain building projects. Some states require the rating system on all state funded buildings; other jurisdictions require them on certain building types and sizes. If a jurisdiction requires the use of a rating system, the code official will typically coordinate with a third-party administrator or verify certain provisions with site inspections. Other jurisdictions have developed their own "green building programs" that must be followed as part of the code process. It is either administered by a code official or through a third party and certain criteria must be met to obtain permits, final approvals, and so forth.

Federal Laws and Regulations

The enforcement of federal laws and regulations such as the Americans with Disabilities Act (ADA) is a little more complicated. Each federal agency enforces its regulations for federal buildings. However, for other types of projects that are not federally owned or funded, there is no clear enforcement procedure. Although these federal laws are mandatory, individual federal agencies do not have the manpower to enforce them in every jurisdiction. And, unless they are adopted as part of the local code (and so become enforceable locally), the code jurisdictions do not review or enforce them either.

For that reason, many state and local jurisdictions formally adopt the federal regulations or create laws that are stricter than the federal requirements so that they can legally enforce them. For example, most states have created their own energy-efficiency laws that meet or exceed federal requirements. In other instances, the federal government will certify a comparable document. For example, in the past, a jurisdiction was able to create a modified version of the *ADA Standards* and have it certified by the Department of Justice (DOJ). This creates a document that can be used for local enforcement. However, this is a long and complicated process; not many jurisdictions have done it. This means that in most cases, there is no review or enforcement process at the local level for the *ADA Standards*. Even though a local jurisdiction does not enforce the ADA or other federal laws, it is the designer's responsibility to know the laws and to incorporate them into projects. (See Appendix A for more information on the ADA.)

THE CODE PROCESS

Although the process for code approval may change slightly, depending on the type of project and the code jurisdiction, the ultimate goal is to meet all the code requirements so that a building permit can be obtained and construction can begin. Most interior projects, unless they consist of minor repairs or minimal finish or furniture selection, cannot be constructed without a permit.

To obtain a permit with minimal delay or difficulty, use the process encouraged by the code officials in the jurisdiction of the project. Learn to work with the code officials while moving through the code process explained in this section. Several steps are done directly by the designer, including the initial code research, preliminary review, and any appeals that may be necessary. The other steps in the process directly affect the construction contractor and include the permit approval, the inspection process, and the final approval, which allows the space to be occupied. Each step is shown in Figure 10.1, which groups the steps into three subcategories: the design process, the permit process, and the inspection process. Refer to the figure as the various items are described below. (Construction documents and liability are explained later in the chapter.)

Code Research and Design

Research should begin by determining the jurisdiction of the project. Remember, the jurisdiction may be a township, city, county, or state. And, in some cases, state and local codes may both apply. (See the sections Code Jurisdiction and Code Enforcement earlier in this chapter.) Contact the local code department to determine which codes and standards are enforced. Since each jurisdiction can make amendments, deletions, and additions that alter the original code publication, these changes need to be determined as well. For example, a jurisdiction that adopts the *International Building Code* may have some local ordinances that override specific *IBC* requirements. Also ask if any other local agency regulations or ordinances will affect the project. For example, local health codes usually apply to projects that include food preparation. It is also the responsibility of the designer to know which federal regulations apply to a project. (See the section Federal Regulations in Chapter 1.)

In addition, it is important to know which edition of the codes is being used and how often new editions are adopted. As described in Chapter 1, most codes and standards have major updates every 3 years and minor changes on a yearly basis. However, jurisdictions are not required to use the updates. Since each jurisdiction adopts these changes on a different schedule, it is important to know when any changes occur. (Some jurisdictions have mailing lists and provide notices when updates occur.) This is especially important if an adoption takes place during the design of a project, since the construction documents must reference the most currently adopted codes when they are submitted for permit. (See also inset titled *Reviewing New Code Editions* on page 437.)

While determining the code publications and the editions required, also determine what is required by the jurisdiction to obtain final project approval. For example, depending on the size and scope of a project, specific floor plans and specifications may be required. For interior projects, the required construction

---

◤ Note

Some projects may require the code official(s) to walk through the building at the beginning of a project to determine code compliance. This is especially important in older buildings that require updating. (See Appendix C.)

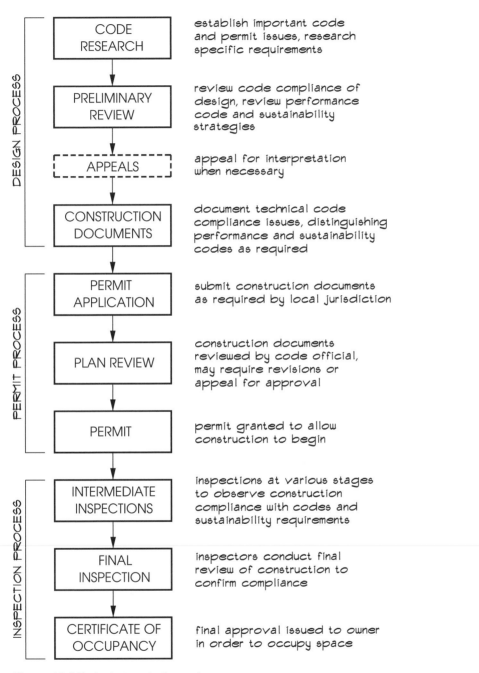

DESIGN PROCESS

CODE RESEARCH — establish important code and permit issues, research specific requirements

PRELIMINARY REVIEW — review code compliance of design, review performance code and sustainability strategies

APPEALS — appeal for interpretation when necessary

CONSTRUCTION DOCUMENTS — document technical code compliance issues, distinguishing performance and sustainability codes as required

PERMIT PROCESS

PERMIT APPLICATION — submit construction documents as required by local jurisdiction

PLAN REVIEW — construction documents reviewed by code official, may require revisions or appeal for approval

PERMIT — permit granted to allow construction to begin

INSPECTION PROCESS

INTERMEDIATE INSPECTIONS — inspections at various stages to observe construction compliance with codes and sustainability requirements

FINAL INSPECTION — inspectors conduct final review of construction to confirm compliance

CERTIFICATE OF OCCUPANCY — final approval issued to owner in order to occupy space

Figure 10.1 Typical steps in the code process.

✍Note

Many code departments
sell copies of the code
publications they have
adopted. These copies
should indicate and/or
include all required
amendments.

documents typically include stamped construction drawings indicating demolition plans, partition plans, reflected ceiling plans, and power and communication plans, as well as required elevations, details, and schedules. The specifications can be part of the drawings or included as a separate document. On certain projects, specific details, stamped engineering drawings, and engineering calculations may be required as well. (See the section Construction Documents later in this chapter.)

Most jurisdictions have strict requirements about who can design a project and what types of drawings are required for an interior project. For example, many drawings must be stamped by a licensed architect and/or engineer registered within the state of the project. In some jurisdictions, a registered interior designer is allowed to stamp drawings as well. Other projects may not require a professional stamp. Projects that require a professional stamp are usually determined by the use, size, and scope of the work being done. If a professional stamp is required, the design and documentation must be done under the direct supervision of the registered professional. To meet these various requirements, many firms employ a variety of design professionals. As an individual, collaboration with others may be required to complete a project.

After determining which codes and standards apply to a project, the specific requirements should be researched, beginning with the occupancy classification. For example, if renovating an existing elementary school, concentrate on the code requirements for Educational occupancies. But if the project includes renovation of the cafeteria, the requirements for Assembly may need to be reviewed as well. Any federal regulations should also be considered. This should be done before starting the project design. A majority of the research should be done in the programming stage of the design process at the same time the client and building information is being collected. The code requirements can then be incorporated into the design from the beginning, which avoids having to redesign to meet the code requirements later. It may be helpful to write down or copy the main sections of the codes that apply to the project and keep them with the project files. (Refer to the section Documentation and Liability later in this chapter.) This documentation, along with the use of the checklists provided in this book, will help track the code issues that affect the design of the project. This can be especially useful if questions arise later.

Later in the design process, additional research may be required as well. For example, when designing the office furniture systems, additional research on minimum aisle widths and accessible clearances may be necessary. Over time, every specific requirement may not need to be checked; however, keep in mind that codes change and the requirements for different project types can be different. For example, the minimum corridor width is typically 44 inches (1118 mm), but for Educational uses it is 72 inches (1829 mm). Doing proper research and

✍Note

A number of Web sites are
available to keep up-to-
date with the codes. These
include www.iccsafe.org
and www.nfpa.org, as
well as many local code
jurisdictions. Frequently
asked questions (FAQs)
are often posted, and chat
rooms may be available.

REVIEWING NEW CODE EDITIONS

When a new edition of a code publication is adopted by a jurisdiction, it is important to take some time and review the differences between the new edition and the previous edition. When a code is updated, both the International Code Council (ICC) and National Fire Protection Association (NFPA) use a similar system to indicate changes that have been made. In the publication, a vertical line in the margin beside the paragraph or table indicates a change such as revised text, relocated sections, and new information. An arrow (ICC) or bullet (NFPA) in the margin indicates where information has been removed from the code. This system allows a quick overview of the changes that have been made. In the sections where significant changes have occurred, it is a good idea to compare them to those in the previous code to become more familiar with the differences.

knowing the codes that apply to a project during design is an important part of getting a project approved by the code official.

Preliminary Review

Most code jurisdictions have some form of preliminary plan review procedure that can occur in the early stages of a project. Although a preliminary review may not be required on all projects, for some projects this may be crucial so that critical items can be finalized before taking the design to the next level. It may be as informal as faxing a floor plan indicating the pertinent code issues or as formal as a meeting with a number of code officials. When arranging a preliminary review meeting, request the presence of the plans examiner, the fire marshal, and any other necessary official so that all code concerns can be addressed at once.

As shown in Figure 10.1, the preliminary review should occur in the early stages of the design process, typically during the schematic design phase. A majority of the code research should have been completed—be prepared to discuss and clarify specific code issues. The preliminary floor plans should be to scale and have enough detail to discuss the major code topics. For example, the overall size of the building or space should be provided, and the division of occupancies and the arrangement of exits should be indicated. If designing only a portion of a building, have a location plan that indicates the layout of the remaining portions of the floor or building.

The purpose of the preliminary review meeting is to review the major code issues and to determine if the conclusions drawn from the research are valid. For example, discuss any code conflicts that may have been found in the research.

> **◀ Note**
>
> If two required codes have conflicting requirements, usually the more restrictive requirement applies. However, the code official has the authority to make the final decision.

Also, ask the code officials if they have any concerns with the design and if they foresee any potential problems. Likewise, if there is a situation that cannot easily meet the requirements of the code, be prepared to present an alternate solution. It is not wise to rely on code officials to solve the problem, because they may come up with a solution that meets the intention of the code but does not fit with the design intentions.

During the meeting, take notes so that the necessary changes can be made to the design. It is also important to prepare a summary of the meeting for the project records. After the meeting, send a copy of the summary to each attending code official and ask him or her either to sign off on the summary, indicating acceptance, or to send written confirmation. On smaller projects, the necessary corrections and notations could be made directly on the preliminary floor plan and ask the code officials to sign their approval on it. In either case, it is important to get all approvals and permissions in writing, since each code official can have a different interpretation of the same code, as discussed in the following section on the Appeals Process.

If a design requires the use of a performance code instead of certain prescriptive requirements, then a preliminary review with the code official is necessary and not optional. In fact, a concept report may need to be submitted before beginning the design, because the code official must agree to the use of the performance criteria in the particular building or space. When using performance codes, the code official must also agree that the design satisfies the code intent before the completion of the construction documents. If this process is not done correctly and the code official rejects the design, a lot of time, money, and energy will be wasted.

Formal reviews for compliance with federal regulations are not normally done for most projects. For example, the DOJ will review projects for compliance, but this is a lengthy process and is usually considered only for very large or public projects. Some federal agencies, such as the Access Board for the *ADA Standards* and the DOE for the EPAct, may provide an interpretation when requested. However, these interpretations are not an official approval. In most cases, a designer must use their best judgment as to whether a design complies with the federal regulation.

It is the responsibility of the designer to know the codes, standards, and federal regulations and to plan a design accordingly. However, it is important to clarify all issues at the beginning of a project, especially code issues. The preliminary code review helps as well. In addition, it typically results in a smoother permit approval. (See the section Plan Review and Permit later in this chapter.) Not only will the necessary requirements be incorporated into the drawings, but the code officials will be familiar with the project before the plans are brought in for review for the construction permit.

Appeals Request

All codes, standards, and federal regulations are written for the safety and protection of the building's occupants. However, they are not always as specific they could be. Often a code provision can have more than one interpretation. Usually these discrepancies can be settled with the help of a code official. Code officials undergo training and attend code review classes and, therefore, can usually provide additional insight into a specific code provision. They also have access to the expertise of other officials.

However, a designer may not always agree with the code official's interpretation. For example, there may be an alternative method of achieving the same code compliance. This will be even truer as more performance codes and/or more green building programs are adopted. (See the inset titled *Performance Codes* on page 452.) In addition, no code will be able to address every design situation. A project may consist of an older building where making changes can be cost-prohibitive, or there may be plans to use a new building material or finish material that is not covered by the code. In most cases, it is beneficial to try to work out a solution with the code official. If a mutual solution cannot be reached or an allowed performance criterion cannot be found, the appeals process may be necessary.

The appeals process is a formal request made in writing either through a code official or directly to a Board of Appeals. Generally, each of the codes provides specific reasons why an appeal can be made. (See the inset titled *Administration Chapter* on page 431.) The codes also regulate who can make the appeal: usually the owner or a representative of the owner. A designer can typically represent the owner and make the appeal to the board. The Board of Appeals consists of a variety of professionals who meet to review conflicts about how a code is interpreted or applied to a specific situation. The board does not have the authority to waive a code requirement. Rather, it is the board's responsibility to review the appeal, listen to both sides, and decide whether the appeal follows the intent of the code. This process can occur in the early review process or when a project fails to be approved for a permit. (This is why an early review can be very important.)

Usually separate appeal requests must be made for building, fire, plumbing, mechanical, and electrical codes. It will depend on the scope of the appeal. Once the Board of Appeals receives the appeal, both the designer (or owner) and the code official are scheduled to present their side of the issue. As the designer, be prepared to explain the current code interpretation and explain how compliance with the code will be met within the design project. If the appeal is accepted, the board grants a variance for that particular project. This variance applies only to the situation at hand; for other projects and even future projects in the same space, similar process must occur.

◢ Note

Often a good source for justifying an appeal is a code publication used by another jurisdiction. For example, the *Life Safety Code* may have an alternative code or method not found in a building code that could be applicable.

◢ Note

The words *variance* and *appeal* are sometimes used interchangeably. However, variances usually apply to local zoning laws and appeals apply to the codes.

Plan Review and Permit

A permit is typically required for any interior project that requires construction. This includes but is not limited to the following:

- ❑ New construction or additions to an existing building
- ❑ Alterations made to a building
- ❑ Change in occupancy
- ❑ Installation of regulated equipment
- ❑ Certain types of repairs or building maintenance

The permit is issued only after a plan review has been completed. The code officials must review and approve the submitted construction documents, which consist of drawings, specifications, and any other documentation that may be required. (See the section Documentation and Liability later in this chapter.) Most of the time, a review is best handled by the local code officials; however, a jurisdiction may use the plan review services of a code organization for an especially large project or when workloads could cause a delay in the permitting process. Sometimes a more formal review service may help identify particular design problem areas. The ICC, for example, will review specific issues of a project—such as means of egress, fire protection, sprinklers and standpipes, lighting and ventilation, and other similar issues. Third-party code consultants who specialize in code review are also available.

It is typically the licensed contractor who submits the documents and obtains the permit for the project. However, some jurisdictions (especially in larger cities) require a independent consultant, known as a code expeditor, to obtain the permit. In some cases, the building owner or a registered design professional can also get the permit. Figure 10.2 is an example a building permit application. Each jurisdiction requires slightly different information. Most jurisdictions also require separate permits for plumbing, electrical, and mechanical work. These are usually obtained by the appropriate subcontractors, since these permits make each subcontractor legally responsible for the specified work.

To obtain the permit, the contractor must submit a permit application and a permit fee along with the construction documents. (Many jurisdictions have online permit applications that can be filed electronically.) Usually, multiple copies of construction documents must be submitted. It is at this stage that the code officials fully review the drawings and specifications. Therefore, it is important that all relevant code correspondence occurring during the preliminary review and any granted appeals be attached to the application or noted directly on the construction drawings. This is especially helpful if the same code officials are not checking the plans in both the preliminary review and the permit plan review.

◀ Note

In some jurisdictions, it is almost imperative that an expeditor be used as a go-between between the contractor and the codes department in order to obtain a permit.

◀ Note

Many jurisdictions have converted to an online permit process and electronic submittals of site inspections. (See the section Code Department earlier in the chapter.)

Application for a Building Permit

Application is hereby made for a building permit to accomplish the work described below. Necessary compliance shall be observed and all requirements of the Codes shall be complied with.

Building Department
123 Main Street
Anywhere, USA 32134
201-345-8532

Date:_____

Property Information:

Project Address: _____ Suite #:_____
Project Name: _____
Subdivision: _____ Lot:_____ Block:_____
Section:_____ Township:_____ Range:_____ Map#:_____
Parcel ID #:_____
Zoning Use:_____ Fire Zone: Y/N Flood Zone: Y/N Landslide Zone: Y/N
Water System:_____ Sewer System:_____
Proposed Use:_____

Owners Information:

Name: _____

Address:_____

City: _____ State:_____ Zip:_____

Phone:_____ Fax:_____ Email:_____

Contractor Information:

Company Name:_____ City Tax ID:_____
Principal Agent:_____ License Number:_____
Phone:_____ Fax:_____ Email:_____

Permit Information:

Work Class:_____ Master Permit Number:_____
Description of Work:_____
_____

Valuation of Work: $_____ Contruction Type: IA, IB, IIA, IIB, IIIA, IIIB, IV, VA,VB
Occupancy Type:
             A1,A2,A3,A4,A5,B,E,F1,F2,H1,H2,H3,H4,H5,I1,I2,I3,I4,R1,R2,R3,R4,M,S1,S2,U
Total Building Sq. Footage:_____ Total Building Height:_____
Sprinkler System: Y/N Permit Area Sq Footage:_____ Floor Number:_____
Soil Erosion Permit #:_____ Sewer Impact #:_____
Report Code:_____ Notes:_____
_____

I hereby certify that I have read this application and that all information contained herein is true.

Date:_____ Signature:_____
Check:_____ Cash:_____   Permit Cost:_____

Figure 10.2 Sample application for a building permit. (Reproduced with permission from the International Code Council.)

The whole process can take 1 day or several weeks, depending on the size of the project, the number of code officials who must check the project, and the workload of the code department. The set of documents is typically checked by both a plans examiner and a fire marshal. Some jurisdictions will have more than one examiner check the drawings. For example, there may be separate building, mechanical, plumbing, and electrical code examiners, as well as other local and/or state code examiners. For certain projects, documents may also need to be sent to a state or local agency, such as the health department, for review. (See the section Code Enforcement earlier in this chapter.)

If there are any code discrepancies on the drawings or in the specifications, the building official will require corrections to be made before the permit is issued. This will necessitate making the appropriate changes and submitting the updated documentation. Upon approval, the code official(s) will stamp or write "Approved" on the drawings. The code department keeps one set of drawings, and at least one set must be kept on the job site at all times. Some jurisdictions will issue a plans approval letter, which should be kept in the project files. In addition, the permit itself must be clearly posted at the job site during construction.

Construction and Inspection

The code process does not stop with the issue of a permit. (See Figure 10.1.) During the construction of a project, a code official must make several inspections of the job site. This is done to guarantee that the work matches what is required by the construction documents and that the work continues to comply with the codes. Inspections must be made at certain intervals during the construction, usually before the work is concealed or covered up by the next phase of construction.

It is typically the responsibility of the contractor to notify the code department when it is time to make an inspection. Depending on the type of interior project, these intervals usually include the following:

1. *Frame inspection:* The walls, ceilings, and floors are usually framed and completed on one side. Gypsum board may be attached to one side of the walls, but all framing must be exposed. The side that is open allows the inspector to check the construction materials and framing.

2. *Systems inspection:* Separate inspections are made for the plumbing, mechanical, and electrical installations. This includes automatic sprinkler systems. Certain jurisdictions may also require an inspection of some communication systems. These inspections can be made at the same time as the framing inspection if these systems are complete. There is usually a preliminary

✑ Note

The *IBC* requires that an approved set of construction documents be stamped "Reviewed for Code Compliance" and that a set be kept at the construction site for review by code officials during construction.

✑ Note

A designer should periodically check the construction of a project to ensure that the project design and code instructions are being followed. This should be part of every project's construction administration.

rough-in inspection before the walls are closed and then a final inspection at the end of construction as part of the final inspection.

3. *Gypsum board/lath inspection:* When all the gypsum board or lathing is in place but before any taping or plastering is done, the inspector will check to make sure that all wall and ceiling assemblies are built to code. Rated assemblies such as fire- and smoke-rated assemblies typically require additional inspections.

4. *Fire- and smoke-resistant penetration inspection:* After the rated assemblies, including walls and floor/ceiling assemblies, are taped and plastered, they are inspected again to confirm that the joints, intersections, and penetrations in the rated assemblies are properly installed and sealed. Any fire-resistant materials sprayed onto structural elements must also be inspected before, during, and after application.

5. *Energy-efficiency inspection:* Items such as the insulation of mechanical ducts, the water heating equipment, and the HVAC system are inspected for compliance with energy standards.

6. *Special inspection:* Certain inspections occur after the construction or installation of a specific design element is complete, such as an elevator, swimming pool, or other special element. In addition, the codes specify when certain products and systems require a separate inspection. These include special wall panels, sprayed fire-resistant material, and smoke control systems. Special inspections may also be required when materials or systems are used in unusual or creative ways, especially as part of a performance approach to the code or when using alternative materials and methods as allowed by the *IBC*. Sustainable-related inspections may also be required. The code official will indicate when a special inspection is required for an individual situation.

At each intermediate inspection, construction can continue only if the inspector grants an approval. If the inspector finds that the project is not acceptable, a correction notice is issued and another inspection is scheduled, allowing the contractor time to correct the problem. If the inspector feels that a condition is unsafe or that the construction is not being carried out in an acceptable manner, a stop work order will be issued. This means that no other work on the site can occur until the specific problem is addressed.

An inspection may not always be done by a code official. Some jurisdictions allow or even require the owner to have the construction process inspected by a separate inspection agency. This is sometimes referred to as a self-inspection. Typically, a third party performs the site inspections and documents the process. In some cases, if approved by the local code jurisdiction, the architect or engineer

◢ Note

Unfortunately, there is no guarantee that preapproved plans or even plans that receive a permit will be approved in the field. An inspector may see a code issue in the field that was missed on the construction drawings. If this occurs, either the designer must work out the discrepancy with the appropriate code official or the contractor must make the changes necessary to comply with the code.

◢ Note

Special inspections might be required when performance codes or unusual construction materials are used. It may be necessary for the actual installation to be observed by the inspector.

for the project can provide the special inspection. The inspection information is submitted to the local code official to verify that inspections are being done. The code official often still performs the final inspection necessary for the final approval and the Certificate of Occupancy.

Sometimes changes must be made to the construction documents after construction begins. For example, a change may be necessary because of a stop work order or to clarify an item on the construction drawings. In other cases, the owner may request a design change. These changes should be submitted to the code department as well as to the construction site. In some cases, the code official will issue a plans approval letter for each revision. The building inspectors will review the project according to the set they have approved. If there is a conflict between their approved set and what is being built, it can delay inspections and approvals.

◢Note

If changes are made to a set of construction documents after a building permit is issued, an amended set of documents must be resubmitted to the code official for approval.

Final Inspection and Approval

◢Note

Most nonresidential building types (including apartment complex common areas) continue to require periodic inspections by building inspectors, fire marshals, and/or the fire department after the building is occupied.

The inspection process is the way the code officials verify that the project is being built according to the most current drawings and that the construction meets the applicable codes. Once the project is complete, the inspector will do a final walk-through to confirm final compliance with codes and to make sure that the space is ready to be occupied. In some jurisdictions, a separate inspection is done by a fire marshal. When the final inspections are completed, the construction of the project is typically considered finished. However, before the occupants can move into the space or building, additional approvals are necessary. The various types are explained below.

Certificate of Completion

A Certificate of Completion is issued when the structure or systems within a space or building are complete. This certificate is usually necessary to connect to local utilities, especially in new construction. However, it does not give the right to occupy the space or building. A Certificate of Occupancy must still be issued to allow the tenant to occupy the space or building.

Certificate of Occupancy

A Certificate of Occupancy (C of O) is issued after the final inspection has been completed. The person who obtained the building permit typically requests the C of O from the code official. This is usually the contractor. If during the final inspection the code inspector, including the fire marshal, is satisfied that the building or space complies with the code and the construction is complete, a certificate is issued. In some jurisdictions, the Certificate of Occupancy is referred to as a Use and Occupancy (U and O) letter. The certificate is typically required before the tenant can occupy the building or space, and it must be posted in a conspicuous location in the building. Once the C of O is issued, the code process is complete.

Temporary Certificate of Occupancy

The client might not want to wait until all portions of the project are completed before occupying the facility. Or a certain aspect of the project cannot be completed because of a delay in the arrival of material or equipment—for example, custom granite countertops or water fountains. In those cases, some jurisdictions will issue a Temporary Certificate of Occupancy. This will allow the project or portions of the project to be occupied as long as the code official feels that the occupants will not be in any danger because the entire project is not complete. The uncompleted work must eventually be inspected before a final Certificate of Occupancy is issued. The Temporary Certificate of Occupancy is also known as a Partial Certificate of Occupancy or a Partial Use and Occupancy Permit. It is usually issued with a time limit, such as 90 days, giving the contractor the time to complete the work.

Some jurisdictions will not issue a temporary certificate because often owners or contractors never request final inspections once they have occupied the space. Not all code departments have a way to track temporary certificates; so, if a final inspection is not requested, they may not know if the final work was done correctly.

Phased Certificate of Occupancy

For a larger project, construction may be done in phases. Often these phases are determined during the design process and incorporated into the construction documents. A Phased Certificate of Occupancy allows the client to occupy the portions of the project that are complete. For example, in the renovation of several floors of a hospital, it may be important to allow the renovated emergency room to be occupied as soon as it is completed without waiting for the renovation of the cafeteria on the floor above to be completed. It also allows code officials to do final inspections on the completed areas. In other cases, each part of a large project could be permitted separately, and then each part would have its own review and inspection process and receive a separate Certificate of Occupancy.

ECONOMIC OPTIONS IN CODES

Thorough code research is imperative for the safety of building occupants, but a number of options are allowed by the code that can affect the cost of the project. These options are frequently overlooked, resulting in needless construction costs. In his book *Building and Safety Codes for Industrial Facilities,* Joseph N. Sabatini lists a number of reasons for overlooked cost savings in industrial buildings. They can be generalized to include all design projects.

1. Options are not clear in the codes. Sometimes options, alternatives, or exceptions are scattered throughout the chapters, and finding them requires familiarity and expertise.

2. Nonfamiliarity and infrequent use of codes lead to poor enforcement. Many designers merely spot-check the codes on an intermittent basis, and therefore miss important details because they do not have the time to review them thoroughly.

3. Some trade-offs are interdisciplinary. Since some designers are scheduled to participate in planning on a staggered basis, poor communication and coordination result.

4. Preliminary meetings do not involve all disciplines. Sound economic decisions can be made only if all disciplines are involved in the early planning stages.

5. Design time is too short. Because of committed investments, interest payments, and the income that a facility will bring as soon as it is in operation, design time is often abbreviated, and therefore comprehensive code reviews are often not done.

6. Overkill. Because of item 5, conscientious professionals use overkill and include items in the design that are not always mandated by the building codes, regulations, and enforced standards.

DOCUMENTATION AND LIABILITY

☰ Note

Some code departments will not issue a permit if a project incorporates more stringent codes not currently enforced by that jurisdiction. If that is the case, document all correspondence.

Building codes and the standards they reference are continually being updated, especially those that pertain to interiors. For example, some of the testing requirements for interior finishes and furniture are fairly recent, and more tests are constantly being developed. Incorporating sustainability into an interior project will also continue to change. (See Appendix B.) In addition, newer federal regulations, such as accessibility or energy regulations, may be mandated. Even if not yet required, some of the updates may benefit the project and its occupants.

It is crucial when designing interior projects to keep current with the codes and regulations. Even if the jurisdiction of a project does not yet require some of the stricter codes or standards, be familiar with them and use them when possible. Not only are people's lives at stake, but a designer may be held liable should an incident occur. It is important to be able to prove that the most advanced tests or strictest requirements available at the time were incorporated into the design. In addition, a jurisdiction (and/or client) may require that a certain level of sustainability and/or energy efficiency is incorporated into the project. It is important to know how to include these aspects while meeting the code requirements.

It is critical to reference specific code sections and standard numbers and note which editions of the publications are used. When conducting a code review, it is a good idea to note the critical chapters and/or sections that apply to the design of the project. On larger projects, a cover sheet can be used to summarize these sections. In addition, collect written evidence of any materials that must meet specific requirments. For example, when requesting the results of a performance test, a product certification, or a product declaration from a manufacturer or an outside source, obtain the results in writing. Equally important is to have the documentation organized to easily show the research done for each code issue.

The development of a checklist or a standard evaluation form is very useful, since the ease of establishing compliance is in direct proportion to the quantity and quality of the documentation. A general checklist, such as the one in Figure 10.3, is also helpful to make sure that each code topic has been covered in every project.

Use this checklist in conjunction with the more specific checklists introduced in each chapter of this book. Add to these checklists as necessary or develop other ones. It is impossible to put every code requirement on a checklist, since the requirements will be different on every project. Instead, the purpose of the checklist is to act as a reminder of the code and standard requirements that must be researched and documented on the drawings and specifications. When necessary, attach the appropriate backup. The backup could consist of a copy of the manufacturer's warranty or specifications, a product evaluation sheet, a product label listing the codes and standards with which the product complies, a copy of a certificate from a testing agency, etc. Attaching reduced floor plans with additional notes might also be helpful. (Also see the sections Future Technology at the end of this chapter and Responsibility for Compliance in Appendix A.)

Documentation to clients is a critical part of a project as well. They need to know how to maintain a building so that it continues to meet codes. For example, if finishes are not cleaned appropriately, they might not retain their fire retardancy or slip resistance. Other maintenance might affect the indoor air quality of the building, energy efficiency of an electrical system, or water conservation of plumbing fixtures. Depending on the size and type of the project, a designer might supply some or all of this information. On larger projects, the project specifications should specify that the contractor supply the client with

◢Note

When using performance codes or alternative methods such those allowed by *IBC Section 104.11*, documentation is very important. All documentation must be clear and designated separately from prescriptive code requirements.

◢Note

Properly and consistently prepared code documentation is imperative should any liability issues occur after a project is completed.

Summary Interior Project Checklist

Project Name: _____ Space: _____ Date: _____

1 DETERMINE WHICH CODES ARE REQUIRED (Chapter 1)

__Building Code
__Energy Code
__Fire Code
__Life Safety Code
__Performance Code
__Sustainability Code/Standard
__Other Code Publications
__Local Codes and Ordinances
__Government Regulations
__Standards and Tests

2 OCCUPANCY REQUIREMENTS (Chapter 2)

__Determine Building Types(s)
__Determine Occupancy Classification(s)
__Calculate Occupant Load(s)
__Adjustments to Occupant Load(s)
__Review Specific Occupancy Requirements
__Compare Code and Accessibility Requirements

3 MINIMUM TYPES OF CONSTRUCTION (Chapter 3)

__Determine Construction Type
__Determine Ratings of Building Elements
__Calculate Maximum Floor Area (as required)
__Calculate Building Height (as required)
__Review Construction Type Limitations

4 MEANS OF EGRESS REQUIREMENTS (Chapter 4)

__Determine Quantity and Types of Means of Egress
__Calculate Minimum Widths
__Determine Arrangement of Exits
__Calculate Travel Distance
__Determine Required Signage
__Compare Code and Accessibility Requirements
__Review Emergency Lighting Requirements

5 FIRE AND SMOKE RESISTANCE REQUIREMENTS (Chapter 5)

__Determine Use of Fire Walls
__ Determine Fire Barriers/Partitions and Horizontal Assemblies
__Determine Smoke Barriers and Partitions
__Determine Location of Opening Protectives
__Determine Location of Through-Penetration Protectives
__Review Types of Fire Tests and Ratings Required
__Determine Sustainability Requirements
__Review Requirements During Assembly Specification
__Review Required Standards

6 FIRE-PROTECTION REQUIREMENTS (Chapter 6)

__Determine Fire and Smoke Detection Systems
__Determine Required Alarm Systems
__Determine Types of Extinguishing Systems and Possible Sprinkler Trade-offs
__Compare Code and Accessibility Requirements
__Coordinate with Engineer (as required)

7 PLUMBING REQUIREMENTS (Chapter 7)

__Determine Types of Fixtures Required
__Calculate Number of Each Fixture Required
__Determine Required Toilet/Bathing Facilities
__Review for Finishes, Accessories, and Signage
__Compare Code and Accessibility Requirements
__Review Water Conservation Requirements
__Coordinate with Engineer (as required)

8 MECHANICAL REQUIREMENTS (Chapter 7)

__Determine Type of Air Distribution System(s)
__Determine Items Affecting Cooling Loads
__Determine Access and Clearance Requirements
__Figure Zoning and Thermostat Locations
__Compare Code and Accessibility Requirements
__Review Energy and Water Efficiency Compliance
__Coordinate with Engineer (as required)

9 ELECTRICAL REQUIREMENTS (Chapter 8)

__Determine Types/Locations of Outlets, Switches, Fixtures
__Determine Emergency Power and Lighting Requirements
__Compare Code and Accessibility Requirements
__Review Energy Efficiency Compliance
__Coordinate with Engineer (as required)

10 COMMUNICATION REQUIREMENTS (Chapter 8)

__Determine Systems Required by Client
__Compare Needs versus Code/Standard Requirements
__Check for Accessibility Compliance and Sustainability Requirements
__Coordinate with Engineer/Consultant (as required)

11 FINISH AND FURNITURE REQUIREMENTS (Chapter 9)

__Review Tests and Types of Ratings Required
__Determine Special Finish Requirements
__Determine Special Furniture Requirements
__Compare Code and Accessibility Requirements
__Review Sustainability Requirements
__Compare Requirements During Selection/Specification
__ Review Required Standards

NOTE: Review all codes and standards required by the local jurisdiction as well as any federal regulations that are applicable. Consult the local code offical at any step in question.

Figure 10.3 Summary interior project checklist.

record drawings (as-builts) of each system installed, as well as operation and maintenance (O & M) manuals that explain how to use and maintain each system and/or material. Client training may also be necessary.

An O & M manual is especially important in performance design and when using alternate materials. Some jurisdictions require them. In addition, an O & M manual is required when using sustainability codes and standards, and must include an operations plan. The plan should include procedures for maintaining indoor air quality, instituting a green cleaning program, and measuring, verifying, and tracking both energy and water use.

The importance of documenting every project in construction drawings, specification books, and project files cannot be stressed enough. Although it has been mentioned throughout this book that the use of performance codes and alternative methods such as those allowed by the *IBC Section 104.11* requires additional research and documentation for approval, all projects must be well documented concerning codes. Even if all the codes were followed throughout an entire project, if it cannot be proven when required, the research was useless. Keep all the research, correspondence with the code officials, and other documentation on file with the project records.

> **◈Note**
>
> The length of time required to keep project records and code documentation is highly debatable. However, many states have a *statute of repose,* which sets a time limitation on how long after a project is completed that a suit can be brought against a designer or design firm.

Construction Documents

Construction documents include drawings, specifications, and any additional documentation required by a code jurisdiction. Having certain information documented on the drawings makes the review by code officials easier. They automatically know which code requirements were considered in the development of the design. It is especially important to use the proper terminology in all documentation. For example, a corridor is an enclosed passageway but an aisle is not enclosed. The code requirements for these two are very different.

> **◈Note**
>
> Although it is rarely done, a permit can be revoked after construction begins if it is discovered that information used to grant the permit was incorrect, even if the error was made by a code official.

Some codes require certain information to be included in the construction documents. Other information is either common design practice or is required by the jurisdiction. This section lists the typical code information that should be included in the construction documents, either on the drawings or in the written specifications. Note, however, that this list is not all-inclusive. Other information, specific to a project type or a jurisdiction, may include requirements from a local or state agency or items specific to a green building program. (See the section Code Enforcement earlier in this chapter.)

Cover Sheet

❏ Applicable code publication(s) and edition(s) (recognize local or state amendments)

❏ Applicable standards and regulations

◀Note

Certain sections in each code indicate specific information that must be included in the construction documents prior to code review. A jurisdiction may have additional requirements.

❏ Name of the design professional responsible for each aspect of the design (plan, electrical, mechanical, etc.)

❏ Construction type(s)

❏ Area of space designed (square footages or square meters)

❏ Building area limitations

❏ Occupancy classification(s)

❏ Sprinkler status of building or space (i.e., sprinklered or nonsprinklered)

❏ Occupant load per floor (or area if necessary)

❏ Identification of any appeals or equivalencies granted

Drawings

❏ Location plan (when designing a portion of a floor or building)

❏ Identification of use of rooms and spaces

❏ Compartmentation of fire areas

❏ Location of rated walls and floor/ceiling assemblies

❏ Location of rated doors, windows, and other through-penetrations

❏ Exit access and exit doors (size, location, swing, hardware, security, etc.)

❏ Egress routes (location, size, and components)

❏ Details of stairs and ramps that are part of the means of egress

❏ Location and heights of electrical devices

❏ Reflected ceiling plan, including lights, emergency lighting, and exit signs

❏ Location of plumbing fixtures (drinking fountains, water closets, lavatories, etc.)

❏ Location and placement of furnishings and finishes

❏ Accessibility clearances and critical dimensions

❏ Sections of rated assemblies (walls, ceilings, etc.)

❏ Details for penetrations (electrical, plumbing, environmental and communication conduits, pipes, and systems)

❏ Elevations (indicating mounting heights and locations of fixtures, equipment, and accessories)

Specifications, Schedules, and Legends

❏ Types of rated wall and floor/ceiling assemblies

❏ Types of rated doors, frames, and hardware

❏ Types of rated windows and through-penetrations

- ❏ Types of electrical outlets, including GFCIs and AFCIs
- ❏ Types of light fixtures, including emergency lights and exit signs
- ❏ Types and locations of regulated finishes and furniture
- ❏ List of required standards and tests

Additional information may be required for review by the code official for approval of the design. This documentation is usually developed by an engineer or other consulting professional. This may include the following:

- ❏ Sprinkler riser diagram
- ❏ Sprinkler coverage calculations
- ❏ Electrical system design and load calculations
- ❏ Lighting power density calculations
- ❏ Mechanical system design and load calculations
- ❏ Plumbing system design and fixture calculations

Performance Design Documentation

When a performance requirement has been used as part of the design, it should be clearly shown in the construction documents. The performance documentation must be distinguished from the rest of the documentation, because often it will require a separate review process. The design and review of the performance portions of a project is more of a team effort than when prescriptive codes are used. The team should include design professionals (architects, engineers and interior designers), special experts, and code officials who are qualified to evaluate the proposed design. In some cases, the code official may choose to have the design reviewed by another consultant who may be more knowledgeable in the review of performance criteria and/or a specific area of design. This is often referred to as contract review. In all cases, the documentation of the design must be acceptable to the code official having jurisdiction.

The documentation of a performance design may include some or all of the information shown below. (See also the inset titled *Performance Codes* on the next page.)

- ❏ Performance criteria
- ❏ Technical references and resources
- ❏ Plans, specifications, and details of the building design
- ❏ Design assumptions, limitations, and factors of safety used
- ❏ Description of the design hazards

> **◀ Note**
>
> If performance-related codes are used on a project, typically only a certain portion of the project will be designed using performance criteria. The prescriptive codes will be used on the rest of the project.

❏ Input information for calculations and computer modeling

❏ Calculations

❏ Computer modeling

❏ Scope of inspection and testing required to demonstrate compliance

❏ Prescriptive requirements used

❏ Maintenance requirements

❏ Reliability of the method of research and process

PERFORMANCE CODES

Whether using a performance code or alternative materials, design, and methods as allowed by the *IBC*, specifying innovative materials and developing unique design solutions for interior projects is an option. These codes can be especially helpful when trying to incorporate sustainable design into a project or when working on an existing building with unusual characteristics. Because they allow for design flexibility, they may also make a project more cost effective. However, it is the designer's responsibility to convince the client and the code official that the proposed situation meets these special code criteria. Additional steps must be taken to prove that the design will provide equivalent safety to the same prescriptive requirements. Examples of additional steps that may be required include:

❏ *Acquire data*. Working with an engineer or other consultant to obtain specific data or develop new data through the use of available design guides, calculation methods, and computer models. These are currently used in supporting fire, smoke, and structural-related scenarios but may have many new applications in the future.

❏ *Obtain reports*. Researching specific materials and assemblies by obtaining reports from product evaluation services (see the inset *ICC Evaluation Services* on page 20) and working with the manufacturer of a particular product. Existing products often have already gone through the necessary testing and have available evaluation reports. But, when developing something new, a manufacturer may be able to obtain the necessary tests and reports.

❏ *Find comparables*. Looking to other buildings and projects with similar situations or a similar use of a product. Contact the designers and contractors involved in those projects for information that could be useful. (This usually cannot be the only supportive documentation.)

In the future, more options will become available to help analyze and support the use of performance codes and alternative methods. The best method to support the solution depends on the extent of the performance criteria as well as the uniqueness of the design. No matter which steps are taken to provide documentation, the ultimate goal is to show that the safety of the building occupants will be maintained. It is also typically necessary to work with the code official early in the design process to establish what criteria will be required for approval.

Depending on which aspect of the building has been designed to meet the performance criteria, the documentation may include drawings, specifications, and additional reports. It might be clearly indicated in the main set of construction documents or be separately documented and cross-referenced to the main set. Additional media, such as computer modeling, may also be part of the documentation.

Once it has been approved, anyone involved in the ownership or management of the building has to be notified that the building was approved based on a performance code. A performance design option is designed for the actual situation. If any aspect of the building is changed during design or after the client occupies the space, it may require reapproval by the local code official. Even the maintenance done by the client after move-in can affect the safety of the building.

Sustainability Design Documentation

Currently, there is not a consistent system in place for documenting sustainable or green design. Until the new sustainability codes and standards are more widely adopted, each jurisdiction has adopted what works best in their area. As mentioned earlier, some require the use of a green rating system, such as LEED or Green Globes, for certain building projects. (See Appendix B.) Others have created their own unique "green building program." As a result, the required sustainability documentation will vary by jurisdiction. In most cases, the relevant sustainability information will need to be distinguished from the rest of the documentation, since, in some cases, this information will be reviewed by a third party. At the very least, the documents should indicate the location, nature, and scope of the proposed green building features. Other documentation may include specific calculations, computer modeling, and certain technical or product details.

When working on an interior project that includes required sustainable features, work closely with the local code officials from the beginning of the project. Similar to performance-based projects, if a building is working toward certification in a green rating system or meeting the requirements of a specific green code/standard, there must be collaboration between the various parties involved. Contact the local jurisdiction to determine what programs are in place and how to document the sustainable features in the project's construction document.

FUTURE TECHNOLOGY

Computers are quickly becoming a powerful force in code research and enforcement. Each code organization sells digital versions of its code publications, many of them now providing search capabilities. For example, a word search can be

✎ Note

Using alternate methods/materials and performance-based codes makes a building unique. It is important to educate the building owner so that the building can be properly maintained to provide optimum health, safety, and welfare to its occupants.

✎ Note

Commissioning is another part of the documentation process for sustainability projects. This process, among other things, verifies and documents that the selected building systems have been designed, installed, and function in accordance with the owner's prerequisites, the construction documents, and the minimum sustainability and other code requirements.

✎ Note

If a jurisdiction mandates sustainable requirements not yet included in the codes, such as the use of a green rating system, ask a code official how this information needs to be documented.

done for a particular code topic or a specific code reference number or table. And, as mentioned earlier, code departments are also incorporating more technology to include online permit applications, electronic plan review, and wireless submittals of site inspections.

In addition, a variety of computer programs are available to the design industry. Some model how different aspects of a building will act in a fire, earthquake, and other emergency situations so that alternatives to existing code solutions can be developed and incorporated into buildings. Others fully simulate a building so that the facility can be viewed three-dimensionally from many different perspectives before it is built. The newest phase of technology, often referred to as Building Information Modeling (BIM), allows a building to be experienced virtually. It simulates the finished product so that it can be analyzed prior to construction to identify potential conflicts or problems. It is also used to predict how the building will operate throughout its life cycle. BIM software crosses over a multitude of applications so that it can be used by everyone involved in the building over its lifetime such as designers, code officials, contractors, facility managers, service technicians, and fire and police departments.

The use of this existing and upcoming technology to enhance a building's performance in code compliance requires training in the software and advanced knowledge of the applicable prescriptive and performance code requirements and criteria. In most cases, it will require a specialist to develop this type of performance data. However, this technology will become more common with the increased use of performance codes as well as alternative materials and methods as found in the *IBC*. This will also become more essential with the development of more complex buildings and spaces. For example, computer models can be used to investigate possible fire scenarios so that the most effective way to address the fire in that specific building and configuration can be incorporated into the design. These computer models then become part of the documentation to support the design.

Other technologies are affecting the construction of the building as well. Increasingly, building systems are being run by computers and integrated together. (See the insets titled *Integrated Alarms* on page 257 and *Building Automation Systems* on page 356.) Devices and methods used to help occupants exit a building are also being reevaluated and updated. As the building industry becomes more complex, with the development of new products and construction techniques, both designers and code officials have to continue to keep up with these new technologies. Although this will ultimately affect the development and enforcement of codes, the code publications and requirements may not always be able to stay current with the changes in technology.

In addition, changes in the way we think about buildings, such as sustainable design and better indoor air quality, will need to be further addressed within the

◈ **Note**

BIM is typically used for large-scale, complex projects. In the future it may become the standard for all types of projects.

◈ **Note**

The ICC continues to develop its software called SMARTcodes™. Made to work with the I-Codes and various BIM options, it will automatically check electronic floor plans for code compliance. Go to www.iccsafe.org for a demonstration using the *IECC*.

codes in the future. Until the newer sustainable codes are more widely adopted, designers need to refer to existing green standards, work with manufacturers and code officials, and be familiar with green rating systems. (See the Appendix B.) For now, the use of new technology, new products, and sustainable design is incorporated into a project through the use of *IBC Section 104.11* or performance aspects of the codes. This will require additional research and documentation and may require additional reviews with the code official before a project can be approved.

Codes, standards, and federal regulations will remain an important part of the design process. Early and comprehensive code research at the beginning of each interior project is crucial to the smooth development of the project, not to mention the safety of the building occupants. In addition, thorough documentation of code issues, research, and design solutions is essential.

Remember, code officials have the same goal as designers—ensuring the health, safety, and welfare of the building occupants. It is important to build a good relationship with the code officials. Since not every jurisdiction is the same, it is important to learn the local system. Learn how to work within the system and with the various personalities. Code officials are a valuable resource. Working together, design solutions that comply with the required codes, standards, and federal regulations are attainable.

ACCESSIBILITY AND THE ADA

As mentioned in Chapter 1, the Americans with Disabilities Act (ADA) is both a federal and a civil law that prohibits discrimination against people with disabilities. Since it is a federal law, the code officials in a jurisdiction cannot make the determination whether or not it applies in their area: The ADA is enforceable throughout the United States. A better question may be: Does the project have to conform to the ADA regulations? And, to what extent must the project meet the accessibility requirements in the ADA standards?

✐Note

Both places of public accommodation and commercial facilities have requirements for compliance with the ADA.

PLACES REQUIRING ACCESSIBILITY

Title III is the segment of the ADA that requires accessibility compliance in places of public accommodation and commercial facilities. The levels of compliance for public accommodations and commercial facilities are slightly different. A place of *public accommodation* is defined by the ADA as any facility that is owned, leased, leased to, or operated by a private entity whose operation affects commerce and falls within one of the 12 categories listed below. Some examples are provided in each category, although other types of facilities may apply as well.

❏ *Place of lodging:* A hotel, assisted living facility, or dormitory (except for owner-occupied establishments renting fewer than six rooms)

❏ *Establishment serving food:* A restaurant, bar, or cafeteria

❏ *Place of exhibition or entertainment:* A sports arena, theater, or concert hall

❏ *Place of public gathering:* An auditorium, convention center, or city hall

❏ *Sale or rental establishment:* A grocery store, clothing store, or shopping center

❏ *Service establishment:* A doctor's office, beauty shop, funeral parlor, pharmacy, or hospital

Note

Federally funded buildings are covered by the Architectural Barriers Act (ABA). Originally required to comply with the requirements of the *Uniform Federal Accessibility Standards (UFAS),* these projects must now meet the requirements of the ABA portion of the 2004 *ADA–ABA Accessibility Guidelines,* known as the *ABA Standards.*

Note

The ADA covers other aspects of accessibility that can affect a project, including employment, communication, and equipment.

Note

Certain Residential occupancies may also need to meet the requirements of the *Federal Housing Accessibility Guidelines (FHAG)* and in some cases the *ADA Standards.* If federally funded, they may also need to meet those of the *UFAS* or *ABA Standards.*

❑ *Station for public transportation:* An airport, train station, or bus stop
❑ *Place of public display:* A museum, library, or art gallery
❑ *Educational facility:* An elementary school, college classroom, or preschool
❑ *Recreation area:* An amusement park, nature park, or zoo
❑ *Place of exercise:* A gym, health spa, or bowling alley
❑ *Social service center:* A homeless shelter, adoption agency, or day care center

A public accommodation must comply with requirements for new construction or altered buildings as defined by the ADA. As a facility that provides services and goods to the public, it must also comply with the ADA requirements that apply to policies, practices, and procedures that affect the ability of a disabled individual to use its services. For example, in a restaurant, the tables are required to be accessible and the servers are required to read a menu to a person who has a sight disability or provide a menu in Braille.

Commercial facilities include nonresidential facilities whose operations affect commerce but are not generally open to the public. Examples include factories and warehouses as well as other businesses that do not typically receive clients or guests, such as a telemarketing office. These facilities must be compliant with the ADA for use by employees. Commercial facilities must meet the requirements for new construction and are not allowed to use some of the alternative requirements for alterations. (The different levels of compliance are discussed later in this appendix.) Some facilities could be considered both a commercial facility and a place of public accommodation. For example, if a commercial facility such as a car factory offers public tours, the path of the tour would then be a place of public accommodation. In addition, the way that the tour is conducted (by guided tour or written instructions, for example) would have to be accessible to persons with disabilities. The employee areas of the facility, however, would need to meet the requirements for commercial facilities. Because the requirements for public accommodation include procedures and policies, it is considered a slightly higher level of overall compliance than commercial facilities. However, the requirements in the *ADA Standards* that affect the actual spaces are similar.

Although almost all places of public activity are included in the definition of a place of public accommodation, there are some types of facilities that are not required to be compliant with the ADA. These include facilities that are owned and operated by religious entities, one- and two-family dwellings, private clubs, and certain government facilities. Those entities or facilities may not be completely exempt from compliance, however, if part of their facility is utilized as a place of public accommodation. For example, if a church rents part of its facility to a day care center during the week and the day care center is not operated by the church, the area that the day care center leases would be required to meet ADA requirements. (Although compliance is technically the day care center's responsibility, this assignment of responsibility may be modified in the landlord-tenant agreement. See Responsibility and Compliance later in this appendix.) Similarly, if part of a private residence is used for a business and it is usual for clients to come there for the operation of the business, the part of the residence that is used for the business would have to meet the requirements even though private residences are exempt from the ADA.

Conversely, an educational facility that is operated by a synagogue, for example, may not be required to conform to the ADA because of the exemption for religious entities. In some cases, it may be clear if a project needs to comply with ADA, whereas in other cases it may need further discussion with the client to determine if the space would be considered a public accommodation or a commercial facility, or if it qualifies for any exemptions. It may be wise to seek an opinion from the Access Board if a project is not clear. (See Appendix E.)

State and local government facilities are also required to be compliant with the ADA under Title II. They must meet the standards of new construction and alterations as well as provide access to all programs that are offered as part of their services. Originally, state and local governments had the choice of following either the *ADAAG* or the *Uniform Federal Accessibility Standards (UFAS)* in order to meet these requirements. However, the *2004 ADA–ABA Accessibility Guidelines* replaces these documents (as explained later).

> **✎Note**
>
> Transportation facilities such as bus stations, subway stations, and airports, must follow the *ADA Standards for Transportation Facilities*. These regulations were approved by the Department of Transportation (DOT) in 2006.

Federal buildings are not required to be compliant with the ADA. Instead, they must comply with the Architectural Barriers Act (ABA) for accessibility. A project for a federal agency or a federally funded project typically requires the use of the UFAS (or the new *ABA Standards*); however, other accessibility standards or guidelines may also apply. (See the section New ADA Standards below.) Federal facilities can include postal facilities, military structures, and other buildings and spaces owned by the federal government. In addition, residential building types owned or developed with federal funding may need to comply with the requirements of the Federal Housing Act (FHA). (See the inset titled *Accessibility Requirements Compared* on page 32.)

ORIGINAL *ADAAG*

The ADA uses guidelines that give designers specific design criteria for accessibility in all aspects of interior and architectural design. The original document is known as the *ADA Accessibility Guidelines (ADAAG)* as published in Appendix A of the Title III Regulations (28 CFR Part 36, revised July 1, 1994) by the Department of Justice (DOJ). First issued by the DOJ in 1991, this document is now referred to as the *1991 ADA Standards*. These standards apply to construction and alterations

✎Note

Differences in the technical and scoping requirements of the 2004 *ADA–ABA Accessibility Guidelines,* the 2003 ICC/ANSI standard, and the newest editions of the *IBC* are minimized because of collaboration between the Access Board, the ICC, and ANSI.

of places of public accommodation and commercial facilities. However, it is important to understand that the requirements in the standards are presented as either scoping requirements or technical requirements. Scoping requirements indicate how many accessible toilets, water fountains, doors, and so on must be included in a project. Technical requirements provide the specific requirements or dimensions that have to be met for the door, sink, millwork, and so on to be accessible. Many of these requirements are discussed throughout this book.

The original *ADAAG* also covers special occupancy sections including restaurants and cafeterias, medical care facilities, business and mercantile, libraries, transient lodging, and transportation facilities. These include both scoping and technical provisions that are specific to the building use. (See Chapter 2 for more information.) The appendix section of the *ADAAG* includes additional information to clarify the requirements and increase accessibility. This information is not mandatory. When required to use *ADAAG* in conjunction other accessibility standards, as well as the accessibility requirements in the building code, the highest level of accessibility should always be provided.

NEW ADA STANDARDS

✎Note

Revisions to the *ADA-ABA Accessibility Guidelines* made by the Access Board are enforceable only when approved by the Department of Justice, or other federal agency.

As mentioned in Chapter 1, the Access Board is responsible for revisions to the guidelines or standards that are used to implement the ADA. The Access Board continues to do research on how to provide for accessibility to the disabled. Once a proposed change is developed, it goes through a thorough process of review by government agencies and the public. In finalizing the proposed change, the Access Board also considers public and industry-related comments that have been submitted and the potential future cost implications of new technical requirements. Even after a change or addition has been finalized and issued by the Access Board, it is still not enforceable as part of the ADA until the DOJ (or another federal agency) approves it and incorporates it into the ADA regulation.

More recently, the Access Board has been working in conjunction with the International Code Council (ICC) and the American National Standards Institute (ANSI), as well as other individuals and organizations, to create a totally new document. The new guidelines update technical requirements, share technical criteria for both the ADA and the ABA, and create more consistency with the requirements of the building codes, such as the *International Building Code (IBC)*, and the ICC/ANSI accessibility standard *ICC/ANSI A117.1.* This revision includes a reorganized format, graphics, and numbering system. Many of the requirements remain the same as in the original *ADAAG*, but there are some differences.

In addition, new topics and accessibility categories have been added. (Refer to Figure 1.4 in Chapter 1.)

The Access Board completed and released the new *ADA–ABA Accessibility Guidelines* in 2004 and has it available on their Web site. Since then, these new guidelines have been adopted by most of the federal agencies, including the Department of Defense (DOD), General Services Administration (GSA) and the United States Postal Service (USPS) for use in the design of federal buildings and spaces under their departments, which can include federal office buildings, buildings owned or leased by the government, and post offices. These new guidelines as adopted by these federal agencies are referred to as the *ABA Standards*. (The *ABA Standards* refer to the ABA application and scoping chapters of the *ADA-ABA Accessibility Guidelines*.) The Department of Transportation (DOT) has also adopted the new guidelines for use in transportation facilities such as airports and train terminals. These standards are referred to as the *ADA Standards for Transportation Facilities*.

ADA-ABA ACCESSIBILITY GUIDELINES ENFORCEMENT

The *ADA–ABA Accessibility Guidelines* was first released by the Access Board in 2004. It combines guidelines for compliance with the federal ADA and the ABA legislation. The ADA and ABA now share the same technical requirements, but have separate application and scoping sections. Therefore, the extent to which the technical requirements are applied will vary depending on whether a project needs to meet ADA or ABA legislation. To be applicable, the governing federal agency has to formally adopt the revised guideline. The following agencies have adopted relevant portions of the *ADA–ABA Accessibility Guidelines* as the *ABA Standards* and the *2010 ADA Standards*.

- ❑ United States Postal Service (USPS)—*ABA Standards* effective October 1, 2005
- ❑ General Services Administration (GSA) — *ABA Standards* effective for construction and alterations that commence after May 8, 2006 and for leases entered into after August 7, 2006
- ❑ Department of Transportation (DOT) — *ABA Standards* effective November 29, 2006
- ❑ Department of Defense (DOD) — *ABA Standards* effective October 31, 2008
- ❑ Department of Justice (DOJ) — *2010 ADA Standards* effective for construction and alterations that commence on or after March 15, 2012. Either the original *ADAAG* (also known as the *1991 ADA Standards*) or the *2010 ADA Standards* can be used if that date is on or after September 15, 2010, and before March 15, 2012.

Note

The federal department of Housing and Urban Development (HUD) enforces Title II of the ADA when it relates to state and local public housing, housing assistance, and housing referrals. (See Chapter 1.) HUD plans to adopt the 2004 *ADA–ABA Accessibility Guidelines* for these types of facilities.

Note

Each standard-setting agency, such as the DOJ, GSA, HUD, and USPS, determines the specific date after which projects must meet the 2004 *ADA–ABA Accessibility Guidelines.*

In 2010, the DOJ, which enforces the ADA, adopted the *ADA–ABA Accessibility Guidelines* for places of public accommodation and commercial facilities. It is referred to as the *2010 ADA Standards* and includes the ADA application and scoping chapters of the guidelines. The DOJ set dates as to how long the original *ADAAG* (or *1991 ADA Standards*) can be used on projects and when the newly adopted *2010 ADA Standards* becomes mandatory for all projects under the ADA. Refer to the inset titled *ADA–ABA Accessibility Guidelines Enforcement* on the previous page for specific enforcement dates. Remember, the local code jurisdiction may also enforce certain accessibility requirements included in the *IBC* and the *ICC/ANSI A117.1*, or their own adopted accessibility standard. Interior projects should be designed to meet all of the requirements using the strictest criteria when appropriate.

It is important to keep up-to-date with changes made to the *ADA–ABA Accessibility Guidelines* and/or the *ADA Standards* to know which requirements apply to a project. The most current information can be found on the Web sites of the Access Board (www.access-board.gov) and the DOJ (www.usdoj.gov). The Access Board also provides email updates upon request, which includes ongoing information about proposed changes to the *ADA Standards*.

LEVEL OF COMPLIANCE

Depending on whether a project involves new construction, an alteration of an existing space, or minor cosmetic changes to an existing facility, the ADA law provides for different levels of required compliance with the *ADA Standards*. Generally, the requirements for new construction are most stringent. When an existing building is being altered for renovation or for accessibility, some alternative solutions are allowed. Below is a general overview of the varying levels of compliance for each type of construction project. The level of accessibility that a project must meet should be established early in the design process.

New Construction

Note

New construction must comply with the *new construction* requirements of the ADA almost without exception.

In most new construction, all aspects of the design will have to comply with the ADA requirements. A project being built from the ground up or a completely new tenant space within an existing building, for example, would both be considered new construction, according to the ADA.

However, even in new construction there are some aspects of a space that may not have to meet the ADA requirements, such as areas used only by employees. For example, the shelves and storage cabinets in a teachers' workroom in an elementary school (used only by teachers) would not all have to be within the reach ranges described by the guidelines. According to the employment sections of the ADA, however, if a disabled teacher was hired, then areas used by that teacher would need to be modified. Other miscellaneous rooms, such as an electrical closet or mechanical room, typically do not have to comply, either.

For areas accessible to the public, the minimum requirement is that everyone must be able to "approach, enter, and exit" each room. For example, even hotel rooms and offices that are not designated as accessible rooms should provide the clearances at the door to allow a visitor in a wheelchair to open the door from the corridor and from inside the room. In areas that will be used by the general public and employees, such as exhibits in a museum, full accessibility must be provided. And in most projects, it is appropriate to make most spaces, even shared work areas, completely accessible according to the *ADA Standards*.

Alterations

In the case of an alteration or renovation to an existing building, rules for compliance are more complex. Changes made to the area must conform to the *ADA Standards* unless existing conditions make compliance impossible. In addition, alterations to one area may require additional changes in adjacent areas. For example, if a "primary function" space, such as a small auditorium in a high school, is altered and made more accessible, the ADA may require that the path to the primary function area and certain support areas, such as the corridors to the auditorium and to the bathrooms, drinking fountains, and telephones, be altered to provide a similar level of accessibility.

> **Note**
>
> An alteration to an existing building must comply with the *ADA Standards* to the *maximum extent possible.* In some cases, an alteration will not have to meet the guideline requirements (e.g., if the change is structurally unfeasible or would cause an unsafe condition).

However, the ADA does provide some options. If it can be proven that the cost of alterations to support areas and the path of travel to them exceeds 20 percent of the cost of the alteration of the primary function area, those changes would not be required. The 20 percent rule may allow alterations for accessibility to be done in increments, but it is not intended to allow building owners to make a series of small alterations to an existing building in order to avoid a more costly accessibility update. To prevent this, the law specifies that the total cost of alterations over a 3-year period may be reviewed in determining if an appropriate allotment of cost has been spent on accessibility updates.

Existing Facilities

Unlike building codes, the ADA also applies to existing buildings even if no alterations or renovations are planned. Owners may seek the advice of a design professional concerning how the ADA applies to them. When the ADA law was originally passed, it allowed a 2-year period for the removal of "architectural barriers" from existing buildings. The intent was to allow building owners to begin to make changes to their existing buildings, such as adding ramps, widening doors, adding power-assisted doors, and eliminating other existing barriers, to bring their buildings into compliance with the law and make them accessible.

Since the initial 2-year period has ended, owners are now expected to have evaluated their facilities and to have removed the architectural barriers that could keep persons with disabilities from using their buildings. Now legal suits can be brought against the owner of a facility that is not compliant. Legal suits are typically filed by persons with disabilities who feel that the building conditions prevent them from gaining services. Existing facilities that were made accessible according to the *1991 ADA Standards* will not be expected to be updated to the *2010 ADA Standards* until some type of alteration is made to the building or space.

There are some options for accommodating the needs of persons with disabilities without making physical changes. However, conforming to ADA regulations should be pursued to the extent of "readily achievable." An accessible path to the building from the exterior, an accessible entrance into the building, an accessible path within the building (to the goods and services), accessible toilet facilities, and then direct access to the actual goods and services is the order of priority that the ADA sets for making changes to an existing building. For commercial facilities, those areas that are required to be accessible should meet the same level of accessibility as "readily achievable." (Additional exceptions are allowed for existing buildings that are deemed historic. See Appendix C for more information.)

To the Maximum Extent Feasible

For all project types, the law requires that an attempt to meet the *ADA Standards* be made "to the maximum extent feasible." If the alterations needed to meet the requirements are not "readily achievable," both structurally and financially, the law allows for exceptions when the alteration could be considered an "undue burden." One example might be that, during the renovation of an auditorium, it is determined that an assistive listening system, although required by *ADA Standards*, exceeds the budget for this phase of the project and is disproportionate to the profit that the owner receives from the auditorium.

Many times these burdens are hard to determine. They are usually decided on a case-by-case basis by the regulating authority or the courts. When determining whether the cost of renovation is not "readily achievable," the financial resources of the facility, the number of employees, and the type of facility are taken into account. The decision to limit the scope of accessibility should be determined by the owner and should be primarily a financial decision, not a design decision.

✎ Note

Existing facilities must be modified as *readily achievable* to meet the requirements of the ADA.

It is typically the owner's responsibility to provide the legal documentation to support this decision.

Another way that the government encourages building owners to make their existing facilities accessible is through tax incentives. Small businesses, in particular, may receive tax credits for architectural and system modifications for accessibility purposes. Other provisions allow expenditures to be treated as a tax deduction instead of as a capital expenditure. Although not within the scope of this book or within the scope of typical design services, designers should be aware that these incentives are available.

REGULATION AND ENFORCEMENT

Often projects must also meet state accessibility requirements as well as accessibility requirements included in the building codes. This may result in conflicts between the different requirements. As mentioned in Chapter 1, the Access Board, the American National Standards Institute (ANSI), and the International Code Council (ICC) continue to work to coordinate the requirements to minimize differences. However, slight differences still exist. In addition, a jurisdiction may be using a different edition of a code or ICC/ANSI standard, including a more current edition which has been updated since the 2004 *ABA-ADA Accessibility Guidelines* were completed. The NFPA codes also include accessibility requirements. In all cases, the highest level of accessibility should be provided. For accessibility requirements included in various codes and standards, what is needed for compliance can be clarified as part of the code review process, but the ADA process is different.

Because the ADA is a civil rights law, it is enforced by the judicial system and through litigation. Currently, enforcement occurs either as a result of a private suit filed by an individual or by legal action taken by a federal agency in support of a discrimination claim. In most cases, there is no local agency that will review a project for compliance with the ADA requirements. The ADA allows states to develop an individual accessibility standard and submit it for review by the DOJ for certification. If the standard is found to sufficiently address accessibility issues consistent with the *ADAAG*, the new standard could be considered *certified*. Projects can then be reviewed by local building officials for accessibility compliance. The *Washington State Regulations for Barrier-Free Facilities*, the *Texas Accessibility Standards*, the Maine Human Rights Act as implemented by the *Maine Accessibility Regulations*, and the *Florida Accessibility Code for Building* are state accessibility standards that have been certified by the DOJ to be consistent with the original *ADAAG*. Others may currently be under review as well. However, as of the printing of this book, no state has received certification

> **⬒Note**
>
> Regulation and enforcement of the *ADA Standards* in design projects is different than the enforcement of code requirements.

⬛Note

When the use of the *2010 ADA Standards* becomes mandatory in March of 2012, any state accessibility document that has been certified by the DOJ will become out-of-date.

according to the *2010 ADA Standards*. This process does not guarantee that the project is in complete compliance with the ADA and its guidelines/standards. Should legal action be taken, the certified document may not be enough to prove compliance.

In many cases, compliance with the ADA requirements will be clearly defined. If not, clarification of specific issues of concern can be requested from the Access Board. In addition, each state now has a central contact to assist with technical questions. A list of these state code contacts can be found on the Access Board's Web site. Projects can also be sent to the DOJ or the Access Board for review, but this process may not be practical except for large projects.

RESPONSIBILITY FOR COMPLIANCE

⬛Note

The Access Board, ICC, and NFPA have all created comparison documents of the accessibility requirements found in each of their respective publications. These documents can be found on their Web sites.

It makes sense that the client, as the owner or tenant of a building, is responsible for compliance with the ADA in their space or building. Even in the design process, they can make decisions about issues that affect the level of accessibility. For example, the client sometimes limits the scope of work because of the budget: They decide what will be changed within an existing building or how much will be constructed. The owner or tenant also maintains the space after construction. All of this affects the accessibility of the building or space.

Typically, the owner of a building and a tenant within a building are responsible for accessibility of the parts of a space that are under their individual control. For example, an accessible entrance into a building would be the owner's responsibility, but the accessibility of a work area within the tenant space would be the tenant's responsibility. The specific responsibilities between owner and tenant can sometimes be allocated by the lease. For example, the lease may state that the owner is responsible for using accessible hardware on tenant corridor doors. However, if a part of the facility is noncompliant, both may be held responsible by law. (But remember, owners or tenants that are a religious entity or a private club may not be required to comply with the ADA.)

⬛Note

Often, additional accessibility requirements, as found in the building codes and the ICC/ANSI standard, will apply to a project. It will depend on the code jurisdiction.

In addition, recent legal cases between the DOJ and design firms suggest that the design professional and potentially others involved in the construction process may hold some legal responsibility for compliance with the ADA. It may be reasonable to assume that the designer is familiar with the ADA requirements in order to apply them to the design. However, the issue of responsibility under the law is sometimes unclear. There have been legal actions that have named the designer as the responsible party for compliance with the ADA. What is clear is that the need for compliance is a joint effort between the client and the designer throughout the development of a design project. Documenting all decisions in drawings and other written documents is important. The clarity of the ADA is still being discovered through the judicial system and the subsequent modifications to the ADA and its requirements.

If a project can be considered a public accommodation or a commercial facility, then the requirements in the *ADA Standards* will apply to the project. (See the exceptions mentioned earlier.) In addition, state and local code jurisdictions may have other accessibility requirements that need to be considered. In cases where the requirements seem to conflict, the requirement that provides for a greater degree of accessibility should be used. If necessary, an opinion from the proper jurisdiction or agency is advisable.

◀Note

Since the level of enforcement and responsibility for compliance with the ADA requirements continue to be developed through litigation, it is important to keep up-to-date by reading articles in professional journals and visiting the DOJ Web site.

APPENDIX B

SUSTAINABILITY

Traditionally, codes and standards concentrated on making a building safe. The goal was to protect the health, safety, and welfare of the building occupant. As a result, many of the code requirements primarily regulated the ways in which the environment affects buildings, protecting occupants from storms, earthquakes, fires, and the like. With the incorporation of sustainability and green practices into the code process, the code requirements have come full circle and now also address how buildings affect the environment. This ultimately makes the building healthier, providing additional benefits to the building occupant.

Codes and standards that address green requirements are relatively new. In the early 1990s, when designers began incorporating more "green" practices and products into their projects, there were very few guidelines. As the desire for sustainable buildings and interiors, from both designers and owners, increased in the market, the industry recognized a need to monitor, track, and verify sustainable projects. Green rating systems, such as Leadership in Energy and Environmental Design (LEED) and Green Globes, are what filled this void. (Green rating systems are explained more next.) They also helped set the foundation for the development of the more recent sustainability codes and standards.

Over time, certain green requirements were incorporated into the codes. For example, when the *International Plumbing Code* was first published in 1995, it included information on water-efficient fixtures and, more recently, waterless urinals. Later in 1998, the *International Energy Conservation Code* was developed. It was the first code document that addressed sustainability more comprehensively, covering energy efficiency throughout the building. It was accompanied by the energy standards *ASHRAE/IESNA 90.1, Energy Standard for Buildings Except Low-Rise Residential Buildings* and *ASHRAE/IESNA 90.2, Energy-Efficient Design of New Low-Rise Residential Buildings.*

Several green codes and standards are now available. For commercial projects there is the *International Green Construction Code (IGCC)* as well as the standard *ASHRAE/USGBC/IES 189.1, Standard for the Design of High-Performance Green Buildings Except Low-Rise Residential Buildings.* Residential projects can use *ICC 700, National*

Note

In the past, the codes and standards concentrated on regulating the ways in which the environment affects buildings. The primary function of the green codes and standards, on the other hand, is to address how buildings affect the environment.

Note

The use of sustainable practices and products must not overshadow the safety of the building occupants. For example, water conservation cannot hinder the effectiveness of fire sprinklers and certain building materials may require fire/flame retardants to meet specific fire ratings.

Note

See Chapter 1 for information on current sustainable codes, standards, and federal regulations. The ICC Web site also includes a section dedicated to green building, providing a wide variety of information and resources. Go to www .ICCsafe.org/green.

Green Building Standard (NGBS). (These documents and many of their requirements have been discussed throughout this book. See Chapter 1 and the Sustainability Considerations sections within each chapter.) As these sustainability documents are adopted by code jurisdictions, they will need to be used in conjunction with the many other codes and standards discussed throughout this book. If a jurisdiction requires the use of a green rating system, the requirements between the codes and the rating system would need to be coordinated within the design.

However, when using the various code documents and green rating systems, it is important to realize that green design and the sustainability industry continues to evolve. For example, the term "green" is often used by both designers and manufacturers to describe many different "sustainable" aspects of a building or product. These terms are often used interchangeably, yet they are very different. *Green* can describe one attribute or multiple characteristics, such as an "energy-efficient building" and a "low-emitting finish." If something is to be considered *sustainable*, it must meet three specific benchmarks: environmental responsibility, economic strength, and social responsibility. (See the section Definitions in the Introduction.)

As the industry works toward true sustainability, new concepts and new tools continue to be developed. The traditional standard that measures a single attribute (e.g., toxicity) will not provide a comprehensive picture of a sustainable product. Instead, more comprehensive multiple-attribute standards are required. (See the section Sustainable Standards and Certification Programs later in this appendix.) More detailed and standardized documentation to allow comparison of various products is also necessary. Examples include life cycle analysis and environmental product declarations (as explained later in this appendix).

This appendix summarizes many of the interior-related green resources available. It begins with a discussion of green rating systems and goes on to explain sustainable product standards, product certification programs, life cycle analysis, product declarations, and other sustainability tools.

> **✎Note**
>
> The sustainable-related catch phrase "triple bottom line" refers to meeting the following three benchmarks: environmental responsibility, economic strength, and social responsibility. Together, these are considered the primary aspects of sustainability.

> **✎Note**
>
> The "three Rs of sustainability" consist of reducing, reusing, and recycling.

GREEN RATING SYSTEMS

The most recognized green rating systems include Leadership in Energy and Environmental Design (LEED) and Green Globes. They are explained in more detail below. Other rating systems are available as well. For example, BRE Environmental Assessment Method (BREEAM), which was originally developed in the United Kingdom, is used more often in other parts of the world. Two rating systems specifically for residential homes that are used more regionally in the United States include GreenPoints Rated by Build It Green, an organization based in California, and EarthCraft House by Greater Atlanta Home Builders Association and Southface. (See Appendix D.)

The rating systems consist of credits and/or points that must be obtained. Specific benchmarks must be met as the building is being designed and constructed. Some of these benchmarks are found within the specification of the rating system, others require the use of specific industry standards or programs. The selection of sustainable building and interior products that are efficient, durable, renewable, and/or recycled is also critical. There are various tools to assist with product selection. These include product certifications, life cycle analysis, and product declarations as well as various industry directories and databases. (These tools are explained later in this appendix.)

There are multiple states, local jurisdictions, and federal agencies that require LEED or Green Globes certification for certain building projects or provide incentives when they are followed. For example, the city of Boston requires new city-owned buildings, including additions and major renovations, to achieve LEED Silver certification and all private buildings over 50,000 square feet to be LEED certified; the state of Washington requires all new state agencies, state colleges/universities, and K–12 school construction and major renovation projects over 25,000 square feet to achieve LEED Silver certification; and the U.S. Department of Veteran Affairs has been using Green Globes to certify its existing medical centers. Contact the local jurisdiction to determine what is required and how to document the information for code review. (See Chapter 10.)

LEED

The Leadership in Energy and Environmental Design (LEED) is a green rating system developed by the U.S. Green Building Council (USGBC). LEED provides a framework for assessing and rating a building's performance and its overall environmental impact. Items that are identified and measured include "energy savings, water efficiency, CO_2 emissions reduction, improved indoor environmental quality, and stewardship of resources and sensitivity to their impacts."

First launched in 2000, LEED was originally developed primarily for the construction of new buildings; multiple programs are now available. Current programs include:

❑ *LEED for New Construction and Major Renovations (LEED-NC)*: used for new construction and major renovations of commercial and institutional buildings; a combination of LEED-CS and LEED-CI, but more comprehensive

❑ *LEED for Core and Shell (LEED-CS)*: used for new construction of the building core and shell for commercial buildings, including the structure, envelope, and building systems

❏ *LEED for Commercial Interiors (LEED-CI)*: addresses the specifics of tenant spaces and the systems within those spaces primarily for commercial and institutional buildings

❏ *LEED for Existing Buildings: Operations & Maintenance (LEED-EB: O&M)*: used for the sustainable operation and upgrades of existing buildings that do not require major renovations

❏ *LEED for Health Care (LEED-HC)*: addresses the distinctive needs of the health care market and can be used for inpatient or outpatient and long-term care facilities, medical offices, assisted living facilities, and medical education and research centers

❏ *LEED for Schools*: addresses the specific need of school spaces

❏ *LEED for Retail*: used for the design and construction of retail spaces

❏ *LEED for Homes*: used for design and construction of residences

❏ *LEED for Neighborhood Development*: integrates the principles of smart growth, urbanism, and green building

The USGBC continues to update their programs and develop new ones. They are currently developing a *Portfolio Program* which will allow building owners and organizations to submit several buildings for certification at once.

Depending on the program selected, buildings are awarded credits for different areas of design. For example, the interiors program (LEED-CI) addresses the selection of sustainable material in tenant spaces, efficiency of water use, energy efficiency of lighting and lighting controls, resource utilization for interior building systems and furnishings, and indoor environmental quality. In some cases an existing sustainability standard, such as *ASHRAE/IESNA 90.1* or ENERGY STAR, is used as the benchmark. When the minimum standards in each category are surpassed, points are earned and the total is used to classify a building into one of four levels: Certified, Silver, Gold, and Platinum.

In 2009, the USGBC introduced a significant update. Known as LEED v3, this new version affects all commercial and institutional building programs. The updated programs, collectively called LEED 2009, include advancements to the existing rating system, incorporating new technology and giving environment issues more weight within the point system of each program. The credits across the different programs were harmonized and aligned so that each program now operates on a standardized 100-point scale with additional points available for "Regional Priority" (depending on the location of the building in the United States) and "Innovation." Going forward, the USGBC plans to update the programs on a more regular development schedule, most likely every 2 to 3 years. (The USGBC is now ANSI accredited so future editions may go through the ANS consensus process. See Chapter 1.)

☝Note

The USGBC assisted in the development of *ASHRAE/ IESNA 189.1*. (See Chapter 1.) This new standard addresses the same main topic areas as the LEED rating systems. In some instances a LEED program will reference this standard.

☝Note

LEED certification can be granted for just the core and shell of the building. In that case, lease spaces that are built out after the initial construction may not be required to meet the same level. However, if it is intended that the interior project be LEED certified as well, then sustainable practices must be incorporated into the design.

☝Note

There is some overlap between the various LEED programs. LEED v3 updated the online tool so that, in addition to managing the application of a specific program, the details of a new project can be entered and it will indicate which program is the best fit.

Another major part of the 2009 update was the introduction of a new building certification model. The USGBC created the Green Building Certification Institute (GBCI) specifically to take over the management of LEED building certification, providing third-party review and verification of LEED projects. The GBCI began with a network of 10 certification bodies that included organizations such as Underwriters Laboratories, NSF International, and Intertek. However, more recently, the GBCI started to phase out the use of the certification bodies and is now directly performing these reviews.

Green Globes

The Green Globes™ rating system originated in Canada in 1996 under the name BREEAM Canada for Existing Buildings. In 2000, when it became an online assessment and rating tool, the name changed to Green Globes. In the United States, Green Globes is owned and operated by Green Building Initiative (GBI). The system can be used for new and existing buildings of all types and includes two programs:

❏ Green Globes for New Construction (or, in Canada, known as Design of New Buildings or Significant Renovation)

❏ Green Globes for Continual Improvement of Existing Buildings (or, in Canada, known as Management and Operation of Existing Buildings)

These programs are based on a 1000-point scale in multiple categories that include energy, indoor environment, site, water, resources, emissions, and project/environmental management.

Unlike LEED, where a specific program needs to be selected based on the type of project (e.g., new, existing, tenant space), Green Globes is more adaptable to a variety of projects. Using a questionnaire-driven assessment, project information is entered online and a rating system is customized to the project. The system is interactive, so that it provides instant feedback as information is entered with advice and resources for improvements where required. All data submitted online is verified by a third party. A preliminary verification is conducted using construction documents, energy and life cycle modeling, as well as other methods and a final verification is made by a site inspection after construction is complete. An approved building can receive a final rating of one, two, three, or four globes.

Green Globes is recognized by many jurisdictions and in some cases may be required as part of the permitting process. In 2005, GBI became the first green building organization to be accredited as a standards developer by the American National Standards Institute (ANSI) in order to establish Green Globes as an official ANS standard. (See Chapter 1 for more information on ANSI.) Completed in March 2010, the standard is titled *ANSI/GBI 01-2010, Green Building Assessment*

⬛Note

Green Globes originated in Canada. When it came to the United States in 2004, the two green rating programs diverged. (www.thegbi.org is the United States Web site and www.greenglobes.com is the Canadian Web site.)

⬛Note

Some of the jurisdictions that have instituted green building programs have used the Green Globes rating system as a model. Some jurisdictions may adopt the new Green Globes standard in the future.

Protocol for Commercial Buildings. This standard includes seven areas of assessment, minimum achievement levels, a water consumption calculator, and the use of Life Cycle Assessments (LCAs, as described later in this appendix). Once a pilot program is completed, Green Globes will be updated to incorporate this standard.

ISO STANDARDS FOR SUSTAINABILITY

The International Standards Association (ISO) is the world's largest developer of voluntary international standards for business, government, and society. Similar to the American National Standards Institute (ANSI) as explained in Chapter 1, ISO establishes procedures which are used by other standards-developing organizations. (See the inset titled *Codes and Standards Changes* on page 14.) Some of ISO's approval procedures are in direct conflict with the ANS process. As a result, ISO standards are not widely used in the United States. However, this is starting to change. (See the inset titled *Codes and Standards in Other Countries* on page 26.) A few are referenced in the model codes.

More recently, ISO has taken the lead in developing sustainability standards. As a result, more standards are being accepted. Some of the ISO standards are specifically to evaluate building products and materials. Other ISO standards assist manufacturers to become more sustainable by setting requirements for environmental management systems and product evaluation. The latter, collectively known as the 14000 series of standards, include:

❏ ISO 14020, Environmental Labels and Declarations—General Principles

❏ ISO 14021, Environmental Labels and Declarations—Self-declared Environmental Claims (Type II Environmental Labeling)

❏ ISO 14024, Environmental Labels and Declarations—Type I Environmental Labeling—Principles and Procedures

❏ ISO 14025, Environmental Labels and Declarations—Type III Environmental Declarations—Principles and Procedures

❏ ISO 14040, Environmental Management—Life Cycle Assessment—Principles and Framework

❏ SO 14044, Environmental Management—Life Cycle Assessment—Requirements and Guidelines (similar to ASTM E1991)

Through these standards, ISO identifies and defines three types of environmental labels, or eco-labels (seals of approval). Type I (*ISO 14024*) is the multi-criteria label which provides third-party verification but does not require a life cycle assessment (LCA). Sustainable product standards and product certification programs fall in this category. Type II (*ISO 14021*) is a self-declared claim made by the manufacturer and does not require a third-party verification or LCA and is not very reliable. Type III (*ISO 14025*) is the strictest with third-party verification, use of an LCA for environmental impacts, and other product performance data. Environment Product Declarations (EPD) are considered a Type III eco-label.

For more information on ISO standards, go to www.iso.org.

SUSTAINABLE STANDARDS AND CERTIFICATION PROGRAMS

Sustainable product standards (SPSs) are similar to other standards used by the codes. However, SPSs are used specifically to determine green and/or sustainable characteristics of building materials and products. Although fairly new to the industry, there are quite a few SPSs now available. Many were discussed in Chapter 1 and within the various Sustainability Considerations sections included throughout this book.

Before reliable SPSs could be developed, however, guiding parameters needed to be created. Internationally, the International Organization for Standardization (ISO) has led the way in creating guiding standards. (See the inset titled *ISO Standards for Sustainability* on the previous page.) In the United States, ASTM International (see Chapter 1) has assumed a leadership role in developing standards related to sustainable development. For example, *ASTM E2432, Standard Guide for General Principles of Sustainability Relative to Buildings* defines in detail the three primary aspects of sustainability as environmental, social, and economic and emphasizes the continual improvement of standards.

Various standards organizations (see Chapter 1), trade associations, and other interested parties have used these guiding standards from ASTM and ISO as they develop new SPSs. These SPSs can be used in a number of ways. They can be:

❏ Referenced by the sustainability codes and standards. A common example is the standard *NSF/ANSI 140, Sustainable Carpet Assessment* (see Chapter 9).

❏ Used by the industry as common practice in the specification of green products, such as *MTS 2006:4, SMART Sustainable Building Product Standard* (see Chapter 5).

❏ Included as part of a green rating system, as a way to benchmark a particular requirement for a LEED credit.

❏ Used as a benchmark for a specific product certification program.

Product certification programs are used to determine the validity of the information supplied by the manufacturer. They were developed in response to "greenwashing." When sustainable building design and the use of green products first began, many manufacturers started advertising their products' eco-friendliness. There ended up being a wide variety of environmental claims with little to back them up. It also made it difficult to compare similar products since there was no consistency in the information. Product

Note

Originally, many of the sustainability standards for finishes and furniture concentrated on emission requirements and VOC criteria. Newer standards are more comprehensive and measure many sustainable attributes.

Note

USGBC approves certain product certification programs as an alternative compliance path. For example, FloorScore® can be used to meet LEED credit EQ4.3 Low-Emitting Materials: Carpet Systems.

Note

Underwriters Laboratories (UL) recently created a sister company, UL Environments™, specifically to provide third-party certification for a variety of sustainability programs. NSF International and ASTM International are other standards organizations that provide independent third-party testing.

certification programs helped solve this problem. In addition, they are typically verified by an independent group (i.e., third-party certifiers) which provides additional authenticity. Examples of third-party certifiers include Scientific Certification Systems (SCS), UL Environments, ASTM International, and NSF International.

Examples of product certification programs include the Forestry Stewardship Council (FSC) program for wood (see Chapter 3) and the Carpet and Rug Institute's Green Label program for carpet, cushions, and adhesives (see Chapter 9). *FSC Certified*, for instance, uses the standard *FSC Principles and Criteria* to evaluate wood forests. The wood from an approved forest is tracked as it is shipped, manufactured, distributed, and sold. Both the *Green Label* and *Green Label Plus* certification programs use the standard *NSF/ANSI 140*. The federal government has two certification programs as well called ENERGY STAR and WaterSense, which use standards set by the U.S. Environmental Protection Agency (EPA). (See the inset titled *Federal Sustainability Certification* on the next page.)

Manufacturers can have their products tested using these SPSs and, in most cases, use third-party certifiers to verify that they meet a specific certification program. Often this information is labeled directly on the product. "FSC Certified," for instance, may be stamped directly on a piece of lumber. These types of labels are known as *eco-labels*. Other eco-label examples include the GreenSeal mark, SMaRT Certified, and *level* conformance mark. The manufacturer typically includes this information on finish samples and product literature as well. For example, the information for the upholstery sample in Figure 9.15 in Chapter 9 indicates that it is certified to meet *GREENGUARD* and *GREENGUARD Children & Schools*SM. Many of the third-party certifiers or the creators of the certification programs will also maintain a database of approved product, which can be accessed by the Internet.

Be aware, however, that there are different levels of product certification programs. First of all, the scope of the program can range from a single product attribute, such as its recycled content or water conservation, to a multiple-attribute focus. Multiple-attribute examples may include toxicity of chemicals and materials, types of energy used, water quality, conservation of natural resources, and recovery and recycling of materials. More comprehensive certification programs concentrate on the entire life cycle of the product and incorporate manufacturer responsibility as well. (Life Cycle Assessments are discussed next.) The second thing to consider is the transparency of information. Some organizations are creating their own certification programs and self-testing products using these program. This may not create as reliable of a process as those organizations that include input from multiple participants and third-party certification.

✎Note

Not all product certification programs are created equal. For example, McDonough Baurngart Design Chemistry (MBDC), which created a certification program known as MBDC Cradle to Cradle, or simply C2C, is one of the few certification programs that are not third-party verified.

✎Note

The EPA currently has two sustainable certification programs: ENERGY STAR and WaterSenseSM. The EPA also has an entire portion of their Web site dedicated to sustainability programs and partnerships (see www.epa.gov/sustainability/).

FEDERAL SUSTAINABILITY CERTIFICATIONS

Some of the first sustainable product certification programs originated with the federal government. ENERGY STAR® was developed by the U.S. Environmental Protection Agency (EPA) in 1992. (See also Chapter 8.) It sets a benchmark for electrical equipment and appliances. Generally, a product will earn an ENERGY STAR label if it uses 20 to 30 percent less energy than the required federal standard. Depending on the type of product, other criteria are required as well and might include maximum power consumption when a unit is turned on, voltage tolerances, sleep mode options, and so forth. In the past, ENERGY STAR was a self-certifying specification where each manufacturer was responsible for testing its own products. However, beginning in 2010, the EPA started verifying all manufacturer reports and requiring independent laboratories to confirm the test results. Many countries outside the United States also use the ENERGY STAR program and label. Some are based on the EPA's criteria while other countries use additional benchmarks.

In 2007, the EPA introduced WaterSense[SM] which is a program that emphasizes water-efficient products and services. Products are tested to ensure sustainable, efficient water use while maintaining a high level of user satisfaction based on several industry standards. WaterSense products are independently tested and certified to meet the criteria in the WaterSense specification for that product as determined by the EPA. The EPA has licensed certain testing laboratories, such as NSF International and Underwriters Laboratories (UL), to do the testing. (The ICC Evaluation Services is also approved to certify products.) If a product passes the specifications set by the EPA, it is considered certified and is allowed to use the WaterSense label. The approved product is also added to the EPA's comprehensive database. A product search can be done at www.epa.gov/watersense/. Example products include high-efficiency toilets and urinals, lavatory faucets and accessories, and showerheads. New specifications for other products are also in development.

More recently, the EPA expanded the ENERGY STAR and WaterSense programs to include certification of new single-family homes. For example, as of January 2011, to receive an ENERGY STAR home label, the energy efficiency of the home must exceed the 2009 *International Energy Conservation Code* by 20 percent. A WaterSense home must follow certain EPA guidelines to receive a label. Upon completion, the home undergoes a certification process similar to that of a green rating system.

LIFE CYCLE ASSESSMENTS

Life Cycle Assessments (LCAs) were developed to provide a more comprehensive view of a sustainable product. It is the assessment of the environmental impact of a given product throughout its lifespan, from the earliest stages of raw material extraction to what happens to it at the end of its life—often coined "Cradle to Grave" or, if more comprehensive, "Cradle to Cradle." An assessment typically includes information on the raw material production, manufacture, distribution, use, and disposal (including all intervening steps).

Most of the sustainable product standards (SPSs) and product certification programs discussed above measure one or more environmental claims. This may indicate the green characteristic of the product or building material. However, in most cases it does not cover a product's overall sustainability. This might provide a benchmark to compare similar products, but it does not take into consideration many other factors; the product may be environmentally harmful in other ways. For example, a product might be made from sustainably harvested wood, but requires shipment over a long distance to the facility; or products are typically tested for the emissions of VOCs, but other semi-volatile compounds, such as phthalates (found in PVC plastics) or halogenated flame retardants, are not taken into consideration. LCAs, on the other hand, measure a wide variety of information. The trend is to incorporate LCAs into more standards and certification programs as well as into green rating systems. In some cases, the LCA incorporates an SPS.

A full product LCA includes 12 environmental impacts as defined by the EPA: global warming, acid rain, water pollution, fossil fuel depletion, indoor air quality, habitat alteration, water use, ambient air pollution, ecological toxicity, human health, ozone depletion, and smog. Currently, there are three recognized standards for measuring the LCA of a product. *ASTM E1991, Standard Guide for Environmental Life Cycle Assessment (LCA) of Building Materials/Products* describes the framework for life cycle analysis rather than the actual techniques in detail. Since an LCA can vary greatly depending on the product and its intended use, additional standards are necessary. The LCA-related standards most widely used are from International Organization for Standardization (ISO): *ISO 14040* and *ISO 14044.* (See the inset *ISO Standards for Sustainability* on page 474.)

LCAs can be used to analyze and optimize the environmental performance of a single product or that of a company. They are typically developed by the manufacturer. Because of the many facets included, software must be used to collect and capture the information. (Manufacturers either use available LCA software or develop their own.) The LCA data is used by the manufacturer internally as a tool to monitor and improve their processes and to market their sustainable practices and products. LCAs are typically available upon request from the manufacturer. Certain LCAs are also available on the Internet in databases such as BEES (Building for Environment and Economic Stability). (See the section Additional Tools later in this appendix.)

Green rating systems are starting to incorporate LCAs. For example, some LEED programs may allow an additional point for conducting an LCA on structural and envelope assemblies; additional interior-related LCAs may be incorporated in the future. Green Globes programs encourage the use of LCAs by offering education credits and providing a software tool. LCAs are also typically required when using the performance option in the sustainability codes and standards. *ASHRAE 189.1*, for instance, includes details for creating an LCA report that must be reviewed by a third party and submitted to the code official as part of the construction documents. Other specific LCA requirements for a manufacturer and/or a product can be included in the specifications of an interior project.

ENVIRONMENTAL PRODUCT DECLARATIONS

An Environmental Product Declaration (EPD) takes Life Cycle Assessment (LCA) and product certification to another level. While an LCA evaluates the environmental impact of a product or company, an EPD includes all the data of an LCA as well as data pertinent to human health, mechanics, and safety. An EPD provides a much higher level of detail and product information with more analysis, transparency, and disclosure of information. More importantly, an EPA must be verified by a third party. Although typically required in a product certification, it is not required for an LCA.

The criteria typically used by manufacturers to develop EPDs are based on standard *ISO 14025* by the International Standards Association (ISO). (See the inset *ISO Standards for Sustainability* on page 474.) More recently, ISO released an additional standard on EPDs titled *ISO 21930, Environmental Product Declarations (EPD) for Building Products*. For a particular product category (e.g. carpet, seating, textiles), Product Criteria Rules (PCRs) are created which all manufacturers must use so that there is consistent data, calculations, and methodologies between similar products. For example, performance information can include environmental impacts, life cycle costs, mechanical resistance, energy efficiency and heat resistance, safety in use, and protection against noise, however, the specific information supplied will vary based on the product category.

An EPD will typically include the manufacturer's LCA information as well as any product certifications the item has passed. The goal of an EPD is to be able to review comparable information on the sustainability and environmental performance of similar products in order to choose the least burdensome—in order to determine what has been coined as an Environmentally Preferable Product (EPP). Manufacturers are beginning to publish EPDs; however, they are fairly new to the industry and may not always be readily available. Similar to material safety data sheets, they should be available upon request or found on the manufacturer's Web site.

☞Note

Environmental Product Declarations were first used in the European Union and Japan. The Green Standard has led the way in instituting an EPD system to support manufacturers in the United States and is developing an interactive software called Gaia Product Profile.

☞Note

Eco-efficiency analysis (EEA) is another tool used to measure and evaluate products. Unlike LCAs, which concentrate on the environmental impacts, EEA also addresses the economic impacts. This tool was developed by NSF International.

ADDITIONAL TOOLS

In addition to the various items discussed above, there are other tools in the industry that can be helpful when using sustainable products and practices for interior projects. Some of these tools are referenced in the codes and include software which helps measure building-related benchmarks. Others are comprehensive lists developed by various sources to help locate green products. Each has their own system of gathering and/or presenting information and may include some or all of the items discussed in this appendix. A few of these resources are briefly explained as follows:

❏ *Building for Environment and Economic Sustainability (BEES):* Developed by the National Institute of Standards and Technology (NIST) Building and Fire Research Laboratory (BFRL), it is software that can be used to help select building products that are cost-effective and environmentally preferable. All products listed are evaluated using the life cycle assessment approach. (The software can be downloaded at no charge from www.bfrl.nist.gov.)

❏ *Pharos Project:* A database developed by Healthy Building Network which presents product information in a graphic wheel format, allowing a quick evaluation of product data and benchmarks against key health, environmental, and social impacts. Also provided are product scores using a 10-point scale within four categories: Indoor Air Quality and Other Toxic User Exposure, Manufacturing and Community Toxics, Renewable Materials, and Renewable Energy. (See www.pharosproject.net.)

❏ *EcoList:* A database developed by The Green Standard and updated four times a year, it lists certified interior products, finishes, and furniture by manufacturer. Information includes product categories, brand names, third-party certifications, and LEED protocol credits. EcoList can be accessed at www.interiorsandsources.com. (Also available is the EcoLibrary which lists various certification programs.)

❏ *CHPS Low-emitting Materials Table:* The Collaborative for High Performance Schools (CHPS) put together a list of materials that are considered low-emitting, organized using the CSI Master Format. Items are tested based on California's Standard *Section 01350* (see Chapters 5 and 9). CHPS has also identified acceptable alternate programs such as FloorScore, Green Label Plus, and Indoor Advantage Gold with low-emitting materials. The list can be found at www.chps.net. (Another CHPS database, called High Performance Products, lists additional performance attributes.)

❏ *ICC-ES SAVE Program:* The Sustainable Attributes Verification and Evaluation (SAVE) program was developed by the ICC Evaluation Services to provide a list of third-party verified sustainable building products as required by the *National Green Building Standard*, LEED, and Green Globes. Manufacturers can elect to have their products evaluated under the SAVE program so they can be included in the directory and use the SAVE mark. (Available at www.icc-es.org/save.)

❏ *EPA Portfolio Manager:* Developed by the Environmental Protection Agency (EPA), it is an interactive energy management tool that can be used to track and assess energy and water consumption and benchmark a building's ENERGY STAR score. (It can be found at www.epa.gov.)

❏ *DOE COMcheck and REScheck:* Software developed by the U.S. Department of Energy for commercial and residential projects, respectively, to simplify compliance with the *International Energy Conservation Code* and *ASHRAE/IESNA 90.1.*

Additional tools are available as well. As the sustainable industry grows, there will continue to be new terminology, methods, and systems put into place. Some will improve upon various items discussed throughout this appendix; others will replace them. Continued research is required to keep up-to-date on the latest information.

✎Note

For a very comprehensive database of sustainable standards and other programs both in the United States and worldwide, check out the *ASTM Sustainability Standards Listing* at www.astm.org/sustainability. (This list is maintained by ASTM Subcommittee E06.71 on Sustainability.)

APPENDIX C

EXISTING AND HISTORIC BUILDINGS

Most of the time, the codes will apply to interior projects in existing buildings and historic buildings the same way that they do for a new building. However, in other cases it may be slightly different. In fact, a different code may even apply. A building can be considered an *existing* building if it falls into one of four categories:

1. A building or structure was erected and occupied prior to the adoption of the most current building code.
2. A permit has been pulled for the construction of the building.
3. A building is currently under construction.
4. The shell of the building is completed but unoccupied, and individual tenant spaces are being constructed.

Eventually every building is considered an existing building. Whether an existing building is *historic* depends on two additional conditions: it must be either listed (or eligible to be listed) in the *National Register of Historical Places* or designated as historic by a specific state or local authority. How the codes apply to both types of buildings is briefly described in this appendix.

When working on interior projects in existing and historic buildings, many of the codes, standards, and federal regulations described throughout this book must still be referenced. The building codes typically have a chapter specifically for existing buildings as well. For example, the *International Building Code (IBC)* has a chapter called "Existing Structures." The NFPA codes, including the *Life Safety Code (LSC)*, have a chapter called "Building Rehabilitation." Each of these chapters includes requirements for historic structures. The *LSC* also has separate requirements for existing occupancies within each of its occupancy chapters.

In 2003, the ICC developed the first *International Existing Building Code (IEBC)*. This code establishes regulations specifically for repairs, alterations, and work performed because of changes in occupancy in existing buildings and historic buildings. It also includes requirements for additions and relocated buildings. The *IEBC* addresses accessibility requirements in these buildings as well. The *IEBC* defines the requirements for existing and historic buildings using both prescriptive-based and performance-based code requirements. There are separate chapters titled "Prescriptive Compliance Method" and "Performance Compliance Method" in the *IEBC* which indicate the level of performance expected in existing buildings that are being modified and how they will be evaluated. In general, the *IEBC* is meant to encourage the reuse of existing buildings by setting realistic standards while still providing for reasonable life safety within an existing building. When working in an existing or historic building, confirm with the local jurisdiction which of the existing building codes will apply.

The alternate means and methods requirements found in the building codes (such as *IBC Section 104.11*) and performance criteria found in the performance codes (such as the *IEBC* chapter mentioned above, and the *ICC Performance Code*) may be useful. These optional methods and criteria set *goals* instead of exact requirements so that alternative solutions can address the unique conditions found in older buildings. If the use of alternate means and methods or performance codes is allowed by the jurisdiction, and performance criteria are used, it is important to work closely with a code official.

Depending on the jurisdiction, sustainability codes and standards may be required as well. In addition, meeting sustainability goals may be requested by the client. Sustainability requirements would apply similarly to new construction; however, there are exceptions. (See the section Sustainability Considerations later in this appendix.) In most cases, the reuse or renovation of an existing building is considered a valuable credit to sustainability codes and rating systems.

As with most projects, some federal guidelines may also apply. For example, many of the Americans with Disabilities Act (ADA) requirements discussed throughout this book will still apply to certain existing and historic buildings. (See Appendix A.) In addition, depending on the use of the project, other federal guidelines may apply, including the Department of Housing and Urban Development's (HUD) *Rehabilitation Guidelines* and the U.S. Department of the Interior's (DOI) *Secretary of the Interior's Standards for Rehabilitation*, written specifically for historic buildings on the *National Register*. (Refer to the Bibliography on the companion Web site for additional sources.)

EXISTING BUILDINGS

Because codes change over time, there are almost always parts of any existing building that do not comply with the most current codes. When a repair, alteration, or addition is made to a portion of an existing building, the codes do not normally require the whole building to comply with the most current building codes; only the area being modified is at issue. However, at times this can be up to the discretion of the code official. Using the *IEBC* or similar existing building requirements helps to define the scope of the work in the area being modified as well as potentially other areas of the building. The *IEBC* (if allowed by the jurisdiction) refers to the *IBC* to set certain code requirements and includes alternate code requirements when meeting a particular *IBC* requirement is not reasonable.

Both the *IBC* and the *IEBC* classify the extent of work occurring within an existing building as repairs, alterations, changes in occupancy, and additions. These levels of work are specifically defined in the chapter on "Classification of Work" within the *IEBC*. These same types of work are repeated in a separate chapter for existing structures in the *IBC*. In the *IEBC*, alterations are further divided into three separate levels. In general, the more work being done in an existing building, the more improvements the code will require. The different levels of work defined in the *IEBC* are discussed next. The NFPA codes use similar categories (repairs, renovations, modifications, reconstructions, and additions); however, some of the details may vary. If working in a jurisdiction that requires the *LSC* in addition to the *IBC* or the *IEBC*, review each publication. Since the *IEBC* and other code requirements for existing buildings are sometimes more lenient, it may be necessary to consult a code official to determine what parts of the projects will need to meet new construction requirements and which can use the alternate requirements found in the existing building code.

◢Note

When renovating an existing building that was originally designed using performance codes, it is important to review existing building documentation. By reviewing existing construction documents and the operations and maintenance manual, it is less likely that a performance-based design will be compromised.

Repairs

According to the *IEBC*, *repairs* include patching or restoration of materials, elements, components, equipment, or fixtures of a building. It is considered the lowest level of change within a building, because in most cases the work is done for maintenance reasons only.

Usually when repairs are made to an existing building, the *IEBC* allows the current conditions to be maintained and does not require the area or materials to be brought up to current code. For example, fire protection, accessibility, and means of egress are allowed to be repaired so that the same level of safety is maintained. In addition, materials that would not typically be allowed in new buildings may be allowed to be used to repair existing conditions. However, there are exceptions. For example, hazardous conditions or materials such as asbestos and lead-based paint cannot be reused; or glazing located in hazardous locations that is being replaced must meet the current requirements for safety glazing. In addition, some system requirements call for increased safety but not to the level of what would be required for new construction. This typically applies to

◢Note

When using the *IEBC*, work is designated as repairs, alterations, change in occupancy, or additions.

the structural, electrical, mechanical, and plumbing systems. Check the specific requirements for each type of system.

Alterations

Typically, work done to a building that is not a repair or an addition is considered an alteration. For *alterations* made to an existing building, the codes typically require only the new work to comply with current code requirements as long as it does not cause other portions of the building to be in violation of the code. For example, the new work cannot demolish an existing fire wall or block an existing exit. However, the *IEBC* creates three levels of alterations. Each represents a different amount of work that is being performed within the building. The more work that is done, the higher the level of compliance with the *IBC* or *IEBC* is required. The *IEBC* refers to the physical scope of the area being altered as the *work area*. Level 1 represents the least amount of work or smallest work area and Level 3 represents the most amount of work. For example, the significant difference between a Level 2 alteration and a Level 3 alteration is the proportion of the building being altered. Below is a brief description of the three levels.

- ❏ *Level 1:* This level of alteration includes the removal and replacement or covering of existing materials, elements, or equipment, using new materials, elements, or equipment. This would include replacing tile in a restroom or a handrail on a stair.

- ❏ *Level 2:* This level of alteration includes modification to the layout of a space, the doors or windows, or a building system. It also includes the installation of new equipment. Alterations considered to be Level 2 may require additional modifications to the *work area* or other areas of the building beyond the initial *work area*.

- ❏ *Level 3:* This level of alteration applies when the *work area* exceeds more than 50 percent of the building area.

Whether or not the *IEBC* is being used in the jurisdiction of a project, if the design calls for a significant change, the code official can require that more of the building be brought up to code. For example, in the renovation of an older building where a large amount of electrical work is being done, the code official can require that the entire electrical service and wiring be updated, especially if more than 50 percent of the system is being changed. In the past, this was referred to as the *50 percent rule*. In all cases, when working on an extensive renovation or alteration, it is important to work closely with a code official to determine what level of compliance will be required for the project and building.

Change in Use or Occupancy

When the purpose or level of activity within a building changes, it is considered a *change in use* or *change in occupancy*. (The NFPA makes the distinction between change in use and change of occupancy. A change in use could be a restaurant changing to a nightclub, which isn't technically a change in the occupancy classification under the NFPA.) A change of occupancy can occur if a new tenant moves into the building or an existing tenant changes its use or classification. (See also the section New versus Existing Occupancies in Chapter 2.) The space must typically meet the most current code requirements for that occupancy. However, other spaces within the building can usually be left alone. The *IEBC* chapter on "Change of Occupancy" discusses to what extent the codes must be met. In most cases, the requirements are based on whether the new occupancy is considered more or less hazardous than the original occupancy.

≇Note

When a change of occupancy occurs in an existing building, a new Certificate of Occupancy may be required to confirm that an acceptable level of code compliance has been achieved.

Additions

According to the codes, an *addition* is an increase in the floor area, number of stories, or height of a building. In most cases, new additions to an existing building must comply with the current building code. In the *IEBC*, most of the requirements focus on how the increase in area or height will affect the structural components of the existing building. Additions to Residential occupancies also require an increase in fire protection. In most cases, additions are required by the codes and the ADA to be fully compliant with the ADA requirements. (See Appendix A for more information.)

≇Note

According to the codes, an *addition* is an increase in the floor area, number of stories, or height of a building.

Accessibility Requirements

In most cases whether an existing building is being repaired or altered, accessibility has to be maintained or increased as changes are made. The *IEBC* includes minimum accessibility requirements for each type of change. A repair must maintain the same existing level of accessibility. An alteration must comply with the accessibility requirements of the *IBC* unless *technically infeasible* and at least to the *maximum extent technically feasible* (as explained in Appendix A). Even when there is a change in occupancy, the *IEBC* sets parameters for accessibility. These include (1) one accessible entrance, (2) one accessible route from the entrance to the primary function area, and (3) the use of accessible signage.

In addition, changes to an existing building must still meet certain requirements in the *ADA Standards* that may be more stringent than the *IEBC*. The *Fair Housing Accessibility Guidelines (FHAG)* may also apply in certain Residential occupancies. Although the ADA specifically states that existing buildings must fully comply with the accessibility requirements as stated in the *ADA Standards*, there are some alternate solutions for existing buildings and for alterations to existing buildings. For example, the ADA does allow exceptions where compliance is either structurally infeasible, too costly, or would cause an unsafe situation. These exceptions must be fully analyzed. Refer to the ADA and other experts when necessary. (See Appendix A for more information.)

HISTORIC BUILDINGS

When working on a project in a historic building, there is an obvious need to balance protecting the historic character of a building or interior space and providing an acceptable level of life safety and accessibility. It is important to know the requirements that apply and the alternative solutions that may be acceptable. As previously mentioned, the *IBC*, the *IEBC*, and the NFPA codes all have special provisions for historic buildings. (The *IEBC* has a separate chapter titled "Historic Buildings.") In addition to codes, many jurisdictions have state or local regulations for historic buildings as well. It is important to check for local regulations before starting a project. For example, some regulations control only the preservation of the exterior of a historic building; however, this may include any interior work that is visible from the exterior of the building.

The key to historic projects is to determine which codes must be met and what approval procedures must be followed. According to the *IEBC*, when a historic building undergoes a repair, alteration, or change of occupancy, a written report may be required to evaluate the condition of the building as it relates to the current codes. It must also identify historic characteristics that may be damaged or destroyed by bringing the building or space up to current codes. Although the code official has the ability to allow alternative solutions or allow aspects of the existing building to remain, any conditions that potentially create a danger to life safety may be required to be modified. Communication with the code department and historic preservation organizations is imperative. Some historic organizations have the power to grant alternatives or waivers to code provisions. For example, some jurisdictions may allow safety equivalencies. In addition, many of the codes include alternative requirements that can be used if approved by the code official. It may also be necessary to apply to the appeals or variance boards in special circumstances. (See Chapter 10.)

Remember that an old or historic building still must be safe. In addition to the codes and documents already mentioned, there are some additional documents that may be required or used to help develop alternatives for safety and accessibility:

❑ *NFPA 914, Code for Fire Protection of Historic Structures*
❑ The Secretary of the Interior's *Standards for Rehabilitation*
❑ *California Historic Building Code*

In most cases, a historic structure will be required to be accessible if used by the public. In some cases, a limited level of accessibility may be allowed by the building codes and the accessibility standards. (See previous section.) The building codes include provisions for accessibility for historic structures. These codes provide minimum requirements and specify alternate solutions when compliance with their accessibility chapters is not feasible. Typically, these alternate solutions and reduced level of accessibility must be approved by the local code official.

The ADA allows exceptions or alternative solutions for historic buildings when a requirement threatens a building's historic significance—for example, where the required change or addition would destroy a historic detail of the building or space. Some of these alternative solutions are stated in the ADA. Others may need to be discussed with the state or local historic preservation official or directly with the Access Board. Remember, though, that approval of an alternative solution for one space or area does not exempt the whole building from meeting other requirements.

The ADA does give minimum requirements that all historic buildings must meet. These include (1) at least one accessible route into the building, (2) at least one accessible toilet when toilet facilities are provided, (3) access to all public areas on the main floor, and (4) accessible displays and written information. There are a number of requirements in the *ADA Standards* that can typically be met without major disruption. Examples include installing compatible offset hinges to widen doorways, adding full-length mirrors and raised toilet seats in restrooms, and replacing door and faucet handles with lever controls. However, all ADA regulations must be followed whenever possible.

When existing conditions seem to make meeting the codes and accessibility requirements difficult, the exemptions allowed for existing and/or historic buildings should be considered. It may be necessary to discuss alternatives with local or federal officials. In other cases, a code variance may be required. However, whether the building is existing or historic, the overall goal when making interior changes is to make the building as safe as possible—and, in the process, as accessible as possible.

SUSTAINABILITY CONSIDERATIONS

Many of the sustainability requirements that apply to new buildings or spaces apply to repairs and alterations in an existing or historic building. However, there are also special provisions in many of the sustainable codes and standards for

⬚Note

The ADA gives minimum accessibility requirements that existing and historic buildings must provide. However, all ADA requirements should be followed whenever possible.

⬚Note

Both the *IGCC* and the *NGBS* provide alternate levels of sustainability compliance for existing building, which can be used in certain situations.

these types of projects. For example, the *International Green Construction Code (IGCC)* has a specific chapter on "Existing Buildings." It sets different levels of compliance based on whether an addition or an alteration is being done. For additions, the requirements for new construction have to be met in the new spaces. When alterations are being made to existing portions or components of a building, the *IGCC* sets minimum energy, HVAC, and water requirements for the building. For lighting issues, the *IGCC* refers to the *International Energy Conservation Code*.

In most cases, there are exceptions to the requirements in the *IGCC* to address unique conditions within an existing building. Additional requirements for existing buildings include maintenance issues and planned phase-out of undesirable use of chemicals and systems that do not contribute to the sustainability of the building. In some cases, an energy audit and report is required to be submitted to the code official to evaluate the green status of the existing building in order to define what requirements need to be met.

A local jurisdiction may require the use of *ASHRAE/USGBC/IES 189.1, Standard for the Design of High-Performance Green Buildings Except Low-Rise Residential Buildings.* However, this sustainability standard does not include specific requirements for existing and/or historic buildings. Instead, the sustainability requirements would typically be applied similar to new construction.

Certain Residential building types may also require the use of the *ICC 700, National Green Building Standard (NGBS)*. If an existing building is renovated or an addition of a limited size is made to a building, specific performance levels are required. These requirements are different from those for new construction. If a larger addition is made, then the requirements for new construction would apply to the whole project. The "Compliance Method" chapter of the *NGBS* specifies how the standard applies to a renovation or addition, how points are allocated, and how threshold environmental performance levels are obtained. Although the usual *NGBS* point allocation is used for existing buildings, there may be special criteria that affect whether specific green practices are mandatory. In addition, special points applicable only to renovations of existing buildings may be available. Both of these affect the building's ability to reach the desired performance levels. Typical criteria include the efficient use and disposal of construction materials, durability of materials, maintenance, material choices, energy efficiency, water efficiency, and indoor air quality.

In addition, the *NGBS* has two levels of compliance depending on when the building was originally constructed. Buildings that were constructed during or after 1980 follow guidelines known as the *Green Building Path*. Buildings constructed prior to 1980 follow either the *Green Remodel Path* or the *Green Building Path*. The *Green Remodel Path* allows a slightly lower level of achievement in some requirements and may make it simpler for existing or historic buildings to reach sustainability goals. (Refer to the standard for specific requirements.)

◤**Note**

A jurisdiction may also require the use of a green rating system as part of their code process. Examples include LEED-EB and Green Globes. (See Appendix B.)

APPENDIX D

FAMILY RESIDENCES

Single-family residences and duplexes are considered Residential occupancies by the building codes. However, there is a separate code publication available specifically for these building types. Published by the International Code Council (ICC), it is called the *International Residential Code (IRC)*. The *IRC* is the main code used for single-family homes, two-family homes, duplexes, and townhouses that have their own means of egress. It is required by many jurisdictions. (Other Residential occupancy types are covered by the building code. See Chapter 2.)

More recently, the ICC collaborated with the National Association of Home Builders (NAHB) to create the first sustainable-related standard specifically for single-family and multiple-family homes. Known as *ICC 700, National Green Building Standard (NGBS* or *ICC 700)*, it was first published in 2008 by the NAHB. (See Chapter 1 and the section Sustainability Considerations later in this appendix.) A state or local jurisdiction may adopt the *NGBS* to be used in conjunction with the *IRC*. A jurisdiction may also adopt the *ASHRAE/IESNA 90.2, Energy-Efficient Design of New Low-Rise Residential Buildings*, which is the energy-efficiency standard specifically for residential homes, or the *International Energy Conservation Code (IECC)*, which includes a chapter on residential buildings.

Unlike codes for other types of projects, which may have separate code publications for building, fire protection, plumbing, mechanical, and electrical code requirements, these are all included in the *IRC* for family residences. In addition, the *IRC* refers to a variety of standards. Although family residences do not have as many interior-related regulations as other buildings, a number of interior codes and standards are still required. Also note that the 2009 edition of the *IRC* was significantly reorganized and updated from the previous edition. Brief descriptions of the most common interior requirements are given in this appendix. (They are listed in the same order as in the rest of the book.) Accessibility and sustainability requirements are discussed towards the end.

✎Note

The National Fire Protection Association (NFPA) does not have a separate code for family residences. Instead, the *NFPA 5000* and the *Life Safety Code (LSC)* each contain a chapter specific to this building type.

✎Note

Another ICC code that includes requirements for residential buildings is the *International Energy Conservation Code (IECC)*. Check to see if this code is required by the jurisdiction.

✎Note

The *IRC* includes an appendix containing provisions for home day care centers operating within a dwelling.

CONSTRUCTION TYPES AND BUILDING SIZE

Unlike the building codes, the *IRC* does not specify different construction types. Family residences are typically wood structures. In some areas, metal framing is also frequently used or required, especially where seismic codes are enforced. However, most houses today still consist of wood framing. Concrete and concrete block are typically used to create the foundation of the structure. Because there are fewer variations in the way a residence is built, the *IRC* specifies both the types of material that can be used and the requirements for proper construction. This includes the foundation, floors, walls, ceilings, and the roof of a residence. Even requirements for exterior materials, such as brick, stucco, and wood siding that are used for aesthetic reasons, are included in the *IRC*. The *IRC* also provides requirements for the construction of interior walls, which generally consist of wood studs with gypsum board, or lathe and plaster in older homes.

Performance-like provisions for the use of alternate construction methods and engineered designs are included in the *IRC* as well. There are additional requirements for residences constructed in areas of the country affected by high winds, seismic forces, and other unique conditions. A code official must approve any alternative materials and construction methods.

Although the total area of a residence is generally not regulated, to be considered a family residence covered by the *IRC*, the structure typically cannot be more than three stories high. (Basements and attics are not included in the number of stories, even if they are habitable.) If it has more than three stories, the building codes will apply. (See the section Understanding Building Height and Area in Chapter 3.) However, the *IRC* does limit the height of each story. It also places minimum square footage (s m) and minimum ceiling height requirements on each habitable room within the residence. For example, the minimum area of a habitable room, except for a kitchen, is 70 square feet (6.5 s m) and at least one room in the home cannot be less than 120 square feet (11 s m). The ceiling height throughout most of the house must be a minimum of 7 feet (2134 mm) above the finished floor.

MEANS OF EGRESS

Because the normal number of occupants in a residence is much less than that in a similarly sized nonresidential space, determining a safe level of means of egress is not as complicated for residences as it is for nonresidential spaces. The *IRC* requires a minimum of one regulated exterior exit door in each residence. It must have a minimum clear width of 32 inches (813 mm) and a clear height of

78 inches (1981 mm) with a specific type of landing on both sides. (Similar to Figure 4.3 in Chapter 4.) Other doors to the exterior are allowed to have smaller widths. All exterior doors must be easily operable without the need for a key to exit. The width of interior doors is not regulated, but the code does set a minimum width for all hallways and exit accesses. The minimum hallway width is typically 3 feet (914 mm). (A larger width may be required by the accessibility standards for accessible houses.)

For all sleeping areas (i.e., bedrooms) within a residence, the *IRC* requires an emergency means of egress. The code typically allows this exit to be an operable window. The bottom of the window cannot be more than 44 inches (1118 mm) above the floor, and the window must have a clear opening of a certain dimension that allows a person to exit through the window in case of a fire or other emergency. If the clear opening of an exterior window is more than 72 inches (1829 mm) above grade, additional requirements must be met.

Stairs and ramps within a residence are also regulated. However, the dimensions are not as strict as those of the building codes. For example, tread depths are allowed to be smaller and riser heights are allowed to be more than those of stairs in nonresidential spaces, and only one handrail is usually required on a stairway. If a basement or attic is habitable, the stairs to these levels must meet the codes as well. Similar to other codes, the *IRC* specifies handrail requirements, such as the mounting height and the handrail grip size. Guards are also required at changes of elevation over a certain height in locations such as porches, balconies, and raised floor areas.

FIRE AND SMOKE RESISTANCE

Fire and smoke separation is required between two or more family dwellings, such as a duplex or a townhouse. Depending on whether they are side by side or above each other, they must be separated by either a fire-resistance-rated wall or a horizontal assembly. The *IRC* references standards *ASTM E119, Standard Test Method for Fire Tests of Building Construction* and *UL 263, Standards for Fire Test of Building Construction and Materials* for the specific requirements. Typically, wall assemblies must extend to the underside of the roof, and floor assemblies must be continuous to each exterior wall. Any required through-penetrations must be firestopped. Draftstops in attic spaces may be required as well. (See Chapter 5.)

In single-family residences, exterior walls in certain locations require fire-resistant construction. However, the most common separation requirement pertains to attached garages. A 1-hour assembly must separate any part of the garage that connects to the house, including walls and ceilings. Any door between the garage and the living space must be fire-rated as well as self-closing and self-latching.

⌐Note

Most homes rely on exterior windows as a means of egress during an emergency. The codes set minimum requirements for the size, height, and operation of these windows.

⌐Note

The *IRC* contains multiple requirements for exterior windows. Consult the various sections in the code for specifics.

⌐Note

Townhouses require stricter separation requirements than two-family dwellings. Some fire and smoke ratings can be reduced when an automatic sprinkler system is installed.

Throughout the family dwelling, fireblocking is required in concealed openings to form an effective fire barrier between each story and the top story and attic space. Examples include concealed spaces in stud walls, duct and wiring penetrations, and openings in the top and bottom of stair stringers. Fireblocking is also required when a clothes dryer exhaust duct penetrates a floor or ceiling membrane. (See Chapter 5 for more information on fireblocking.) Other fire code requirements are specified for items such as fireplaces and wood-burning stoves.

FIRE PROTECTION

Previously, fire detection and suppression in family residences consisted primarily of smoke detectors and manual fire extinguishers. However, as of the 2009 edition of the IRC, an automatic fire sprinkler system is required in new homes. (Similar requirements have been part of the NFPA codes for family residences since the 2006 edition of the codes.) The IRC references either the plumbing section of the code or the standard NFPA 13D, *Installation of Sprinkler Systems in One- and Two-Family Dwellings and Manufactured Homes.* Although the sprinkler system is required throughout the residence, certain areas, such as closets and pantries, are exempt. (See also the section Sprinkler Systems in Chapter 6.)

Smoke alarms are required by the IRC as well. All new homes must have smoke alarms that consist of smoke detection and an alarm-sounding appliance. They must be interconnected and tied into the electrical system with battery backup. Typically, smoke alarms are required in each sleeping room, outside each sleeping area, on all inhabitable floors (including attics), and in basements and garages. These detectors are required to be interconnected so that if a detector indicates smoke in one area, all of the detectors will sound. The IRC also references the household fire-warning equipment provision of the *National Electrical Code (NEC)* for the installation of these systems. If a significant renovation or addition is being made to an existing residence or if a bedroom is added to an existing residence, the code typically requires that an interconnected smoke-detecting system be added to the entire house. Older homes require at least battery-operated detectors.

Although not a component of fire protection, carbon monoxide alarms are also now required by the 2009 edition of the IRC in certain instances. They are required when the residence includes a "fuel-fired" appliance (gas furnace, gas water heater, etc.) or an attached garage. (See the inset titled *Carbon Monoxide Detection* on page 250.) These single station alarms must comply with the standard UL 2034, *Standard of Safety for Single and Multiple Station Carbon Monoxide Alarms.* In new construction, when required, a carbon monoxide alarm must be installed directly outside each separate sleeping area. Any renovation made to an existing residence that requires a permit, whether the work affects the interior or the exterior of the house, must also add carbon monoxide alarms to meet these requirements.

PLUMBING

The minimum requirements for plumbing fixtures in family residences typically include one kitchen sink, one water closet, one lavatory, one bathtub or shower unit, and one washing machine hookup. (In a duplex residence, one washing machine hookup may be adequate if it is available to both units.) In addition, each water closet and bathtub or shower must also be installed in a room with privacy. Some jurisdictions may require additional plumbing fixtures, based on the number of bedrooms.

The *IRC* generally specifies the size, clearances, installation requirements, and finishes for most fixture types. For example, a shower must have a minimum floor area of 900 square inches (0.581 s m), have a minimum dimension of 30 inches (762 mm) in one direction and a minimum height of 70 inches (1778 mm), and be surrounded by nonabsorbent materials. Sometimes these dimensions are less that those required by the *International Plumbing Code (IPC)* for other buildings. Other dimensions such as clearances for water closets, bidets, and lavatories match those of the *IPC*.

For each type of plumbing fixture, additional standards are referenced as well. This includes faucets that regulate the maximum temperature of water. In most cases, the manufacturer will have produced the fixture to meet the applicable standards for its use or the contractor will be aware of its proper installation; however, check the requirements for each type of fixture, especially in custom design. If accessible plumbing facilities are required, the appropriate accessibility document must be referenced. (See the section Accessibility Considerations later in this appendix.)

MECHANICAL

Ventilation in a family residence is directly related to the size and number of exterior windows and how much natural ventilation they supply. For example, the *IRC* specifies that a bathroom should have an operable window of a certain size. If it does not have a window, an exhaust fan with a duct leading directly to the exterior of the building is required. Another important ventilation requirement

✎Note
Most carbon monoxide poisoning in single- and multi-family homes occurs as a result of faulty fuel-fired appliances, such as a gas water heater, or automobile exhaust.

✎Note
Plastic (i.e., PVC) plumbing pipes are not allowed in some jurisdictions.

✎Note
Beginning in 2006, the *IRC* no longer allows "green gypsum board" as backer behind tiled bath and shower walls. Instead, cement, fiber-cement, or glass mat gypsum backers must be used.

✎Note
Limits on the length of certain ventilation and exhaust pipes may dictate the location of an appliance, such as a clothes dryer or vented stove top. In some cases a ventless or ductless appliance may be used.

has to do with the venting of certain common appliances such as clothes dryers, range hoods, fireplace stoves, and heating, ventilating and air conditioning (HVAC) equipment. For example, a clothes dryer must typically be ducted to the outside. Since the *IRC* limits the maximum length of the duct, it may restrict the location of a laundry room within the house. (Some jurisdictions may allow the use of a condensing [ductless] dryer.)

The mechanical system of a house must be able to maintain a specific room temperature in all habitable rooms. Because the size of a house can vary greatly, a wide variety of systems can be used. Some examples include air units, heat pumps, radiant heat, and baseboard heating. The *IRC* requires all HVAC equipment and appliances to meet certain standards and have a factory-applied label, and they must be located where they are easy to access and maintain. Other requirements are specifically for the ducts and piping needed to run the HVAC systems.

Additional mechanical requirements can be found in the *IECC*. The *IECC* contains detailed requirements for air sealing and insulation throughout the residence, including the insulation used for supply and return ducts. This in turn will affect the building's heating load and the type of HVAC equipment required. ENERGY STAR equipment and a programmable thermostat may be required.

ELECTRICAL AND COMMUNICATION

Although the *IRC* has several chapters dedicated to electrical requirements, including energy-efficiency-related items, it also refers to the NFPA's *National Electrical Code (NEC)*. Some of these requirements were discussed in Chapter 8. Examples include all electrical outlets must be certain distances apart (see Figure 8.3); GFCI outlets must be used in wet areas, garages, and basements; and AFCI outlets are required in bedrooms as well as living areas, hallways, and closets.

Other electrical requirements are more specific to residential homes. For example, all inhabitable rooms require a wall switch to control lighting, and all stairways must include at least one light fixture with a wall switch at each floor level. Certain types of light fixtures are limited by the code as well. However, the 2009 *IRC* allows the use of LED luminaires in locations approved for incandescent fixtures, including clothes closets. In addition, if using the *IECC*, it requires that high-efficacy lamps (see Glossary) must be used in at least 50 percent of the permanently installed light fixtures in residences.

A number of interior appliances must also meet certain electrical code requirements as well as minimal federal energy standards, including ENERGY STAR® compliance. These include ranges and ovens, open-top gas broiler units, clothes washers and dryers, HVAC units, and water heaters. The *IECC* includes specific appliance requirements as well. In addition, the ENERGY STAR program includes a home label that can be used to certify an entire residence. (See the inset titled *Federal Sustainability Programs* on page 477.)

Communication systems in single-family homes have few code-related requirements. However, the *NEC* does require that all cables be listed and that at least one telephone outlet be wired in each residence. The industry standard most commonly used is *TIA/EIA-570, Residential Telecommunication Cabling Standards.* Others are available as well. (See also Chapter 8.)

FINISHES AND FURNITURE

Requirements for finishes and furniture in private residences are not as strict as those in other occupancies. For example, floor finishes are not typically regulated by the *IRC*. However, carpet and rugs must meet the federally required *Pill Test.* The *IRC* does require that wall and ceiling finishes, except for materials that are less than 0.036 inch (0.90 mm) thick, have at least a Class C rating using the *Steiner Tunnel Test.* The *Room Corner Test* is also allowed as an alternate. (These tests are discussed more fully in Chapter 9.) Because of their thickness, the most popular residential finishes, paint and typical wallpapers, are both exempt from these requirements.

Typical wood trims used throughout the residence, such as baseboards and crown moldings, are not regulated by the *IRC*. However, if the trim is made of foam plastic, it cannot constitute more than 10 percent of the specific wall and ceiling area of a room or space. Other wood finishes, such as wood veneer and hardboard paneling, must conform to other standards. Finishes in shower and bath areas are also regulated. These areas must have finishes with a smooth, hard, nonabsorbent surface (e.g., ceramic tile, marble, or vinyl tile). If glazing is used (e.g., shower walls), safety glass is typically required. (This applies to certain size mirrors as well.)

Although furniture for private residences is not currently regulated by the codes, the federal government does require all mattresses sold in the United States to meet certain standards. In addition, multiple industry standards are available that can be used to increase the flame resistance of specified upholstered furniture and mattresses. These are explained in detail in Chapter 9. Also refer to the section Pretested Finishes and Furniture in Chapter 9 for more information on the UFAC hang tag used on furniture sold in the United States. This tag indicates furniture with higher cigarette-ignition resistance.

ACCESSIBILITY CONSIDERATIONS

The Americans with Disabilities Act (ADA) does not typically apply to private residences. Instead, the Fair Housing Act (FHA) sets most of the accessibility

Note

The *IRC* requires that a "permanent energy certificate" be posted on the main electrical panel to provide energy conservation–related information such as insulations used in construction assemblies and ducts, ratings of windows and doors, and equipment efficiency.

Note

All states in the United States have enacted "fire-safe cigarette" laws, which require cigarettes to self-extinguish when not being actively smoked, hoping to reduce fire-related deaths, especially in Residential occupancies. They are required nationwide in Canada as well. (See www.firesafecigarettes.org.)

Note

Although the *IRC* does not regulate floor finishes, all carpets and certain rugs must still meet the requirements of the *Pill Test.* (See Chapter 9.)

Note

If part of a private residence is used for business, that part of the residence may need to meet the requirements of the *ADA Standards.*

Note

The 2004 *ADA–ABA Accessibility Guidelines* includes requirements for dwelling units throughout its text. Although not typically required for private residences, they can be referenced when designing an accessible home.

standards for residences, yet it pertains mostly to multi-unit housing. (See Chapter 1.) In addition, the ICC/ANSI accessibility standard, *ICC/ANSI A117.1,* has a section dedicated to dwelling units.

Most private residences are not required to be accessible. However, housing built with government funds may require partial or full accessibility. Other interior projects may require a house to be "adaptable." This means that the house could easily be converted to be accessible. An adaptable house may include such things as adjustable counters, movable cabinetry, structurally reinforced walls for future grab bars, and specific fixtures and equipment, such as wall-mounted water closets and a stove with front controls. The additional maneuvering space would also have to be designed into the layout of the dwelling. When a private residence is *required* to be accessible, the requirements of the *FHA Accessibility Guidelines (FHAG)* must be met.

SUSTAINABILITY CONSIDERATIONS

Note

In addition to setting requirements for new home construction, the *NGBS* also addresses renovations and additions to existing homes and other Residential occupancies. (See Appendix C.)

The *IRC* includes a chapter on energy efficiency. Many of the provisions in this chapter are similar to those in the *International Energy Conservation Code's (IECC's)* chapter on residential energy efficiency, some of which were explained earlier. Check with the local jurisdiction to determine which document should be referenced. A jurisdiction may also require the use of the standard *ASHRAE/ IESNA 90.2* for energy-efficiency requirements (see Chapter 1).

If a jurisdiction requires the ICC 700, *National Green Building Standard,* there are additional sustainability requirements to be considered. As discussed in Chapter 1, this standard is specifically for Residential occupancies, including single-family homes. It includes minimum requirements as well as performance thresholds similar to a green rating system.

Note

If a homeowner or builder wants to use the *NGBS* but the jurisdiction has not adopted it, an approved third-party verifier can be used to administer, rate, and certify the project. Go to www.nahbgreen.org for more information.

For home interiors, the *NGBS* includes sections with requirements for resource efficiency, water and energy efficiency, and indoor environmental quality (IEQ). Resource efficiency includes using salvaged materials, recycled-content building materials, renewable materials, resource-efficient materials, and indigenous materials. For example, when installing hardwood floors, points could be earned by using salvaged hardwood or by using resource-efficient engineered wood. Water and energy efficiencies are accomplished similar to other occupancies as discussed in Chapters 7 and 8. For instance, occupancy sensors can be used and ENERGY STAR appliances are required. Points earned for IEQ cover everything from properly venting fireplaces and fuel-burning appliances to reducing emissions in wood materials (e.g., cabinetry) and finishes (e.g., carpet, paints, wallcoverings).

Another section of the *NGBS* requires a building owner's manual to address the operation and maintenance of the residence as well as training for the building owner. For example, the manual must at least include a list of the residence's green building features and the manufacturer's product manuals. Training must include how to operate equipment and control systems. Ultimately, the code official will check a project for the compulsory minimum requirements as well as confirm that the appropriate threshold level was achieved in each section of the code so that the home can receive one of four levels: Bronze, Silver, Gold, and Emerald.

Some jurisdictions may also require the use of a green rating system for residential homes. For example, many jurisdictions in and around California use the system GreenPoints Rated, which is maintained by Build It Green, an organization based in Berkeley, California. (It can be used for new and existing homes.) In the southeast United States, some jurisdictions require the use of the EarthCraft House rating system, developed by Greater Atlanta Home Builders Association and Southface. Other jurisdictions may require the use of the U.S. Green Building Council's (USGBC's) LEED for Homes program. (See Appendix B.) If a jurisdiction requires a rating system, it is important to determine the minimum certification level the project must attain as well as how to incorporate the information into construction documents as required for permitting (see Chapter 10).

✎Note

Additional sources for designing sustainable homes include the *Model Green Home Building Guidelines,* developed by the NAHB and ICC, and www.greenhomeguide.org, developed by the USGBC.

✎Note

The EPA's WaterSense program also now has a certification program for new single-family homes. (See the inset titled *Federal Sustainability Certifications* on page 477.)

BIBLIOGRAPHY (BY TOPIC)

The bibliography for this book is organized by the following topics and can be found on the companion Web site at www.wiley.com/harmon.

ACCESSIBILITY

CODE, STANDARDS, AND CODE OFFICIALS

COMMUNICATION REQUIREMENTS

CONSTRUCTION TYPES AND BUILDING SIZES

ELECTRICAL CODES AND ENERGY EFFICIENCY

EXISTING AND HISTORIC BUILDINGS

FINISHES AND FURNISHINGS

FIRE AND SMOKE PROTECTION

FIRE AND SMOKE RESISTANT ASSEMBLIES

MEANS OF EGRESS

MECHANICAL CODES

OCCUPANCY CLASSIFICATIONS

PLUMBING CODES AND WATER CONSERVATION

RESIDENTIAL—ONE- AND TWO-FAMILY

SUSTAINABILITY

GLOSSARY

ACCEPTABLE METHODS When using performance codes, these are the design, analysis, and testing methods that have been approved for use in developing design solutions for compliance with a code requirement.

ACCESSIBLE As it applies to accessibility, a building, room, or space that can be approached, entered, and used by persons with disabilities. Also generally applies to equipment that is easy to approach without locked doors or change in elevation or to wiring that is exposed and capable of being removed.

ACCESSIBLE MEANS OF EGRESS See Means of Egress, Accessible.

ACCESSIBLE ROUTE A continuous and unobstructed path connecting all accessible elements and spaces of a building, including corridors, floors, ramps, elevators, lifts, and clear floor spaces at fixtures.

ACCESSIBLE UNIT A dwelling unit or sleeping unit that meets all the requirements for accessibility.

ACCESSORY When discussing plumbing requirements, refers to miscellaneous equipment and/or devices found within a typical toilet or bathing facility. (See also Occupancy, Accessory)

ADDITION An expansion, extension, or increase in the gross floor area of a building, the number of stories, or the height of a building.

AFTER FLAME When an item continues to hold a flame after the source of ignition is removed.

AISLE An unenclosed path of travel that forms part of an exit access or the space between elements such as furniture and equipment that provides clearance to pass by and/or use the elements.

AISLE ACCESSWAY The initial portion of an exit access that leads to an aisle.

ALARM NOTIFICATION APPLIANCE A part of the fire alarm system that notifies occupants that a fire has been detected; can include audible, tactile, visible, and/or voice instruction.

ALARM SYSTEM See Emergency Alarm System and Fire Alarm System.

ALARM VERIFICATION A feature of a fire alarm system that delays notification of occupants in order to confirm the accuracy of the smoke or fire detection.

ALLEY See Public Way.

ALTERATION Any construction or modification to an existing building or facility other than a repair or addition.

ALTERNATE METHODS Refers to methods, materials, and systems used other than those specifically mentioned in the codes; use of these alternates requires prior approval from the authority having jurisdiction. (See also Equivalency.)

ANNULAR SPACE The opening around a penetrating item.

ANNUNCIATOR A device with one or more types of indicators, such as lamps and alphanumeric displays, that provides status information about a circuit, condition, or location.

APPROVED Acceptable to the code official or Authority Having Jurisdiction (AHJ).

ARC-FAULT CIRCUIT INTERRUPTER A device that disconnects the electrical power to the circuit when it detects an unexpected electrical surge (or arc); typically required in sleeping rooms; commonly known as AFCI.

AREA, FIRE The aggregate floor area enclosed and bounded by fire walls, fire barriers, exterior walls, and/or fire-rated horizontal assemblies of a building.

AREA, GROSS FLOOR The area within the inside perimeter of a building's exterior walls, exclusive of vent shafts and interior courts, with no deduction for corridors, stairs, closets, thickness of interior walls, columns, toilet rooms, mechanical rooms, or other unoccupiable areas.

AREA, GROSS LEASABLE The total floor area designated for tenant occupancy and exclusive use measured from the centerlines of joint partitions to the outside of the tenant walls; includes all tenant areas as well as those used for storage.

AREA, NET FLOOR The area actually occupied within a building, *not* including accessory unoccupied areas such as corridors, stairs, closets, thickness of interior walls, columns, toilet rooms, and mechanical rooms.

AREA OF REFUGE A space or area providing protection from fire and/or smoke where persons who are unable to use the stairways can remain temporarily to await instruction or assistance during an emergency evacuation; protection can be created by rated enclosures and/or an approved fire-protection system. (Code term.)

AREA OF RESCUE ASSISTANCE An area that has direct access to an exit where people who are unable to use stairs may remain temporarily in safety to await further instructions or assistance during emergency evacuations. (Accessibility term.)

AREA, WORK The portion of a building affected by renovation or modification based on work indicated on construction documents. In some jurisdictions, the work area may also include incidental areas not included in the permit but affected by the work.

AS-BUILT DRAWINGS See Record Drawings.

ASSEMBLY, CONSTRUCTION Building materials used together to create a structure or building element.

ASSEMBLY, FIRE DOOR Any combination of a door, frame, hardware, and other accessories that together provide a specific degree of fire protection to the opening in a rated wall.

ASSEMBLY, FIRE-RATED A combination of parts (including all required construction materials, hardware, anchorage, frames, sills, etc.) that, when used together, make up a structural or building element that has passed various fire tests and has been assigned a fire rating; includes fire-resistant assemblies and fire-protection assemblies. (See also Rating, Fire-Resistance and Rating, Fire-Protection.)

ASSEMBLY, FIRE WINDOW Any combination of glazing or glass block, frame, hardware, and other accessories that together provide protection against the passage of fire.

ASSEMBLY, FLOOR FIRE DOOR Any combination of a fire door, frame, hardware, and other accessories installed in a horizontal plane that together provide a specific degree of fire protection to a through-opening in a fire-rated floor.

ASSEMBLY, HORIZONTAL A continuous fire-resistance-rated assembly of materials designed to resist the spread of fire in which openings are protected; includes floor/ceiling assemblies and floor/roof assemblies. (See also Barrier, Fire.)

ATRIUM A roofed, multi-story open space contained within a building that is intended for occupancy.

ATTIC The space between the ceiling joists of the top story and the roof rafters above.

AUTHORITY HAVING JURISDICTION (AHJ) Used by the codes to indicate organizations, offices, or individuals that administer and enforce the codes. See also Code Department, Code Official, and Jurisdiction.

AUTOMATIC CLOSING An opening protective (e.g., door, window) that has a closure activated by smoke or heat, causing it to close in an emergency to prevent the spread of fire and smoke.

BACKCOATING The process of coating the underside of a fabric or finish to improve its durability and/or serve as a heat barrier.

BACKDRAFT An explosive surge in a fire caused by a sudden mixture of air with other combustibles. (See also Flashover.)

BALLAST A magnetic coil that adjusts current through a fluorescent tube, providing the current surge to start the lamp.

BANDWIDTH Refers to the capacity for communication cabling to move information; for telephone cabling it is measured in cycles per second (Hz), and for data cabling it is measured in bits per second (bps).

BARRIER Any building element, equipment, or object that restricts or prevents the intended use of a space and/or protects one building material or finish from another.

BARRIER, FIRE A continuous fire-resistance-rated vertical wall assembly consisting of materials designed to resist the spread of fire in which openings are protected. (See also Assembly, Horizontal and Partition, Fire.)

BARRIER, SMOKE A continuous vertical or horizontal membrane, such as a wall, floor, or ceiling assembly (with or without protected openings), that is designed and constructed to restrict the movement and passage of smoke. (See also Partition, Smoke.)

BASEMENT Any story of a building that is partially or completely below grade level, located so that the vertical distance from the grade to the floor below is greater than the grade to the floor above.

BATHING FACILITY A room containing a bathtub, shower, spa, or similar bathing fixture either separately or in conjunction with a water closet and lavatory. Also sometimes called a bathroom.

BENCHMARKING A term used when tracking a building's energy use and water consumption as well as other measurable building uses.

BIO-BASED MATERIAL A commercial or industrial material or product that is composed of or derived from living matter such as plant, animal, and marine materials, or forestry materials.

BORROWED LIGHT An interior stationary window that allows the passage of light from one area to the next.

BOX, ELECTRICAL A wiring device that is used to contain wire terminations where they connect to other wires, switches, or outlets.

BOX, JUNCTION An electrical box where several wires are joined together.

BRANCH A horizontal pipe that leads from a main, riser, or stack pipe to the plumbing fixture or sprinkler head.

BUILDING Any structure usually enclosed by walls and a roof used or intended for supporting, sheltering, enclosing, or housing any use or occupancy, including persons, animals, and property of any kind. Includes private buildings (not open to the public) and public buildings.

BUILDING CODE Regulations that stress the construction of a building and the hazardous materials or equipment used inside.

BUILDING CORE A building element that is vertically continuous through one or more floors of a building, consisting of shafts for the vertical distribution of building services. (See also Shaft.)

BUILDING ELEMENT Any building component that makes up a building, such as walls, columns, floors, and beams, and can include load-bearing and non-load-bearing elements; known as structure elements in some older codes. (See also Structural Element.)

BUILDING ENVELOPE Term used by energy codes to refer to the element of a building that encloses conditioned spaces through which thermal energy is capable of being transferred to or from the exterior or other spaces not inside the shell of the building envelope.

BUILDING, EXISTING Any structure erected and occupied prior to the adoption of the most current appropriate code, or a structure for which a construction permit has been issued.

BUILDING HEIGHT See Height, Building.

BUILDING, HISTORIC A building or facility that is either listed in or eligible for listing in the *National Register of Historic Places* or that is designated as historic under a state or local law.

BUILDING OFFICIAL See Code Official.

BUILDING TYPE A specific class or category within an occupancy classification.

CABLE A conductor, consisting of two or more wires combined in the same protective sheathing and insulated to keep the wires from touching.

CEILING HEIGHT See Height, Ceiling.

CEILING RADIATION DAMPER See Damper, Ceiling Radiation.

CHANGE IN USE or OCCUPANCY See Occupancy, Change in Use.

CHILDREN As defined by the codes, people 12 years old and younger (i.e., elementary school age and younger).

CIRCUIT The path of electrical current that circles from the electrical source to the electrical box or fixture and back to the source.

CIRCUIT, BRANCH A circuit that supplies electricity to a number of outlets or fixtures.

CIRCUIT INTERRUPTER A safety device that opens or disconnects a circuit to stop the flow of electricity when an overload or fault occurs.

CIRCULATION PATH An interior or exterior way of passage from one place to another such as walks, corridors, courtyards, stairways, and ramps.

CLEAN OUT An access opening in the drainage system used to remove obstructions.

CLEAR FLOOR SPACE The minimum unobstructed floor or ground space required to accommodate a single stationary wheelchair and its occupant.

CLOSED-CIRCUIT TELEPHONE A telephone with a dedicated line, such as a house phone, courtesy phone, or phone that must be used to gain entrance to a facility.

CODE DEPARTMENT A local government agency that administers and enforces the codes and standards within a jurisdiction; also sometimes referred to by the codes as Authority Having Jurisdiction, or AHJ.

CODE OFFICIAL An officer or other designated authority charged with the administration and enforcement of the codes, standards, and regulations within a jurisdiction; also known as a building official and sometimes referred to by the codes as Authority Having Jurisdiction, or AHJ.

CODE, PERFORMANCE A code that is generally described and gives you an objective but not the specifics of how to achieve it. The focus is on the desired outcome, not a single solution, and compliance is based on meeting the criteria established by the performance code; engineering tools, methodologies, and performance criteria must be used to substantiate the use of the code requirement.

CODE, PRESCRIPTIVE A code that provides a specific requirement that must be met for the design, construction, and maintenance of a building. The focus is on a specific solution to achieve an objective or outcome based on historic experience and established engineering.

CODE VIOLATION Not complying with a code as stated in a code book or required by a jurisdiction, whether the noncompliance is deliberate or unintentional.

C.O.M. An acronym for "customer's own material"; refers to fabrics that are ordered separately from the furniture that they will cover.

COMBINATION FIRE/SMOKE DAMPER See Damper, Combination Fire/Smoke.

COMBUSTIBLE Refers to materials, such as building materials or finishes, that are capable of being ignited or affected by excessive heat or gas in a relatively short amount of time.

COMMON PATH OF TRAVEL That portion of an exit access along which occupants are required to travel before two separate and distinct paths of egress travel to separate exits are available. Paths that merge are also considered common paths of travel.

COMMON USE See Use, Common.

COMPARTMENTATION The process of creating confined spaces or areas within a building for the purpose of containing the spread of fire or smoke.

COMPARTMENT, FIRE A space within a building enclosed by fire barriers on all sides, including the top and bottom.

COMPARTMENT, SMOKE A space within a building enclosed by smoke barriers on all sides, including the top and bottom.

CONCEALED Items in a building rendered inaccessible by the structure or finish of the building.

CONDITIONED SPACE An area, room, or space being heated and/or cooled, containing uninsulated ducts, and/or with a fixed opening directly into an adjacent conditioned space.

CONDUCTOR A cable or wire that carries and distributes electricity.

CONDUIT, ELECTRICAL A raceway or pipe used to house and protect electrical wires and cables.

CONDUIT, PLUMBING A pipe or channel for transporting water.

CONSTRUCTION ASSEMBLY See Assembly, Construction.

CONSTRUCTION DOCUMENTS Written, graphic, electronic, and pictorial documents prepared or assembled for describing the design, location, and physical characteristics of the elements of the project necessary for obtaining a building permit; includes construction drawings, specifications, and any other required code information.

CONSTRUCTION DRAWINGS The floor plans, elevations, notes, schedules, legends, and other drawing details used to convey what is being built and included as part of the construction documents.

CONSTRUCTION TYPE The combination of materials and assemblies used in the construction of a building based on the varying degrees of fire resistance and combustibility.

CONSULTANT An individual who provides specialized services to an owner, designer, code official, or contractor.

CONTRACT REVIEW Similar to a plan review but performed by a consultant who is retained by the code department for that purpose. (See also Plan Review.)

CONTROL AREA A building or portion of a building where hazardous materials are allowed to be stored, dispensed, used, or handled in maximum allowable quantities.

CORRIDOR A passageway that creates a path of travel enclosed by walls, a ceiling, and doors that lead to other rooms or areas or provides a path of egress travel to an exit.

COURT See Egress Court.

DAYLIGHT ZONE See Zone, Daylight.

DAMPER, CEILING RADIATION A listed device installed in a ceiling membrane of a fire-resistance-rated floor/ceiling or roof/ceiling assembly to automatically limit the radiative heat transfer through an air inlet/outlet opening.

DAMPER, COMBINATION FIRE/SMOKE A listed device that meets the requirements of both a fire damper and a smoke damper.

DAMPER, FIRE A listed device installed in ducts or air transfer openings that automatically closes upon detection of heat to interrupt migratory air flow and restrict the passage of flame.

DAMPER, SMOKE A listed device installed in ducts and air transfer openings that is designed to resist the passage of air and smoke during an emergency.

DEAD-END CORRIDOR A hallway in which a person is able to travel in only one direction to reach an exit.

DEAD LOAD The weight of permanent construction such as walls, partitions, framing, floors, ceilings, roofs, and all other stationary building elements and the fixed service equipment of a building. (See also Live Load.)

DECORATIVE MATERIAL Any material applied over an interior finish for decorative, acoustical, or other effect.

DELUGE SYSTEM An automatic sprinkler system connected to a water source that delivers a large amount of water to an area upon detection of fire by a separate automatic detection system.

DEMARK The point in a communication room or other location in a building where the wiring from the utility company enters the building and is connected to the building wiring.

DESIGN DOCUMENTS See Construction Documents.

DETECTABLE WARNING A standardized surface texture applied to or built into a walking surface to warn visually impaired people of hazards in the path of travel.

DETECTOR, FIRE A device that detects one of the signatures of a fire and initiates action.

DETECTOR, HEAT A fire detector that initiates action when it senses heat due to abnormally high temperature and/or a specific rate of rise.

DETECTOR, SMOKE A device that detects the visible or invisible particles of combustion and initiates action.

DEVICE A unit of an electrical system that is intended to carry but not utilize electric energy.

DISABLED A person who has a condition that limits a major life activity. This can include the inability to walk and difficulty in walking, reliance on walking aids, blindness and visual impairment, deafness and hearing impairment, uncoordination, reaching and manipulation disabilities, lack of stamina, difficulty in interpreting and reacting to sensory information, and extremes in physical size. (See also Severe Mobility Impairment.)

DRAFTSTOP A continuous membrane used to subdivide a concealed space within a building (such as an attic space) to restrict the passage of smoke, heat, and flames.

DRAIN PIPE Any pipe that carries wastewater in a building. (See also Soil Pipe.)

DUCT An enclosed rectangular or circular tube used to transfer hot and cold air to different parts of a building; can be rigid or flexible.

DWELLING Any building that contains one or two dwelling units to be built, used, rented, leased, or hired out and intended for living purposes. (See also Living Space.)

DWELLING UNIT A single unit providing complete independent living facilities for one or more persons, including permanent provisions for living, sleeping, eating, cooking, and sanitation.

EGRESS A way out or exit.

EGRESS COURT An outside space with building walls on at least three sides and open to the sky that provides access to a public way.

ELEVATOR A hoistway and lowering mechanism equipped with a car or platform that moves on glides in a vertical direction through successive floors or levels. (See also Hoistway.)

ELEVATOR LOBBY A space directly connected to the doors of an elevator.

EMERGENCY ALARM SYSTEM A system that provides indication and warning of emergency situations involving hazardous materials and summons appropriate aid. A signal may be audible, visual, or voice instruction.

EMPLOYEE WORK AREA As used for accessibility purposes, any or all portions of a space used only by employees and only for work; excludes corridors, toilet facilities, breakrooms, and so forth.

ENERGIZED Electrically connected to a source of voltage.

ENERGY The capacity for doing work in various forms that is capable of being transformed from one into another, such as thermal, mechanical, electrical, and chemical.

ENERGY ANALYSIS A method for determining the annual (8760 hours) energy use of the proposed design and standard design based on hour-by-hour estimates of energy use.

ENERGY EFFICIENCY Refers to products or methods designed to reduce energy or demand requirements without reducing the end-use benefits.

ENERGY, RENEWABLE Includes energy derived from natural daylighting and photosynthetic processes and other solar radiation sources such as wind, waves, tides, and lake or pond thermal differences, as well as from the internal heat of the earth, such as nocturnal thermal exchanges.

ENERGY, SOLAR Source of natural daylighting and thermal, chemical, or electrical energy derived directly from the conversion of solar radiation.

ENTRANCE Any access point into a building or portions of a building used for the purpose of entering.

ENTRANCE, PUBLIC An entrance that is not a service entrance or a restricted entrance.

ENTRANCE, RESTRICTED An entrance that is made available for common use on a controlled basis, but not public use, and that is not a service entrance.

ENTRANCE, SERVICE An entrance intended primarily for the delivery of goods and services.

EQUIVALENCY Term used by the codes to indicate alternate systems, methods, and/or devices that are allowed because they have been determined by a code official to meet or exceed a specific code requirement.

ESSENTIAL FACILITIES See Facilities, Essential.

EXHAUST AIR Air removed from a conditioned space through openings, ducts, plenums, or concealed spaces to the exterior of the building and not reused.

EXISTING BUILDING OR STRUCTURE See Building, Existing.

EXIT The portion of a means of egress that leads from an exit access to an exit discharge and is separated from other interior spaces by fire-rated construction and assemblies as required to provide a protected path of travel.

EXIT ACCESS The portion of a means of egress that leads from an occupied portion of a building to an exit.

EXIT DISCHARGE The portion of a means of egress between the termination of an exit and the public way.

EXIT ENCLOSURE Similar to an exit passageway but can be in a vertical or horizontal direction.

EXIT, HORIZONTAL A fire-rated passage that leads to an area of refuge on the same floor within a building or on the same level of an adjacent building.

EXIT PASSAGEWAY A fire-rated portion of a means of egress that provides a protected path of egress in a horizontal direction to the exit discharge or public way.

EXIT, SECONDARY An alternative exit, not necessarily required by codes.

EXPANDED VINYL WALLCOVERING A wallcovering that consists of a woven textile backing, an expanded vinyl base coat layer, and a nonexpanded vinyl skin coat distinguishing it from standard vinyl wallcovering; typically requires a more stringent finish test.

FACILITIES, ESSENTIAL Buildings or other structures that are intended to remain operational in the event of extreme environmental loading from flood, wind, snow, or earthquake.

FACILITY All or any portions of buildings, structures, site improvements, elements, and pedestrian or vehicular routes located on a site.

FAMILY TOILET FACILITY A single-toilet facility that provides additional space to allow for someone to assist in the room.

FAUCET A fitting that controls the flow of water at the end of a water supply line.

FEEDER A conductor that supplies electricity between the service equipment and the branch circuits.

FENESTRATION Term used by energy codes to include skylights, roof windows, vertical windows (fixed and operable), opaque doors, glazed doors, glass block, and combination opaque/glazed doors. (See also Opaque Area.)

FIRE ALARM SYSTEM A system that is activated by the detection of fire or smoke or by a manual pull station that sends a signal to the occupants of a controlled area that a fire has been detected; it may also be activated by an extinguishing system.

FIRE AREA See Area, Fire.

FIRE BARRIER See Barrier, Fire.

FIRE BLOCKER Fire-rated material used to protect materials that are not fire rated.

FIREBLOCKING A building material (such as caulk or expandable foam) installed to resist the free passage of flame to other areas of the building through concealed spaces.

FIRE COMMAND CENTER The principal location where the status of various detection, alarm, and other control systems is displayed and can be manually controlled.

FIRE COMPARTMENT A space within a building enclosed by fire barriers on all sides, including the top and bottom.

FIRE DAMPER See Damper, Fire.

FIRE DEPARTMENT CONNECTION A hose connection at grade or street level for use by the fire department for the purpose of supplying water to a building's standpipe and/or sprinkler system.

FIRE DOOR ASSEMBLY See Assembly, Fire Door.

FIRE EXIT HARDWARE Similar to panic hardware but additionally provides fire protection, since it is tested with and included as part of a fire door assembly.

FIRE EXTINGUISHING SYSTEM, AUTOMATIC An approved system that is designed and installed to automatically detect a fire and discharge an extinguishing agent without human intervention to suppress and/or extinguish a fire; can consist of carbon dioxide, foam, wet or dry chemicals, a halogenated extinguishing agent, or an automatic sprinkler system.

FIRE LOAD See Fuel Load.

FIRE MODEL A structured approach using engineering analysis and quantitative assessments to predict one or more effects of a fire.

FIRE PARTITION See Partition, Fire. (See also Fire Wall.)

FIRE PROTECTION Refers to assemblies and opening protectives that have been chemically treated, covered, or protected so that they prevent or retard the spread of fire and smoke.

FIRE-PROTECTION RATING See Rating, Fire-Protection.

FIRE-PROTECTION SYSTEM Approved devices, equipment, and systems or combinations of systems that are intended to protect the life safety of the occupants and the structural integrity of the building in the event of a fire; includes fire and smoke detectors, fire alarms, and extinguishing systems.

FIRE RATING The time in minutes or hours that materials or assemblies have withstood a fire exposure, as established by a standard testing procedure; includes fire-resistance and fire-protection ratings.

FIRE-RESISTANCE RATING See Rating, Fire-Resistance.

FIRE RESISTANT Refers to construction materials, assemblies, and textiles that prevent or retard the passage of excessive heat, hot gases, or flame.

FIRE-RETARDANT-TREATED WOOD Pressure-treated lumber and plywood that exhibit reduced surface burning characteristics and resist fire development.

FIRE RISK The probability that a fire will occur, with the accompanying potential for harm to human life and property damage.

FIRESTOP An assembly or material used to prevent the spread of fire and smoke through openings in fire-resistive assemblies.

FIRE SUPPRESSION SYSTEM See Fire Extinguishing System.

FIRE WALL A fire-rated wall having protected openings, which restricts the spread of fire and extends continuously from the foundation to or through the roof with sufficient structural stability under fire conditions to allow collapse of construction on either side without collapse of the wall.

FIRE WINDOW ASSEMBLY See Assembly, Fire Window.

FLAME RESISTANT Refers to finishes or furniture that prevent, terminate, or inhibit the spread of a flame upon application of a flame or nonflaming ignition source with or without removal of the ignition source.

FLAME RETARDANT A chemical or other treatment used to render a material flame resistant.

FLAME-RETARDANT TREATMENT A process for incorporating or adding flame retardants to a finish or other material.

FLAME SPREAD The propagation of flame over a surface or the rate at which flame travels along the surface of a finish.

FLAMMABILITY The relative ease with which an item ignites and burns.

FLAMMABLE Capable of being ignited.

FLASHOVER A stage in the development of a contained fire in which all exposed surfaces reach ignition temperatures more or less simultaneously and fire spreads rapidly throughout the space.

FLIGHT A continuous run of rectangular treads, winders or combination thereof, from one landing to another.

FLOOR AREA The amount of floor surface included within the exterior walls. (See also Area, Net Floor and Area, Gross Floor.)

FLOOR FIRE DOOR ASSEMBLY See Assembly, Floor Fire Door.

FLUE A passageway within a chimney or vent through which gaseous combustion products pass.

FUEL LOAD Amount of combustible material present in a building or space that can feed a fire, such as combustible construction materials, paper, books, computers, and furniture.

FULL-SCALE TEST The simulation of an actual fire condition, such as for a full-size room or a full-size piece of furniture with all its contents.

FUSE A safety device that contains metal that will melt or break when the electrical current exceeds a specific value for a specific time period, causing the flow of electricity to stop.

FUSIBLE LINK A connecting link of a low-melting alloy that melts at a predetermined temperature, causing separation.

GLAZING The process of installing glass into frames; sometimes refers to the glass itself.

GRADE The average of the finished ground level where it adjoins the building at the exterior wall.

GRAYWATER Any nonindustrial wastewater generated from domestic processes such as dishwashing, laundering, or bathing.

GREEN DESIGN The practice of increasing the efficiency of a building so that less resources (e.g., materials, energy, water) are used, while reducing the building's impact on human health and the environment. (See also Sustainable Design.)

GROUNDED As it relates to electrical work, connected to the earth.

GROUND-FAULT CIRCUIT INTERRUPTER A device that detects small current leaks and disconnects the electrical power to the circuit or appliance, should a current leak occur, for the protection of the user; often required in areas with water; commonly known as GFCI or GFI.

GUARD A system of rails or other building components located near open sides of elevated walking surfaces that minimizes the possibility of a fall. (Previously known as a guardrail.)

GUEST ROOM or SUITE An accommodation that combines living, sleeping, sanitation, and storage facilities within a compartment or a contiguous group of rooms. (NFPA term.)

HABITABLE SPACE A room or enclosed space in a building used for living, sleeping, eating, or cooking but excluding bathrooms, toilet rooms, closets, halls, storage or utility spaces, and similar areas.

HANDICAPPED See Disabled.

HANDRAIL A horizontal or sloping rail intended for grasping by the hand for guidance or support.

HAZARDOUS MATERIAL A chemical or other substance that is a physical or health hazard, whether the material is in usable or waste condition; includes combustible or flammable materials, toxic, noxious, or corrosive items, or heat-producing appliances. (See also Toxic Material.)

HEAT BARRIER A liner or backcoating used between upholstery and the filling underneath to prevent the spread of flame or smoldering heat.

HEIGHT, BUILDING The vertical distance from the grade plane to the average height of the highest roof surface.

HEIGHT, CEILING The clear vertical distance from finished floor to finished ceiling directly above.

HEIGHT, STORY The clear vertical distance from finished floor to the finished floor above or finished floor to the top of the joists supporting the roof structure above.

HIGH-EFFICACY LAMPS Compact fluorescent lamps, T-8 or smaller diameter linear fluorescent lamps, or other types of lamps with specific lumens per watt.

HIGH-RISE BUILDING A structure with a floor used for human occupancy more than 75 feet (22,860 mm) above the lowest level of fire department vehicle access.

HISTORIC BUILDING See Building, Historic.

HOISTWAY A vertical shaft for an elevator or dumbwaiter.

HOME RUN Refers to wiring that is continuous from a device directly back to a main electrical panel or communication equipment without any interruptions or intermediate connections.

HORIZONTAL ASSEMBLY See Assembly, Horizontal.

HORIZONTAL EXIT See Exit, Horizontal.

HORIZONTAL PASSAGE Allows movement between rooms or areas on the same floor or story—for example, a door, archway, or cased opening.

INCIDENTAL USE A small area, space, or room that exists within another larger occupancy or building type that is considered more hazardous than the rest of the occupancy or building. (See also Occupancy, Accessory.)

INDIGENOUS MATERIAL Material that is originated, produced, or grows/occurs naturally in a region, typically within 500 miles (804.7 km) of a construction site.

INDOOR AIR QUALITY (IAQ) A general term used to describe the relative health of the air in an indoor environment which can be negatively impacted by volatile organic compounds (VOCs), such as those that off gas from building materials, finish, furniture, and cleaning products, and other pollutants.

INDOOR ENVIRONMENTAL QUALITY (IEQ) Includes indoor air quality as well as other interior elements that affect a building occupant's well being such as daylighting, thermal comfort, and acoustics.

INGRESS An entrance or the act of entering.

INITIATING DEVICE A component of the fire-protection system that is the initial notification of fire, such as a smoke detector or a manual fire alarm box.

INSANITARY A condition that is contrary to sanitary principles or injurious to health.

INSPECTION When a code official visits a job site to confirm that the work complies with the project's construction documents and required codes.

INTERIOR FINISH Any exposed interior surface of a building, including finished ceilings, floors, walls, window treatments, and decorative trim, as well as other furniture and furnishings.

INTERIOR ROOM Any enclosed space or room within the exterior walls of a building.

JURISDICTION A legally constituted governmental unit, such as a state, city, or municipality, that adopts the same codes, standards, and regulations; often referred to by the codes as Authority Having Jurisdiction, or AHJ.

LABELED Refers to any equipment or building material and assemblies that include a label, seal, symbol, or other identification mark of a nationally recognized testing laboratory, inspection agency, or other organization acceptable to the jurisdiction concerned with product evaluation, which attests to the compliance with applicable nationally recognized standards. (See also Listed.)

LANDING, DOOR A level floor surface immediately adjacent to a doorway or threshold.

LANDING, INTERMEDIATE A level floor surface between two flights of stairs or ramps.

LIFE CYCLE ASSESSMENT (LCA) A technique to evaluate the relevant energy and material consumed and environmental emissions associated with the entire life of a building, product, process, activity, or service. It considers raw material acquisition through manufacturing, construction use, operation, demolition, and disposal.

LIGHT-DIFFUSING SYSTEM A system in which light-transmitting plastic is positioned below independently mounted electrical light sources (or natural light sources) to create a light feature, not including similar plastic lenses, panels, grids, or baffles used as part of the electrical or light fixture.

LIGHT FIXTURE A complete lighting unit consisting of at least one lamp (and ballast when applicable) and the parts required to distribute the light, to position and protect the lamp, and to connect the lamp to the power supply (with a ballast when required). Also referred to as a luminaire.

LIMITED COMBUSTIBLE Refers to material that is not considered noncombustible, yet still has some fire-resistive qualities; a term used by the National Fire Protection Association.

LINTEL The member that is placed over an opening in a wall to support the wall construction above.

LISTED Refers to equipment or building materials and assemblies included in a list published by a nationally recognized testing laboratory, inspection agency, or other organization acceptable to the jurisdiction concerned with product evaluation that periodically tests the items to confirm that they meet nationally recognized standards and/or have been found suitable to be used in a specified manner. (See also Labeled.)

LIVE LOAD Any dynamic weight within a building, including the people, furniture, and equipment, and not including dead load, earthquake load, snow load, or wind load. (See also Dead Load.)

LIVING AREA See Dwelling Unit.

LIVING SPACE A normally occupied space within a dwelling unit other than sleeping rooms utilized for things such as living, eating, cooking, bathing, washing, and sanitation purposes.

LOAD-BEARING ELEMENT Any column, girder, beam, joist, truss, rafter, wall, floor, or roof that supports any vertical structural element in addition to its own weight; also known as a bearing element.

LOW-VOC (PRODUCTS) Products or materials with volatile organic compound (VOC) emissions equal to or below the established thresholds established by a code or industry standard.

LOW-VOLTAGE LIGHTING Lighting equipment that is powered through a transformer such as a cable conductor, rail conductor, or track lighting.

LUMINAIRE See Light Fixture.

MAKEUP WATER The water temporarily supplied by a municipality (either reclaimed or potable) when onsite nonpotable water supply systems, such as graywater and rainwater systems, are not available.

MAIN, WATER The principal artery of any continuous piping or duct system to which branch pipes or ducts may be connected.

MAKEUP AIR Air that is provided to replace air being exhausted.

MANUAL FIRE ALARM A manual device used to signal a fire; usually used by an occupant.

MARK An identification applied to a product by a manufacturer indicating the name of the manufacturer and the function of the product or material. (See also Labeled.)

MASONRY The form of construction composed of stone, brick, concrete block, hollow clay tile, glass block, or other similar building units that are laid up unit by unit and set in mortar.

MASS NOTIFICATION SYSTEM A system that integrates fire, security, and communication systems to provide emergency notification to occupants in a building, in multiple buildings, or in a much larger area.

MEANS OF EGRESS A continuous and unobstructed way of egress travel, both horizontally and vertically, from any point in a building to a public way; it consists of the exit access, the exit, and the exit discharge.

MEANS OF EGRESS, ACCESSIBLE A continuous and unobstructed way of egress travel from any accessible point in a building to a public way.

MEANS OF ESCAPE A way out of a building that does not conform to the strict definition of a means of egress but does provide an alternate way out.

MEMBRANE PENETRATION An opening created in a portion of a construction assembly that pierces only one side (or membrane) of the assembly.

MEZZANINE An intermediate floor level placed between a floor and the ceiling above in which the floor area is not more than one-third of the room in which it is located.

MOCK-UP, FURNITURE A full or partial representation of a finished piece of furniture that utilizes the same frame, filling, and upholstery as the finished piece.

NATURAL PATH OF TRAVEL The most direct route a person can take while following an imaginary line on the floor, avoiding obstacles such as walls, equipment, and furniture to arrive at the final destination.

NET-ZERO ENERGY Refers to a building that produces at least as much energy as it consumes and derives such energy from renewable on-site sources, not outside sources.

NOMINAL DIMENSION Not the actual size, it is the commercial size by which an item is known. For example, the nominal size of a stud is 2 × 4 inches and the actual size is 1½ × 3½ inches.

NONCOMBUSTIBLE Refers to material, such as building materials and finishes, that will not ignite, burn, support combustion, or release flammable vapors when subject to fire or heat.

NON-LOAD-BEARING ELEMENT Any column, girder, beam, joist, truss, rafter, wall, floor, or roof that supports only its own weight; also known as a nonbearing element.

NONPOTABLE WATER Water that is not safe for drinking, cooking, or personal use.

NOSING The leading edge of the tread on a stair and of the landing within a stairwell.

NUISANCE ALARM An alarm indicating a problem with a building system due to mechanical failure, malfunction, improper installation, or lack of proper maintenance; an alarm activated by an unknown cause.

OCCUPANCY The use or intended use of a building, floor, or other part of a building.

OCCUPANCY, ACCESSORY An occupancy that exists with another occupancy in the same space or building but is much smaller than the main occupancy. (See also Incidental Use.)

OCCUPANCY, CHANGE IN USE A change in the purpose or level of activity within a building that involves a change in application of code requirements.

OCCUPANCY, MIXED A building or space that contains more than one occupancy; in some cases, parts of the common egress paths are shared by the occupancies.

OCCUPANCY, MULTIPLE A more general term that includes any building used for two or more occupancy classifications.

OCCUPANCY SEPARATION A multiple occupancy where the occupancies are separated by fire-resistance-rated assemblies.

OCCUPANT The person or persons using a space, whether they are tenants, employees, customers, or other.

OCCUPANT CONTENT A term used by some of the older codes, it is the number of total occupants for whom exiting has been provided. This is the maximum number of persons who can occupy the space.

OCCUPANT LOAD Refers to the number of people or occupants for which the means of egress of a building or space is designed; total number of persons who may occupy a building or space at any one time.

OCCUPIABLE SPACE Refers to a room or enclosed space designed for human occupancy that is equipped with means of egress, light, and ventilation as required by the codes. (See also Regularly Occupied Space.)

OPAQUE AREA Term used by energy codes to refer to all exposed areas of a building envelope that enclose conditioned space except openings for windows, skylights, doors, and building service systems. (See also Fenestration.)

OPENING PROTECTIVE Refers to a rated assembly placed in an opening in a rated wall assembly (such as a fire door or window) or rated ceiling assembly (such as a floor fire door) designed to maintain the fire resistance of the wall assembly.

OUTLET, FIXTURE An electrical box in which electrical wiring is connected to a light or the light switch; can also be called a lighting outlet.

OUTLET, RECEPTACLE An electrical box in which electrical wiring allows the connection of a plug-in appliance or other equipment.

OWNER Any person, agent, firm, or corporation having a legal or equitable interest in the property.

PANIC HARDWARE A door latching assembly that has a device to release the latch when force is applied in the direction of exit travel. (See also Fire Exit Hardware.)

PARAPET The part of a wall entirely above the roof line of a building.

PARTITION A nonstructural interior space divider that can span horizontally or vertically, such as a wall or suspended ceiling.

PARTITION, FIRE A continuous fire-resistance-rated vertical assembly of materials designed to restrict the spread of fire, in which openings are protected; typically used to separate areas on the same floor of a building but not between floors; usually less restrictive than a fire barrier. (See also Barrier, Fire.)

PARTITION, PARTIAL A wall that does not extend fully to the ceiling and is usually limited by the codes to a maximum height of 72 inches (1830 mm).

PARTITION, SMOKE A continuous membrane that is designed to form a barrier to limit the transfer of smoke; usually less restrictive than a smoke barrier. (See also Barrier, Smoke.)

PASSAGEWAY An enclosed path or corridor.

PATH OF TRAVEL A continuous, unobstructed route that connects the primary area of a building with the entrance and other parts of the facility.

PERFORMANCE CODE See Code, Performance.

PERFORMANCE TEST The check of a component for conformity to a performance criterion or standard, performed during manufacturing, at the site during or after installation, or at a certified testing agency.

PERMANENT SEATING Any multiple seating that remains at a location for more than 90 days.

PERMIT An official document issued by code jurisdiction (or AHJ) that authorizes performance of a specified activity.

PHOTOLUMINESCENT Having the property of emitting light that continues for a length of time after the normal light source has been removed.

PHYSICALLY DISABLED or CHALLENGED See Disabled.

PICTOGRAM As it relates to accessibility, a pictorial symbol that represents activities, facilities, or concepts.

PLAN REVIEW The review of construction documents by code official(s) to verify conformance to applicable prescriptive and performance code requirements.

PLASTIC See Thermoplastic and Thermoset Plastic.

PLATFORM A raised area within a building used for worship or the presentation of music, plays, or other entertainment; considered temporary if installed for not more than 30 days.

PLATFORM LIFT A type of elevator, typically used when a ramp is not possible, to transport people short vertical distances.

PLENUM SPACE A chamber that forms part of an air circulation system other than the occupied space being conditioned; includes the open space above the ceiling, below the floor, or in a vertical shaft.

PLUMBING CHASE An extra-thick wall consisting of studs with a space between them to create a wall cavity allowing for wide plumbing pipes.

PLUMBING FIXTURE Any receptacle, device, or appliance that is connected to a water distribution system to receive water and discharge water or waste.

POST-CONSUMER RECYCLED CONTENT Waste material generated by consumers or facilities after it is used and that would otherwise be discarded.

POST-INDUSTRIAL RECYCLED CONTENT See Pre-consumer Recycled Content.

POTABLE WATER Water that is satisfactory for drinking, cooking, and cleaning and that meets the requirements of the local health authority.

PRESCRIPTIVE CODE See Code, Prescriptive.

PRE-CONSUMER (POST-INDUSTRIAL) RECYCLED CONTENT Proportion of recycled material in a product diverted from the waste created during the manufacturing process.

PROTECTED Refers to a building or structural element that has been covered (or protected) by a noncombustible material so that it obtains a fire-resistance rating.

PUBLIC ENTRANCE See Entrance, Public.

PUBLIC USE See Use, Public.

PUBLIC WAY Any street, alley, or other parcel of land open to the outside air leading to a street, permanently appropriated to the public for public use, and having a clear and unobstructed width and height of no less than 10 feet (3048 mm).

RACEWAY An enclosed channel designed to hold wires and cables.

RADIANT HEAT The heat that is transmitted through an object to the other side.

RAMP A walking surface that has a continuous slope steeper than 1 in 20 (5 percent slope).

RAMP, CURB A short ramp cutting through a curb or built up to it, usually used on the exterior of a building.

RATING, FIRE-PROTECTION The period of time a fire opening protective assembly (fire door, fire damper, etc.) will maintain the ability to confine a fire when exposed to a fire as determined by a test method.

RATING, FIRE-RESISTANCE The period of time that a building element, component, or assembly (wall, floor, ceiling, etc.) will withstand exposure to fire in order to confine a fire or maintain its structural function as determined by a test method.

READILY ACHIEVABLE A term used by the Americans with Disabilities Act (ADA) to indicate a change or modification that can be done without difficulty or large expense.

RECEPTACLE As it applies to electrical work, a contact device installed at the outlet for the connection of an attachment plug.

RECLAIMED WATER Water that, as a result of treatment of waste, is suitable for a direct beneficial use or a controlled use that would not otherwise occur, but does not meet the definition of potable water and, therefore, is not suitable for drinking purposes. Also known as recycled water.

RECORD DRAWINGS Drawings that document the location of all devices, appliances, wiring, ducts, or other parts of various building systems; often referred to as as-built drawings.

REFLASH The reignition of a flammable item by a hot object after the flames have been extinguished.

REFRIGERANT A substance utilized to produce refrigeration by its expansion or vaporization.

REGULARLY OCCUPIED SPACE A room or enclosed space which is regularly occupied for at least 1000 daytime hours per year. Restrooms, corridors, stairwells, and mechanical and electrical equipment rooms, are not considered to be regularly occupied. Dwelling units and sleeping units are considered to be regularly occupied.

REHABILITATION Any work undertaken to modify an existing building.

RENEWABLE ENERGY See Energy, Renewable.

REPAIR The reconstruction or renewal of any part of an existing building to good and sound condition for the purpose of its maintenance.

RESTRICTED ENTRANCE See Entrance, Restricted.

RETURN AIR The air removed from a conditioned space through openings, ducts, plenums, or concealed spaces to the heat exchanger of a heating, cooling, or ventilation system; either recirculated or exhausted.

RISER, PLUMBING A water pipe that runs vertically one full story or more within a building to supply water to branch pipes or fixtures.

RISER, STAIR The vertical portion of a stair system that connects each tread.

RISK FACTORS Conditions of the building occupants or space that can potentially cause a hazardous situation.

ROUGH-IN The installation of all parts of a system that can be completed before the installation of fixtures such as running pipes, ducts, conduit, cables, and the like.

SALLY PORT See Security Vestibule.

SECURITY BOLLARD Any device used to prevent the removal of products and/or shopping carts from store premises.

SECURITY GRILLE A metal grating or gate that slides open and closed, either vertically or horizontally, for security and protection.

SECURITY VESTIBULE An enclosed compartment with two or more doors where only one door is released at a time to prevent continuous passage for security reasons.

SEISMIC Refers to that which is a result of an earthquake.

SELF-CLOSING As applied to a fire door or other opening, equipped with an approved device (e.g., closer) that will ensure closing after having been opened. (See also Automatic Closing.)

SELF-LUMINOUS A fixture illuminated by a self-contained power source and operating independently of an external power source.

SERVICE ENTRANCE See Entrance, Service.

SEVERE MOBILITY IMPAIRMENT The ability to move to stairs without the ability to use the stairs.

SHAFT An enclosed vertical opening or space extending through one or more stories of a building connecting vertical openings in successive floors or floors and the roof. (See also Building Core.)

SIDE LIGHT A frame filled with glass or a solid panel that is attached to the side of a door frame.

SIGN or SIGNAGE A displayed element consisting of text or numbers or verbal, symbolic, tactile, and pictorial information.

SILL The horizontal member forming the base of a window or the foot of a door.

SITE A parcel of land bounded by a property line or a designated portion of a public right-of-way.

SLEEPING UNIT A room or space used primarily for sleeping that can include provisions for living, eating, and either sanitation or kitchen facilities but not both. A sleeping room or space that is part of a dwelling unit is not a sleeping unit.

SMOKE ALARM An alarm that responds to smoke and is not connected to another system; can be a single-station or multiple-station alarm.

SMOKE BARRIER See Barrier, Smoke.

SMOKE COMPARTMENT A space within a building enclosed by smoke barriers on all sides, including the top and bottom.

SMOKE DAMPER See Damper, Smoke.

SMOKE DETECTION SYSTEM, AUTOMATIC A fire alarm system that has initiation devices that utilize smoke detectors that provide early warning for protection of a room or space from fire.

SMOKE PARTITION See Partition, Smoke.

SMOKEPROOF ENCLOSURE An exit consisting of a vestibule and/or continuous stairway that is fully enclosed and ventilated to limit the presence of smoke and/or other products of combustion during a fire.

SMOKESTOP An assembly or material used to prevent the passage of air, smoke, or gases through an opening in a smoke barrier.

SMOLDERING Combustion that occurs without a flame but that results in smoke, toxic gases, and heat, usually resulting in a charred area.

SOIL PIPE A pipe that carries sewage containing solids. (See also Drain Pipe.)

SOLAR ENERGY See Energy, Solar.

SPACE A definable area such as a room, corridor, entrance, assembly area, lobby, or alcove.

SPECIFICATIONS Written information that is a part of or an addition to construction drawings that logically communicates the requirements of the construction and installation as part of the overall construction documents.

SPRINKLERED Refers to an area or building that is equipped with an automatic sprinkler system.

SPRINKLER HEAD The part of a sprinkler system that controls the release of the water and breaks the water into a spray or mist.

SPRINKLER SYSTEM, AUTOMATIC A system using water to suppress or extinguish a fire when its heat-activated element is heated to a specific temperature or above.

STACK PIPE A vertical main that can be used as a soil, waste, or venting pipe.

STAIR A change in elevation consisting of one or more risers.

STAIRWAY One or more flights of stairs with the required landings and platforms necessary to form a continuous and uninterrupted vertical passage from one level to another.

STANDPIPE SYSTEM A fixed, manual extinguishing system, including wet and dry systems, with outlets to allow water to be discharged through hoses and nozzles for the purpose of extinguishing a fire.

STORIES, NUMBER OF Typically counted starting with the primary level of exit discharge and ending with the highest occupiable level.

STORY See Height, Story.

STRUCTURAL ELEMENT Any building component such as columns, beams, joists, walls, and other framing members that are considered load-bearing and are essential to the stability of the building or structure.

STRUCTURE See Building.

STRUCTURE ELEMENT See Building Element.

SUPPLY AIR The air delivered to a conditioned space through openings, ducts, plenums, or concealed spaces by the air distribution system, which is provided for ventilation, heating, cooling, humidification, dehumidification, and other similar purposes.

SUSTAINABLE DESIGN More encompassing than green design, sustainability typically includes three main tenets: environmental responsibility, economic strength, and social responsibility. Buildings and spaces that incorporate sustainable design are designed to lessen their impact on the environment, stimulate the economy, and provide improvements to those who use and surround the building.

TACTILE Describes an object that can be perceived by the sense of touch.

TECHNICALLY INFEASIBLE A change or alteration to a building that has little likelihood of being accomplished due to existing structural conditions that would affect an essential load-bearing element or because other existing physical constraints prohibit modification or addition of items that are in full and strict compliance with applicable codes and/or accessibility requirements.

TELEPHONE BANK Two or more adjacent public telephones, often installed as one unit.

TENANT A person or group of persons that uses or occupies a portion of a building through a lease and/or payment of rent.

TENANT SEPARATION See Occupancy Separation.

TEXT TELEPHONE Similar to computers with modems, a type of keyboard input and visual display output that provides telephone communications for persons with hearing or speech impairments, also known as a TDD or TTY.

THERMOPLASTIC Plastic material that is capable of being repeatedly softened by heating and hardened by cooling and in the softened state can be repeatedly shaped for molding and forming.

THERMOSET PLASTIC Plastic material that, after having been cured, cannot be softened again.

THERMOSTAT An automatic control device triggered by temperature and designed to be responsive to temperature.

THROUGH-PENETRATION An opening created in a portion of a horizontal or vertical construction assembly that fully passes through both sides of the assembly.

THROUGH-PENETRATION PROTECTIVE A system or assembly installed in or around a through-penetration to resist the passage of flame, heat, and hot gases for a specified period of time; includes firestops, draftstops, and dampers.

TOILET FACILITY A room containing a water closet and usually a lavatory but not a bathtub, shower, spa, or similar bathing fixture. Also known as a single-toilet facility. A room with multiple water closets is known as a multiple-toilet facility.

TOWNHOUSE A single-family dwelling constructed in attached groups of three or more units in which each unit extends from foundation to roof and is open to space on at least two sides.

TOXIC MATERIAL A material that produces a lethal dose or lethal concentration as defined by the codes and standards.

TRANSIENT LODGING Facilities other than medical care and long-term care facilities that provide sleeping accommodations.

TRANSOM An opening above a door that is filled with glass or solid material.

TRAP A fitting or device that creates a liquid seal at a plumbing fixture to prevent the passage of odors, gases, and insects back into the fixture.

TREAD, STAIR The horizontal portion of a stair system that connects each riser.

TRIM Picture molds, chair rails, baseboard, handrails, door and window frames, and similar decorative or protective materials used in fixed applications.

TURNSTILE A device used to control passage from one area to another, consisting of revolving arms projecting from a central post.

UNDUE HARDSHIP A term used by the Americans with Disabilities Act (ADA) to mean "significantly difficult or expensive"; also known as undue burden.

UNISEX TOILET FACILITY A single-toilet facility that is intended for use by both males and females.

UNPROTECTED Refers to materials in their natural state that have not been specially treated.

UNSANITARY See Insanitary.

USE, COMMON As it refers to accessibility, the interior or exterior circulation paths, rooms, spaces, or elements that are not for public use but are instead made available for use by a restricted group of people.

USE GROUP or TYPE Sometimes referred to as building type, use group usually gets more specific and can be a subclassification within a building type. (See also Building Type.)

USE, PUBLIC Interior or exterior rooms, spaces, or elements that are made available to the general public.

VALVE A device used to start, stop, or regulate the flow of liquid or gas into piping, through piping, or from piping.

VARIANCE A grant of relief from certain requirements of the code that permits construction in a manner

otherwise prohibited by the code where strict enforcement would require hardship.

VENEER A facing attached to a wall or other structural element for the purpose of providing ornamentation, protection, or insulation, but not for the purpose of adding strength to the element.

VENTILATION The process of supplying or removing conditioned or unconditioned air by natural or mechanical means to or from a space.

VENTILATION AIR The portion of supply air that comes from outside the building plus any recirculated air that has been treated to maintain the desired quality of air within a space.

VENT, MECHANICAL The part of the air distribution system that dispenses and collects the air in a space, including supply diffusers and return grilles.

VENT PIPE A pipe that provides a flow of air to the drainage system and allows the discharge of harmful gases to prevent siphonage or backpressure. (Also called a flue.)

VERTICAL OPENING An opening through a floor or roof.

VERTICAL PASSAGE Allows movement from floor to floor—for example, a stairway or an elevator.

VOLATILE ORGANIC COMPOUND (VOC) A class of carbon-based substances and organic compounds that readily release gaseous vapors at room temperature causing indoor pollutants and sometimes ground-level ozone when in contact with certain exterior pollutants. (See also Low-VOC.)

WALL, CAVITY A wall, typically built of masonry or concrete, arranged to provide a continuous air space within the wall. (See also Plumbing Chase.)

WALL, DEMISING A wall that separates two tenant spaces in the same building, typically requiring a fire rating. (See also Occupancy Separation.)

WALL, EXTERIOR A bearing or nonbearing wall that is used as an enclosing wall for a building other than a party wall or fire wall.

WALL, FIRE A fire-rated wall that extends continuously from the foundation of a building to or through the roof with sufficient structural stability to allow collapse of one side while leaving the other side intact, typically requiring a 3-hour to 4-hour fire rating.

WALL, PARAPET The part of any wall that extends above the roof line.

WALL, PARTY See Fire Wall.

WASTE The discharge from any plumbing fixture that does not contain solids.

WHEELCHAIR LIFT See Platform Lift.

WHEELCHAIR SPACE A space for a single wheelchair and its occupant. (See also Area of Refuge.)

WIRELESS SYSTEM A system or part of a system that can transmit and receive signals without the aid of a wire.

WORK AREA See Area, Work.

WORKSTATION An individual work area created by the arrangement of furniture and/or equipment for use by occupants or employees.

ZONE CABLING A ceiling distribution method for communication cables in which ceiling spaces are divided into sections or zones so that cables can be run to the center of each zone, allowing for flexible, changeable cabling of open office areas; also called zone distribution.

ZONE, DAYLIGHT In general, an area below a skylight or adjacent to a vertical fenestration which receives daylight through the fenestration.

ZONE, FIRE A protected enclosure within a building created by rated walls or a contained fire suppression system that can be controlled separately from other areas of the same building.

ZONE, HVAC A space or group of spaces within a building with heating or cooling requirements that are similar and are regulated by one heating or cooling device/ system.

ZONE, NOTIFICATION An area within a building or facility covered by notification appliances which activate simultaneously.

INDEX